Issues in Economics Today

Today **Third Edition**

Issues in Economics Today

Third Edition

ROBERT C. GUELL
Indiana State University

 **McGraw-Hill**
Irwin

Boston   Burr Ridge, IL   Dubuque, IA   Madison, WI   New York
San Francisco   St. Louis   Bangkok   Bogotá   Caracas   Kuala Lumpur
Lisbon   London   Madrid   Mexico City   Milan   Montreal   New Delhi
Santiago   Seoul   Singapore   Sydney   Taipei   Toronto

McGraw-Hill
Irwin

ISSUES IN ECONOMICS TODAY

Published by McGraw-Hill/Irwin, a business unit of The McGraw-Hill Companies, Inc., 1221 Avenue of the Americas, New York, NY, 10020. Copyright © 2007 by The McGraw-Hill Companies, Inc. All rights reserved. No part of this publication may be reproduced or distributed in any form or by any means, or stored in a database or retrieval system, without the prior written consent of The McGraw-Hill Companies, Inc., including, but not limited to, in any network or other electronic storage or transmission, or broadcast for distance learning.

Some ancillaries, including electronic and print components, may not be available to customers outside the United States.

This book is printed on acid-free paper.

1 2 3 4 5 6 7 8 9 0 DOW/DOW 0 9 8 7 6 5

ISBN-13: 978-0-07-313752-0
ISBN-10: 0-07-313752-9

Editorial director: *Brent Gordon*
Publisher: *Gary Burke*
Executive sponsoring editor: *Lucille Sutton*
Editorial assistant: *Jackie Grabel*
Senior marketing manager: *Martin D. Quinn*
Lead producer, Media technology: *Kai Chiang*
Project manager: *Kristin Bradley*
Production supervisor: *Debra R. Sylvester*
Senior designer: *Kami Carter*
Photo research coordinator: *Kathy Shive*
Photo researcher: *Mary Reeg*
Lead media project manager: *Becky Szura*
Cover design: *Jillian Linder*
Cover image: *Getty*
Typeface: *10/12 Times New Roman*
Compositor: *International Typesetting & Composition*
Printer: *R. R. Donnelley*

Library of Congress Cataloging-in-Publication Data

Guell, Robert C.
    Issues in economics today / Robert C. Guell.—3rd ed.
       p. cm.
    Includes index.
    ISBN-13: 978-0-07-313752-0 (alk. paper)
    ISBN-10: 0-07-313752-9 (alk. paper)
    1. Economics. I. Title.
  HB87.G83 2007
    330—dc22   2005054116

www.mhhe.com

To Susan, Katie, and Matt

About the **Author**

Dr. Robert C. Guell (pronounced "Gill") is an associate professor of economics at Indiana State University in Terre Haute, Indiana. He earned a B.A. in statistics and economics in 1986 and an M.S. in economics one year later from the University of Missouri–Columbia. In 1991, he earned a Ph.D. from Syracuse University, where he discovered the thrill of teaching. He has taught courses for freshmen, upper-division undergraduates, and graduate students from the principles level, through public finance, all the way to mathematical economics and econometrics.

Dr. Guell has published numerous peer-reviewed articles in scholarly journals. He has worked extensively in the area of pharmaceutical economics, suggesting that the private market's patent system, while necessary for drug innovation, is unnecessary and inefficient for production.

In 1998, Dr. Guell was the youngest faculty member ever to have been given Indiana State University's Caleb Mills Distinguished Teaching Award. His talent as a champion of quality teaching was recognized again in 2000 when he was named project manager for the Lilly Project to Transform the First-Year Experience, a Lilly Endowment–funded project to raise first-year persistence rates at Indiana State University. He has since become Coordinator of First-Year Programs.

Dr. Guell's passion for teaching economics led him to request an assignment with the largest impact. The one-semester general education basic economics course became the vehicle to express that passion. Unsatisfied with the books available for the course, he made it his calling to produce what you have before you today—an all-in-one readable issues-based text.

Brief **Contents**

Table of **Contents**

The **Preface**

This book is designed for a one-semester issues-based general education economics course, and its purpose is to interest the nonbusiness, noneconomics major in what the discipline of economics can do. Students of the "issues approach" will master the basic economic theory necessary to explore a variety of real-world issues. If this is the only economics class they ever take, they will at least gain enough insight to be able to intelligently discuss the way economic theory applies to important issues in the world today.

Until the first edition of this book was published, instructors who chose the issues approach to teaching a one-semester general economics course have had to compromise in one of the following ways: they could (1) pick a book that presents the issues but that is devoid of economic theory; (2) pick a book that intertwines the issues with the theory; (3) ask students to buy two books; or (4) place a large number of readings on library reserve.

Each of these alternatives presents problems. If the course is based entirely on an issues text, students will leave with the incorrect impression that economics is a nonrigorous discipline that offers opinions devoid of a theoretical basis. A book that intertwines issues and theory implicitly assumes that all the issues are relevant to all students in the course. In fact, some issues are not relevant to some students and others are relevant only when the issue makes news. For example, at Syracuse my students never understood why farm price supports were interesting, whereas at Indiana State no student that I have met has ever lived in a rent-controlled apartment. Other issues are of interest only at particular times. Oil prices were of little consequence to students during the bulk of the 1990s, but students are very interested today. Student interest in Social Security rose during 2005 when President Bush pushed his version of reform but may again wane. Similarly, the minimum wage is of interest to students when there is a debate over an increase. Finally, some issues are white hot for a brief moment in time, like the 2003–2005 housing bubble, and do not survive the lead time necessary to make it into a regular economics text.

The problem associated with using multiple books is the obvious one of expense. Having multiple reserve readings, still a legitimate option, requires a great deal of time on the part of students, teachers, and librarians, and it is usually not convenient for students. This book meets both student and instructor needs simultaneously. By regularly updating the material, regularly adjusting the portfolio of topics, and using a Web platform for "white hot" issues and as an archive of discarded issues, this book allows instructors of economics to keep students interested.

HOW TO USE THIS BOOK

Issues in Economics Today includes eight intensive core theory chapters and 33 shorter issues chapters. The book is designed to allow faculty the flexibility in approach as well. Some colleagues like to intertwine theory and issues while others like to lay the theoretical foundation first before heading into the issues. Some faculty will choose to set a theme for their course and pick issues consistent with that theme while others will let their students decide what issues interest them. There is no right way to use the book except that **under no circumstances is it imagined that the entire book be covered.**

I believe that an issues-based course must have the virtue of being both timely and flexible. As a result, this book presents a wealth of issues from which instructors or students can pick and choose. This book also has the benefit of having timely Web-available chapters that allow students to study issues as they happen. Between the time the first edition went to press and this edition became available, the accounting scandals of 2002 occurred. During the book's first year the United States went to war in Iraq. Before this edition hit college bookstores, the housing bubble was of significant concern. Chapters discussing the economic impact of these events were available within a month of these events. I am committed to providing balanced and timely chapters for the Web so that instructors and students have the latest available information.

There are 33 issues chapters that I have divided into the following categories: Macroeconomic Issues, International Issues, Externalities and Market Failure, Health Issues, Government Solutions to Societal Problems, Discrimination Issues, Price Control Issues, and Miscellaneous Markets. These groupings will be helpful as you navigate through the Contents looking for a particular topic. To help you decide which issues chapters to cover, see the table on page xxii, entitled "Required Theory Table." It shows at a glance which theory chapters need to be covered before pursuing each of the issues chapters. On page xxi, the table entitled "Issues for Different Course Themes" includes my recommendations for courses that focus on social policy, international issues, election year issues, or business.

The format of this book, as well as the tools I've mentioned, are meant to provide you the maximum flexibility in choosing issues chapters for your course.

NEW TO THE THIRD EDITION

- **New Chapters:** In its third edition, *Issues in Economics Today* introduces new chapters that examine the economic impact of Wal-Mart, the economic impact of casino gambling, why college textbooks cost so much, and the housing bubble. These chapters, originally posted as Web chapters to accompany the second edition, have been updated and expanded for inclusion in the textbook. Chapter 37, "The Cost of War" uses the example of the recent war on Iraq and updates the material to focus on the occupation costs rather than simply the invasion. Similarly, Chapter 38, "The Economics of Terrorism" uses the example of the September 11 attacks to examine the effects of terrorism on the national economy and how the government responded. In its revised form it uses subsequent terrorist acts, like the London bombings of July 2005, to emphasize important points.

- **Combined Chapters:** In response to reviewer feedback, the gender and race and affirmative action chapters from the second edition have been combined as Chapter 26, "The Economics of Race and Sex Discrimination." Many readers felt they belonged together. In addition, the content of the chapter on the Consumer Price Index was folded into Chapter 6's discussion of problems with the measurement of inflation.

- **Kick It Up A Notch:** This new feature to the second edition has been expanded to more chapters. This encourages students to challenge themselves with slightly more advanced concepts. For those who want extra practice with this section, additional material can be found in the Study Guide.

- **All New Quiz Yourself Questions:** Because fraternities, sororities, clubs, and organizations are notorious for maintaining homework banks, the Quiz Yourself, Talk about This, and Think about This questions have been changed for chapters that date back to the first edition.

- **Frequent Web Updates:** Because new economic issues arise all the time, Web chapters are posted to the Web site during the life of the edition. In 2005, a housing bubble chapter was added there. The author's pledge is to continue posting issues.

FEATURES

- *A conversational writing style* makes it easier for students not majoring in economics to connect with the material. The book puts students at ease and allows them to feel more confident and open to learning.

- *Chapter Outline and Chapter Objectives* set the stage at the beginning of each chapter to let the student see how the chapter is organized and anticipate the concepts that will be covered.
- *Key Terms* are defined in the margins, recapped at the end of the chapters, and included in the Glossary.
- *Summaries* at the end of each chapter reinforce the material that has been covered.
- *Issues Chapters You Are Ready For Now* are found at the end of each theory chapter, so students can go straight to the issues chapters that interest them once they've mastered the necessary theoretical principles.
- *Quiz Yourself* presents questions for self-quizzing at the end of each chapter.
- *Think about This* asks provocative questions that encourage students to think about how economic theories apply to the real world by putting themselves in the economic driver's seat. For example, one Think about This asks, "Suppose you buy a new car. What is the opportunity cost of doing so?" This feature facilitates active learning so that the students will learn the concepts more thoroughly.
- *Talk about This* includes questions designed to trigger discussion.
- *For More Insight See* sends the students to Web sites and publications to find additional material on a given topic. Since economic issues are particularly time-sensitive, this feature not only helps students learn to do research on the Web, but also keeps the course as fresh and current as today's newspaper.

SUPPLEMENTS

The supplements for *Issues in Economics Today* provide some wonderful teaching resources for instructors and learning resources for students.

FOR THE INSTRUCTOR

Instructor's Manual/Test Bank

In addition to a traditional outline of each chapter's content and updated Web references to data sources for each chapter, the Instructor's Manual offers key-point icons to emphasize the importance of particular concepts. Another distinctive feature is that each figure is broken into subfigures with explanations that can be offered at each stage. The Test Bank includes 60 to 100 multiple-choice questions for the core theory chapters and 40 to 70 multiple-choice questions for the issues chapters. These questions test students' knowledge of key terms, key concepts, theory and graph recognition, theory and graph application, and numeracy, as well as questions about different explanations given by economists regarding particular economic phenomena.

COMPUTERIZED TEST BANK

The Computerized Test Bank makes the test bank questions available electronically in a Word for Windows format.

PowerPoint Presentations

Approximately 20 slides are available per chapter. **Website (www.mhhe.com/economics/ guell3)**
The password-protected Web site contains downloadable instructor supplements including the Instructor's Manual, downloadable PowerPoints, and grading guidelines for the Web-based issues offered on the student side.

FOR THE STUDENT

Study Guide

The Study Guide, like the text, is divided into theory chapters and issues chapters, with a slightly different format for each. The theory chapters include the major points of the chapter, a chapter outline, key terms with definitions, and problems. This is followed by a self-test of multiple-choice and true/false questions. The issues chapters include the major points of the chapter, a chapter outline, key terms with definitions, discussion questions, and Web-based questions. Additional material to correspond with the new Kick It Up A Notch section is now available. Answers to all problems are included.

Website (www.mhhe.com/economics/guell3)

On the student side of the Web site, you will find chapter summaries, viewable PowerPoints, chapter quizzes, Web questions, key terms, and links to additional resources.

ACKNOWLEDGMENTS

This text would not have been possible but for the efforts of a number of people. I would like to thank Indiana State University and its Department of Economics for their continued support of this project. In particular, I would like to thank my chair, John Conant, for his unflagging support, both moral and material. I am indebted to the personnel of McGraw-Hill/Irwin for their work in gathering and compiling peer reviews. Jackie Grabel, my development editor, and Lucille Sutton, my editor, were always encouraging and willing to help at every stage. I would also like to thank the Associate Vice President of Academic Affairs of Indiana State University, Rebecca Libler, for granting me the time and access to student workers who, through their hard work allowed me to complete this project while continuing to coordinate First-Year Programs. One student worker, Brian Heaton, graded everything in sight which enabled me to keep teaching. It is not an exaggeration to say that without the other student, Kylie Douglas, neither the second nor third edition would have happened. She scoured every table, graph, and sentence and brought every reference up to date. Her "what's next" attitude, her willingness to put everything aside for the sake of the book, and her ability to stay several days ahead of me regardless of the toll made it such that I never had to stop. For this she got the typical pittance that universities pay students and asked for only one other thing . . . so here it is: Kylie, You Continue to Rock!

I also want to thank the following peer reviewers whose insight substantially enhanced this book:

William Candley	Lemoyne-Owen College
Thomas W. Dolislager	University of Central Arkansas
Ralph Gamble	For Hays State University
Daphne Greenwood	University of Colorado—Colorado Springs
Bin Wang	Minot State University

Issues for **Different Course Themes**

Social Policy

16. Tobacco, Alcohol, Drugs, and Prostitution
18. Health Care
19. Government-Provided Health Insurance
20. The Economics of Prescription Drugs
21. The Economics of Crime
22. Education
23. Poverty and Welfare
25. Head Start
26. The Economics of Race and Sex Discrimination
29. Rent Control
40. The Economic Impact of Casino Gambling

International Issues

10. Federal Deficits, Surpluses, and the National Debt
13. International Trade
14. The International Monetary Fund
15. NAFTA, CAFTA, GATT, WTO
16. Tobacco, Alcohol, Drugs, and Prostitution
17. The Environment
18. Health Care
27. Farm Policy
33. Energy Prices
37. Cost of War
38. The Economics of Terrorism

Election Year

9. Federal Spending
11. Fiscal Policy
13. International Trade
17. The Environment
18. Health Care
21. The Economics of Crime
22. Education
24. Social Security
26. The Economics of Race and Sex Discrimination
28. Minimum Wage

Business Issues

9. Federal Spending
12. Monetary Policy
13. International Trade
18. Health Care
20. The Economics of Prescription Drugs
30. Ticket Brokers and Ticket Scalping
31. Personal Income Taxes
32. Antitrust
33. Energy Prices
35. The Stock Market and Crashes
36. Unions
39. Wal-Mart

Required Theory Table

Core Theory Required								
1	2	3	4	5	6	7	8	
X								9. Federal Spending
					X		X	10. Federal Deficits, Surpluses, and the National Debt
					X		X	11. Fiscal Policy
					X		X	12. Monetary Policy
X	X	X						13. International Trade: Does It Jeopardize American Jobs?
X					X			14. The International Monetary Fund: Doctor or Witch Doctor?
X	X							15. NAFTA, CAFTA, GATT, WTO
X	X	X						16. Tobacco, Alcohol, Drugs, and Prostitution
X	X	X	X	X		X		17. The Environment
X	X	X						18. Health Care
X	X	X						19. Government-Provided Health Insurance
X	X	X	X	X				20. The Economics of Prescription Drugs
X	X	X				X		21. The Economics of Crime
X						X		22. Education
X								23. Poverty and Welfare
						X		24. Social Security
X						X		25. Head Start
	X							26. The Economics of Race and Sex Discrimination
X	X	X						27. Farm Policy
X	X	X						28. Minimum Wage
X	X	X						29. Rent Control
	X		X	X				30. Ticket Brokers and Ticket Scalping
						X		31. Personal Income Taxes
	X	X	X	X				32. Antitrust
	X	X	X	X				33. Energy Prices
X						x		34. If We Build It, Will They Come? And Other Sports Questions
						X		35. The Stock Market and Crashes
	X	X	X	X				36. Unions
X			X				X	37. Cost of War
X						X	X	38. Economics of Terrorism
x	x	x	x	x				39. Wal-Mart
x	x	x	x	x				40. Casino Gambling
x	x	x	x	x				41. Cost of Textbooks

Issues in Economics Today

Third Edition

Chapter 1

Economics: The Study of Opportunity Cost

Chapter Objectives

After reading this chapter you should be able to

Define the key terms of economics and opportunity cost and understand how a production possibilities frontier exemplifies the trade-offs that exist in life.

Distinguish between increasing and constant opportunity cost and understand why each might happen in the real world.

Appreciate the meaning of thinking economically, and recognize its inherent traps.

Chapter Outline

Economics and Opportunity Cost

Modeling Opportunity Cost Using the Production Possibilities Frontier

Attributes of the Production Possibilities Frontier

Thinking Economically

Kick It Up A Notch: Demonstrating Constant and Increasing Opportunity Cost on a Production Possibilities Frontier

Summary

This chapter lays the foundation for understanding how to think like an economist. It begins by defining the discipline of economics and its most basic concept: opportunity cost. Opportunity cost is modeled and further explained through the use of a diagram called a production possibilities frontier. The chapter continues with a discussion of what "thinking economically" means. To understand this concept, we look at why economists use marginal analysis and explore the difference between positive and normative analysis as well as examining economic incentives. We conclude by examining logical traps that obstruct our path to such economic thinking.

ECONOMICS AND OPPORTUNITY COST

Economics Defined

economics
The study of the allocation and use of scarce resources to satisfy unlimited human wants.

Some define **economics** as a hard requirement for general education or a major; others, a "dismal science"; and still others, the study of the allocation and use of scarce resources to satisfy unlimited human wants. The reality is that economics is all three. It deserves its reputation as a difficult course, its practitioners are always disappointing the public by insisting that there is a cost to everything, and it really is a social science dealing with the fact that humans want more than resources are capable of satisfying.

On another level, the study of economics is the application of complicated jargon and graphs to common sense. You already know a lot of economics. You know, for instance, that choices have consequences; that having more money is more fun than having less; and that even though you are rich relative to a starving refugee, you are less rich than you would like to be. Of course there are many other economic lessons that you learn simply by being alive. What you do not have is a systematic way of thinking about those economic ideas, and that is what this course and this book provide.

The definition illustrates a couple of things. First, in this book all jargon with special meaning to economists will be in **bold,** with its definition, sometimes also in jargon, close by in the text as well as in the margin. If the definition is in "econ-speak" rather than common-sense English, you will also find an English translation nearby. Two terms in this definition need clarification because they have special meaning to economists. First, you find the word "scarce." Something is **scarce** when there is not a freely available and infinite source of it. Second, a **resource** is anything we either consume directly or use to make things that we will ultimately consume.

There are four basic resources that society can allocate: land, labor, capital, and the entrepreneurship of its people. Any other resource, like oil, steel, or corn, is made available to a society when it allocates one or more of the basic resources to uncover, create, or harvest it.

scarce
Not freely available and lacking an infinite source.

resource
Anything that is consumed directly or used to make things that will ultimately be consumed.

opportunity cost
The forgone alternative of the choice made.

Choices Have Consequences

In this course and with this book you will be faced with choices: Do you read and study, or do you sleep and party? Fortunately, this choice illustrates the first and most basic concept of economics: opportunity cost. **Opportunity cost** is the forgone alternative of the choice made.

Translated into English, opportunity cost is "what you would have done had you not done what you did." It is important to keep in mind that the "forgone alternative" is the next best choice. It is not all the things "you could have done had you not done what you did," but it is the best of these alternatives because presumably that is "what you would have done."

If, for example, you decide at some point before finishing your assigned reading to put down this book, you will be implicitly saying that you would rather do something other than read this book. In terms of the course you are taking, the "opportunity cost" of such a poor decision could well be the lower grade that results from lost understanding.

Unfortunately, no matter what you do, you cannot escape opportunity cost. If you stay responsible and continue to read your text, the opportunity cost would be what you would do with the time saved. You are giving up the opportunity to watch *American Idol* or *Survivor,* to sleep, or to study something else. To you, the preferred one of these would be the opportunity cost of reading.

MODELING OPPORTUNITY COST USING THE PRODUCTION POSSIBILITIES FRONTIER

The Intuition behind Our First Graph

The concept of opportunity cost can be further illustrated by looking at something called a **production possibilities frontier.** This graph, Figure 1.1, is the first of more than 100 that you will see in this book. It is an example of a **model,** a simplification of the real world that we can manipulate to explain the real world. This particular one relates the amounts of different goods that can be produced in a fully employed society.

production possibilities frontier
A graph which relates the amounts of different goods that can be produced in a fully employed society.

Because chalkboards and book pages have only two dimensions, our explanation is limited. This gives us the first opportunity to introduce something called a **simplifying assumption.**

FIGURE 1.1

Production possibilities frontier: the starting point.

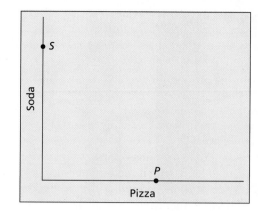

model

A simplification of the real world that can be manipulated to explain the real world.

simplifying assumption

An assumption that may, on its face, be silly but allows for a clearer explanation.

A simplifying assumption is one that may, on its face, be silly but allows for a clearer explanation. A good one also has the characteristic that the conclusions that spring from it are valid in its more complicated scenario. For our production possibilities frontier we will make several simplifying assumptions. We will assume that there are only two goods in the world, that these goods are pizza and soft drinks, and that these goods will be produced with a fixed number of resources and fixed technology.

For another simplification, suppose that there are five types of people in the world: (1) those really good at producing pizza but lousy at producing soda; (2) those pretty good at producing pizza and not so good at producing soda; (3) those sort of OK at both; (4) those good at producing soda and not so good at producing pizza; and (5) those really good at producing soda but lousy at producing pizza.

The Starting Point for a Production Possibilities Frontier

If we imagine that our resource is the time of our workers, it can be consumed directly in the form of their leisure or it can be combined with other resources to produce goods and services. This resource is also scarce because there is not an infinite number of people to work, those people can do only so much work, they will not work without being paid, and there is only so much soda that can be produced—even if all the people on the planet devote their lives to the production of soda. Of course this point also holds if we apply the scarce resource to the production of pizza. There is only so much pizza that can be produced even if everyone on the planet is producing pizza. This notion of scarcity gives us a starting point and an ending point for Figure 1.1

Point S in Figure 1.1 represents the situation where all resources are devoted to the production of soda; point P represents the situation where all resources are devoted to the production of pizza. In both cases all the resources in the world are devoted to the production of a specific good and production is still limited. It is limited by the ability of people and by the number of people and machines we have to help those people do their jobs. So that it is clear, remember that the production possibilities frontier is giving us a series of choices. We can pick only one of them. We cannot have both S sodas and P pizzas; thus, it is an either–or situation.

Points between the Extremes of a Production Possibilities Frontier

We can have some soda and some pizza, so many points between S and P are possible; we need to determine them. To proceed, assume you want something to eat with your soda, and ask yourself what kind of people you would remove from soda production to foster pizza production. Clearly, you would remove those who are not contributing much to the soda production but would contribute greatly to pizza production. That is, those with the attributes of people in group 1 above: really good at pizza, lousy at soda.

FIGURE 1.2 Production possibilities frontier: moving pizza chefs to their rightful place.

FIGURE 1.3 Production possibilities frontier: moving to even more pizza production.

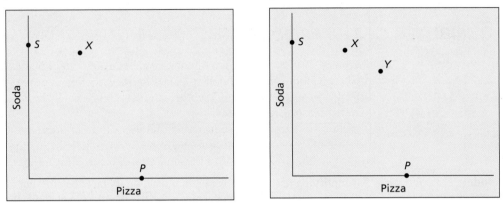

Figure 1.2 shows us what happens if we go ahead and move that group. As you see, this increases pizza production to a respectable level while not costing society much soda. Point *X* in Figure 1.2 represents that new soda–pizza combination. There everyone except those whom we will call the "pizza chefs" are still making soda, and the pizza chefs are efficiently cranking out as many pizzas as they can on their own. The thing is, though we gained a great deal of pizza production, we lost some soda production. That's why point *X*, while to the right of point *S*, is also lower than point *S*.

If we continue this process further, we are not blessed with a similar effect. The reason is that if we move toward greater pizza production, we do not have those pizza chefs to call on; instead we have our group 2, who are pretty good at pizza and not so good at soda. What that means is that even though pizza production rises, it does not rise as much as it did before. On top of that, our soda production falls more than it had before because when we moved the pizza chefs, they were "lousy" at soda. Now we are moving workers who are simply not so good at soda. Our soda losses are growing at an increasing rate. Thus we have point *Y* in Figure 1.3.

Going further, point *M* in Figure 1.4 results from moving the workers from group 3 (OK at both) from soda to pizza, point *Z* results from moving group 4 workers to pizza, and point *P* results from moving group 5 workers to pizza.

FIGURE 1.4 All points on a production possibilities frontier.

FIGURE 1.5 A fully labeled production possibilities frontier: the case when people are different.

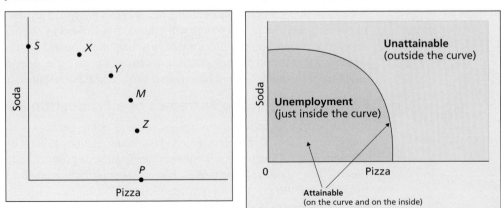

Connecting points like this creates Figure 1.5: a production possibilities frontier. This curve represents the most pizza that can be produced for any given amount of soda or, interpreted differently, the most soda that can be produced for any given amount of pizza.

ATTRIBUTES OF THE PRODUCTION POSSIBILITIES FRONTIER

unemployment
A situation that occurs when resources are not being fully utilized.

attainable
Levels of production that are possible with the given resources.

unattainable
Levels of production that are not possible with the given resources.

Of course, if you can produce on the curve, you can produce less than that as well. If you do produce at points inside a production possibilities frontier, there are unemployed resources, or **unemployment** for short. Therefore, all points on or inside the production possibilities frontier are **attainable.**

Conversely, since the production possibilities frontier represents the maximum amount of one good that you can produce for a given level of production of another, those points outside the production possibilities frontier are **unattainable.** This means that currently available resources and technology are insufficient to produce amounts greater than those illustrated on the frontier. On the graph, everything beyond the frontier is unattainable.

The preceding discussion illustrates something you need to be wary of in this book. Words you think you know may mean something entirely different to economists. Thus far we have at least three such words: unemployment, frontier, and good. You think of unemployment as the condition of someone wanting a job but not having one. Economists do not disagree but expand that definition to resources other than labor. For example, on the interior of the production possibilities frontier there is unemployment, but that unemployment may be of capital. The word "frontier" is used to describe the boundary of production, not a wooded area with bears to avoid. The word "good," to an economist, is a generic term for anything we consume. In the example, soda and pizza are goods.

In the soda and pizza example there were people of different talents at soda and pizza production. The pizza chef had far different skills from the soda master. If, on the other hand, everyone were identical in their soda and pizza production capabilities, then points would fall on the line, as seen in Figure 1.6.

Increasing and Constant Opportunity Cost

Figures 1.5 and 1.6 have important similarities and differences. In both, the points on the production possibilities frontier are the most of one good that can be produced for a given amount of the other good. In both, the points on the curve and inside it are attainable and those on the outside of it are unattainable. In both, the opportunity cost of moving from one

FIGURE 1.6
A fully labeled production possibilities frontier: the case when people are the same.

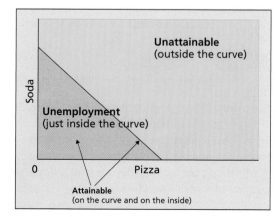

point to another is the amount of one good you have to give up to get another. They differ in one important way, however: whether opportunity cost is increasing or constant.

If the production possibilities frontier is not a line but is bowed out away from the origin, then opportunity cost is increasing. The reason for this is that as we add more resources to the production of pizza, we are using fewer resources to produce soda. Compounding that problem, at each stage as we take the resources away from soda and put them into pizza, we are moving workers who are worse at pizza production and better at soda production than those moved in the previous stage. This means that the increase in pizza production is diminishing and the loss in soda production is increasing. An economist would call this an example of **increasing opportunity cost.**

If the production possibilities frontier is a straight line that is not bowed out away from the origin, then opportunity cost is constant. If every worker possesses identical skill, though you still have to give up some soda to get pizza, this is not compounded by anything. The resources you put into producing more pizza are just as good as the resources used to get you to that point and the resources taken away from the soda are similarly just as good as the resources used up to that point. An economist would call this an example of **constant opportunity cost.**

THINKING ECONOMICALLY

Marginal Analysis

optimization assumption
An assumption that suggests that the person in question is trying to maximize some objective.

One of the central tools of economics is marginal analysis. Economists typically look at problems by analyzing the costs and benefits of various solutions. When people buy something they have to compare the value of what they purchase to the value of what they give up. When companies produce goods for sale, they have to compare the money they generate from sales to the costs they will incur from the production process. When you clean up your dorm room, you weigh the cleanliness gained against the time required to clean it.

Economists generally make an **optimization assumption.** This is an assumption that suggests that the person in question is trying to maximize some objective. For example, consumers are assumed to be making decisions that maximize their happiness subject to a scarce amount of money. Companies are assumed to maximize profits. People are assumed to clean things until the benefits of cleaning more are not worth the time or effort.

marginal benefit
The increase in the benefit that results from an action.

marginal cost
The increase in the cost that results from an action.

Economists see that all of these problems can be looked at using the same framework. Economists compare the **marginal benefit** of an action with its **marginal cost.** Something is worth doing only if the increase in benefits equals or exceeds the increase in costs. If the marginal benefit of an action steadily decreases and the marginal cost of an action steadily increases, then a person maximizes **net benefit** by doing that action until the marginal benefit equals the marginal cost. This is the essence of marginal analysis, and we will see it in action throughout this book.

net benefit
The difference between all benefits and all costs.

Positive and Normative Analysis

positive analysis
A form of analysis that seeks to understand the way things are and why they are that way.

When people look at the world they often see things as they are and compare the way things are to the way they think things should be. They see a major league shortstop sign a contract for a quarter of a billion dollars over 10 years while their high school teachers make less than $40,000 a year. Economists, and social scientists in general, distinguish views of "the way things are" from "the way things should be," calling the former **positive analysis** and the latter **normative analysis.** Although there are economists who utilize both forms of analysis, more economists are comfortable explaining why things are the way they are than are comfortable suggesting the way things should be. Some critics look at this as self-delusion on the part of economists, using the argument that we choose which information to weigh more heavily based on normative beliefs.

normative analysis
A form of analysis that seeks to understand the way things should be.

Economic Incentives

What kinds of choices we make as individuals and as a society depend on our preferences. Returning to the soda and pizza example, whether we like soda or pizza, or in what combinations we most like them, will have an important impact on what we choose to produce and consume. But also high on the list of things that determine what combinations of things we will produce and consume are **incentives.** Something is an incentive if it influences a decision we make. Some incentives are part of a market, like prices. Others are put on by an outside force like a government, and they can positively reinforce behaviors that are desired or deter behaviors that are not. What this means is that you are still able to produce and consume what you want, but something—perhaps a tax or a government regulation—is encouraging a particular choice. For example, by taxing beer and not soda, the government encourages you to steer toward soda and away from beer.

On a deeper level, an incentive may motivate you to do something you would not ordinarily do. For instance, many incentives are offered in the tax system. Tax credits and deductions for college tuition are considered incentives that will persuade people to get an education. For many people who would go to college anyway, these are not incentives. However, to some people who were perhaps considering college but had not made a decision, any influence these tax benefits would have on the decision would constitute an incentive.

An important and sometimes unfortunate aspect of incentives is that they create unintended consequences. Taxes are an area where some argue that the unintended consequences can be predicted from the incentives that arise out of programs. If welfare payments were reduced when the recipient found part-time employment, some predict the result that the recipient would not look for part-time employment.

incentives

Something that influences a decision we make.

Fallacy of Composition

One of the key traps to thinking economically is assuming that the total economic impact of something is always and simply equal to the sum of the individual parts. The **fallacy of composition** is an important logical trap to avoid because invalid economic conclusions will inevitably be drawn.

Outside of economics, cake constitutes a famous illustration of why the fallacy of composition is just that—a fallacy. Imagine a cake. Now imagine the ingredients that go into making the cake. Imagine eating the cake and the satisfaction you get from that. Now compare that level of satisfaction to what you would have if you separately poured flour, sugar, and baking powder down your throat, washed it down with a couple of raw eggs and some cooking oil, and then stuck your head in an oven. The baked combination is obviously better than its individual parts.

As an example within economics, we will learn in Chapter 5 that when many farmers are making high profits, others will want to join in. If they do join in, will all of the old and new farmers be making high profits? We will see that the new farmers' extra production will ultimately drive prices down so far that neither the older nor the newer farmers make money.

What this means is that when we are making economic judgments, we must do so with care. The sums of the individual parts must not be confused with the whole. The two can be, and often are, different.

fallacy of composition

The mistake in logic that suggests that the total economic impact of something is always and simply equal to the sum of the individual parts.

Correlation ≠ Causation

When people are attempting to think economically, another trap they may fall into is assuming that because two variables changed simultaneously, one caused the other to happen.

For instance, if you weighed all people under age 30 and also asked them how many dates they have had in their lifetime, you would find a **direct correlation,** meaning that it appears

direct correlation

A higher level of one variable is associated with a higher level of the other variable.

causation
A change in one variable makes another variable change.

inverse correlation
A higher level of one variable is associated with a lower level of the other variable.

that the more people weigh, the more dates they have had. This does not imply **causation.** Heavier people do not necessarily get more dates and dating does not make us gain weight. In this case the two variables happen to be correlated with age. People in their twenties weigh more and have had a longer opportunity to have dates than have teens, preteens, and young children.

When politicians attempt to take credit for good economic times with the claim that their policies caused the good economic times to happen, we must be suspicious. Of course we must be equally suspicious if they attempt to pin the blame on their incumbent opponent if bad economic times existed in their opponent's time in office. While their claims may be true, it is perfectly plausible that the policies and the economy were unrelated, or that the economy did well or did poorly despite the policies.

Sometimes two variables move in opposite directions. This **inverse correlation** can also be misinterpreted as being causal. If you were to get season tickets to your college's football games and observe the amount of skin (bare arms, legs, and midriffs) showing on the fans and compare that to the amount of hot chocolate sold during the game, you would find that when people show more skin they also consume less hot chocolate. If you came to the conclusion that one caused the other to happen you would, of course, be wrong. Obviously, the weather caused each to occur.

Kick It Up A Notch — DEMONSTRATING CONSTANT AND INCREASING OPPORTUNITY COST ON A PRODUCTION POSSIBILITIES FRONTIER

Economists use the production possibilities frontier to show the concepts of increasing and constant opportunity cost. If we start with no pizza and only soda but then move in increments to change our mix there is opportunity cost. Just how much depends on whether it is increasing or constant.

Demonstrating Increasing Opportunity Cost

For example, in Figure 1.7 if we go from the point on the graph where we are producing no pizza to the point where we are producing a single unit, a unit whose numbers could be in the billions, our opportunity cost would be characterized by lost units of soda. On Figure 1.7, the opportunity cost of going from 0 units of pizza to 1 unit of pizza is one unit of soda. Moving from 1 unit of pizza to 2 units has an opportunity cost that is 3 units of soda. Similarly, moving from 2 to 3 units of pizza has an opportunity cost of 6 units of soda. As is visually obvious, the opportunity cost of going from 0 to 1 is smaller than going from 2 to 3. This is why we say that the opportunity cost is increasing.

Demonstrating Constant Opportunity Cost

Similarly, we can use Figure 1.8 to show constant opportunity cost. The opportunity cost of moving from producing no pizza to 1 unit is 3 units of soda. Moving from 1 unit to 2 units and from 2 to 3 units also has an opportunity cost of 3 units of soda. In this case the opportunity cost of going from 0 to 1 is the same as going from 2 to 3. This is why we say that the opportunity cost is constant.

FIGURE 1.7 Illustrating increasing opportunity costs.

FIGURE 1.8 Illustrating constant opportunity costs.

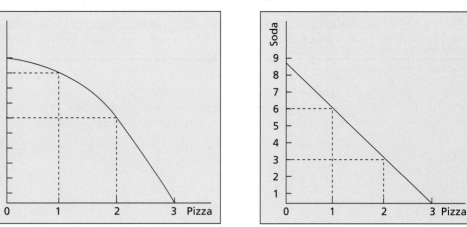

What this all means is simple: choices have consequences. Sometimes those consequences are great and sometimes they are small. If studying for five hours moves you from an F to a B on a test, then the higher grade has a low opportunity cost in terms of lost television watching. Viewed from the other side, the opportunity cost of another five hours of television watching (instead of studying to get a good grade) could be substantial. Opportunity cost is everywhere and is a consequence of every decision you make.

Summary

In this chapter we learned the definition of economics, that choices have consequences, and that those consequences are called opportunity cost. We learned how to model choices using a production possibilities frontier. We also learned that, depending on our assumptions, opportunity cost can be increasing or constant. Last, we explored the meaning of thinking economically by examining marginal analysis, positive and normative analysis, incentives, and the flaws of logic that may get in the way of economically accurate thinking.

Key Terms

attainable, 5
causation, 8
direct correlation, 7
economics, 1
fallacy of composition, 7
incentives, 7
inverse correlation, 8
marginal benefit, 6

marginal cost, 6
model, 3
net benefit, 6
normative analysis, 6
opportunity cost, 2
optimization
   assumption, 6
positive analysis, 6

production possibilities
   frontier, 2
resource, 2
scarce, 2
simplifying
   assumption, 3
unattainable, 5
unemployment, 5

Issues Chapters You Are Ready For Now

Federal Spending, 104

Poverty and Welfare, 248

If We Build It, Will They Come? And Other Sports Questions, 353

Quiz Yourself

1. Scarcity implies that the allocation scheme chosen by society can
   a. Not make more of any one good.
   b. Always make more of any good.
   c. Typically make more of a good but at the expense of making less of another.
   d. Always make more of all goods simultaneously.

2. A production possibilities frontier is a simple model of
   a. Scarcity and allocation.
   b. Prices and output.
   c. Production and costs.
   d. Inputs and outputs.

3. The underlying reason that there are unattainable points on a production possibilities frontier diagram is that there
   a. Is government.
   b. Are always choices that have to be made.
   c. Is a scarcity of resources within a fixed level of technology.
   d. Is unemployment of resources.

4. The underlying reason production possibilities frontiers are likely to be bowed out (rather than linear) is
   a. Choices have consequences.
   b. There are always opportunity costs.
   c. Some resources and people can be better used producing one good rather than another.
   d. There is always some level of unemployment.

5. The optimization assumption suggests that people make
   a. Irrational decisions.
   b. Unpredictable decisions.
   c. Decisions to make themselves as well off as possible.
   d. Decisions without thinking very hard.

6. Imagine an economist ordering pizza by the slice. When deciding how many slices to order she would pick that number where the enjoyment of the _____ equals the enjoyment she could get from using the money on another good.
   a. First slice.
   b. Last slice.
   c. Average slice.
   d. Total number of slices.

7. Of course, all individual students are better off if they get better grades. If you were to conclude that all students would be better off if everyone received an "A" you would
   a. Have fallen victim to the fallacy of scarcity.
   b. Be right.
   c. Have fallen victim to the fallacy of composition.
   d. Be mistaking correlation with causation.

8. If you were to conclude, after carefully examining data and using proper evaluation techniques, that a tax credit for attending college benefits the poor more than a tax deduction (of equal total cost to the government) would, you would have engaged in _____ analysis to reach that conclusion.
   a. Negative.
   b. Positive.
   c. Normative.
   d. Creative.

Think about This

What was your opportunity cost of attending college?

Think about the most expensive thing you have ever purchased. What could you have done with the money? Which outcome would have made you better off; what you did or what you could have done?

Think about the last time you took a series of tests during a short period of time (high school or college finals work here). How did you decide how much time to spend on each subject? How might the study of economics help you make that allocation decision in the future?

Talk about This

Discuss whether you believe people make rational decisions based on the optimization assumption.

Discuss what kinds of noneconomic (that is something you would normally not think of as an economic decision) trade-offs could be modeled with a production possibilities frontier?

Appendix **1A**

Graphing: Yes, You Can.

Whether you like it or not, graphing is an important part of "getting" economics. If you have ventured to this appendix it is likely that your instructor agrees and wants you to have a firm foundation for what you are about to do. This appendix is geared to the student who never understood what a graph was trying to tell them; to those poor souls who look at a complex diagram and see a bunch of stray lines that have no meaning. In the movie *Jerry Maguire,* Tom Cruise bursts into his home to offer a long heartfelt apology to his wife, who finally interrupts him to say "You had me at 'Hello.'" Those of us who teach economics have often lost our students at "Hello," or at least at the moment we went to the board to draw a graph. Let's get off on the right foot with learning what a graph is and what it can tell us.

CARTESIAN COORDINATES

origin
The point on the graph where both the variables are zero (0,0).

y-axis
The vertical axis.

x-axis
The horizontal axis.

slope
The increase in the value of the y-axis variable for a one unit increase in the value of the x-axis variable.

x-intercept
The value of the x-axis variable when the y-axis variable is zero.

y-intercept
The value of the y-axis variable when the x-axis variable is zero.

As unpleasant as the subheading suggests, Cartesian coordinates are named for their inventor, Frenchman René Descartes. As the legend goes, he was staring at the ceiling and began following the path of a fly. He discovered that he could use just two numbers to pinpoint the placement of the fly on the ceiling every time it landed. So lie back for a moment and look at the ceiling.

Now pick a corner of the room where the ceiling meets two walls; that will be your reference point. (In math it is called the **origin.**) Assuming the walls are square to one another, call the wall that runs on your left the **y-axis** and the wall on your right the **x-axis.** Now find a spot on the ceiling that stands out; a spider, a small stain, a vent, anything. Draw the shortest possible imaginary line from your spot to the ceiling to the wall on the right. Call that point A. Do the same thing for the wall on the left and call that point B. You can identify that point on the ceiling using just two numbers. The first number is the distance along the *x*-axis from the corner to A and the second is the distance along the *y*-axis from the corner to B. In Fig 1A.1 the point that is marked is 9 units along the *x*-axis and 11 along the *y*-axis, so it is shown as (9,11)

PLEASE! NOT *Y = MX + B*. . . . SORRY.

Whether you want to recall the experience or not, you were first exposed to the **slope, x-intercept,** and **y-intercept** of a line and the dreaded $y = mx + b$ form of the line in your first algebra class. Whether that was in 7th, 8th, 9th, or 10th grade, enough time has passed that a refresher on the ideas is in order. The equation $y = mx + b$ is a line because if you get all of the x, y combinations that come about from plugging in random values of x and computing what you get for y and then graph them, they end up in a line. That line will cross the *y*-axis at b, because if you plug in 0 for x in the $y = mx + b$ equation, mx is 0 (because anything times 0 is 0), so all you are left with is b. Therefore b is the *y*-intercept. It will cross the *x*-axis at $-b/m$. Therefore, the *x*-intercept is $-b/m$. As you will (perhaps not so vividly) recall, the slope is the "rise over the run." That means it is the amount by which y rises divided by the amount by which x rises. Suppose

FIGURE 1A.1
Graphing a point.

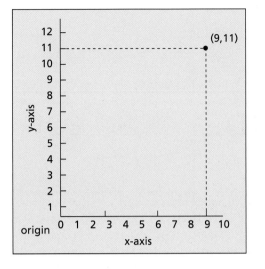

FIGURE 1A.2
Graphing a line
$y = mx + b$
$m > 0, b > 0$.

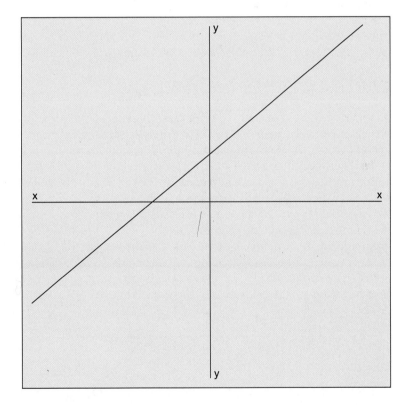

we let x start at 3 and rise to 4. If that happens, then y goes from $m3 + b$ to $m4 + b$. y therefore rises by m. The rise is m, the run is 1, so the slope is m. There is nothing magic about the choice of 3; we could have used any number and we would have gotten the same result. The slope is m.

If m and b are positive, you get a graph like Figure 1A.2. If m is positive and b is negative, you get something like Figure 1A.3. If m is negative and b is positive you get a graph like Figure 1A.4, and finally if they are both negative, you get something like Figure 1A.5. If m is large and positive, that means the line is upward sloping and steep; small and positive means that it is

FIGURE 1A.3
Graphing a line
$y = mx + b$
$m > 0, b < 0.$

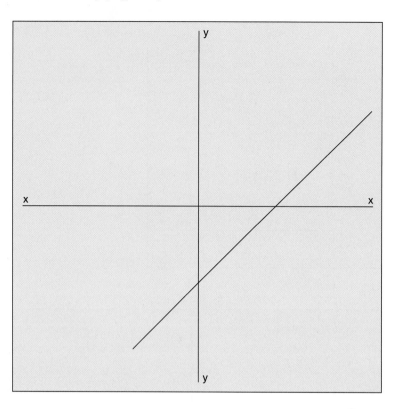

FIGURE 1A.4
Graphing a line
$y = mx + b$
$m < 0, b > 0.$

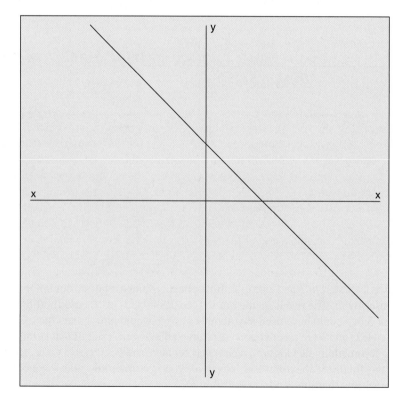

FIGURE 1A.5
Graphing a line
$y = mx + b$
$m < 0, b < 0.$

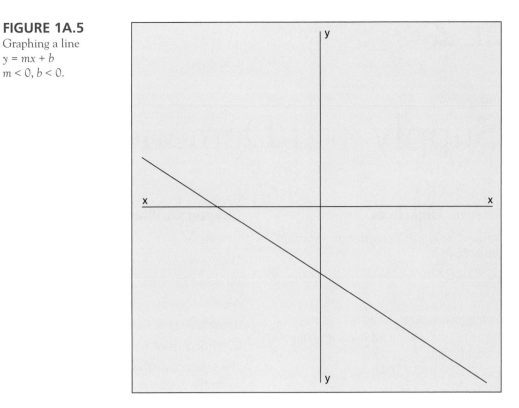

upward sloping and relatively flat. If *m* is really negative, then the line is downward sloping and steep, and if it is slightly negative, then the line is downward sloping and flat.

WHAT ON GOD'S GREEN EARTH DOES THIS HAVE TO DO WITH ECONOMICS?

To simplify things some, the only things that matter on our graphs will be those things that happen in the first quadrant (where both *x* and *y* are positive). We will have downward-sloping lines and upward-sloping lines. We will have some lines that are steep and some that are flat. Often, what we graph will not be a line at all but a curve (such as Figures 1.5 and 1.7). That is less important than this: An upward-sloping line or curve means that as the variable on the *x*-axis increases, so does the variable on the *y*-axis; a downward-sloping line or curve means that as the variable on the *x*-axis increases, the variable on the *y*-axis decreases.

This will become apparent when we talk about supply and demand in Chapter 2 and costs of production in Chapter 4. As you will see in Chapter 2, economists put price on the vertical axis (the *y*-axis) and the amount people want to buy or firms want to sell on the horizontal axis (the *x*-axis.) The upward-sloping line will be supply and will suggest that companies will produce more stuff if you pay them more for each one, and the downward-sloping line will be demand and will suggest that consumers will buy less stuff when the price per unit rises.

We will also make a big deal out of two lines or curves crossing. When supply crosses demand in Chapter 2, when marginal revenue crosses marginal cost in Chapter 5, and when aggregate demand crosses aggregate supply in Chapter 8, this is going to have particular significance. It is important that when you get there and you don't understand why two lines crossing matters at all . . . **ASK!**

Chapter 2

Supply and Demand

Chapter Objectives

After reading this chapter you should be able to

Understand the economic model of supply and demand.

Define many terms, including supply, demand, quantity supplied, and quantity demanded.

Use the intuition behind the supply and demand relationships as well as the variables that can change these relationships to manipulate the supply and demand model.

Chapter Outline

This is the make-or-break chapter of the book: you cannot understand economics without understanding supply and demand. Only if you understand this complicated topic will you be able to read the issue chapters with a good level of comprehension.

You probably are familiar with the words "supply and demand" through television, newspapers, or conversation. Unfortunately the phrase frequently is used by people in a way an economist would not use it. This chapter is intended to keep you out of that crowd. It will help you understand the supply and demand model enough so that you will be able to use it when we discuss a variety of other economic issues.

Arriving at that level of understanding will take some time. We begin by setting out some of the language we will be using. It may be tempting for you to read too fast, to skim through, figuring that you have heard all the words before. Don't. As we discussed in Chapter 1, the language has precise meaning to economists, and it is not necessarily the same as the meaning you have associated with it before.

Our next move is laying out the supply and demand model itself, starting with brief explanations of the term "demand" and then the term "supply." We then put them together on one graph to form our first look at the model and our first look at what economists call equilibrium. We then step back a moment to examine in detail demand and then supply.

With a rudimentary understanding of the supply and demand model we explore what happens in it when demand changes and then explore what happens in it when supply changes. Our last step shows why supply or demand changes require a change in the equilibrium.

DEFINITIONS

Markets

supply and demand
The name of the most important model in all of economics.

price
The amount of money that must be paid for a unit of output.

output
The good or service produced for sale.

market
Any mechanism by which buyers and sellers negotiate an exchange.

consumers
Those people in a market who want to exchange money for goods or services.

producers
Those people in a market who want to exchange goods or services for money.

equilibrium price
The price at which no consumers wish they could have purchased more goods at the price; no producers wish that they could have sold more.

equilibrium quantity
The amount of output exchanged at the equilibrium price.

quantity demanded
Amount consumers are willing and able to buy at a particular price during a particular period of time.

quantity supplied
Amount firms are willing and able to sell at a particular price during a particular period of time.

Supply and demand is the name of the most important model in all of economics. Economists use it to provide insight on the movements in **price** and **output.** Remember from Chapter 1 that a model is a simplification of a complicated real-life phenomenon. This model assumes that there is a **market** where buyers and sellers get together to trade. **Consumers** are assumed to bring money to the market, whereas **producers** are assumed to bring goods or services to the market. Consumers want to exchange their money for goods or services while producers want to exchange the goods or services they have for money.

It is important that you understand that the word "market" has a very specific meaning to economists and that it is very different from the business idea of "marketing." A market exists anywhere that buyers and sellers negotiate price and perform an exchange. Therefore, they have to be able to communicate and they have to be able to exchange. Take, as an example, the market for used midsized sedans. There are people who are looking to buy them and people who are looking to sell them. Prior to the Internet, most of the communication was geographically constrained. Buyers went to used-car lots or read ads in the newspaper. People who wanted to unload a car advertised by word of mouth, by newspaper, or sold to a dealer. With the Internet, the market is greatly expanded because communication (autotrader.com; Ebay.com, etc.) is easier but you still are unlikely to buy a car in Seattle if you live in Miami because the cost of getting the car from Seattle is prohibitive. Finally, "marketing" is what the used-car sales staff does to convince you to buy their cars. Try not to confuse the two.

The supply and demand model assumes that there are many consumers and producers, so that no one of them can dictate price. There is a price at which neither consumers nor producers leave with less value than they came with; no consumers wish they could have purchased more goods at the price; no producers wish that they could have sold more at that price—in short, everyone is better off for participating. Economists call such a price an **equilibrium price** and the amount that consumers buy from producers an **equilibrium quantity.** The nuts and bolts of this model are the supply and demand curves. The demand curve shows the relationship between the price consumers have to pay and how much they "want to buy," whereas the supply curve shows the relationship between the price firms receive and how much producers "want to sell." Economists refer to the amount that consumers want to buy at any particular price as the *quantity demanded* and the amount that firms want to sell at any particular price as *quantity supplied.*

People participate in markets because markets make their participants better off. Markets evolved because our ancestors recognized that self-sufficiency, though possible, did not allow people to take advantage of their particular skills. A social creation of humans, markets have been shaped by humankind to bring people together to exchange goods and services and because these exchanges have always been voluntary, participants have always left them content that they have gained from the market's existence. Thus markets have endured as a useful social institution because they continue to advance our individual and societal standard of living.

Quantity Demanded and Quantity Supplied

This is one place where everything you have read, heard, or seen in newspapers, on radio, or on TV will confuse you because economists use these terms very differently from the way they are used outside of economics. Economists insist on highlighting the difference between demand and quantity demanded. If you look carefully at the paragraph that is two above, the **quantity demanded** is how much consumers are willing and able to buy at a particular price during a particular period of time. Demand, on the other hand, shows how much consumers want to buy at all prices. An identical distinction exists with supply. **Quantity supplied** is

Markets Box

Markets exist whether the underlying economic system is capitalist, socialist, or communist. A **capitalist** economy is so-named because in addition to there being free markets in most goods and services, there are free markets in financial capital. Whether people have money to lend because they have saved it or inherited it, in a capitalist system, they control it. The profit that the capital generates goes to the owner of the capital. In a **communist** system, capital and the profit that it generates is controlled by a government authority. The government authority decides how the money is used. In a **socialist** system, a significant part of the profit generated by financial capital goes to the government in the form of taxes. The government then uses the tax money to counter the wealth impacts of the distribution of profit. No country is completely capitalist and few (possibly North Korea) are completely communist. Each country exists along a spectrum. The politically conservative Heritage Foundation, in conjunction with the *The Wall Street Journal*, developed an Index of Economic Freedom that measures the degree to which countries have free capital flows, minimal government regulation of business and labor, minimal limits on trade, and a legal system conducive to business. Selected countries are listed in the table below.

Heritage Foundation's Index of Economic Freedom

Free	Mostly Free	Mostly Unfree	Repressed
Hong Kong	Germany	Lebanon	Tajikistan
Singapore	Austria	Guyana	Haiti
Ireland	Belgium	Sri Lanka	Venezuela
New Zealand	Italy	Tunisia	Uzbekistan
United Kingdom	Taiwan	Bosnia	Iran
Denmark	Latvia	Guatemala	Cuba
Iceland	Norway	Colombia	Laos
Australia	Spain	Ukraine	Turkmenistan
Chile	Czech Republic	Brazil	Zimbabwe
Switzerland	Israel	Philippines	Libya
United States	Hungary	Kenya	Burma
Sweden	Slovak Republic	Georgia	North Korea
Finland	Portugal	Mozambique	
Canada	Japan	Egypt	
Netherlands	Poland	Tanzania	
	Uruguay	Honduras	
	France	Paraguay	
	South Korea	China	
	Bolivia	Turkey	
	Kuwait	Algeria	
	Peru	Argentina	
	South Africa	India	
	Greece	Indonesia	
	Cambodia	Rwanda	
	Mexico	Russia	
	Nicaragua	Romania	
	Albania	Ethiopia	
	Macedonia	Pakistan	
	Malaysia	Sierra Leone	
	Thailand	Republic of Congo	
	Saudi Arabia	Vietnam	
	Senegal	Bangladesh	
		Belarus	

http://www.heritage.org/research/features/index/.

how much firms are willing and able to sell at a particular price during a particular period of time, whereas supply alone shows how much firms want to sell at all prices.

Ceteris Paribus

Social scientists in general, and economists in particular, believe in something called the "scientific method," one aspect of which suggests that to isolate the effect of one variable on another you have to separate out the impacts of everything else. Unlike chemistry or biology, though, economists are rarely able to put their subjects (people) into a lab and experiment on them. For instance, economists cannot create a capitalist system in one area of town, a socialist system in another, and a communist system in a third so as to test which economic system serves society best. Economists have to observe in the context of their models. So, even though life does not progress one change at a time, our model allows us to focus on one change at a time. This brings us to the only Latin most economists know: **ceteris paribus,** which means other things equal.

Demand and Supply

For our demand curve we want to know what the relationship is between price and quantity demanded. Determining this relationship is difficult because the relationship depends on such things as whether people are rich or poor, whether the good is in or out of fashion, or how much rival goods cost. To get around this we assume we are looking at the relationship between price and quantity demanded in such a way that none of the other things are changing. Thus, **demand** is the relationship between price and quantity demanded, ceteris paribus.

Precisely the same logic applies to supply. There are many things upon which the relationship between price and quantity supplied depends: how much workers must be paid, the cost of materials, or the availability of technology. Again we assume these things do not change, so **supply** is the relationship between price and quantity supplied, ceteris paribus.

ceteris paribus
Latin for other things equal.

demand
The relationship between price and quantity demanded, ceteris paribus.

supply
The relationship between price and quantity supplied, ceteris paribus.

THE SUPPLY AND DEMAND MODEL

Demand

We have put it off long enough—let's look at the model. To plot a demand curve let's first tell ourselves a reasonable story and put the relevant information in a table. Suppose we are looking at soft drinks sold at a football game. There are obviously lots of things that will affect the supply and demand for soft drinks at a football game, but for the moment we are going to assume they are held constant.

We start this inquiry with the price of soft drinks at zero and ask how many will be wanted. Probably a lot, but not as many as you might think. You go to a game to see the game, not to drink (soft drinks at least), so you might get one at the beginning of the game, one at the end of the first quarter, one at halftime, one at the end of the third quarter, and one as you leave to go home. That would be five. Presuming that you do not differ from the rest of the crowd (of 10,000), that would mean that with a price set at zero, there would be a quantity demanded of 50,000 drinks.

Suppose the price were raised to 50 cents per drink. You might forgo the end-of-game drink so you (and everyone else) would want to buy four and the quantity demanded would be 40,000. Another 50-cent increase might have you cut out the first-quarter drink and the quantity demanded would continue to fall to three for you and 30,000 for the crowd. At $1.50 you might cut out the third-quarter drink and you would be down to two for you and 20,000 for the crowd. At $2.00 you might only get a halftime drink and you would be down to one for you and 10,000 for the crowd. Finally, at $2.50 you might not drink at all. Table 2.1 depicts the options we have just suggested in the form of what is called a **demand schedule.** A demand schedule presents the price and quantity demanded for a good in a tabular form.

demand schedule
Presentation, in tabular form, of the price and quantity demanded for a good.

TABLE 2.1

Demand schedule for soft drinks at a football game.

Price ($)	Your Quantity Demanded	Crowd Quantity Demanded (10,000 fans just like you)*
0	5	50,000
0.50	4	40,000
1.00	3	30,000
1.50	2	20,000
2.00	1	10,000
2.50	0	0

*This is ceteris paribus at work, holding the number and type of fans constant.

FIGURE 2.1

The demand curve.

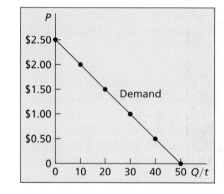

This information can also be displayed on a graph. As a matter of fact, that is how you will nearly always see it from now on. Figure 2.1 is a graph of a demand curve. Note that the vertical axis is labeled *P* for price and the horizontal axis is labeled *Q/t* for quantity per unit time. You probably anticipated the first label, but the second may require a short explanation. Quantity per unit time is that number of drinks that the 10,000 people will want during that particular game. There always has to be a time reference for quantities demanded and for quantities supplied. The dark dots represent the points from our demand schedule, and when we connect the dots we have a demand curve.

Supply

Now, using the same sporting event example, let's think about the sellers of soft drinks. Suppose for the sake of this example that the different concession stands are not required to charge the same price for sodas; that is, they are independent businesses. Also assume that there are 10 such stands around the stadium. Now ask yourself how many soft drinks a business would attempt to sell at various prices. Obviously they would not want to give any away, so at a price of zero, quantity supplied would be zero. Even at a very low price, such as 50 cents a cup, they might not want to sell any because the cost of hiring a worker to fill and sell drinks and the cost of the drinks themselves might be more than the 50 cents a cup they would get. As prices go up they would probably be willing to put forth more and more effort to make more and more money. For the sake of this example we will assume that at $1.00 per cup each business will want to sell 1,000 cups. At $1.50 we will assume they will each want to sell 2,000. At $2.00 we will assume it is 3,000 and at $2.50 we will assume it is 4,000. Table 2.2 displays this information in what is called a **supply schedule,** which presents in tabular form the price and quantity supplied for a good.

supply schedule
Presentation, in tabular form, of the price and quantity supplied for a good.

TABLE 2.2

Supply schedule for soft drinks at a football game.

Price ($)	One Concession Stand's Quantity Supplied	The Stadium's Quantity Supplied (all 10 concession stands)
0	0	0
0.50	0	0
1.00	1,000	10,000
1.50	2,000	20,000
2.00	3,000	30,000
2.50	4,000	40,000

FIGURE 2.2

The supply curve.

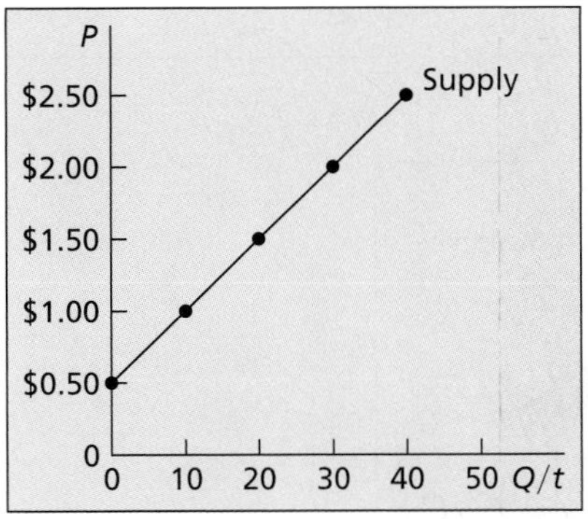

equilibrium

The point where the amount that consumers want to buy and the amount firms want to sell are the same. This occurs where the supply curve and the demand curve cross.

shortage

The condition where firms do not want to sell as many goods as consumers want to buy.

surplus

The condition where firms want to sell more goods than consumers want to buy.

excess demand

Another term for shortage.

excess supply

Another term for surplus.

This information can also be displayed on a graph. Figure 2.2 shows the supply curve with the axes labeled the same as Figure 2.1: price and quantity over time. Here the dark dots represent the points from our supply schedule. When we connect the dots we have a supply curve.

Equilibrium

Table 2.3 combines the supply schedule and the demand schedule into a single schedule and Figure 2.3 combines the supply curve and demand curve on one diagram. They both show us that at prices below $1.50 consumers want more soft drinks than concession stand operators are willing to provide and that at prices above $1.50 they want fewer soft drinks than concession stand operators are willing to sell. Where the supply and demand curves cross, the amount that consumers want to buy and the amount firms want to sell are the same. This is called an **equilibrium.**

Shortages and Surpluses

When the price is too low we have a **shortage.** Firms do not want to sell as many goods as consumers want to buy. When the price is too high we have a **surplus.** Firms want to sell more goods than consumers want to buy.

Imagine that the concession stands start to run out of soft drinks at our mythical football game. There is an obvious shortage of soft drinks. According to the model of supply and demand, this will have occurred because the price was too low. With long lines of people wanting to buy sodas in front of them, the vendors will see that in the face of a shortage, or **excess demand,** they can raise the price and still sell their product. The opposite will occur if there is a surplus, or **excess supply.** If the price is too high, the vendors will want to sell more soft drinks than consumers will want. Instead of long lines there will be excess inventory and firms will see that in the face of a surplus they should lower the price to get rid of it.

TABLE 2.3   Supply and demand schedules with shortage and surplus.

Price ($)	Individual Quantity Demanded	Crowd Quantity Demanded	One Concession Stand's Quantity Supplied	The Stadium's Quantity Supplied	Shortage (excess demand)	Surplus (excess supply)
0	5	50,000	0	0	50,000	
0.50	4	40,000	0	0	40,000	
1.00	3	30,000	1,000	10,000	20,000	
1.50	2	20,000	2,000	20,000		
2.00	1	10,000	3,000	30,000		20,000
2.50	0	0	4,000	40,000		40,000

FIGURE 2.3
The supply and demand model and equilibrium price and quantity.

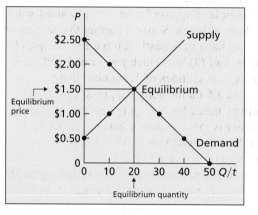

With self-interested sellers, shortages and surpluses are short-lived. Firms react to changes in inventories by changing the price they charge. They react to shortages with price increases and surpluses with price cuts, and as a result either situation is temporary.

ALL ABOUT DEMAND

The Law of Demand

We know from this chapter's section on definitions that demand is the relationship between price and quantity demanded, ceteris paribus, and we followed a reasonably believable story about soft drinks at a football game. That story implied that there was a negative relationship between price and quantity demanded. Because of the relationship, the demand curve we drew was downward sloping. The negative relationship between price and quantity demanded is called the **law of demand.** This "law" is not really a law but is common sense applied to the following rather constant observation: when prices are higher, we tend to buy less.

Why Does the Law of Demand Make Sense?

Why do we see this negative relationship so often? There are three distinct reasons. First, when you go to the store and find that the good you want is highly priced, you search for an acceptable substitute that costs less. If you buy something else, you are substituting another good for

law of demand
The statement that the relationship between price and quantity demanded is a negative or inverse one.

substitution effect
Purchase of less of a
product than originally
wanted when its price is
high because a lower
priced product is
available.

real-balances effect
When a price increases
your buying power is
decreased, causing you
to buy less.

the one that you originally wanted because its price was too high. Economists say that this is a **substitution effect.** You buy less of what you originally wanted when its price is high because you use something else instead.

Second, suppose you cannot find an acceptable substitute. In this case you are stuck buying less of the good because you cannot afford as much. What has happened is that your real buying power has fallen (even though the money you have in your wallet is the same) because prices have risen. This does not necessarily work for all goods (especially basic necessities like water), but generally economists call this a **real-balances effect** because when a price increases it decreases your buying power, causing you to buy less.

The third reason we see a negative relationship between price and quantity demanded can be explained with either great detail, or a useful lie. You are in this course and your professor has chosen this book because you do not need the great detail, so you will get the useful lie.[1] It starts from the premise that what you are willing to pay for something depends on how many you have recently had. With this in mind, consider the following very silly but illustrative example. Suppose I give you $10 and I want to know how much you would pay for pizza slices at lunch. Suppose further that as part of this experiment you are given truth serum so you have to honestly tell me two things: (1) on a scale from 1 to 10, how happy your belly is; and (2) how much you valued each slice in terms of money. Starting hungry at a belly happiness index of 1, suppose that you eat one slice and tell me that it was worth $3 and rated a 5 on the belly happiness index. Now you eat another slice and tell me it wasn't worth as much because you were not as hungry, so you say it was worth $2 and your belly happiness index rose to 8. You eat the third slice and tell me that because you were somewhat full at the time you ate the third slice your belly happiness index only rose to 9 and the slice was only worth $1.

In this scenario each time you consume a slice, the value you place on the next slice falls. This means that the value you place on a good depends on how many you have already had. Economists refer to the amount of extra happiness[2] that people get from an additional unit of consumption as **marginal utility** and say that it decreases as you consume more. This **law of diminishing marginal utility** suggests that the amount of additional happiness that you get from an additional unit of consumption falls with each additional unit. Stated more simply, because each additional slice increases your happiness less than the previous slice, the most you would be willing to pay for each additional slice is less than before. The third reason why a demand curve is downward sloping, then, is that for most goods there is diminishing marginal utility.

marginal utility
The amount of extra
happiness that people
get from an additional
unit of consumption.

**law of diminishing
marginal utility**
The amount of
additional happiness
that you get from an
additional unit of
consumption falls with
each additional unit.

It is often helpful to view the demand curve as more than a way of finding how much of a good a person wants at a particular price. In addition, you can use it to find out how much a person is "willing to pay" for a particular amount of the good. Whenever you come across this phrase, think "the most they would be willing to pay." Of course you would always want to pay less, but looked at this way the demand curve also represents the most you would be willing to pay for different amounts of the good, ceteris paribus.

---

[1]Before you get too upset about the notion of useful lies think about stories we tell our children. Age 3: "Santa will not come if you do not go to bed"; age 8: "You always subtract the smaller number from the bigger number"; age 15: "You can't take the square root of a negative number."

[2]Here lies the useful lie. Most economists do not believe that you can measure happiness in the same way that you measure distance or temperature. This means that though you can say you are happier in one circumstance than in another, you cannot say how much happier you are. All is not lost, though, because we can get the same idea through the concept of indifference. The reason no one-semester course textbooks explain the downward-sloping nature of demand using the concept of indifference is that it takes too long and gets you no further in your understanding than the last two paragraphs have. Thus the lie of marginal utility nets the same result in a lot less time and is judged by most teachers of one-semester economics courses as useful.

ALL ABOUT SUPPLY

The Law of Supply

We also know from our section on definitions that supply is the relationship between price and quantity supplied, ceteris paribus, and we followed an equally reasonably believable story about how many soft drinks a business would want to sell at a football game. That story implied that there was a positive relationship between price and quantity supplied. Because of that the supply curve we drew was upward sloping. The positive relationship between price and quantity supplied is called the **law of supply.** Like all other laws in economics, this one isn't a law either but is more like a hypothesis that is supported by nearly all the evidence nearly all the time. Stated more simply: when prices are higher, firms tend to want to sell more.

law of supply
The statement that there is a positive relationship between price and quantity supplied.

Why Does the Law of Supply Make Sense?

Though believable intuitively, the technical reason that a supply curve is upward sloping takes up much of Chapters 4 and 5. What follows is a simplified (though probably not simple) explanation that will be repeated and expanded in Chapters 4 and 5.

Suppose the stadium at which we are selling soft drinks has three levels. Suppose our stand is on the first level with most of the fans, that we would have to walk up a moderately long set of steps to get to the second level and they were somewhat more dispersed, and finally, to get to the third level we would have to walk up a very long set of steps and nearly no one was up there. Even at relatively low prices it would be worth it to sell in the stands to the folks in the first level, but unless prices rose it would not be worth the effort to sell in the upper levels. We can imagine that if we could charge somewhat higher prices, it would be worth it to make it to the second level and that if prices were quite a bit higher we might venture into the nose-bleed territory to sell.

What this means, and what Chapters 4 and 5 attempt to demonstrate in detail, is that the reason the supply curve is upward sloping is that it costs more per unit to sell more units. In this example, the soft drink was not any more expensive, but the cost of transporting it was higher when we sold to more remote areas.

DETERMINANTS OF DEMAND

In the previous section we talked about holding other things constant. Now is the time to consider what happens when things change. As we alluded to in the section on definitions, there are many things that affect the demand relationship for a good. These include how much the good is liked, how much income people have, how much other goods cost, the population of potential buyers, and the expectations of the price in the future. These variables will change how much of the good is wanted as well as how much someone is willing to pay for it. Again "willing to pay" is shorthand for the most someone is willing to pay. If people want more of the good, this also translates into willingness to pay prices that they would not have paid before.

Taste

Taste is the word that economists use to describe whether the good is in fashion or whether conditions are right for many people to want the good. A high level of taste means that the good is in fashion or highly desired; a low level of taste means that few people want it. It works on demand in an obvious way: the more people like the good (the higher the taste for the good), the more they are willing to pay higher prices for any particular amount and the more of it they will want.

Determinants of Demand

Taste
> Determinant of whether the good is in fashion or whether conditions are right for many people to want the good.

Income
> **Inferior goods:** You buy less of a good when you have more income.
> **Normal goods:** You buy more of a good when you have more income.

Price of other goods
> **Substitute:** Goods used instead of one another.
> **Complement:** Goods that are used together.

Population of potential buyers
> The number of people potentially interested in a product.

Expected price
> The price that you expect will exist in the future.

Income

How much **income** people have to buy the good also matters but not always in a positive way. Consider a couple of staples in the college diet, instant ramen noodles and macaroni and cheese. No matter which of these you eat, you can fill your belly for under 50 cents. Now ask yourself how many pouches, boxes, or bags of this stuff you would buy if your grandmother died and left you $25,000. Answer: not many, particularly if you have been eating them because you could not afford other things to eat. This example shows you that it is not always the case that the more you make, the more you buy. In cases where you buy less of a good when you have more income, economists call the good **inferior.** If the good is inferior and your income rises, you are able to buy more but you want to buy less of the good and you will need lower prices to induce you to buy any particular quantity.

On the other hand, for most goods an increase in income will lead to an increase in the amount that consumers want. In cases where you buy more of a good when you have more income, economists call the good **normal.** If the good is normal and your income rises, you are able to buy more and you want to buy more of the good and you are willing to pay more for it.

Price of Other Goods

Similarly, there is no straightforward answer to the question of how you will change your willingness to purchase a good if the price of another good rises. It is possible that if the price of a good like Pepsi rises, you will switch to Coke. In that case you would be willing to pay more for Coke and want to buy more of it. Likewise, if the price of hot dogs increases, you will decide to buy fewer of them. Since hot dog buns have little good use other than to surround hot dogs, you will need fewer of these too. Economists say that goods used instead of one another e.g., Coke and Pepsi) are **substitutes** and that goods that are used together (e.g., hot dogs and hot dog buns) are **complements.**

Examples of substitutes and complements abound. Peanut butter and jelly are often considered complements because they are typically used together to produce sandwiches. Pepperoni and sausage might be considered substitutes because they are alternative meats for a pizza. To confuse matters, though, goods can be substitutes to some and complements to others. My father-in-law considers peanut butter and jelly to be equally good bagel spreads so to him they are substitutes. The Meat Lover's Pizza by Pizza Hut includes both sausage and pepperoni so to people who like this pizza the two may be complements.

Population of Potential Buyers

The number of people potentially interested in a product will clearly have an impact on the demand for the product. For instance, in the dark ages of the 1970s, when there were only a few computer-literate people, only a few people were interested in buying computers. Then schoolchildren, and especially college students, began to rely on computers for their school-work, creating a group of potentially interested customers when they graduated. Economists shorten this concept of the number of people potentially interested in a product to call it the **population.**

Expected Price

Last, when the **expected price of a good** rises, this induces a stock-up effect. Smokers stock up when a tax increase is expected. Frugal drivers buy gas on Wednesdays, before the nearly universal weekend price increase. If there is an expectation that an increase in price is imminent, consumers will be willing to pay more and they will want to buy now rather than later.

The Effect of Changes in the Determinants of Demand on the Supply and Demand Model

Tables 2.4 and 2.5 summarize how the determinants of demand work on the supply and demand diagram. Table 2.4 indicates the impact of increases in the variables listed above, whereas Table 2.5 indicates the impact of decreases in those variables. The final column of each table refers to the figure corresponding to the change. Figure 2.4 shows the impact of an increase in demand while Figure 2.5 shows the impact of a decrease in demand. In each figure, the original supply and demand curves are shown in black and the new demand curve is shown in the blue color. The original equilibrium is shown with the big black dot, and the new equilibrium is shown with the big blue-colored dot.

TABLE 2.4   Movements in the demand curve: increases in the values of the determinants.

An Increase in	Causes Demand to	Causes the Demand Curve to Move to the	And Is Shown in Figure
Taste	Increase	Right	2.4
Income, normal good	Increase	Right	2.4
Income, inferior good	Decrease	Left	2.5
Price of other goods, complement	Decrease	Left	2.5
Price of other goods, substitute	Increase	Right	2.4
Population	Increase	Right	2.4
Expected future price	Increase	Right	2.4

TABLE 2.5 Movements in the demand curve: decreases in the values of the determinants.

A Decrease in	Causes Demand to	Causes the Demand Curve to Move to the	And Is Shown in Figure
Taste	Decrease	Left	2.5
Income, normal good	Decrease	Left	2.5
Income, inferior good	Increase	Right	2.4
Price of other goods, complement	Increase	Right	2.4
Price of other goods, substitute	Decrease	Left	2.5
Population	Decrease	Left	2.5
Expected future price	Decrease	Left	2.5

FIGURE 2.4 The effect of an increase in demand on the supply and demand model.

FIGURE 2.5 The effect of a decrease in demand on the supply and demand model.

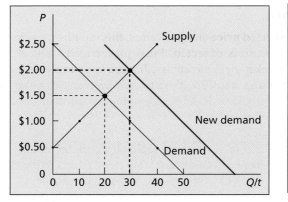

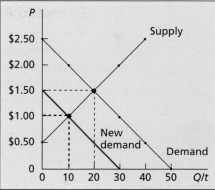

DETERMINANTS OF SUPPLY

Again, the definitions section alluded to the types of things that can change the supply relationship. They include changes in the price of inputs, technology, price of other potential output, the number of sellers, and expected future price. Again we are assuming that other things are held constant.

Price of Inputs

The **price of inputs** refers to the costs to firms of all the things necessary to produce output. If an input is used to make a product, then the input costs money and therefore has a price even though its name may change. Obvious examples of inputs are raw material, labor, and equipment. The price of a raw material is simply its price. (Though this sounds like a circular definition, think about our soft drink example. The cups, the carbonated water, and syrup canisters have a price.) The price of labor is the wage + benefit cost to employers associated with hiring a person. (Everything that employers pay for that is not paid directly to workers—health insurance, unemployment insurance, worker's compensation, and so on, are defined as benefits.) The price of equipment can affect supply but just as often what matters is the rental cost of leased equipment or the interest + depreciation rates that must be paid on the equipment bought with

Determinants of Supply

Price of inputs: Costs to firms of all the things necessary to produce output.

Technology: The ability to turn input into output.

Price of other potential output: When firms have to decide which good to produce they will want to produce the one that makes them the most money.

Number of sellers: The number of firms competing in the same market.

Expected future price: Firms want to hold back sales to wait for higher prices and unload inventory before prices fall.

borrowed money. (Interest is the price of borrowed money, and depreciation is the rate at which machines lose value owing to wear and tear.)

Technology

Within economics, the word **technology** refers to the ability to turn input into output. In our previous example of selling sodas at a football game a technological advance that would allow workers to fill a cup with Diet Coke without having to wait several seconds for the foam to settle would reduce wasted employee time. This technology would increase output and lower costs. As we are using it here, the technology variable can change because of increases in the ability of employees to work harder and smarter, or it can change because new devices make employees more efficient.

Another example of how increases in technology change markets can be seen in the *very illegal* term paper business. If you wanted to buy term papers in the 1960s you would have had to pay people to go to the library to look stuff up in card catalogs of alphabetized index cards and indices of periodicals to find source material. Because access to copy machines was limited, they would have then had to read the material in the library. Finally, they would have had to type the paper on a typewriter, and they would have been able to fix mistakes only with a pasty liquid called White-Out. Paying people to do this would be expensive.

In the 1970s all the steps were the same except copy machines would have allowed the people you hired to read source material in their homes. In the 1980s primitive computers would have allowed them to gather limited quantities of source material on a computer and to write the paper using a hard-to-use, not very flexible word processor. By the 1990s writers of term papers could look up material on the Internet, print it, read it, and write the paper, all from the comfort of their own bedrooms. In each of these periods producers of such contraband had to find a way to sell their papers. Often informal networks had to be created and payment had to be in cash. Today, you can go to any number of term paper sites on the Internet and download a paper by simply entering a credit card number. You, of course, would never do this because your college can easily catch you and throw you out of school. But because it is easier to produce papers in less time than used to be the case, sellers of term papers can charge lower prices and produce more papers.

Price of Other Potential Outputs

The **price of other potential output** refers to the idea that when firms have to decide which good to produce they will want to produce the one that makes them the most money. If the price of one falls, they will want to produce less of the cheaper good and use the resources to produce

TABLE 2.6 Movements in the supply curve: increases in the values of the determinants.

An Increase in	Causes Supply to	Causes the Supply Curve to Move to the	And Is Shown in Figure
Price of inputs	Decrease	Left	2.7
Technology	Increase	Right	2.6
Price of other potential outputs	Decrease	Left	2.7
Number of sellers	Increase	Right	2.6
Expected future price	Decrease	Left	2.7

more of the other good. When farmers are choosing planting options for the growing season, they want to make as much money as possible. If they are grain farmers, they will have to decide which fields will be planted in corn and which will be planted in soybeans.[3] If the price of corn falls, they will change planting decisions to plant less corn and plant more soybeans.

Number of Sellers

The **number of sellers,** that is, the number of firms competing in the same market, is important because the more firms there are, the greater is total market production. Using the soft drink example, we assumed that there were 10 different concession stands at this game. If these concession stands are all making a profit, it is likely that other entrepreneurs will want to set up their own stands. This raises total market supply. Similarly, if there were losses, some of those concession stands may close, reducing total market supply.

Expected Price

The **expected future price** should sound familiar because it is also something that will change demand. In the context of supply, it refers to a firm's desire to hold back sales to wait for higher prices and its desire to sell its goods and thus lower its inventory before prices fall. Firms want to sell their goods when they can make the most money regardless of when that time is. A warning that a hurricane is coming will bid up the current price of gas-powered generators because firms will want to retain those they have in stock to sell at high prices after the hurricane hits. Conversely, if firms figure that the goods they hold will be out of fashion soon, they will want to get rid of them now.

The Effect of Changes in the Determinants of Supply on the Supply and Demand Model

Tables 2.6 and 2.7 summarize how determinants of supply work on a supply and demand model. Table 2.6 indicates the impact of increases in the variables listed above, whereas Table 2.7 indicates the impact of decreases in those variables. It is important to understand that on the supply side an increase in supply is shown by a movement to the right in the supply curve and that a decrease in supply is shown by a movement to the left in the supply curve. As with Tables 2.4 and 2.5 the final columns of Tables 2.6 and 2.7 refer to the figures corresponding to

---

[3]Typically that decision is based on what was planted the year before. Crop rotation is key because more corn can be harvested from a field that produced soybeans in the previous year than from a field in which corn had been grown the previous year.

TABLE 2.7   Movements in the supply curve: decreases in the values of the determinants.

A Decrease in	Causes Supply to	Causes the Supply Curve to Move to the	And Is Shown in Figure
Price of inputs	Increase	Right	2.6
Technology	Decrease	Left	2.7
Price of other potential outputs	Increase	Right	2.6
Number of sellers	Decrease	Left	2.7
Expected future price	Increase	Right	2.6

FIGURE 2.6   The effect of an increase in supply on the supply and demand model.

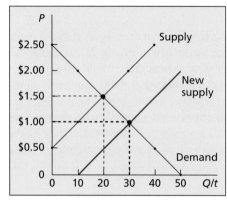

FIGURE 2.7   The effect of a decrease in supply on the supply and demand model.

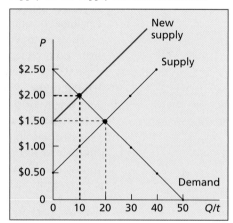

the changes. Figure 2.6 shows the impact of an increase in supply while Figure 2.7 shows the impact of a decrease in supply. Just as it was for Tables 2.4 and 2.5 and Figures 2.4 and 2.5, the original supply and demand curves are shown in black and the original equilibrium is shown with the big black dot. This time the new supply curve is shown in the rust color with the new equilibrium shown with the big blue-colored dot.

THE EFFECT OF CHANGES IN PRICE EXPECTATIONS ON THE SUPPLY AND DEMAND MODEL

If you have not already noticed, expected future price shows up in both the determinants of demand and the determinants of supply. This means that if the expected future price changes, both the supply and demand curves change as well. If the expected future price rises, consumers will want to stock up, thereby increasing demand. Firms, on the other hand, will want to hold back their inventory to wait for the price increase, thereby decreasing supply. In this case we do not know what will happen to equilibrium quantity because the demand shift will, by itself, increase quantity, whereas the supply shift will, by itself, decrease quantity. Whether there is a net increase or decrease in equilibrium quantity depends on which shift is greater. On the other hand, the effect on price is known, and it amounts to a self-fulfilling prophecy because a credible prediction of a future price increase will lead to an actual current price increase.

When expected prices rise we know that the current price will rise but we do not know what will happen to the quantity. This is because we do not know whether firms' desire to wait for price increases will be stronger than consumers' desire to stock up. When the price is expected to fall, firms will want to get rid of their inventory and consumers will want to wait for the new lower prices.

When expected prices fall we know that the current price will fall but we again do not know what will happen to the quantity. This is because we do not know whether firms' desire to unload inventory will be stronger than consumers' desire to wait for lower prices.

Kick It Up **A Notch**

WHY THE NEW EQUILIBRIUM?

When either the supply curve or the demand curve shifts, the equilibrium has to change. If it does not, one of two things will happen: There will be a shortage where consumers want to buy more than firms want to sell, or there will be a surplus where firms want to sell more than consumers want to buy.

To show that this is the case imagine that there is an increase in the demand for a good and firms do not increase the price. As shown in Figure 2.8, keeping the price at the old equilibrium would set up a situation where consumers would want more (40) than firms would be willing to sell (20). The resulting shortage would not be eliminated unless there was an increase in the price.

A somewhat different problem would happen if firms did not lower their price in the face of decreased demand. Figure 2.9 shows that keeping the price at the old equilibrium with a decrease in demand would set up a situation where consumers would want fewer (0) than firms would be willing to sell (20). The resulting surplus would not be eliminated unless there was a decrease in the price.

Just as we needed a new equilibrium when there was a change in demand, we need one when there is a change in supply. Figure 2.10 shows that keeping the price at the old equilibrium when supply increases sets up a situation where consumers want fewer (20) than firms are willing to sell (40). The resulting surplus will not be eliminated unless there is a decrease in the price.

Finally, if firms do not raise their prices in the face of decreased supply, there will be a shortage. Figure 2.11 shows that keeping the price at the old equilibrium in the face of decreased supply sets up a situation where consumers want more (20) than firms are willing to sell (0). The resulting shortage will be eliminated unless there is an increase in the price.

FIGURE 2.8   The shortage that is created when demand increases if price and quantity do not.

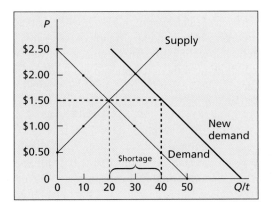

FIGURE 2.9   The surplus that is created when demand decreases if price and quantity do not.

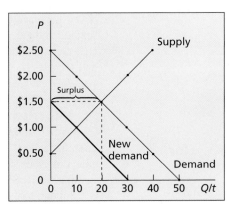

FIGURE 2.10   The surplus that is created when supply increases if price and quantity do not.

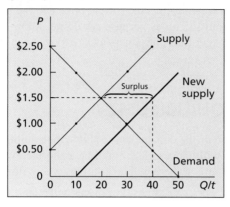

FIGURE 2.11   The shortage that is created when supply decreases if price and quantity do not.

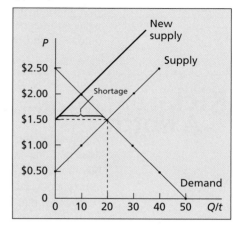

What lesson can you draw from all of this? A change in either the supply or demand curve will change the price at which the quantity consumers want to buy equals the quantity that firms want to sell. If the price does not change, either a surplus or a shortage will ensue.

There are circumstances when a new equilibrium will not be achieved. For instance, **price gouging** is the name given to the situation in which a rapid increase in demand is followed by a rapid increase in price. When demand increases, firms do not have to raise prices to cover costs; they raise prices because they can. Laws preventing price gouging are relatively common.

If you sell ice and have a freezerful to sell, in many states you are not allowed to raise the price of it more than a specified percentage if your community loses electrical power. Economists call the maximum price allowed by law a **price ceiling.** Once the price hits that level, it cannot rise further and you have a shortage for that good. Other examples of price ceilings involve rent control and laws that prevent ticket scalping.

Similarly, equilibrium will not be achieved if there is a **price floor.** This exists when a price may not fall below a certain legally proscribed level. In that circumstance, there is a surplus of the good. Examples of this include farm price supports and the existence of the minimum wage.

price gouging
The pejorative term applied to the circumstance when firms raise prices substantially when demand increases unexpectedly.

price ceiling
The level above which a price may not rise.

price floor
Price below which a commodity may not sell.

Summary

The supply and demand model is the single most important model in economics. More than half the issues that you deal with in the latter part of this book will rely on your ability to put an economics problem into the context of this model. In the course of this chapter we explained the supply and demand model by providing all of the language up front. We explained both supply and demand in isolation and then put them together in the form of a coherent model. We then talked about what variables might change demand and then which ones might change supply. We showed that prices and quantities sold would have to change to maintain an equilibrium.

Key Terms

capitalism, 18
ceteris paribus, 19
communism, 18
consumers, 17

demand, 19
demand schedule, 19
equilibrium, 21
equilibrium price, 17

equilibrium quantity, 17
excess demand, 21
excess supply, 21
law of demand, 22

Issues Chapters You Are Ready For Now

Quiz Yourself

1. The supply and demand model examines how prices and quantities are determined
    a. In markets.
    b. By governments.
    c. By churches.
    d. By monopolists.

2. On the Heritage Foundation's scale of "economic freedom," the least "free" country
   would be that one who's economic system was purely
    a. Capitalist.
    b. Socialist.
    c. Unitarian.
    d. Communist.

3. When an economics student draws a supply and demand diagram to model an increase
   in the income, she is assuming this change happens
    a. Semper fidelis.
    b. Ceteris paribus.
    c. Ipso facto.
    d. De facto.

4. If the supply and demand curves cross at a price of $2, at any price above that there
   will be
    a. An equilibrium.
    b. A surplus.
    c. A shortage.
    d. A crisis.

5. If the supply and demand curves cross at a quantity of 100, then the price necessary to
   get firms to sell more than that will have to be_____equilibrium.
    a. Above.
    b. At.
    c. Below.
    d. Within 10 percent either way of.

6. An increase in which of the following determinants of demand will have an ambiguous
   (uncertain) effect on price?
    a. Taste.
    b. Price of a complement.
    c. Income.
    d. Price of a substitute.

7. Which of the following will impact both supply and demand?
   a. A change in price.
   b. A change in quantity.
   c. A change in expected future price.
   d. A change in income.

8. An increase in the income of consumers will cause the
   a. Supply of all goods to rise.
   b. Demand for all goods to rise.
   c. Supply of all goods to fall.
   d. The demand for some goods to rise and for others to fall.

9. Without an increase in price, an increase in demand will lead to
   a. A shortage.
   b. A surplus.
   c. Socialism.
   d. Equilibrium.

10. The underlying reason for the upward-sloping nature of the supply curve is that
    a. The production of most goods comes with increasing marginal benefits.
    b. The production of most goods comes with increasing marginal costs.
    c. The consumption of most goods comes with decreasing marginal utility.
    d. The consumption of most goods comes with increasing marginal utility.

Think about This

Using simple supply and demand analysis, think about the system of allocating human kidneys. The law that forbids the sale of human organs but allows their voluntary donation means that there is a bigger shortage of kidneys than there otherwise would be. Does this fact alter your view of the law forbidding the sale of human organs? How about blood?

Talk about This

Are markets always right? List some markets that you think get the production or price of a good wrong. What do these goods have in common?

Chapter **3**

The Concept of Elasticity and Consumer and Producer Surplus

Chapter Objectives

After reading this chapter you should be able to

Understand that "elasticity," the responsiveness of quantity to changes in price, is an important concept in economics.

Recognize the relationship between the concept of elasticity and the appearance of the demand curve.

Understand and show that a market equilibrium provides both buyers and sellers with benefits. Consumers pay less than they are willing to pay and producers make a profit. Economists call the former "consumer surplus" and the latter, "producer surplus."

Recognize "deadweight loss," a circumstance which comes into play when prices that are too high or too low create inefficiencies.

Chapter Outline

We now change gears a bit and reconsider the individual supply and demand curves. Our focus here is on the ability of consumers and producers to react to price changes with changes in the amounts they wish to buy or sell. That ability to react, called *elasticity*, will be very important to us as we prepare to use the supply and demand model for issues. We will see how differently shaped demand curves will reflect the degree to which price changes affect quantity.

The last third of the chapter is central in our analysis of several issues. We will see how the supply and demand model can be used to explain why markets are effective in pleasing both consumers and producers. Though we know that consumers long for low prices and producers for high prices, we will see that when a consumer buys something from a producer, both can be pleased with the outcome. We will also see why the net benefit to society is lower when prices are not at equilibrium than it would be if equilibrium were at work.

ELASTICITY OF DEMAND

Intuition

In the previous chapter we saw that a change in supply or demand changes the equilibrium price–quantity combination, but we did not discuss which one changes more. For instance, if costs to a firm go up, it is reasonable to ask whether the firm will pass that price increase on to consumers or be willing to accept lower profits. Exploring this question brings in the concept of elasticity.

If the good is one that you need to survive and that has no good substitutes, or if it is one that you spend very little money on, the firm may be able to pass on its increased costs to you in the form of higher prices. On the other hand, if it is a luxury, that is, a good you can do without, if there are many other things that will serve just as well, or if you already spend a lot of your income on it and could not afford a price increase, you may buy a lot fewer. In this case the firm's profits are eaten up.

elasticity
The responsiveness of quantity to a change in another variable.

price elasticity of demand
The responsiveness of quantity demanded to a change in price.

price elasticity of supply
The responsiveness of quantity supplied to a change in price.

income elasticity of demand
The responsiveness of quantity to a change in income.

cross-price elasticity of demand
The responsiveness of quantity of one good to a change in the price of another good.

Definition of Elasticity and Its Formula

There are many kinds of elasticity. In general, **elasticity** is the responsiveness of quantity to a change in another variable. The two most commonly referred to elasticities are the **price elasticity of demand** and the **price elasticity of supply.** Respectively, these are the responsiveness of quantity demanded to a change in price and the responsiveness of quantity supplied to a change in price. Other elasticities include the **income elasticity of demand** and the **cross-price elasticity of demand.** The former measures the responsiveness of quantity to changes in income, and the latter measures the responsiveness of quantity to changes in the price of another good.

The price elasticity of demand is measured by looking at how a percentage change in price affects the percentage change in quantity demanded. The formula for elasticity is

$$\text{Elasticity} = \frac{\%\Delta Q}{\%\Delta P} = \frac{\Delta Q/Q^*}{\Delta P/P^*}$$

where

$\%$ = percent
Δ = change
P^* = price (read as "P star")
Q^* = quantity (Q star)

The other elasticities are similar in that the percentage change in either quantity demanded or quantity supplied is in the numerator and the percentage change in the price, income, or other price is in the denominator. Because the bulk of the issues that deal with elasticity deal with price elasticity of demand, we focus here on this particular form of the concept.

From here there are two ways of proceeding: We can explain everything in a great deal of mathematical detail or not. Guessing that the chorus is singing "not," we will skip the math.

elastic

The circumstance when the percentage change in quantity is larger than the percentage change in price.

inelastic

The circumstance when the percentage change in quantity is smaller than the percentage change in price.

unitary elastic

The circumstance when the percentage change in quantity is equal to the percentage change in price.

You will need now to follow the "English" explanations to understand and accept the conclusions about elasticity.

When you use the elasticity of demand formula you will always get a negative number for it. For our purposes we will simplify things by ignoring the negative sign. The negative sign appears because the demand curve is downward sloping, and an increase in price will therefore cause a decrease in quantity. To illustrate, if a 5 percent increase in price leads to a 10 percent decrease in quantity, the elasticity fraction is $-0.10/.05$. Since the important thing about elasticity is the value of the fraction itself, it is acceptable and less complicated for us to ignore the minus sign.

Elasticity Labels

This brings us to an important distinction that will be vital when we look at issues that hinge on whether demand is elastic or inelastic—for example, whether increasing the tax on cigarettes leads to decreases in teen smoking. Economists say that demand is **elastic** when the percentage change in quantity is larger than the percentage change in price and **inelastic** when the percentage change in quantity is smaller than the percentage change in price. Looking at the formula, if the computed elasticity is greater than 1, then demand is elastic; when it is less than 1, then demand is inelastic. When the percentage change in quantity is the same as the percentage change in price (the computed elasticity is exactly 1), demand is **unitary elastic.**

ALTERNATIVE WAYS TO UNDERSTAND ELASTICITY

To see this more clearly let's look at it using three different thought processes. First we look at elasticity using the graph of our demand curve. Then we look at it using only words. Last, we look at it in terms of how much money is spent on the good.

The Graphical Explanation

We first examine the elasticity phenomenon using graphical skills. Figure 3.1 shows that the flatter the demand curve, the greater the elasticity. This is *not* to say that slope and elasticity are the same thing; it just means that slope matters. To see that slope matters look at Figures 3.1 and 3.2. Though they are in separate diagrams, both go through the point $P = \$8$, $Q = 4$. Suppose you were to ask how much price would have to rise in order to induce a reduction in quantity demanded to 3. In Figure 3.1 you can see that it would take an increase to \$9, whereas in Figure 3.2 it would require an increase to \$12. What that implies is that on the steeper curve (Figure 3.2) demand is less elastic and on the flatter one (Figure 3.1) it is more elastic. In Figure 3.1, a 12.5 percent increase in prices results in a 25 percent reduction in quantity.[1] In Figure 3.2 it takes a 50 percent increase in price to generate a 25 percent decrease in quantity.

Figure 3.3 shows that the higher the price, the greater the elasticity. The price increase from 2 to 3 causes a decrease in quantity from 11 to 10. The same size increase in price from 8 to 9 causes the same size decrease in quantity from 4 to 3. This is because the slope of this demand curve is the same at all those points. Looking at the formula again, we see it is the percentage changes that matter and not just the size of those changes. Even though the price increases and quantity decreases are the same, the percentage changes are very different.

From point D to C the percentage change in price from 2 to 3 is a sizable 50 percent while the percentage change in quantity from 11 to 10 is negligible, only 9.1 percent. Since the percentage change in the price is greater than the percentage change in the quantity, demand is inelastic here (elasticity is low). On the other hand, from point B to A the percentage change in price from 8 to

---

[1]A price increase from 8 to 9 is a 12.5 percent increase because it is the fraction 1/8. It is a 25 percent decrease in quantity because it went from 4 to 3 (1/4).

FIGURE 3.1 At a given price, a flatter demand curve is more elastic than a steeper one.

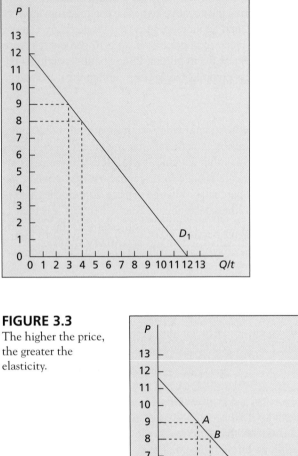

FIGURE 3.2 At a given price, a steeper demand curve is more inelastic than a flatter one.

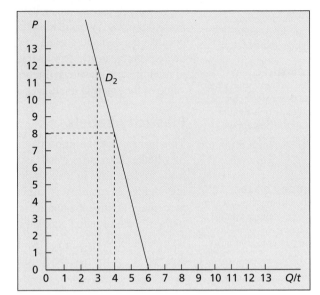

FIGURE 3.3
The higher the price, the greater the elasticity.

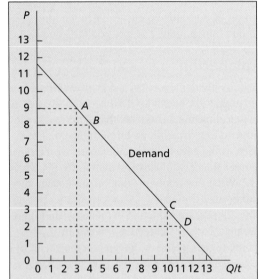

9 is only 12.5 percent whereas the percentage change in quantity from 4 to 3 is large (25 percent, visually about 33 percent). As a result, demand here is elastic (elasticity is high).

The Verbal Explanation

Although the graphical explanation of elasticity is highly accurate, if it does not make sense to you, it is useless. Recall the original definition of elasticity (the reaction of quantity to a change in price). If you really need a product because there are no good substitutes (like insulin to a diabetic), you will hardly change the amount you buy when the price changes. Thus there is

Determinants of Elasticity of Demand

Number and closeness of substitutes: The more alternatives you have, the less likely you are to pay high prices for a good and the more likely you are to settle for an adequate alternative.

Time: The longer you have to come up with alternatives to paying high prices, the more likely it is you will shift to those alternatives.

little, if any, reaction of quantity to changes in price. The demand curve for a good you "need" is going to be rather steep. If the good is a luxury item, you are more likely to eliminate it from your budget if it becomes overly expensive. In this case there is a substantial reaction of quantity to a change in price. The demand curve for a luxury is likely to be flatter.

In addition, price changes for goods that take up little of your income (like drinking water) are not likely to lead to big quantity changes. This is because even if their price increases greatly, you can easily afford those price increases. Goods that take up a significant portion of your income are more likely to have elastic demand because you are less able to afford large price increases. In this case goods with low prices are likely to have inelastic demand and goods with high prices are likely to have elastic demand.

Seeing Elasticity through Total Expenditures

total expenditure rule
 If the price and the amount you spend both go in the same direction, then demand is inelastic, whereas if they go in opposite directions, demand is elastic.

If we wanted to, we could use math to show that if the price and the amount you spend both go in the same direction, then demand is inelastic. If they go in opposite directions, however, demand is elastic. This **total expenditure rule** of elasticity also allows us to quickly judge whether demand is elastic or inelastic. For instance, when the price of cigarettes goes up, smokers usually have to spend more on them. When the prices of luxuries go up, many of us spend less on them (because we do without them). In this way we can find out for ourselves whether our demand for a good is elastic or inelastic. All we need to do is to ask ourselves whether a price increase will cause us to spend more on that good.

MORE ON ELASTICITY

Determinants of Elasticity

Key factors of the three elasticity explanations are important in determining whether a good is elastic or inelastic. The first is the **number and closeness of substitutes.** When there are many substitutes that all serve nearly as well as the good in question, demand is likely to be more elastic because price increases induce changes to other goods. Whether price increases can be easily absorbed into a person's budget also matters. If price increases cannot be absorbed, it is likely that when they occur, significant quantity reductions will follow. And although timing was not mentioned above, given **time,** close substitutes can be found or invented, or methods to avoid the price increase will be developed.

Elasticity and the Demand Curve

Elasticity is important because supply changes will have very different results depending on the elasticity of demand. As you can see from the figures on the next page, an identical supply change can affect only price (Figure 3.4), only quantity (Figure 3.5), price much more than quantity (Figure 3.6), or quantity much more than price (Figure 3.7).

FIGURE 3.4   Perfectly inelastic demand.

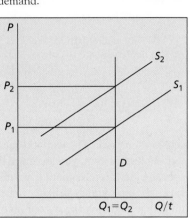

FIGURE 3.5   Perfectly elastic demand.

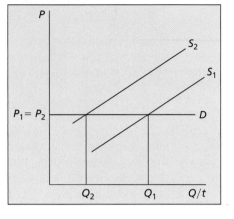

FIGURE 3.6   Inelastic demand.

FIGURE 3.7   Elastic demand.

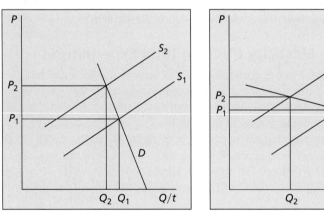

perfectly inelastic
The condition of demand when price changes have no effect on quantity.

perfectly elastic
The condition of demand when price cannot change.

In Figure 3.4 the demand curve is **perfectly inelastic** because price changes have no effect on quantity. In Figure 3.5 the demand curve is **perfectly elastic** because price cannot change. As we saw in Figures 3.2 and 3.3, a linear demand curve is elastic at high prices and inelastic at low prices. In Figure 3.6 demand is inelastic over the entire range shown because at every point the percentage change in price is larger than the percentage change in quantity. This will be true when the demand curve is nearly vertical. In Figure 3.7 demand is elastic over the entire range, because at every point the percentage change in price is smaller than the percentage change in quantity. This will be true when the demand curve is nearly horizontal.

If we look back at the elasticity formula, we can use this explanation to compute the appropriate elasticity numbers for each of these elasticity labels. For perfectly elastic demand the computed elasticity is ∞ (infinity), while for perfectly inelastic demand the computed elasticity is 0 (zero). Remembering that unitary elastic demand computes to 1 (one), it makes sense that elastic demand will compute to greater than 1 but less than ∞ and inelastic demand will compute to less than 1 but greater than 0.

Elasticity: Some Illustrative Examples

Sometimes it is easier to see the importance of elasticity with particular goods. There are economists who spend their days and nights estimating the elasticity of demand for particular goods. This is not because they have nothing else to do. It is because the elasticity of demand for a good is important information to have if you are interested in the impact of a price increase or a tax on that good. For instance, if you take up the chapter on tobacco, alcohol, drugs, and prostitution later in the course, you will find that the question of how much impact a tax on cigarettes will have in decreasing smoking depends greatly on the elasticity of demand for cigarettes.

Consider the goods listed at right and their elasticities. You should be able to tell a story about why short-run gasoline demand is less elastic than long-run gasoline demand. You should be able to figure out why demand for foreign travel is quite elastic while demand for salt is not. The key to the question of whether a good is elastic or not is whether there is an acceptable substitute.

Inelastic Goods	Price Elasticity
Eggs	−0.06
Gasoline (short-run)	−0.08
Gasoline (long-run)	−0.24
Highway and bridge tolls	−0.10
Unit Elastic Good (or close to it)	
Shellfish	−0.89
Elastic Goods	
Luxury car	−3.70
Foreign air travel	−1.77

Sources: "Bridge and Tunnel Toll Elasticities in New York; Some Recent Evidence." *Transportation; May 1995,* vol. 22; Ira Hirschman, Claire McKnight, and John Pucher, Economic Research Service/ USDA, *Food Demand and Nutrient Elasticities*/TB-1887 www.globefish.org/publication/specialseries/vol09/SSE0803.htm; Bruce Schaller. *Transportation* 26: 283–297, 1999; Rolando F. Pelaez, *The Price Elasticity for Gasoline Revisited,* Dept. of Economics, University of St. Thomas, Houston, Texas; Robert F. Bordley, "Estimating Automotive Elasticities from Segment Elasticities and First Choice/ Second Choice Data," *The Review of Economics and Statistics* 75, no. 3 (August, 1993), pp. 455–462; Hendrick S. Houthakker and Lester D. Taylor, *Consumer Demand in the United States, 1929–1970* (Cambridge: Harvard University Press, 1966, 1970).

SAMPLE STORY 1

There are few substitutes to driving to and from work. Though you may or may not be able to take public transportation or carpool, though you may or may not be able to trade in your SUV for a fuel-efficient car, it would take a substantial change in the price of gasoline to cause you to make the substitution immediately upon seeing an increase in gas prices. This is especially true if you did not anticipate that prices would remain high. On the other hand, if you did see that gasoline prices were going to remain high, you might, over the next year or so, consider trading in the gas guzzler for something more miserly.

SAMPLE STORY 2

Suppose you wanted to take your family on an interesting vacation. Suppose further that your family had narrowed its choices to hiking in the Grand Canyon or seeing the sights in Paris. Given the acceptability of the substitute, a relatively small change in the price of flights and accommodations for the trip to France would have a significant impact on your choice.

CONSUMER AND PRODUCER SURPLUS

Consumer Surplus

Most people think that when consumers buy goods only the firm is better off for the exchange. They do not often acknowledge that consumers are also better off. It turns out that consumers often get much more value than they part with. Look back to "All about Demand" in Chapter 2 and recall that the demand curve represents the marginal utility of the good. This means that the amount each additional unit of the good is worth to the consumer can be read from the demand curve.

Figure 3.8 indicates that if the demand curve represents your individual demand for water and you have none, you would value it at (be willing to pay) $2 for the first glass. If you had the first glass in hand (or you already had drunk it), you would value the second glass at $1.50, and so on. If you only had to pay 50 cents, you would buy four, but, more important, you would be getting value that you did not have to pay for. You would be getting $2 worth of value for 50 cents; then you would be getting $1.50 worth of value for only 50 cents. It is only when you pay 50 cents for

Comparing the Gain to the Gainers with the Loss to the Losers

When there are win–win scenarios such as the case outlined, economists generally favor uninhibited exchange. When there are losers, economists look to consumer surplus–producer surplus analysis to weigh the gain to the gainers against the loss to the losers. To you, whether free trade is a good thing or not depends on whether you are a Kia owner who saved several thousand dollars on your car or an unemployed United Auto Workers union member. Whether a new Wal-Mart Supercenter is good for your town depends on whether you are a consumer paying lower prices for steak or a union meat cutter unemployed because the Kroger that you worked for closed. Generally, but by no means universally, economists favor market outcomes because they make the calculation that the gain to the gainers outweighs the loss to the losers. Whether it is trade between the United States and Korea or Wal-Mart outcompeting Kroger, free-trade economists insist that lower prices generate a gain in consumer surplus that is greater than the net loss in producer surplus.

consumer surplus
The value you get that is in excess of what you pay to get it.

the fourth one that the value will not exceed what you would have paid to get it. Economists call the value you get that is in excess of what you pay to get it **consumer surplus.**

When the good is infinitely divisible (in this case, you can buy water in any fractional amount like 2.63478956 glasses of water) the consumer surplus is the area between the demand curve and the price line. In Figure 3.8 the consumer surplus is the triangle between the demand curve and the 50 cent price line and is $4 [($2.50 – $0.50) × 4 × 1/2].

Producer Surplus

Firms also benefit from exchange. In the Chapter 2 section "All about Supply" the supply curve is upward sloping because it is the marginal cost curve and marginal cost is increasing. In Figure 3.9 the firm's cost of producing the first unit of its product is $1. The cost of producing the second, given that it already produced the first (its marginal cost), is $1.50. The cost of producing the third, given that it already produced two, is $2, and so on. Because it is getting $1.50 for each unit it sells, the firm makes money on the first and second units. Again, as long as the good is infinitely divisible, the money that the firm makes over its costs is the area between the price line and the supply curve. Economists call the money the firm gets that is in excess of its marginal costs **producer surplus.** In Figure 3.9 the producer surplus is $1 [($1.50 − $.50) × 2 × 1/2].

producer surplus
The money the firm gets that is in excess of its marginal costs.

FIGURE 3.8 Consumer surplus.   **FIGURE 3.9** Producer surplus.

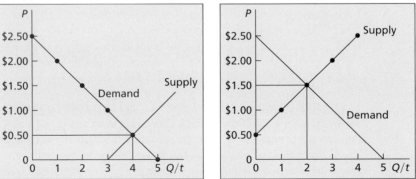

market failure
The circumstance where the market outcome is not the economically efficient outcome.

exclusivity
The degree to which the consumption of the good can be restricted by a seller to only those who pay for it.

rivalry
The degree to which one person's consumption reduces the value of the good for the next consumer.

purely private good
A good with the characteristics of both exclusivity and rivalry.

purely public good
A good with neither of the characteristics of exclusivity or rivalry.

excludable public good
A good with the characteristic of exclusivity but not of rivalry.

congestible public good
A good with the characteristic of rivalry but not of exclusivity.

Because in this example the producer surplus is $1 and the consumer surplus is $1 [($2.50 − $1.50) × 2 × 1/2], both demonstrably benefit from the trade. The money that consumers pay firms is simultaneously more than it costs firms to make the good and less than consumers value the good. This is the underlying reason that free enterprise works as well as it does—all the participants leave the market at least as happy as they were when they came to it.

Market Failure

Reread the last sentence of the preceding paragraph. It seems to suggest that the market works perfectly and that there is never cause for government to intervene. Intuitively you know that is not true. A market can fail for a number of reasons: The actions of a consumer or producer can harm an innocent third party, a good may not be one for which a company can profit from selling even though society profits from its existence, the buyer may not be able to make a well-informed choice given the complexity of the decision, or a buyer or seller may have too much power over the price. Each of these problems leads to **market failure**—the circumstance where the market outcome is not the economically efficient outcome. In the issue chapters to come you will explore each of these types of market failures.

Broadly speaking, goods can be classified into four categories on the basis of the degree to which the consumption of the good can be restricted by a seller to only those who pay for it—called **exclusivity,** and the degree to which one person's consumption reduces the value of the good for the next consumer—called **rivalry.** Goods, like a slice of pizza have a high degree of both qualities; the pizza joint can easily prevent you from consuming their pizza if you do not pay for it and once you have eaten a pizza, that particular pizza is not available to others. As a result, economists would label pizza as a **purely private good.** On the other hand, the army protects all citizens from foreign invasion regardless of how much they pay in taxes and their success at doing so is not diminished at all by how many people they have to defend. Economists label national defense as a **purely public good** because it is one for which there is neither rivalry nor exclusivity.

In addition to those extremes, there are goods that have a high degree of one characteristic and a low degree of the other. Cable companies can easily exclude their consumers from getting HBO but one consumer's viewing of HBO does not affect another's viewing. HBO is excludable but there is no rivalry. Economists call such goods **excludable public goods.** Similarly, a city street is an example of a good for which it would be nearly impossible to prevent usage by citizens and one for which rivalry is common (think traffic jams).[2] Such goods are what economists call **congestible public goods.**

---

[2]While you may think license plates allow for exclusivity, they do not serve the entire function in that once you have a licensed car it is very difficult to charge you based on usage. As technology increases, GPS receivers and transmitters may make it possible to charge drivers based on where and when they drive.

Kick It Up A Notch CONSUMER AND PRODUCER SURPLUS IN A SUPPLY AND DEMAND MODEL

As we move through the issue chapters you will see this kind of analysis over and over again. Since we will often be using letters instead of numbers in our examples, it will be useful to get some practice now. If you struggle with the letters, use the shaded areas in Figures 3.11 through 3.15. Figure 3.10 shows us that the value that consumers get from their purchase of Q^* of the good is the area under the demand curve, $0ACQ^*$ or the shaded area in Figure 3.11. The money that consumers pay firms is the rectangle $0P^*CQ^*$ (Figure 3.12). The variable cost to firms to make Q^* is the area under the supply curve $0BCQ^*$ (Figure 3.13). The consumer surplus is the triangle P^*AC (Figure 3.14), while the producer surplus is the triangle BP^*C (Figure 3.15).

FIGURE 3.10   Consumer and producer surplus.

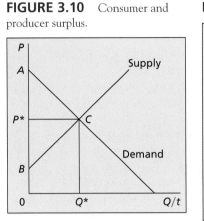

FIGURE 3.11   Value to the consumer.

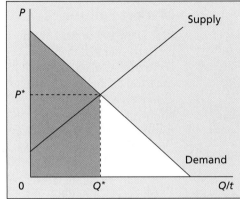

FIGURE 3.12   Money consumer pays producer.

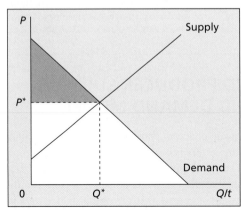

FIGURE 3.13   Variable cost to producer.

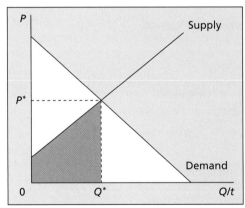

FIGURE 3.14   Consumer surplus.

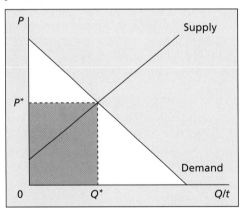

FIGURE 3.15   Producer surplus.

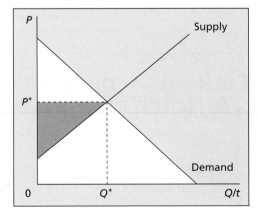

Without the sale of Q^* goods for P^* dollars, neither the consumer surplus nor the producer surplus would exist. This means that we can measure the benefit that society gets from the market as the triangle that is made up by the sum of the producer and consumer surplus, *BAC*.

DEADWEIGHT LOSS

When the market is not at equilibrium the consumer surplus plus the producer surplus will not be as large. This triangle, *ABC*, is as big as it can be. If consumption is more than Q^*, then consumers are paying more than they think a product is worth, or producers are not meeting their marginal costs, or both. If consumption is less than Q^*, the consumers wish they could buy more (and they would get more consumer surplus), or firms wish they could sell more (and they would get more producer surplus), or both. If the triangle is smaller than *ABC*, then there is **deadweight loss**. This deadweight loss is the measure economists use to discuss the inefficiency of markets when a problem like air pollution exists or when government establishes an impediment to a free floating price, such as the minimum wage.

deadweight loss
The loss in societal welfare associated with production being too little or too great.

To see how deadweight loss fits our supply and demand diagram suppose that for some reason the price cannot be at P^* but is instead at P' (pronounced "*P* prime"). Figure 3.16 shows the impact of this when P' is greater than P^*, and Figure 3.17 shows the impact when P' is less than P^*. In either circumstance the new quantity will be less than equilibrium because consumers will not be willing to buy more than Q' (pronounced "*Q* prime") at the higher P' in Figure 3.16 and producers will not be willing to sell more than Q' in Figure 3.17 at the lower P'.

In Figure 3.16 the price is higher than P^*. At that higher price, though producers will want to sell many more than the previous equilibrium quantity, consumers will want to buy fewer. Unless the consumers are compelled to buy things they do not want, they will buy only Q'.

Given that we can find the consumer and producer surplus in this market and compare it to what it was in Figure 3.10. The area under the demand curve represents the value to the consumer of Q' goods and this is $0AEQ'$. The price P' times the quantity Q' is the amount of money consumers will pay to get Q', and this is represented by the area $0P'EQ'$. The difference between these, $P'AE$, is the consumer surplus. It costs the producer $0BFQ'$ in terms of variable costs to make these goods. The difference between the money consumers pay them and their costs, $BP'EF$, is the producer surplus. The sum of consumer and producer surplus in this case is $BAEF$, but this is less than ABC, which is what this sum was in Figure 3.10. This means that

FIGURE 3.16 Deadweight loss with a price higher than P^*.

FIGURE 3.17 Deadweight loss with a price lower than P^*.

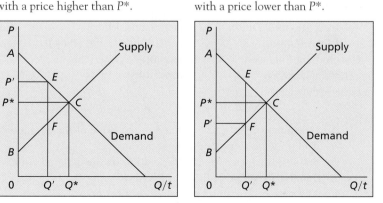

the area *FEC* is lost as a result of being at *P'* instead of *P**, and this is what economists call the deadweight loss of being at *P'* instead of *P**.

In Figure 3.17 the price is lower than *P**. At that lower price, though, producers will not want to sell as much as they did at the previous equilibrium and consumers will want to buy more. Unless producers are compelled to sell things they do not want to sell, they will produce only *Q'*. Again we can find the consumer and producer surplus in this market and compare it to what it was in Figure 3.10. The area under the demand curve still represents the value to the consumer of *Q'* goods and is still *0AEQ'*. The price *P'* times the quantity *Q'* is still the amount of money consumers will pay to get *Q'*, but this is now represented by the area *0P'FQ'*. The difference between these, the consumer surplus, is now *P'AEF*. Whereas the costs of the producer, *0BFQ'*, remain the same, the revenue has fallen so the producer surplus falls to *BP'F*. The sum of consumer and producer in this case is also *BAEF*, and this is still less than it was in Figure 3.10. The deadweight loss is again represented by the area *FEC*.

Summary

This chapter expanded on the supply and demand model by showing the importance of the responsiveness of quantity to changes in price and how the model can be used to show that market exchange results in mutually beneficial results for consumers and producers.

In discussing elasticity we began by introducing the formula, defining the terms *elastic* and *inelastic,* and exploring why demand for some goods may be elastic while others may be inelastic. We then considered how elasticity of demand is determined by the number of close substitutes and the time available to generate them.

To conclude the chapter we discussed how we could use the supply and demand model to show that consumers and producers each benefit from a market transaction, and we showed how to measure the benefit each gets by defining consumer and producer surplus. Finally, we showed how we measure the inefficiency of being away from equilibrium by defining and illustrating the concept of deadweight loss.

Key Terms

Issues Chapters You Are Ready For Now

Quiz Yourself

1. The elasticity of demand is related to the slope of the demand curve
   a. And only the slope of the demand curve.
   b. But also the (price, quantity) position on the demand curve.
   c. But also the slope of the supply curve.
   d. And whether the good is normal or inferior.

2. Suppose a firm cannot figure out whether the demand for the good it sells is elastic or inelastic but discovers that every time it raises its price, its total revenue declines. Their
   a. Demand is unit elastic.
   b. Demand is elastic.
   c. Demand is inelastic.
   d. Demand is perfectly inelastic.

3. Suppose you observe that minor changes in supply seem to cause dramatic changes in price, you would conclude that
   a. Demand is unit elastic.
   b. Demand is elastic.
   c. Demand is inelastic.
   d. Demand is perfectly inelastic.

4. The fact that the demand for eggs is inelastic should not surprise you because
   a. They are a very cheap food.
   b. The demand for nearly all food products is inelastic.
   c. The supply of eggs is inelastic.
   d. They are so expensive.

5. Combined the consumer surplus and producer surplus at equilibrium is
   a. Lower than it would be at prices below equilibrium.
   b. Lower than it would be at prices above equilibrium.
   c. Typically negative.
   d. As big as it can get.

6. If supply and demand are lines, then at equilibrium both consumer and producer surplus are
   a. Equal.
   b. Shown as squares.
   c. Shown as trapezoids.
   d. Shown as triangles.

7. When looking at the impact of a change in trade policy economists use consumer and producer surplus to look at the winners and losers. Free-trade economists insist that
   a. No one loses.
   b. Everyone loses.
   c. There are winners and losers but that the gain to the winners is greater than the loss to the losers.
   d. There are winners and losers but that the loss to the losers is greater than the gain to the winners.

8. When a satellite television company gains a subscriber there is no impact on existing subscribers. That is, there is no rivalry in the consumption for their service. This is an example of a
   a. Purely private good.
   b. Purely public good.
   c. Congestible public good.
   d. Excludable public good.

9. Policy makers have considered putting computer chips in cars that would allow tax collectors to charge people on the basis of how often they drive during rush hours. These policy makers are dealing with the fact that public roads are
   a. Purely private goods.
   b. Purely public goods.
   c. Congestible public goods.
   d. Excludable public goods.

Think about This

Suppose both gasoline supply and demand are highly inelastic. Knowing that a change in the expected price of gasoline will shift both supply and demand, explain how these combined facts can lead you to an understanding of wildly changing gasoline prices.

Talk about This

Talk about your alternative choices for colleges. What schools did you consider? Was tuition a consideration? Does your college's proximity to other schools imply anything about your school's ability to raise revenue by raising tuition?

Behind the Numbers

"Highway and Bridge Toll Elasticities," *Transportation; May 1995,* vol. 22.
Ira Hirschman, Claire McKnight, and John Pucher,

Food Demand and Nutrient Elasticities—www.globefish.org/publication/specialseries/vol109/SSE0803.htm.

Transportation Elasticities: Bruce Schaller. *Transportation* 26: 283–297, 1999.

Gasoline Elasticities: *The Price Elasticity for Gasoline Elasticity Revisited* by Rolando F. Pelaez (Department of Economics, University of St. Thomas, Houston, Texas).

Chapter 4

Firm Production, Cost, and Revenue

Chapter Objectives

After reading this chapter you should be able to

Understand the relationship between production and costs and the relationship between sales and revenues.

Recognize that models of production are based on the assumption that firms seek to maximize profit.

See how profit maximization dictates that firms set production so that marginal cost equals marginal revenue.

Chapter Outline

Production

Costs

Revenue

Maximizing Profit

Summary

---

profit

The money that a firm makes: revenue − cost.

cost

The expense that must be incurred to produce goods and services for sale.

revenue

The money that comes into the firm from the sale of goods and services.

The business of business is making money, and the money business makes is called **profit.** How it makes that profit is by selling its goods for more than it costs to make them. For this chapter (and for most of this book) we make the simplifying assumption that nothing influences business other than maximizing profit. Although this is an exaggeration, it is reasonably close to the truth, and accepting it as the truth simplifies our task considerably. Nothing about this chapter is simple, but you may be comforted by the knowledge that it could be more complicated (of course you may not be).

With the simplifying assumption of myopic profit maximization in place, we can break things down into the cost side and the revenue side. **Cost** is the expense that businesses must incur to produce goods for sale. **Revenue** is the money that comes into the firm from the sale of the goods.

It is important to understand why economists focus on costs that are incurred rather than simply those costs that must be paid. Accountants focus only on expenses that must be paid for a business to produce, but economists also consider the *opportunity cost* of choices. To fully understand the concepts of **economic cost** and **accounting cost,** consider an upstart business whose owner quits a $50,000 a year job and cashes in a $100,000 CD (earning 6 percent) to get it off the ground. An accountant would not consider the $50,000 of forgone job-related income or the $6,000 per year in forgone interest as costs of the business. An economist would. For the remainder of this chapter and all of the next, all costs refer to economic costs.

economic cost

All costs of a business: those that must be paid as well as those incurred in the form of forgone opportunities.

accounting cost

Only those costs that must be explicitly paid by the owner of a business.

With that said, since profit is the difference between revenues and costs, we will be able to use what we have developed in these areas to find how much production our profit-maximizing firm will choose. We then explore the production process and the costs that it generates, move on to discuss the revenue side, and then put the two together to show how, under different circumstances, firms choose their production levels. To pull all that off, we carry one example from the beginning of this explication to the end. Let's assume that the industry we are talking about is the computer memory industry, the industry that makes the chips that enable computers to use and quickly access information. Let's suppose that the production of computer memory requires three things: expensive machines, highly trained people, and very inexpensive plastic and metal from which the chips are made. To make things even easier, let's assume that the plastic and metal used to make the chips are free.

So far we have had a section entitled "Kick It Up A Notch" in some chapters. The problem with this chapter is that material presented is already "kicked up" plenty. Complicating matters further, some students need a verbal explanation, some need to "see" it in the form of a graph, while still others can only get their arms around a concrete numerical example. To deal with that, we go through each of them once using just words, once using graphical explanation, and then again with a numerical example.

PRODUCTION

production function

A graph that shows how many resources are needed to produce various amounts of output.

cost function

A graph that shows how much various amounts of production cost.

fixed inputs

Resources that do not change.

variable inputs

Resources that can be easily changed.

Just Words

To get a handle on costs we need to know how much money it takes to produce goods. First we need to know what resources are necessary for production. Then we can construct an input–output relationship called a **production function,** and we will do this in the form of a graph. Our graph will show how many resources we need to produce various amounts of output. From that production function we can find out how much various amounts of production cost. From this resulting **cost function** we will be able to figure out how much each one costs on average and how much each additional one costs.

Of course, this is putting the cart before the horse. Before the firm decides how many to produce, it has to decide what to produce. In our example, the memory chip firm did not decide to make chips for the fun of it. Early computer designers decided that their computers would work better if they had a short-term place to store and quickly retrieve information. Chip-making companies came into existence to provide the computer industry with the parts to make short-term storage of data possible. For the remainder of this section and this chapter we assume that the firm is up and running and is simply trying to figure out how many chips to make at any given time.

To make any product you typically have **fixed** and **variable inputs.** That is, you have resources that you cannot change and resources that you can. In our example, the plant and the equipment in the plant are called fixed inputs because they are not easily changed, added to, or subtracted from. On the other hand, the person power to operate those machines is easily changed. You can hire and fire more easily and quickly than you can replace a machine. People and other resources that can be easily changed are called variable inputs.

The first step in our process of figuring out how many memory chips to make is to map out how many resources are needed to produce various numbers of these chips. Of course, without any personnel there is no production. If there are only a few workers, as at point *B* in Figure 4.1, production is not very great because workers are not able to specialize in particular parts of the production process. They waste time moving from one part of the process to another, and they take time to build momentum, working at each stage of production only to find that when they get good at it, it is time to move on to another stage.

FIGURE 4.1   A production function.

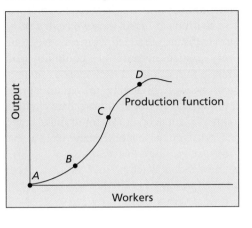

TABLE 4.1   Numerical example: production function.

Labor	Total Output	Extra Output of the Group
0	0	
1	100	100
2	317	217
3	500	183
4	610	110
5	700	90
6	770	70
7	830	60
8	870	40
9	900	30
13	1,000	

division of labor
Workers divide the tasks in such a way that each can build momentum and not have to switch jobs.

The addition of a few more workers solves that problem and production levels increase greatly. Workers divide the tasks in such a way that each can build momentum and does not have to switch jobs. This specialization is called the **division of labor,** and its impact is such that for a small increase in labor we can get a dramatic increase in output.

At some point, though, there are enough workers to get the job done, as at point *D,* and more workers do not add much to production. Some jobs, too, just cannot be easily divided. Although it is usually the case that having more workers increases output, workers find that the existing plant and equipment are too limiting for them to get the most out of new employees. As a result, output increases but not as fast as it had before. This phenomenon, referred to by economists as **diminishing returns,** is a central assumption of this chapter as well as the next.

diminishing returns
The notion that there exists a point where the addition of resources increases production but does so at a decreasing rate.

Graphical Explanation

Using the same ideas just presented, let's walk through Figure 4.1. Point *A* begins at the origin because, as was pointed out in the preceding section, if you have no workers you have no output. Where there are too few workers to staff the plant they have to waste time moving from one stage of production to the next, so the increase in production associated with the first group of workers is relatively low. That gives us point *B.* The curve is bowed to the right between points *A* and *C* because of the division of labor. That is, as you add the same number of workers, you get the benefits from those workers specializing and production increases at an increasing rate. Once you get to point *C,* though, there is not enough plant and equipment to accommodate more workers efficiently. The curve is then bowed to the left because of diminishing returns to the existing plant and equipment.

Numerical Example

Now, let's consider the same concept using the numbers that comprise Table 4.1. Continuing with the memory chips example, suppose the first column represents the groups of workers, the second column represents the total output produced, and the third column represents the extra output added with the inclusion of the group. Because memory chips cannot make themselves, zero labor corresponds to zero output. Suppose that the first group of workers hired initially produces 100 units but when a second group is added a total of 317 units is produced.

That is, the second group adds 217 units to production. Suppose the third group adds somewhat less, 183 units, so that the total becomes 500. If it takes 5 groups of workers to produce 700, 9 to produce 900, and 13 to produce 1,000, then we have a story similar to what we saw in the graphical explanation. That is, as we added workers we got more production. The first group of workers was not very efficient because they could not specialize, whereas the second group was efficient because they could. In each case as more groups were added, efficiency waned because the workers were limited by the existing plant and equipment.

We have now explained production in terms of how a varying number of workers can be combined with a fixed amount of plant and equipment to make computer memory chips. We work next on how much it costs to hire those workers and pay for that machinery.

COSTS

Just Words

fixed costs

Costs of production that cannot be changed.

variable costs

Costs of production that can be changed.

marginal cost (MC)

The addition to cost associated with one additional unit of output.

average total cost (ATC)

Total cost divided by output, the cost per unit of production.

average variable cost (AVC)

Total variable cost divided by output, the average variable cost per unit of production.

average fixed cost (AFC)

Total fixed cost divided by output, the average fixed cost per unit of production.

Once we know how many workers it takes to produce our memory chips we can find out how much it costs to make those chips. The first thing to consider is that there are costs of production that we cannot change. In our example these **fixed costs** are the costs of the plant and equipment that we own. Costs that we can change, like the number of workers we hire for our plant, are called **variable costs.** The task now is to compare the number of memory chips we make against the costs of making those chips.

To accomplish this we need four cost concepts: marginal cost, average total cost, average variable cost, and average fixed cost.

Marginal cost (MC) is the increase in cost associated with a one-unit increase in production. Because total cost always rises, marginal cost is always positive. Because total cost rises quickly at low levels of output, marginal cost is high at low levels of output; however, total cost rises much more slowly at moderate levels of output, so marginal cost is much lower there. Last, because a rapid rise in total cost resumes at high levels of output, marginal cost is high in this range. Thus marginal cost starts high, decreases for a while, and then increases again.

Average total cost (ATC) is the per-unit cost of production. Because this includes fixed cost, which can be very high, average total cost will be high at low levels of production. It will shrink as production gets more efficient and the fixed costs become spread over greater levels of output. As production rises to higher levels where marginal costs are increasing, these two effects will begin to counteract each other and the drop in average total costs will slow. Eventually the increases in marginal cost will overwhelm the effect of spreading fixed costs over higher levels of output and average total cost will rise again.

The **average variable cost (AVC)** is dictated by the same changes in efficiency that gave us the marginal cost curve. Because it is an average, however, the movements are dampened; the highs are not as high and the lows are not as low.

Average fixed cost (AFC) falls continuously because the fixed costs of production are being spread over greater and greater levels of production. In addition, graphically, average fixed cost is the vertical distance between average total cost and average variable cost.

These cost concepts serve as the basis for much of what follows in this chapter, the next one, and our subsequent study of issues.

Looking back at Figure 4.1, you can see that at point *A* we will not have to pay anything to our workers (because we have no workers to pay), but we still have to pay fixed costs. As a result, point *A* in Figure 4.1 corresponds to point *A* in Figure 4.2. We have workers at point *B* whom we have to pay, and they are not all that productive. Remember that this is not their fault, because there are too few of them to allow specialization. Point *B* in Figure 4.2 is therefore higher than point *A* (because we have to pay them) but not much further to the right (because they are not making that many chips).

FIGURE 4.2   Total cost function.

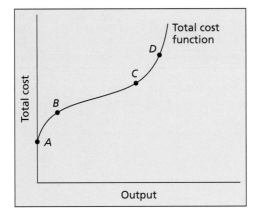

FIGURE 4.3   Marginal cost, average total cost, and average variable cost.

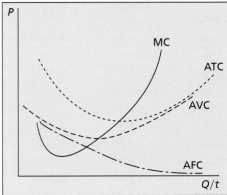

Point C in Figure 4.1 indicates that the workers were quite productive; so for the same amount of an increase in our costs we see a significant increase in production. Thus point C in Figure 4.2 is also higher than point B but is significantly further to the right. Point D in Figure 4.1 shows us where extra workers did not add much to production. Again they cost money, so point D in Figure 4.2 is higher than point C but is not that much further to the right. Connecting these points we have a total cost function. Our graph shows how the function helps us understand and make decisions about the cost of production and the amount produced.

Thus far we have focused on finding the total cost of producing various amounts of output. When we get total revenue, we will be able to find the profit. Before we go there, though, we are going to need four other cost functions: marginal cost, the average variable cost, the average fixed cost, and the average total cost. In higher-level economics courses, students are required to derive these other cost functions from the total cost function. When you derive one function from another you graphically manipulate the parent function (in this case total cost) to draw its descendants (in this case marginal cost, average variable cost, and average total cost).

Numerical Example

Again we are dealing with concepts that may be easier to comprehend when there are numbers attached. Following the numerical example used in Table 4.1, consider Table 4.2. The first column represents output. The second, Total Variable Cost, is based on the $2,500 per unit of labor from Table 4.1 that is required to produce that output. The third, Total Fixed Cost, is the cost of plant and equipment and is unchanging. The fourth, Total Cost, is the sum of total variable cost and total fixed cost. The fifth, Marginal Cost, is the increase in total cost from each level of production. The sixth, Average Total Cost, is the per-unit cost, the seventh, Average Variable Cost, is per-unit variable cost, and the eighth, Average Fixed Cost, is per-unit fixed cost.

These derivations take economics majors several class periods to understand. We'll skip that but outline why Figure 4.3 looks the way it does. Starting with the easiest one, average fixed cost, it is constantly decreasing because the same costs are being spread over more and more output. Marginal cost, average total cost, and average variable cost all start high, decrease, and then increase. The manner in which they do that, though, is somewhat complicated.

Marginal cost is the increase in costs associated with a one-unit increase in production. That means it is the "rise over the run" in the total cost curve, which means it is the slope of the total cost curve. You can see in Figure 4.2 that total cost rises rapidly at the beginning, flattens out, and then rises rapidly again.

TABLE 4.2   Numerical example: cost functions.

Output	Total Variable Cost	Total Fixed Cost	Total Cost	Marginal Cost*	Average Total Cost	Average Variable Cost	Average Fixed Cost
0	0	8,500	8,500				
100	2,500	8,500	11,000	25	110	25	85
200	3,800	8,500	12,300	13	62	19	43
300	4,800	8,500	13,300	10	44	16	28
400	6,000	8,500	14,500	12	36	15	21
500	7,500	8,500	16,000	15	32	15	17
600	9,500	8,500	18,000	20	30	16	14
700	12,500	8,500	21,000	30	30	18	12
800	17,000	8,500	25,500	45	32	21	10.6
900	22,500	8,500	31,000	55	34	25	9.4
1,000	32,500	8,500	41,000	100	41	32.5	8.5

*Change in total cost/change in output.

Average total cost and average variable cost are both U-shaped because they start high and decrease. The difference between the two curves is average fixed costs. Because average fixed cost diminishes as production increases, the gap between the two curves diminishes. They are both cut from below by the marginal cost curve at their respective minimums. This happens when, because of diminishing returns, marginal costs increase to the point where, first average variable cost, then average total cost, start to rise as well.

To see how each column in Table 4.2 is computed, let's look at a production increase from 400 to 500. The variable costs associated with producing 400 are $6,000. Variable costs rise to $7,500 when output rises to 500. Fixed costs are $8,500 in both cases. That means that total cost is $14,500 ($6,000 + $8,500) for 400 and rises to $16,000 ($7,500 + $8,500) for 500. The increase cost for the increase of 100 units is $1,500, so each one increased cost by $15, so marginal cost is $15. Average total cost for 400 units is $36 ($14,500/400) and $32 ($16,000/500) for 500 units. The average fixed cost is $21 ($8,500/400) for 400 units and $17 ($8,500/500) for 500 units.

If you plot the last four columns against output, you will see that the curve for marginal cost is indeed check-shaped, that those for average total cost and average variable cost are both U-shaped, and that average fixed cost decreases steadily. You can also see that at 300 units of output marginal cost is at its minimum. Further, you can see that the curve depicting marginal cost cuts average variable cost at its minimum (at 500 units of output) and that the marginal cost curve cuts the average total cost curve at its minimum (at 700 units of output).

REVENUE

Just Words

The other side of any production decision is the amount of money that will come in from the sale of the goods. To get a handle on this revenue side we will need to know whether the business has competition and if so, how much. For instance, if a business faces many other competitors that produce goods like the ones it produces, its behavior will be different from what it would be if it had the market to itself.

In some industries, like agriculture, the price that the firm receives remains unchanged regardless of how much it has to sell. In other industries, like those that supply electric power, the amount

FIGURE 4.4   Setting the price when there are many competitors.

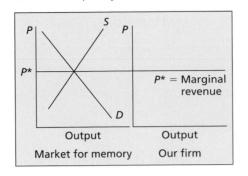

Market for memory · Our firm

FIGURE 4.5   Marginal revenue when we have no competitors.

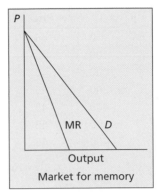

Market for memory

sold affects the price. To explore this difference let's first assume our memory chip maker is one of many chip makers. Then we will see what happens when we assume that it is the only one.

If our chip-making firm has many competitors, the price is set in a market that it cannot control. The supply of and the demand for chips determine how much the firm can charge for its chips. To see the futility of trying to set its own price, imagine that it tried to have a price higher than the market price. If it did, computer makers could and would buy all their chips from our firm's competitors. The firm could, of course, set a price lower than the market price. If it did, it would get to sell all it produced. On the other hand, it could do that at the market price. Because our firm wants to maximize profit and because it can always sell as much as it wants at or below the market price, it will always want to charge the market price.

Figure 4.4 shows how the market generates the price for the firm. This price also happens to be the additional revenue the firm receives from the sale of each unit. To see why this **marginal revenue (MR)** is the same as the price, consider a thought experiment. If the market price is 5, how much will revenue be if our firm sells one? Answer: 5. How much will revenue be if it sells two? Answer: 10. The increase in revenue associated with any sale is therefore 5. This is true whether you let the price be 5, 10, or 600; the price is the marginal revenue.

If, on the other hand, we are the only ones selling computer chips, computer makers have to buy their memory chips from our firm. This situation is quite different from the case where there were many competitors. Instead of just taking a price given to it by the market, it is setting the price. Instead of being a small, insignificant part of the market, it is the market. Unfortunately, to sell more, the firm has no recourse other than lowering the price it charges. For instance, if it is currently selling 1 million chips a week and it wants to increase its sales to 2 million a week, it must lower the price to everyone, even those who would have bought 1 million at the higher price. This means that in Figure 4.5 the marginal revenue is not graphed with a flat line; it falls as we increase sales.

marginal revenue (MR)

Additional revenue the firm receives from the sale of each unit.

Numerical Example

Using the same numerical example that we have been using, suppose that our firm is one of many and has no control over price. Suppose further that the price in the market for memory is $45 per unit. This means that the total revenue (TR) increases by $45 for each unit sold and the marginal revenue is thus $45 for each unit sold. This is illustrated in Table 4.3.

If there are no competitors, then the market demand for memory is simply the demand for our firm's memory. This means that our firm must lower its price to induce consumers to buy more memory. Another way of looking at precisely the same thing is to notice that a firm

TABLE 4.3 Numerical example: revenue when there are many competitors.			
Q	Price	TR	MR*
0	45	0	
100	45	4,500	45
200	45	9,000	45
300	45	13,500	45
400	45	18,000	45
500	45	22,500	45
600	45	27,000	45
700	45	31,500	45
800	45	36,000	45
900	45	40,500	45
1,000	45	45,000	45

*Change in total revenue/change in output.

TABLE 4.4 Numerical example: revenue when there are no competitors.			
Q	Price	TR	MR*
0	75	0	
100	70	7,000	70
200	65	13,000	60
300	60	18,000	50
400	55	22,000	40
500	50	25,000	30
600	45	27,000	20
700	40	28,000	10
800	35	28,000	0
900	30	27,000	−10
1,000	25	25,000	−20

*Change in total revenue/change in output.

without competition can force the price higher by restricting its output. As before, total revenue is price times quantity, but because price does not remain the same, the marginal revenue falls. This is illustrated in Table 4.4.

MAXIMIZING PROFIT

Graphical Explanation

perfect competition
A situation in a market where there are many firms producing the same good.

monopoly
A situation in a market where there is only one firm producing the good.

As mentioned, the level of output for the business that will maximize profit very much depends on whether the business is in **perfect competition**—that is, one of many producing the same thing—or is a **monopoly**—that is, it has no competitors. Regardless of whether it has many competitors or it has the market to itself, we assume firms produce and sell the amount that will make them the most money possible. In economic terms this ends up meaning that every firm should produce an amount such that marginal revenue equals marginal cost (MR = MC). Recall the Chapter 1 concept of marginal analysis; this is our first opportunity to see it at work.

This is not as difficult as it seems. Remember that marginal revenue is the amount the firm brings in from selling one more, and the marginal cost is the amount of money that it costs to produce one more. To illustrate, suppose you start by selling a fixed number, say, 10. If you sell an eleventh and you make money on that sale (MR > MC), you should do it again and sell at least one more. If you sell an eleventh and you lose money on that sale (MR < MC), you should reduce sales by at least one. Since marginal revenue is less than marginal cost for the eleventh chip, you should not have produced it. To maximize profit you could repeat this one-by-one process until you have found the production that makes the most money. On the other hand, you now know that it is only when marginal cost equals marginal revenue that you have exhausted the profit potential on the good you are trying to sell.

Of course it is possible that our entire business is a loser. In the age of word processors and cheap personal computers, the manual typewriter business would be a loser even if ours were the only firm in this industry. The exception to the rule that a firm should produce where marginal cost equals marginal revenue occurs when the best alternative is to do nothing; that is, sometimes the best decision is to shut down the business. This occurs when the amount that you sell a good for is not enough to cover the variable costs that went into the production of the good. The firm should shut down if the price is less than the average variable cost (*P* < AVC).

The Rules of Production

- A firm should produce an amount such that marginal revenue equals marginal cost (MR = MC).
- A firm should shut down if the price is less than the average variable cost ($P <$ AVC) at the quantity where marginal revenue equals marginal cost.

Numerical Example

To illustrate profit maximization when there are many competitors, we need to combine the information in Tables 4.1 and 4.3; when there are no competitors, we need to combine the information in Tables 4.3 and 4.4. In either case we need to pick a quantity to maximize profit. This is done where marginal cost equals marginal revenue. Table 4.5 illustrates this for the case where there are many competitors, and Table 4.6 does it for the case where there are no competitors. In Table 4.5 we see that the firm that has many competitors has its profit maximized at $10,500, and this happens when the firm produces 800.[1] In Table 4.6 we see that the firm that has no competitors has its profit maximized at $9,000, and this happens when it produces 600.

TABLE 4.5

Numerical example: profit maximization when there are many competitors.

Q	Price	TR	TC	MR	MC	Profit
0	45	0	8,500	0	0	−8,500
100	45	4,500	11,000	45	25	−6,500
200	45	9,000	12,300	45	13	−3,300
300	45	13,500	13,300	45	10	200
400	45	18,000	14,500	45	12	3,500
500	45	22,500	16,000	45	15	6,500
600	45	27,000	18,000	45	20	9,000
700	45	31,500	21,000	45	30	10,500
800	45	36,000	25,500	45	45	10,500
900	45	40,500	31,000	45	55	9,500
1,000	45	45,000	41,000	45	100	4,000

TABLE 4.6

Numerical example: profit maximization when there are no competitors.

Q	Price	TR	TC	MR	MC	Profit
0	75	0	8,500	0	0	−8,500
100	70	7,000	11,000	70	25	−4,000
200	65	13,000	12,300	60	13	700
300	60	18,000	13,300	50	10	4,700
400	55	22,000	14,500	40	12	7,500
500	50	25,000	16,000	30	15	9,000
600	45	27,000	18,000	20	20	9,000
700	40	28,000	21,000	10	30	7,000
800	35	28,000	25,500	0	45	2,500
900	30	27,000	31,000	−10	55	−4,000
1,000	25	25,000	41,000	−20	100	−16,000

[1] In the next chapter we will see that firms with many competitors see their profits disappear because new firms enter, thereby increasing market supply and lowering the price.

Summary

This chapter has illustrated production, costs, revenues, and profit maximization. For each concept and relationship we considered both graphical explanations and numerical examples. We assumed that businesses choose production to maximize profit, and that as a result they set it where marginal cost equals marginal revenue.

Key Terms

accounting cost, 50
average fixed cost (AFC), 52
average total cost (ATC), 52
average variable cost
  (AVC), 52
cost, 49
cost function, 50

diminishing returns, 51
division of labor, 51
economic cost, 50
fixed costs, 52
fixed inputs, 50
marginal costs (MC), 52
marginal revenue (MR), 55

monopoly, 56
perfect competition, 56
production function, 50
profit, 49
revenue, 49
variable costs, 52
variable inputs, 50

Quiz Yourself

1. When firms add workers and get more efficient they are benefiting from
   a. The division of labor.
   b. Diminishing returns.
   c. The law of large numbers.
   d. Diminishing marginal utility.
2. When firms add workers and find that the additional workers add less to output than their predecessors did, they are experiencing
   a. The division of labor.
   b. Diminishing returns.
   c. The law of large numbers.
   d. Diminishing marginal utility.
3. Suppose a firm has $1,000,000 in fixed costs and variable costs equal to $100 for every unit they produce,
   a. Their marginal costs are decreasing.
   b. Their fixed costs are decreasing.
   c. Their average costs are decreasing.
   d. The marginal costs are increasing.
4. The average total cost curve will be cut by the marginal cost curve from below as long as
   a. Fixed costs are rising.
   b. Average costs are decreasing.
   c. Marginal costs eventually increase.
   d. Marginal costs continually decrease.
5. Whether marginal revenue is constant or decreasing depends on
   a. Whether the firm is benefiting from the division of labor.
   b. Whether the firm is dealing with diminishing returns.
   c. How much the firm sells.
   d. Whether the firm faces competition.
6. When a firm chooses to shutdown, it is
   a. Making a poor decision because it should always produce where marginal cost equals marginal revenue.
   b. Making a poor decision because it should always produce where average costs exceed average revenue.
   c. Making a good decision as long as the price it is getting is less than its average costs.
   d. Making a good decision as long as the price it is getting is less than its average variable costs.

7. The result that a firm should produce where MC = MR except when the shutdown condition is met is based on the assumption that it is attempting to
   a. Maximize profit.
   b. Maximize market share.
   c. Minimize marginal costs.
   d. Minimize average costs.

Think about This
Why is it that when a firm has no competition it typically must lower the price to all consumers in order to sell more? What would have to happen for it to be able to lower the price only to new consumers?

Talk about This
We assume that the price to all consumers is the same. List the cases where the price to one person is different than the price to another. Why might a firm do this?

Chapter **5**

Perfect Competition, Monopoly, and Economic versus Normal Profit

Chapter Objectives

After reading this chapter you should be able to

Distinguish between perfect competition and monopoly and between normal and economic profit.

Understand why economic profit disappears under perfect competition but not under monopoly.

Know why, under perfect competition, the supply curve from Chapter 2 is marginal cost.

This chapter builds on Chapter 4 to describe firms in different competitive situations; show why, when there are many firms competing against one another, substantial profits are unsustainable; and conclude by demonstrating why the supply curve from Chapter 2 was upward sloping.

Some firms, such as family farms, are among millions of firms in an industry, whereas other firms completely dominate their industry. In the middle of this continuum are numerous firms with definable sets of competitors. Some industries lend themselves to many competitors while others lend themselves to only a few, and we explore examples along this continuum.

In Chapter 4 we operated under the assumption that firms were out to maximize profits. What we want to do now is to determine how well various-sized firms will manage. For instance, we may want to know why it is that family farmers cannot seem to make consistently high profits, whereas Microsoft can. We approach this by separating profit into two categories: the profit that is necessary for firms to stay in business and the profit that is above that level.

Last, we see that the supply curve laid out in Chapter 2 was indeed upward sloping for a reason. We will show that under perfect competition, an upward-sloping supply curve stems from the check-shaped marginal cost curve from Chapter 4.

FROM PERFECT COMPETITION TO MONOPOLY

As we discussed in Chapter 4, the shape of the marginal revenue curve depends on whether there are many competitors or no competitors. Figure 5.1 lays out these extreme cases. On the left, the cost curves from Figure 4.3 are applied to the marginal revenue curve from the case where there are many competitors. On the right we see the same for the case where there are no competitors. The amount they pick in each case is labeled Q^*. The price they charge is labeled P^*.

Perfect Competition

The key difference between the cases just outlined is the number of competitors. When the number of competitors is large, the firm (e.g., a dairy farm) simply has to take the market price as given but can sell as many goods as it wants at that price. When there are no competitors, the firm (e.g., Microsoft) can set any price it wants but can sell only the number that consumers want to buy at that price. Of course not every firm is faced with the stark either–or difference. Some firms (e.g., Exxon) have only a few competitors in markets of similar or identical products, and other firms (e.g., McDonald's) have many competitors in markets where each has its own signature brand.

When a firm faces a large number of competitors, such that no one firm can influence the price, when the good a firm sells is indistinguishable from those its competitor sells, when firms have good sales and cost forecasts, and when there is no legal or economic barrier to its entry into or exit from the market, then we have what economists call *perfect competition*.

Monopoly

Monopolies exist at the other end of the spectrum, when we have markets in which there is only one firm. The important thing to know about the concept of monopoly is that the existence of many firms does not necessarily mean the firms are in competition. For instance, Consolidated Edison was the exclusive provider of residential electrical power to New York City and Commonwealth Edison still is the exclusive provider of residential electrical power to Chicago. There are hundreds of power companies in the United States but very few of them compete with one another. They are not competitors because they cannot sell in another's area. Another way of looking at this is to say while there are many power companies, they are not competing in the same market. The reason is that it costs the companies too much to get the electricity to the consumer in the distant market. Just as a cement contractor in Little Rock, Arkansas, is not competing with a cement contractor in Miami for roadwork in south Florida

FIGURE 5.1

Picking the quantity to maximize profit.

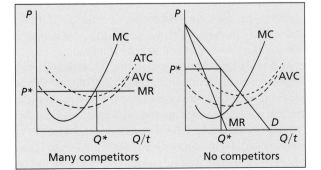

Characteristics of Perfect Competition

- A large number of competitors, so that no one firm can influence the price.
- The good a firm sells is indistinguishable from those its competitor sells.
- Firms have good sales and cost forecasts.
- There is no legal or economic barrier to entry into or exit from the market.

because of transportation costs, electric companies do not compete with one another because they cannot access the same buyers. For monopoly, all that is necessary is that one firm and only one firm sells to the customers in a given market.

Some firms get their monopoly power because the law prevents others from entering the market. An example of a legal barrier to entry is a patent. For example, the manufacturer of Clarinex is the only firm that can produce and sell this drug. On the other hand, some firms get their monopoly power by attaining such a huge size that competing against them is impossible. An example of this type of monopoly is Microsoft's near-exclusive corner on the sale of PC-based operating systems.

Monopolistic Competition

monopolistic competition

A situation in a market where there are many firms producing similar but not identical goods.

One of the areas of middle ground is **monopolistic competition,** in which many firms sell slightly different products. In the fast-food market there are quite a few firms (McDonald's, Wendy's, Burger King, etc., in burgers; KFC, Taco Bell, etc., in various niches), but they do not sell exactly the same good. McDonald's has a monopoly on the Big Mac and Happy Meal, but its competitors offer many close substitutes. This means that each firm has a monopoly on its particular menu, but the demand curve for the product is quite elastic. (Remember from Chapter 3 that the number of close substitutes determines elasticity.)

Oligopoly

oligopolistic market

A situation in a market where there are very few discernible competitors.

Another area of middle ground between perfect competition and monopoly is **oligopolistic markets,** in which there are very few discernible competitors. In the satellite TV business, for example, there are companies like Direct TV and the Dish Network. In the soft drink business there are Coke and Pepsi. In some markets firms sell exactly the same thing, whereas in other markets firms sell close substitutes. In either case, firms are acting in oligopolistic ways and referred to as *oligopolies.*

Which Model Fits Reality

Tables 5.1 and 5.2 summarize these market forms by providing examples and distinguishing characteristics of each type. That does not mean we will spend a great deal of time in the issues chapters worrying about market forms. Recall that in Chapter 2 we implicitly assumed that all markets were perfectly competitive. It turns out that very few markets meet the extreme criteria necessary to be labeled perfect competition. Most of the products that meet the criteria of perfect competition are agricultural; few products outside this area can make that claim. It may strike you, then, as somewhat curious that we will assume that most markets are perfectly competitive when we move into the issues. We do this because the supply and demand model is simple enough so that it can be used to explain and describe most markets where there are several competitors and the products are similar. You should understand that your instructor and I (the author) make this simplifying assumption reluctantly but knowingly.

TABLE 5.1
Examples of different market forms.

Perfect Competition	Monopolistic Competition	Oligopoly	Monopoly
Agricultural products	Fast food	Cars and trucks	Operating systems
Lumber	Long-distance service	Soft drinks	Local residential electric power

TABLE 5.2
Distinguishing characteristics between market forms.

Characteristic	Perfect Competition	Monopolistic Competition	Oligopoly	Monopoly
Number of firms	Many (often thousands or even millions)	Several*	Few* (usually two to five)	One
Barriers to entry	None	Few	Substantial	Insurmountable, at least in the short run
Product similarity	Identical	Similar but not identical	Similar or identical	NA

*There is dispute about the line that separates monopolistic competition and oligopoly.

Finally, you should be prepared for a high level of ambiguity in how particular markets fit into these forms. For instance, long-distance telephone service used to be a monopoly, became an oligopoly in the 1980s, and saw significant expansion in the number of companies offering service in the 1990s. Perhaps now it fits best under monopolistic competition. They all sell essentially the same thing but have a monopoly over their brand. Similarly, if you want to fly from New York to Los Angeles you have a number of alternatives. Perhaps not so many that it would be perfect competition but certainly enough to classify this service as monopolistic competition. On the other hand, if you wanted to fly directly from Indianapolis to Phoenix you have two choices (America West and American Trans Air). If you want to fly directly from Syracuse to Detroit you only have one choice (Northwest). Where airline travel fits depends greatly on where, and from where you are traveling. In particular, it depends on who has a hub in the respective airports.

Further, there is no magic line that separates oligopoly from monopolistic competition. Economists who study these things will often look to something called a "**concentration ratio**" that measures the percentage of total market sales for the top firms (from 4 firms to 100 firms). So even though there are several tobacco companies selling cigarettes, one company, Phillip Morris, holds nearly half the market and the top four hold all but 1 percent of the market. Several equally competitive firms would suggest monopolistic competition, but this concentration ratio data suggests oligopoly may be a better fit. Table 5.3 presents 4-, 8-, and 50-firm concentration ratios for specific industries.

concentration ratio
A measure of the market power held by the top firms in an industry. For a specific number of firms (n) it is the percentage of total sales in the industry accounted for by top n firms.

SUPPLY UNDER PERFECT COMPETITION

Normal versus Economic Profit

Let's return to the example we used in Chapter 4: the business of selling memory chips. If we are one of many firms competing in this industry, it stands to reason that making money will be difficult. Because of our assumption of free entry into and exit from this market, any time there are abnormally large profits, other firms will want to start making memory chips. Remember that Chapter 2 presented evidence that an increase in the number of sellers will move the supply curve to the right, thus lowering market price. If that happens, our marginal

TABLE 5.3

Concentration ratios for various manufacturing industries.

Industry Group	Concentration Ratios		
	4 Largest Firms	**8 Largest Firms**	**50 Largest Firms**
Breakfast cereals	82.9%	93.5%	100.0%
Ice cream	32.3	48.7	88.3
Beer	89.7	93.4	96.7
Clothing	17.6	23.2	38.8
Computers and peripherals	37.0	52.1	86.3
Furniture	11.2	17.6	37.2
Long distance	47.0	74.9	95.4
Cellular service	51.4	74.6	88.0

Sources: http://www.census.gov/epcd/www/concentration.html; http://www.census.gov/epcd/www/pdf/97conc/c97s51-sz.pdf.

TABLE 5.4

Return on equity for corporations in various industries, 1997.

Industry	Rate of Return*
Agriculture	8.2%
Manufacturing	14.5
Transportation and public utilities	9.3
Wholesale and retail trade	13.3

*Rate of Return = Net income/(Assets − Liabilities).

Source: *Statistical Abstract of the United States*
(http://www.census.gov/prod/2001pubs/statab/sec17.pdf).

normal profit

The level of profit that business owners could get in their next best alternative investment.

economic profit

Any profit above normal profit.

revenue curve will fall. As a matter of fact, it will fall all the way to where profit is normal. **Normal profit** is the level of profit that business owners could get in their next best alternative investment. The next best alternative would be whatever investment an owner would choose if he or she decided to go out of business. Any profit above normal profit is called **economic profit.**

Table 5.4 summarizes profit levels for different industry types. It is important to note that these levels are accounting profits rather than economic profits and though the rates of return shown are for just one year, 1997, they do reflect the reality that accounting profits are lower in markets, such as agriculture, where perfect competition dominates than in other markets.

If business owners do not make their normal profit, they will quit the business and move into another. This means that we might think of normal profit as the salary the business owners pay themselves and, as such, part of the "cost of doing business." If they make less than normal profit, then the salary they can pay themselves is too low to keep them in the industry. On the other hand, if profits are routinely more than that, others will want to enter the industry. This means that in the long run profit will shrink to normal levels.

When and Why Economic Profits Go to Zero

Fortunately for our chip maker, although the firm cannot make long-run economic profits, it is not going to lose money for long either. When firms lose more money than their fixed costs, they shut down. In the short run firms will continue to produce when they lose less than their fixed costs, but as time passes these firms will also want to shut down. So, though our chip maker can make economic profit in the short run and lose money in the short run, the effect of free entry and exit in this market will cause the marginal revenue curve to settle at the minimum of the U-shaped average total cost. What this means in everyday English is that any short-run profit or loss will evaporate in the long run because new competitors will come in or old ones will leave. This will drive the price toward the minimum of average total cost where profit is normal.

Though profit also shrinks to its normal level under monopolistic competition, there is no mechanism for profits to shrink to normal levels under oligopoly or monopoly. This is because the mechanism that shrinks profit is entry. Because entry is almost insurmountable under monopoly and substantially difficult under oligopoly, new firms do not come in to put the pressure on the price to fall.

At this point we need to back off our discussion to define more explicitly what economists mean by short run and long run. To an economist the distinction between the two centers on the ability of a firm to change its fixed inputs. We have assumed all along that we cannot change things like plant and equipment, and this is true in what we call the **short run.** In the **long run** there is enough time to change plant and equipment. We can either buy more plant and more equipment, or we can sell what we have. The distinction is thus not one of time but of flexibility; in the long run we are more flexible and in the short run less flexible.

short run

The period of time where a firm cannot change things like plant and equipment.

long run

The period of time where a firm can change things like plant and equipment.

Why Supply Is Marginal Cost under Perfect Competition

Showing that, under perfect competition, supply and marginal cost are interchangeable is important for several of the issues that follow but it is also notoriously difficult. That is why we will go back to the three approaches used in Chapter 4. We'll do the "Just Words," and "Numerical Example" approaches first and end with the "Graphical Explanation."

Just Words

In order to see that, under perfect competition, supply and marginal cost are interchangeable, you need to recall two key facts from Chapter 4: (1) all profit-maximizing firms will choose to produce where marginal cost equals marginal revenue (as long as price is greater than average variable cost); and (2) under perfect competition price and marginal revenue are the same. With that in your head, imagine that a firm is trying to decide how much to produce. It will take the price that is given to it by the market (which is also the firm's marginal revenue) and set production where that price equals its marginal cost. If the price rises or falls, it will do the calculation again. In every case, the quantity at which marginal revenue equals marginal cost is the same as the quantity at which price equals marginal cost. That means that in every case the relationship between quantity produced and the marginal cost of producing it (the marginal cost curve) is the same as the relationship between the quantity produced and the price at which it is sold (the supply curve). So, under perfect competition, supply and marginal cost are interchangeable.

Numerical Example

Using the memory chips example again, you can see from Table 4.2 that the average variable cost reaches a minimum at $15 per unit at the quantity of 500 units. This is important because at any price below $15 the firm will choose not to produce. To see that, suppose the price were $12 per unit. Marginal cost equals marginal revenue ($12) at 400 units, but at 400 units the firm's total revenue will be $4,800 ($12 × 400) while its total cost will be $14,500 and it will lose more money ($9,700 = $14,500 − $4,800) than it would if it simply shut down ($8,500).

At every price above $15 the firm either makes money or at least loses less than $8,500, and therefore it makes sense for the firm to produce where marginal cost equals marginal revenue. If the price were exactly $15, the firm would produce 500 units, have $7,500 ($15 × 500) in total revenue, $16,000 in total cost, and lose exactly its fixed costs. If the price were $20, the firm would produce 600 units, bringing $12,000 in revenue while costing $18,000, and the loss is $6,000. The firm would rather lose $6,000 than $8,500, so it produces 600 units.

As the price rises to $30, it produces 700 units, has both revenue and cost of $21,000, and breaks even. At a price of $45 it produces 800 units, has revenue of $36,000, costs of $25,500, and makes a profit. At a price of $55 it produces 900 units, has revenue of $49,500, costs of $31,000, and its profit increases. Finally, at a price of $100, it produces 1,000, has revenue of $100,000, costs of $41,000, and its profit increases further. Putting it all together, the firm's supply curve is its marginal cost curve (out of the minimum of average variable cost) because it sets production by noting the price and using the marginal cost figure to set production. Therefore, the relationship between its marginal cost and its production (its marginal cost curve) is the same as the relationship between the price it will receive and its production (its supply curve).

Graphical Explanation

Figure 5.2 shows our ATC-AVC-MC cost curve diagram with four potential marginal revenue curves. For each, if there is pressure on the price to change in the short run, this is indicated with a short arrow in the direction of the pressure. If there is long-run pressure, this is indicated with a long arrow. At the first price–marginal revenue, MR_1, the loss is so big that firms want to leave in both the short and the long run. This will reduce the number of sellers and the market price will rise in both the short run and the long run. At MR_2 the chip maker is losing money but not enough for it to close down. So, though the firm does not want to shut down in the short run, it will want to shut down rather than invest money in new equipment as the old equipment wears out. Therefore, the long-run pressure is for the price to rise. At MR_4 our chip maker is making an economic profit. If this happens, others will want to join the chip-making industry and there will be short- and long-run pressure for the price to fall. It is only when the price is at MR_3 that there is no pressure on the price.

Now to why under perfect competition a firm's supply curve is its marginal cost curve out of the minimum of its average variable cost. In Figure 5.3 the arrows from Figure 5.2 have been taken away and the points where the firm will produce are indicated by a dot. These points appear where marginal cost crosses marginal revenue, a circumstance that will come about only if firms do not shut down.

FIGURE 5.2

In perfect competition the market price is under pressure to move to where economic profit is zero.

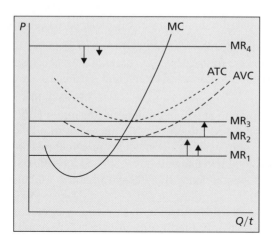

FIGURE 5.3   Points where MC = MR in perfect competition.

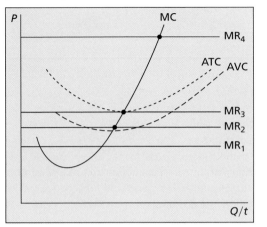

FIGURE 5.4   Derivation of supply: marginal cost out of the minimum of average variable cost.

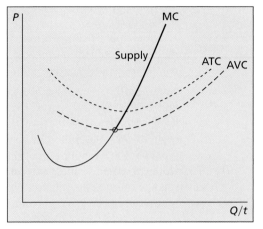

In our final manipulation of the figure we get one of the most important implications of perfect competition. Connecting the dots of Figure 5.3 makes clear the relationship between the price of the chips our firm is selling and the number of chips our firm is willing to produce. If that sounds familiar, it is because that is exactly the definition of supply. As a result we now know that supply, under perfect competition, is marginal cost out of the minimum of average variable cost. This, of course, also demonstrates why the supply curve is upward sloping: marginal cost is increasing.

Although more difficult to show than it is worth, it is important to state that there is no supply curve under monopolistic competition, oligopoly, or monopoly. To understand the reason, note that Figure 5.4 generates the supply curve by finding the production levels with a variety of different prices. Recall from Figure 4.4 that these horizontal price lines also represent perfectly elastic demand curves for a particular firm's output. This same derivation does not work for the other market forms because the elasticity of demand for a firm's output is not perfectly elastic and demand curves of different elasticities result in different profit-maximizing firm output.

Summary

This chapter built on the previous one in which costs and revenues were defined and illustrated. We saw the distinction between perfect competition and monopoly and that they are the endpoints of a continuum. We said that most markets operate somewhere in the middle of this continuum. Further, we distinguished between normal and economic profit, and showed why economic profit disappears under perfect competition but not under monopoly. Last, we saw that under perfect competition, the supply curve from Chapter 2 is the part of the check-shaped marginal cost curve from Chapter 4 that is above average variable cost and is therefore upward sloping.

Key Terms

concentration ratio, 63
economic profit, 64
long run, 65

monopolistic
  competition, 62
normal profit, 64

oligopolistic market, 62
short run, 65

Issues Chapters You Are Ready For Now

Antitrust, 331
Energy Prices, 339
The Economics of
  Prescription Drugs, 218

Ticket Brokers and Ticket
  Scalping, 312
Unions, 375
Walmart, 398

Casino Gambling, 404
Cost of Textbooks, 408

Quiz Yourself

1. An industry in which there are many competitors with specific marketing niches is likely to be characterized by
   a. Monopoly.
   b. Oligopoly.
   c. Monopolistic competition.
   d. Perfect competition.

2. An industry in which there are a very limited number of large firms is likely to be characterized by
   a. Monopoly.
   b. Oligopoly.
   c. Monopolistic competition.
   d. Perfect competition.

3. Owing to it's usefulness and relative simplicity of the supply and demand model is often used
   a. Because nearly every major industry in the United States is governed by perfect competition.
   b. Because nearly every major industry in the United States is governed by monopoly.
   c. Even though, strictly speaking, few industries in the United States are governed by perfect competition.
   d. Even though it has no connection to economic reality.

4. Whether a firm stays in business or shuts down depends heavily on the concept of
   a. Economic profit.
   b. Actual profit.
   c. Market share.
   d. Concentration ratios.

5. Economic theory would suggest that the profitability of an industry would be
   a. Directly related to the number of firms competing in the industry.
   b. Inversely related to the number of firms competing in the industry.
   c. Unrelated to the number of firms competing in the industry.
   d. Zero in the long run, regardless of market structure.

6. Under perfect competition, the supply curve is
   a. The marginal cost curve for all price quantity combinations.
   b. The marginal cost curve, but only that portion that is downward sloping.
   c. The marginal cost curve, but only that portion that is upward sloping.
   d. The marginal cost curve, but only that portion that is above the minimum of average variable cost.

7. An indicator of the degree of competition in an industry is the concentration ratio. It measures
   a. The percentage of sales in the industry by the largest firms.
   b. The percentage of profit in the industry by the smallest firms.
   c. The sales in the industry as a percentage of all consumption in the United States.
   d. The profitability of the industry.

8. Local telephone service was once an area in which consumers had no choices. Many young people no longer use "land lines" preferring instead to use their cellular phones. This means that the market has moved toward
   a. Monopoly.
   b. Oligopoly.
   c. Perfect competition.
   d. Monopsony.

9. In a diagram of perfect competition, the marginal revenue line moves up and down when there is exit and entry, respectively, because
   a. The market demand for the good rises and falls when there is exit and entry, respectively.
   b. The market demand for the good rises and falls when there is entry and exit, respectively.
   c. The market supply for the good rises and falls when there is exit and entry, respectively.
   d. The market supply for the good rises and falls when there is entry and exit, respectively.

10. If MR > MC then when an additional unit is sold the firm's
   a. Profit will be positive.
   b. Profit will increase.
   c. Profit will be negative.
   d. Profit will decrease.

Think about This

One of the concerns about Wal-Mart's entry into the grocery business in the latter part of the 1990s was that it would set low prices, drive little stores out of business, and then raise prices to monopoly levels when it had no competition. That hasn't happened but that doesn't mean it couldn't happen. Under what conditions, and in what industries, might such a strategy work?

Talk about This

List the monopolies that used to exist when you were growing up that are now facing increased competition. Compare that list to a list provided by your instructor (who is presumably older than you). What current monopolies are likely to be threatened with entry in the future?

Behind the Numbers

Concentration ratios for largest four and eight firms in various industries— http://www.census.gov/epcd/ www/concentration.html.

Concentration ratios for 50 largest firms in various industries— http://www.census.gov/epcd/www/pdf/97conc/c97conc/c97s51-sz.pdf.

Chapter **6**

Every Macroeconomic Word You Ever Heard: Gross Domestic Product, Inflation, Unemployment, Recession, and Depression

Chapter Objectives

After reading this chapter you should be able to

Use the basic vocabulary of macroeconomics.

Understand how the economy is measured.

Understand that gross domestic product is our national measure of output and that inflation is calculated using a price index.

See that real gross domestic product is adjusted for inflation and as such is the accepted measure of the economy's health.

Understand how unemployment is measured and be familiar with the types of unemployment that economists recognize.

Use the vocabulary of the business cycle.

Chapter Outline

Measuring the Economy

Real Gross Domestic Product and Why It Is Not Synonymous with Social Welfare

Measuring and Describing Unemployment

Business Cycles

Kick It Up A Notch: . . . But the Bureau of Labor Statistics Isn't Stupid

Summary

microeconomics
That part of the discipline of economics that deals with individual markets and firms.

macroeconomics
That part of the discipline of economics that deals with the economy as a whole.

We shift gears now to talk about the economy as a whole rather than the consumption or production of specific goods. What we covered in Chapters 2 through 5 is called **microeconomics,** because it deals with individual markets and firms. The prefix *micro,* meaning small, applies here because of the narrow scope of microeconomics. The opposite prefix, *macro,* means large, so **macroeconomics** deals with the economy as a whole. When you read or hear "economic news" you more often than not get macroeconomic news. In that context you hear the same words over and over again. This chapter attempts to define and explain the vocabulary of macroeconomics.

We begin the chapter by examining the methods by which we measure the macroeconomy. In that process we define and explain gross domestic product, inflation, and how and why the gross domestic product is adjusted for inflation. We move from there to explain how unemployment is measured, and we finish with a discussion of the business cycle. You will see that all of these economic measures have flaws that economists recognize and study and that though real gross domestic product is an accepted measure of the economy's health, it is not a perfect measure of our nation's overall health.

This is by far the most easily understood chapter of all the theory chapters, but you should make sure that you understand the terms and the concepts behind them thoroughly. Chapter 8 and the more macro-oriented issues chapters rely on them heavily.

MEASURING THE ECONOMY

Measuring Nominal Output

gross domestic product (GDP)
The dollar value of all of the goods and services produced for final sale in the United States in a year.

To keep tabs on how well or how poorly the economy is doing, we measure economic activity by adding up the dollar value of all of the goods and services produced for final sale in the United States in a year. The **gross domestic product (GDP)** is the primary measure of the health of the economy, and some important concepts within this definition need to be highlighted:

1. This measure is a dollar measure that is subject to price variability.
2. Only "final" sales are counted.
3. The goods that are studied must be goods produced within the United States.

The fact that the GDP is influenced by changes in prices must be dealt with at length, but this discussion must be delayed until we explore inflation at length. Moreover, besides inflation, two other fairly straightforward issues should be addressed. The first of these is the issue of double-counting intermediate sales; the second is how to count the production of multinational companies.

To avoid the double-counting of certain economic activity, only final sales are counted. Suppose that you are talking about the production and sale of two loaves of bread. Suppose the first loaf is produced by a woman who grows and grinds the wheat, mixes the dough, bakes the loaf, and sells it all by herself. Suppose another loaf begins with a farmer who grows the wheat and sells it to a miller, who grinds it into flour and sells the flour to a baker, who mixes the dough, bakes the loaf, and sells the loaf to a retailer, who sells the loaf to a customer. If both loaves are of equal quality, then both should be sold for the same price; say one dollar. Clearly both loaves contribute the same to the amount of bread available to society, so both should count the same when we measure economic activity. If you summed all sales along the way, however, the second loaf would count more than the first.

The other aspect of this measure is that it counts production only if it takes place within the borders of the United States. This means the Fords produced in Mexico are not counted in the U.S. GDP but the Hondas produced in Ohio are.

The actual computation of the GDP is done in two distinct ways. One way is to count all those things for which people pay money. This is called the *expenditures approach.* The expenditures approach adds up all of the following: consumption, investment, government spending on goods and services, and exports; then it subtracts imports. The other approach, which counts all those ways in which people earn money, is called the *income approach.* This approach adds up employee compensation, interest, rents, profits, and depreciation and then subtracts income earned in other countries and indirect business taxes (such as sales taxes). Both approaches yield the same result because the money that the buyer "spends" is, by definition, the seller's "income." Therefore, adding up everyone's income and everyone's spending yields the same sum.

The sources that the government uses to compute this information are wide and varied. They are known as the National Income and Product Accounts, and compiling them is complicated and time-consuming. For instance, while the government knows quickly and reliably how much it spends on goods and services, nearly every other piece of information included in the GDP has to come from forms that businesses send to the government: tax forms, unemployment insurance forms, reports of sales and sales taxes, and other documentation. It is therefore obvious, but it warrants noting, that trying to produce the final GDP quickly is difficult. What actually happens is that government economists use sampling techniques to produce preliminary estimates that are repeatedly updated as more information is submitted. When all information is in, sometimes more than a year after the first preliminary estimate is made, a final GDP value is published.[1]

Measuring Prices and Inflation

As we said in the previous section, measuring price changes is important. Whether price changes account for changes in the GDP or whether actual production changes account for those changes is vital to the question of whether we are better off in one period than we were in a previous period. A GDP number that increases because prices rise is less desirable than a GDP that increases because people are actually buying products in greater quantities. For instance, let's make the simplifying assumption that there is only one good in society, cheese, we produce 10 trillion tons of cheese in one year, and cheese is sold at a price of $1/ton. That is vastly better than if we produce only one ton of cheese and it is sold at a price of $10 trillion. Clearly, to discuss the value of production we have to discuss how we measure prices.

market basket
Those goods that average people buy and the quantities they buy them in.

The way that government economists measure prices is intricate. Under their direction, employees of the Bureau of Labor Statistics go shopping for a **market basket** of goods and services in an effort to see if the total cost of that market basket has changed in the current year from what it was in the previous year. To do this they have to establish what should go into that market basket through a process of figuring out what average people buy and in what quantities they buy it. This market basket then makes up a kind of "grocery list" of things that government employees go out and find prices on. Because the average person's buying pattern changes over time, the contents of the market basket, though they remain the same for a period of years, are modified when changes are observed in the fundamental things that people buy.

For the years in which a given grocery list is in effect, government employees go out every month and find the prices of the items that are on the list. The list is very specific, not only indicating what model number or UPC code to look for, but also specifying stores in which the goods need to be located. Frequently, especially with electronic equipment, the item that the employee is supposed to find no longer exists or no longer exists at the specified store. In that case employees must use their best judgment to find a suitable substitute.

base year
Year in which the market basket is established and year to which all other prices are compared.

For each month for which the list is in effect, including the first month of the first year, called the **base year,** Bureau of Labor Statistics employees find the prices of everything on the list. When they finish, a national average is computed. The result constitutes the first key

---

[1]Even then some components are estimates.

price of the market basket in the base year
National average of the total cost of the market basket, abbreviated P_{MB}^{BY}.

piece of information necessary to compute future inflation: it is the national average of the total cost of the market basket. It is called the **price of the market basket in the base year,** and it is abbreviated P_{MB}^{BY}. In succeeding months a revised national average is generated on the basis of new information on prices.

To use this information to measure any inflation that may have arisen in any given year, we have to go through three distinct steps:

1. We find the price of the market basket in the relevant years.
2. We compute a price index for the relevant years.
3. We compute the percentage of change in the relevant price indices.

After arriving at the price of the market basket in the base year, we also have to get the price of the market basket in any of the other years in question. For instance, if you ultimately wanted to know the inflation rate for 2004, you would need the price of the market basket in the base year, 1998; the price of the market basket at the beginning of 2004; and finally the price of the market basket at the beginning of 2005.

price index
A device that centers the price of the market basket around 100.

Next, a **price index,** which centers the price of the market basket around 100, is computed for the beginning of 2004 and 2005. For instance, the **consumer price index (CPI)** for 2004 is

consumer price index (CPI)
The price index based on what average consumers buy.

$$\text{CPI in 2004} = \frac{\text{Price of the market basket in 2004}}{\text{Price of the market basket in the base year of 1998}} \times 100$$

This formula can be interpreted to mean that in the base year the CPI is 100. At other times, as prices rise, the CPI will rise above 100. If prices eventually become twice what they were in the base year, the CPI will be 200.

The last step is to compute the percentage change in the price index. To do this, you take the CPI at the beginning of the year and the CPI at the beginning of the next year and plug them into the formula

$$\text{Inflation during 2004} = \frac{\text{CPI on January 1, 2005} - \text{CPI on January 1, 2004}}{\text{CPI on January 1, 2004}} \times 100\%$$

inflation rate
The percentage increase in the consumer price index.

As a practical matter the CPI is important for another reason. For economists it is important because it is used to generate not only an **inflation rate,** the percentage increase in the CPI, but also the **cost-of-living adjustment,** or **COLA.** This adjustment compensates people for the fact that changes in inflation also change the spending power of their income. For social security recipients and others on pensions that pay a COLA, as well as union members with contracts that are tied to a COLA, this represents the extra income they get each year to compensate them for inflation. Table 6.1 presents a historical picture of the CPI.

cost-of-living adjustment (COLA)
A device that compensates people for the fact that changes in inflation change the spending power of their income.

Problems Measuring Inflation

We now have a measure of inflation that gives us helpful information on how the total price of a given market basket changes. For several reasons, however, it does not do a very good job in measuring the true impact of inflation. The first way in which the CPI can estimate inflation inaccurately derives from the infrequent changes in the market basket. Because it changes only once a decade, large price decreases that occur in the first few years after the introduction of a product are ignored. For instance, VCRs and personal computers did not come into the market basket until 1987. Moreover, until 1997 the market basket did not include cellular phones or DVD players. It still does not include PDAs, IPods, flat-screen TVs, or my favorite invention of the last few years, TiVo boxes. In all of these cases large price

TABLE 6.1
CPI and inflation in
selected years,
1920–2004; base years
1982–1984.

Year	CPI	Inflation Rate (%)	Year	CPI	Inflation Rate (%)	Year	CPI	Inflation Rate (%)
1920	19.4		1983	101.3	3.8	1994	149.7	2.7
1930	16.1		1984	105.3	3.9	1995	153.5	2.5
1940	14.1		1985	109.3	3.8	1996	158.6	3.3
1950	25.0		1986	110.5	1.1	1997	161.3	1.7
1960	29.8		1987	115.4	4.4	1998	163.9	1.6
1970	39.8		1988	120.5	4.4	1999	168.3	2.7
1978	67.7		1989	126.1	4.6	2000	174.0	3.4
1979	76.7	13.3	1990	133.8	6.1	2001	176.7	1.6
1980	86.3	12.5	1991	137.9	3.1	2002	180.9	2.4
1981	94.0	8.9	1992	141.9	2.9	2003	184.3	1.9
1982	97.6	3.8	1993	145.8	2.7	2004	190.3	3.3

Note: CPI is year-end figure.

Source: ftp://ftp.bls.gov/pub/special.requests/cpi/cpiai.txt.

decreases and significant quality improvements occurred long before their inclusion in the market basket. Flat-screen TVs used to be priced at more than $10,000 and can be found now for less than $500. Though the CPI methodology will eventually pick up the final fall in prices once they are included, it will fail to pick up the initial drop in price. Further, even if we ignore, for a moment, that PCs available in 1987 were 10 times faster than those in 1982, they were also less than half the price. In each case the CPI's adoption of these goods occurred well after their actual adoption rates justified it and well after significant price decreases. Therefore, in significant areas the CPI overstates the impact of inflation by failing to capture decreases like those we just described.

The second way in which the CPI may assess inflation inaccurately relates to quality improvements in electronics, which may occur so quickly that by the third or fourth year of the market basket, the good that was originally included no longer exists. The best example of this is the personal computer. Since 1982 PC speeds have doubled every two years. In the two most recent market baskets, by the time the baskets changed, the computer types described in the basket no longer existed.

Third, people have significantly changed the places in which they buy goods. For instance, in the 1950s television sets were, by and large, purchased in department stores or small-appliance stores. Although the personal service customers received during this period undoubtedly exceeded the level of service we now get at large discount stores or warehouse clubs, the price we pay when we make our purchases at discount stores is also much lower. Today we buy from stores where service is low but prices are also very low. If you remember, the government employees who go looking at prices do so at the specific stores designated at the beginning of the life of the market basket. Because they change the store to match consumer behavior only when they change the market basket, they may fail to capture a significant source of price decreases.

Fourth, when prices change dramatically people look for substitutes. Because the market basket is fixed for a long period, it is implicitly assumed that people mindlessly buy exactly the same amount of everything, every period, regardless of prices. This is surely a silly assumption for economists, given that much of Chapter 2 was devoted to how people react to price changes. For an example of how failing to account for substitution can overstate the effects of an increase in the price of one good, consider energy prices.

Inflation's Winners and Losers

An interesting aspect of inflation is that it creates its own set of winners and losers. People living on fixed incomes will be highly sensitive to inflation, and because people who borrow money are paying it back with dollars that are less valuable than the money they borrowed, both they and the lending institutions from whom they borrow will have a stake in the rate of inflation.

Anyone receiving a fixed amount of money per month or per year through an investment or having a fixed amount of cash that they must stretch over a long period of time will be unambiguously hurt by inflation. They will see their buying power drop incrementally over time. To see how important that is, suppose a 65-year-old new retiree sets up an annuity so that she gets $20,000 a year until she dies. If she lives 20 additional years and inflation is running at 5 percent per year, the buying power of that money will be 62 percent lower. Even if inflation is running at a modest 2 percent per year, her buying power will be 33 percent lower. While good financial planners will account for this when setting up such annuities for their clients, retirees who forgo investment advice can get caught in this trap.

In the arena of borrowing and lending there are also winners and losers. Here the important question is not necessarily whether there is inflation but whether inflation is greater than was expected by the respective parties. If inflation is greater than was expected when the interest rate on the loan was established, then borrowers are winners because they are paying the loan back using less valuable dollars than they anticipated. If borrowers are the winners, then lenders are clearly the losers in that they are receiving less valuable dollars in return. Of course, each "dollar" is still worth a dollar, but with inflation running above expectations, each dollar buys less than it was expected to be able to buy when the loan was set up.

On the other hand, if inflation runs less than was expected, the lender is the winner and the borrower is the loser. The borrower is paying the loan back with dollars that have more spending power than they were anticipated to have and the lender is receiving those more valuable dollars.

In the 1970s when energy prices quadrupled, the market basket proportion of energy remained unchanged even though substitutions were made. People changed to more efficient cars and furnaces, drove less, turned their heat down, and installed insulation. Similar actions took place in the last few years as gasoline prices have increased from less than $1 in 1999 to more than $3.00 in some places in 2005. These actions changed what people bought, but the market basket did not reflect these changes until the basket was altered.

REAL GROSS DOMESTIC PRODUCT AND WHY IT IS NOT SYNONYMOUS WITH SOCIAL WELFARE

Real Gross Domestic Product

GDP deflator (GDPDEF)
The price index used to adjust GDP for inflation, including all goods rather than a market basket.

real gross domestic product (RGDP)
An inflation-adjusted measure of GDP.

Having examined inflation and how it is measured, we can now come back to gross domestic product. As we said, one of the concerns with GDP measurement is that changes in prices can affect the GDP just as easily as changes in output. To cleanse our GDP measure of the price changes, we use a price index called a **GDP deflator (GDPDEF).** This inflation-adjusted measure of GDP is called the **real gross domestic product (RGDP).** Real GDP is computed by taking current production of goods and services and multiplying those by their previous year prices and then adding these up across different goods and services. The current production of new goods and services is then added to this figure. This process is different from that which creates the CPI in that the market basket changes from year to year so the choice of a base year is somewhat arbitrary. Still, it allows for a comparison of total production from one year to the next while eliminating the effects of inflation. Further, many economists feel more

FIGURE 6.1

Post–World War II real gross domestic product by quarter, billions of 2000 dollars.

Source: http://www.bea.doc. gov/bea/dn/gdplev.xls.

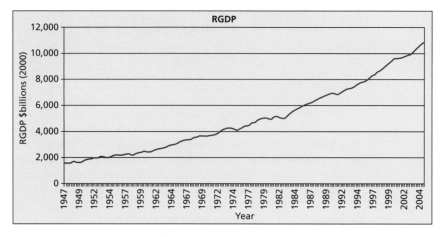

comfortable computing inflation using the GDP deflator approach (which is the annual percentage increase in the GDP deflator) than the CPI approach (which is the annual percentage increase in the CPI). Figure 6.1 shows the trajectory of real GDP since World War II using 2000 as the base year.

Problems with Real GDP

Even with its adjustments, real GDP does not do everything right. Besides having the GDP deflator suffer from many of the problems that the CPI suffers from, real GDP has several other problems.

First, it does not give your mother or father much credit. When either one does things around the house—laundry, cooking, yard work, and the like—the value created in the process is not counted in GDP. It is not counted because it is not sold. Much work gets done and much value is created without sales. I, for instance, installed a large wooden fence around my backyard. Had I gotten a contractor to do it, it would have cost $8,000. Since I built it myself, it cost only $3,000 for supplies and the GDP missed as much as $5,000 of the value that was created.

Second, real GDP does not see that leisure is valuable. If we all worked ourselves to the bone and never took days off, we would cause GDP to rise, but we would be worse off for it. Clearly, in a fully employed society, people who retire voluntarily reduce GDP by the amount of work they would have done. Just as clearly, people retire voluntarily because they are happier fishing, golfing, lollygagging, or volunteering than working.

Third, what people buy is not considered important in the computation of GDP. The substantial increase in government spending on homeland security that resulted from the terrorist attacks of 2001 and beyond were quite likely necessary given the threat, but we are not better off as a society for having to spend this money. We spend it in an attempt to recreate the old sense of security. Spending more money on something that used to require less does not make us better off.

Fourth, the population of the United States is always growing. If real GDP does not grow at the rate that the population does, then the per capita real GDP (the inflation-adjusted goods and services going to the average person) will fall.

Fifth, we can sacrifice environmental quality of life for economic gain, but again we would not necessarily be better off. There is untapped crude oil under the coral reefs off the coast of Florida and under the vast tundra of northern Alaska. We would increase real GDP if we pumped this oil, but the price of doing so would have to include its impact on the environment.

Sixth, just as the laundry and yard work your parents do does not count because the service does not get sold in a market, goods or services sold under the table do not get counted either.

The illegal drugs that people buy do not get recorded anywhere. Similarly, if you mowed lawns or babysat as a teenager, it is unlikely you reported any of that income to the government. If you do not report the income on your taxes and your employer does not either, this economic activity does not appear as part of the GDP. This omission is especially important when it comes to the effect of higher tax rates. Studies reflect the obvious: when taxes are higher, people do more of their work under the table.

For all of these reasons, real GDP cannot be considered a perfect measure of social welfare. Still it remains the primary measure of the economic health of the country. Any attempt to account for the problems outlined above would subject the measure to value judgments about the intrinsic worth of certain goods for which there is little agreement. Therefore, economists generally accept real GDP for what it can tell us while remaining aware of its limitations.

MEASURING AND DESCRIBING UNEMPLOYMENT

Measuring Unemployment

Losing one's job is the most traumatic thing that a person can go through short of the loss of a loved one. Economists therefore consider the unemployment rate to be one of the most important indicators both of the economy and of well-being in general. When people who want and need to work cannot find suitable employment, they lose not only income but also self-esteem. The problem for economists is distinguishing in a meaningful way between stay-at-home parents who might work outside the home if they were paid $50,000 a year and unemployed auto workers who refuse to go from $20 an hour assembling cars to $6 an hour flipping burgers. At what point does the lack of a job go from being the economy's fault for not generating good jobs to being the person's fault for not having realistic expectations? This is an important question, but it is nearly impossible to answer.

The government measures unemployment by conducting phone surveys. The first thing the people making the surveys do is to make sure they are speaking to a person 16 or over. (This is because people under 16 are not counted, whether they are working or not.) Second, they ensure that the person they are talking to is not in the military. (Such people are not counted either.) Third, they ask if the person has done work for pay or worked more than 20 hours a week in a family business during the previous week. If the answer to that question is yes, then the person is considered employed. If the answer to that question is no, then the person is asked if he or she looked for work during the week, that is, whether he or she filled out an application or made a job inquiry. If the answer to that question is yes, then the person is considered unemployed.

work force
All those nonmilitary personnel who are over 16 and are employed or are unemployed and actively seeking employment.

From those surveys the government creates two numbers, the work force and the unemployment rate. The **work force** is generated by adding the employed to the unemployed. The **unemployment rate** is the unemployed divided by the work force and should be interpreted as the percentage of people in the work force who do not have jobs and are actively seeking them. Both of these numbers are announced on the first Friday of every month.

unemployment rate
The percentage of people in the work force who do not have jobs and are actively seeking them.

Problems Measuring Unemployment

This measure of the unemployment rate has some flaws. First, it does not count as unemployed any people who are so discouraged that they stop looking for work. Second, it counts as unemployed those people who are (correctly or incorrectly) encouraged by positive economic news to look for work before there really is any work. Third, it fails to recognize the plight of workers who are working significantly below their skill level or those who would like to work full time but are stuck in part-time jobs. Those suffering from either of these last two problems are referred to as **underemployed**.

underemployment
The state of working significantly below skill level or working fewer hours than desired.

FIGURE 6.2

Post–World War II unemployment rates: the civilian unemployment rate (UR) and the rates as they would be if we include discouraged workers (DW) and the underemployed.

Source: http://stats.bls.gov/ webapps/legacy/cpsatab8.htm. http://data.bls.gov/cgibin/surve ymost?ln
Series: LNS12000000; LNS 14000000; LNS12032194; LNU05026645

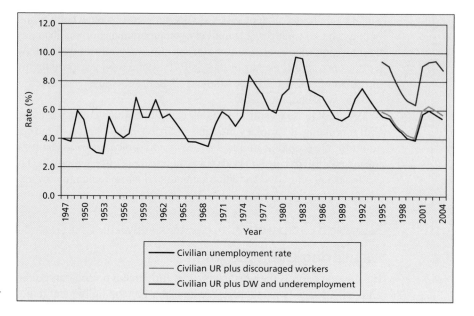

Year

Civilian unemployment rate
Civilian UR plus discouraged workers
Civilian UR plus DW and underemployment

discouraged-worker effect

Bad news induces people to stop looking for work, causing the unemployment rate to fall.

encouraged-worker effect

Good news induces people to start looking for work, causing the unemployment rate to rise (until they succeed in finding work).

cyclical unemployment

State that exists when people lose their jobs because of a temporary downturn in the economy.

seasonal unemployment

State that exists when people lose their jobs predictably every year at the same time.

structural unemployment

State that exists when people lose their jobs because of a change in the economy that makes their particular skill obsolete.

The first two flaws are important because they subject the unemployment rate to incorrect interpretation. For example, if there are 10 people, 8 who work and 2 who are looking, then the unemployment rate is 20 percent. If things turn bad, so that one of the two decides to stop looking, the unemployment rate falls to 11 percent (1/9). Thus bad news in this case causes the unemployment rate to fall. This is called the **discouraged-worker effect,** a process that can be reversed. That is, good news causes people to look for work before there is any, and the unemployment rate rises back to 20 percent. This is called the **encouraged-worker effect.** Figure 6.2 offers a historical perspective on unemployment.

Types of Unemployment

Economists further divide the unemployed by reasons for unemployment. If people lose their jobs because of a temporary downturn in the economy, economists call them **cyclically unemployed.** The **seasonally unemployed** are those people who lose their jobs predictably every year at the same time, like lifeguards in Michigan.

A third type of unemployment is more problematic and permanent. If people lose their jobs because of a change in the economy that makes their particular skill obsolete (either because the industry ceases to exist or because it moves to another country), they are referred to as **structurally unemployed.** These are typically the most difficult people to re-employ because their wage expectations are higher than the positions that remain in the economy that they can fill.

Conversely, a fourth type of unemployment often results from good things in the economy. If things are going well and people get better jobs or at least are encouraged to go out and look for better jobs, they sometimes add to the unemployment rate. For instance, if people hear there are better jobs out there and quit their jobs to devote time to looking for them, they might be surveyed when they are unemployed. Still others may be part of a two-earner family where one gets a promotion that requires that the family move to another city and the spouse who does not get promoted quits to find work in the other city. During the time that such people are looking for work they are categorized as **frictionally unemployed.** These people are unemployed for a short time, but they have skills that employers will want. It just takes time to find the appropriate job. Thus, this type of unemployment exists in any smoothly functioning economy as long as it takes time to find similar or better work.

frictional unemployment
Short-term unemployment during a transition to an equal or better job.

Typically between a quarter and a third of unemployed people are laid off subject to recall (cyclically unemployed), an equal number voluntarily leave their jobs (frictionally unemployed), and the remainder are let go involuntarily without being subject to recall (though not all of this latter group should be referred to as structurally unemployed).

BUSINESS CYCLES

business cycle
Regular pattern of ups and downs in the economy.

trough
The lowest point in the business cycle.

recovery
The part of the growth period of the business cycle from the trough to the previous peak.

expansion
The part of the growth period of the business cycle from the previous peak to the new peak.

peak
The highest point in the business cycle.

recession
The declining period of at least two consecutive quarters in the business cycle.

Over the years there has been such a regular pattern of ups and downs in the economy that economists have put a name to it: the **business cycle.** Figure 6.3 shows the general pattern of the economy over time. Though the general trend is up, you can see that the path is rarely a straight line. With real gross domestic product on one axis and time on the other, you can see that a business cycle has five main components. The **trough** is the lowest point in the business cycle. The **recovery** is the period of growth in RGDP from the trough to the previous peak, that is, the period where RGDP gets back to where it was before the recession began. The **expansion** is the period of growth in RGDP from the previous peak to the new peak. The **peak** is the period where the growth in RGDP slows and eventually stops. A **recession** is a period of at least two consecutive quarters when the RGDP falls and finally works itself back to another trough.

Between 1950 and 2005 there were eight recessions that lasted an average of nine and a half months. Some economists have argued that absent a major precipitating event, such as the September 11 terrorist attacks, the potential for a recession has been lessened by the globalization of the U.S. economy. Typically, a recession is accompanied by a steep rise in the unemployment rate, a moderation in the inflation rate, and a reduction in real gross domestic product in the range of 2 percent to 3 percent. Many times in the last half-century economists have wondered whether the business cycle had been "repealed" only to find that it had not. The worst recession since World War II occurred in the early 1980s. At that time the unemployment rate went from around 7 percent to nearly 11 percent and the inflation rate went from 13 percent to less than 4 percent. The recession that occurred in 1990 as a result of Iraq's invasion of Kuwait had muted effects, in that it lasted only eight months. Its effect on unemployment, inflation, and output was not nearly as stark as the recession of 1981–1982. The recession of 2001 began with the uncertainty of the 2000 presidential election and ended in November of 2001. Figure 6.4 shows the two-plus business cycles from 1982 to 2005.

The potential for a recession has been lessened in some economists' eyes by the globalization of the U.S. economy. Those who argue from this point of view suggest that with greater international trade, countries moving into recessions are bolstered by international demand for their products. Conversely, countries that are in strong recoveries have that impact dampened because purchases that were once domestic often are made from foreign sources.

FIGURE 6.3
The business cycle.

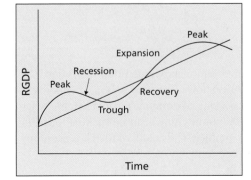

If Inflation Is Bad, How Can Deflation Be Worse?

From 1970 through the late 1990s the predominant concern over prices was their propensity to rise too rapidly. Inflation concerns reached their peak in the late 1970s and early 1980s as prices were rising at or near 10 percent per year. Given that, why would it be a problem for prices to decline? The answer is actually somewhat simple. People delay buying big ticket items when they are certain it will be cheaper if they are patient.

When inflation is running between 1 and 2 percent per year, it is not in anyone's interest to not buy things in hopes that prices will decline because they won't. On the other hand, if prices are falling then there is such a motivation. If consumers do not buy goods in anticipation of price declines, then the people who make those goods will see demand fall. They cut costs by cutting wages and benefits, or worse, by laying people off. When profits decline, the value of stocks declines. With less wealth, stockholders spend less on consumer goods. The final straw is when housing prices start to fall. When that happens people can easily owe more on their house than their house is worth. That results in a dramatic contraction in their willingness to maintain it and the elimination of their ability to borrow money against its equity (since they now have none).

Since the late 1980s Japan has experienced a significant **deflation** in asset prices. The Japanese stock market, as measured by its principal index, the Nikkei 225, fell from nearly 40,000 to less than 10,000 and has struggled to maintain even that level. Japanese real estate values also plummeted during this period. So though Japan's economy was once the envy of the Western world, now some economists are concerned that the United States may follow Japan's lead into a deflation-led 20-year economic slump. That's how deflation can be worse than inflation.

deflation
A general reduction in prices.

FIGURE 6.4

An example of two business cycles: 1981 to 2004.

Source: http://www.bea.gov/bea/dn/gdplev.htm.

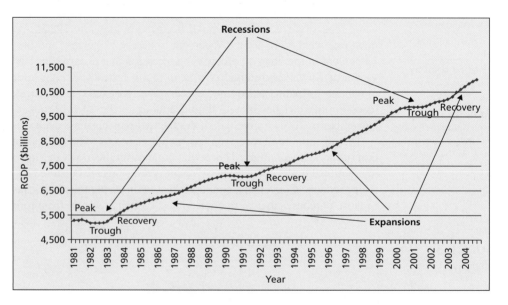

On the other hand, other economists warned that the Asian–Russian–Latin American financial crisis of the late 1990s shows how one region's economy can begin a domino effect that is destabilizing. Just as a string of dominoes is more stable when barriers are strategically placed between dominoes, economies may be more stable if the troubles in one country are insulated from the troubles in another. The health of the U.S. economy during the period did, in the end, stabilize the world economy.

depression

Severe recession typically resulting in a financial panic and bank closures, unemployment rates exceeding 20 percent, prolonged retrenchment in RGDP on the magnitude of 10 percent or more, and significant deflation.

A phenomenon that has not visited the United States in nearly 60 years is **depression.** Although there is no formal economic distinction between a recession and a depression, there certainly is little doubt that we have not experienced a depression since the 1930s. Depressions are severe recessions usually characterized by any one of the following problems: financial panic and bank closures, unemployment rates exceeding 20 percent, prolonged retrenchment in RGDP on the magnitude of 10 percent or more, and significant deflation.

Lessening the likelihood of depression are the economic and social safety nets (e.g., unemployment insurance, welfare) that exist in most modern economies. The recessions that occur when people lack the confidence to buy things can be prevented from becoming depressions by governments that move to alter interest rates and government spending policies. Further, as things worsen and unemployment rises, unemployment insurance and other policies exist now to lessen the effect. Thus people who are unemployed at the beginning of the twenty-first century have much more spending power than those unemployed at the beginning of the twentieth century. This in turn lessens the likelihood that a recession will turn into a depression.

Kick It Up A Notch   . . . BUT THE BUREAU OF LABOR STATISTICS ISN'T STUPID

In 1996, the Boskin Commission established that measuring inflation the way we do probably overstates the true inflation rate by 1.1 percentage points. In response to this criticism and in recognition of these problems, the Bureau of Labor Statistics began an effort to correct some of these flaws.

First, they make an explicit effort to account for the consumer electronics quality problem. Instead of attempting to price out-of-date computers, for instance, they create an index of quality and then try estimate price changes for a good of fixed quality.

Second, they have created a chain-based version of the consumer price index that essentially reestablishes the market basket every year. This allows for new goods to enter the market basket much more quickly and have their initial drops in price count. It also allows them to account for substitution between goods when there are long-term changes in prices, such as the increase in gas prices between the late 1990s and the early part of this decade. While this **chain-based index** is not the one that you hear reported on the news, it still represents progress as far as economists are concerned.

chain-based index

A price index based on an annually adjusted market basket.

Still, these efforts have not solved the problem. In a summary of the issues, Lebrow and Rudd reported that the degree of error in the consumer price index has been cut to less than a percentage point. Though better than before, their 0.8 percentage point estimate for the overstatement is significant. Over the course of 30 years, tax brackets and CPI-adjusted benefits will be overadjusted by 27 percent.

Summary

This chapter presented the basic vocabulary of the macroeconomy and explored many of the measures of it—measures that are not without flaw. We saw that the measure of output is gross domestic product, that prices and inflation are measured using a price index, and that the most frequently referred to price index is the CPI. Moreover, we discussed why

GDP is adjusted for inflation to create real GDP and that this, though also flawed, is a key measure of economic health. Further, the chapter explained how unemployment is measured, that this measure is subject to some concern, and that economists divide the unemployed into types depending on how they got that way. We concluded by discussing the language of the business cycle.

Key Terms

base year, 72
business cycle, 79
Chain-based index, 81
consumer price index
  (CPI), 73
cost-of-living adjustment
  (COLA), 73
cyclical unemployment, 78
deflation, 80
depression, 81
discouraged-worker
  effect, 78
encouraged-worker
  effect, 78

expansion, 79
frictional unemployment, 79
GDP deflator
  (GDPDEF), 75
gross domestic product
  (GDP), 71
inflation rate, 73
macroeconomics, 71
market basket, 72
microeconomics, 71
peak, 79
price index, 73
price of the market basket in
  the base year, 73

real gross domestic product
  (RGDP), 75
recession, 79
recovery, 79
seasonal
  unemployment, 78
structural
  unemployment, 78
trough, 79
underemployment, 77
unemployment rate, 77
work force, 77

Quiz Yourself

1. In measuring gross domestic product, goods produced by foreign firms in the United States are
   a. Counted, and so are goods produced by American firms in foreign countries.
   b. Counted, but goods produced by American firms in foreign countries are not counted.
   c. Not counted, but goods produced by American firms in foreign countries are counted.
   d. Not counted, and goods produced by American firms in foreign countries are also not counted.

2. Gross domestic product is counted using two methods: one which counts all the ways people _____ money and another which counts all the ways people _____ money.
   a. Earn, spend.
   b. Spend, save.
   c. Earn, save.
   d. Loan, borrow.

3. Inflation is measured using _____ in a price index.
   a. The absolute increase.
   b. A multiyear weighted average increase.
   c. The percentage year-to-year increase.
   d. Logarithm adjusted absolute increase.

4. In early 2005, inflation increased unexpectedly because of an increase in oil prices. This helped
   a. Borrowers.
   b. Lenders.

    c. People on fixed incomes.

    d. Workers.

5. The consumer price index (CPI) is a heavily criticized measure of inflation because

    a. The government does nothing to fix its known deficiencies.

    b. It consistently understates the increase in the cost of living.

    c. It consistently overstates the increase in the cost of living.

    d. The government constantly makes adjustments in it without warrant.

6. One problem with using real gross domestic product as a measure of social welfare is that

    a. It fails to count home production.

    b. It fails to count services, a growing part of the economy.

    c. It double, triple, and sometimes quadruple counts goods that are produced in stages.

    d. It fails to account for imports, a growing part of the economy.

7. In 2005, General Motors announced a 20 percent reduction in its staffing levels and the closure of many assembly plants. Those laid off as a result would likely be classified as

    a. Seasonally unemployed.

    b. Cyclically unemployed.

    c. Frictionally unemployed.

    d. Structurally unemployed.

8. On a graph of real gross domestic product over time, recessions appear as

    a. Relatively short and shallow drops on an otherwise increasing path.

    b. Long, sharp declines on an otherwise increasing path.

    c. The dips on a path that increases and decreases equally.

    d. The periods where the rate of growth, while still positive, slows.

9. Of these, economists consider this the worst

    a. Inflation of 5 percent.

    b. Recession.

    c. Deflation of 5 percent.

    d. Depression.

Think about This

Economists have argued for many years that the CPI overstates the cost of living. The degree of that overstatement has been the subject for significant economic research. Part of the problem in resolving the agreed-upon problems is that any correction has the effect of reducing Social Security checks and increasing taxes. Should economic measures be subject to political debate?

Talk about This

Economist Joseph Schumpeter once argued that people are too often lulled into an unproductively comfortable state when they have continuous employment. His conclusion was that recessions (more accurately, depressions, in his era) were good because they forced people to be creative and entrepreneurial. He labeled this "creative destruction." Do you agree with the premise of his argument? Do you agree with his conclusion?

For More Insight See

Hausman, Jerry, "Sources of Bias and Solutions to Bias in the Consumer Price Index," *Journal of Economic Perspectives* 17, no. 1, pp. 23–44.

LeBow, David E., and Jeremy B. Rudd, "Measurement Error in the Consumer Price Index: Where Do We Stand?" *Journal of Economic Literature* XLI, pp. 159–201.

Behind the Numbers

U.S. Gross Domestic Product 1947–2003—http://www.bea.doc.gov/bea/dn/gdplev.xls.

CPI and inflation for selected years—ftp://ftp.bls.gov/pub/special.requests/cpi/cpiai.txt.

Unemployment rate 1947–2002—http://stats.bls.gov/webapps/legacy/cpstatab8.htm.

Recessions 1980–2003—http://www.bea.gov/bea/dn/gdplev.xls.

Chapter **7**

Interest Rates and Present Value

Chapter Objectives

After reading this chapter you should be able to

Understand what interest rates are. Realize why economists delineate nominal from real interest rates and how these ideas are vital to the concept of present value.

Recognize why present value is a tool to use when thinking about economic decisions where the costs and benefits of the decisions happen at different times.

Chapter Outline

Interest Rates

Present Value

Kick It Up A Notch: Risk and Reward

Summary

Many economic decisions take place over time. That is, the time at which the benefits of a given decision are gained is different from the time the costs are incurred. For instance, when you save money, you put off the ability to buy something now so that you have even more money to spend in the future. When you borrow, you get to consume a good before you have sufficient means to pay for it. Thus we agree to give up a single sum now for a larger amount that we will receive later, or we agree to pay a certain amount per month over a series of months rather than pay a single sum now. As it is in any market, there is a price and there is a quantity, and there is a buyer and there is a seller. In this chapter we explore borrowing, lending, investing, and saving decisions.

We begin by exploring interest rates, the price of money, and how they are determined. We look at the importance of anticipated inflation in this decision so as to draw a distinction between nominal and real interest rates, a distinction that is important to economists.

We conclude by looking at financial decisions. We will see that any particular decision to borrow, save, lend, or invest depends on what economists call present value. We will examine scenarios in which we save or borrow a sum of money now in order to get a larger sum of money later. We will also provide more complicated examples in which the payments we make or receive are spread over time.

INTEREST RATES

The Market for Money

interest rate
The percentage, usually expressed in annual terms, of a balance that is paid by a borrower to a lender that is in addition to the original amount borrowed or lent.

When people lend or borrow money, we call the price at which they do this the **interest rate.** A useful way to think of this market for money is to imagine yourself renting a moving van. When you rent such a vehicle, the owner is letting you use it for a predetermined period of time at a predetermined price. Now, instead of renting a van, think about renting money. The owner of the money is letting you use the money for a period of time at a predetermined price. The period of time is typically denoted per year and so the price is an annual interest rate. This means that when you are borrowing money to buy a car or home or seeking money from investors, you must pay interest.

Of course you could be on the other side and be the owner of money that you put in a bank or used to buy a bond. You are now "renting" the money to someone else. In all cases the rate of interest is an important component in your transaction. In this market that we are discussing, the seller is the one with money and the buyer is the one seeking the money.

Figure 7.1 depicts a market like one we saw in Chapters 2 and 3. Here, though, the price is the interest rate and the quantity is the amount that the lender/saver extends to the borrower. The supply curve is upward sloping because the lender/saver will be motivated to lend more if he or she can get a higher return, and the demand curve is downward sloping because at higher interest rates the borrower will view borrowing as less advantageous. As in any other market, an equilibrium interest rate and amount borrowed or lent will result.

The equilibrium interest rate will depend on a number of factors. For instance, the interest rate for people with good credit histories is typically lower than it is for people with poor ones. The bank interest rate for car loans is usually higher than the interest rate for home loans. Credit card interest rates are very high. The reason for this is the degree of risk. A lender cannot assume that a borrower will pay every loan back in full. Lenders are taking a risk and part of what goes into their decisions is the likelihood that the borrowers will pay back the loans and the consequences if they do not. Credit cards are typically not secured by anything, and as a result credit card interest rates are higher than home loans. If a buyer defaults on a home loan, the lender can take possession and ultimately sell the house.

Nominal Interest Rates versus Real Interest Rates

nominal interest rate
The advertised rate of interest.

When the interest rate for a certificate of deposit (CD) or car loan is advertised publicly, that is referred to by economists as the **nominal interest rate.** Though this is the rate of interest referred to in Figure 7.1, it is not as interesting to economists as what they refer to

FIGURE 7.1
The market for money.

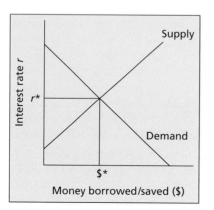

real interest rate

The rate of interest after inflation expectations are accounted for; the compensation for waiting to consume.

as the **real interest rate.** The real interest rate is the rate of interest after inflation expectations have been taken into account. Inflation, which was explained in Chapter 6, is the increase in prices in percentage terms. Inflation matters for our discussion of interest rates because both borrowers and lenders consider the benefits and costs of their decisions in terms of the consumption gained and lost. Since the borrower is presumably going to take the money to buy something now and pay the money back later to a lender who will then buy something with the money, the change in prices is important. Let's consider a concrete example.

Suppose you agree to lend a friend $100 if he agrees to pay you back next year with 10 percent interest. This means that next year you will get $110. Suppose that both of you will end up buying portable mp3 players with the money and that today it costs exactly $100. If the price of these players goes up to $115 by the time you get your money, then you have lost out. He got his player and you did not have enough for one even after waiting a year to get it. On the other hand, if mp3 players increased only to $105, then you could afford one when you got your money and would have $5 extra for waiting the year to get it. What this means is that inflation matters in this borrowing/lending decision. This is especially true if we know what the rate of inflation will be.

Although no one knows for sure what inflation will be in the coming year, people are able to use recent experience as a guide. As a result borrowers and lenders form inflation expectations. If you require $10 compensation for waiting a year to buy your mp3 player and you expect the price to increase by $10, then you will require $120 be paid to you. The first $10 compensates you for the higher prices that will exist when you go to buy yours and the second $10 compensates you for waiting the year to buy it.

What this means for economists is that the nominal interest rate is equal to the sum of inflation expectations and the real interest rate.[1]

PRESENT VALUE

It is easy to see that $100 is more than $50. It is much more difficult to compare $50 today against $100 six years from now. To put dollar values on an even playing field, we compare monies using a concept called **present value.** Using an appropriate interest rate, though, you can compare money paid at two different times. We say that two amounts paid apart from one another in time are equal in present value if the money paid now could be invested at an appropriate interest rate and generate an amount that turns out to be equal to a higher amount that is paid later.

present value

The interest-adjusted value of future payment streams.

Simple Calculations

The math required to fully understand present value is somewhat complicated and is displayed below.

$$\text{Present value} = \frac{\text{Payment}}{(1 + r)^n}$$

where

$$\text{payment} = \text{payment to be received in the future}$$
$$r = \text{interest rate}$$
$$n = \text{number of years before payment is received}$$

Fortunately, the concept and its conclusions are not as complicated as the math. The idea is that the payment in the future needs to be deflated by a factor equal to 1 plus the interest rate

---

[1]There is a mathematical cross-product term as well but it is very small when the inflation and real interest rates are low.

Year	Interest Rate (%)				
	20	**10**	**5**	**2**	**1**
30	237.38	17.45	4.32	1.81	1.35
10	6.19	2.59	1.63	1.22	1.10
5	2.49	1.61	1.28	1.10	1.05
1	1.20	1.10	1.05	1.02	1.01

for every year that is to pass before the payment is made. If the interest rate is 10 percent and 10 years is to pass, then the payment is deflated 10 times by 1.10.

To use a particular example, consider what $200 paid 10 years from now is worth in present value if the interest rate is 10 percent. To compute this we need to multiply 1.1 by itself 10 times. The result is 2.5937, so the present value is $200/2.5937, or approximately $77.11. This means that if you had $77.11 today, and you invested it at 10 percent interest for 10 years, you would have $200. Stated differently, if 10 years from now you were going to receive $200 and wanted to borrow against it and the going rate was 10 percent, you could borrow only $77.31.

As mentioned, the factor 2.5937 was computed by multiplying 1.1 by itself 10 times. Table 7.1 provides factors for several different interest rates for several different periods. The interest rate appears at the top, and the left column indicates the number of years between the time when the borrower gets the money and the time he or she pays it back. The body of the table displays how much money the borrower will have to pay back for every dollar borrowed. For instance, every dollar you borrow on a 20 percent credit card that you fail to pay back within five years costs you $2.49, the original dollar plus $1.49 interest.

Mortgages, Car Payments, and Other Multipayment Examples

We can use this concept to calculate how much house or car we can afford. Here, instead of borrowing a single sum and paying it off with a single payment, we are borrowing a single sum and paying it off in small increments. Of course we could think of situations where we save in small increments to generate a single sum, like saving for a vacation, or situations where we save in small increments to generate other increments, like saving for retirement and getting a monthly check in retirement. These are simply extensions of the same principle.

For each of these examples there is a wonderfully elegant formula that would allow us to plug in various numbers and get results. These formulas, while interesting to those who study financial management issues, are not necessary for us to understand how we might use the present value idea in these other contexts.

For that, let's turn to Figure 7.2, where we will try to evaluate whether a particular business deal is a good idea. Suppose that an investment of $100 each year for five years will, starting in the sixth year, return a payout of $100 a year that will continue for the next seven years. Suppose the appropriate interest rate is 10 percent. In the figure, the down arrows indicate payments being made and up arrows indicate payments being received. The value of each of these payments is shown both with the formula and as the result of that formula. If you add the results, you get the present value, which in this case is negative. A positive present value indicates a good business deal and a negative value indicates a bad one. In this example the present value is negative, which means that this would not be a good business deal.

FIGURE 7.2 Present value of payments.

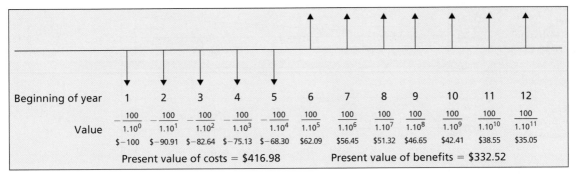

Beginning of year	1	2	3	4	5	6	7	8	9	10	11	12
Value	$-\dfrac{100}{1.10^0}$	$-\dfrac{100}{1.10^1}$	$-\dfrac{100}{1.10^2}$	$-\dfrac{100}{1.10^3}$	$-\dfrac{100}{1.10^4}$	$\dfrac{100}{1.10^5}$	$\dfrac{100}{1.10^6}$	$\dfrac{100}{1.10^7}$	$\dfrac{100}{1.10^8}$	$\dfrac{100}{1.10^9}$	$\dfrac{100}{1.10^{10}}$	$\dfrac{100}{1.10^{11}}$
	$-100	$-90.91	$-82.64	$-75.13	$-68.30	$62.09	$56.45	$51.32	$46.65	$42.41	$38.55	$35.05

Present value of costs = $416.98   Present value of benefits = $332.52

TABLE 7.2

Monthly payments required on a $1,000 loan for various interest rates and various loan durations.

	Interest Rate (%)				
Year	20	10	5	2	1
30	16.71	8.78	5.37	3.70	3.22
10	19.33	13.22	10.61	9.20	8.76
5	26.49	21.25	18.87	17.53	17.09
1	92.63	87.92	85.61	84.24	83.79

All mortgages and car payments are similarly calculated, though these are somewhat more simple because there is only one up arrow, the value of the house or car loan, and the multiple down arrows, the payments that are required. To give you some perspective on how much you would have to make in monthly payments on a variety of loans consider Table 7.2, a very abbreviated set of present value factors. Again at the top are the various yearly interest rates and in the left column are the various loan durations. Thus a $1,000 computer purchased on a 20 percent interest credit card will cost the buyer $26.49 every month for five years. This translates into $1,589.63 in total payments over the five-year loan.

We can use Table 7.2 to figure out what typical monthly payments will be on purchases that you might make in the coming years. We just saw that if you purchase a $1,000 computer using a typical credit card, you will have to pay $26.49 per month for five years to pay off the loan. If you buy a $30,000 car with a five-year payoff period and get a 10 percent interest bank loan, you will have monthly payments of $637.50 (30 × $21.25). If you buy the same car during a financing promotion where the car company loans you the cost of the car at only 2 percent interest, your payments will be only $525.90 (30 × $17.53) per month. Last, if you purchase a $100,000 home with a 30-year mortgage at 5 percent interest, it will cost you $537 (100 × 5.37) per month.

Kick It Up A Notch   RISK AND REWARD

risk
The possibility that the investor will not get anticipated payoffs.

Investing is risky business. Some investments do not pay off as expected. Economists look at **risk** as the possibility that the investor will not get those anticipated payoffs. There are two basic types of risk, the **default risk,** where the borrower doesn't pay the debts and **market risk** where the market value of a stock or bond changes in an unanticipated manner. To compensate the investor, a greater reward is offered. Economists call that greater

FIGURE 7.3
Yield curve for
U.S. Treasuries,
January 2005 with
maturities to 2035.

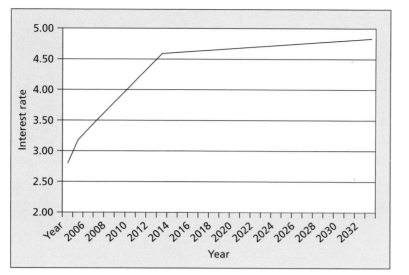

default risk
The risk to the investor
that the borrower will
not pay.

market risk
The risk that the
market value of an asset
will change in an
unanticipated manner.

risk premium
The reward investors
receive for taking
greater risk.

yield curve
The relationship
between reward and the
time until the reward is
received.

reward the **risk premium.** Because longer-term predictions are often less accurate than shorter-term ones, there is also a relationship between the reward an investor receives and the length of time the investor must wait to get that reward. Economists call that relationship between reward and the time you have to wait to get it, the **yield curve.** A sample yield curve for loaning money to the federal government is shown in Figure 7.3.

Summary

This chapter introduced the concept of interest rates and showed that the market for money is no different conceptually from the market for any other good. The interest rate was explained as the price of borrowing money. The difference between real and nominal interest rates was explained, highlighting the notion that real interest rates account for anticipated inflation. These concepts were expanded to explain present value and how that concept can be used to evaluate economic decisions where payments are made or received over a span of time.

Key Terms

Issues Chapters You Are Ready For Now

Quiz Yourself

1. When evaluating a business decision, an economist will often resort to the use of present value because
   a. The profits may not be large enough to warrant the time and attention of the investor.
   b. The investment occurs in one time period and the profits in another.
   c. The investment is often in one currency and the profits in another.
   d. The investment is often under one set of managers and the profits under another.

2. In the market for loanable dollars, an increase in the profitability of investments overall will be revealed in
   a. An increase in the supply of loanable dollars.
   b. An increase in the demand for loanable dollars.
   c. A decrease in the supply of loanable dollars.
   d. A decrease in the demand for loanable dollars.

3. When evaluating whether or not to make an investment one should focus on the _____ because doing so takes into account anticipated inflation.
   a. Nominal interest rate.
   b. Real interest rate.
   c. Exchange rate.
   d. Junk bond rate.

4. Suppose your grandmother told you (today) that she had set aside an amount of money in a savings account bearing 3 percent interest that was sufficient to give you a $5,000 graduation present in exactly four years. How much would she have had to set aside?
   a. $5,000.
   b. $5,000 $\times$ $(1.03)^4$.
   c. $5,000 / (1.03)^4$.
   d. $5,000 / (1 + 0.034)$.

5. Using an interest rate of 5 percent, which figure has the largest present value?
   a. $5,000.
   b. $5,050 to be received two years from now.
   c. $5,075 to be received three years from now.
   d. $5,500 to be received 10 years from now.

6. Using an interest rate of 5 percent, which figure has the smallest present value?
   a. $5,000.
   b. $5,050 to be received two years from now.
   c. $5,075 to be received three years from now.
   d. $5,500 to be received 10 years from now.

7. The present value of a $1,000 payment received two years from now at 5 percent annual interest will be less than $900 because of
   a. Taxes.
   b. Compounding.
   c. Withholding.
   d. Double jeopardy.

8. A 60-month car loan (where no down payment was made) with a 6 percent interest rate and a monthly payment of $500 would allow the borrower to buy a
   a. $35,500 car.
   b. $30,000 car.
   c. $25,863 car.
   d. $28,200 car.

Think about This

The amount of principal paid in the early stages of a mortgage is relatively modest. On a $100,000 loan, at 6 percent for 360 months, the first payment is almost exactly $600 with $500 going for interest and $100 going toward principal. Many new homebuyers are getting "interest-only" mortgages. Suppose that means that for the first five years of the mortgage they are paying only $500 per month. After that they have to pay $644. Do you think this is a good idea?

Talk about This

College students and young people generally get themselves into credit problems because they do not fully understand the consequences of borrowing and overestimate their ability to pay loans back. Should your college censor campus bulletin boards and remove credit card offers from mail you receive in residence halls?

Bankruptcy laws prevent people from defaulting on student loans which means even if you do declare bankruptcy on your credit card debt, you can not get out from money you owe in student loans. Were you aware of this when you took out a student loan and would that impact your decision to take out a student loan?

Chapter **8**

Aggregate Demand and Aggregate Supply

Chapter Objectives

After reading this chapter you should be able to

Understand and manipulate the aggregate supply and aggregate demand model of macroeconomics.

Recognize why the aggregate demand curve is downward sloping and why there is controversy over the shape of the aggregate supply curve.

List the variables that shift these curves and understand how the shifting translates into price and output impacts.

See the difference between demand-pull and cost-push inflation.

Understand what is meant by supply-side economics.

Chapter Outline

Now that we have laid out the language of macroeconomics and some of the measurement issues, it is time that we turn our attention to modeling the macroeconomy. Just as we used the supply and demand model in Chapter 2 to help us understand what would happen in a particular industry if certain variables changed, we use the aggregate supply and aggregate demand model to help us understand how other variables affect the economy as a whole.

Remember that models are not perfect. They rest on simplifying assumptions that allow us to boil down the essentials of what we are looking at in a way that clarifies the big picture. In microeconomics, supply and demand is a well-understood and relatively well-accepted framework to look at particular industries. Regrettably, in macroeconomics no such comparable model exists.

The closest we come to finding a workable model that is relatively easy to use and that is flexible enough to encompass a variety of differing viewpoints is the aggregate supply and aggregate demand model. It also has the virtue of mirroring the supply and demand model that we studied in Chapter 2, so the concepts are less foreign than they would be with a completely new model.

The reason for caution with regard to macro models is that, unlike microeconomic models, where there is only one market, many interrelated goods and services are combined. Whereas we can readily list five important things that influence the price of apples, we would need more than five pages to list the important things that affect the economy as a whole. The macroeconomy is just much bigger and much more complex than any particular market. With this caution in mind we proceed in this chapter with the aggregate supply–aggregate demand model knowing that, although not perfect, it is reasonably suited to the purpose at hand.

Following the method of presentation in Chapter 2, we explain this model by first examining aggregate demand and aggregate supply individually. Then we look at them together, as part of one model. Just as in Chapter 2, where we then looked at why supply and demand might change, we examine why aggregate supply and aggregate demand might change and what happens when they do. Last, we use the aggregate supply–aggregate demand model to explain, albeit very briefly, supply-side economics.

AGGREGATE DEMAND

aggregate demand (AD)

The amounts of real domestic output that domestic consumers, businesses, governments, and foreign buyers collectively will desire to purchase at each possible price level.

Definition

Aggregate demand (AD) is a measure of the amount of goods and services that will be purchased at various prices. It shows the quantities of real domestic output which domestic consumers, businesses, governments, and foreign buyers collectively will desire to purchase at each possible price level. As a practical matter we map this on a graph (Figure 8.1) with our measure of real goods and services sold, real gross domestic product (RGDP), on the horizontal axis and our measure of all prices, the price index (PI), on the vertical axis.

Just as in Chapter 2, when we asserted that the demand curve was downward sloping and then discussed why this makes sense, we do the same now. As shown in Figure 8.1, the aggregate demand curve does, in fact, relate all prices to real output in a negative or inverse manner. This makes sense for three reasons: the real-balances effect, the foreign purchases effect, and the interest rate effect.

FIGURE 8.1

Aggregate demand.

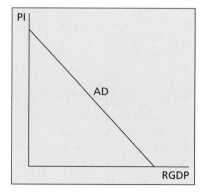

Why Aggregate Demand Is Downward Sloping

real-balances effect
Because higher prices reduce real spending power, prices and output are negatively related.

The **real-balances effect** is the idea that any wealth that you may have in the form of cash or securities becomes less valuable as prices rise. Also, if you have less ability to buy real goods and services when prices are higher, then the two are negatively related.

The second reason why the aggregate demand curve is downward sloping is the **foreign purchases effect.** The argument here is that as prices rise in the United States, Americans will be more willing to buy imports and less willing to buy American-made goods. Foreigners will also be less willing to buy U.S. goods, thus reducing our exports to them. If you remember the expenditures approach from Chapter 6, you will recall that any increase in imports reduces U.S. GDP.

foreign purchases effect
When domestic prices are high relative to their imported alternatives, we will export less to foreign buyers and we will import more from foreign producers. Therefore, higher prices lead to less domestic output.

The **interest rate effect** is that higher prices lead to inflation. This in turn leads to less borrowing and a lowering of RGDP. The definition of aggregate demand will help explain the significance of interest rates as they relate to the downward-sloping nature of the aggregate demand curve. Recall from Chapter 6 that, using the expenditure approach, aggregate demand is calculated by adding total consumption, business investment, government spending on goods and services, and exports and then subtracting imports from that sum. Two of those items, consumption and business investment, are interest-sensitive. When people buy homes, cars, home furnishings, or any good expected to last longer than three years (what economists call *durable goods*), they often do it by borrowing the money. When interest rates are high, the payments people can expect to make on the consumption of these goods will be higher than they are when interest rates are lower. When businesses borrow money to build a new plant or buy new equipment, the payments they must make to their creditors are also determined by the interest rate. Any time the interest rate rises, the volume of both large-dollar-item consumption and business investment will fall because the interest rates have caused costs to be greater. Recall from Chapter 7 that inflation increases interest rates, so if prices rise, inflation rises; if inflation rises, interest rates rise; if interest rates rise, consumption and investment fall; if consumption and investment fall, then RGDP falls.

interest rate effect
Higher prices lead to inflation, which leads to less borrowing and a lowering of RGDP.

AGGREGATE SUPPLY

Definition

aggregate supply (AS)
The level of real domestic output available at each possible price level.

Aggregate supply (AS) is a measure of the level of real domestic output available at each possible price level. The accommodations for differing viewpoints take place in the aggregate supply curve. The differing viewpoints hinge on what is called full employment. Most economists say that full employment exists when cyclical unemployment is zero, so that there are still unemployed people at "full employment." Specifically, the so-called structurally unemployed, the people whose industry has moved or no longer exists, are without work. In addition, the frictionally unemployed, those who quit because they are looking for better jobs or because their spouse found a better job in a new location, are out of work during what is referred to as "full employment." These differences of opinion are displayed in the various ranges of the aggregate supply curve shown in Figure 8.2.

Competing Views of the Shape of Aggregate Supply

We have a serious divergence of opinion among macroeconomists on several important definitions. The following questions separate the two main camps of economists: What constitutes full employment and how are voluntary unemployment and involuntary unemployment defined? While what follows may seem like "airing out dirty laundry in public," it also serves as an excellent "teachable moment" in your general education curriculum.

FIGURE 8.2
The aggregate supply curve.

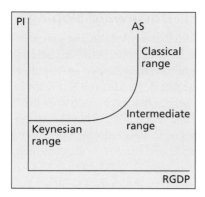

Profound differences of opinion exist in all disciplines, and one of the most profound differences of opinion in macroeconomics centers on these issues. Accepting that there is not a single right answer to every question is an important step in becoming an educated person. So, given that caution. . . .

Classical economists believe in the ability of all markets to generate good outcomes without government involvement. They believe that if minimum-wage jobs are available and unemployed steel workers choose not to take them, they are not involuntarily unemployed, just deluded about their prospects. As a result, they believe that cyclical unemployment is zero and therefore we will, by definition, always be at full employment because changes in the labor market will ensure that each person who wants a job will have one. If people are not willing to work for the market equilibrium wage, then they do not count anyway—at least within the definition of full employment held by classical economists.

Keynesian economists take the opposite view. These economists, followers of the early 20th-century economist John Maynard Keynes, argue that there are always more people willing to work than there are jobs available and that, as a practical matter, we have never actually reached full employment. To Keynesians the concept of full employment is irrelevant. Thus, however many people are employed, Keynesians argue there could always be more and increases in aggregate demand are needed to employ them.

To depict these differing views on a graph, classical economists believe that the aggregate supply curve is vertical all the time. They believe that prices and wages will constantly equilibrate all markets, so increases in aggregate demand will only bid up prices, and the underlying real gross domestic product will remain unchanged. As an example, recall the memory chip-making firm we studied in Chapters 4 and 5. Suppose it has many competitors that are identical to it. If aggregate demand increases leading to an increase in demand for computers and therefore memory chips, our firm will want to expand output. Classical economists argue that since all markets are at full employment to begin with, our firm will have to raise the wage it pays to attract more employees to produce those extra chips. Whether or not the firm succeeds in luring away the workers from the competition, total industry output will remain the same, since the total number of workers will not have changed. The only thing that will change if the classical economists are right is that prices will rise.

On the other hand, Keynesian economists believe that prices and wages are rigid and that unemployment results from that fact. The only way to employ these people, so the Keynesians' argument goes, is to increase aggregate demand. Moreover, since prices do not change, the aggregate supply curve should be thought of as horizontal. Again, using our chip maker as an example, if there are many unemployed workers available for hire into the chip-making business, then increasing output to meet increased demand does not require that wages rise.

A reasonable middle ground between these two models is that some industries are at full employment while other industries are not. If this is the case, an increase in aggregate demand may simply bid up prices in some industries and simply increase output in others. Thus, in the aggregate, real GDP rises a little and prices rise a little. If some industries, like computer chip makers, are at full employment and others, like steel, are not, then an increase in aggregate demand that increases demand for these two products will cause only inflation in the chip industry and only an increase in output in the steel industry.

The aggregate supply curve and the differences among economists are shown in Figure 8.2. As you can see, the vertical portion corresponds to what classical economists believe and is so indicated because any increase in aggregate demand will simply increase prices and not output. Similarly, the horizontal region corresponds to what Keynesian economists believe and is labeled as such because any increase in aggregate demand will simply increase output and not prices. The middle ground, labeled the intermediate range, connects the two ideological extremes and does so on the assumption that the classical economists may be right for some industries and the Keynesians for others.

You should understand that the representation of aggregate supply in Figure 8.2 is not one that most economists would embrace as perfect. For our purposes, though, it allows us to deal with the differences of opinion among the major schools of thought within macroeconomics in a way that is as uncomplicated as it can be. (This is not to say that you will necessarily find it to be uncomplicated.)

SHIFTS IN AGGREGATE DEMAND AND AGGREGATE SUPPLY

Variables That Shift Aggregate Demand

Just as we saw in Chapter 2, where there were factors that shifted demand, there are factors that will shift aggregate demand. If you look at the elements of aggregate demand, you will find clues to what these might be. Anything that affects people's willingness to consume, government's desire or need to spend money on goods and services, business's desire to invest in new plant and equipment, or net exports (exports minus imports) will affect aggregate demand.

For instance, taxes on personal or business income will affect consumption and investment, respectively. With higher tax rates, consumers have less take-home income to spend on things. With higher business or corporate tax rates, prospective business ventures are not as attractive as they might otherwise be. Thus any increase in personal or business taxes will lower aggregate demand, shifting it to the left on the graph, and any increase will raise it, shifting it to the right on the graph.

Any increase in interest rates will have a similar effect. As we saw in Figure 7.1 and as we described in the previous discussion on the interest rate effect, increases in interest costs diminish individuals' and businesses' willingness to borrow money. The result is that aggregate demand decreases and moves to the left on the graph.

Any increase in business and consumer confidence will be followed by an increase in, and a movement to the right in, aggregate demand. This result occurs because as consumers become more confident in their own financial situation, they are more willing to take on debt to buy durable goods. As businesses have more confidence in their ability to sell their products, they will invest more in their productive capacity. Any reduction in that confidence will, of course, have the opposite effect. It will lessen aggregate demand and move the curve to the left on the graph.

The effect of foreign exchange rates on aggregate demand is complicated by the fact that though exchange rates are widely published, the fashion in which they are published is

Why a Strong Dollar Isn't Necessarily Good

There is something vaguely unpatriotic about saying there are problems with a "strong dollar." Nevertheless, it is true. As an example take the euro (€)–dollar($) relationship and apply it to the hypothetical case where a German and an American are car shopping. Suppose each person is looking to buy a midsized sedan and each is comparing a German-made car with an American-made alternative. Each, after extensive research has decided they are of equal quality and overall appeal and that each will simply buy which ever one is cheaper.

Keeping in mind that the euro was created in the 1990s to replace various European currencies and its value was originally pegged to equal one U.S. dollar, then if they are of equal value, the exchange rate is 1–1 (one euro equals one U.S. dollar). That would mean that if each of the cars was equally priced in both the United States and Germany, both cars would cost $30,000 in the United States and both cars would cost 30,000€ in Germany.

Now suppose that American dealers of German cars must buy those cars from Germany for 25,000€ and that German dealers of American cars must buy those cars from the United States for $25,000. That means that American dealers pay $25,000 to a bank to get 25,000€ and German dealers pay 25,000€ to a bank to get $25,000.

If the dollar gets substantially stronger so that the exchange rate moves to 1–.75 (one euro equals 75 cents), then German dealers of American cars would have to pay 33,333€ to a bank to get $25,000 to buy the car from America. To maintain the 5,000€ margin they had been making at the old exchange rate, they would have to raise the price of American cars in Germany to 38,333€. The American dealer of German cars would now need only $18,750 to get the 25,000€ and could therefore maintain the $5,000 margin by charging a price of $23,750 for German cars. Thus, the American is now more likely to buy the imported (German) car and the German is more likely to buy the domestic (German) car. Thus, a stronger dollar increases imports and decreases exports in the United States.

---

often confusing. The Japanese yen typically is expressed in terms of how many yen it takes to buy a U.S. dollar, whereas the British pound typically is expressed in terms of how many dollars it takes to buy the pound. It is as if you went into one bakery looking to buy a dozen donuts and they quoted prices in terms of the number of donuts you can buy for a dollar and another bakery quoted prices in terms of the money you needed to buy a single donut. With a bit of arithmetic you can do the comparison; it just takes a minute. This aside, we can say that if the dollar becomes stronger, exports will fall and imports will rise. Thus a strong dollar reduces aggregate demand, moving it to the left on the graph. Of course, a weaker dollar has the opposite impact. Aggregate demand increases and moves the curve to the right on the graph.

The only variable that impacts aggregate demand directly, one that needs little explanation, is government spending. Because government spending on goods and services is a direct part of the addition that makes up aggregate demand, the impact is direct. An increase in government spending causes an increase in aggregate demand, and a decrease in government spending causes a decrease in aggregate demand. Therefore, an increase in government spending will move the aggregate demand curve to the right and a decrease in government spending will move the curve to the left.

These impacts are summarized in Table 8.1. The effect of an increase in aggregate demand is shown in Figure 8.3, and the effect of a decrease in aggregate demand is shown in Figure 8.4.

TABLE 8.1
Determinants of
aggregate demand.

Variable	Part of Aggregate Demand Affected	Effect of an Increase in Variable on the Movement of Aggregate Demand	Effect of a Decrease in Variable on the Movement of Aggregate Demand
Taxes	Consumption Investment	Decreases AD so curve moves left	Increases AD so curve moves right
Interest rates	Consumption Investment	Decreases AD so curve moves left	Increases AD so curve moves right
Confidence	Consumption Investment	Increases AD so curve moves right	Decreases AD so curve moves left
Strength of the dollar	Exports and imports	Decreases AD so curve moves left	Increases AD so curve moves right
Government spending	Government spending	Increases AD so curve moves right	Decreases AD so curve moves left

FIGURE 8.3   Aggregate demand increases, causing it to move to the right on the graph.

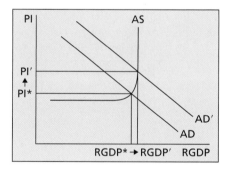

FIGURE 8.4   Aggregate demand decreases, causing it to move to the left on the graph.

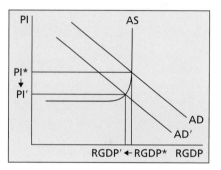

Variables That Shift Aggregate Supply

Just as there are factors that will change aggregate demand, there are important factors that will change aggregate supply. These are factors that are important to business. Any change that increases business costs will be important in terms of aggregate supply. Other factors that matter are government regulations and factors affecting productivity.

Any factor that will increase costs of production will hurt aggregate supply. That is, an increase in labor costs or other input costs will decrease aggregate supply and shift the curve to the left, whereas a decrease in those costs will increase aggregate supply and move the curve to the right. Along with any or all other costs of doing business, interest rates also impact the aggregate supply curve in that they affect borrowing costs on lines of credit used to keep cash-flow problems at a minimum.

Similarly, if government regulations increase costs of production in some way, then aggregate supply will decrease and the curve will shift to the left. Deregulation will have the opposite impact because firms can eliminate costs of complying with regulations. Last, if firms become more productive perhaps through the use of better technology, then aggregate supply will increase and the curve will shift to the right.

Table 8.2 summarizes these impacts; Figures 8.5 and 8.6 summarize the impacts of these shifts on an aggregate supply–aggregate demand diagram. Figure 8.5 shows the impact of an increase in aggregate supply, and Figure 8.6 shows a decrease in aggregate supply.

TABLE 8.2
Determinants of
aggregate supply.

Variable	Effect of an Increase in the Variable on the Movement of Aggregate Supply	Effect of a Decrease in the Variable on the Movement of Aggregate Supply
Input prices	Decreases AS so curve moves left	Increases AS so curve moves right
Productivity	Increases AS so curve moves right	Decreases AS so curve moves left
Government regulation	Decreases AS so curve moves left	Increases AS so curve moves right

FIGURE 8.5   Aggregate supply increases, causing it to move to the right on the graph.

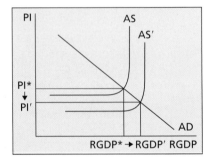

FIGURE 8.6   Aggregate supply decreases, causing it to move to the left on the graph.

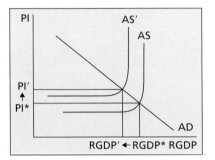

CAUSES OF INFLATION

demand-pull inflation

Inflation caused by an increase in aggregate demand.

cost-push inflation

Inflation caused by a decrease in aggregate supply.

As can be seen in Figures 8.3 and 8.5, increases in prices can result from demand-side impacts or supply-side impacts. Anything that causes the aggregate demand curve to move to the right increases prices. Economists refer to the inflation caused for this reason as **demand-pull inflation.** Anything that causes the aggregate supply curve to move to the left also increases prices. Economists refer to the inflation caused for this reason as **cost-push inflation.**

Many of the things that move the aggregate demand curve to the right are things that government manipulates. If government spending is increased or taxes are decreased, aggregate demand is increased and demand-pull inflation occurs. In addition, monetary policy—government decisions about the money supply—purposefully influences interest rates. If the impact of that policy is the lowering of the rates, then the aggregate demand increases as a result of the increase in interest-sensitive consumption and investment.

During the 1960s, when President Lyndon Johnson was simultaneously carrying on the Vietnam War and attempting to wage a war on poverty, there was a substantial concern of demand-pull inflation. Government spending was increasing rapidly, and though taxes during this period also increased, inflation increased from 1 percent in 1965 to 6 percent in 1970.

Input costs are important influences on the aggregate supply curve. For example, an increase in wages that comes about either because of market actions or legislation will move the aggregate supply curve to the left, thereby increasing prices. Increases in such things as oil prices will have a similar effect on the aggregate supply curve.

The inflation of the late 1970s was largely attributable to increases in oil prices. Oil, a significant input to production throughout the economy, increased from $5.21 per barrel in 1973 to $35.15 per barrel in 1981. This is turn contributed to inflation rising from 3 percent in 1972 to 18 percent in the first quarter of 1980.

HOW THE GOVERNMENT CAN INFLUENCE (BUT PROBABLY NOT CONTROL) THE ECONOMY

In looking at the determinants of aggregate demand and the determinants of aggregate supply, it is clear that government can influence the economy in a number of ways. Taxes, interest rates, the strength of the dollar, and government spending make up four of the five determinants of aggregate demand outlined in Table 8.1, and these are quite clearly areas where the government can exert influence. Input prices and government regulation show up as determinants of aggregate supply in Table 8.2. The latter is quite obviously under the control of government, and there are aspects of the former in which influence is possible.

Demand-Side Macroeconomics

While Chapters 11 and 12 offer more detail on how government policy makers can influence the economy via the demand side, it is worth mentioning here as well. By raising or lowering taxes or by raising or lowering spending, Congress and the president can influence aggregate demand and thereby influence prices and output. Similarly, by raising or lowering target interest rates, the Federal Reserve can influence aggregate demand. To a lesser extent governments, through their ability to buy or sell world currencies, can influence the value of their own currency. These are the means by which government can steer an economy out of a recession. The 13 reductions in interest rates that occurred between January of 2001 and the summer of 2003 and the increase in the child-tax credits in 2001 and 2003 as well as the tax rebate checks they generated were all attempts to jump-start the economy on the demand side.

Supply-Side Macroeconomics

During the late 1970s a new way of thinking about government's ability to influence the economy began to arise. Basically, the new way of thinking involved policy actions that would influence the aggregate supply curve. We have already seen that government spending and interest rate policy influence the aggregate demand curve. Figures 8.3 and 8.4 show that any movement in the aggregate demand curve will either increase RGDP but also increase inflation, or it will decrease RGDP but also decrease inflation. Movements in the aggregate supply curve to the right have only good consequences: inflation is reduced and RGDP is increased.

supply-side economics
Government policy intended to influence the economy through aggregate supply by lowering input costs and reducing regulation.

Supply-side economics involves influencing the aggregate supply curve by lowering input costs and reducing regulation. Though advocates of supply-side economics usually advocate for changes in the tax code, such changes are not necessary. Only some of the actions the Reagan administration (1981–1989) took are properly understood as supply-side actions: tax cuts aimed at businesses (the investment tax credit and accelerated depreciation schedules), attempts at deregulation and lax enforcement of existing regulations, and vetoing of increases in the minimum wage are clearly supply-side policies. On the other hand, the large tax cut to individuals and the larger defense buildup are properly thought of as typical aggregate demand-side policy.

The biggest supply-side impact in the 1980s was that the price of a barrel of oil fell from $40 to less than $10. More recently, the tax cuts proposed by President Bush in 2003 to eliminate the taxation of corporate dividends are properly thought of as supply-side economics.

The argument he was making was that eliminating the double taxation of corporate dividends would stimulate businesses to invest in productivity increasing assets. Whether or not his logic was on target or flawed, the 2003 tax cut did not eliminate double taxation, though it did reduce the top tax rates on capital gains, an objective of supply-side economists.

Summary

This chapter introduced the aggregate demand and aggregate supply model that we will use when discussing the macroeconomy and macroeconomic issues. We first examined aggregate demand and aggregate supply in isolation, explaining why aggregate demand is downward sloping. We also looked at the shape of the aggregate supply curve in the context of the differences between classical and Keynesian views of both aggregate supply and full employment. When they were combined as one, we were able to show what happens when certain macroeconomic variables change. In that way we used them to explain the concepts of cost-push and demand-pull inflation and of supply-side economics.

Key Terms

aggregate demand (AD), 94
aggregate supply (AS), 95
cost-push inflation, 100

demand-pull inflation, 100
foreign purchases effect, 95
interest rate effect, 95

real-balances effect, 95
supply-side economics, 101

Issues Chapters You Are Ready For Now

Federal Deficits, Surpluses, and the National Debt, 114

Fiscal Policy, 126
Monetary Policy, 136

Quiz Yourself

1. Any event that creates a "crisis in confidence" is likely to lead to
   a. Higher aggregate prices.
   b. Higher aggregate output.
   c. Lower aggregate prices.
   d. Inflation.
2. Use the aggregate supply–aggregate demand model to determine which of the following will lead to higher prices.
   a. A tax increase.
   b. A fall in world oil prices.
   c. An increase in interest rates.
   d. An increase in government spending.
3. Use the aggregate supply–aggregate demand model to determine which of the following will lead to higher aggregate output.
   a. A tax increase.
   b. A spike in world oil prices.
   c. A cut in interest rates.
   d. A cut in government spending.
4. Congress and the president have control of the tax system and government spending. As a result their policies will directly impact
   a. Aggregate supply.
   b. Aggregate demand.

c. Residual demand.

d. The demand for loanable dollars.

5. The Federal Reserve has indirect control over short-term interest rates and as a result their ability to control economic activity is through

a. Aggregate supply.

b. Aggregate demand.

c. Residual demand.

d. The exchange rate.

6. An economist worrying about the economic impact of environmental regulations would model that impact with a

a. Decrease in aggregate supply.

b. Increase in aggregate supply.

c. Decrease in aggregate demand.

d. Increase in aggregate demand.

7. Disagreements about the shape of the aggregate supply curve focus on the degree of _____ in the economy.

a. Unemployment.

b. Inflation.

c. Fraud.

d. Confidence.

8. The use of a backward-L–shaped aggregate supply curve allows us to _____ in a way that other shapes would not.

a. Consider various levels of prices.

b. Consider different macroeconomic points of view.

c. Deal with shifting curves.

d. Create an equilibrium.

Think about This

President Harry Truman once lamented that he wanted a "one-handed economist" because we economists have a tendency to say "on the one-hand. . . but on the other hand. . . ." Economists have never made very good presidential aides because we respect the uncertainty of things; we rarely give straight answers because there are rarely simple, straight answers to give. Macro-economics generally, and the aggregate supply–aggregate demand model specifically, embraces that uncertainty. If you were a political leader, would you want a "one-handed" economist?

Talk about This

The aggregate supply–aggregate demand model can be useful in predicting macroeconomic consequences of policy actions (like tax cuts, government spending increases, regulatory actions, interest rate adjustments). It does not tell you about the distributional aspects of policy actions. For instance, a regulatory requirement that all employers offer health insurance would shift the aggregate supply curve to the left, increasing prices and decreasing real GDP. Does that make it a bad idea? Would the impact of such a regulation on health care availability counteract these macroeconomic consequences in your mind?

Chapter 9

Federal Spending

This unmanned reconnaissance aircraft, Predator B, was paid for by the federal government.
Source: Nasa

Chapter Objectives

After reading this chapter you should be able to

Understand the process that goes into creating the federal budget of the United States.

Recognize that mandatory spending—the portion of the budget that is devoted to spending on items for which no annual vote is taken—has steadily increased because of various entitlement programs and interest on the national debt.

See how 30 percent of the federal budget is allocated almost equally to domestic spending and defense, with a relatively small amount going for foreign aid and for dues to international organizations such as the United Nations.

Understand how to use marginal analysis when looking at federal spending.

Distinguish between current-services and baseline budgeting.

See that the idea of opportunity cost is at the heart of federal spending.

Chapter Outline

A Primer on the Constitution and Spending Money

Using Our Understanding of Opportunity Cost

Using Our Understanding of Marginal Analysis

Budgeting for the Future

Summary

The federal government of the United States of America spends more than $2.5 trillion each year on everything from welfare to national defense. This chapter focuses attention on how the government spends that money, a perfect example of how, in public policy, we use the concept of opportunity cost that was introduced in Chapter 1.

We start with a brief primer on what the Constitution requires before money can be spent. We then discuss the difference between mandatory and discretionary spending and how the balance between the two has shifted over the years. Next we lay out where the money was budgeted in the 2006 fiscal year, how that budget reflects on our priorities, and how the shift in distribution over the years reflects a shift in priorities. We focus our attention, in particular, on the health, Social Security, and defense spending, which make up the bulk of the federal budget. We use the Chapter 1 notion of marginal analysis to discuss both the size of federal spending and the distribution of it among various programs. Finally, we describe baseline and current-services budgeting and use Medicare and defense to discuss the differences.

As can be seen in Figure 9.1, federal spending as a percentage of GDP stayed between 18 percent and 22 percent for 28 years. After peaking in 1952 as a result of the Korean War, this measure trended up from 16 percent in 1955 to its modern peak at 22.5 percent in 1982 as spending on social programs increased. The Reagan years saw a slow decline only to rebound in the George Herbert Walker Bush years as billions were spent in a bailout of failed savings and loan associations. Since that time the size of the federal government, measured as a percentage of GDP, had fallen to its lowest point in 25 years only to rise again in the wake of the September 11, 2001 attacks, and the subsequent wars in Afghanistan and Iraq.

A PRIMER ON THE CONSTITUTION AND SPENDING MONEY

What the Constitution Says

According to the Constitution of the United States of America, "No money shall be drawn from the treasury, but in consequence of appropriations made by law." This means that unless Congress passes an appropriations bill and the president either signs it or has a veto overturned, no money can be spent. The president and Congress thus must reach either an agreement or a compromise on spending priorities so that Congress will pass an appropriation bill that the president will sign.

Under normal procedures, the president sends a proposed budget to Congress in late winter or early spring. The Congress often uses that budget as a blueprint upon which it bases a budget plan of its own. It uses its version as it debates and negotiates with the executive branch of government. When both sides reach agreement on a final budget, Congress passes appropriations bills to actually spend the money that has been budgeted.

All of this work must be completed by October 1 because the government's fiscal year starts then and goes to September 30 of the following year. (So the 2006 fiscal year began October 1, 2005, and ended September 30, 2006.) When these bills are passed and signed by the president they become law and money can be spent. Otherwise, money cannot be spent.

Shenanigans

This process has a myriad of places for shenanigans. Chief among these are actions taken by the various subcommittee and committee chairs and in the House–Senate conferences. The chairs of the appropriations subcommittees and the chairs of the full committees can and do influence how much gets spent and where it gets spent. Whereas spending on social insurance

FIGURE 9.1 Federal spending as a percentage of GDP.

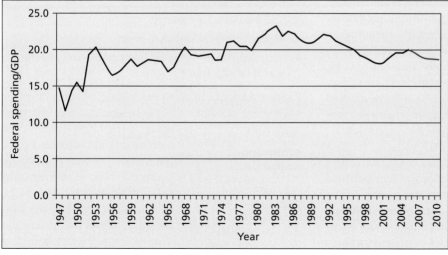

programs like Medicaid, Medicare, and Social Security cannot be easily altered, highway and defense spending are prime targets for spending on items of local rather than national interest. The chair of a subcommittee like the one on highway spending can fund the building of bridges and highways in his or her district much more easily than anyone else can. As with roads and bridges, defense is also an area where the powerful chairs of the subcommittees and the full committees work to ensure that federal money is spent in their districts. Recent history is replete with examples of weapons systems that are not wanted by the military but that are being built anyway because the production facilities are in districts or states of powerful members of Congress.

Even worse, members of the conference committees, who are charged with putting together good compromise bills, have been known to spend significant time making sure money is included for their states or districts and less time making sure the bill is a good one for the country. Members of Congress who have seniority over other members are the ones who are assigned to such committees. Such appointments are considered rewards for years of service. The most egregious products of the conferences are usually found in parts of the final bill that were not in the original House or Senate version of the bill. These are items that conference members knew they could not get passed in their own houses. Knowing they were going to end up on a conference committee, they just waited and made the inclusion of the item they wanted passed a condition of their support for the bill in conference.

Another element of budgetary shenanigans comes when members of Congress agree to support spending programs in each other's districts. This vote trading,

logrolling

The trading of votes used to generate sufficient support for projects that are not in the general interest of the country.

called **logrolling** among economists, increases spending in ways that raise eyebrows. A senator from Vermont got his colleagues to declare Lake Champlain a Great Lake so that it would qualify for an environmental program. The emergency spending legislation approved after the attacks of September 11, 2001, included billions for wholly unrelated items. Bridges, roads, university studies, and memorials to obscure local celebrities tend to grow on spending bills in direct proportion to the need to move the legislation quickly as members of Congress take advantage of the situation and agree to spending that would otherwise require extensive review.

Dealing with Disagreements

The appropriations process seldom moves smoothly, and the process is particularly rough when the political party in control of the White House is not in control of Congress. Disagreements abound when this is the case, and rarely can one party "have its way" with the budget. The Clinton administration's first budget for the 1994 fiscal year passed by one vote in each house, even though there were solid Democratic majorities in both houses. President Clinton enjoyed a Democratic Congress for only two of his eight years. Within a few months of his inauguration, George W. Bush's functioning Senate majority was gone and only a slim majority remained in the House. While slim Republican majorities were reestablished after the 2002 congressional elections, the tax cut of 2003 was less than half the size and quite a bit different in focus than the president originally sought. This was mostly because moderate Republican senators joined their Democratic colleagues in insisting on a trimmed-down version. Even after the 2004 elections, in which President George W. Bush enjoyed an expanded majority in both houses, Congress and the president battled over budget issues. Specifically, Congress passed a highway construction bill that was far beyond what the president wanted. It has been a truly rare circumstance in recent American history where a president had sufficient political party and ideological majorities in Congress to get his way. Thus the usual case for much of the late 20th century featured long and protracted budget debates.

When Congress either does not pass appropriations bills that are acceptable to the president or passes bills the president does not want, there are only four choices:

1. Congress can give in.
2. The president can give in.
3. The government can shut down.
4. Congress can pass a continuing resolution and the president can sign it.

If either side gives in, a bill gets passed. Shutting down the government becomes a battle of chicken until the sides reach compromises. A continuing resolution constitutes an

continuing resolution

A bill passed by Congress and signed by the president that allows the government to temporarily spend money in a fashion identical to the previous year.

agreement to disagree that lets the government continue functioning.

Specifically, a **continuing resolution** is a bill passed by Congress and signed by the president that allows the government to spend money temporarily in a fashion identical to the previous year. This usually happens when Congress does not meet the October 1 deadline. More often than not, it is for only a few of the 13 appropriations bills and for only a few weeks, but in 1983 there was so much disagreement between Republican President Reagan and a Democratic Congress that the entire fiscal year 1984 budget was passed in the form of a continuing resolution.

USING OUR UNDERSTANDING OF OPPORTUNITY COST

The federal budget of the United States is an object lesson in opportunity cost. Whenever money is spent in one area, it cannot be spent in another. Although more money can be spent in all areas, this also has an opportunity cost. When money is taken from taxpayers, their ability to enjoy private consumption is reduced. Deficit spending is also not without opportunity cost. Interest payments add up into the future and money for private investment is reduced.

Some economists argue that the opportunity cost of government deficit spending is such that for every dollar the federal government borrows and spends, a dollar is removed from private investment. If these economists are correct, this phenomenon, called

crowding out

The opportunity cost of government deficit spending is that private investment is reduced.

crowding out, is an example of opportunity cost at work: Government cannot just spend money and make everyone better off. In the process, someone is being made worse off. Other economists suggest that the crowding out is less than complete, which means that for every dollar of government spending something less than a dollar of private spending is lost. In either case there is an opportunity cost to the money spent.

The remainder of this section describes the choices that must be made by Congress and the president when setting out a spending plan.

Mandatory versus Discretionary Spending

Although the actual budget proposal of the president runs to more than 1,000 pages and is incredibly detailed and precise, Figure 9.2 offers its basic distribution of

mandatory spending

Budget items for which a previously passed law requires that money be spent.

spending. You can see that the broadest of its distinctions is the difference between mandatory and discretionary spending. **Mandatory spending** delineates those items for which a pre-

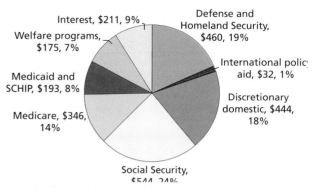

FIGURE 9.2 Fiscal Year 2006 spending (in billions) and percentage of federal budget.

Interest, $211, 9%

Welfare programs, $175, 7%

Medicaid and SCHIP, $193, 8%

Medicare, $346, 14%

Defense and Homeland Security, $460, 19%

International policy aid, $32, 1%

Discretionary domestic, $444, 18%

Social Security, $544, 24%

Source: http://www.whitehouse.gov/omb/budget/fy2006/pdf/hist.pdf

discretionary spending

Budget items for which an annual appropriations bill must be passed so that money can be spent.

viously passed law requires that money be spent while **discretionary spending** is subject to annual appropriations decisions. For instance, current law states that people are entitled to certain benefits that must be paid without regard to any other budget details. Future laws could overturn those now in existence, but the benefits that are currently provided through Social Security, Medicare, Medicaid, and welfare are so firmly entrenched in our society that in reality the money spent on them is untouchable. These four areas of the budget are often referred to as **entitlement** spending because the people for whom they are intended are entitled to the money they receive

entitlement

A program where if people meet certain income or demographic criteria they are automatically eligible to receive benefits.

based on their poverty or age. Entitlement spending is a subset of mandatory spending, which also includes interest on the national debt.

The appropriations for defense, student loans, the courts, and so on, occur annually. While these budgets rarely change drastically from the previous year, a failure to pass an appropriations bill can significantly affect the operations in these areas.

On the discretionary side of the budget there are three main components: defense, international policy and foreign aid, and everything else (broken out in Table 9.1). The most misunderstood and controversial of these is international policy. Of the 32 billion spent in this area, 15 billion is spent to maintain the State Department and

TABLE 9.1   Nondefense domestic discretionary spending, Fiscal Year 2006.

Category of Domestic Discretionary Spending	2006 Spending ($ billions)
Science and space	$24
Natural resources/environment	31
Agriculture	26
Transportation	71
Education and training	89
Veterans	68
Justice	43

Source: http://www.whitehouse.gov/omb/budget/fy2006/pdf/hist.pdf

its embassies in other countries and to pay our dues to the UN and other international organizations. The remaining 17 billion goes to other countries in foreign aid.

As you can see from Figure 9.3, the proportion of the budget devoted to discretionary spending has decreased from over 65 percent to just over 30 percent, while the proportion devoted to mandatory spending has skyrocketed. This led President Clinton in 1993 to decry the fact that under projections valid at the time, by 2010 Congress would convene each year to debate less than 10 percent of the annual budget. Although this trend was halted in the late 1990s, it is now projected to resume.

This brings us back to the inescapable notion of opportunity cost. Every time a new entitlement program comes on board, such as the prescription drug coverage for Medicare recipients, it not only costs money now and

in the future but also reduces the amount of flexibility of future Congresses and presidents as less and less of the budget can be devoted to other priorities.

Where the Money Goes

As you can see from Figure 9.2, defense, Social Security, Medicare, Medicaid, and net interest take up $1.75 trillion of the $2.6 trillion spent each year. The rest is either in the form of other welfare programs such as Temporary Assistance for Needy Families (TANF) or food stamps, or it is spent in the relatively smaller amounts listed in Table 9.1. The biggest of these areas of spending are under the Department of Education and its education and training programs. Of the $89 billion spent on education and training, $45 billion is spent on student loans, grants, and the federal work–study program. The remainder is spent as a supplement to state and local spending on primary and secondary education. Smaller amounts are spent on veterans' benefits ($68 billion), building new highways ($71 billion), the federal justice system ($43 billion), and other programs.

Figure 9.4 indicates that the mix of spending has dramatically changed over the years. Half or more of the federal budget once was devoted to national defense; today the amount is approximately 17 percent (although it rose briefly in 2003 and 2004 to 20 percent.) While Social Security once took up only 15 percent of the budget, today it is approaching 21 percent. Net interest paid increased from less than 10 percent to more than 15 percent only to fall to 7 percent as a result of the surpluses of the late 1990s and early 2000s and the historically low interest rates of

FIGURE 9.3   Mandatory and discretionary spending as a percentage of total federal spending, 1962–2008.

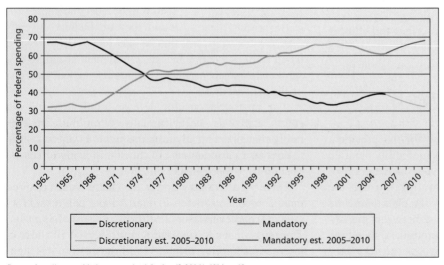

Source: http://www.whitehouse.gov/omb/budget/fy2006/pdf/hist.pdf

FIGURE 9.4   Composition of federal spending.

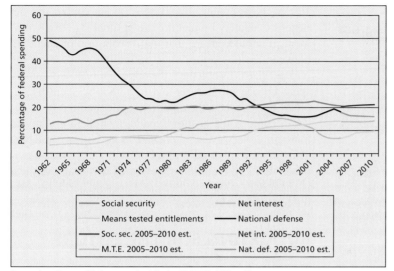

Source: http://www.whitehouse.gov/omb/budget/fy2006/pdf/hist.pdf

FIGURE 9.5   Real health spending by the federal government, 1962–2010, billions of 1982–1984 dollars.

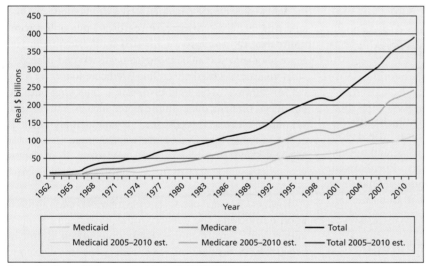

Source: http://www.whitehouse.gov/omb/budget/fy2006/pdf/hist.pdf

2001 through 2004. With significant deficits and increasing interest rates in 2004 and 2005, this figure rebounded and will soon exceed 10 percent.

An area of spending that has increased remarkably since 1970 is federal spending in support of health care. As seen in Figure 9.5, adjusted for inflation, federal spending on health care has risen 1,000 percent over that time. This is because Medicare and Medicaid spending have risen dramatically. When these programs were introduced in the late 1960s, spending on both was trivial. In the 2006 federal budget more than $192 billion is spent on Medicaid and the State Children's Health Insurance Programs, and $340 billion on Medicare. Together this is more than is spent on any program other than Social Security.

Again we are faced with the fact that there are always trade-offs. The trade-offs that we have made until now have clearly been in favor of entitlements. Social Security, Medicare, Medicaid, and various welfare programs have driven the budget for many years. The combined budget for all nondefense domestic spending, which includes

TABLE 9.2   International comparisons of defense spending, 2002.

Country	Defense Spending/GDP
United States	4.0
France	2.1
United Kingdom	2.5
Germany	1.3
Japan	1.1

Source: http://www.census.gov/prod/2004pubs/04statab/intlstat.pdf.

everything from the federal judiciary to student loans, is exceeded by just one program, Social Security. The choice that we have made, to ensure that elderly people and persons who are disabled have steady and reliable incomes, comes at a cost.

Another choice that we have made is to exercise our military power in other parts of the world. Though some would argue that we had no real choice being the world's only superpower, it does, nonetheless, absorb resources and have an opportunity cost. As can be seen from Table 9.2, we spend a higher percentage of our GDP on military expenditures than our allies.

USING OUR UNDERSTANDING OF MARGINAL ANALYSIS

Federal spending is a prime arena to utilize marginal analysis. We can use this form of thinking to discuss whether the federal government spends too little or too much and whether the distribution of spending on various spending priorities is appropriate. Recall from Chapter 1 that marginal analysis compares the marginal benefit of an action with its marginal cost. In particular, that marginal cost is its opportunity cost.

The Size of the Federal Government

In judging the proper size of the federal government, an economist using marginal analysis would attempt to decide if the benefits resulting from additional tax money would outweigh the benefits that would otherwise accrue to private citizens if they were not taxed that amount. A government that purports to be "of, by and for the people" should seek to take only that money needed to fund programs whose marginal benefit is greater than or equal to their marginal cost. Thus it is not enough to say that we are getting $2.5 trillion in value for our $2.5 trillion; we need to be able to say that we are getting a dollar's worth of value for the last dollar of those $2.5 trillion dollars.

The Distribution of Federal Spending

Just as government should seek to maximize the net benefit to society by picking the optimal size of government, it should ensure that the distribution of spending between various priorities is optimal as well. Once the optimal size is established, the opportunity cost of money spent by one program is that it cannot be spent by another. For instance, the choice to build an aircraft carrier could come at the cost of expanding student grants and loans to cover several thousand more college students. Thus money spent on a program with only modest evidence of success could be viewed as wasteful, even if it is spent with good intentions and does no harm, because the money could be spent elsewhere to greater effect.

BUDGETING FOR THE FUTURE

Baseline versus Current Services Budgeting

The yearly budget debate in Washington is replete with claims about who is making what cuts. For instance, during the debate over the 1996 budget, Republicans suggested that spending on Medicare increase yearly at a rate of 9 percent rather than the 14 percent requested by President Clinton. Since another aspect of their program was a broad-based tax cut, they were accused of "cutting Medicare to pay for a tax cut for the rich." This kind of debate is annoying because politicians often redefine simple words such as "cut" or simple phrases such as "broad-based" to suit their argument. It is indisputable that Democrats wanted more money for Medicare and Republicans less. Moreover, Republicans wanted a reduction in taxes in rough proportion to taxes paid and Democrats did not.

Had each side used straightforward and agreed-upon definitions, the debate would have been easier to understand. For instance, Democrats often define a broad-based tax cut as one that goes to everyone equally, whereas Republicans define it as one that goes proportionally to those who pay income taxes. Republicans argue that most of a tax cut should go to those making the most money since they pay the most taxes. (See Chapter 31 on personal income tax.) Democrats, on the other hand, define broad-based tax cuts as those that are given to everyone in similar amounts.

The language problem on spending cuts is equally exasperating. The problem is that when you formulate a budget and you compare it to other years, there is an open question as to how the comparison should be done. If you simply look at last year's budgeted figure and compare it to this year's budgeted figure, you are engaging in what is referred to as **baseline budgeting.** If you are budgeting more than you did last year, that is an increase; if you are budgeting less, that is a decrease. This is a commonsense approach and it is one that Republicans typically take.

baseline budgeting
Using last year's budgeted figure to set this year's budgeted figure.

This approach, however, misses an important point that is vital to interests Democrats support. They wish to ensure that government services are available to everyone who is eligible to receive them. There is no guarantee that baseline budgeting will provide enough money. A reasonable question to ask in budgeting is one that Democrats tend to ask: "How much will it cost to perform services this year in a manner identical to last year?" This is referred to as **current-services budgeting.**

current-services budgeting
Using an estimate of the costs of providing the same level of services next year as last.

Current-services budgeting takes into account such things as overall inflation, inflation in the specific sector, and an increase in the number of people being served. If you want to guarantee enough money to provide identical services in the future, then merely starting with the previous year's baselines may not work. This has been particularly true in the health care field because new, more effective treatments become available. Thus the question is whether the new spending required to meet the old standard of care will be sufficient to meet the new standard.

Using current-services budgeting, President Clinton criticized Republicans in 1995 for their plan to "cut Medicare." Republicans countered, using baseline budgeting, that there was no cut at all. By using jargon with technical definitions to further their own positions, each party was telling the truth. In this case the truth depended on the standard that had been set. If the agreed-upon standard had been baseline budgeting, then the Republicans were right; if it had been current services, then the Democrats were right. Because a standard had not been set, they were both right and they were both wrong.

Spending before and after September 11, 2001

The attacks of September 11, 2001, changed many things, not the least of which was the pattern of federal spending. In 1999, defense spending was on a trajectory such that by 2010 it would have been at its lowest percentage of GDP since World War I. From 1999 to 2001 defense had received 5.5 percent annual increases. Before the attacks, federal law enforcement agencies were receiving modest 4.4 percent per year increases. In fiscal years 2002, 2003, and 2004 defense received 14, 16, and 13 percent increases, respectively, while federal law enforcement agencies received average increases of 15 percent between 2002 and 2005. Overall, the nondefense, non-law-enforcement "on-budget" increases were 4.6 percent before the attacks and 9.7 percent after. As can be clearly seen in Figure 9.6, relative to what spending was in 1999

FIGURE 9.6   Budgetary impact of September 11, 2001, and the subsequent wars in Iraq and Afghanistan.

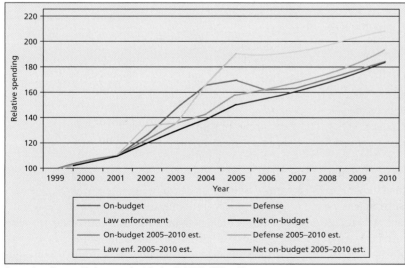

Source: http://www.whitehouse.gov/omb/budget/fy2006/pdf/hist.pdf

for the "on-budget" side of things, for defense, for federal law enforcement, and for the "on-budget" side net of these two categories, overall spending and spending on these areas increased steadily from 1999 to 2001 but rose much more briskly for 2002 and 2005. The rates of growth in all federal spending, even that spending having nothing to do with the 2001 attacks or the wars in Afghanistan and Iraq, increased at a much faster pace after the attacks than before. The federal spending spree continued in 2005 in the aftermath of hurricanes Katrina and Rita as Congress passed more than $60 billion in immediate aid. Such emergency spending is rarely followed by a counteracting cut in another program or tax increase.

Summary

You now understand the process that goes into creating the federal budget of the United States. You know that in percentage terms a large and increasing part of the budget is devoted to spending on items for which no annual vote is taken. You now see that this mandatory spending goes mostly to Social Security, Medicare, Medicaid, various welfare programs, and the costs of interest on the debt. You understand that the rest goes almost equally to spending on domestic concerns and spending on defense.

You see that a relatively small amount goes for foreign aid and other obligations to international organizations such as the United Nations. You understand the difference between current-services and baseline budgeting and why this difference is at the heart of many political debates. Most important, you now understand that the idea of opportunity cost—choices have consequences, and money spent in one area cannot be spent in another—is at the heart of budgeting.

Key Terms

baseline budgeting, 111
continuing resolution, 106
crowding out, 107

current-services budgeting, 111
discretionary spending, 107
entitlement, 107

logrolling, 106
mandatory spending, 107

Quiz Yourself

1. Federal spending is typically_____ percent of GDP
   a. Less than 10.
   b. Between 18 and 22.
   c. Between 25 and 30.
   d. More than 30.

2. The FY 2006 federal budget was around
   a. $2.5 million.
   b. $2.5 billion.
   c. $2.5 trillion.
   d. $2.5 quadrillion.

3. Disagreements between the Congress and the president about the federal budget occur frequently. When they cannot agree on a budget but want to keep the government running they
   a. Use the president's budget.
   b. Use Congress's budget.

   c. Use a budget created by an independent budget commission.
   d. Pass a continuing resolution.

4. Mandatory spending implies spending that is
   a. Required by a previously passed set of laws.
   b. Required by the U.S. Constitution.
   c. Needed more than discretionary spending.
   d. Off-limits for any cuts at any time.

5. The largest single item in federal spending is
   a. International aid.
   b. Welfare.
   c. Defense.
   d. Social Security.

6. Total federal spending on health care, after adjusting for inflation, has been
   a. Growing.
   b. Relatively constant.

c. Declining slowly.

d. Declining rapidly.

7. In determining whether the federal government is the right size, an economist would determine whether
   a. The first dollar spent produced $1 worth of social good.
   b. The average dollar spent produced $1 worth of social good.
   c. The last dollar spent produced $1 worth of social good.
   d. $2.5 trillions of social good was created with the $2.5 trillion spent.

8. In determining whether the distribution of federal spending among various agencies was correct, an economist would want to make sure
   a. That each agency manager got what (s)he thought was needed in that area.
   b. That the last dollar spent in each area produced the same amount of social good.
   c. That the average dollar spent in each area produced the same amount of social good.
   d. That the total amount of money spent in each agency produced the same level of social good.

9. If a program's cost rises only with inflation and increases in those that qualify for the program, this represents
   a. An increase in spending using baseline budgeting.
   b. A decrease in spending using current services budgeting.
   c. No increase or decrease in spending using current services budgeting.
   d. *a* and *c* are both correct.

10. After September 11, 2001, and the subsequent wars in Afghanistan and Iraq, spending on defense and homeland security rose at a much faster rate than before. Between 2002 and 2006 spending on other government programs
    a. Rose faster than for defense and homeland security.
    b. Rose, but at a slower rate than defense and homeland security.
    c. Was frozen.
    d. Was cut.

Think about This

The Medicare prescription drug benefit passed during 2003 comes at a significant long-term cost (at least $720 billion over 10 years). Consider the opportunity cost of this spending in terms of tax cuts, deficit reduction, or spending on other priorities. Would you have committed the federal government to this spending?

Talk about This

When Congress and the president do not agree on a spending package and cannot agree on a continuing resolution, the government shuts down all but emergency services. What, in your mind, should be considered under the umbrella of "emergency."

For More Insight See

Lee, Ronald, and Jonathan Skinner, "Will Aging Baby Boomers Bust the Federal Budget?" *Journal of Economic Perspectives* 13, no. 1 (Winter 1999).

Lynch, Thomas, *Public Budgeting in the United States* (Englewood Cliffs, NJ: Prentice Hall, 1979).

Behind the Numbers

Historical data.
   Federal spending 1947–2004.
   Mandatory and discretionary spending 1962–2010 est.
   Composition of federal spending 1962–2006.
   Federal government health spending 1962–2010 est.
      Budget of the United States Government, 2006; historical tables—http://www.whitehouse.gov/omb/budget/fy2006/pdf/hist.pdf

Fiscal Year 2006.
   Fiscal Year 2006 spending.
   Nondefense domestic discretionary spending.
      Budget of the United States Government, 2006.

International comparisons of defense spending, 2002.
   Statistical Abstract of the United States; comparative international statistics—http://www.census.gov/prod/2004 pubs/04statab/intlstat.pdf
   World Bank; data and statistics—http://www. worldbank.org/data/databytopic/GDP_PPP.pdf.

Chapter **10**

Federal Deficits, Surpluses, and the National Debt

Senator Kent Conrad D-N.D. responds to Congressional Budget Office budget surplus projections. *Source: AP Wide World Photo*

Chapter Objectives

After reading this chapter you should be able to

Understand how economists look at the federal budget deficits and surpluses and the national debt.

See that deficits frequently are caused by wars.

See that economists are interested less in raw numbers than in more sophisticated measures of the burdens that deficits and debt place on us.

Recognize that the U.S. national debt-to-GDP ratio is relatively moderate when compared to U.S. history and to other countries.

See that the federal government owns much of the debt.

Understand why economists are divided on the issue of a balanced-budget amendment to the U.S. Constitution.

See how the debt picture has changed substantially and why deficit projections are so often wrong.

Chapter Outline

Surpluses, Deficits, and the Debt: Definitions and History

How Economists See the Deficit and the Debt

Who Owns the Debt?

A Balanced-Budget Amendment

Projections

Summary

In the 1980s and early 1990s this chapter would have had a simpler title: "Deficits and the National Debt." That's because prior to 1998, deficits were the rule of the day. You had to go back to 1969 to find a year when there was a surplus and back to 1960 to find a second one. Between 1998 and 2001 it looked as though surpluses would be the rule for more than a decade. Since then five things have served to change that expectation again: dramatic stock market declines in 2000–2001 and stagnation through 2005, the recession of 2001 and anemic growth in 2002, the two substantial Bush tax cuts in 2001 and 2003, the impact on military and domestic security spending resulting from September 11th and the wars in Afghanistan and Iraq, and finally the significant increases in non-defense-related spending.

The purpose of this chapter is to discuss the history of the deficits, the surpluses, and the national debt of the U.S. federal government. After a brief history of these, we discuss the main causes of deficits and debt through time. We examine how economists look at the federal debt and how they compare the current state of affairs with other countries and U.S. history. When we discover who actually owns the federal debt, you will be surprised to see that nearly a quarter of it is owned by the federal government itself. We discuss whether a balanced-budget amendment to the U.S. Constitution makes sense as economic policy, and we conclude by looking at the rosy projections of surpluses and the national debt made by the Office of Management and Budget and the Congressional Budget Office and comparing them with much less rosy projections made by others.

SURPLUSES, DEFICITS, AND THE DEBT: DEFINITIONS AND HISTORY

Definitions

budget deficit
The amount by which expenditures exceed revenues.

budget surplus
The amount by which revenues exceed expenditures.

national debt
The total amount owed by the federal government.

Defining **budget deficit, budget surplus,** or **national debt** ought to be simple, but because of the way the federal government does its accounting, the definitions are not as simple as they could be. For instance, you would think that if you did the math, a surplus would result when the total amount of tax revenue that came in was greater than the total amount that you spent. If spending exceeded the revenue, the result would be a deficit, and the debt would be the sum of the deficits minus the sum of the surpluses.

The problem is, the usual definitions are not quite right, and it is because the deficit or surplus for a year is the combination of what are referred to as the off- and onbudget deficits and surpluses. Social Security, Medicare, and other parts of the budget that have trust funds attached to them

off-budget
Parts of the budget designated by Congress as separate from the normal budget. Programs that operate with their own revenue sources and have trust funds; Social Security, Medicare, and the Postal Service are examples.

on-budget
Parts of the budget that rely entirely or mostly on general revenue.

complicate the matter because they are considered **off-budget.** The part of the federal budget that operates from year to year without a trust fund is **on-budget.** So, in 1998, when revenues exceeded expenditures and there was a $60 billion surplus for the total budget, we still added to our national debt because of a deficit in the on-budget part of the equation. Whenever we have an on-budget deficit, we have more debt. Since the off-budget part of the system had a greater surplus than the on-budget part had a deficit, the total budget was in net surplus, yet our debt grew.

History

The annual budget of the United States is never actually balanced. The closest we ever came to a strictly balanced budget was a $3,800 deficit in 1835. Why is the budget not ever balanced? Congress passes the budget *before* it knows exactly how much money is going to come in. When the United States operated under the Articles of Confederation, before the Constitution was ratified, the country had a considerable debt (more than $75 million) from the American Revolutionary War and no money to pay it off. In fact, because the Continental Congress had no power to tax during the war, almost all of the money necessary to fight and win it was borrowed. In the first 58 years of constitutional government in the United States, from 1791 to 1849, there were more years of surplus (36) than deficit (23), and over that time the country ran a net surplus of $60 million. As a matter of fact, in 1836 the debt had all been repaid and President Andrew Jackson got Congress to give states money. Congress missed the mark and gave away $37,000 too much. The only alternative to giving the money to the states—investing in the private sector—was considered inappropriate.

The American Civil War ended notions that the country would ever again go without a national debt. Two billion dollars was borrowed to fight that war, and even though in the 35 years after the war there were more years with a surplus (21) than a deficit (14), the debt remained at $2 billion by 1900. As a matter of fact, in the first 30 years of the 20th century there were almost as many years of surplus (13) as deficit (17). The debt during that period grew because the deficits during the two-year U.S. involvement in World

FIGURE 10.1   The total and off-budget deficits and surpluses since 1940, in billions of 1996 dollars.

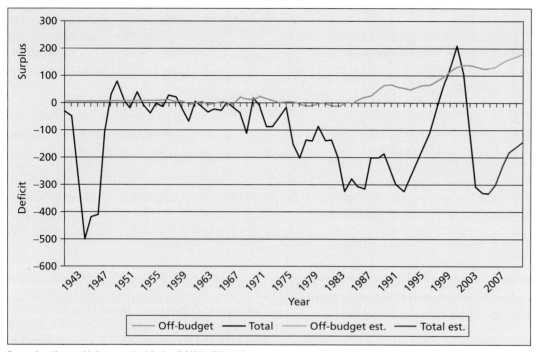

Source: http://www.whitehouse.gov/omb/budget/fy2006/pdf/hist.pdf

War I were twice the size of the combined surplus in the other years. The longest uninterrupted period of debt reduction began just after World War I and lasted until 1930, the first full year of the Great Depression. Surpluses ruled for 11 consecutive years. In general, U.S. economic history prior to the Great Depression can be summarized as one in which the expenses of wars created the debt and steady efforts were made to eliminate the debt when the wars ended.

Since 1930, however, deficits have been more the rule than the exception. During the 76 years from 1930 to 2005, there were only 11 years with surpluses (three years in the 1940s, three in the 1950s, two in the 1960s, two in the 1990s, and two in the 2000s), whereas there were 65 with deficits. Also during that time the national debt grew from $50 billion to $8.0 trillion. Adjusting the deficits and surpluses for inflation, we can compare the relative size of the various years, and this is shown in Figure 10.1.

Figure 10.1 also portrays an important division between the total budget and the off-budget surpluses and deficits. Recall that the total budget is the combination of the on- and off-budget numbers. In recent times, especially after changes in Social Security in 1982 that saw a hefty increase in taxes in anticipation of the large number of retirements among baby boomers, the off-budget surplus has

been substantial. In all but 12 of the 76 years depicted in Figure 10.1, the off-budget part of the system was in surplus, and 9 of these were from the late 1970s and early 1980s, before Social Security taxes were raised substantially. This continues to be the case with the surpluses in the Social Security system. These off-budget surpluses masked the severity of budget deficits in the late 1980s and created the illusion of surpluses in the late 1990s. It was only in fiscal years 1999 and 2000 that the on-budget side was showing a surplus. Since then the on-budget deficit has ballooned to more than $558 billion.

Figure 10.2 displays the trend in deficits as a percentage of GDP. On the left side of the graph the large annual deficits were for the expenses of war, just as 19th-century deficits were. In addition to all of the other upheaval caused by the Great Depression and World War II, budget deficits, measured in 1992 dollars in Figure 10.1 and measured as a percentage of GDP in Figure 10.2, peaked at more than $400 billion a year, or nearly a third of GDP.

The deficits of the 1980s and 1990s were caused by a confluence of events. In 1981 President Ronald Reagan took office on a platform dedicated to decreasing the size of the federal government and to lessening the threat of communism. Part of this meant that he worked to reduce federal income taxes. Tax rates were slashed and

FIGURE 10.2   Deficits as a percentage of GDP: 1940–2004.

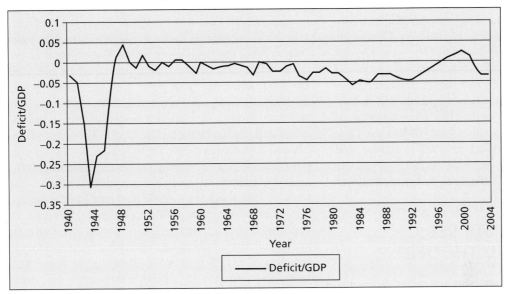

Source: http://www.whitehouse.gov/omb/budget/fy2006/pdf/hist.pdf

important deductions and exemptions were indexed[1] for inflation to prevent bracket creep[2] from raising taxes later. The part of the equation that focused on quelling communism resulted in an increase in federal spending on national defense from $157 billion in 1980 to $303 billion in 1988. All of this might have meant a budget with historically typical deficits had President Reagan been successful in convincing Congress to cut or even substantially slow the rate of increase in domestic spending. Though the rate of increase in spending on those programs that were on-budget did slow, they did not slow enough. In addition, spending on Social Security and Medicare increased substantially faster than before. While revenues grew quickly despite the cut in income taxes, this growth was insufficient to keep pace with the spending increases. With spending growing in nearly all sectors of the budget and revenues not keeping pace, the deficits during this period were, inflation-adjusted, larger than the deficits it took to win World War I but smaller than the deficits it took to win World War II.

Despite incurring the huge deficits, many argue in President Reagan's defense that the victory over the Soviet Union in the Cold War and the **peace dividend** (money that was freed up for other spending priorities when the Cold War was over) that ensued was worth the investment. To back up this position, they claim that the inflation-adjusted military budget in 2000 was smaller than at any-other point since World War II and about half of its 1980s peak. If you accept the proposition that the Reagan defense buildup caused, or at least contributed to, a more rapid ending of the Cold War, then those responsible for allowing the deficits of the 1980s are no more to be criticized than those responsible for the deficits from either of the two world wars.

peace dividend
Money that was freed up for other spending priorities when the Cold War was over.

The dramatic turnaround in the deficit picture that occurred between 1996 and 2001 resulted from a nearly 50 percent increase in taxable income. About a third of that increase resulted from a skyrocketing stock market. From 1991 to 2000 taxable capital gains income increased from just over $100 billion to more than $630 billion. As a result a deficit that had been approaching $300 billion in 1992 turned into a $236 billion surplus in 2000.

Beginning in 2000 things began to unravel. In March, the stock market reached its peak (12,000 on the Dow Jones and 5,000 on the NASDAQ) and began a two-and-a-half year decline (7,500 on the Dow and 1,200 on the

---

[1]Recall from Chapter 6 that indexing is adjusting a dollar amount for inflation. It is called indexing because an index, in this case the consumer price index, is used to perform the adjustment.

[2]When inflation occurs and incomes rise exactly in line with inflation then, unless the tax brackets are adjusted for inflation, people pay a higher percentage of that income in taxes even though the real spending power of their income has remained unchanged. This is called bracket creep.

NASDAQ). Taxable capital gains income was cut by more than half in that time. In November of 2000 we had an election where it took a month of court battles to decide who won the presidency. By the time George W. Bush took office, the economy was in recession and unemployment was on the rise. He delivered on a promised tax cut in the spring of 2001 that further diminished revenues. The attacks of September 11th resulted in vast increases in government spending for reconstruction as well as military and domestic security. More tax cuts, undisciplined federal spending unrelated to defense, and the wars in Afghanistan and Iraq further swelled the deficit such that by 2005 the total budget deficit was more than $400 billion.

HOW ECONOMISTS SEE THE DEFICIT AND THE DEBT

As you know by now, economists see things differently from the way many other people see them. Nothing is more emblematic of that different viewpoint than the way economists look at deficits and the national debt. When noneconomists see that we have spent more than we have paid in taxes, they see it as a problem. Only a minority of economists believe that the current U.S. national debt represents a significant threat to current or future economic health. This differs substantially from the position most economists took in the early 1990s when the deficit was large and growing and the debt and its interest obligations were becoming rapidly burdensome. We next examine why economists hold differing views on this matter.

Operating and Capital Budgets

To see things from an economist's perspective, consider first that the debt is made up of a series of budget deficits over time. The next thing to realize about the budget is that, again from an economist's viewpoint, it is figured all wrong. It should be divided between **operating** and **capital budgets.** Things that

operating budget
That part of the federal budget devoted to spending on goods and services that will be used in the current year.

capital budget
That part of the federal budget devoted to spending on goods that will last several years.

are big, expensive, and will last several years ought not be accounted for in the same way as federal purchases of toilet paper. Highways, dams, and buildings are certainly going to be around for a while, and it makes little economic sense to account for them as though they are going to disappear at the end of the year.

Away from government, what businesses normally do with such large investments is to create a *capital budget.* An investment in an asset with a long life simply has to be able to generate profits over the years that are more than sufficient to make payments on the asset. The expenses of the business that go to pay for items that are used up soon after they are paid for, like labor, paper, and phone calls, go into an *operating budget.* As long as the revenue of the firm is sufficient to cover the operating budget and make the appropriate payments on the capital previously purchased, the business is fine, even if it is carrying a large debt. If big corporations did their accounting the way the federal government does, they would rarely show a profit. When they did show a profit, it would be a great deal smaller than usual.

One problem with separating a capital budget from an operating budget is trying to figure out what spending is an investment that should go into the capital budget and what spending is not. Liberal politicians tend to argue that nearly all social spending should be included in the capital budget. Conservatives, on the other hand, usually say that nearly all military spending should be included in the capital budget. Each would label its spending recommendations as investments in the future and the other's as spending on today. This distinction is important because getting the budget to balance is harder as more goes into the operating side. Moreover, balancing the operating budget is more a political shell game than an exercise grounded in fundamental economic principles.

Cyclical and Structural Deficits

Another way in which economists look at the deficit differently from other people is that we divide it between its structural and cyclical components. In Chapter 6 we broke unemployment into three parts—frictional, cyclical, and structural. We can do a similar thing here. The part of the deficit that is attributable to the economy's not being at full employment is called the

cyclical deficit
That part of the deficit attributable to the economy's not being at full employment.

structural deficit
That part of the deficit that would remain even if the economy were at full employment.

cyclical deficit, and the part of the deficit that would remain even if we were at full employment is called a **structural deficit.** If the deficit is large because the economy is not doing well, then the whole economy is the issue, not the deficit. If the deficit is large even when the economy is doing relatively well, then the deficit is a problem. Economists who think deficits can be used to stimulate a

FIGURE 10.3   Debt as a percentage of GDP: 1940–2010.

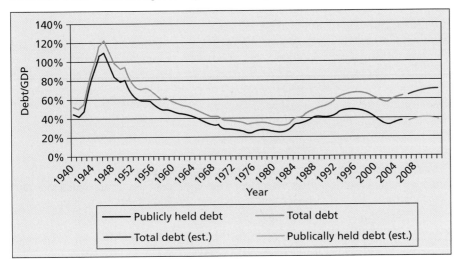

Source: http://www.whitehouse.gov/omb/budget/fy2006/pdf/hist.pdf

functional finance
That part of the budget attributable to programs designed to get an economy out of a recession.

lackluster economy consider that part of the deficit attributable to the "stimulus package" useful and label it **functional finance.**

The Debt as a Percentage of GDP

There are other reasons why most economists do not view the national debt as all that troubling. Among these is that as a percentage of national income, the national debt is not anywhere near as high as it has been. If you look at Figure 10.3, you will see that the ratio of national debt to the GDP has been greater than 1 and, while it increased to near .70 in the 1990s, it fell sharply when, in the late 1990s deficits turned into surpluses. Of course, that lasted only a short time as burgeoning deficits resumed bringing the debt-to-GDP ratio back near the 70 percent level.

Gross domestic product measures what we can afford as a nation, and Figure 10.3 shows that we are in a position that is similar to the average of our recent history.

International Comparisons

There is an even more compelling argument that the current state of the national debt is not out of line. The current U.S. debt-to-GDP ratio is well within the norms of the rest of the world, as seen in Table 10.1. Though this ratio was growing quickly throughout the 1980s and early 1990s, it is currently well below that of Italy, Germany, and Canada, and just above that of the United Kingdom. The country that was once held up as an example of fiscal rectitude,

TABLE 10.1   International comparisons of gross debt-to-GDP ratios.

Year	Canada	U.S.	U.K.	Germany	Italy	Japan
1970	54.1	44.5	78.0	17.5	38.1	10.6
1975	44.9	42.8	62.1	23.1	57.4	20.2
1980	45.6	39.8	54.5	30.2	58.0	47.9
1985	66.3	53.5	59.4	41.6	82.1	64.2
1990	74.5	66.6	33.0	41.5	103.7	68.6
1995	100.3	74.2	52.7	57.2	125.5	87.1
2000	81.8	58.3	45.9	60.9	124.7	134.0
2001	81.0	57.9	41.2	60.4	123.9	142.3
2002	77.7	60.2	41.5	62.9	122.6	149.4
2003	73.3	62.6	42.0	67.0	120.1	154.6
2004	71.5	63.4	44.2	70.1	118.6	157.6

Source: http://www.oecd.org.

Japan, has seen its national debt balloon from 10.6 percent of GDP to more than 150 percent.

Generational Accounting

Some economists look at the deficit and surplus in a completely different fashion. These economists, led by Alan Auerbach and Laurence Kotlikoff, argue that instead of looking at the deficit as a meaningful number we should look at the "net tax rate" that the current policies imply for future generations. To understand their argument, recall the discussion of present value from Chapter 7. These economists and others argue that if you look at the

FIGURE 10.4   Who owns our debt? Percentage of the debt held by the public, trust funds, and the Federal Reserve.

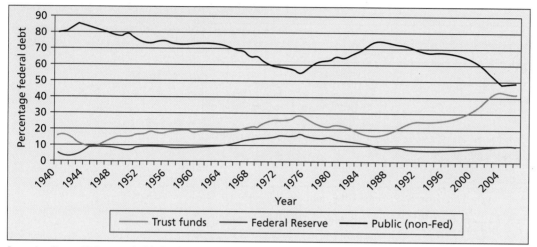

Source: http://www.whitehouse.gov/omb/budget/fy2006/pdf/hist.pdf

difference between the present value of what people of different generations pay in taxes and the transfers that they get in government benefits, you can compute a net tax rate. They claim that this number has been getting steadily worse for younger generations, and that future generations will face a terrible tax burden because of the deficits of the 1980s and 1990s and the entitlement crises of Social Security and Medicare.

WHO OWNS THE DEBT?

The question of who owns the bonds that a nation sells to finance its debt is an important aspect of any nation's debt. Although this may seem like an irrelevant issue, you may be surprised to know that the U.S. government owes itself more than a quarter of the debt. That is what separates the "Total" and "Public" debts in Figure 10.3 and is the point of Figure 10.4. There are two ways in which the federal government lends itself money:

1. The Federal Reserve uses federal debt for purposes of open-market operations.
2. The federal trust funds invest their money by lending it to other parts of the federal government.

As you may see in the issue chapter on monetary policy, the Federal Reserve of the United States (the Fed) has three options for moving the economy: open-market operations, changing key interest rates, and changing the reserve ratio. Open-market operations are

activities that result in the Fed buying or selling bonds. To get money into the economy it buys bonds, and to remove money from the system it sells bonds. Since the role of the Federal Reserve is to keep inflation on an even keel, it must steadily increase the money supply to keep pace with the growth in the economy. Doing so requires that the Fed constantly buy bonds. In this way the federal government owes itself a growing amount of money. If you think that is silly, consider that when the federal government borrows money from itself it also pays itself interest, and as a matter of fact in the early 1990s it was borrowing money from itself to pay interest to itself.

The government also owes itself money through the various trust funds it maintains for Social Security, Medicare, highways, airports, and other smaller parts of the government entities. By law, these trust funds are allowed to invest their money in federal bonds only. Given that these bonds are the safest investment on the planet, this makes sense, but the bonds also return among the lowest interest rates available. In any event, when these programs bring in more money than they spend, the excess is lent to other parts of the government and is money that the government will not have to borrow on the open market.

From Figure 10.4 we see that the amount of federal debt that is held by the public tends to fall unless the deficit and debt are rising quickly. When these are rising quickly, the Federal Reserve is reluctant to buy a great amount of debt in a short period of time because injecting large quantities

FIGURE 10.5   U.S. debt owed to foreign entitites.

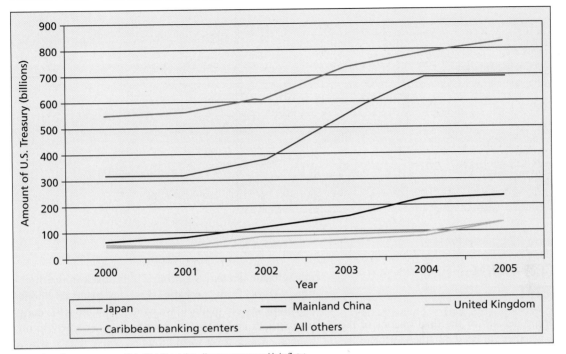

Source: http://www.ustreas.gov/tic/mfhhis01.txt; http://www.ustreas.gov/tic/mfh.txt.

of new money in the system can create inflation. Any time large deficits are rung up, they have to be sold to the public, and the overall proportion held by the public rises. When the deficit is not large or we have a surplus, the percentage held by the public will fall. It is conceivable that if we ran many years of large surpluses, the bulk of the debt would be owed to the government itself.

On a more dreary note, we should remember that the portion of the debt that the Social Security system owns will have to be sold to the public beginning in about 2010. That is when the amount going to Social Security's beneficiaries will exceed the tax payments that fund it. That debt will be transferred to the Treasury and then sold to the public. During that time we can expect that the portion of the debt held by the public will rise. Because of the way we do the accounting now, the national debt will not rise but the amount that is important, the amount held by the public, will.

Externally Held Debt

A concern that has arisen from time to time is the degree to which our national debt is owed to foreigners. At various points in American history our national debt has been owed to citizens of other nations. While we could consider this flattering, in that these non-Americans view the U.S. as a safe place for their savings, it can also be a problem if too much of our debt is owed to foreigners.

Figure 10.5 demonstrates that, in large measure, the Japanese and Chinese have loaned us much of the money we have used to go on the federal spending and tax cut spree of this decade. Our debt to citizens of Japan has more than doubled since 2000 while our debt to Chinese citizens has quadrupled. Of the nearly $8 trillion in debt, about half is owed to real people and of that more than one-third is owed to non–U.S. entities.

This presents a problem for the future in that eventually these investors will want their money back in the form of goods and services. Foreigners are no different than the rest of us: they save in order to buy something later. When one U.S. citizen owes another U.S. citizen money, the future state of the economy is not necessarily threatened. On the other hand, when the U.S. taxpayer owes money to foreign investors, part of the taxes that we pay in the future will go to pay them interest rather than to pay for schools, defense, or our criminal justice system.

FIGURE 10.6   Built-in stabilizers at work.

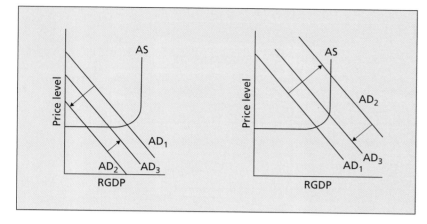

A BALANCED-BUDGET AMENDMENT

One of the important debates of the final quarter of the 20th century was whether we need an amendment to the U.S. Constitution requiring a balanced federal budget. Economists are on both sides of this issue, but the majority believe it is not a good idea. Those who are opposed reason that an inflexible amendment could cause recessions to turn into depressions because the provisions of the amendment would mandate tax increases and spending cuts at precisely the time when just the opposite would be needed. Those in favor of the amendment argue that the politicians' performance in the latter half of the 20th century is evidence of Congress's inability to show the discipline necessary to bring budgets into balance. Balancing the federal budget, it is argued, is necessary to generate low interest rates, which bring about long-term, investment-led growth.

Opponents of balanced budgets and of a constitutional amendment that makes them mandatory offer their best argument against a balanced-budget amendment by appealing to the aggregate supply–aggregate demand model that was explained in Chapter 8. The left panel of Figure 10.6 depicts this model and what would happen if we entered a recession. If aggregate demand were to shrink from AD_1 to AD_2 and a balanced-budget amendment were not required, two things would happen: (1) people would make less money and therefore pay less in taxes and (2) people would require more assistance from government and spending would have to rise. This would happen without any new laws having to be passed. This nondiscretionary fiscal policy is built into the system and is called a *built-in stabilizer*. This stabilizer would result

in aggregate demand's getting a boost back in the direction it came from, perhaps AD_3. If a balanced-budget amendment were in place, we would be without the built-in stabilizer and the movement back to AD_3 would not happen. A recession would thus be worse than it would be if it were to come along now.

Of course the opposite could happen, and the right side of Figure 10.6 depicts that eventuality. Because spending on welfare programs and unemployment benefits would fall and tax revenues would rise, an increase in aggregate demand would result in surpluses. Without a balanced-budget requirement (that might force the money to be spent or taxes cut), aggregate demand would fall back to AD_3. With such a requirement, aggregate demand would not bounce back and the economic boom would be more extensive than otherwise. What this means is a balanced-budget amendment would be **procyclical** because good times would be even better and bad times even worse than they would be without such a requirement. This "boom or bust" phenomenon was part of the economic landscape of the 19th century. Avoiding that outcome has been one of the successes of the economics profession in the post–World War II era.

procyclical
Situation that renders good times better and bad times worse.

The best argument for mandating a balanced budget in some way, however, is that an elimination of federal borrowing would go a long way to reducing interest rates. The results of the 1990s support the idea that reducing the deficit can create a virtuous cycle in which lower deficits create lower interest rates. With lower interest rates the economy grows, tax revenues increase, the deficit decreases even more, and so on. While this

FIGURE 10.7   Deficit and surplus projections of the past.

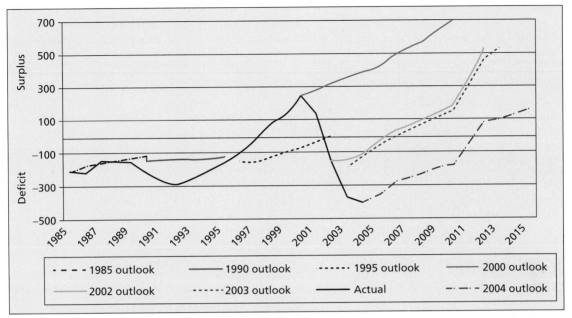

Source: "The Budget and Economic Outlook: An Update," 1985–2005, http://www.cbo.gov.

occurred without a balanced-budget amendment in the late 1990s, the 1960s through the early 1990s was a period of extensive borrowing with little fiscal discipline by either political party.

In the 1990s both the Republican and Democratic parties claimed that reducing the federal deficit was important. Both parties, under President Bush (George Herbert Walker) with a Democratic Congress and President Clinton with a mostly Republican Congress, attempted to reduce the deficit. Each did it with means consistent with their own party's philosophy. They were successful because a reduction in the demand for loanable funds by the federal government translated into lower interest rates. In particular, mortgage interest rates were lower during this period than they had been in 30 years. Lower interest rates meant more business investment as well. What ensued was the most dramatic drop in the deficit and the longest peacetime expansion since the end of World War II.

Both proponents and opponents of such an amendment point to the behavior of the states during the 1990s and early 2000s. Opponents note that the fiscal crises the states experienced between 2002 and 2005 were a direct result of the constitutional requirements to have balanced budgets. Though the constitutions of the states are varied in this regard, they generally suggest that they can spend no more than the revenue for that year plus their built-up reserve. This essentially requires that they have a cyclically balanced budget, one that is in balance over the business cycle.

An annual balanced-budget requirement would not let a state create or utilize a reserve. What occurred in many states, though, was that the shortfall in revenues lasted longer than the reserve. Many states raided their state employee pension funds and delayed payments to local school districts and state universities forcing them to borrow to meet their needs, all in an effort to have a "balanced budget." Opponents argue that governments will resort to these and other "smoke and mirror" tactics when forced to render any balanced-budget amendment meaningless.

Proponents of a federal balanced-budget amendment suggest that most states were doing very well until 1999 and 2000 when they had built up substantial reserves. Had the recession begun two years earlier, most states would have been in a good position to withstand it. Unfortunately, once the recession began in 2001, they had already frittered most of it away on tax cuts and new spending.

PROJECTIONS

In the movie *Major League,* a 1989 baseball comedy, the character played by real-life Milwaukee Brewers announcer Bob Uecker suggests that a pitch that ends up in the stands was "juuuuuust a bit outside." In terms of projecting the deficit/surplus picture the Congressional Budget Office and the Office of Management and Budget have similarly missed the target. In 1990 both were projecting "deficits as far as the eye could see." In 1995 they each projected a shrinking deficit. Five years later they projected that "we would be debt free by 2010." Two years after that it was deficits now, surpluses later.

Figure 10.7 illustrates the rapidly changing projections, but the year 2005, in particular, illustrates the degree of misestimation. In 2000, the prediction for 2005 was that there would be a surplus approaching $402 billion. In 2002 the projection was for a $39 billion deficit. The year actually came to a close with a deficit of more than $400 billion. As a result, the estimates produced in 2000 missed the mark by $800 billion (or one-third the size of the federal government.)

How could they get it so wrong, so often, and still be given any credibility? In an April 2003 report, the Congressional Budget Office makes a pretty good case that it wasn't their fault. They argue that taking into account the things that occurred during this period, they did a pretty good job in short-term projections. They also argue that longer term projections are given more weight than they are due.

Consider these factors: No one foresaw that the economy would grow at twice the projected rates in the late 1990s. No one projected that the stock markets would grow as quickly as they did during this period such that taxable capital gains income would increase 700 percent. No one projected that the 2000 presidential election would insert so much uncertainty into the economy and push it into a recession in 2001. They had no way of knowing in 1995 that George W. Bush would take over as president and get a tax cut enacted in 2001 and 2003. They certainly could not have taken into account in 2000 that Al-Qaeda would attack the United States or that we would respond by going to war in Afghanistan and Iraq in 2002 and 2003. Still, the "outlook" lines on the graph are all upward sloping meaning that the OMB and CBO are always projecting a better future when the reality is that there are ups and downs.

Summary

You now understand how economists look at federal budget deficits and surpluses and the national debt. You know that deficits have been more often than not caused by wars and that economists are less interested in the raw numbers of the debt and deficits than in more sophisticated measures of them. You now are aware of U.S. economic history and that comparisons with other countries indicate that the United States has a relatively moderate national debt-to-GDP ratio. You know that the federal government actually owns much of the debt and you should understand why economists are divided on passing an amendment to the U.S. Constitution that would mandate that it maintain a balanced budget. Finally, you now see that the deficit-surplus picture changed substantially between 1996 and 2001 and changed again as a result of the 2001 recession, the September 11, 2001, terrorist attacks, and the wars in Afghanistan and Iraq.

Key Terms

budget deficit, 115
budget surplus, 115
capital budget, 118
cyclical deficit, 118

functional finance, 119
national debt, 115
off-budget, 115
on-budget, 115

operating budget, 118
peace dividend, 117
procyclical, 122
structural deficit, 118

Quiz Yourself

1. In 2005 the national debt was approximately
   a. $8 million.
   b. $8 billion.
   c. $8 trillion.
   d. $8 quadrillion.

2. The off-budget–on-budget distinction
   a. Is important because two large programs, Social Security and Medicare, largely run off-budget.
   b. Is a historical fiction.

    c. Deals with long-lasting products of government
(like roads and bridges).

    d. Is important because defense is run off-budget.

3. The U.S. budget

    a. Is required to be balanced.

    b. Is never truly balanced but historically surpluses
are more common than deficits.

    c. Is never truly balanced but historically surpluses
are less common than deficits.

    d. Is typically balanced except in time of war.

4. The $400 billion deficits of 2005 were

    a. Accurately forecast by the Office of Management
and Budget in 2000.

    b. Accurately forecast by the Office of Management
and Budget in 2002.

    c. Accurately forecast by the Office of Management
and Budget in 2003.

    d. Much higher than any previous Office of
Management and Budget forecast.

5. The portion of the national debt owed to citizens of
other countries

    a. Is economically irrelevant however big it is.

    b. Is economically important but it has been falling
in recent years.

    c. Is economically important and it has been rising
in recent years.

    d. Is practically inconsequential because it is so small.

6. When looking at a balanced-budget amendment to
the U.S. Constitution, economists

    a. Are universally opposed to it.

    b. Are universally in favor of it.

    c. Are of two minds with opponents concerned
about its pro-cyclical nature.

    d. Are of two minds with proponents excited about
its pro-cyclical nature.

7. By way of international comparison, recent U.S.
deficits have increased the ratio of debt to GDP

    a. Such that the U.S. has the highest ratio in the
industrialized world.

    b. But every other industrialized nation's ratio is
much worse.

    c. But the U.S. ratio is still lower than that of
Germany, Canada, and Japan.

    d. Such that only Japan's ratio is worse.

Think about This

The U.S. and China have had foreign policy disputes in
the past. The most problematic situation could arise over
the status of Taiwan. Does owing Chinese investors
nearly $250 billion make this problem more or less likely
to come to a head? Does economic interdependence promote peace?

Talk about This

What is the opportunity cost of running a high deficit?
How might this opportunity cost depend on the shape
of supply curve for loanable funds? What does it tell
you about the supply curve for loanable funds when interest rates remained low even while the U.S. went
from a $200 billion surplus to a $400 billion deficit
over five years?

For More Insight See

Journal of Economic Perspectives 10, no. 1 (Winter
1996). See articles by Alan J. Auerbach, Ronald Lee and
Jonathan Skinner, and Douglas Bernheim. Lee, Ronald,
and Jonathan Skinner "Will Aging Baby Boomers Bust
the Federal Budget?" *Journal of Economic Perspectives*
13, no. 1 (Winter 1999).

Behind the Numbers

Total U.S. off-budget, on-Budget and total deficit,
surplus, debt, debt sources 1940–2006.
    Budget of the United States Government, historical
        tables—http://www.whitehouse.gov/omb/budget/
        fy2006/pdf/hist.pdf

U.S. GDP 1940–2004.
    Bureau of Economic Analysis—http://www.bea.gov.

International comparisons of gross debt-to-GDP ratios.
    Statistical Abstract of the United States; comparative
    international statistics—http://www.oecd.org.

CBO projections.
    Congressional Budget Office; The Budget and
    Economic Outlook: an update, multiple years—
    http://www. cbo.gov.

Chapter 11

Fiscal Policy

Members of Congress convene at a Joint Session on Capitol Hill. Source: *AP Wide World Photo*

Chapter Objectives

After reading this chapter you should be able to

Understand discretionary and nondiscretionary fiscal policy and how the aggregate supply and aggregate demand model can be used to demonstrate how they work.

Distinguish between aggregate demand and aggregate supply shocks.

See that there are considerable problems associated with discretionary fiscal policy but that nondiscretionary fiscal policy is a mainstay of our current macroeconomic system.

Chapter Outline

Nondiscretionary and Discretionary Fiscal Policy

Using Fiscal Policy to Counteract "Shocks"

Evaluating Fiscal Policy

Kick It Up A Notch: Aggregate Supply Shocks

Summary

When you want government to "do something" about the economy, you are typically referring to **fiscal policy,** which was considered a vital tool in macroeconomics at one time. Fiscal policy is the purposeful movements in government spending or tax policy designed to direct an economy. In the United States, fiscal policy is determined by the Congress and the president.

Fiscal policy is not simply one idea; it is really two. **Discretionary fiscal policy** consists of actions taken at the time of a problem to alter the economy of the moment.

fiscal policy
The purposeful movements in government spending or tax policy designed to direct an economy.

discretionary fiscal policy
Government spending and tax changes enacted at the time of the problem to alter the economy.

nondiscretionary fiscal policy
That set of policies that are built into the system to stabilize the economy.

Nondiscretionary fiscal policy is that set of policies that are built into the system to stabilize the economy when growth is either too fast or too slow.

Discretionary and nondiscretionary fiscal policy are described first. Then we consider the benefits of nondiscretionary fiscal policy and explain why some argue that discretionary fiscal policy cannot claim similar benefits. We use that discussion to examine why policy makers had abandoned discretionary fiscal policy for many years. We finish by discussing the two Bush tax cuts, and specifically the child-credit rebates, in the context of reviving discretionary fiscal policy.

NONDISCRETIONARY AND DISCRETIONARY FISCAL POLICY

How They Work

The difference between nondiscretionary and discretionary fiscal policy is that one is automatic and the other is not. Nondiscretionary fiscal policy, for example, includes government policies that stimulate the economy when it needs stimulus and dampen it when it needs to be dampened. Under discretionary fiscal policy Congress and the president agree on a course of action to stimulate or dampen the economy at a specific time.

Nondiscretionary fiscal policy is at work every day as a result of policies enacted years ago. Every time you get a raise, move to a better job, or make a killing in the stock market, the government takes a portion of your improved income in taxes. The effect on your assets becomes more pronounced as you advance in the tax brackets, because when you make more money you pay a higher percentage of that income in taxes. If you happened to have been a welfare recipient and you have found a job, the effect is even greater. Not only is the government now not providing you with money; it is withholding taxes from your pay. In both cases, the effect of nondiscretionary fiscal policy is dampening the increase in your income.

Of course, nondiscretionary fiscal policy can have the opposite effect as well. If you lose your job, get demoted, or lose a lot of money in the market, your tax burden falls. If you lose your job and go back on welfare, the effect is again magnified. The government is not taking money from you but is giving money to you. This stimulates the economy somewhat, and it thus has the effect of helping to counteract the loss you incurred.

Because our progressive income tax system increases the percentage that you pay in taxes as you make more money and because federal and state programs are in place that offer economic assistance when you need it, nondiscretionary fiscal policy is constantly working to stabilize the economy. No one has to use any discretion—that is, make any decisions—to make it work. Therefore, it is called nondiscretionary fiscal policy. Because the actions are built into the system, nondiscretionary fiscal policy is often referred to as a *built-in stabilizer.*

With discretionary fiscal policy, on the other hand, action is required by Congress and the president. When each decides that the economy is in need of a specific action that will properly stimulate or dampen it, the usual actions that they consider involve changes in taxes or spending policies. Historically, fiscal policy has been used to stimulate an economy in recession but rarely to dampen an economy that is running too hot.[1]

The specific policy actions used in the past were tax cuts and funding of public works projects to give jobs to people who were unemployed. In the middle 1970s, for example, President Gerald Ford sought to provide each taxpayer with a tax rebate of $50. During the Great Depression many unemployed workers found jobs in government programs that built roads, dams, and bridges.

During his 2000 campaign President George Bush promised a broad-based tax cut. Shortly after being determined the victor, he began to discuss the economic slowdown that seemed to be going on. He used this slowdown as an argument for immediate passage of his plan. Part of what emerged was a tax rebate mailed out during the late summer of 2001. This rebate, $300 for singles, $500 for single parents, and $600 for married couples, was intended to stimulate an economy that was in recession in 2001. In 2003, when the economy was growing at a rather anemic pace, a similar plan was enacted. Tax rebate checks of $400 per child were sent to those parents who had paid federal income taxes in 2002.

Using Aggregate Supply and Aggregate Demand to Model Fiscal Policy

Our aggregate supply and aggregate demand model is a useful tool for examining the effect of both forms of fiscal policy. Both discretionary and nondiscretionary fiscal policy work to move the aggregate demand curve. Figure 11.1 shows the effect of expansionary fiscal policy and Figure 11.2 shows the effect of contractionary fiscal policy. *Expansionary* fiscal policy options, such as increased government spending and decreases in taxes, are reflected in an aggregate demand curve that moves to the right. *Contractionary* fiscal policy options, including decreased government spending and increases in taxes, are seen in an aggregate demand curve that moves to the left.

---

[1]A one-year 10 percent surtax was added to income taxes in the Lyndon Johnson administration. Some justified this action as an effort to combat inflation.

FIGURE 11.1 Expansionary fiscal policy.

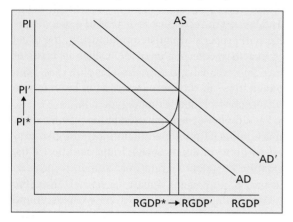

FIGURE 11.2 Contractionary fiscal policy.

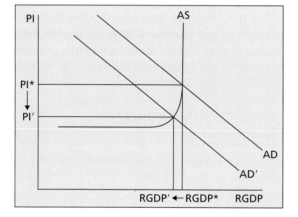

It should be noted that there is considerable debate over whether any fiscal policy will have a real impact on the economy. A useful but relatively simplistic way of thinking about this argument is to frame it in terms of where on the aggregate supply curve the economy lies. Those who believe that we are on the vertical portion of the curve argue that any expansionary fiscal policy will be completely ineffective. It will merely create inflation without bolstering output.

It is worth mentioning that the money necessary to engage in expansionary fiscal policy does not come out of thin air. The increased government spending and the reduced tax revenue generate a shortfall that must be made up with either borrowing or printing the requisite money. Economists do not consider the latter option a good one in that inflation is nearly always the result. Thus deficits financed through borrowing money tend to be the result of expansionary fiscal policy.

USING FISCAL POLICY TO COUNTERACT "SHOCKS"

Aggregate Demand Shocks

Neither expansionary nor contractionary actions happen in a vacuum. They happen because the economy moves unexpectedly to make RGDP much higher or much lower than policymakers think is healthy. Figures 11.3 and 11.4 show the impact of these

shock
Any unanticipated economic event.

shocks, or unexpected moves. In each we suppose that aggregate demand is what moves unexpectedly, and in each we start with it at AD_1. Because of a shock it unexpectedly moves to AD_2. If a slump in aggregate demand causes a recession, like Figure 11.3, then the aggregate demand curve moves from AD_1 to AD_2. When people lose their jobs, welfare spending will have to rise and tax revenue will fall. As Figure 11.5 shows, this nondiscretionary fiscal policy moves the aggregate demand curve partially back to AD_3. Expansionary discretionary fiscal policy (either increases in government spending or decreases in taxes) can move aggregate demand all the way back to AD_1.

If a jump in aggregate demand causes an overheated economy, like Figure 11.4, then the aggregate demand curve moves from AD_1 to AD_2. When people get better jobs or raises, welfare spending will fall and tax revenue will rise. As Figure 11.6 shows, this nondiscretionary fiscal policy moves the aggregate demand curve partially back to AD_3. Contractionary discretionary fiscal policy (either decreases in government spending or increases in taxes) can move aggregate demand all the way back to AD_1.

FIGURE 11.3 A negative aggregate demand shock.

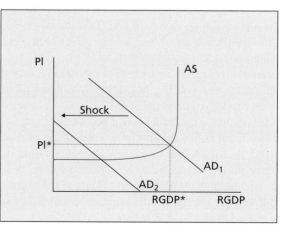

FIGURE 11.4 A positive aggregate demand shock.

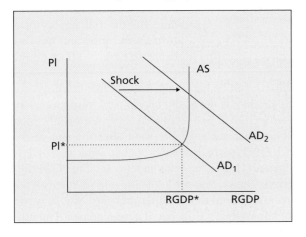

FIGURE 11.5 Nondiscretionary and discretionary fiscal policy as it combats a recession.

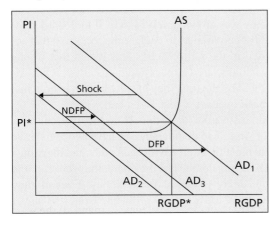

FIGURE 11.6 Nondiscretionary and discretionary fiscal policy as it combats an overheated economy.

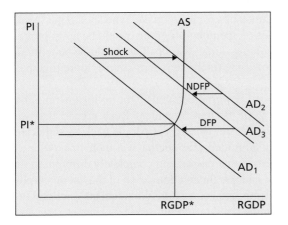

Nondiscretionary fiscal policy (NDFP) moves it back toward AD_1 to AD_3, and discretionary fiscal policy (DFP) can move it all the way back to AD_1 again. In theory, whether the economy experiences a positive demand shock or a negative one, the government can use both discretionary and nondiscretionary fiscal policy to return us to a healthy economy.

We need to ask at this point how it is that aggregate demand can move unexpectedly. There are a number of reasons and each involves the reaction of people to their predictions of the future. If people's positive view of the health of the economy spurs them to buy new cars or furnishings, an aggregate demand curve will move to the right. If the opposite happens and people decide to delay buying these expensive items because of negative feelings about the economy, the aggregate demand curve will move to the left. Tracking the "feeling" that people

aggregate demand shock

An unexpected event which causes aggregate demand to increase or decrease.

have about the economy is not easy and therefore large, unexpected swings can upset the economy. Economists call these swings **aggregate demand shocks.**

Aggregate Supply Shocks

Along with aggregate demand shocks we must also deal with the problem of aggregate supply shocks. Usually an

aggregate supply shock

An unexpected event which causes aggregate supply to increase or decrease.

aggregate supply shock involves an important natural resource. It should come as no surprise that recent supply shocks have all involved the price of oil. During the 1973

Arab–Israeli war, for example, the price of oil climbed dramatically. During the Iran–Iraq war, the price of oil fell dramatically as both sides increased production to pay for war material. Whether drastic changes are positive or negative, policy makers may wish to use discretionary fiscal policy to counter an aggregate supply shock.

EVALUATING FISCAL POLICY

Nondiscretionary Fiscal Policy

Nondiscretionary fiscal policy serves to get output moving back toward the desired level, RGDP*, but it works much better when the shock is to aggregate demand rather than to aggregate supply. In addition, even though previous Congresses and presidents developed tax and spending policies to get the country out of a recession, such discretionary fiscal policy just does not work as well as does nondiscretionary policy.

Since the Great Depression of the 1930s the U.S. economy has successfully avoided the sorts of boom and bust cycles that plagued the 19th century. The degree to which the built-in stabilizing effect of a welfare state and a progressive tax system generated this state of affairs is debated by economic historians. The recession of 1982, the worst since World War II, was far less onerous than any of the financial panics of the 1800s.

The Mistiming of Discretionary Fiscal Policy

You might think that discretionary fiscal policy would work as well. If you did, you would be wrong, but you would be in good company. By the 1950s and 1960s most economists were confident that discretionary fiscal policy would essentially eliminate the instability of recessions. By 1980 most economists had given up on discretionary fiscal policy. Coincidentally or not, during the 20 years that followed, the United States experienced half the usual number of recessions.

What transformed economists from overconfident discretionary fiscal policy champions in the 1960s to ardent detractors in the 1980s was the very poor performance of these policies during the 1970s. The preceding aggregate demand and aggregate supply analysis is nice to look at, and the nondiscretionary fiscal policy part does work as advertised, but discretionary fiscal policy was more of a fantasy of economists. In the 1950s and 1960s economists were confident that Congress could know exactly how much stimulus or dampening would be necessary to get the economy back to a desired level of RGDP. Congress would then pass a bill that the president would sign to implement that policy. As a practical matter, it just did not work in the ways economists predicted it would.

The reasons discretionary fiscal policy does not work can be attributed to lags in recognizing, administering, and operating fiscal policy. The first, the **recognition lag,** is that the economy in general, and RGDP in particular, is measured with a considerable lag. The second, the **administrative lag,** results because it takes time for Congress and the president to agree on a course of action. The

recognition lag
The time it takes to measure the state of the economy.

administrative lag
The time it takes for Congress and the president to agree on a course of action.

operational lag
The time it takes for the full impact of a government program or tax change to have its effect on the economy.

third, the **operational lag,** results because it takes quite a while for the full impact of a government program or tax change to have its effect on the economy.

The recognition lag results from the fact that gross domestic product is not easily and immediately measured. Quarterly GDP is first estimated using reasonably good predictors that are available soon after the end of the quarter. Later, more data are brought to bear and GDP is reestimated. Only after many months is a final GDP figure given. Thus we do not know for sure whether we are in a recession until months after it begins. Similarly, we do not know when we are out of a recession until months after it ends. The problem this creates was highlighted by the recession we experienced in 2001. That recession began in the first quarter of 2001, and it ended in the third quarter of 2001. We did not know for sure that it was a recession until the late fall of 2001. At the recession's end the economy was growing very slowly. It took until summer 2003 for economists to declare the recession had actually ended in the fall of 2001. This meant that by the time they had declared a recession had started, it was almost over and by the time they had declared it over, it had actually been over for a year and a half.

The administrative lag results from the inherent inefficiency of American democracy. We have two legislative bodies that must first agree with each other and then must agree with the president. The president, the House, or the Senate can delay or derail fiscal policy. Even if they choose to work on a given problem, Congress never solves a problem without disagreements. They may agree, for example, that we are in a recession but will not be able to decide whether to engage in discretionary fiscal policy through tax cuts or through spending programs. Even when they agree on that, they may argue over the kinds of tax cuts to make, who should get them, what kinds of spending programs would be appropriate, and the congressional districts that should be benefitted. By the time they finally agree, of course, more time has passed.

This is quite well illustrated by the political wrangling over the 2003 tax cut. President Bush argued that we needed the tax cut to help put people back to work. He originally submitted a tax cut that was more than twice as big as the one that passed and completely different in its focus. He had sought an elimination of the tax on corporate dividends and got a cut in individual tax rates and increases in the child tax credit.

The operational lag offers the final roadblock to effective discretionary fiscal policy. Even supposing that Congress and the president agree on time that a policy is needed and they agree on the type of policy, it takes months, if not years, for discretionary fiscal policy to have its desired effects.

If the discretionary fiscal policy takes the form of increases in highway construction, a program that increases the numbers of jobs available, federal contracts usually do not pay the entire amount up front. Contractors are paid in the stages of building, and it takes quite a while to go from the beginning of a large construction project to its end. As with changing tax laws, much of the money in the contract may hit the economy well after it is needed. The 2001 and 2003 summer rebate checks are evidence that tax cuts can make their way into the economy somewhat more quickly. In both cases the laws generating the rebates were passed in late spring and the checks were sent out in late summer. How quickly that money was spent is not yet known but will surely be the subject of intense economic research.

The Political Problems with Fiscal Policy

Another argument against discretionary fiscal policy is that even if it worked, vote-obsessed politicians would not use it properly. Aside from the bias toward expansionary fiscal policy alluded to in the introduction, there is the question of who will be affected by any changes in taxation or spending policies. In addition, there is the complication caused by politicians too concerned with reelection. They seek to expand the economy in presidential election years only to act responsibly after the election.

The first of these issues raises questions of political motivation. Whether large-scale, federally funded building projects are needed is one question; where they will go is quite another. For instance, whether the revamped Boston mass transit system, referred to by many as the "big dig," was motivated by purely engineering reasons or because influential members of Congress lived in the area is debatable. Similarly, critics have charged that political influence alone was behind the placement of a majority of highway demonstration projects in the early 1990s in West Virginia. While these are examples of Democrats engaging in steering tax dollars, Republicans too have engaged in such practices. Between 1995 and 2001, the GOP majority leader and the chair of the Senate Appropriations Committee made certain that disproportionate dollars were spent in their home states. Noted

economist James Buchanan and others have suggested that all federal spending, but in particular that spending that is done in the name of fiscal policy, is susceptible to this kind of problem.

There is also the problem of the **political business cycle.** It is suggested that politicians, particularly presidents, will add new spending and tax policies to their preelection-year budgets to boost the economy in time for their own or their party's reelection. Table 11.1 suggests that this might be the case, given that the average of growth rates in the fourth year of presidential terms of office is slightly higher than that of first-year growth rates.

> **political business cycle**
> Politically motivated fiscal policy used for short-term gain just prior to elections.

The Rise, Fall, and Rebirth of Discretionary Fiscal Policy

In the 1970s it became apparent to policy makers that discretionary fiscal policy was not up to the task of stabilizing the economy. The lags were just too important to ignore, and the recessions of the 1970s had been too short for these recessions to be recognized, laws to be passed, and money spent in time to have any effect on them.

Despite the preceding cautions about the effectiveness of discretionary fiscal policy, its arguments have been used to bolster particular programs. President Clinton used the discretionary fiscal policy argument in 1993 to bolster a $16 billion investment program. Critics defeated his proposal, suggesting that we were already out of the recession and its size was too small to have any impact.

An odd coincidence happened on the way to grave for discretionary fiscal policy. When the 2001 Bush tax cut passed in May of that year it was not known then that we were already in a recession. In addition, instead of implementing the tax cut prospectively, it was made retroactive to the beginning of the year, and instead of having taxpayers wait until they filed their tax forms in 2002 to claim their money, rebate checks were sent out in anticipation of those cuts. These checks started arriving in August and September of that year and were nearly fully dispersed when the terrorist attacks of September 11th occurred. Together with a series of interest rate cuts, these tax cuts had the fortunate coincidence of stimulating the economy at precisely the time the stimulus was needed.

When the economy had not picked up much steam through early 2003, President Bush proposed another tax cut. What he proposed was not at all what passed, but

TABLE 11.1   Real growth rates by presidential terms.

President	First Year	Second Year	Third Year	Fourth Year
Truman	−0.5	8.7	7.7	3.8
Eisenhower I	4.6	−0.7	7.1	1.9
Eisenhower II	2.0	−1.0	7.1	2.5
Kennedy/Johnson	2.3	6.1	4.4	5.8
Johnson	6.4	6.5	2.5	4.8
Nixon I	3.1	0.2	3.4	5.3
Nixon II/Ford	5.8	−0.5	−0.2	5.3
Carter	4.6	5.6	3.2	0.2
Reagan I	2.5	−1.9	4.5	7.2
Reagan II	4.1	3.5	3.4	4.1
Bush GHW	3.5	1.9	−0.2	3.3
Clinton I	2.7	4.0	2.5	3.7
Clinton II	4.5	4.2	4.4	3.7
Bush GW I	0.8	1.9	3.0	4.4
Average	3.3	2.8	3.8	4.0

Source: http://www.bea.doc.gov/bea/dn/gdplev.xls.

FIGURE 11.7   Did the 2003 rebate work?

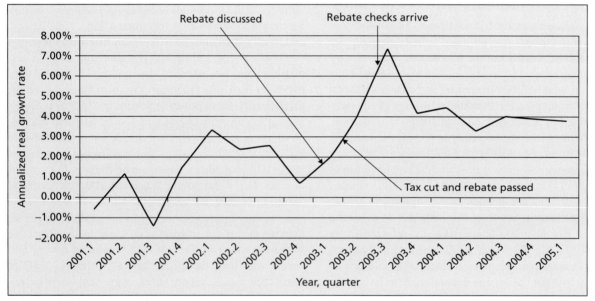

Source: http://www.bea.doc.gov/bea/dn/gdplev.xls.

what did pass was remarkably similar to what had passed in 2001. Again, rebate checks began arriving in taxpayers' mailboxes in late summer 2003.

Whether this apparent rebirth of fiscal policy is found by economists to be effective, only time will tell. The 2003 rebate could be used as evidence (see Figure 11.7) either in support of, or opposition to, discretionary fiscal policy. Supporters would argue that the checks arrived and had their hoped-for impact. Opponents would argue that by the time the checks arrived, the economy was already on the rebound and risked overheating the economy.

Kick It Up A Notch   AGGREGATE SUPPLY SHOCKS

In both Figures 11.8 and 11.9 we start out with AS_1 crossing AD_1 so that prices are at PI* and output is at RGDP*. A hypothetical shock moves aggregate supply to AS_2. If the supply shock is negative and it raises input prices substantially, as in Figure 11.8, people will lose their jobs as RGDP falls. Nondiscretionary fiscal policy will kick in at this point, though, because the loss of jobs will mean an increase in welfare spending and a decrease in taxes. This will cause aggregate demand to shift to the right to AD_2. If the president and Congress then decide to go further with discretionary fiscal policy in an effort to get output back to RGDP*, they will have to cut taxes or raise spending to do so.

The problem is that the shock itself and the nondiscretionary fiscal policy that was implemented has already created high inflation. Discretionary fiscal policy can only serve to worsen the problem.

On the other hand, if the supply shock is that input prices have fallen, as depicted in Figure 11.9, output increases. Nondiscretionary fiscal policy is such that taxes go up and welfare spending goes down. When this happens aggregate demand falls to AD_2. In this case there is no need for discretionary fiscal policy, because, even though there is a shock, it is only for the good. Both the shock and the nondiscretionary fiscal policy also serve to calm inflation.

FIGURE 11.8   Nondiscretionary and discretionary fiscal policy in the wake of a negative aggregate supply shock.

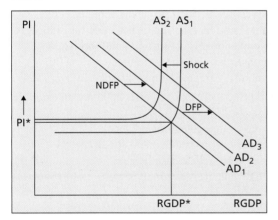

FIGURE 11.9   Nondiscretionary fiscal policy in the wake of a positive aggregate supply shock.

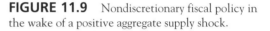
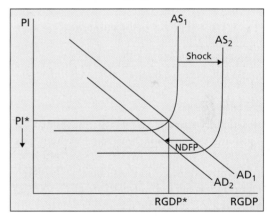

Summary

You now understand the difference between discretionary and nondiscretionary fiscal policy and know how to model them using an aggregate supply and aggregate demand diagram. You understand that different policies are used to counteract aggregate demand and aggregate supply shocks. You also now understand that though there are considerable problems associated with discretionary fiscal policy, it has seen a recent revival. Still, nondiscretionary fiscal policy remains a mainstay of our current macroeconomic system.

Key Terms

administrative lag, 130
aggregate demand shock, 129
aggregate supply shock, 129
discretionary fiscal policy, 126

fiscal policy, 126
nondiscretionary fiscal policy, 126
operational lag, 130

political business cycle, 131
recognition lag, 130
shock, 128

Quiz Yourself

1. The existence of the federal income tax and the welfare system serve as the primary elements of
   a. Discretionary fiscal policy.
   b. Nondiscretionary fiscal policy.
   c. Monetary policy.
   d. Exchange rate policy.

2. Adjustments to tax and spending policies serve as primary elements of
   a. Discretionary fiscal policy.
   b. Nondiscretionary fiscal policy.
   c. Monetary policy.
   d. Exchange rate policy.

3. Discretionary fiscal policy is the purview of
   a. Congress only.
   b. The president only.
   c. Congress and the president collectively through law.
   d. The Federal Reserve.

4. Nondiscretionary fiscal policy has its impact by
   a. Magnifying the economic ups and downs already occurring.
   b. Purposefully adjusting interest rates.
   c. Congress focusing it's constant attention.
   d. Dampening the economic ups and downs already occurring.

5. The aggregate demand–aggregate supply model examines the impact of discretionary fiscal policy and nondiscretionary fiscal policy by focusing on movements of
   a. Interest rates.
   b. Aggregate supply.
   c. Aggregate demand.
   d. Regulatory policies.

6. One typical response to a recession for those interested in discretionary fiscal policy is to
   a. Raise taxes and cut spending.
   b. Lower taxes and cut spending.
   c. Raise taxes and increase spending.
   d. Lower taxes and increase spending.

7. One typical response to an overheated economy for those interested in discretionary fiscal policy is to
   a. Raise taxes and cut spending.
   b. Lower taxes and cut spending.
   c. Raise taxes and increase spending.
   d. Lower taxes and increase spending.

8. Discretionary fiscal policy as a tool for making things better is
   a. Universally applauded as being helpful.
   b. Universally derided for never being effective.
   c. Considered by many to be effective but subject to several concerns over timing and motive.
   d. Inconsistent with the aggregate demand–aggregate supply model.

9. The oil price increases of 2002–2005 are an example of a
   a. Positive aggregate demand shock.
   b. Negative aggregate demand shock.
   c. Positive aggregate supply shock.
   d. Negative aggregate supply shock.

Think about This

Concerns over the recognition, administrative, and operational lags as well as the concern that discretionary fiscal policy is subject to political biases have caused some economists to believe Congress and the president should do nothing in the face of a recession. Even if they are correct, is it realistic to expect the public to embrace elected officials who do nothing?

Talk about This

The third and fourth year of presidential terms have higher average rates of real growth than the first and second years.

Do you think this is a coincidence or is it a reflection of political reality that politicians are more concerned about re-election than creating long-run economic growth.

For More Insight See

Journal of Economic Perspectives 14, no. 3 (Summer 2000). See articles written by Alberto Alesina, John B. Taylor, Alan Auerbach and Daniel Feenberg, and Douglas Elmendorf and Louise Sheiner.

Any textbook entitled *Intermediate Macroeconomics* will have a chapter on fiscal policy.

Behind the Numbers

Gross domestic product.

U.S. Bureau of Economic Analysis; gross domestic product; historical data—http://www.bea.doc.gov/bea/dn/gdplev.xls

Early estimates of GD.

U.S. Bureau of Economic Analysis; news release—http://www.bea.gov/bea/rels.htm.

Chapter 12

Monetary Policy

Federal Reserve Board Chairman Alan Greenspan testifies before the Senate Budget Committee. *Source © Reuters NewMedia Inc./CORBIS*

Chapter Objectives

After reading this chapter you should be able to

Understand the role of the Federal Reserve of the United States.

Recognize that macroeconomic stability is the Fed's primary goal, but controlling inflation has become the way it measures its success.

Know the tools of monetary policy, understand how they work, and be able to apply that knowledge to an aggregate supply–aggregate demand model.

See how the recent history of monetary policy has shaped the Federal Reserve's current emphasis on inflation.

Understand that the wisdom of the emphasis on inflation has been the subject of substantial debate among economists.

Chapter Outline

Goals, Tools, and a Model of Monetary Policy

Central Bank Independence

Modern Monetary Policy

Summary

The role of the Federal Reserve—usually called the Fed—in shaping the economy of the United States and the rest of the world is as mysterious as it is important. No more important aspect of our daily lives is run by people with as little accountability as those who are its executive officers. The Federal Reserve began in 1913 as a response to the boom and bust nature of the financial world of the late 19th and early 20th century. It has become a government institution every bit as important in the lives of people as the three branches of government we learn about in school. In the matter of a couple of hours, one person, the chairman of the Federal Reserve Board, can influence stock prices by 5 percent, cause mortgage interest rates to rise or fall by a full percentage point, and set in place a course of action that will raise or lower the unemployment rate by a point or more. The chairman can do this, moreover, without the approval of or even consultation with any elected person. Fortunately, the chairmen appointed by presidents and confirmed by the Senate have all been people of impeccable character. Even if their wisdom has been clouded at some points, a hint of corruption in this area of government would be devastating to world financial markets in particular and, by extension, to the whole world economy.

We begin by discussing the goals and tools of monetary policy. We consider why it exists and why its independence from political winds is important. Next we review some of the history of the modern use of monetary policy. Last, we focus on an important ongoing debate about inflation. Has the Federal Reserve's policy of keeping growth slow during the 1990s to combat potential inflation been prudent or needlessly cautious?

GOALS, TOOLS, AND A MODEL OF MONETARY POLICY

Goals of Monetary Policy

The most important historical role for monetary policy and its implementing institution, the Federal Reserve, has been to prevent boom and bust cycles by regulating banks and other financial institutions. While the role of dampening the boom and bust cycle remains an important part of the job, the mechanism has changed dramatically. At first the Fed simply ensured the financial soundness of institutions. Now it also directly manipulates interest rates to change the borrowing habits of banks, businesses, and consumers.

Tools of Monetary Policy

The tools that the Fed has at its disposal are the direct buying and selling of government debt, the changing of the interest rate at which banks borrow from the Fed, and the changing of the proportion of deposits that all banks must hold in reserve in their regional Federal Reserve bank.[1]

The Fed uses these tools to keep its "target" within the range it sets. The target of the Federal Reserve can be either a key interest rate (usually the federal funds rate) or

monetary aggregate
A measure of the quantity of money in the economy.

M1
Cash + coin + checking accounts.

M2
M1 + saving accounts + small CDs.

M3
M2 + large CDs.

federal funds rate
The rate at which banks borrow from one another to meet reserve requirements.

a **monetary aggregate**—a measure of the quantity of money in the economy. Three classes of assets comprise the monetary aggregate: **M1**—cash and checking accounts; **M2**—M1, savings accounts, and small certificates of deposit (CDs); and **M3**—M2 and large CDs.

For a look at how the Fed has operated in the past consider the following. In the 1970s the target was the **federal funds rate**—the rate at which banks borrow from one another to meet reserve requirements. As inflation heated up in the late 1970s, targeting the federal funds rate proved to be impossible. Keeping the rate down required a continuous increase in the supply of money. As more money chased limited goods, those increases created even greater inflation. This caused interest rates to rise rather than fall. In October 1979, as the rate of inflation continued to rise, the Fed formally gave up on the federal funds rate as its target. In its place the Fed set as its target the monetary aggregate M2, the sum of all bill and coin currency in circulation, plus the amount in check-accessible accounts, plus the amount in small short-term certificates of deposit. By the summer of 1982, inflation had subsided just as M2 became unstable and too difficult to target. In response the Fed reverted to targeting the federal funds rate.

Whatever is targeted, the mechanism by which the Fed keeps day-to-day tabs on the target is the **open-market operations.** Open-market operations result when the

---

[1]There are 12 regional Federal Reserve banks. They are located in Boston, New York, Philadelphia, Richmond, Atlanta, Cleveland, St. Louis, Kansas City, Chicago, Dallas, Minneapolis, and San Francisco.

open-market operations

The buying and selling of bonds, which, respectively, increases or decreases the money supply, thereby influencing interest rates.

Fed buys and sells government debt. The Fed owns approximately half a trillion dollars of the national debt, and it sells a portion of that reserve of bonds when it wants to get money out of the system. It buys bonds when it wants to add to the money that is in circulation.

The way open-market operations affect the interest rate is by affecting the supply of loanable funds. The left panel of Figure 12.1 shows that if the Federal Reserve buys bonds, it increases the amount of money that banks and other financial institutions can loan. The increase in the supply of loanable funds decreases the interest rate. The Fed can just as easily have an opposite desire and want to increase interest rates. The left panel of Figure 12.2 shows what happens when the Fed sells bonds in an effort to increase interest rates. The increase in interest rates is accomplished when the Fed reduces the supply of loanable funds.

Because the federal funds rate is determined by market forces between banks and is not determined directly by the Fed, the way the Fed can influence that rate is by increasing or decreasing the supply of generally available funds for loans. Its rationale is that this action will indirectly influence the federal funds rate. There is enough linkage between the quantity of money that is generally available for loans and the interest rate that banks charge each other so that this seems to work fairly well.

discount rate

The rate at which the Fed itself loans money to banks.

Prior to 2003 the Federal Reserve utilized another key interest rate to signal its intentions, the **discount rate.** This was the

interest rate at which the Fed itself loaned money to banks. Banks can borrow directly from the Fed, something they usually do by selling the Fed a loan they have made. The Fed used this discount rate to compute how much it would pay for that purchased loan.

Even though banks can still borrow from the Fed, since 2003 the Fed has changed the system by which it loans money directly to banks. Before the change, the discount rate was around half a percentage point below the federal funds rate. Banks could borrow from the Fed but were reticent to do so because it brought with it the potential for extra scrutiny from auditors.

Lombard System

Federal Reserve system where the discount rate is set above the federal funds rate and (subject to creditworthiness) banks can borrow freely.

primary credit rate

The rate at which banks with excellent credit can borrow from the Federal Reserve.

Since 2003, the Fed has adopted the **Lombard System** whereby banks, with sufficient creditworthiness, can borrow unlimited amounts from the Fed at the **primary credit rate.** The primary credit rate functions like the old discount rate except it is now set above the federal funds rate and applies only to banks with excellent credit ratings. Banks with lesser credit ratings face higher rates.

reserve ratio

The percentage of every dollar deposited in a checking account that a bank must maintain at a Federal Reserve branch.

The last way that the Federal Reserve can impact interest rates is by altering the proportion that the bank can lend from the deposits it takes in. The **reserve ratio,** at 10 percent in 2000, requires that a specific percentage of every dollar deposited be placed in a Federal Reserve bank. If the ratio is lowered, the bank has more money

FIGURE 12.1   Expansionary monetary policy: buying bonds, lowering the discount rate, or lowering the reserve ratio.

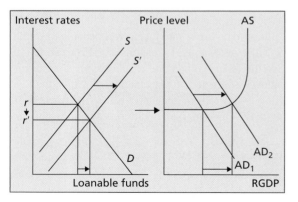

FIGURE 12.2   Contractionary monetary policy: selling bonds, raising the discount rate, or raising the reserve ratio.

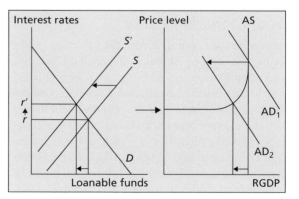

Money Creation

One of the lessons that economists routinely teach students in courses designed for economics and business majors is the notion of "money creation." The banking system can create more "money" than physically exists in the form of coin and cash. This was implied in our definitions of the monetary aggregates (M1, M2, etc.) because if money were only currency, then there would be no need to add checkable accounts and CDs.

The banking system creates money by a series of loans. To see how, let's assume that there are several people (John, Paul, George, Ringo, Justin, Lance, Chris, JC, and Joey) and several banks (1st National, 2nd National, 3rd National, and 4th National [the Midwest is home to an actual bank called "Fifth-Third"]). Suppose John makes a $1,000 deposit at 1st National, and that bank loans Paul $900 (10 percent, or $100, must be held as part of the required reserve). Suppose Paul buys something from George, who deposits that $900 at 2nd National. Then suppose that Ringo borrows $810 (again 10 percent, or $90, must be held at the Fed) from 2nd National to buy something from Justin, who deposits that money in 3rd National. If Lance borrows $729 (10 percent, or $81, must be held at the Fed) from 3rd National to buy something from Chris and Chris deposits that money in 4th National and. . . . You get the point—this could go on forever. In the end there are deposits totaling $10,000 ($1,000 + $900 + $810 + $729 + . . .) that resulted from that initial $1,000).

to lend and the supply of loanable funds moves to the right, as it does in the left panel of Figure 12.1. If the ratio is raised, the bank has less money to lend and the supply of loanable funds moves to the left, as is indicated in the left panel of Figure 12.2.

Modeling Monetary Policy

The impact of monetary policy on the overall economy can be seen in the right panels in Figures 12.1 and 12.2. As you saw in Chapter 8, one of the determinants of aggregate demand is interest rates. The influence of interest rates stems from the fact that investors want to borrow more to buy plant and equipment when interest rates are lower. In addition, consumers are more willing to buy expensive durable goods like cars and home furnishings when interest rates are lower. For the person who pays cash, the lower interest rate effect is indirect in that buyers sacrifice less in-

terest income when they take money out of savings to buy something. The person who buys a car and gets a shiny new payment book with the shiny new car is more likely to buy that car and more likely to buy a nicer, more expensive car because of the lower interest rate.

A loosening of the money supply or a lowering of the federal funds or discount rate allows banks to make more loans. These are loans that they can make only if they lower interest rates to ordinary borrowers. The lowering of interest rates causes the aggregate demand curve to rise as a result of increases in investment and interest-sensitive consumption. This is shown in the right panel of Figure 12.1. An identical but opposite story can be told concerning a tightening of the money supply. Less is available for banks to lend, a circumstance that allows them to raise the interest rates they charge to ordinary borrowers. Raising such rates causes a reduction in investment and interest-sensitive consumption. This in turn causes aggregate demand to fall, as is shown in the right panel of Figure 12.2.

It should be noted that economists disagree about the effectiveness of monetary policy, especially its effectiveness in the long run. Whereas there is some doubt among economists about whether the Fed has the ability to alter short-term economic outcomes, the doubt is much more widely held concerning its long-term ability to increase output through sustained increases in the money supply. The underlying reason for the skepticism is that sustained increases in the money supply will be factored in by investors, who will anticipate that substantial inflation will result from such a policy. Thus, though it may look as if the Fed could use the logic from Figure 12.1 to continuously foster long-run rapid growth, not many economists believe the Fed has this power. As a result, Figures 12.1 and 12.2 should be taken as relevant only in the short term.

CENTRAL BANK INDEPENDENCE

The Fed's power over the economy is substantial because it can do what it thinks is best without fear of being contradicted. Its independence from political control gives it awesome power and awesome responsibility to use that power judiciously. The Fed is so independent that it can slow growth or even put the nation into a recession in an effort to stamp out inflation. Economists generally agree that the Fed must be free from political control in order to take the necessary action to fight inflation. Experience across nations

The Role of Money

Imagine a world without money. While you may think that would be utopian, it would actually be a pain in the neck. Money allows us to exchange the goods or services we have to offer so that we may get the goods or services we want. Without it we would have to barter. Money allows us to avoid this by serving as a medium of exchange.

Money also holds its value. Suppose the good you had to offer was subject to spoilage. If you could not find someone who had a good you wanted and wanted what you had to offer within a short period of time, your goods would be worthless. With money you can sell your goods and hold on to the cash until such time that you find the goods you want to buy.

in the latter half of the 20th century provides rather powerful evidence that this is true.

Long-run economic growth requires that the financial markets have faith that money invested in a country will not lose value as a result of excessive inflation. When people are concerned about inflation, interest rates increase. Higher interest rates make investments more expensive. Since growth occurs only when investments in the future take place, long-term growth depends on the existence of a believable monetary authority. Monetary authority, by the way, is the general name for institutions like the Federal Reserve. While a politically controlled monetary authority could generate that faith if it never wavered from potentially unpopular policies, experience tells us this does not happen. We know this because those countries with a history of independent monetary authorities have experienced lower inflation rates, lower interest rates, and higher real growth rates than countries without that history of independence. The United States, Germany, Switzerland, Japan, Canada, and the Netherlands are examples of countries with such independence, whereas Spain and Italy are examples of countries without it. For the stability we enjoy, we are willing to accept the risk of having an independent monetary authority.

It is worth a small historical interlude to note that Congress could, by simply passing a law, regain complete control over the Federal Reserve. Article I, Section 8, of the U.S. Constitution gives the Congress control over the power to coin money. It never took the role of monetary policy very seriously, however, and before the

Civil War paper money was usually a bank note, typically backed by gold, of an individual private bank. With its authorizing of the printing of money during and after the Civil War, prices fluctuated so fast that three significant financial panics in the span of 60 years convinced Congress to create the Federal Reserve. If Congress became sufficiently motivated, it could return to the business of controlling the supply of money and, indirectly, interest rates.

MODERN MONETARY POLICY

The Last 30 Years

The history of monetary policy in the second half of the 20th century is one of increasing importance and self-confidence, and its effect on interest rates can be seen in Figure 12.3. In the late 1970s the Fed attempted to combat the oil-price shocks and a stagnating economy with increases in the money supply. Unfortunately, these efforts served only to add to inflation. In 1981 the Fed changed course with a high-stakes war on inflation. It sent interest rates soaring. Its grip on M2 was such that the federal funds rate went to nearly 20 percent while the discount rate went to 13 percent. By most measures the resulting recession of 1981–1982 was the worst in post–World War II history. The unemployment rate peaked higher, real GDP fell more, and the reduction in inflation was greater than in any of the other post-1946 recessions. It also had the distinction of being the only recession caused intentionally by the Fed.

Since that time the Fed has had a little better luck and has learned from its mistakes. For one thing, since the recession of 1982 it has not had to fight a significant inflation battle. In part this has been because it has been vigilant about not contributing to inflation. After 1984 the highest inflation rate has been 5 percent. Not having to wring out double-digit inflation but only having to keep it under control has made the Fed's job a little easier. In 1988, 1995, and again in 1999 and 2000, the Fed preemptively kept inflation in check by quickly increasing interest rates to slow an economy on the verge of creating inflation. It also worked to prevent a recession in 1994 by quickly pushing interest rates down.

Its response to the 1990 recession was slow, but it was probably forgivably slow. In the months leading up to Iraq's invasion of Kuwait, real GDP growth was slow, inflation was picking up, and consumer indebtedness was starting to peak. On top of that, the Fed was determined to wait for the outcome of a budget deal. At the time, the federal deficit was more than $250 billion, it was headed toward

FIGURE 12.3   Key interest rates from 1955 to 2004.

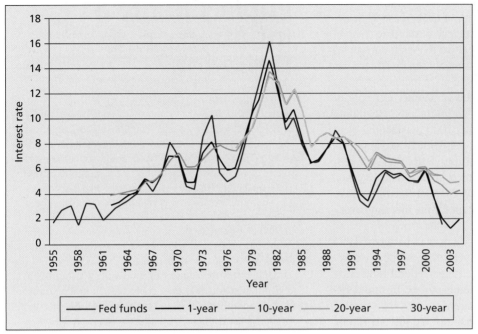

Source: http://www.federalreserve.gov/releases/h15/data.htm.

$400 billion, and the Fed wanted to hold President Bush's (George Herbert Walker) and the Democratic leadership in Congress's collective feet to the fire and force them to act.

Unfortunately Saddam Hussein's Iraq did not wait for the completion of the budget deal. After the invasion of Kuwait, gasoline prices increased sharply, and these circumstances precipitated an equally sharp decline in consumer confidence. Had the Fed acted immediately, it might have had better success keeping the United States out of the 1990–1991 recession, but its focus was on the deficit. It was also wary of duplicating the mistakes of the late 1970s by trying to battle cost-push inflation (inflation caused by movements in aggregate supply to the left) with increases in the money supply.

Whether explicitly or by chance, the Fed simply let the recession happen. It appeared to decide that there was little it could or should do to prevent it. Fortunately, however, the 1990–1991 recession was one of the shortest and the least disruptive recessions on record. Inflation never became a significant problem in part because consumer credit card debt was so high. Thus, except for a short spike in gas prices, inflation was negligible during this period. Unemployment rose but it came nowhere near 1982's modern record of 11 percent. During the first 18 months of the recovery, from June 1992 through the end of 1993, the economy was so weak, however, that it was unclear at the

time whether it was a recovery or just an extension of the recession. In 1992 and 1993 the Fed stepped in with a significant reduction in interest rates, and by the last quarter of 1994 the economy was humming along nicely.

From 1994 on, the Fed kept a vigilant eye on inflation. Where necessary, as in 1995, the Fed let its guard down enough to prevent a slowdown from becoming a recession. By 1998 Fed governors were feeling rather proud of themselves. Unemployment was at a 30-year low, inflation was nowhere in sight, and longtime Fed chairman Alan Greenspan had successfully kept the stock market in check by offering advice against "irrational exuberance." In 1998 the economy was doing fine. It was in no need of increases or decreases in interest rates. Then the Asian financial crisis hit.

Explained in further depth in Chapter 15, on the International Monetary Fund, the Asian financial crisis resulted from a series of bad loans made in the Pacific Rim nations of Thailand, Malaysia, South Korea, and Indonesia, and from failed attempts by these countries to hold their foreign exchange rates constant.

The Fed's response to the crisis was guarded at first. It wanted to prevent the crisis from spreading but did not want its action to have the effect of importing the crisis to the United States. Stock prices in the United States did fall 20 percent in three months and many economists began to predict that a recession would occur in the United States within a year. The Fed lowered interest rates a full percentage point, enough of an action to increase U.S. demand for imported goods. This helped to stabilize Asia. In turn the dollar got so strong relative to Asian currencies that the relative price of imports purchased by Americans fell enough to offset any domestic price increases.

The recession of 2001 served as another example of monetary policy, its uses and its limitations. Beginning with the ambiguous nature of the 2000 presidential election, the recession of 2001 was met with 12 separate cuts in interest rates by the Federal Reserve. By 2003 the federal funds rate was at its lowest level in more than 40 years. For a time, in the spring of 2003, 30-year fixed mortgage interest rates were below 5 percent for the first time ever.

As can be seen from Figure 12.4 the crowning period of this aggressive monetary policy was between 1999 and 2005. The Federal Reserve Board's Open-Market Committee, aggressively moved their federal funds rate target to combat economic circumstances. In mid-1999 the Fed aggressively raised interest rates six separate times to combat what Greenspan termed the "irrational exuberance" of the stock markets. These actions had little impact themselves in stemming the overheated stock market. The tech-stock bubble burst on its own in 2000 prompting the Fed to begin to lower interest rates.

The Fed was in the process of easing credit conditions in 2001 when the attacks of September 11, 2001, occurred. When stock markets opened the following Monday it was with a Federal Reserve announcement that it was aggressively moving interest rates lower. With 13 rate cuts in a period of two-and-one-half years, the sluggish economy slowly rebounded through 2002 and picked up considerable steam through 2003 and 2004. In response, the Fed raised interest rates to more normal historical levels in ten steps through mid-2005.

Economists will debate whether these interest rate changes had the desired impact, but consider this: Between June 2003 and June 2004, the Fed was pretty much out of bullets. Had growth not picked up, at 1 percent the federal funds rate was about as low as the Fed could make it. The Fed can't make businesses borrow money to invest in new plant and equipment and can't make consumers borrow to buy expensive consumer durables. Once the interest rate has been driven to nearly zero, these decisions to borrow money are determined by the confidence that the borrower has in his or her ability to pay the money back.

Also worth noting was the Federal Reserve's difficulty in "talking down" skyrocketing home prices and questionable home lending practices in 2005. Fed increases in

Public Enemy #1: Inflation or Deflation?

In the late 1980s and through the decade of the 1990s, criticism started to be heard from the left and right that the Fed was overly concerned about the reappearance of inflation and not sufficiently concerned about the average person. Whether it has admitted it in public or not, since the late 1970s and early 1980s the Fed had considered inflation public enemy number one. This had been true whether inflation was really a problem, as it was in 1979 and 1980; had the possibility of being a problem, as in 1988, 1995, and 1999–2000; or was just a theoretical threat on the distant horizon.

Only when the country or the world was in trouble and inflation was less than 3 percent, as in the United States in 1993 and 2001 and the world in 1994, has the Federal Reserve relaxed its vigilance against inflation. In being focused on inflation it has cut recoveries short or starved them of sufficient cash to really get going.

In late 2002–early 2003, a new public enemy number one had begun to come into view: deflation. Recall from Chapter 6 that deflation is the opposite of inflation but is no less of a concern. Deflation has the effect of encouraging people not to buy now. This is because they know that if they wait, they will save money. This can be self-perpetuating in that by not buying consumers force businesses to cut prices. This causes profits to fall and layoffs to occur, and buying diminishes even further. Even moderate deflation is worse than inflation in this regard. The Japanese experience with deflation in the late 1980s and 1990s offered very slow growth and stagnant employment. The Fed understood this potential quite well in 2003 when it again began to consider further interest rate cuts.

short-term interest rates during 2005 had little impact on mortgage rates, which remained low during that year.

Though Figure 12.3 makes it look like short- and long-term interest rates move in lockstep, they do not. Though they typically move together, its useful to remember Chapter 7's definition of the yield curve. Figure 12.5 notes yield curves from different periods of recent history. What appears is that at times the yield curve is upward sloping (the usual case), while at other times it is flat and at still other times it is downward sloping.

FIGURE 12.4   Aggressive monetary policy between 1999 and 2005.

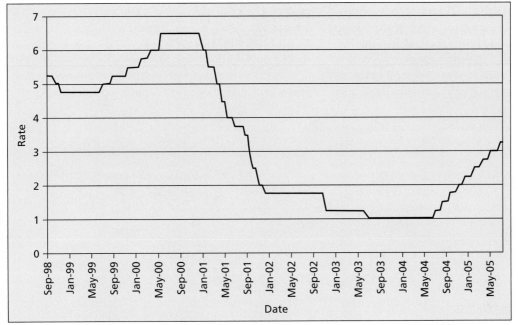

Source: http://www.federalreserve.gov/fomc/fundsrate.htm.

FIGURE 12.5   Selected yield curves on federal funds and U.S. debt.

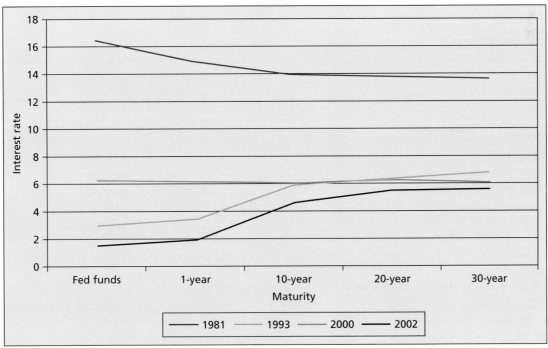

Source: http://www.federalreserve.gov/releases/h15/data.htm.

Summary

With your newfound wealth of knowledge you now understand the role of the Federal Reserve of the United States and its primary goal to be macroeconomic stability. You see that the Fed's own apparent measure of success in meeting this goal has been the ability to control inflation. You know the tools of monetary policy, understand how they work, and are able to apply that knowledge to an aggregate supply–aggregate demand model. You know the recent history of monetary policy and know how it has shaped the Federal Reserve's current fixation with inflation. Finally, you understand the debate among economists over whether inflation or deflation is a greater concern.

Key Terms

discount rate, 138
federal funds rate, 137
Lombard System, 138
*M*1, 137

*M*2, 137
*M*3, 137
monetary aggregate, 137
open-market operations, 137

primary credit rate, 138
reserve ratio, 138

Quiz Yourself

1. The Constitution of the United States grants to Congress the power of monetary policy in Article 1, Section 8. Since 1913, Congress has
   a. Jealously guarded this power.
   b. Granted this power to the president.
   c. Delegated this power to the Federal Reserve.
   d. Ignored this power.

2. When engaging in monetary policy, the impact of expansionary policy on an aggregate demand–aggregate supply model is to
   a. Increase aggregate demand.
   b. Increase aggregate supply.
   c. Decrease aggregate demand.
   d. Decrease aggregate supply.

3. The most precise tool of monetary policy is
   a. The adjustment of the federal funds target.
   b. The adjustment of the discount rate.
   c. The adjustment of the reserve requirement.
   d. The use of open-market operations.

4. Federal Reserve independence is
   a. Completely fictitious.
   b. Totally complete.
   c. Subject to Congress's desire to keep it independent.
   d. Subject to the Supreme Court's desire to keep it independent.

5. The "creation" of money is
   a. Entirely the purview of Congress.
   b. Entirely the purview of the Federal Reserve.

   c. Formally the purview of the Federal Reserve, constitutionally the purview of Congress, but banks have a practical means of creating money.
   d. Entirely subject to the whims of the banking system.

6. During 1999 through 2005 the Federal Reserve
   a. Was passive and simply let things happen.
   b. Reacted actively to quell potentially inflationary expansions but did nothing to deal with the recession.
   c. Reacted actively to deal with the recession but did nothing to quell potentially inflationary expansions.
   d. Reacted actively to deal with the recession and to quell potentially inflationary expansions.

7. The ability of the Federal Reserve to control interest rates is
   a. Limited almost entirely to short-term rates.
   b. Limited almost entirely to long-term rates.
   c. Limited almost entirely to intermediate-term rates.
   d. Unlimited.

8. Which of the following tools would have likely had the impact of raising short-term interest rates the most?
   a. Cutting the federal funds target by one-quarter point.
   b. Buying $1-million in bonds.
   c. Raising the reserve requirement from 8 percent to 15 percent.
   d. Raising personal income tax rates by 1 percentage point each.

Think about This

Because the chairs of the Federal Reserve Board can have an enormous impact on policy decisions of the Fed and thereby the economy, their selection has been subject of great political interest. Politically motivated monetary policy could be ruinous economic policy. Previous Fed chairs have understood that their functional independence from congressional interference depends on the apolitical nature of their decisions. What would the economic consequences be if this balance was upset by a president who nominated a Fed chair dedicated to protecting the president's political party?

Talk about This

Presidents tend to nominate Fed chairs on the basis of advice from those working daily in the financial markets. Who should have an impact on the choice of the Fed chair? Specifically, Fed policy can favor financial interests or the interests of workers. Should unions or others with a claim to represent workers have an impact on the selection of the Fed chair?

For More Insight See

Colander, David, "The Stories We Tell: A Reconsideration of AS/AD Analysis." *Journal of Economic Perspectives* 9, no. 3 (Summer 1995), pp. 169–188.

Ramo, Joshua Cooper, "The Three Marketeers," *Time,* February 15, 1999, pp. 34–42.

Steiger, Douglas, James H. Stock, and Mark W. Watson, "The NAIRU, Unemployment and Monetary Policy," *Journal of Economic Perspectives* 11, no. 1 (Winter 1997), pp. 33–50.

Behind the Numbers

Consumer price index and historical U.S. inflation rates.
    Bureau of Labor Statistics—ftp://ftp.bls.gov/pub/special. requests/cpi/cpiai.txt.
U.S. interest rates 1955–2005.
    Federal Reserve Board; statistics: releases and historical data—http://www.federalreserve.gov/releases/h15/ data.htm.

Chapter 13

International Trade: Does It Jeopardize American Jobs?

A container terminal awaits its next voyage on Kobe Port Island, Japan. *Source: © Photodisc/Getty Images.*

Chapter Objectives

After reading this chapter you should be able to

Understand with whom we trade, in what goods we trade, and that international trade benefits both trade partners and why.

Know the principles of absolute and comparative advantage and why they are important in proving the benefits from trade.

See that there are reasons for limiting trade and know the mechanisms for doing so.

Understand that limiting trade protects some industries and jobs, but at a very high cost.

See that the use of trade as a diplomatic weapon has been largely a failure.

Chapter Outline

What We Trade and with Whom

The Benefits of International Trade

Trade Barriers

Trade as a Diplomatic Weapon

Kick It Up A Notch: Costs of Protectionism

Summary

One of the more important economic developments of the last 20 years is the increased globalization of our economy. Whereas the world used to be made up of more than 150 countries whose economies were mostly independent of one another, nearly all of the economies of the nations of the world now depend heavily on one another.

As you can see from Figure 13.1, in 2004 some 10.6 percent of the U.S. economy was made up of exports. You can also see that for the last 30 years the United States has imported more than it has exported. The increasing importance of the international sector has led some to worry about whether this trend is a good one. Are American jobs being unfairly taken by workers from

146

other countries? If so, is this trend toward globalization avoidable?

We address these questions first by explaining why economists generally believe that international trade is good for both parties. Then we discuss the reasons for limiting international trade, distinguishing between reasons that economists embrace and those that they do not. Next we discuss the methods by which trade is limited. To wrap up, we consider whether trade can be used as a tool in political or diplomatic disagreements.

WHAT WE TRADE AND WITH WHOM

Trade in the United States is not only growing, it is also encompassing a diverse area of goods and services, as seen in Table 13.1. We trade in the obvious goods and the not so obvious goods. We import TVs, computers, and other electronics, as well as cars and oil. We export agricultural products and airplanes. You probably would have guessed this. We simultaneously export and import large quantities of chemicals, automobiles, computers, and services. While that may sound somewhat odd, it is not as strange as it may sound. There are myriad types of chemicals, and we are importing some and exporting others. Similarly, though we export and import computers, this also shows the degree to which many products are made all over the globe.

If you open up any computer, you will find components that were made in a variety of places. The memory comes from one country, the hard drive from another, and the CPU from still another. Your computer may have been assembled in the United States, but it was made from components that could have been produced in

FIGURE 13.1 Increasing importance of international trade.

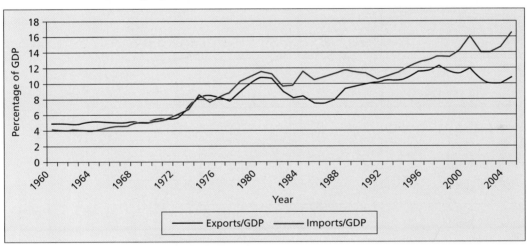

Source: http://www.ita.doc.gov/td/industry/otea/usfth/aggregate/H04t01.html.

TABLE 13.1 U.S. exports and imports of goods and services, 2004.

Exports		Imports	
Good	**Exports (billions)**	**Good**	**Imports (billions)**
Chemicals	108.5	Chemicals	108.8
Food and agricultural products	59.8	Computers and electronics	249.1
Computers	164.2	Petroleum and coal products	39.9
Aerospace products and parts	52.3	Audio and video equipment	32.1
Motor vehicles and parts	72.1	Motor vehicles and parts	201.6
Services	338.6	Services	256.3
Total	1,146.1	Total	1,763.9

Sources: http://ita.doc.gov/td/industry/otea/usfth/aggregate/H04t35.pdf; http://ita.doc.gov/td/industry/otea/usfth/aggregate/H04t01.html; http://ita.doc.gov/td/industry/otea/usfth/aggregate/H04t36.pdf; http://ita.doc.gov/td/industry/otea/usfth/aggregate/H03T38.html; http://ita.doc.gov/td/industry/otea/usfth/aggregate/H03T39.html.

TABLE 13.2   U.S. exports, imports, and trade balances of goods with selected countries and regions of the world, 2004.

Country	Exports ($ billions)	Imports ($ billions)	Balance ($ billions)
Canada	$160.8	$ 210.6	$ −49.8
Mexico	97.5	134.7	−37.2
Japan	51.4	121.5	−70.1
China	22.1	125.2	−103.1
Middle East	18.9	34.4	−15.5
Other Asia	101.1	175.2	−74.1
Western Europe	157.1	246.3	−89.2
Africa	10.7	22.2	−11.5
World	693.5	1,163.6	−470.1

Source: http://www.census.gov/foreign-trade/balance/c5830.html.

FIGURE 13.2   Trade balances with selected partners.

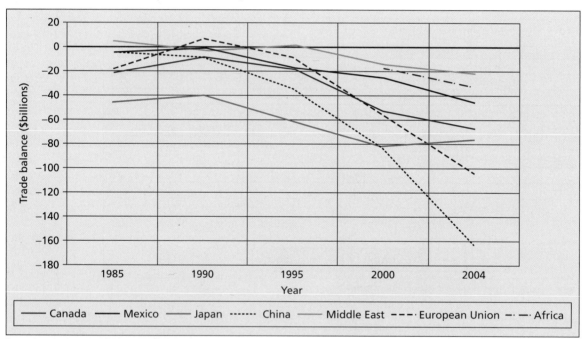

Source: http://www.census.gov/foreign-trade/balance/c5830.html.

10 other countries. You can see that it is difficult to decide where it was really made.

The final item in Table 13.1 might seem out of place. How do you trade in services? It is hard to imagine that we would import babysitting and lawn-mowing services, but it is much more plausible in areas of financial services and, specifically, in insurance. An American insurance company can easily sell life insurance to Canadians, and vice versa. Services make up a large and rapidly growing area

of trade, and it is one area where the United States has a substantial trade surplus.

Table 13.2 may also surprise you in that few Americans realize how important Canada is as a U.S. trading partner. In trade it is roughly equal in importance to all of western Europe. What probably does not come as a particular surprise is that nearly half of the large U.S. trade deficit stems from Asia. Figure 13.2 shows the degree to which these deficits continue to burgeon.

THE BENEFITS OF INTERNATIONAL TRADE

Comparative and Absolute Advantage

To illustrate the benefits of trade it is useful to distinguish between two kinds of "advantages" that people can have. Consider a brain surgeon and her secretary. Suppose that the surgeon worked her way through school by typing papers and that she types faster than her current secretary. If she is better at both typing and surgery, would it be better for her to do both and fire her secretary? The answer is no; she will be better off having her slow-typing secretary do the typing. Making the decision relies on the notion of opportunity cost that we discussed in Chapter 1.

To review, opportunity cost is what you give up by making the choices that you do. In the case of the secretary and the surgeon, if the surgeon does her own typing, she must give up at least some of her lucrative surgeries. On the other hand, if she delegates the typing, she will pay the secretary only a small fraction of the money she would earn doing extra surgeries. In this case she has an **absolute advantage** in both surgery and typing, though, because she is better at both things than the competition. Her secretary has a **comparative advantage** at typing because the secretary has a lower opportunity cost of doing the typing than does the surgeon.

absolute advantage
The ability to produce a good better, faster, or more quickly than a competitor.

comparative advantage
The ability to produce a good at a lower opportunity cost of the resources used.

As a simple example of how this applies to international trade consider Tables 13.3 and 13.4. We can illustrate comparative and absolute advantage and the benefits from trade for each of two countries relating their individual production of two goods. We will suppose that the two countries are Italy and Germany and the two goods are beer and sausage.

In Table 13.3 we will suppose that Italy is better at producing sausage than it is at producing beer and Germany is better at producing beer than it is at producing sausage. We will assume that a single unit of labor is capable of producing two units of sausage in Italy but only one unit of beer. In Germany that situation is reversed. A unit of labor produces two units of beer but only one of sausage. Clearly, since a unit of labor in Germany can produce more beer than a unit of labor in Italy, Germany has the absolute advantage in beer. Similarly, it is clear that Italy has an absolute advantage in sausage.

TABLE 13.3   Production: absolute and comparative advantage are the same.

	Sausage	Beer
Germany	1	2
Italy	2	1

TABLE 13.4   Production: absolute and comparative advantage are not the same.

	Sausage	Beer
Germany	3	2
Italy	2	1

To analyze comparative advantage we need to measure what is given up when the two countries allocate a unit of labor. For instance, when Germans produce an additional unit of sausage they are giving up two beers. When Italians produce an additional unit of sausage they are giving up only one-half a unit of beer. Italians therefore have the lower opportunity cost of producing sausage. Similarly, when Germans produce an additional unit of beer they give up one-half a unit of sausage, and when Italians do so they give up two units of sausage. As a result Germans have a lower opportunity cost for beer. What this means is that in addition to having an absolute advantage in sausage, Italians also have a comparative advantage in sausage. Similarly, Germans have a comparative advantage as well as an absolute advantage in beer.

These advantages need not be in line. Consider Table 13.4, which shows where the Germans are assumed to have an absolute advantage in the production of both goods. A single unit of German labor can produce more beer and more sausage than a single unit of Italian labor. As a result, Germans have an absolute advantage in the production of both goods. Comparative advantage is another story. The opportunity cost of an additional unit of sausage to Germans is two-thirds of a unit of beer. For Italians the opportunity cost of an additional unit of sausage is only half a beer. Thus Italians have the lower opportunity cost of producing sausage and therefore have a comparative advantage in sausage. In beer production the Germans have an opportunity cost of one and a half units of sausage while the Italian opportunity cost is two units of sausage. Germans therefore have the lower opportunity cost of beer production and, as a result, the comparative advantage in beer.

Demonstrating the Gains from Trade

In either case the gains from trade can be illustrated. Starting with the situation where the gains from trade are more obvious, look back at Table 13.3. If Germans focus their production on beer and Italians on sausage, then for every unit of labor that Germans move to beer and Italians move to sausage there is a worldwide increase in total production of one beer and one sausage.

To see that each is better off with trade than without it, suppose there is a total of 30 units of labor in each country and each prefers beer and sausage in equal amounts. Before trade there will be 10 Germans producing 20 units of beer and 20 Germans producing 20 units of sausage. Similarly there will be 10 Italians producing 20 units of sausage and 20 Italians producing 20 units of beer.

To see that trade makes both better off we need to know how the **terms of trade,** the amount of one good required to get the other, between the two countries will come out. If we suppose that it comes to one unit of beer for one unit of sausage, then we have our answer. The Italians will produce only sausage and make a total of 60 units, and the Germans will produce only beer and pro-

duce 60 units. The Italians will ship 30 units of sausage to Germany in exchange for 30 units of beer, and in the end each will be able to consume 30 units of each and be better off with trade than without it.

Trade is also beneficial when one country has the absolute advantage in both goods. Turning back to Table 13.4 we can show that there are gains from trade here as well. Prior to trade the Italian situation is unchanged from the preceding example but the German situation is such that 12 are producing 24 units of sausage and 8 are producing 24 units of beer. Again if both focus entirely on the good for which they have a comparative advantage, sausage for Italians and beer for Germans, and the terms of trade remain one-for-one, then the Germans will again ship 30 beers to Italy for 30 sausages, and both will be better off.

Production Possibilities Frontier Analysis

We can show the gains using our Chapter 1 production possibilities frontier as well. Recall that a production possibilities frontier shows the output combinations that a country can accomplish on its own. If we assume either of the scenarios presented above, then the production possibilities frontiers for the two countries, shown in Figure 13.3, would

FIGURE 13.3   Increased consumption possibilities with trade.

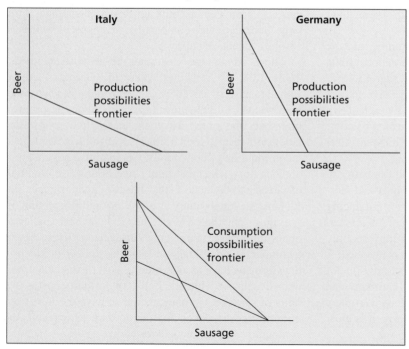

have different slopes. The Italian production possibilities frontier would be flatter and Germany's steeper.

If we again assume the one-for-one terms of trade, perfect specialization would improve the situation for both the Germans and the Italians, in that the Germans would now have to give up only one unit of sausage to get a unit of beer instead of the two they had to give up before. The Italians would benefit, too. They would have to give up only one unit of beer instead of two to get a unit of sausage.

This is specifically illustrated in the bottom panel of Figure 13.3, which uses the production possibilities frontier of both to create a new line that shows the consumption possibilities with trade. We saw in Chapter 1 that a production possibilities frontier further away from the origin implies that more production is possible. You can see that the consumption possibilities with trade are greater for both the Italians and the Germans than their individual production possibilities without trade. When the Italians concentrate on sausage and the Germans concentrate on beer, and they trade, each country is better off. Each produces what it produces best and trades for what it does not produce particularly well.

Even though we have seen that both countries are clearly better off than before, there still are people who would not necessarily like the development of trade. Specifically, German sausage makers and Italian beer brewers would not necessarily find the idea of trade good. International trade would cause workers in these industries to lose their jobs because the competition would drive their employers out of business. This simple model assumes that the unemployed could find new work in the expanding industries in their respective countries. This assumption, however, while not bad in the long run, ignores the pain of people losing their jobs and needing to attain new skills.

TRADE BARRIERS

Reasons for Limiting Trade

Because it is possible that with free trade some businesses go under and some workers lose their jobs, it is useful to summarize some of the questionable and some of the good reasons to limit trade. The questionable reasons begin with protecting jobs within the industries that are being affected by better or cheaper imports. The good reasons are as numerous as they are narrow. We may choose not to trade with other countries in certain goods because those goods may be important to our national

security or national identity. Producing such goods at home is therefore important in and of itself. We may choose not to trade with countries that gain their comparative advantage through lax worker safety rules, lax environmental laws, or because they allow businesses to employ child labor.

Though there are clearly short-run costs to free trade, when people lose their jobs to foreign competition and need retraining to get new ones, the long-term benefits usually outweigh these. When labor unions argue against free trade, it is often because the industry that they represent has lost its comparative advantage to other countries. Though this comparative advantage is sometimes lost because of labor or environmental protections, it is usually because the other country has come up with a better or more cost-effective method of producing the good. Protecting an industry in such circumstances is not beneficial for two reasons:

1. For capitalism to work, not only must success be rewarded, but failure must be punished. If companies see that the government will prevent international competition, they will become lax, and they will not produce the best goods for the lowest prices.

2. If other countries see that we protect our firms from competition, they will certainly feel free to do the same. Instead of everyone benefiting from trade, we will return to the days before trade and lose consumption possibilities. We will lose our ability to export our goods to countries where our products are better and cheaper than domestic goods.

The preceding points notwithstanding, there are still good and legitimate reasons for limiting trade even when other countries produce better or cheaper goods. If, for instance, a country other than the United States produced the best and cheapest combat aircraft and it also happened to be a potential wartime enemy of the United States, the United States would be seriously misguided to shut down its own combat aircraft industry and buy planes from the other country. For national security reasons, guaranteed access to war material is important for countries.

Countries also limit trade for reasons that are similar to national defense. If a nation's identity is tied to a particular commodity the way the Japanese identity is tied to rice, for example, it makes sense for the government to limit imports of the commodity so that its domestic producers can survive. Though there is enough productive capacity in the south central United States to supply the entire rice consumption needs of Japan, and though the Japanese continue to pay more than five times the world market price for rice to maintain a domestic industry, this economically inefficient trade restriction can be justified on two grounds. First, Japan without a rice industry is not Japan, and second, in case of a naval war in the Pacific, it is hard to imagine the United States or any other country devoting significant naval resources to protect rice shipments to Japan. It is not a coincidence that as the Cold War waned, the Japanese began to allow at least limited rice imports.

A final reason for limiting trade is that other countries may get their comparative advantage by using production processes that indirectly harm other countries or that other countries find offensive. If a country lowers its production costs, for example, by polluting in a way that would not be allowed in the United States, the United States might reasonably decide not to let that country sell its products here. This is especially true if the pollution ultimately causes health problems here. The United States thus might not want to allow the importation of chemicals and other environmentally onerous products from Mexico if, as a by-product of their manufacture, they pollute the Rio Grande.

In addition to environmental objections, countries may find certain labor practices so immoral that they do not allow importation of goods from countries that engage in them. For instance, it is against U.S. law to import any good made with slave labor or with prison labor. Additionally, the United States will not knowingly allow the importation of goods made with forced or indentured child labor, and the U.S. government requires that its contractors certify that no child labor was used in the production of its goods.[1] Several countries allow children as young as eight to work in factories several hours a day. For example, if you own a soccer ball, it was probably made outside the United States, and the production involved at least one child who would not be allowed to work in the United States. The garment industry joins sporting goods in utilizing child labor and engaging in other labor practices that are not legal in the United States. Child labor has existed in nearly every country at some point, and its use is attributable almost entirely to high rates of poverty. In addition, some economists argue that laws outlawing child labor are not necessarily good for the children involved if their only alternative is abject poverty. Despite this, many see the issue less in economic terms and more in moral ones.

Other reasons for limiting trade have appeal to only a limited number of economists. The first of these, the infant-industry argument, says that trade protection is required to give an industry in a country time to get on its feet. In theory, there may be an argument for temporary shelter from competition, but in practice, it often happens that trade is permanently limited.

The second of these limited-appeal arguments is the antidumping argument. **Dumping** occurs when international competitors charge less than their cost in order to drive out competition. The argument is that competitors do this to gain a monopoly in the long run. The problem with this argument is ascertaining the true marginal cost of the international competitor. Inefficient domestic producers' assertions of dumping often hinge on the notion that since they cannot produce at such low costs, it must be impossible. The crux of the dumping argument is the attempt at generating a monopoly, and there are few if any industries in which such a strategy has prevailed.

dumping
The exporting of goods below cost to drive competitors out of business.

Methods of Limiting Trade

Once a nation has decided to limit trade it must choose a method. There are three main methods for limiting trade. A country can put a tax on imported goods, limit the quantity of a good that can be imported, or put regulations on goods that are imported to make it more difficult for the goods to be imported.

The most widely used method for limiting trade is the use of a tax on imports, called a **tariff.** Figure 13.4 shows that if a country wants to limit the amount of a good imported to Q_{limit}, a tax can be put on the good that is sufficient to move the supply curve to where it intersects the demand curve at that output. With such a tariff the price increases to P_{limit}, where domestic producers have a better chance of competing. In addition, the government gets $CP_{limit} AB$ in tax revenue that it can use to retrain workers or to provide other sorts of compensation.

tariff
A tax on imports.

The second method of limiting trade, a **quota,** places a legal restriction on the quantity of a good coming into the country. Also shown in Figure 13.4, this method is popular in that it has the effect of raising the price that domestic producers can charge to P_{limit}. The

quota
A legal restriction on the amount of a good coming into the country.

[1]See Executive Order 99-06-12, Executive Order on Child Labor, http://www.fedworld.gov/pub/w-house/0616-3.txt.

FIGURE 13.4   The effect of tariffs and quotas.

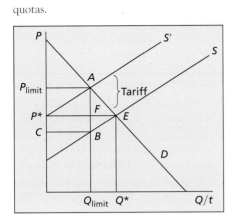

main difference between a quota and a tariff is that with a quota the government of the importing country receives no tax revenue. Importers get to raise their prices and they get to keep the extra money as profit. Even though it appears this method would seem to be much worse than a tariff for the importing country, quotas sometimes provide political advantages. Often it is less of a diplomatic problem for a country to impose a quota on the imports of another country. Also, as has happened before in the automobile business, it is sometimes possible to get an exporting country to agree to limit its exports voluntarily. While this operates exactly like a quota, the exporting country retains the power to end the action rather than ceding that power to the importing country. In the early 1980s Japan willingly limited exports of cars to the United States when congressional action was threatened.

The final method by which a country can limit the imports of another country utilizes a recognized right of a country to inspect goods coming in. If you do not want a particular good coming into the country, you can set up rules for its import that effectively make the importation too costly. This method is effective, it is nearly impossible to get around, and it becomes apparent only when the rules become silly. The method is seen mostly with the importation of agricultural products. Although it is perfectly legitimate for a country to want to inspect a shipment to look for certain diseases, bugs, or parasites, countries will sometimes use such inspection as an excuse to limit imports. Because the goods themselves are usually perishable, this can raise the cost to prohibitive levels and effectively prevent any attempts to break into a new market.

nontariff barriers
Barriers to trade resulting from regulatory actions.

Many examples of these **nontariff barriers** exist. Some are perfectly logical; others are

dubious. An outbreak of mad cow disease began to affect English herds in 1999, resulting in a ban on English beef sold in Europe. A concern over the potential of allergic reactions in genetically altered corn resulted in a similar European ban on Starlink corn. The European ban on milk from cows that had been given bovine growth hormone (BGH) and the Japanese ban on American apples in the 1980s appear to be examples of the use of nontariff barriers for strictly protectionist reasons.

TRADE AS A DIPLOMATIC WEAPON

There are countless examples in the last 45 years of international trade being used to make a diplomatic point or to solve a diplomatic problem. Since the late 1950s, the United States has imposed trade sanctions against Cuba to destabilize Fidel Castro. In 1979, in response to Iran's refusal to free American diplomats being held hostage in its embassy, the United States made it illegal to trade with Iran. In 1980, in response to the Soviet invasion of Afghanistan, the United States imposed a grain embargo, making it illegal to sell wheat to Russia. In the middle 1980s, in response to a series of terrorist acts by the Libyan government and its surrogates, the United States declared it illegal to buy Libyan oil. In the early 1990s, after Iraq invaded Kuwait, the United Nations imposed economic sanctions against Iraq in hopes that Iraq would retreat. Iraq did not retreat, the Gulf War was fought, and afterward, further economic sanctions were used in attempts to pressure Iraq into giving up its weapons of mass destruction. This too failed.

Manipulating trade simply has not been particularly effective as a method of influencing diplomacy. Castro has outlasted nine U.S. presidents; the Iranians did not buckle to such pressure; the Soviets, the Libyans, and the Iraqis followed their lead. The main reason that cutting off trade has not worked as a diplomatic tool is that it has been impossible to implement adequately. There have always been other avenues that the countries in question could use for trade. The Iranians had never sold much oil to the United States, and they found few problems selling their output to other countries. Argentinean and Australian farmers were only too happy to sell their grain to the Soviets, and the Libyans and the Iraqis had few problems breaking the sanctions imposed on them because many other countries felt free to break them. In theory, the limiting of trade appears to be a powerful diplomatic tool. In reality, it has not been very effective.

Kick It Up
A Notch

COSTS OF PROTECTIONISM

Reasons and mechanisms for limiting trade are available, but their use incurs substantial economic costs. We can examine those costs using Figure 13.4 and our consumer and producer surplus analysis from Chapter 3. Whatever the mechanism is for limiting trade, if the price of the imported good increases to P_{limit} and the quantity is reduced to Q_{limit}, then there are winners and losers from the protectionist measures. The losers are consumers because their consumer surplus falls by $P^*P_{limit} AE$. Domestic producers are winners because they get a higher price, and foreign producers are losers because their sales are limited. The net gain to producers from a quota, or alter- natively the net gain to producers plus the tariff revenue to the government, is $CP_{limit} AB - BFE$. In any event there is a net loss to society from the protectionist meas- ures of *ABE*.

In practice this loss can be very substantial. Table 13.5 illustrates the net loss to the United States from trade pro- tection in certain industries. It also demonstrates the net loss per job that the protectionist measures save. This table clearly shows the efficiency costs to American con- sumers from tariffs and quotas. We pay a few dollars more for many goods, but these figures add up to more than $32 billion to save 191,664 jobs. At $169,000 per job saved, trade protectionism is one of the worst jobs programs in place.

TABLE 13.5   Total cost of trade protectionism.

Industry	Total Cost to Consumers ($ millions)	Jobs Saved	Cost per Job Saved ($)
Food and beverage	$ 2,947	6,035	$488,000
Textiles and light industry	26,443	179,102	148,000
Chemical products	484	514	942,000
Machinery	542	1,556	348,000
Miscellaneous	1,895	4,457	425,000
Total	32,311	191,664	169,000

Source: Gary Hufbauer and Kimberly Elliott, *Measuring the Costs of Protection in the United States.* Washington, D.C.: Institute for International Economics, 1994.

Summary

You now understand that the United States trades in many goods and with many partners, that we have a massive trade deficit, but that both we and our trading partners benefit from our international trade. You are now able to use the principles of absolute and comparative advantage as well as a production possibilities frontier to demonstrate why that is the case. You know the reasons for limiting trade and al- ternative mechanisms for doing so and that limiting trade comes at a very high cost. Last, you now see that the use of trade as a diplomatic weapon has been largely a failure.

Key Terms

absolute advantage, 149
comparative advantage, 149
dumping, 152

nontariff barriers, 153
quota, 152

tariff, 152
terms of trade, 150

Quiz Yourself

1. America's most significant trading partner is
   a. Saudi Arabia.
   b. Canada.
   c. China.
   d. Japan.

2. In 2005, which country had the largest trade surplus with the United States?
   a. Saudi Arabia.
   b. Canada.
   c. China.
   d. Japan.

3. Theoretically speaking, all trade is based on
   a. Comparative advantage.
   b. Absolute advantage.
   c. Numerical advantage.
   d. Political advantage.

4. The trends in U.S. international trade are such that
   a. Imports are increasing and exports are decreasing.
   b. Imports are decreasing and exports are increasing.
   c. Both imports and exports are decreasing.
   d. Both imports and exports are increasing.

5. Using simple linear production possibilities frontiers in a simple two-good, two-country model, comparative advantage is evident when
   a. One country can make more of both goods than the other.
   b. The slopes of the two production possibilities frontiers are identical.
   c. The slopes of the two production possibilities frontiers are different.
   d. One country is incapable of producing one good.

6. Using simple linear production possibilities frontiers in a simple two-good, two-country model, absolute advantage is evident when
   a. One country can make more of a good than the other country can.
   b. The slopes of the two production possibilities frontiers are identical.
   c. The slopes of the two production possibilities frontiers are different.
   d. One country is incapable of producing one good.

7. Of the following justifications for limiting trade, which one would economists be least likely to endorse? Some goods should not be imported because
   a. They are important for national defense (e.g., tanks, fighter airplanes).
   b. They are important for national identity (e.g., television programs).
   c. Their production employs many people (e.g., cars).
   d. Other countries use child labor to gain a comparative advantage (e.g., clothing).

8. When choosing to limit trade, a country can impose a tax on imported goods. This is called
   a. An estate tax.
   b. A tariff.
   c. A quota.
   d. A capital gains tax.

9. Economists are concerned about nontariff (regulatory) barriers when they are used to prevent imports when a good
   a. Is produced via questionable means (e.g., banning milk produced from cows injected with bovine growth hormone).
   b. Is produced via more efficient use of labor.
   c. May spread disease (e.g., banning beef from countries that have experienced Mad Cow).
   d. Violates local standards for decency.

Think about This

Today's transportation infrastructure makes international trade more efficient than intra-U.S. trade was 100 years ago. What this means is that it is easier today for a shirt made in China to get to California than it was for a shirt made in Georgia to make it to Missouri in 1900. The U.S. Constitution has always banned states from regulating trade between states. This amounted to a within United States free-trade agreement. Can we use the experience of the United States between 1900 and 2000 to predict what would happen in world trade if there was free trade across the globe?

Talk about This

Simple trade theory suggests that a country should not import and export the same good. It should either import the good or export the good, but not both. Reality is that intraindustry trade is common. What might explain this?

For More Insight See

Journal of Economic Perspectives 12, no. 4 (Fall 1998). See articles by Dani Rodrik; Maurice Obstfeld; and Robert C. Feenstra and Jeffrey G. Williamson, pp. 3–72.

Journal of Economic Perspectives 9, no. 3 (Summer 1995). See articles by J. David Richardson and Adrian Wood, pp. 57–80.

Krugman, Paul R, "Is Free Trade Passé?" *Journal of Economic Perspectives* 1, no. 2 (Fall 1987), pp. 131–144. Any text with a title like *International Economics*.

Behind the Numbers

Historical data.
   Gross Domestic Product 1940–2004.

Budget of the United States Government, 2006; historical tables—http://www.gpoaccess.gov/usbudget/fy06/pdf/hist.pdf.

U.S. trade, overall and by Industry, 2004.
   U.S. foreign trade highlights—http://www.ita.doc.gov/td/industry/otea/usfth/tabcon.html.

International Comparisons of Exports and Imports, 2004.
   U.S. foreign trade highlights—http://www.ita.doc.gov/td/industry/otea/usfth/tabcon.html.

Chapter **14**

The International Monetary Fund: Doctor or Witch Doctor?

Top officials of the International Monetary Fund discuss global trade issues at a meeting in Prague. *Source: AP Wide World Photo*

Chapter Objectives

After reading this chapter you should be able to

Understand what the IMF is and how and why it came into existence.

See how foreign exchange markets work to facilitate trade.

Understand the role of the IMF and how it makes decisions.

Apply your knowledge of the IMF to the Asian financial crisis of the late 1990s.

Chapter Outline

Before the IMF and Its Birth

Foreign Exchange Markets

Today's IMF

The Asian Financial Crisis

Summary

One economic news story dominated the front pages in 1998: the year-long Asian financial crisis that threatened the health of the world economy. The Asian crisis introduced much of America to the International Monetary Fund (IMF), which attempted to cure the economic disease that plagued Asia, Russia, and Latin America. Rarely heard from at one time, this institution was simultaneously being praised for doing a masterful job of preventing worldwide depression and castigated for causing the Asian crisis in the first place. We cannot present a consensus view, because no consensus exists, but we will use the Asian economic crisis of 1997 and 1998 as our primary example.

We start by looking at the world before the IMF came into existence, examining why it was needed in that world. We describe what the IMF does and who funds it. We consider how the Asian financial crisis started, and we outline how the IMF responded to it.

Last, we survey the debate over the successes and failures of the IMF. We try to decide whether it serves as a doctor who administers needed economic medicine or a witch doctor who administers more pain than cure.

BEFORE THE IMF AND ITS BIRTH

In the Great Depression of 1929, world financial markets began a three-year collapse that brought about a worldwide deflation of 48 percent and a reduction in world trade of 63 percent. Even now not all economists agree on the causes of the Great Depression. However, at the end of World War II in 1945, governments around the world agreed that if the new understandings of macroeconomics could be used to prevent another depression, it was worth a try. Thus, along with a new currency exchange system, a new organization came into being: the International Monetary Fund, or IMF.

The IMF was the brainchild of John Maynard Keynes, the same economist who lent his name to the aggregate supply curve's Keynesian range. The IMF was not designed simply to operate as a lender to countries in financial turmoil. It was also intended to be a center for macroeconomic expertise for member nations to consult, one that would help to prevent economic turmoil from beginning or to deal with it when it arrived. Its role as a lender has gotten more headlines lately, but its role as adviser is still important to its mission.

The Great Depression began as a financial crisis and became a goods and assets crisis as mistake after mistake was made by country after country. Many nations, for example, saw tax revenues fall and responded by raising taxes to keep budgets balanced. Many others saw exports fall while their competitor nations scrambled to export to them. In response, many nations raised tariffs and other trade barriers, and in doing so nations entered a race to close their economic borders to outside goods. These actions, taken in the short-term economic and political interest of each nation's people, deepened and lengthened the Great Depression. The world economy was not fully back on its feet until 1940, when World War II created a high demand by governments for armaments and soldiers. It was not until the 1950s that the world economy was back to consistent growth that was grounded in peace.

Trade, whether it be city to city, state to state, or nation to nation, is vital to the growth of an economy. Without it people produce only what they themselves can consume. Thus they lose benefits from **economies of scale,** the aspect of production where per-unit costs

economies of scale
The aspect of production where per-unit costs decrease as production increases.

decrease as production increases. For trade to work, each party must believe that it is getting something at least as valuable as it is giving up. **Barter,** the direct trade of goods for other goods and without money, serves this purpose, but barter is inefficient and unpredictable. When you use money you do not need to find someone with some "thing" that you want; you only have to find someone with money. In trade that goes from city to city or from state to state, the logistics of this are simple. International trade becomes complicated by the introduction of foreign exchange.

barter
The direct trade of goods for other goods and without money.

FOREIGN EXCHANGE MARKETS

To understand the importance and the complexity of dealing with foreign exchange consider the simple act of buying a Creative Labs Zen portable media player (if you haven't seen them, they allow you to listen to MP3s and watch computer or TiVo recorded television shows on the go). When you plunk down $500 or so at a local store, the $500 goes several places. The first place it goes is to the store owner, who uses some of it to pay employees and other business expenses, and some of it to pay the Creative Labs distributor. The rest is profit. The distributor bought the player from Creative Labs which is based in Singapore, and here is where the issue of **foreign exchange** comes up. Those in Singapore want to be paid in their Singapore dollars, rather than U.S. dollars, so the distributor has to make arrangements to get Singapore dollars. Much of the manufacturing of Creative Labs products no longer takes place in Singapore but now takes place in countries like China. If your player was made in China, the Chinese manufacturer has employees who want to be paid in neither U.S. nor Singapore dollars but want yuan, the home currency of China (to say "yuan," say "u-wan").

foreign exchange
The conversion of the currency of one country for the currency of another.

Let's look at the first of these exchanges, the U.S. dollar-for-Singapore dollar exchange. Figure 14.1 looks like any ordinary supply and demand diagram except that the labels are more confusing. The confusion stems from the fact that in a typical market you are exchanging a form of currency for a good or a service. Here you are exchanging a form of currency for another form of currency. In this particular case the demand for Singapore dollars is also the supply of U.S. dollars and the demand for U.S. dollars is really the supply of Singapore dollars. The price is confusing. Typically the price is quoted in terms of dollars per

FIGURE 14.1   Singapore dollar-to-U.S. dollar exchange.

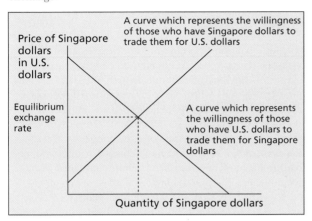

Price of Singapore dollars in U.S. dollars

A curve which represents the willingness of those who have Singapore dollars to trade them for U.S. dollars

Equilibrium exchange rate

A curve which represents the willingness of those who have U.S. dollars to trade them for Singapore dollars

Quantity of Singapore dollars

unit of the good. Here it is U.S. dollars per unit of Singapore dollar. It could just as easily be Singapore dollars per unit of U.S. dollars. For this reason we have renamed the curves using somewhat roundabout language.

The vertical axis of Figure 14.1 is labeled "Price of Singapore dollars in U.S. dollars" because it is the number of U.S. dollars that must be given up to get a quantity of Singapore dollars. The horizontal axis is the amount in Singapore dollars exchanged. What would normally be called a demand curve is the "Curve which represents the willingness of those who have U.S. dollars to trade them for Singapore dollars." It is downward sloping because people would be less willing to trade their U.S. dollars for Singapore dollars if they have to give up more U.S. dollars to do it. What would normally be called a supply curve is the "Curve which represents the willingness of those who have Singapore dollars to trade them for U.S. dollars." It is upward sloping because people would be more willing to trade their Singapore dollars for U.S. dollars if they could get more dollars from it.

The U.S. dollar can get stronger or weaker relative to the Singapore dollar if either the desire of Singapore dollar holders to acquire U.S. dollars changes or the desire of U.S. dollar holders to acquire Singapore dollars changes. An increase in the desire of either to have U.S. dollars rather than Singapore dollars would strengthen the U.S. dollar, causing the price of Singapore dollars—the U.S. dollar-to-Singapore dollar exchange rate—to fall. A decrease in the desire of either to have U.S. dollars will weaken the U.S. dollar, causing the price of Singapore dollars—the U.S. dollar-to-Singapore dollar exchange rate—to rise.

Going back to our portable media player example, you can see that even for such simple foreign trade to take place, a number of different currencies must be exchanged. If currency exchange is as easy as going to the bank with a 20-dollar bill and asking for 20 one-dollar bills, then foreign exchange is not an obstacle to trade. In most of the Western world it is a relatively simple proposition for a corporation to get the currencies it needs. There are foreign exchange markets in all large cities that have stock markets. If you need a special permit to exchange currency, however, the transaction is far more cumbersome. Moreover, if that special permit is given only to those who support the ruling party, the ease of trading ranges from difficult to nearly impossible.

Who gets hurt by such obstacles to trade? Lots of people. With too many barriers your portable media player either will not be manufactured or will cost much more. You will be forced to choose to pay more or to do without it. The store owner will lose profit and the store salesperson will lose commissions. The distributor, Creative Labs, and the Chinese worker will be hurt too; one will not make a sale, the other will not have a job.

The IMF tries to ensure that the world is as free and open to world trade as possible. It has no enforcement mechanism other than an ability to persuade and the ability to withhold lending if it so chooses. The preferred IMF role is simply to watch for signs of trouble, to deal with trouble when it arises, and to advise countries on keeping their exchange rules easy to follow.

TODAY'S IMF

How the IMF Works

The IMF is a collective of 184 countries, each of which contributes an amount of money based on its ability to pay. In return, each member country receives free access to the best economic wisdom of the other members and assistance in the form of loans if its economy suffers. The IMF differs from the World Bank in that the loans the World Bank gives are long term and go exclusively to developing countries for projects aimed at boosting them out of poverty. The IMF gives short-term loans designed to bridge rough economic waters.

Each member contributes its quota of money to the IMF so that this can be loaned to members in temporary economic distress. Although a country's quota must be paid before it can borrow, the payments do not all have to be in "real" currency. Many countries have currency controls that prevent people from converting their currencies to others. Such currencies, of course, have little value on the world market because the countries that print them

The World Bank

The World Bank's job is to finance growth-enabling investment in the poor countries of the world. Bridges, wells, roads, irrigation systems, communication systems, and health systems are all projects that are funded by the World Bank in its pursuit of reducing worldwide poverty.

If you have tackled Chapter 23, "Poverty and Welfare," you know that what qualifies as "poor" is in some dispute. Intuitively, you might choose to use the U.S. poverty line for income. While few serious economists use that standard for judging world poverty rates, doing so places a sizable majority of the world population in "poverty." The World Bank itself uses the percentage of a country's population that lives on less than $2 per day and less than $1 per day. For a host of technical reasons you may wish to explore on the World Bank Web site (http://www.world.bank.org), even this very low standard is in dispute. In any event, in 2004 using the $2 per day standard suggests that nearly half of the more than 6 billion people in the world are poor. Even worse, 20 percent of the world's population lives on less than $1 a day.

Poverty at this level can be self-perpetuating. Every year 100 million children do not attend school because their families are too poor not to have each child working. The cycle of poverty continues as these children grow up with no ability to earn a living sufficient to offer their own children a better living through education. Further, because these countries have few viable export goods and have no history of paying their international debts, traditional banks will not lend them money to engage in structural changes necessary to bring vitality to their economies.

The World Bank, though charged with tackling this problem, is poorly named because by its own admission it is not a bank in the conventional sense. It takes no deposits. Developed countries funnel some of their taxes to it and the World Bank makes interest-free long-term (35 or more years) loans with lenient terms (up to 10 years of a grace period on paying off the loan) that are designed to allow those countries to build the infrastructure necessary for growth. In 2004, the International Development Association, that part of the World Bank charged with providing loans to the most impoverished countries, provided $9 billion to finance 158 projects in 62 countries.

A separate division, the International Bank for Reconstruction and Development, borrows money using its excellent credit rating to loan it out to countries that could borrow from traditional banks but only at prohibitively high interest rates. These countries may have had previous difficulties meeting their debt obligations or have faced recent political difficulties causing private banks to shy away from granting them credit directly. In this area, the World Bank operates as a guarantor of loans. A third division provides insurance to private businesses that invest in volatile parts of the world. This insurance allows private corporations to invest in politically unstable countries by minimizing the economic consequences of political unrest.

The World Bank has its share of critics in large part because dictators, tyrants, and politicians on the take have managed to pilfer significant amounts of this aid for their own personal use. Still the World Bank's work cannot go unnoticed. Whether it is combating AIDs in Africa, educating young women in Bangladesh, or helping rebuild war-torn Bosnia, the resources are used to help the poor in developing countries build better lives.

will not honor them for anything but exports from the countries that issue them. The official exchange rates that these countries pretend exist between their own and **hard currencies,** currencies easily converted to U.S. dollars or gold, dramatically overstates the value of their own currencies. For this reason, at least 25 percent of all quotas must be paid in gold or hard currency while the remainder can be paid in local currency.

hard currencies
Currencies easily converted to U.S. dollars or gold.

The fact that countries that have currency controls can pay 75 percent of their quota in money of questionable value means that though the IMF may theoretically have

$327 billion to lend, only about half of that has real value. In a typical year only about 20 world currencies are borrowed, and the vast majority of them are dollars, euros, pounds, and yen.

As an example, though Albania is a member of the IMF and has a quota of a little more than $50 million, almost $40 million of it is paid in a currency that no one but Albanians would ever use. Moreover, it is not really worth the $40 million that the Albanian government says it is. If it were convertible on the world market to dollars, then the IMF could theoretically exchange it for dollars and lend those dollars. It is not convertible, so the IMF cannot exchange it for dollars or any other hard currency.

In theory all currency is convertible to hard currency, but it is not convertible at the exchange rate claimed by the issuing country. If the IMF chose to convert these currencies at the lower realistic values, this would create a balance sheet problem. In the Albanian case, the $40 million worth of Albanian currency would be turned into something like $10 million. This would mean that the IMF would have to admit the fact publicly that countries were not really paying their quotas. Since the IMF views itself as a problem-solving institution, creating a political problem by using realistic exchange rates to determine quotas is not worth the cost.

How IMF Decisions Are Made

The IMF decision-making process resembles a democracy that is based on a rule that is not one country–one vote but roughly 100,000 SDRs to 1 vote. **Special drawing rights (SDRs)** are currency invented by the IMF and composed of a weighted average of the four major currencies of the world. It is 40 percent U.S. dollar, 35 percent euro, 13 percent yen, and 12 percent British pound. Though the exchange rates of the various currencies change their dollar equivalencies, a decent rule of thumb is that one SDR is worth $1.45.

special drawing rights (SDRs)
A made-up currency of the IMF that is comprised of a weighted average of the four major currencies of the world.

Table 14.1 indicates that not only do the major industrialized nations have a disproportionate obligation in terms of quotas; they also have a disproportionate say in the policies of the IMF. A similar arrangement funds the World Bank, and the World Bank is always run by an American. The IMF's managing director has always come from one of the other four major nations listed in Table 14.1. The day-to-day operation of the IMF is, for practical purposes, run by 24 executive directors who are drawn from the five major nations, Russia, China, and Saudi Arabia. There are sometimes formal votes that involve the ministers of finance, including the U.S. secretary of the Treasury. A rotating set of 16 others represents other parts of the world.

THE ASIAN FINANCIAL CRISIS

The Cause

Although there is still significant disagreement over what caused the Asian financial crisis, one of the most plausible scenarios is the following. Growth in Japan and Europe was relatively slow for some time, and this caused interest rates and investment opportunities in these countries to be low. Investors, seeking a place to put their money, saw Asian countries such as South Korea, Malaysia, Thailand, Indonesia, and Singapore as offering high-return possibilities. Banks and brokerage houses in these countries borrowed hard currencies from Japan, Europe, and elsewhere. They did it without making sure they could exchange their own money for hard currency when the time came to repay the loans. They used the money to make risky loans. Some of the loans turned out bad. At the same time the Thai government decided it could no longer maintain an exchange rate it had fought to defend. This caused a steep devaluation of the baht.

Thai and other Asian financial institutions could not pay back the money they owed because many loans they had made turned out to be bad. Combined with the devalued currency, it was doubly difficult for them to pay

TABLE 14.1   Distribution of quotas and votes in the IMF.

Nation	Quota (SDRs in millions)	Percentage of Votes
United States	37,149	17.5
Japan	13,313	6.3
Germany	13,008	6.1
United Kingdom	10,739	5.1
France	10,739	5.1
Other major Western nations (Belgium, Netherlands, Canada, Italy, Russia)	29,146	13.3
Other major non-Western nations (China, India, Saudi Arabia)	17,513	8.1
Rest of the world	99,384	46.6

Source: International Monetary Fund, http://www.imf.org.

back the debts they were required to pay in hard currency. Not only were banks unable to pay off the loans they owed to foreign banks, but they were unable to fund the new loans that good businesses needed to maintain production. The previous loans of once-sound companies could not be paid, and the problem just continued to spiral. Although each of the steps in the Asian financial crisis warrants its own thick book, we will try to examine them in enough detail to be of some value.

First, the growth rate in Japan had slowed substantially from its 1970s and early 1980s levels and had been in recession or slow-growth recovery for nearly a decade. European nations, though not in recession, were experiencing relatively slow growth. Investors throughout the globe were looking for high-opportunity places to put their money, and Asia was an attractive sight. Except for Japan, growth rates in the major nations of Asia had exceeded the world average for years, and it appeared at the time that this would continue. Together, these phenomena contributed to form the first ingredient in the crisis: a large supply of available hard currency.

Second, financial institutions in these countries did something that looked like a pretty good gamble at the time. They borrowed the money and exchanged it with their governments for their own currency without **hedging.** Hedging would have amounted to ensuring that they could exchange their own currencies for hard currency at a guaranteed exchange rate when the loans were due. Financial institutions normally hedge when they are concerned about a fluctuating currency, but these banks believed their governments' assurances that they would maintain current exchange rates. Since hedging costs money, the banks decided to avoid the cost and take the risk. The failure to hedge put the second ingredient in place: banks unprepared to repay loans with hard currency.

hedging

Taking an investment position so that changes in prices or exchange rates do not alter the advisability of a business decision.

Third, when the financial institutions lent money to businesses, they were confident of repayment. For a variety of reasons, unfortunately, the banks' confidence was misguided. Some companies, for example, generated the confidence with fraudulent financial statements. Some were thought to be "too big to fail"—people expected that their government would bail them out. Others had influence within their governments. At any rate, the businesses used the borrowed local currency to pay workers and to get hard currency from their governments to buy equipment for their plants. We know, also, that some of it was used to pay off corrupt politicians. Regardless of how it was spent, its spending constituted the third ingredient, one that meant there was little margin for error if things started to go badly: most of the hard currency was gone.

Fourth, two things happened together that set off a slide: More than the expected number of businesses failed and the Thai government lost its battle to hold the line on the exchange rate. Businesses fail all the time but, in combination with an untenable exchange rate, the failures at this time set off the first pebble in the economic landslide. Governments of emerging countries, like Thailand, attempt to foster growth in their industries by pegging their currency to another country's currency. To do this when the currency is too strong is quite simple: the government prints more money and exchanges it for hard currency. This sounds appealing but it is also almost never the problem. When the currency is too weak to maintain the peg on its own, the government has to step in and use gold or hard currency to buy it up so as to make it more scarce. When a government runs low on hard currency and gold it can no longer maintain the exchange rate. Even worse, investors often take this as a signal that the country cannot maintain even a lower exchange rate. If the country is, in fact, completely out of hard currency and gold, it cannot maintain the exchange rate and it may fall even further. Thailand gave up just as it was running out of hard currency, and other countries followed suit by reducing the value of their own currency before they were in similar trouble. Because the financial institutions had not hedged, they did not have enough local money to exchange at the new, unfavorable exchange rate, and the banks had to turn to their governments to bail them out. The governments had no hard currency left to pay off those debts because they had already used it all in the failed attempt to maintain the exchange rate peg.

As these banks went under, they lost the ability to make loans to businesses that could have survived the onslaught with small loans, and even the relatively healthy businesses also started to go under. This further weakened the banks and the Asian currencies. The slide did not stop until most investors in Asian businesses with paper assets denominated in Asian currencies had lost 75 percent or more of their investment. This all happened between the late summer of 1997 and the winter of 1998–1999.

The IMF to the Rescue?

The IMF came to the rescue with a package of routine and not-so-routine assistance. It also came armed with conditions, and that is what puts the question mark on whether the assistance was helpful or not. With even a moderate amount of economic distress, any nation can lay claim to the 25 percent of its IMF quota that it puts up in hard currency. In last-ditch attempts to prop up the Asian currencies this amount was given, and it was gone in a few days. To qualify for three times its quota, the maximum allowed under normal IMF rules, countries had to agree to certain conditions. When the problem revealed itself to be more systemic, the IMF brought out the big money. The IMF feared the problem might spread to Russia, Latin America (especially Brazil), and then to the rest of the world.

The usual job of the IMF is to offer short-term loans of three- to five-year duration to keep a nation's temporary downturn from becoming permanent and to keep it from spreading. It applied this by first bringing in $35 billion worth of SDRs and a set of conditions to which governments had to agree to get it. These conditions were at the same time helpful and unhelpful, wise and unwise, popular and unpopular.

The conditions attached required some governments to give up on favorite industries and pet projects. Corrupt siphoning of resources was identified, and ending this was made a first condition of aid. In this arena a terribly corrupt and ruthless president, Suharto of Indonesia, was forced aside by internal pressure that began, not because the IMF insisted upon it, but as an inevitable consequence of the discovery that Suharto had siphoned off billions in previous IMF funds for his own purposes.

Other conditions required that countries completely relinquish exchange controls that had allowed only the elite to escape with hard currency. Still other conditions put forth a set of accounting principles that would reveal any future balance sheet fraud.

While conditions such as ending corruption had popular support, there were others that caused a great deal of short-term pain and probably made the problem worse. The IMF insisted, for example, on a tightening of monetary policy, the closing of what it termed "unviable financial institutions," and the tightening of controls for other, weaker institutions. This made loans either unavailable to semistable businesses or so costly that businesses that might have weathered the storm went under.

runs
Panicked withdrawal of money by worried depositors.

The closure of the "unviable" institutions generated **runs** (panicked withdrawal of money by worried depositors) on weaker institutions, and they too became unviable. When the semistable businesses began to fold the crisis worsened, and it did so because of the conditions the IMF had imposed.

What should the IMF have done? If it had done nothing, simply letting the problems sort themselves out, it is certain that things would have been bad. Whether what it did was the right solution is certainly debatable. If it had come in and saved all the financial institutions, it would have created a situation where it was guaranteeing stupidly risky investments. This would have signaled to other countries that they did not have to reform and that the IMF would always be there to bail them out.

Let's consider the title of this section, "The IMF to the Rescue?" and the subtitle of this chapter, "Doctor or Witch Doctor?" The problem the IMF faces is that fixing the short-term crisis and dealing with its long-term causes often require different actions. Because the IMF has nearly no leverage in good times and a great deal of leverage in bad times, it has tended to impose what it sees as a long-term solution. It is analogous to a patient who listens to what his doctor says only when he is in the hospital. The long-term problem is that a poor diet and no exercise has caused a short-term health crisis, say, a heart attack.

It is pretty clear in a medical scenario that it would be bad practice for the doctor to order the patient to immediately go out and run five miles. This is essentially what the IMF did. It made a short-term crisis worse than it would have been if it had simply shored up the problem financial institutions. On the other hand, some of the prescriptions it offered for long-term economic health, like requiring more accessible financial statements, were probably necessary.

Of course, all of this must be compared to the outcome that would have resulted had the IMF done nothing. While doing nothing is always an option, it begs the question "Why have an IMF if it won't act during a crisis?" Had the IMF done nothing, it may well have been the case that things would have been better in the short term. There would be no reason to believe, however, that there would have been a solution to either the political corruption or the financial mismanagement that were at the root of the crisis to begin with.

The success of the IMF's intervention will be debated by economists for many years as we try to learn from this event. Ordinary citizens of countries around the world will also debate the issue of allowing international organizations to influence local economies. (See the "International Protests" box in the next chapter.) The conclusion of that debate may also determine whether countries in trouble in the future will put their faith in the policy prescriptions of the IMF.

Summary

You now understand what the IMF is and how and why it came into existence. You understand what foreign exchange markets are and how they work to facilitate trade.

You understand the IMF's role and how it makes decisions. You should now be able to apply this knowledge to the Asian financial crisis of the late 1990s.

Key Terms

barter, 158
economies of scale, 158
foreign exchange, 158

hard currencies, 160
hedging, 162

runs, 163
special drawing rights (SDRs), 161

Quiz Yourself

1. Exchange rates reflect
   a. The price of one indexed good in terms of the domestic currency.
   b. The price of one indexed good in terms of a foreign currency.
   c. The price of one indexed service in terms of a foreign currency.
   d. The price of one currency in terms of another currency.

2. In a supply and demand diagram for a (dollar–yen) foreign exchange market, the supply of dollars can also be viewed as
   a. The demand for yen.
   b. The demand for SDRs.
   c. The supply of yen.
   d. The supply for SDRs.

3. The IMF was a creation of the
   a. Industrial victors after World War II.
   b. Major economic powers after World War I.
   c. United States after the Great Depression.
   d. European Union after the Asian financial crisis of 1998.

4. The World Bank has a different mission than the International Monetary Fund. The World Bank focuses on
   a. Loans to industrialized countries whereas the IMF focuses on developing countries.
   b. Loans to developing countries whereas the IMF focuses on industrialized countries.
   c. Loans and grants to build infrastructure in developing nations whereas the IMF focuses on currency and economic stabilization.
   d. Being the "Fed" for developing countries.

5. The exchange rate between the dollar and the euro is determined by
   a. The IMF.
   b. The World Bank.
   c. The United Nations.
   d. The forces of supply and demand.

6. The influence that countries have over the policies of the IMF are based on
   a. The provisions of its originating treaty.
   b. The quota of contributions of hard-currency equivalents (SDRs) each country must make.
   c. The gross domestic product of each country.
   d. The population of each country.

7. The track record of the International Monetary Fund in providing advice and funds to stabilize currencies is
   a. Unblemished.
   b. Viewed by economists as being nearly perfectly wrong in all circumstances.
   c. Debated by economists but usually viewed as better than nothing.
   d. Debated by economists with most thinking it does more harm than good.

8. The International Monetary Fund's track record is hard to judge because
   a. It has no authority to require adherence to its advice even when it allocates money.
   b. It deals only with countries that are having trouble after they have gotten themselves into trouble.
   c. It deals only with countries that are not in any trouble. The World Bank deals with countries in trouble.
   d. It has no authority to require adherence to its advice. Only those nations that take the IMFs money must heed their advice.

Think about This

The International Monetary Fund cannot require countries to adopt policies it prefers. For years China pegged the value of the yuan to the U.S. dollar. Because this peg was typically at an exchange rate that undervalued the yuan, this led to substantial U.S. deficits with China and to the potential for a hard crash of the dollar. In July 2005 it began pegging the yuan's value to a market basket of currencies. When China finally releases its currency's value to the forces of supply and demand the IMF may have to play an important role in smoothing the transition. Should the IMF have more authority to prevent problems or should it simply be in a position to react to problems?

Talk about This

The world political and economic systems are governed by treaties written 60 years ago. At that time China, India, and South Korea were politically and economically less important than they are today and the United Kingdom and France were more important than they are today. Should these agreements be entirely renegotiated to reduce the influence of Europe and the United States? Should the president of the World Bank always be an American and the president of the IMF always be a European?

The IMF is predominantly interested in stabilization rather than promoting economic growth. It can be argued that this bias is in the interest of wealthy nations at the expense of poorer ones. Do you agree?

For More Insight See

Driscoll, David, "What Is the International Monetary Fund?" http://www.imf.org/external/pubs/ft/exrp/ what.htm.

IMF, "The IMF's Response to the Asian Crisis," http://www.imf.org/external/np/exr/facts/asia.htm.

Krugman, Paul. *What Happened to Asia* (Cambridge, MA: MIT) (mimeo), http://web.mit.edu/krugman/www/DISINTER.html.

Ramo, Joshua Cooper, "The Three Marketeers." *Time,* February 15, 1999, pp. 34–42.

Stiglitz, Joseph, "Bad Private-Sector Decisions." *The Wall Street Journal,* February 4, 1998, p. A22.

World Bank
　　Roles and country activities (see About Us and Countries and Regions)—http://www.worldbank.org.

Behind the Numbers

Distribution of Quotas and Votes in the IMF
　　International Monetary Fund; About the IMF—http://www.imf.org/external/np/exr/facts/sdr.htm.

World poverty rates.
　　World Bank; data and statistics; data by topic; poverty—http://www.worldbank.org/data/databytopic/poverty. html.

Chapter **15**

NAFTA, CAFTA, GATT, WTO: Are Trade Agreements Good for Us?

Protestors filled the streets of Seattle during an anti–World Trade Organization demonstration in 1999.
Source: AP Wide World Photo

Chapter Objectives

After reading this chapter you should be able to

Understand why economists generally believe free trade is better than restricted trade.

See how trade agreements facilitate the opening of trade and why such agreements are sometimes necessary.

Be familiar with NAFTA, GATT, and WTO as trade agreements and institutions.

Know some of the thinking on whether trade agreements are working as advertised.

Understand the economic and political concerns that free-trade agreements generate.

Know why the bottom line for most economists is that trade agreements are good policy.

Chapter Outline

The Benefits of Free Trade

Why Do We Need Trade Agreements?

Trade Agreements and Institutions

Economic and Political Impacts of Trade

The Bottom Line

Summary

One of the central tenets of economic policy during the Clinton administration was that free trade is good for the United States. The reasoning was that Americans can and routinely do outcompete their international trade partners. The jobs that were gained and the increases in living standards from such trade would thus outweigh any losses. The foundation for this argument relies heavily on the theory of international trade that we addressed in Chapter 13, "International Trade: Does It Jeopardize American Jobs?"

NAFTA, the North American Free Trade Agreement, **CAFTA,** the Central America Free Trade Agreement, **GATT,** the General Agreement on Tariffs and Trade, and the **WTO,** the World Trade Organization, are the spearheads of this free-trade policy. This chapter explains the purposes of each and reviews the arguments for and against them. As a first step we summarize the theoretical argument for free trade. We then explicate some of the details of the three agreements just mentioned. Finally, we examine, in some detail, the effect of these agreements on trade, income inequality, workers' wages, and environmental health.

NAFTA

North American Free Trade Agreement involving the United States, Mexico, and Canada.

CAFTA

The Central America Free Trade Agreement involving the United States and five Central American countries: Costa Rica, El Salvador, Guatemala, Honduras, and Nicaragua.

GATT

General Agreement on Tariffs and Trade, a world trade agreement.

WTO

The World Trade Organization, an institution that arbitrates trade disputes.

THE BENEFITS OF FREE TRADE

The economic benefits from trade are so often assumed to be obvious that economists do not feel the need to explain them. Most noneconomists, however, assume that trade is a zero-sum game that can be characterized by the phrase "your win is my loss." Nothing could misrepresent trade more thoroughly. Nowhere in the field of economics is there such a discrepancy between what economists know and what noneconomists consider to be the conventional wisdom. If the explanation that follows does not lay out the economists' argument on the benefits of international trade in sufficient detail, you will find additional information in Chapter 13, "International Trade."

Suppose that the United States and Mexico are the only countries in the world and that they produce only two goods: low-tech (LT) and high-tech (HT). Further, suppose that U.S. workers can make both LT and HT more quickly and in greater numbers than Mexican workers. Why would the United States want to trade with Mexico when it can produce both goods itself? To see the possibilities, assume that workers in the United States and Mexico are divided between high skill and low skill and that everyone is fully employed in both countries. To see how effective they are, assume that Table 15.1 represents the number of workers needed to produce specific amounts of each good in each country.

Table 15.1 shows that it takes one high-skill U.S. worker to make one high-tech good, that one high-skill Mexican worker can produce three low-tech goods, and so on. The suggestion here is that high-skill workers in the United States are more proficient than anyone else at all forms of production and that Mexican low-skill workers are less proficient across the board. The low-skill American worker is assumed to be better at high-tech production than the high-skill Mexican worker (perhaps because the American is working with better machines), but the two are equal in low-tech production.

If 100 American low-skill workers were to shift from the production of low-tech (LT) to the production of high-tech (HT) and 120 Mexican workers were to shift from HT to LT, then there would be 50 more high-tech goods and 300 fewer low-tech goods produced in the United States. In Mexico there would be 40 fewer high-tech goods and 360 more low-tech goods produced. The world (limited in this case to the United States and Mexico) would have a net addition of 10 high-tech goods

TABLE 15.1   Production of workers: number of workers needed to produce a number of goods.

	High Tech		Low Tech	
	High Skill	**Low Skill**	**High Skill**	**Low Skill**
United States	1 produces 1	2 produce 1	1 produces 4	1 produces 3
Mexico	3 produce 1	4 produce 1	1 produces 3	1 produces 1

and 60 low-tech goods. Given a fair distribution of these gains from trade, each side would be better off.

As a result of the increased competition from Mexican low-tech firms, the workers in low-tech firms in the United States would lose their jobs. They would quickly get new jobs in the high-tech firms, however, as increased demand for American high-tech goods increases demand for laborers capable of such production. While there are more than a few places where the argument that trade is good for all can be criticized, it remains the basic position of economists. Most economists are convinced that trade provides increased standards of living and regardless of how many workers are displaced, they will always be absorbed into the growing industries.

WHY DO WE NEED TRADE AGREEMENTS?

You may instinctively distrust this economists' view of trade. You may be asking, If free trade is so good, why do we need agreements to keep it in place? The answer is twofold: one economic, the other political.

Strategic Trade

Strategic trade policies are policies designed to get more of the benefits from trade in a country than would exist under free trade. On the economic front, there are circumstances under which a country can increase its share of the free-trade benefits. That is, a country can increase its benefits from trade by putting on tariffs, quotas, and the like; if it does, however, the sum of the benefits from trade to the two trading partners deteriorates.

strategic trade policies
Policies designed to get more of the benefits from trade in a country than would exist under free trade.

Although the circumstances under which strategic trade is better for a country than free trade are somewhat complicated, one example might shed some light. Suppose a large country is the dominant world player in the production of a particular good and another large country is a much smaller player. The monopoly power of the large company can overwhelm the other country's small company. Economists have shown that, at least theoretically, the country with the small company can subsidize its exports and increase its profits by more than the subsidy. The typical example of this has been the Boeing–Airbus competition in the manufacture of large aircraft. In practical terms, Airbus's subsidy from France and Britain has been greater than its profits.

Special Interests

Whenever there is trade, there are individuals who see themselves as the losers. Typically, these are the folks who are the most visible. When a plant closes in an American town to move production to a facility in another country, the job losses from trade are obvious for all to see. The jobs created by trade are more difficult for the average worker to see. As a result, workers left with pink slips become vocal opponents of trade, and those who benefit from it do not see that they benefit from it.

An even greater political problem occurs if the loser from trade has sufficient political strength to convince elected officials that restricting trade is in the officeholders' electoral interest. Again, because many of the beneficiaries of free trade—consumers paying lower prices and workers having better jobs—do not see these gains as attributable to trade, they are far less vocal in favor of trade. There are two groups whose voices are typically raised in favor of trade, business interests and farmers. As a result, it appears to the political world as though free trade is a battle between workers on one side and big business and farmers on the other. In such a circumstance, though free trade is rather obviously the better outcome to economists, it is not so obvious to elected officials.

What Trade Agreements Prevent

To see how misplaced self-interest can lead to a deterioration of trade benefits let's return to our hypothetical example of trade between Mexico and the United States. If the low-skill, low-tech workers in the United States fear that trade will cost their jobs, they can seek a **tariff** (a tax on imports) or a **quota** (a limit on imports) from the U.S. government. Each would raise the price of imported goods and the former would bring tax revenue to the U.S. government.

tariff
A tax on imports.

quota
A limit on imports.

If Mexico does not retaliate by levying its own tariffs or quotas, our exports of high-tech goods will remain unchanged. This will be good for the United States, but less so than it will be bad for Mexico, and it will be worse for the world as a whole. If Mexico does retaliate, it can make itself better off than if it does not retaliate. It will do so with tariffs or quotas of its own. Again, the degree to which

Mexico will make itself better off is outweighed by the damage done to the United States, which will retaliate further. Soon there will be no gains from trade because there will be no trade.

Trade agreements prevent countries from starting on the slippery slope of trade retaliation. Because a country is better off with free trade than with no trade, free trade wins. The problem is that countries will always be tempted to raise some barriers in hopes no one will retaliate. When countries get into a tariff war and retaliation is met with more retaliation, not only are any small advantages lost, but all other advantages from trade are lost. Countries thus need trade agreements to keep themselves from the temptation of creating trade barriers.

The history and politics of trade are somewhat strange. The first Republican president, Abraham Lincoln, ran for his first U.S. House seat on a platform that called for high tariffs. Such protectionist trade policy was a staple of Republican political philosophy, and it was exemplified by the disastrous Smoot-Hawley tariff law of the 1930s. Not until the 1950s did Republicans begin to change and to embrace free trade, and they did so because their constituents in business argued that they could be more profitable with trade than without it. During the same time, Democrats, the party most identified with labor unions, switched from being the free-trade party to the protectionist party, and they did so because the unions saw trade hurting their members. In 1993, Democratic President Bill Clinton started to move his party back to a free-trade position just as some Republicans were moving back to their traditional protectionist position. In 2005, most Democrats in Congress remained sympathetic to the protectionist concerns of labor and most Republicans remain free traders. It was in this context that President George W. Bush brought the CAFTA to Congress with an eye toward spreading the idea of free trade throughout the Americas. It passed by one vote.

TRADE AGREEMENTS AND INSTITUTIONS

Alphabet Soup

The North American Free Trade Agreement, NAFTA, was first proposed by President Ronald Reagan, negotiated by President George Bush (George Herbert Walker), and, after being amended, pushed through Congress and signed by President Bill Clinton. It created a geographical area of free trade in which the United States, Canada, and Mexico agreed to (1) very low tariffs and (2) procedures whereby some tariffs could remain in place. An important element in the agreement was a formalized grievance process whereby disputes could be aired.

The General Agreements on Tariffs and Trade, GATT, is another agreement negotiated across the terms of many presidents. GATT set out the conditions under which signatory nations could set tariffs and quotas. GATT came into existence just after World War II, but its most recent version, the Uruguay Round, has had the greatest free-trade bent. Even under stretched definitions, GATT cannot be called a free-trade agreement, but it has moved nations in that direction. In reality it simply makes the rules for tariffs and retaliation more explicit.

The rules of GATT require that retaliation be proportional. When in 1999, for example, much of western Europe gave favorable treatment in banana sales to its former colonies, the United States, at the behest of major fruit companies like Dole, retaliated by threatening a tariff on European leather goods. Although the connection between bananas and purses is tenuous, it was deemed acceptable retaliation under GATT. It makes sense under GATT because the trade in question is roughly the same. In operational terms GATT is an agreement that says "here are ways you can impose tariffs and other ways you cannot impose them."

The Uruguay Round also took up the issue of intellectual property rights and restrictions. The laws of China, South Korea, and other Asian nations at this time had not recognized the right of people to own ideas the way that copyright and patent laws allowed them to in Western countries. They engaged in copying and selling copyrighted materials like CDs, books, and computer software with impunity. In addition, much to the consternation of the U.S. government and the industries whose markets were affected, many nations whose television and movie industries were unable to compete with Hollywood limited the importing of American shows and movies.

On the issue of copyright infringement, Asian governments promised a crackdown on entrepreneurs' openly making and selling copies of widely distributed music and software CDs. At one time there were more illegal than legal copies of Windows 95 (the predecessor of 98, NT, ME, 2000, and XP) in China. It was the position of the United States that this represented a theft from American artists, producers, record companies, and software producers and, as such, it should be banned. On this issue, GATT recognized copyright infringement as an area worthy of tariff retaliation.

Another priority for the United States was the distribution of American-made movies and television shows. The American entertainment industry sells its output throughout the world, and shows like *Baywatch* got very high ratings in Europe during the 1990s. Many countries, however, have "domestic content" rules that require that at least a certain percentage of all movies shown in a theater and programs shown on television be produced (1) in the home country and (2) with domestic actors. The United States objects to these rules because they have the effect of limiting U.S. exports. Even though movies and television programs represent an important area of American export, the final negotiations leading up to the conclusion of the Uruguay Round of GATT in 1997 did not ultimately resolve this issue in favor of the United States.

One aspect of GATT that did go our way was the power given to the WTO, the World Trade Organization. Until 1997 trade disputes involving countries reverted to no more than "yes it is fair" versus "no it is not fair" spats. There were no institutions charged with the task of finding the truth in such disputes. The WTO's job is now to resolve those disputes. Although the WTO has no greater power than to suggest who is in the right and who is not, it is hoped that complaints with and without merit will be separated and that disputes will be resolved more easily.

Are They Working?

From the outcomes of NAFTA, GATT, and the WTO it is hard to tell which side was more wrong in its predictions, those who suggested a "giant sucking sound" would be heard as jobs left the country or those who suggested a great export employment boom would result. While trade has grown rapidly among the United States, Canada, and Mexico after NAFTA, it had grown rapidly before NAFTA. While some jobs were lost as firms left to go to Mexico, the overall economy created more jobs in a shorter period than at any time in U.S. history. So what was the impact of these agreements?

From late 1995, when NAFTA was fully in place, until late 1998 trade between the United States and Canada and between the United States and Mexico has increased 30 percent and 60 percent, respectively. These increases are somewhat misleading, however, in that trade had increased 50 percent and 75 percent, respectively, in the five years leading up to NAFTA. The increases in trade left what had been a small deficit for the United States with respect to Canada unchanged. On the other hand, it converted a small U.S. surplus with Mexico into a substantial U.S. deficit with Mexico.

The impact that NAFTA has had on jobs is also in dispute. The U.S. Department of Labor has certified more than 100,000 workers as eligible for retraining benefits as a result of NAFTA-induced job losses, but these figures are hotly debated. Some argue that these figures are inflated and represent jobs that would have been lost to non–NAFTA-related competition. Others suggest that the secondary effects of these estimates understate the true impact of job losses due to NAFTA.

ECONOMIC AND POLITICAL IMPACTS OF TRADE

Of much greater concern to those objecting to free-trade agreements than its effects on trade in general is its impact on workers' wages, wage inequality, labor treatment in general, and the environment. Before we discuss whether worries about these variables have been borne out as a result of the trade pacts we have been discussing, it will be useful to look at them individually to explain the specific concerns.

Average manufacturing wages in the United States are substantially higher than those in Mexico, Canada, and nearly every other nation. If the productivity of workers were the same worldwide, you would expect that corporations would move their operations to places where there is cheaper labor. As long as the cost reduction to a company exceeds the increased costs of shipment and as long as there are not any trade barriers, you would expect jobs to leave the United States.

If workers in the United States are more productive but are not sufficiently more productive to make up for the difference in wages, then it is still the case that companies will make more money producing elsewhere and importing the goods into the United States. This can be prevented if trade protections are in place to prevent or to at least discourage imports. For the workers whose livelihoods are tied to the exiting industry, it is nearly impossible to argue that they will not be hurt by free trade. What advocates of free trade suggest is that there are enough gains from trade to finance a retraining program for workers who are displaced.

We need only to look at the number of workers and the quantity of imports in certain industries to get an idea of the magnitude of worker displacement that is involved. Since 1960 industries involved with cars, car parts, steel, electronics, apparel, and textiles have lost significantly to imports. Unfortunately, these industries (with the exception

International Protests

Wherever IMF officials, trade negotiators, or G-8 political leaders meet protestors are sure to gather. So it was for four days in late November–early December 1999 when demonstrators battled Seattle police in what became known as the Battle in Seattle. The demonstrators were protesting at a meeting of the World Trade Organization. They spanned the political spectrum. Some were environmentalists protesting what they saw as the threat that trade agreements posed to the health of the environment. Others were labor activists protesting what they saw as the threat what globalization and the increase in international competition meant for wages and job security. Still others were right-wing anti-internationalists who saw the WTO as an attack on American sovereignty. Of the estimated 35,000 protestors, more than 500 were arrested over the four-day period. Whether as a result of the protests or not, the meeting ended without an anticipated accord and without even an agreement on when the next meeting would take place. Though the move toward globalization did not end as the protestors wanted, leaders around the world were given an abrupt wake-up call to the potential political consequences of their actions.

More recently at the G-8 summit in July 2005, protestors and Scottish police clashed when a violent incident prompted police to cancel a previously approved march. The protestors tried to disrupt the meeting and were met with police batons and dogs. These protestors had differing objectives, from African aid policies, to global warming and other environmental concerns, to general discontent with what they see as corporation-driven trade policies that harm workers and the environment.*

It is a sign of modern times, that international interconnectedness is not always welcomed with open arms. One need only look at the defeat of the proposed European Union Constitution in France and the Netherlands to note that though trade and technology are making us more connected with people around the world, we are not always comfortable with that trend.

*These July 2005 G-8 summit protests were banished from the headlines when terrorists struck the London mass transit system with four, nearly simultaneous bomb blasts.

tion.[1] Using the CPI, real wages for production workers in the United States have fallen since 1970[2] while wages for high-skill workers increased. This increasing gap between the haves and the have-nots has increased the tension concerning trade tremendously.

Free trade benefits workers only if they keep their jobs. By and large the educated have kept their jobs and even gotten better ones. For such people the prices of goods they purchase are cheaper than they would be if they were produced in the United States, and, with jobs that pay well, they have enjoyed a sharp increase in their standard of living. Many people who have lost their jobs, in comparison, have found new ones, but the new ones do not allow them to maintain their previous standard of living. The loss of steel production in Pennsylvania, auto production in the Midwest, and electronics production throughout the United States has seriously lessened the number of high-paying jobs. It is therefore not surprising that professionals and some highly educated people are in favor of free trade and that people who have been hurt by it, frequently those without a college education, are against it.

If our trade policy is to move forward on the premise that everyone can be a winner, we will have to ensure retraining benefits are available to those who lose out. To do this, some of the benefits accruing to those who benefit from trade will have to be transferred in the form of spending on temporary income assistance and retraining for the unemployed.

Another area of significant concern with regard to trade agreements is the treatment both of child labor and of labor in general. If industries that were once in the United States have to compete with industries that hire eight-year-olds and pay them a dollar or less an hour, then either American workers have to be 10 times more efficient or the industry will move. Many Americans not only consider child labor immoral, but they think anything that promotes its existence is immoral as well. If they perceive free trade as responsible for promoting child labor, they may very well consider free trade itself to be immoral.

It is not just the treatment of children that is of concern. Labor costs are kept down in impoverished countries in large part because workers fear losing even a bad job. The concentration of wealth is so great among the few people who control the industries that employers can

of textiles) provided the best paying low- to semiskilled jobs around, and their loss contributed to one of the main problems of the second half of the 20th century, the lack of employment prospects for people without a college educa-

---

[1]The extent to which trade exacerbates this is debated because this trend may have been inevitable.
[2]This is accurate unless you modify the CPI as suggested in Chapter 6, in which case the real wages for production workers have risen slightly.

get away with threatening workers with an inability to work anywhere. The employers collude to keep wages down. Workers have few rights and, even if they have legal rights, they are unwilling to invoke them against an employer for fear that they will lose the job they have. Such fundamental rights as freedom from physical torture, breaks for regular meals or bathroom visits, a 40-hour work week, and collective bargaining are but dreams to many of the world's work force.

Free trade gives countries with such a paucity of workers' rights a competitive advantage against American and European firms that must pay higher wages and accord workers with better rights. To compete, these Western firms must have efficiencies that their competitors cannot achieve with a poorly trained work force. This is not difficult for high-skill areas such as software development, but it is nearly impossible for textile and apparel production. When a job takes very little skill or is not intellectually challenging, then a poorly treated, poorly trained, or poorly paid worker can keep up. It is only when the job requires complex thinking that workers who are well-treated, highly trained, and handsomely paid are going to outproduce the poorly treated, poorly trained, and poorly paid by enough to justify those who hire them keeping production in the United States.

A last area where free-trade agreements are criticized is the environment. The maquiladoras, concentrations of industries on the Mexican side of the border with the United States, produce some of the most toxic substances in the world. Those toxic substances are produced wherever the manufacturing takes place, but their handling, an important factor, differs. For instance, in the United States the wastewater from these manufacturing plants would have to be cleaned to a near-drinkable standard. In Mexico, however, less than 10 percent of industrial wastewater is treated with that degree of stringency. This is an obvious example of how the comparative advantage gained and exploited through free trade is not wanted or good. Since much of the waste travels along the Rio Grande and affects Texans directly, it would be better for them if production were in the States, even though it would cost more.

Free-trade agreements can deal with these issues. Whereas it is impossible to impose U.S. labor and environmental standards on other countries, it is possible to set forth principles in the accords that require that the less developed countries continually increase standards in designated areas. Although neither NAFTA nor CAFTA does all of this, they do work toward that end. And GATT, while less strict than either NAFTA or CAFTA, also requires that

signatories adhere to the international treaties on labor rights that they have already signed.

THE BOTTOM LINE

The bottom line on international trade pacts is this: most economists favor them for two basic reasons:

1. Economists generally favor allowing people to buy what they want from whom they want and to sell what they want to whomever they want, without restriction, as long as doing so does not harm an innocent third party.
2. More to the point of this chapter, they favor trade pacts because, if they are negotiated with care, such pacts enhance global economic well-being.

While free trade eliminates some jobs in some areas, it creates more jobs in other areas. Some countries with high poverty rates and low wages will gain jobs in areas where training and education are relatively unimportant. Other countries, including the United States, will benefit by being able to sell goods that require highly skilled workers to produce.

With regard to free trade, what economists insist is true is that with income support and retraining, the gains from trade are nearly always sufficient to offset the losses of the people made worse off by trade. What we need to understand is that if the people who gain from trade get all of the benefits and the people who get laid off are forgotten, then free trade is going to be seen and will in fact become just another way the rich get richer and the poor get poorer.

One interesting spin on those who lose their jobs is the notion of **creative destruction** introduced by Joseph Schumpeter. Schumpeter's thesis is that workers' desire for job security and their complacency when they have it is such that they do not seek out better opportunities unless they are forced to. If this logic is to be believed, then free trade does such people a favor by sending them into unemployment. Because most economists firmly believe that people do what they think is in their best interests, it may be that they know that there are better opportunities out there but are simply more comfortable where they are. This would suggest that unemployment is not really a favor. However, it is just not as bad as many fear because the massive and burgeoning service sector in the United States has absorbed many of those whose jobs were lost due to trade.

creative destruction
The notion that people need to lose their jobs involuntarily in order to seize better opportunities.

Whether or not we have NAFTA, CAFTA, GATT, or any other trade agreement, what labor unions, workers, and young people in general have to understand is that the days are over when a high school diploma ensured the holder of a job that earned middle-class wages. The trends toward more mechanized manufacture are inexorable. The jobs that are available now are in operating or designing the new machines. These jobs, moreover, require training and higher education.

In addition to the economic side, NAFTA's diplomatic benefits cannot be missed. Not since the Panama Canal treaty has Latin America been treated as well by the United States as it has as a result of negotiations with NAFTA. In the past the sovereignty of Latin American countries was threatened by the United States on more than a few occasions. Now NAFTA implicitly recognizes Mexico as a partner with both the United States and Canada in the development of the Western hemisphere.

Summary

As a result of completing this chapter you now understand that economists generally see that free trade is better than restricted trade and that trade agreements that facilitate the opening of trade are seen by most economists as a good thing. You understand why economists insist that free trade is good and why it is that agreements to maintain it are sometimes necessary. You are familiar with NAFTA, CAFTA, GATT, and the WTO as trade agreements and institutions and you know some of the thinking about whether they are working as advertised. You understand the economic and political concerns that free-trade agreements generate, and you know that the bottom line for most economists is that such agreements are good policy.

Key Terms

CAFTA, 167

creative destruction, 172

GATT, 167

NAFTA, 167

quota, 168

strategic trade policies, 168

tariff, 168

WTO, 167

Quiz Yourself

1. Trade agreements are often necessary because
   a. Free trade is in no one's best interest.
   b. Limiting trade is in no one's best interest.
   c. Limiting trade helps those doing the limiting but typically by less than it hurts those whose are limited.
   d. Limiting trade helps those doing the limiting and typically by more than it hurts those whose are limited.

2. Trade agreements are enforced
   a. Militarily by the United States.
   b. Militarily by the United Nations.
   c. By the consent of the parties to abide by the judgment of the arbitrators.
   d. Only by the willingness of the parties to respond favorably to each other.

3. Which concept from Chapter 1 can be used to explain how it is possible for it to be in the individual interest of each nation to engage in protectionist policies but for everyone to be worse off if they all engage in protectionist policies?
   a. The fallacy of composition.
   b. That correlation does not necessarily equate to causation.
   c. That all resources are scarce.
   d. That the right policy option is one chosen at the "margin."

4. Free-trade agreements
   a. Are just that, about tariff and quota-free trade.
   b. Have very little to do with the trade of goods and services and more to do with currency exchange.

  c. Are about making trade freer than it was before
     and rarely about making it completely free.
  d. Only impact the trade of goods and rarely impact
     the trade of services.

5. When one country objects to the trade restrictions of
   another, the provisions of trade treaties typically
   a. Allow it to militarily exact retribution against the
      offending party.
   b. Require that it submit its objections to an adjudi-
      cation body to determine whether the practice is
      allowed.
   c. Require that the offending country immediately
      stop the action pending a review of the case by an
      adjudication body.
   d. Provide no form of relief.

6. The World Trade Organization governs the provisions of
   a. NAFTA.
   b. GATT.
   c. CAFTA.
   d. SHAFTA.

7. From the perspective of the United States, a major
   accomplishment of the 1999 round of GATT was
   a. The complete banning of "domestic content"
      provisions in movie and television production.
   b. The creation of major restrictions on child labor.
   c. The worldwide adoption of U.S. environmental
      practices.
   d. The recognition of copyright protection for
      software, music, and movies.

8. The consensus among economists is that NAFTA's
   impact on the U.S. economy is
   a. Enormously positive.
   b. Enormously negative.
   c. Marginal in net though it has increased both
      imports and exports.
   d. Marginal in net because it has affected neither
      imports nor exports.

9. Joseph Schumpeter coined the phrase "creative
   destruction." The idea of creative destruction is that
   a. People need to be forced from their comfort zone
      in order to make crucial decisions that enhance
      their economic prospects.

  b. Unemployment affects society more negatively
     than thought because it breeds social
     discontent.
  c. Unemployment is good because it keeps prices
     down.
  d. Competition for resources is inherently
     destructive.

Think about This

Look at the ingredients list on the next nondiet soda you
buy. The second ingredient behind water, is high-fructose
corn syrup. If you do the same thing in Canada or Mexico,
the second ingredient is sugar. The reason for the difference
is that the U.S. imposes a quota on cane sugar imports (to
protect beet sugar growers in Minnesota and California). Is
this good policy?

Talk about This

Protesters insist that the economic benefits of trade
have social costs that go unrecognized. Whether or not
you agree with them, make a list of those social costs.
Open your closet and look at the labels on your clothing. Look for the labels on your consumer electronics
to see where they were made. Are you, individually,
better off with cheap clothing and electronics? In that
context do we owe something to those who bear those
social costs?

For More Insight See

"China and the WTO," *Economist,* April 3, 1999,
pp. 14–15.

Husted, Steven, and Michael Melvin, *International
Economics* (Reading, MA: Addison-Wesley, 1997), esp.
Chapter 8.

Krugman, Paul R., and Maurice Obstfeld, *International
Economics: Theory and Policy* (Reading, MA: Addison-
Wesley, 1997), esp. Chapter 11.

The Seattle Times, December 4, 1999, and the *Seattle Times*
WTO Web page, http://seattletimes.nwsource.com/wto/.

Whitelaw, Kevin, "Banana-Trade Split," *U.S. News & World
Report,* January 11, 1999, p. 49.

Chapter 16

Tobacco, Alcohol, Drugs, and Prostitution

Red-light districts are often centers of illegal activity.
Source: © L. Clarke/CORBIS

Chapter Objectives

After reading this chapter you should be able to

Understand how we can apply a supply and demand model and the concepts of consumer and producer surplus to tobacco, alcohol, drugs, and prostitution.

See that economists endorse interference in a market for reasons related to the information and costs to innocent third parties.

See how the elasticity of demand for tobacco and alcohol determines who gets hurt by taxes on these goods.

Understand the impact of drug legalization.

Chapter Outline

An Economic Model of Tobacco, Alcohol, Drugs, and Prostitution

Why Is Regulation Warranted?

Taxes on Tobacco and Alcohol

Why Are Drugs and Prostitution Illegal?

Summary

Let's face it. No mother wants her child to start smoking or drinking, use drugs, or engage in prostitution. These are not healthy activities. Nevertheless, economists are generally reticent to suggest that a good or service should be banned outright just because it is not good for you. This chapter uses the tools of supply and demand, elasticity, and consumer and producer surplus to look at these particular goods and services and the reason some are regulated, some are taxed, and still others are illegal.

Twenty-three percent of the American population smokes, and the average American consumes nearly 32 gallons of beer a year. With that much smoking and drinking going on, tobacco and alcohol are obviously important parts of the American economy. The tobacco industry employs 33,000 people a year, and it has annual sales of $86 billion. The alcohol industry employs 64,000 people, and its annual sales amount to $29 billion. Because drug use and prostitution are illegal, it is impossible to know exactly how much money is spent on those activities or how many people are employed in them. What is known is that nearly half of all adults under 35 have tried marijuana and one in seven has tried cocaine. The data on the number of prostitutes is far less precise, but anywhere from 200,000 to more than 1 million sell sexual services in a year. Every year, billions of dollars are spent on these activities.

Before looking closely at the economics of these goods and services, we will review the fundamentals of supply and demand to remind ourselves of how equilibrium within a market serves the interests of both the consumer and producer. Then we will turn to reasons why selling and using these goods are regulated, taxed, or banned and why economists might back such restrictions. Along the way, we'll focus not only on secondhand smoke, drunk driving, the spread of STDs, and increases in crime but also on the issues of age restrictions, warning labels, and prohibition. After a brief discussion of the importance of elasticity, we'll use the concept within our supply and demand model to indicate who gets hurt by the considerable taxes that are levied on both tobacco and alcohol. Finally, we'll discuss why tobacco and alcohol are legal, why certain drugs and prostitution are not, and what decriminalization of these goods and services would likely bring.

AN ECONOMIC MODEL OF TOBACCO, ALCOHOL, DRUGS, AND PROSTITUTION

We'll use the market that was presented in Chapter 2 as the basis for our analysis of tobacco, alcohol, drugs, and prostitution. As we did with the market in that chapter, we will assume that there are many buyers and sellers, that the demand curve for each is downward sloping, and that the supply curve for each is upward sloping. For the time being, we will pretend that there are no negative consequences to innocent third parties. We will also pretend that all the people who engage in these activities know exactly what they are getting themselves into. While these are fanciful assumptions, the approach gives us a

FIGURE 16.1   Market for an offending good.

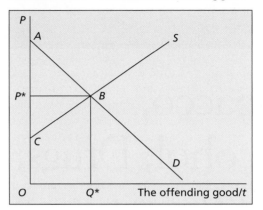

jumping-off point that we can use to look at these markets. To prove that the markets benefit both the consumers and the producers, we have to refer to the consumer and producer surplus analysis that was presented in Chapter 3.

We start with a few facts that are presented in Figure 16.1. Consumers buy Q^* goods and pay P^* for each. This means that consumers pay producers an amount of money that is simultaneously less than the value the consumers place on the good and more than it cost the producers to provide it. That is, consumers are happier with the good or service than they were with the money they gave up, and producers make a profit. The gain to the consumers is P^*AB and is called their consumer surplus. The profit to the producer is CP^*B and is called their producer surplus.

As a result of this analysis, we can state that the sale of these goods or services make drinkers, beer companies, smokers, tobacco companies, drug users, drug dealers, and prostitutes and the people who frequent them better off than they would have been without those sales. The sum of the consumer surplus and the producer surplus is CAB. If it were illegal to buy and sell these goods and services, and if everyone obeyed the law, all of the above-named parties would be worse off. Before you have a fit at this conclusion, though, remember that it was arrived at only after we made some fanciful assumptions.

WHY IS REGULATION WARRANTED?

It is now time to recognize reality and to deal with the very real problems of tobacco, alcohol, illegal drugs, and prostitution. The goods themselves are very addictive. There are harmful effects to innocent third parties from secondhand smoke, drunk driving, and the spread of sexually transmitted diseases. Their presence has caused experts in public health to persuade legislators to implement restrictions, regulations, taxes, or outright bans.

When people argue for government intervention in a market, they do so from many points of view. Economists, who tend to decry unwarranted intervention, generally categorize reasons into three broad areas. First, they deem it possible for people to suffer from a lack of knowledge or an inability to think clearly. When that is the case, it may be appropriate for the government to step in with information or with warnings of danger. It may even be appropriate for government to make decisions for people. Second, they accept that the good or service may have adverse impacts on people other than the consumer or producer. Those costs, which are ignored in a market, must be taken into account by the government. Last, and least appealing among economists, is that consumption or production of the good may be immoral. That is, even though buying or selling the good may not hurt anybody in a physical sense, its production or consumption hurts society in general.

Whaaazzup, Joe Camel, and the Information Problem

For legal goods, advertising is intended to draw people to a product, and advertisers want their ads to be memorable. When the advertising is for products like tobacco and alcohol, we sometimes bemoan the effectiveness of the ads. From the frogs, to "Whaaazzup" to "How you doin'," Anheuser-Busch's series of Budweiser ads have been very effective, memorable Super Bowl highlights for decades. Their catch phrases continue to enter the everyday language of our children. Similarly, the Joe Camel advertising campaign raised the market share of Camel cigarettes substantially during the middle- to late-1990s.[1] Since children cannot legally consume either product, it was of particular concern to people that the respective ads were able to capture the attention of young people.

For illegal goods, advertising is not an issue; the real "information" problem is the degree to which people do not adequately weigh the likelihood or impact of addiction. Government's reaction to this can be one of education, one of restriction, or one of prohibition. In the United States we use education to dissuade young people from using drugs and reinforce that with prohibition. In all but certain counties in Nevada, the government's response to prostitution is simply one of prohibition.

The addiction argument clearly applies to cocaine, ecstacy, and methamphetamine. The reasoning is that potential users may not know or fully comprehend that these drugs can be addictive and what the impact of that addiction will be on users. The argument as it applies to prostitution is somewhat different. When prostitutes get started in the sex business, they may not fully realize the consequences of their actions. Some advocacy groups that seek to maintain and strengthen the ban on prostitution, for instance, claim that prostitutes generally begin their trade as children. (Estimates place the number of U.S. prostitutes under the age of 18 at between 300,000 and 600,000.) As such, they do not know that they will likely be raped on a regular basis, nor do they know that their pimp will likely attempt to get them hooked on an illegal drug in order to control them and keep them dependent. These groups also make the point that more than 80 percent of prostitutes were the victims of incest in childhood and that the industry capitalizes on this sense of degradation.

In general, then, economists suggest that the information problem can be dealt with using education, age restrictions, or prohibition. The appropriate tool depends on the degree of the problem. For example, the government requires that packages of cigarettes and bottles of alcohol display warning labels that describe the consequences of smoking and drinking. Thus, requiring warning labels and banning tobacco or alcohol advertising on the grounds that these promotions serve only to cloud the judgment of consumers is acceptable to economists. We take the "providing knowledge" a step further when we ensure that every new generation knows the addictive nature of smoking and drinking through programs in the schools.

Of course, there are times when we simply do not trust young people to make good decisions, even when they have all the information. In these cases we either make it illegal to buy the goods or services or we require that people reach a certain age before they can buy them. Economists are not at all uncomfortable forbidding children from consuming tobacco products for two reasons. First, the vast majority of smokers began their nicotine addictions well before becoming adults. Second, there is evidence that the tobacco companies aided their becoming addicted through their marketing efforts. Because only a tiny fraction of smokers began smoking as adults, preventing children from having ready access to cigarettes is in society's interest and in the child's long-term interest.

Ultimately, the reason many economists embrace the prohibition of cocaine, ecstacy, and methamphetamine is that for these the addiction problem is often permanent.

---

[1]Tobacco advertising on billboards and in magazines ended with the 1998 Tobacco Settlement between the large tobacco companies and the states.

External Costs

Few economists object when government interferes in a market in which someone other than the consumer or producer is hurt by the consumption or production of a good. These externalities are important considerations for market regulation because the point of market efficiency is that everyone either benefits from, or is left unaffected by, a transaction. If that does not happen, then standing by and allowing the market to take care of itself is not always acceptable.

The externalities that result from the use of tobacco are the illnesses and deaths associated with secondhand smoke and the increased health care expenditures incurred by people who do not smoke but must pay increased premiums for health insurance to cover the expenses of smokers. It is not the concern of most economists that (knowledgeable) smokers hurt themselves by smoking. It is the concern of economists that those smokers tend to pass on costs to others.

The sale of drugs often affects someone other than the buyer or seller of the drug. As a result, at least some of the costs of that market are not being accounted for by the buyer or seller. If addicts are more likely to commit crime than nonaddicts, then neither the addict nor the dealer is accounting for the rising number of innocent victims when they sell their goods. Similarly, if a person gets a venereal disease from a visit to a prostitute and passes that disease on to an unsuspecting third party, then there is an external cost. Someone who is not part of the original transaction is being affected because of the transaction.

Establishing who should be counted as an innocent victim, though, is not as easy as it might sound. Children clearly are innocent victims, but are nonsmoking spouses? Some economists suggest that as part of the give and take of a marriage, smokers and their nonsmoking partners negotiate the rules for smoking in a household. If they decide it is all right for one to smoke and the other to be negatively affected, then smoking and its implications do not constitute an externality; it is simply one of the costs of the marriage. Other economists disagree. They suggest that regulations are needed to protect any people who are not consumers themselves.[2]

---

[2]This is the same argument that some economists use to suggest that government need not regulate workplace safety. Risk-takers must be compensated adequately or they would not take the risk.

Examining the Externalities

There are a few facts on crime that we ought to consider when dealing with drugs in particular. First, 28 percent of all violent crimes (44 percent for rapes) are committed while the perpetrator is on drugs. Second, 55 percent of inmates in jail, detention, or prison used drugs during the month leading up to their arrest. Last, we spend $1.9 billion on drug interdiction and $49 billion on incarceration in this country every year. More than half of those incarcerated now are there for drug-related offenses. What effect would legalization have on these statistics? We would save a lot of money—half of the incarceration costs and all of the interdiction costs. If overall use increased, as it probably would, violent crime would increase as those who were not addicts before legalization became addicts after legalization and, once addicted, became violent.

BATTLING NEGATIVE EXTERNALITIES WHILE CREATING OTHER PROBLEMS

Solving the externalities associated with a good by enforcing a prohibition strategy creates a problem. Sometimes the solution can be worse than the problem it was intended to solve. Much drug violence exists only because of laws criminalizing drug use. If cocaine, methamphetamine, and marijuana were legal and inexpensive, there would be less of a need for addicts to rob in order to get money to buy them. There would be no drive-by shootings to protect turf. There would be no need for the hundreds of thousands of prison beds devoted to drug offenders. It is for this reason that you find a significant number of economists, even very conservative economists, favoring drug legalization. They appreciate that drugs carry with them externalities but see the solution as worse than the problem.

However you decide the issue of who is an innocent victim, those who are subjected to secondhand smoke have higher rates of lung-related illness than exist in the general population. Children in the presence of smokers are much more likely to die from sudden infant death syndrome (SIDS), asthma, and other lung illnesses. Airline cabin crews, servers in restaurants, bartenders, and a variety of others who have been exposed to others' smoke also report rates of lung illness that are not only higher but beyond those that might have occurred by chance. The costs of treating these innocent victims are ignored by both smokers and tobacco companies. Economists abhor ignored costs. Whether economists support corrective actions when there are such costs depends on the degree of those costs and whether eliminating them is worth the loss of private benefits. In addition, there are more smokers on Medicaid than their proportion within the general population warrants. They, of course, produce some rather substantial costs to the program. If they were not smoking, Medicaid would cost taxpayers less. Here the innocent victim is the taxpayer.

Externalities also exist in less likely places. Since smokers typically die 5 to 10 years earlier than comparable nonsmokers, if they have group life insurance policies whose rates are the same for both smokers and nonsmokers, the expected net payout for smokers' beneficiaries is more than for nonsmokers' beneficiaries. Life insurance rates are therefore higher for nonsmokers than they should be and the rates for smokers are lower than they should be.[3]

These facts combine to suggest that when smokers buy cigarettes, the full cost of their smoking not only is not paid at the cash register but is not even fully incurred by the smoker. Most estimates of the external expenses that are paid by the general public come to around a dollar per pack of cigarettes.

This is not to say that economists hold unanimous opinions in these matters. Some suggest that there is a benefit to nonsmokers when other people smoke. These benefits come from two separate but related aspects of smoking. First, as mentioned previously, people who smoke for long periods of time die several years earlier than comparable people who never smoked. Smokers and nonsmokers pay more into Social Security and other pension plans, but nonsmokers have some of their retirement essentially subsidized by smokers, because the smokers died before they had collected the benefits to which they were entitled.

A second form of subsidy that smokers grant nonsmokers is that they not only die early, but they die more suddenly than nonsmokers. When smokers over the age of 60 become ill, their lifetime of smoking has so depressed their immune systems that they die of illnesses that nonsmokers are more likely to survive. They also succumb to those

illnesses much faster and less is spent attempting to save them. Even though the money is spent sooner, it is much less. It is grimly ironic then that by dying more quickly than nonsmokers, smokers sometimes cost the health system less than do nonsmokers. By dying early and quickly, smokers avoid expenses that nonsmokers eventually need to pay. Because more than half of Medicare expenses are incurred during the last year of elderly people's lives, hastening their deaths saves money. If this gruesome fact is taken into account, the net external costs of smoking become negligible in the eyes of some economists.

Though there is a morbid economic upside to smoking, there is no such benefit to drunk driving. There are more than 1 million arrests a year for driving under the influence of alcohol. While that number has come down substantially over the last decade, it is still more than high enough to represent a significant problem. Of the roughly 37,000 accidents that result in 42,000 traffic fatalities each year, 40 percent involve at least one person whose blood alcohol level is over the legal limit. Another 10 percent involve someone who has a legal, but still measurable, blood alcohol content. Even when someone does not die, alcohol is a contributing factor in nearly a half million automobile accidents a year.

Despite these troubling statistics, it is time to try to look at the issue from a dispassionate viewpoint. To model the problem of the externalities that are associated with people who drive under the influence of alcohol, we need to alter our supply and demand diagram to account for the extra costs for which their behavior is responsible. To understand Figure 16.2 , you need to recall that under perfect competition the supply curve is the marginal cost curve to the firms in the business. Any costs that are borne by neither the seller nor the buyer must be added

FIGURE 16.2   Modeling externalities.

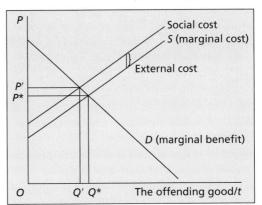

---

[3]This externality is avoided when life insurance companies differentiate their premiums for smokers and nonsmokers. The degree of the employer subsidy would have to depend on this as well.

to these costs to create the social cost of the good. On the assumption that the only people who benefit from the consumption of the good are the consumers themselves, the demand curve is the social benefit curve. So instead of coming to the market solution of a price–quantity combination $P*$-$Q*$, the socially optimal combination is P'-Q'. That is, if there is a market for a good where some of the costs spill over to others, then the market will produce too much of the good and charge too little for it.

Morality Issues

We have looked now at the first two circumstances under which economists consider it acceptable for government to intervene in the market. Besides lack of information and externalities in which innocent people may be harmed, a final reason why government might regulate a free market is that the market may be for a good or service that is considered to be immoral. For believers in certain major world religions, alcohol, tobacco, drugs, and prostitution are accorded this status. While appeals to righteousness are not particularly meaningful to economists on an academic level, they are certainly important to many other people. Many religions consider drinking a sin and a few feel the same way about smoking.

TAXES ON TOBACCO AND ALCOHOL

Modeling Taxes

To correct an externality, we can tax the offending good, we can limit its use, and we can forbid its use. Of these options, taxes are the most appealing to economists, as they allow people who are willing to pay all of the costs of their consumption to go ahead and consume. Using taxes in this way has the positive effect of discouraging those people who are not willing to pay the costs from becoming consumers of the undesirable or unhealthy good.

The taxes that the United States imposes on tobacco and alcohol are a 39-cent per pack tax on cigarettes and a 32-cent per six-pack tax on beer. The federal taxes on tobacco raise approximately $7.4 billion a year, while the taxes on alcohol raise $6.7 billion. States also tax these goods, finding them to be a significant source of revenue, as they are for the federal government.

Figure 16.3 shows that the effect of the federal taxation on cigarettes and alcohol is to raise the price from $P*$ to P' and to lower consumption from $Q*$ to Q'. An important thing to notice about this effect is that smok-

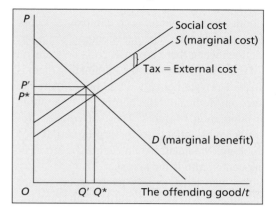

FIGURE 16.3   Modeling taxes.

ing and drinking do not stop. This means that the deleterious effects of secondhand smoke and drunk driving do not stop either. They are simply reduced. If the tax is set equal to the dollar value of such externalities, then in theory the tax revenue raised is sufficient to cover the costs of the externalities. One problem, though, is that the tax hits the considerate and rude alike. Smokers who light up alone do not cause secondhand smoke, whereas smokers who blow it in your face do. A per-pack tax hits both equally.

In any event, a policy short of prohibition implies that there is an economically acceptable number of expected drunk driving deaths and of childhood secondhand-smoke-induced illnesses. The idea is that as long as we have an adequate sum of money available to compensate the people who are affected, it is acceptable for smokers to smoke, for drinkers to drink, and for people to be influenced in negative ways by their behavior.

People who are not economists have a very difficult time with the "acceptability" of deaths and illnesses. The basic idea is that people drink and smoke because they enjoy doing so. If we take taxing and regulating too far, the reduction in enjoyment by users would outweigh the effect of the reduction on innocent victims.

The notion of acceptable deaths is a difficult one for many to accept. Consider this though: The Brain Injury Association reports that approximately 15 children die each year on playgrounds as a result of falls and other injuries. We continue to send our children out on recess because we weigh what is to be gained with what is to be lost and judge the risk of injury or even death to be tolerable. We drive to work because we see that what is gained—income—is greater than what is lost—a small risk of injury or death.

The Tobacco Settlement and Why Elasticity Matters

For quite some time legislators have given particular consideration to raising the taxes on tobacco. The settlement between several states and the big tobacco companies that was reached in 1998 requires that the companies pay the states more than $250 billion over 20 years to compensate them for Medicaid expenses the states paid that were created by smoking. The companies will then pass on those taxes to the smokers who buy their products. To see how a sequence like this works, we need to look at the supply and demand curve for tobacco.

First, it should be remembered that when someone is addicted to a product, as smokers are to cigarettes, the demand curve for the good is highly inelastic. If you look at Figure 16.4, you see that a tax will again raise the price from $P*$ to P'. If you compare the size of the tax (P'' to P') to the amount of the price increase, you see that smokers will be paying for most of this tax increase and that tobacco companies will pay comparatively less ($P*$ to P' versus $P*$ to P''). Since smokers are far poorer than the average of the general population, this tax is as regressive as any tax we can imagine. Since consumption falls only from $Q*$ to Q', it is also disturbing that the tax will not have a significant influence on how much people smoke either.

When you look at teen smoking, the picture is not quite so bleak. Because the habit of smoking takes up a much larger portion of teenagers' than adults' incomes, the elasticity of demand for cigarettes by young people is much greater. That is, demand is more elastic and the demand curve is flatter. If you were to draw such a demand curve, you would see that the burden of the tax would still fall mainly on consumers. You would also see that tobacco companies would be paying a greater proportion of

the amount of compensation. Further smoking, at least teen smoking, would be reduced by more. Still, economists' best estimates are that elasticities for cigarettes are as low as .2 for adults and as high as .5 for children. This means that an increase of a dollar in cigarette prices would diminish adult smoking by 10 percent, but it would diminish smoking by children by 25 percent. A study of the elasticity of demand for beer put it at 2.53, which suggests a tax that adds 10 percent to the price of a six-pack would reduce consumption by 5.3 percent.

WHY ARE DRUGS AND PROSTITUTION ILLEGAL?

The debate over whether drugs and prostitution should be legal usually comes down to a comparison of the negative consequences of what is currently legal, tobacco and alcohol, with what is currently illegal. Clearly a case can be made that the aggregate impact of tobacco and alcohol is much greater than the aggregate impact of illegal drugs and prostitution. As you can tell by now, economists are less interested in "aggregate" impacts than "marginal" ones. Here, the case can be made that the negative externalities associated with one person purchasing one more unit of the illegal goods is greater than the negative externalities associated with one person purchasing one unit of a legal good. The other argument that could be made to justify the current state of the law is that the unknown or underestimated consequences to the consumer of using drugs or engaging in prostitution are substantially greater than those with regard to alcohol. Of course, the opposite case could be made as well.

The Impact of Decriminalization on the Market for the Goods

Given the previous discussion, suppose a good or service is currently illegal. What would result from making it legal? The first thing that would likely happen as a result of making a good legal is that the concerns of both consumers and producers about getting caught would evaporate. Because getting caught would not be a problem any longer, any shift to the left of supply that resulted from clandestine operation would cease to exist. Similarly, any shift to the left in the demand curve by those who might have wanted to partake of the illicit good but did not because it was illegal would cease to exist. The net result of legalizing a previously illegal activity would be a movement in the demand curve to the right and a movement in the supply curve to the right.

FIGURE 16.4   Tax on tobacco with inelastic demand.

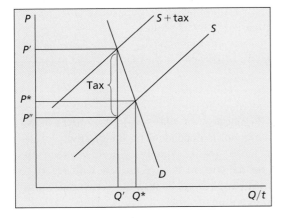

FIGURE 16.5   Making an illegal good legal or vice versa.

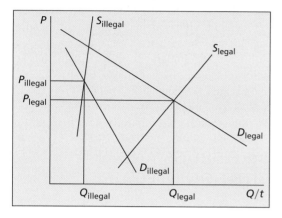

Another impact of decriminalization would occur on the elasticity of demand and, to a lesser degree, supply. When a good is illegal, it is often the case that the consumers of the good are addicted to it in some sense. The demand curve for a good for which a consumer is addicted is likely to be very inelastic. Similarly, once people have made the decision to become a seller of an illicit good, the price they sell it for is not usually a stimulus to sell it in great quantities. This is because the risks of getting caught may prevent sellers from expanding their operation quickly as prices rise. Therefore, from either side, the supply and demand curves are less elastic when the good or service is illegal than when it is legal. The net result here is that both curves flatten out when the good is made legal. Figure 16.5 depicts the effect of legalizing a previously illegal good. The demand curve flattens and moves right, and the supply curve flattens and moves right. If the supply curve movement is more than the demand curve movement, as it is in Figure 16.5, the net result is a lowering of price. Not shown, but equally plausible, is the case where the demand curve

movement is greater than the supply curve movement and the price rises.

Thus, the direction of a price change as a result of decriminalization depends on whether the reduction in risk to dealers or prostitutes is greater than the increase in interest by consumers. Because the conventional wisdom is that legalization would lower the price, conventional wisdom is just that: The supply curve shift will be greater than the demand curve shift.

The External Costs of Decriminalization

Ultimately, whether legalization makes sense to you depends on whether you believe the external costs of these activities are significant enough to pay the significant costs of punishing users and dealers. One potential solution that many pro-legalizers suggest is that we tax and regulate drug sales and prostitution in order to take into account and pay for the externalities.

Looking back to Figure 16.3, you see that we simply added a tax equal to the external cost that was examined in Figure 16.2 to get the P', Q' result. That is, a proper taxation scheme can make up for the problems of an externality. There is money to educate against the use of the illicit good or to compensate victims of users of the questionable good.

The problem is that if the external costs are very great, the tax will have to be very high. If the tax is very high, there will be a motivation to have a black market in untaxed goods. As evidence of this, consider that in Canada a prohibitively high tax created a black market for cigarettes. In this case people drove to the United States, bought cigarettes, took them back to Canada, and sold them. In another similar case, while prostitution is legal in Nevada, it is highly regulated. That regulation leads to prostitutes' avoiding regulation by working on their own outside the regulated brothels. Whenever a tax is too high or regulation too severe, a black market will exist beside a legal market.

Summary

You now understand how we can apply a supply and demand model and the concepts of consumer and producer surplus to tobacco, alcohol, drugs, and prostitution. You understand that there are reasons that economists endorse interference in a market, reasons that have to do with information and costs to innocent third parties. You have seen how the question of who gets hurt by taxes on tobacco and alcohol is dependent on the elasticity of demand for these goods. Finally, you have seen the argument for the current state of the law with regard to the treatment of these goods and the economic consequences of decriminalization.

Quiz Yourself

1. When examining the question of tobacco taxes, economists focus almost entirely on
   a. The cost to cigarette companies of production.
   b. The cost to cigarette smokers for the cigarettes themselves.
   c. The cost to cigarette smokers for their extra health care expenses.
   d. The costs to nonsmokers (like secondhand smoke).

2. When discussing an addictive drug, an economist is likely to focus on
   a. Both the external costs and the "information problem" associated with addiction.
   b. The moral costs totally.
   c. The cost of the drug to the user.
   d. The costs of production.

3. If you became convinced that marijuana was neither addictive nor contributed to externalities, then banning it creates
   a. A social benefit without social cost.
   b. What economists call deadweight loss.
   c. What economists call a vacuum.
   d. A social benefit with an exact countering social cost.

4. Decriminalizing a drug is likely to lead to a price decrease if
   a. The anticipated supply effect is greater than the anticipated demand effect.
   b. The anticipated demand effect is greater than the anticipated supply effect.
   c. The anticipated demand effect is exactly equal to the anticipated supply effect.
   d. Both demand and supply decrease.

5. Compared to a recreational user of a drug, an addicted user's elasticity of demand is
   a. Much more elastic.
   b. Much less elastic.
   c. Much less.
   d. Flatter.

6. If policy makers were to attempt to set a tax equal to the external costs of alcohol, one would have to evaluate
   a. The cost of production.
   b. The price paid by consumers.
   c. The value of innocent lives lost to drunk driving.
   d. The value of the shortened lives of alcoholics.

7. When examining the "right tax" on a good that produces an externality, the tax should be such that
   a. It is greater than the externality.
   b. It is less than the externality.
   c. It is exactly equal to the externality.
   d. It makes consumption prohibitively expensive for anyone.

8. One unsettling consequence of setting a tax on tobacco sufficiently high to reduce consumption would be
   a. It would likely reduce Medicare costs.
   b. It would likely increase tobacco revenues to farmers.
   c. It would likely increase tobacco company profits.
   d. It would make Social Security's financial outlook worse.

Think about This

There are considerate smokers and inconsiderate smokers. Secondhand smoke is not an issue when smokers are considerate (in that they smoke where no one is around to breathe it). Should these smokers be taxed when they are producing no harm to society?

Talk about This

As unsavory as it sounds, there are travel agents who book "sex tours" in parts of Asia. Travelers visit prostitutes in various locations. While some of the brothel operators mandate "safe" practices, others allow the patrons to pay extra if they wish to participate in "unsafe" practices. Should you be able to pay someone to risk their lives in this manner?

For More Insight See

Grossman, Michael, Jody Sindelar, John Mullahy, and Richard Anderson, "Alcohol and Cigarette Taxes." *Journal of Economic Perspectives* 7, no. 4 (1993), pp. 211–222.

Thorton, Mark, *The Economics of Prohibition* (Salt Lake City: University of Utah Press, 1991).

Behind the Numbers

Drugs and crime.
   Violent crimes and drug use.
      U.S. Dept. of Justice; Criminal Victimization in the U.S., 2003; statistical tables—http://www.ojp.usdoj.gov/bjs/ cvict.htm.

Federal Spending on Crime Control.
> Federal drug control spending, 2002.
> Federal Drug Control Budget, 2004.
>> Office of National Drug Control Policy; drug control funding tables—http://www.whitehousedrugpolicy.gov/publications/policy/06budget/.

Traffic Fatality and Blood Alcohol Statistics, 2003—http://www-nrd.nhtsa.dot.gov/pdf/nrd-30/ NCSA/ TSF2003/809767.pdf.

Taxes on Beer and Cigarettes, 2004—http://www.atf.treas.gov/alcohol/stats/historical.htm.
> Statistical Abstract of the United States; federal receipts—http://www.ttb.gov/statistics.htm.

Chapter 17

The Environment

These giant redwoods in northern California might be in jeopardy if they weren't federally protected.
Source: © Royalty-Free/CORBIS

Chapter Objectives

After reading this chapter you should be able to

Understand how to use marginal analysis to answer the question of how clean is clean enough.

Use the concept of externalities to explain why pollution warrants government intervention in the market.

See why pollution is much more likely to occur on publicly owned property than on private property.

Understand the variety of environmental problems that exist in the world as well as the economic solutions that exist to address these problems.

Chapter Outline

How Clean Is Clean Enough?

The Externalities Approach

The Property Rights Approach

Environmental Problems and Their Economic Solutions

Summary

Few political issues are as popular with people as cleaning up the environment. On the surface the solution to the problem is rather simple: stop polluting. For an economist, though, not only is the problem more complicated, but so also is its solution. The environmental problems of modern society are substantial and varied: pollution of the water and air, the potential extinction of 1,100 species of plants and animals, acid rain that puts forests and fish in jeopardy, and greenhouse effects that are probably responsible for rapidly rising global temperatures.

To most environmentalists solving these problems involves strict questions of right and wrong. Economists, on the other hand, want to look also at costs and benefits. Economics may be central to solving environmental problems because in dealing with the environment we will need to reallocate our resources in directions that generally move from consuming and growing in positive economic ways to preserving and living with economic slowdowns. Where economics can be particularly helpful is in the area of efficiency. Coming up with a plan that reduces pollution is not difficult, but it is hard to come up with a plan that reduces pollution in a way that will min-imize the economic costs. That is what economists are good at.

HOW CLEAN IS CLEAN ENOUGH?

When you were 10 your bedroom was a wreck. I know this because I was 10 and I have two teenage children. When asked whether a room is clean, a 10-year-old will respond with a reply that is pure economics: "clean enough." With that reply, 10-year-olds are say-ing that to them, further cleaning is simply not worth the effort. In the language of economics, children are saying that the marginal benefit of cleaning more (the value they place on additional cleanliness) is less than the marginal cost of cleaning more (the value they place on IM time).

Economists apply the same standard to environmental issues—merely on a larger scale than a child's bedroom. The opportunity cost of a cleaner environment is lost eco-nomic satisfaction. We can use marginal cost–marginal benefit analysis to look at this problem, but only if we make some simplifying assumptions.

Let's assume for the moment that we have a gener-ally accepted measure of environmental quality. Let's further assume that the really dirty stuff is relatively easy to clean up but that achieving higher levels of cleanliness is harder and harder. Using the dirty room analogy, you know that the quickest way to make your room look cleaner is to pick up the dirty clothes, which can be done in seconds. Once you get down to straight-ening and dusting the knick-knack shelves, the benefits

are slight and the time required is great. What this implies is that the marginal cost of achieving greater cleanliness is increasing while at the same time its mar-ginal benefit is decreasing. As shown in Figure 17.1, this means that the maximum net benefit of environ-mental cleanup is *EQ**, where the marginal benefit equals the marginal cost.

THE EXTERNALITIES APPROACH

We created many environmental problems in the first place when we produced and consumed goods and were concerned only with the costs and benefits that directly affected us. As we saw in Chapters 2 and 3, doing this is usually fine, but problems often arise when the actions we take impose costs on or present benefits to others. Economists call costs or benefits that are incurred by someone other than the pro-ducer or consumer **externali-ties.** We begin this chapter by reviewing why a market without externalities serves everyone. We then explore why there is a problem with markets when externalities are present. After that, we examine the specific environmental prob-lems discussed above. We conclude with a look at what economics can offer in the way of solutions.

externalities
Effects of a transaction which hurt or help people who are not a part of that transaction.

When the Market Works for Everyone

As we learned in Chapter 3, a market works very well in a world where all the costs and benefits of production are confined to producers and consumers. Figure 17.2 depicts in graphical form that the market price–quantity combina-tion, *P*–Q**, provides benefits to consumers, *OABQ**, at a cost to them of *OP*BQ**. The difference, *P*AB*, is called *consumer surplus;* that is, what consumers get in net ben-efits. Similarly, for the producer, the variable costs of pro-duction, *OCBQ**, are lower than revenue generated from sales, *OP*BQ**. The difference, *CP*B*, is called the *pro-ducer surplus*. Thus when the market does not generate costs or benefits to anyone other than consumers and pro-ducers, both benefit and no one loses.

When the Market Does Not Work for Everyone

The main problem with the model just described is that it does not take into account that there are nearly al-ways indirect costs to others in either the production or

FIGURE 17.1 Clean enough.

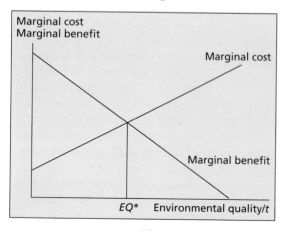

FIGURE 17.2 When the market works.

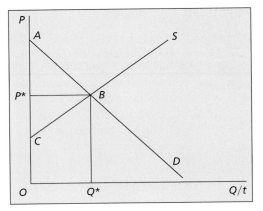

FIGURE 17.3 When a market does not work.

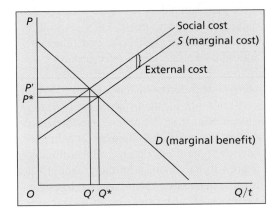

consumption of a good. There are, for example, very few goods that do not require some form of energy for their production. Whether that energy is generated from the direct combustion of a steel mill's smelting facility or electricity generated from burning coal, some fossil fuel is used in nearly all production. Even when the power is hydroelectric, nuclear, wind, or solar, there are environmental and possibly aesthetic costs that are not always considered.

Using fossil fuels like oil or coal creates a number of environmental problems from beginning to end. In each of the stages of getting energy to the user, people or animals are affected. In extraction, land is either temporarily or permanently altered. Transporting oil, natural gas, and coal consumes energy. Transporting the first two carries with it the potential for an environmental catastrophe like the rupturing of the *Exxon Valdez* disaster and the resulting massive oil spill in Alaska's Prince William Sound. By far the greatest problem, though, is created when fossil fuels are burned. Particulate matter creates breathing problems that are unpleasant for some and life-threatening for others. Burning coal releases sulfur into the air and it produces acid rain. If current scientific predictions of the United Nations Intergovernmental Panel on Climate Change are found to be true, greenhouse gases will cause significant changes in the world's climate.

You may believe that alternatives like nuclear, hydroelectric, wind, or solar power offer externality-free energy, but, like fossil fuels, each has its own problems. Nuclear power, though potentially clean, is also potentially damaging, and there are impassioned debates going on about how to store nuclear waste. Hydroelectric power requires the

destruction of river valleys, eliminating habitat as rivers flood the area behind the dams. While wind and solar power are clean in that they do not pollute the air or water, the sheer number of collectors needed to produce an amount of electricity that is equal to the amount produced by coal at the present time is vast. Therefore, this option has the potential of destroying thousands upon thousands of acres of land that we now consider to have great scenic beauty.

Figure 17.3 depicts the problem as an economist would see it. Whereas firms pay attention to the costs of production of their goods, unless forced to, they tend to ignore the environmental costs of their production. Similarly, consumers pay attention to how much a good costs them, but it often serves their purposes to ignore the costs to those around them. Costs to people other than the producers and consumers are considered to be unaccounted for costs in the market. The existence of such costs is unacceptable to an economist. The fundamental flaw with the market is that unless all costs are accounted for, it will produce too much and charge too little. To find the true cost of production and consumption of a good that in-

social cost
The true cost of production and consumption of a good that includes the effects on innocent bystanders.

cludes the effects on innocent bystanders, called the **social cost,** you need to add the external cost to the private costs (measured on the supply curve). When these costs are accounted for, the price is to be *P′* rather than *P**, and the amount produced is *Q′* rather than *Q**.

Unless you believe that a pristine environment is a matter of right and wrong, allowing no compromises to your position, you will have to accept the existence of some environmental problems even when you account for all the costs. For example, Figure 17.2 does not display a thoroughly clean environment, but it does show how the costs of pollution are weighed against the benefits of consumption. We may decide, for instance, that even though some pesticides threaten certain species, they so enhance food production that using them is worth the cost. The species are still threatened, but at least the cost is recognized. Similarly, we may decide that reformulating gasoline to reduce emissions by 80 percent is worth 20 cents per gallon but that reducing it another 10 percent is not worth the dollar a gallon it would take to accomplish that level of reduction. Here the costs of pollution are weighed, but so are the benefits of consumption. There are substances for which the optimal level is zero. This occurs when the marginal benefit of the production or use of even one drop of the good is less than its social cost.

THE PROPERTY RIGHTS APPROACH

A Nobel Prize–winning economist by the name of Ronald Coase came up with a completely different method of dealing with pollution. His widely cited theorem states that markets with externalities can be made to be efficient. This can be done by simply assigning rights to the polluted property, but it requires that bargaining costs be reduced to zero. To see why this is so we need to first look at why ownership matters.

Why You Do Not Mess Up Your Own Property

Consider a relatively simple problem. Why is it that you are much more willing to litter in a park than you are to litter in your own residence hall, apartment, or house? The reason is that you have property rights in the place you live and you make your own place less valuable when you litter in it. You do not own the park. Though your littering diminishes the value of the park, it does not diminish your own wealth.

This explains why people treat many forms of common property worse than they treat their own. If you have ever lived on a cul-de-sac you will have noted that the circle of grass in the center of the turn-around was in demonstrably worse shape (or at least less well landscaped) than the surrounding lawns. People tend to treat their own property better than they do public property.

Why You Do Mess Up Common Property

common property
Property that is not owned by any individual but is owned by government or has some other collective ownership.

Common property is property that is without a discernible individual owner. This property is usually owned by the government, a neighborhood association, or some other collective group. The problem with common property is that even though it may be worth a great deal to the group, the benefits of treating the property well are not worth the costs to any one individual. Economists refer to this as the "tragedy of the commons."

Consider again the problem of a neighborhood park. Suppose that a city agrees to pay the up-front costs of a park for a neighborhood of 100 homes. It buys the playground equipment, plants trees and grass, but then turns the park over to the neighborhood. What happens when the grass needs to be cut, a tree falls and needs to be taken out, or the surface under the playground equipment needs to be rejuvenated? While each neighbor may consider the individual benefit to be worth one one-hundredth of the cost of this regular maintenance, often no one will view maintenance for the entire neighborhood as worth the time or money. The ultimate problem is that no one owns the property. As a result, while the social benefit of the maintenance is greater than its cost, the benefit to an individual is much lower than its cost to that individual.

Natural Resources and the Importance of Property Rights

Economists use many of the same tools to explore the use of natural resources as we use when dealing with pollution. Whether the resource in question is mineral, timber, energy, or the oceans' bounty, economists note that the extraction, cutting, removal, or harvesting imposes costs on someone other than the producer or consumer. It doesn't matter whether this results from the fact that the land is owned by the government or not owned by anyone at all, or because the process of garnering the resource is itself polluting. What matters is that all of the costs must be acknowledged.

Economists also bring another element to the table: the notion of present value. The value of an untapped resource to its owner is the present value of the profit associated with exploiting it over a period of time. In this way there is an optimal rate of exploitation, which is the rate that maximizes the present value. Suppose you owned a resource such as a forest of timber. You could clear-cut it and sell all of it at once. Then you would have to plant new trees, wait for the trees to grow tall enough to harvest, and repeat the cycle. On the other hand, you could cut only those trees that had achieved an optimal height and leave the rest for another year. In this way you would have a few trees to cut every year. An economist would look at this and say that whichever rate of exploitation maximizes the present value of the profit emanating from that timber would be the optimal exploitation rate. Assuming that no timber company can influence prices, then there is no value to waiting to harvest trees unless some are relatively immature. The motivation to wait comes from the fact that trees grow and, thereby grow more valuable. If the interest rate is high (and exceeds the rate of tree growth), then that favors the cut-it-now rate, while if the interest rate is low, that favors the let-them-grow rate.

The problem comes when no one owns the resources that are being harvested. For instance, the oceans are notoriously overfished because there is no value to leaving the fish to grow bigger. Similarly, when logging companies buy the right to harvest trees on federal land, those contracts need to be well specified and well enforced or the company will have no motivation to leave the smaller trees for a later date, especially if the contract expires before the trees grow to maturity. This is much less of a problem on private property because the owner must weigh the present value of the profit from taking an immature tree against the present value of the profit from taking it a few years later. It is often the case that the logging company that owns the property it is working on will leave the smaller trees because it is in its interest to do so.

ENVIRONMENTAL PROBLEMS AND THEIR ECONOMIC SOLUTIONS

Environmental Problems

We face many environmental problems, some obvious and others not so obvious. Specific problems include water and air pollution, plant and animal species that face extinction, the effects of acid rain, landfills that are overflowing, limited natural resources that are being used up, and global warming. In this section we look briefly at each.

When humans are affected by the economic activity of other humans, the problem is relatively easy to solve. People complain when they are being hurt. When producers pollute the air or water, there are concerned people who have to breathe the affected air or want to drink or swim in the affected water. They will lobby their representatives for pollution regulations. In fact, the Environmental Protection Agency was created in 1969 in response to pleas that environmental regulations be enforced. The Clean Air Act of 1970 and the Clean Water Act of 1972 were additional responses to people's perceptions that problems existed and desire to have them addressed.

By most measures, these laws have been effective. The nation's air and water are much cleaner than they were 30 years ago. Air pollution has been addressed with regulations that range from requirements that smoke stack emissions be "scrubbed" before being released to requirements that cars have catalytic converters and burn unleaded gasoline. Since the Clean Air Act's inception the amount of sulfur dioxide in the air has been reduced by 40 percent, carbon monoxide by 25 percent, particulate matter by 25 percent, and lead by 97 percent.

In the area of water pollution, municipal wastewater facilities now have to return untreated water to rivers and streams in nearly drinkable form. Companies can no longer discharge waste materials into rivers or lakes, either. Though some of the damage to these bodies of water is permanent, most are improving. Classic examples of this include the Cuyahoga River near Cleveland, Ohio, which was so polluted that it once actually caught fire. Now it is clean enough so that people can eat its fish. Other areas, though, have not yet fared as well. On the bottom of Onondaga Lake in Syracuse, New York, for example, there remains several feet of toxic sludge, and, on the official map of the city, there is a piece of shoreline labeled the "Allied Waste Beds," where Allied Chemical simply dumped its toxic waste.

When air and water are unacceptably dirty the problem is fairly obvious. However, it is more difficult to see damage to wildlife and it is harder to address the problem. Plants and animals do not object as they become extinct. Fortunately for them there are scientists who monitor their health. To illustrate the difficulty of convincing people of problems with wildlife, though, it took the threatening of our national symbol, the bald eagle, to bring about legislative action. The Endangered Species Act of 1973 has resulted in lists of plants and animals that are either threatened or, more serious, endangered. Currently there are in the United States alone 129 threatened and 388 endangered animal species, as well as 147 threatened and 599 endangered plant species. Since the inception of the act 11 species have been removed from the lists and a number, including the bald eagle, downlisted from endangered status to threatened status.

Although 34 North American species of birds and mammals have become extinct since the 1500s, none that has been listed since 1973 has succumbed. Some species would have become extinct without the help of humans, but the rate of extinction is estimated to have increased at least tenfold since the time of the first known human. It is discouraging, moreover, that for the listed species whose habitat is government land, there are 1.5 on the decline for every 1 on the rebound. On private land, where regulation is less stringent, the figure is 9 to 1.

The key to keeping plant and animal life from extinction is to prevent the loss of habitat. This is why the Endangered Species Act is a problem for economic growth. The lost logging associated with preserving a single mating pair of spotted owls in the American Northwest amounts to $650 million. While strict environmentalists push for the preservation of species, regardless of the economic costs of doing so, the costs are foremost in the minds of the people whose livelihoods are threatened by this law's requirements.

A piece of environmental legislation that combines protections for both wildlife and habitat is the Clean Air Act of 1990. In this legislation, the targeted problem is acid rain. Acid rain is created when power plants burn highsulfur coal and the sulfur dioxide (SO_2) emissions from that burning combine in the atmosphere with various nitrogen oxides (NO_2, NO_3, etc.) to create a dilute form of sulfuric acid. In particular, the coal that is burned in the Midwest creates an acid that travels to the northeastern states in clouds, and the rain that subsequently forms has caused trees to die and lakes to become deadly for fish.

The legislation limits the quantity of sulfur that industry can put into the air. To comply with the law's provisions, firms can buy more expensive low-sulfur coal, they can buy equipment to clean up the emissions, or they can buy another firm's pollution permits. Offering options like the trading of pollution permits is considered to be very innovative. It allows companies to clean up the environment in the cheapest way possible, and, as we will discuss later, this innovative way of dealing with pollution has earned economists a place at the table in discussing environmental problems.

An additional environmental problem is that landfill space is being used up faster than new space is created. The problem here is less an environmental problem than a location problem. Modern landfills are required to prove that no contamination leaks into groundwater. No homeowners want garbage in their neighborhoods, and Congress has steadfastly refused to allow states to keep others from exporting their garbage. A consequence of this stance is that more New York City garbage is put in out-of-state landfills than in those in New York. Because the interstate commerce clause of the U.S. Constitution prevents states from refusing to let out-of-state garbage in, and because of the way the U.S. population is distributed, the burden of siting new landfills has shifted from the East to the Midwest.

The economic implications of changes in Earth's climate are what we will discuss last in this chapter. It is fairly well settled scientific fact that the globe is warming. The warmest years on record are concentrated in the 1980s and 1990s. The problem is that unless they were told by a scientist that this is bad, most people would neither have noticed nor objected to the change in temperature. Though summers have been somewhat warmer, winters—especially at night—have been still warmer. Who is likely to object if winter weather is milder than usual?

Meteorologists tell us that the Earth's temperature has risen about 1.5° Fahrenheit in the entire 20th century. The average, though, is 2.5° higher in 1999 than it was in 1970. It is a change, however, that is simply too small for the typical person to detect. Over time, however, the problems with global warming will become more obvious. With temperatures that are anywhere from 5 to 10° higher by the end of the 21st century, several things may happen. The bad things include a thawing of the polar ice caps, which scientists say will be accompanied by a flooding of coastal cities and islands. Soils may become dry, making it more difficult to grow grains. People will use more refrigerants for air conditioning. Warm-weather diseases like malaria and yellow fever may proliferate, and certain areas of the world will become deserts, in a process labeled with the frightening word "desertification." Going further, the particularly active hurricane seasons of 2004 and 2005 were blamed by some meteorologists on uncharacteristically warm water in the Atlantic and Caribbean. If these scientists are correct, and these were at least partially related to global warming, then our global consumption of energy and its effect on the environment has a tremendous dollar-denominated cost. Taken together 2004's hurricanes Ivan, Charlie, Frances, and 2005's Katrina and Wilma represent five of the top six costliest storms ever.

On the other hand, some good things will happen if global temperatures rise. Growing seasons will lengthen in northern climates, less energy will be needed to heat homes and businesses in those areas, and the impact of cold-weather diseases like colds and the flu will diminish. A good way of imagining the positive impact is to realize that though there will be places where the climate will get "too hot," some places that were once "too cold" will now be "just right."

This is not to suggest that there will necessarily be an even-up trade by any means. While temperature zones will change relatively quickly, forests can move only extremely slowly. Thus some forests whose trees require a specific temperature band to be healthy will die out long before new ones appear. There is also new research suggesting that only about half of the increased carbon dioxide, which may be good for some species of plant life, can be absorbed.

Economic Solutions: Using Taxes to Solve Environmental Problems

To solve the environmental problems that we face we have to encourage or require clean behaviors, or we must discourage unclean behaviors or render them illegal. To varying degrees all these methods work. America's history of environmental regulations clearly indicates that we have been moving successfully from forms of regulation that concentrate on punishing people to forms where we provide incentives that make clean behavior profitable.

Most environmental regulation still prohibits certain actions that damage the air, water, or wildlife. For instance, the Clean Water Act prohibits dumping of untreated industrial waste into a river. Mandating that the environment be protected, however, is not necessarily the best way to deal with all environmental issues. For instance, it is hypothetically possible that production of a cure to a terrible disease may turn out to be very dirty. In such a case it might be in society's best interest to sacrifice the environment. Instead of an outright ban, a polluting activity could be heavily taxed. Activities that were sufficiently profitable to cover whatever tax was levied could continue.

A tax could conceivably be used to discourage any polluting activity, including the creation of garbage or the use of fossil fuels. As Figure 17.4 indicates, a tax would be set that was equal to the external cost, that is, the dollar-denominated value of the pollution. Production of the good would fall to Q', its socially optimal level, and the price would increase to P'. There would be enough tax revenue to compensate those affected by the pollution resulting from a garbage dump or, perhaps, to fund research on

FIGURE 17.4   Solving the problem with a pollution tax.

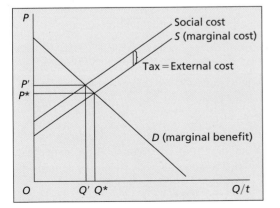

nonpolluting technologies. Assuming a connection between energy use and global warming and between global warming and hurricane flooding, such a fund might also be used to deal with flood-relief from hurricanes.

Economic Solutions: Using Property Rights to Solve Environmental Problems

Coase's theorem holds that it does not matter if you grant the property right to the polluter or the victim of the pollution. If you say that people have a right to clean air, then Coase suggests that the polluter would buy the right to pollute from the people; if you say that polluters have the right to do what they want, then Coase suggests that the people will pay polluters to be cleaner. Either way, the right amount of production and pollution will result.

An interesting adaptation of Coase's ideas was the Clean Air Act of 1990 and its use of effluent[1] permits. The law provides that each emitter of certain restricted pollutants can be granted a fixed number of permits ceding the right to pollute a specific amount. In 1990 the quota of polluted emissions was slightly less than the historical levels of pollution. Any firm that polluted less than that amount could sell its remaining rights to pollute to those that polluted more than their permits allowed. In 2000, in the second phase of the Clean Air Act of 1990, emission rights were reduced further, and when the act is reauthorized, it is likely that further reductions will be required. In this way pollution is reduced over time, while polluters have options that allow them flexibility in meeting the reductions.

The allocation of the pollution rights ensures that we get the most economically efficient pollution reduction. Specifically, we get the most output (usually electrical power) subject to our societal goal of pollution reductions. This happens because power companies have different opportunity costs associated with reducing pollution. Those that have a high opportunity cost will buy permits from those that have a low opportunity cost. Consider the following uncomplicated example. Suppose there are only two electrical companies and both have older, coal-powered generators that generate a great deal of pollution. Each one will have to reduce pollution slightly unless it wishes to buy permits from the other. Suppose one is close to a natural gas pipeline, but the costs of switching to cleaner-burning natural gas have been heretofore just beyond what would have made economic sense for the firm. Suppose the options to the other are much more prohibitive. Suppose, finally, that electrical power demand is increasing so each will be expected

---

[1]Effluent is the general term for the stuff that comes out of a smoke stack.

to produce more electricity and will therefore generate more pollution in the future. Because they cannot both increase pollution, the firm that has the lower cost option of reducing pollution will do so and be compensated for doing so by selling its permits to the firm with the higher cost option. In this way, society's goal of both meeting the increase in electrical demand and reducing pollution is furthered.

Under the Clean Air Act each permit grants its holder approximately a ton of sulfur dioxide (SO_2) emissions. Total emissions of SO_2 over the life of this provision of the 1990 act have been cut nearly in half, to 5.3 million tons per year. Surprising as it may seem, the price of those emission permits has fallen from more than $200 each to around $100 each. This is because power companies have found it a profitable sideline to find ways to reduce pollution. And though the reduction in the number of available permits and the increase in electrical power demand put pressure on the permit prices to rise, electric utilities are using new, cleaner technologies to either reduce the number of permits they have to buy or to make money selling their rights. Thus the pressure on the price of these permits to decrease that has resulted from this innovation has greatly outweighed the pressure to rise.

Another area where economists use the property right idea to help with air pollution is with the automobile. Cars pollute, and old cars pollute much worse than newer ones. California faces the problem of meeting certain air quality standards or mandating that gas stations in parts of the state provide a cleaner form of gasoline, which is more expensive to produce. One way that California has addressed the problem has been to require that all cars meet a minimum air quality standard. The problem with this solution is that older cars are typically owned by people who cannot afford the repairs necessary to meet the standard. This is the case even though the law allowed for the repair to be deferred for a year if it cost more than $500. To meet the air quality standard and to ease the burden on the poor of California, the state has from time to time made a blanket offer to buy all cars made prior to a particular year for more

than they are worth. In the summer of 2000 it was paying $1,000 per car. This innovative solution has the effect of reducing pollution in a very effective way. By saying that drivers have a right to pollute for a year but then turning around and offering them a reward for not polluting, the state of California is using Coase's idea effectively.

Economists influence environmental regulations and legislation precisely because we offer suggestions like the concept of issuing emission permits and the buying up of clunkers, thus aligning self-interest with environmentalism.

No Solution: When There Is No Government to Tax or Regulate

Let's assume that the problems of global warming exceed the benefits. What can be done? When an environmental problem is confined to one jurisdiction, the government, whether it be local, state, or national, can enact legislation to tackle the problem. When the problem is international, such as with global warming, there is no government to impose a regulatory or tax-based solution.

The Kyoto Protocol is a treaty to which the United States is a signatory. Such treaties require U.S. Senate approval, so President Clinton's signature was pointless from the start because there were not 20 votes for ratification and he knew that when he signed it. Shortly after his election, President Bush formally pulled the United States out of the agreement noting the significant economic impact compliance would have. He also noted that the agreement did not limit China or India, two rapidly growing energy consumers, in any meaningful way. Regardless of whether Clinton or Bush was right, the issue illustrates the intractability of international environmental problems. There is no motivation for a single country to impose high economic costs on itself, and there is no world government to impose those high costs on everyone. As a result, if those warning of the consequences of global warming are correct, this could be one of the more calamitous examples of the Chapter 3 notion of market failure.

Summary

You now understand how to use the concept of externalities to explain why pollution warrants government intervention in the market. You understand why pollution is much more likely to occur on publicly owned property than on private property and you have a cursory understanding of the variety of environmental problems that exist in the world. You now also have an understanding of some economic solutions to these problems.

Key Terms

common property, 188   externalities, 186   social cost, 187

Quiz Yourself

1. The notion of "clean enough" is
   a. Appealing to an economist thinking about average benefit and average cost.
   b. Appealing to an economist thinking about marginal benefit and marginal cost.
   c. Appealing to an economist thinking about total benefit and total cost.
   d. Completely rejected as a concept by an economist.

2. If a chemical does environmental damage but is used in the production of a good that provides satisfaction to the consumer and profit to the producer an economist
   a. Will insist that the market be left alone.
   b. Will insist that the chemical be completely banned.
   c. Will seek to impose a tax on the good so that the net benefit to society (including the environmental damage) is maximized.
   d. Will suggest that consumers voluntarily cut back their consumption.

3. An example of an externality that we see every day is
   a. People paying high prices for gasoline.
   b. People enjoying their ability to drive to work.
   c. Oil companies making record profits.
   d. The emissions from a car's tailpipe.

4. When tackling local environmental problems, taxes and regulations can be useful. The reason that global problems (like global warming) are more difficult to control is
   a. It is in every countries' aggregate interest to ignore the problem.
   b. It is in no country's interest to address the problem.
   c. There is no ability to enforce those taxes or regulations.
   d. The "marginal" country is unknown.

5. Overfishing certain parts of the ocean and certain species of fish has been a problem for centuries with countries actually going to war over fishing disputes. Ronald Coase would suggest that there would be no the problem if
   a. Someone owned (and could control) the ocean.
   b. People stopped eating fish.

   c. People reacted according to the golden rule.
   d. Countries agree to voluntary restrictions on fishing.

6. The evidence on most environmental pollutants (lead in the air and water, sulfur in the air, etc.) is that
   a. They are not nearly as harmful as once thought.
   b. They are increasing at an alarming rate.
   c. They have decreased substantially in the last 20 years.
   d. They have stabilized in the air at their all-time high.

7. If made "King of the World" an environmental economist would
   a. Eliminate fossil fuel consumption.
   b. Impose per gallon a tax on gasoline equal to the environmental damage caused by a gallon of gasoline.
   c. Impose per gallon a tax on gasoline greater than environmental damage caused by a gallon of gasoline.
   d. Suggest voluntary limits on driving.

Think about This

Fossil fuels were the "clean" alternative to wood burning and only overcame wood as a source of fuel when it became cheaper to use than wood. If left unchecked, this will happen to fossil fuels as well because this limited resource will eventually become more scarce than its alternative (solar-, wind-, hydroelectric-, or biomass-generated power). Should we just wait it out?

Talk about This

Every power source entails some environmental consequence. Nuclear power leaves behind waste that is dangerous for thousands of years. Hydroelectric power destroys the habitat of valley-dwelling animals. Wind and solar power require vast spaces for collection devices. Combustible fuels typically leave a heat-trapping gas. Currently, the U.S. dominant fuel sources are fossil-based (coal, oil, natural gas). While other countries have turned toward nuclear power, we have not. Given that our power needs are continuously growing, what are your solutions?

For More Insight See

Joskow, Paul L., A. Denny Ellerman, Richard Schmalensee, Juan Pablo Montero, and Elizabeth M. Bailey, *Markets for Clean Air: The U.S. Acid Rain Program* (Cambridge, MA: Cambridge University Press, 2000).

Journal of Economic Perspectives 12, no. 3 (Summer 1998). See articles by Gardner M. Brown, Jr., and Jason F. Shogren; Andrew Metrick and Martin Weitzman; Robert Innes, Stephen Polasky, and John Tschirhart; and Richard Schmalensee, pp. 1–88.

Journal of Economic Perspectives 9, no. 4 (Fall 1995). See articles by Michael E. Porter and Claas van der Linde; Karen Palmer, Wallace E. Oates, and Paul R. Portney, pp. 97–132.

Journal of Economic Perspectives 7, no. 4 (Fall 1993). See articles by Richard Schmalensee; William D. Nordhaus; John P. Weyant; James M. Poteba and Gacielka Chichilinsky; and Geoffrey Heal, pp. 3–86.

Behind the Numbers

Air quality and emissions data.
  Outdoor air pollution
    Environmental Protection Agency; environmental indicators—http://www.epa.gov/Envindicators/roe/pdf/tdAir.pdf.
  Emissions prices and trading.
    Environmental Protection Agency; clean air markets—http://www.epa.gov/airmarkets/.

Global temperatures.
  History and projections.
    Environmental Protection Agency; global warming—http://yosemite.epa.gov/oar/globalwarming.nsf/content/.
  Average surface temperature.
    World Meteorological Association—http://www.wmo.ch/web/Press/Press670.html.

Threatened, endangered, and delisted species.
    U.S. Fish and Wildlife Service; publications—http://endangered.fws.gov/.

Hurricane Costs
    http://wwwnhc.noaa.gov/gifs/table3a.gif.

Chapter **18**

Health Care

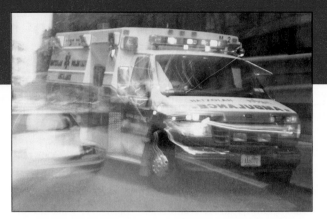

An ambulance rushes to an accident scene. *Source: © Photolink.Getty Images.*

Chapter Objectives

After reading this chapter you should be able to

Understand how the system of health care finance seriously alters the market for health care services.

See why in the United States 46 percent of the health care tab is picked up by the taxpayer with the remainder being paid either directly by patients or by their insurance companies.

Look at health care using the supply and demand tools discussed earlier even though it is not like most other goods that economists study.

Understand that taxpayer-financed health care as well as private insurance plans increase the overall price of health care.

State some advantages and disadvantages of a single-payer, taxpayer-financed health care system.

Chapter Outline

Where the Money Goes and Where It Comes From

Insurance in the United States

Economic Models of Health Care

Comparing the United States with the Rest of the World

Summary

Health care in the United States has two characteristics that seem to be fundamentally inconsistent. No other country on earth can match the United States in terms of the quality of care that is available, but no developed country has our infant mortality rate. Additionally, in no other country are doctors as skilled, and in no other country are doctors as highly paid. In no other country is the quality of care as high, but in no other developed country is care denied so often because patients are unable to pay for it. At its root, the problem of having high-quality care that is not available to everyone who needs it is attributed only to the way we finance health care.

In this chapter we explain health care in the United States by first detailing the money spent and by whom it is spent. We discuss how private and public insurance work in the United States and discuss the problems associated with each. We then turn to why the economics of health care differs so much from the economics of any other good. Last, we compare our health care financing system with the model used in most other developed countries.

WHERE THE MONEY GOES AND WHERE IT COMES FROM

In defeating the health care plan that the Clinton administration attempted to implement, Republicans claimed that Democrats were trying to take over one-seventh of the economy. Indeed, while in 2003 one-seventh of the gross domestic product ($1.7 trillion of $11.2 trillion) was spent on health-related goods and services, the government's portion was already almost half (46 percent, or $766 billion) of health care expenditures. President Clinton and his Democratic supporters were merely attempting to federalize the private portion of health care expenditure.

Of the $766 billion that government spent on health care in the United States in 2003, some $278 billion was

Medicare

Public health insurance in the United States which covers those over age 65.

Medicaid

Public health insurance in the United States which covers the poor.

spent on **Medicare** (the government health insurance program for the elderly) and $278 billion was spent on **Medicaid** (the government health insurance program for the poor). The remainder was spent by all levels of government on local, state, and veteran's hospitals and in support of medical research.

Of the $913 billion that was spent on health care in the private sector in 2003, some $582 billion came from premiums paid to insurance companies and by the money that insurance companies realized from their investments. People paid an additional $231 billion in out-of-pocket expenditures, and the remainder was spent by private medical research companies.

In general, of the $1.7 trillion spent on health care in the United States in 2003, $515 billion went to hospitals and $370 billion went to doctors. Drugs accounted for $179 billion and medical research spending accounted for $40 billion.

INSURANCE IN THE UNITED STATES

Most people in the United States are covered by some form of health insurance for at least part of the year. In 2004, for example, 82 percent of the 292 million people in the United States had coverage all year, another 8 percent had coverage for part of the year, and 10 percent had no coverage at all. The coverage during that year came from a variety of sources. The largest group, 175 million people, was covered by group insurance policies, 24 million had individual policies, 41 million were on Medicare, 40 million were on Medicaid, and 6 million were on both.

How Insurance Works

Whether we are discussing health insurance, life insurance, or auto insurance, private insurance of any kind works like this. There is a small chance that something bad will happen to you and there is a large chance that nothing bad will happen to you. You spend a little money on insurance that will cushion the effects of the bad prospect, should it occur. In other words, you pay a premium so that if the bad thing happens, the insurance provider (whether it be the government or an insurance company) will pay to make things better. In the case of health insurance, people pay premiums so that when they get sick their provider pays most of the expense of dealing with their illnesses.

It is perfectly rational to buy insurance even when the average expense you would face is less than the cost of

risk averse

A characteristic of a person who would pay extra to guarantee the expected outcome.

the insurance. The reason is that most people are **risk averse:** they prefer to be guaranteed a particular outcome, even when the odds are that for the average person, over an average lifetime, insurance is more expensive than the problem they are insuring themselves against. As an example, suppose there is a 1 percent chance that you will have a major health-related expense of $100,000 and a 99 percent chance that

risk neutral

A characteristic of a person who would not pay extra to guarantee the expected outcome.

you will have only $1,000 of typical health expenses. A **risk-neutral** person would look at the expected expense, $1,990,[1] and not be willing to pay any more than that for full insurance coverage. People who are risk averse, on the other hand, would be willing to pay more than that to guarantee themselves that they would not have to pay any more.

Nearly all private health insurance plans have a number of characteristics in common. You owe a premium that, for most Americans, is paid partly by you and partly by your employer.[2] Insurance companies use premiums for three things: (1) to pay doctor and hospital bills of

---

[1]$.99 \times 1,000 + .01 \times 100,000 = 1,990$.

[2]This aspect is actually an artifact of World War II. Because of inflation fears during that time, it was against the law to raise wages to attract workers. Instead, companies increased benefits in the form of group insurance subsidies, and the practice survived the war.

their patients, (2) to cover administrative expenses, and (3) to provide profit for the owners (usually shareholders) of the insurance company.

If you get sick and have a health expense, it is usually the case that both you and your insurance company will pay part of the bill. There are four key pieces of vocabulary that determine who pays how much. The **deductible** is the amount of health spending a year that you have to pay before the insurance company pays anything. This very much depends on the type of plan you have but can be as low as nothing and as high as several thousand dollars. Typically, the deductible for a plan is between $200 and $300 per person and between $600 and $1,000 per family per year. For instance, if you have an insurance plan with a $200 deductible and you have a covered medical expense that totals $500, you will have to pay $200 before your insurance company pays anything.

deductible
The amount of health spending a year that you have to pay before the insurance company pays anything.

The **copayment** is either a set amount or the percentage of the bill after the deductible has been taken out that you have to pay. This also has a wide range. Some plans have no copayment, others as much as 30 percent. The **maximum out of pocket** is the most that a person or family will have to pay over a year for all covered health expenses. This means that a $500,000 health expense will not bankrupt the typical person because the maximum out of pocket is usually between $2,000 and $6,000 a year.

copayment
Either a set amount or the percentage of the bill after the deductible has been taken out that you have to pay.

maximum out of pocket
The most that a person or family will have to pay over a year for all covered health expenses.

Last, the **lifetime maximum** is the most that an insurance company will pay on your health expenses over your lifetime. This protects the insurance company against any one person's health expenses getting so great that it jeopardizes the plan for everyone else in it. The amount of an insurance policy's lifetime maximum is usually a million dollars or more.

lifetime maximum
The most that an insurance company will pay on your health expenses over your lifetime.

Varieties of Private Insurance

There are several types of private insurance plans out there, but they boil down to three large groups: (1) fee for service, (2) health maintenance, and (3) preferred provider. A fee-for-service provider allows sick people to go to any doctor they want, wherever they want, for whatever ails them. The doctor then bills the insurance company, the insurance company pays its share, and the doctor bills the patient for the remainder. Because there are few controls on spending in a system like this, it is very costly. Patients and doctors, however, have few complaints.

A health maintenance organization (HMO) requires that people see specific doctors at the beginning of any problem. These doctors are referred to as **primary care physicians (PCP)** or, familiarly, as *gatekeepers*. Patients can see specialists only after their primary care physician makes a referral, and the PCP, or gatekeeper, has the job of making sure that his or her patients get the appropriate care as inexpensively as possible. Usually HMO PCPs receive a fixed fee for every patient assigned and specialists are either salaried or also have fixed fees for every referral. Patients and doctors complain about the controls on spending in HMOs, but these serve to keep costs down.

primary care physician (PCP)
Physician in managed care operations charged with making the initial diagnosis and making referrals. Also called a *gatekeeper*.

A preferred provider organization (PPO) is somewhat of a hybrid. People can choose the doctor they want from a list of doctors. The doctors agree to charge a specific amount per procedure or disease, and they take a lower fee than usual in order to be guaranteed a large number of potential patients.

Table 18.1 outlines the advantages and disadvantages of each of these private insurance options from the patient's standpoint.

Public Insurance

Public insurance, provided by the government, is divided into three main programs, Medicare, Medicaid, and the Children's Health Insurance Program. Medicare is available to eligible citizens who are 65 years old and older. It works very much like a generous fee-for-service health insurance plan, except that the burden for high premiums is placed on the taxpayer rather than the patient or the patient's employer. The tax that funds Medicare appears on your paycheck in the same place your Social Security tax does; they are both under FICA (Federal Insurance Contributions Act). The portion that is used for Medicare is 1.45 percent of your salary, wages, and tips; you and your employer each pay that rate. For part of Medicare, money is also taken from the general tax revenues of the government.

TABLE 18.1   Advantages and disadvantages to patients of different forms of private insurance.

Insurance Type	Advantages	Disadvantages
Fee for service	Maximum physician choice Little insurance company meddling in doctors' decisions	Highest premiums, deductibles, and copayment rates because of little control over expensive and unnecessary procedures
HMO	Maximum control over expensive and unnecessary procedures so premiums, deductibles, and copayment rates are low	Minimal physician choice Significant meddling in physician decisions, especially when differing procedures have significant cost differences
PPO	Some physician choice Moderate premiums, deductibles, and copayment rates Some control over expensive procedures Minor meddling in physician decisions	

Source: www.medicare.gov

Medicare is generous in the following sense: By private health care standards its premiums are very low, and the copayments and the deductibles are also low. In truth Medicare is really two programs, a compulsory program that covers hospital-related expenses and a voluntary program that covers doctors' charges. In 2005 those who were eligible for the compulsory version, Medicare Part A, and worked fewer than 40 quarters paid a $175 monthly premium. To those who worked more than 40 quarters it was free. The voluntary version, Medicare Part B, cost beneficiaries $78.20 a month and covered doctor-related expenses. Elderly people who are eligible for the primary welfare program for the old and poor, Supplemental Security Income, have Medicaid pick up the Part A premium and often the Part B premium as well.

In contrast with Medicare, Medicaid is a no-premium, no-deductible, very low or no copayment health plan for the poor.[3] Under Medicaid, doctors are reimbursed at rates that are low relative to what Medicare pays and extremely low relative to what private insurance pays. Hospitals and doctors can and do refuse to treat Medicaid patients when they judge the reimbursement rates to be too low.

In 2004 there were 43 million Americans who survived, at least part of the year, without any health insurance at all. Many of these are people who move from one job to another and whose insurance runs out while they are unemployed.[4] On the other hand, a 1994 study by Katherine Swartz indicated that 21 million Americans were without

any health insurance for more than a year. Of the uninsured, 18 million are between the ages of 18 and 34. Their lack of insurance may be voluntary in the sense that they may be able to afford insurance but are healthy and therefore choose not to purchase it. A recently emerging group of people without health insurance is those who retire early and are waiting for Medicare to kick in when they turn 65. Most disturbing among the uninsured are the nearly 9.5 million who are under 18.

It was in reaction to this phenomenon of children living without health insurance that the Children's Health Insurance Program was created in the 1990s. Its function is like that of Medicaid, but it is focused, as the names suggests, on children who live in families where the breadwinners do not have insurance through their employer and do not make enough to purchase it themselves.

ECONOMIC MODELS OF HEALTH CARE

We can use our supply and demand model to look at what happens when the good in question is not something tangible, like an apple, but intangible, like health care. Additionally, in the context of this model, we can explore how the health care finance system alters people's behavior.

Why Health Care Is Not Just Another Good

Health care is not like any other good. You can look at an apple grown in 1998 and say that it is comparable to an apple grown in 1995 or 1885. An apple is pretty much the same through time. On the other hand, health care tends

---

[3]States may impose small copayments to discourage abusive overuse.
[4]Workers have the right to continue their employer-sponsored health insurance even after they quit or are fired. The problem is that most employers do not continue subsidizing the premiums, which means people are not likely to be able to afford to exercise this right.

to be changeable. The medical CPI has risen at or above the overall rate of inflation for several years. However, we cannot be sure how much of this increase is an increase in prices, how much is an increase in quality, and how much is the availability of new procedures or treatments.

To illustrate, let's discuss the treatment of acquired immunodeficiency syndrome (AIDS). In 1985 there was no standard treatment for AIDS. Morphine was sometimes given to ease pain—a terribly ineffective but "cheap" treatment compared to today. In 2001 the treatment became a "drug cocktail" of zidovudine (AZT) and a group of protease inhibitors. Together these drugs cost more than $12,000 a year, but they can sustain a good quality life for several years. Which "treatment" costs more? You do not have to answer the question because you know that you are not pricing the same thing. The quality of the treatment has improved so greatly that to say that the price of the treatment has increased is simply wrong. The quality of the treatment has improved, and because there was no effective treatment to compare the current one to, the "price" has fallen from infinity.

Many of the complaints about the increase in the cost of health care over the past few years are misdirected. The cost of things that do not change in quality (syringes, bandages, etc.) have surely gone up. But, just as surely, we cannot measure the price of things whose quality is constantly changing. A night in a hospital, for instance, is not the same in 2005 as it was in 1985. Though some definitions are the same (semiprivate has meant and still means two beds in a room, for example), other aspects of the night's stay are different. Today television sets and other creature comforts and sophisticated medical equipment, including beds that monitor vital signs, are standard. Not long ago these were either optional or simply unavailable.

Another key problem with using a supply and demand model for health care services is that one of the assumptions that we made for such a model to work was perfect knowledge. One of the reasons we go to the doctor in the first place is that we do not know what is wrong with us. We go not only to stop the pain but also to find out why the pain exists. This is distinctly different from buying an apple. We know what an apple is, we know why we want it, and we know what it costs to get one. In health care we have to trust the seller (the doctor) to tell us what we need and how much it will cost.

Implications of Public Insurance

Though considerations such as these are important, we can still examine the effect of our financing system on the supply and demand model for health care services. As

FIGURE 18.1   Health care: who gets it without subsidies.

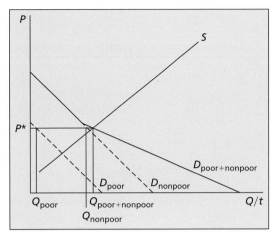

you can see in Figure 18.1, if there were no program to provide health care services to the poor, the nonpoor would get many services and the poor few. If D_{poor} is the demand for health care by the poor and $D_{nonpoor}$ is the demand for health care by the nonpoor, then $D_{poor + nonpoor}$ is the market demand for health care services. This is arrived at by adding the two demand curves together horizontally. Specifically, at each price, the quantity demanded of the poor is added to the quantity demanded of the nonpoor. If the supply curve is as shown, then the price is P^* and the poor consume Q_{poor}, much less than the nonpoor $Q_{nonpoor}$.

On the other hand, if the poor were to get the services at no cost, then the situation might be quite different. Figure 18.2 shows that in this case, the market demand is the amount that the poor would consume if it were free to them, Q_{poor}, plus the demand by the nonpoor. As you can see, the poor would consume much more, Q_{poor}, while the nonpoor would consume less. Prices would also be higher.

Efficiency Problems with Private Insurance

What private insurance does to the market for health care is as disruptive as public insurance. Recall the idea of copayments: after the deductible is met, for every dollar of covered medical expense, a low percentage (usually 20 percent) is paid by the patient and the remainder is paid by the insurance company. How does that affect the demand for health care? For simplicity's sake, assume the deductible has either been met or is zero.

FIGURE 18.2   Health care: who gets it with subsidies.

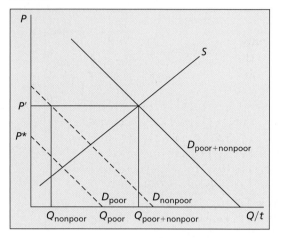

FIGURE 18.3   The effect of co-payments on the market for health care.

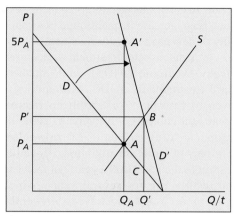

Figure 18.3 shows that the demand curve will rotate out to the right and that this will cause a greater consumption of health care services and higher prices. Let's look at why the curve rotates out to the right. Take the equilibrium point prior to any insurance; call that point A. A person is willing to pay P_A and consumes Q_A medical services prior to insurance. Suppose that person now has insurance with a 20 percent copayment rate. If that is the case, that person would be willing to consume Q_A medical services even if the price were five times that of P_A. This is because the effective price to the insured person is 20 percent of $5P_A$, or just P_A. The reason it rotates out of the horizontal intercept of the demand curve is that if health care services were free, the effect of co-payments would not matter. Twenty percent of nothing would be nothing and five times of nothing would still be nothing.

Whenever there is a situation where someone other than the consumer is paying the bill, economists call this other

third-party payer
An entity other than the consumer who pays part of the costs.

entity a **third-party payer.** When this happens, the usual role of keeping costs down is taken out of the hands of the consumer.

Since our demand curve rotates out, we buy more health care services and pay more for them. The good news here is that this effect is lessened if the underlying demand curve D is itself inelastic. It can certainly be argued that the demand for health care services is relatively inelastic, and the evidence from an extensive study started in the late 1970s and published in 1987 suggests just that. This is because we would not have an unnecessary operation even if it got less expensive, and most people will have a necessary operation

even if the price is high. This study suggests that patient sensitivity to price is greater for visits to doctors than for hospitalizations. Overall health elasticity estimates from this study indicate that a 10 percent increase in the out-of-pocket expenses of the patient is associated with a 1 percent to 3 percent reduction in health care utilization.

The increase in health care utilization also has an efficiency implication. Recall from the Chapter 3 discussion of consumer and producer surplus that the deadweight loss is the yardstick by which economists measure inefficiency. Here the triangle ABC is the amount of the inefficiency.

Another area of inefficiency with health care insurance in particular comes in the

moral hazard
Having insurance increases the demand for the insured good.

form of **moral hazard.** People who have insurance consume more health care. This is a problem with all forms of insurance, and the clearest example is in automobile insurance. If you drive more recklessly when you have insurance than when you do not, having insurance makes you more likely to need insurance. In the field of health care, if having insurance makes you more likely to get tested for certain diseases, or even worse, fail to exercise or eat right, then moral hazard is a problem.

The HMO Debate

Though we described HMOs previously, the current debate over this element of private insurance warrants further discussion. The HMO was created to combat the escalating costs of health care by dealing specifically with efficiency problems. To control the impulse to overconsume health care, some new form of insurance was needed to encourage cost-consciousness on the part of consumers, physicians, or insurance companies.

Take the example of an uncomplicated birth. Most women are physically capable of leaving the hospital within 24 hours of such a birth. Though they are eager to get home, many women want an extra day in the hospital to recover in an environment free of other obligations. On the medical side, many complications for the mother and child are discovered in the first 48 hours. If a new mother had to pay all of the costs of her delivery and stay in a hospital, she would weigh the costs to her against the benefits to herself and her baby. If she has a fee-for-service insurance plan that covers 80 percent of the costs of that extra day, she is much more likely to take the extra day. Having a third-party payer can significantly increase the amount of health care consumed.

Many of the original HMOs were collectively owned by the participating physicians. Here the cost-conscious party would be doctors, because it would be in their personal financial interest to recommend earlier discharges. The problem with this was that it was only indirectly in their financial interest. Though profits of the HMO would rise with an earlier discharge, if there were many physicians in the HMO, the profit to the doctor doing the early discharge would only be a few dollars. Many physicians were not willing to appear uncaring or penurious for only a few dollars. Physician-owned HMOs thus tended to become unprofitable.

Subsequently, many HMOs have been taken over by insurance companies. They have started controlling costs by enforcing cost-saving rules, such as paying for only the first 24 hours after a birth. In cases like this, the HMO is effectively making the decision, rather than the patient or the doctor. If, in doing so, the HMO rulemakers enforce rules that are in line with what their clients would do if they had to pay all of the costs of their own health care, then the HMO is enhancing the efficiency of the health care system. If the HMO rulemakers enforce rules that reduce health care consumption from what it would have been if patients paid the whole bill, then we are exchanging one form of inefficiency with another.

As a result, HMOs have not solved the insurance problem with health care to everyone's satisfaction. Fee-for-service plans are flawed because of overconsumption and HMOs are flawed because of restrictions that can be excessive. Which one is better? The jury is still out.

The Blood and Organ Problem

One problem associated with our current system is the scarcity of blood and organs. To an economist, the shortage of blood and organs is directly and unambiguously determined by the fact that it is illegal for people to sell these items for medical use. The ban on the sale of blood and organs for medical use is almost entirely justified on moral grounds. For instance, it is not illegal to sell your blood for use in cosmetics.

If a price can be forced to be zero, the quantity supplied will be reduced and the quantity demanded enhanced. This offers another moral dilemma. If a market were allowed, there would be people who would not be able to pay the price for a needed organ, and, as a result, they would die while someone else who could afford that organ would live. On the other side of that moral debate, though, is the fact that if there were a legal market, more organs would become available and more people would live.

Note that although both the supply and demand for organs is inelastic, neither is perfectly inelastic.[5] There are people who would choose not to pay an exorbitant price to live and there are people who would be more likely to sign their donor cards if there were a high reward that they could bestow on their heirs by doing so.

The downside of such a market is similar to the downside of the market for tobacco. Poor information can cause people to make life-altering mistakes. For instance, you can live on one kidney, and therefore you could sell the other if the price were right. However, you might underestimate the likelihood that you will ultimately need that other kidney. The sale of organs may be a poor idea, but selling blood may not. There is little economic reason to ban the sale of blood for medical purposes because, unlike organs, blood is self-replenishing.

COMPARING THE UNITED STATES WITH THE REST OF THE WORLD

Every industrialized nation on earth has a distinct health care system. The one thing that is common throughout the rest of the developed world, though, is that government is the health care provider, insurer, or insurer of

single-payer system
The government collects (usually very high) taxes to pay for everyone's health care.

last resort. There are distinct advantages to the way the rest of the world does this, but there are disadvantages as well. Having a **single-payer system,** where

---

[5]If both were perfectly inelastic at different quantities, there would be no market-clearing price.

TABLE 18.2   International health care finance schemes.

Country	Public Expenditures as a Percent of Total, 2003	Hospitals	Physicians	Function of Prviate Insurance
Australia	67.5	Mostly public	A	a
Canada	69.9	Mostly private	A, B	a
France	76.3	Mostly public	A	b
Germany	78.2	Mix of public and private	A	a
Japan	81.5	Mostly private	A, B	None
United Kingdom	83.4	Mostly public trusts	C	a
United States	44.4	Mostly private	A	c

A—mostly private fee for service.

B—government-imposed fee schedule.

C—public employees.

a—option to purchase private insurance for all expenses.

b—option to purchase private insurance for noncovered expenses.

c—all non-Medicare, non-Medicaid.

TABLE 18.3   International comparisons of health expenditures, infant mortality, and life expectancy.

Country	Health Expenditures/ GDP, 2001	Infant Mortality Rate per 1,000 Births, 2003	Life Expectancy, 2003	Five-year Survival Rates, %	
				Prostate Cancer	Breast Cancer
United States	13.9	6.8	77.1	81.1	82.8
United Kingdom	7.6	5.3	78.2	44.3	66.7
France	9.5	4.4	79.3	61.7	80.3
Germany	10.7	4.2	78.4	67.6	71.7
Japan*	7.6	3.3	80.9		

*Japan's health expenditure data is from the year 2000.

Source: http://www.census.gov/prod/2004pubs/04statab/intlstat.pdf.

the government collects significantly high taxes to pay for everyone's health care, benefits those who could not afford health care any other way. It creates serious shortages as well.

In Canada, England, and much of Europe, being a citizen of the country grants you unlimited rights to necessary health care that is either free or close to it. While the financial arrangements (shown in Table 18.2) in these countries differ, the citizenry need not worry about access to basic health care regardless of their ability to pay. This helps explain the very low occurrences of infant mortality and relatively long life spans in these countries, as seen in Table 18.3. The unemployed and

the employed, the working and the retired, the young and the old, the rich and the poor, are treated with a degree of equality that cannot be claimed in the United States. In addition, because the doctors are paid salaries by the government instead of fees for seeing patients, they do not have an incentive to order expensive tests and perform costly surgeries. Further, as government employees, they are usually protected from lawsuits. Thus universal access is accomplished at lower overall costs than in the United States.

This, however, comes at a cost. These countries have severe doctor shortages because, in an effort to keep costs down, physicians are paid much less than they are paid in the United States. One principal reason why you see many foreign-born physicians in the United States is that they can make a great deal more money here than in their own countries. Additionally, there is no monetary incentive to become a doctor when you cannot get rich by being one. The effect of having doctors on salary also is seen when these doctors are reluctant to put in long hours. Physicians are among the hardest-working people in the United States. You can also see the effect of this public health provision in the five-year survival rates of breast and prostate cancers. The United States enjoys the highest survival rates among these countries. Another factor weighing in favor of the U.S. system is immediate access to procedures that require long waiting periods elsewhere.

In the United States a 50-year-old man with blocked arteries is hospitalized and operated on within hours of being admitted, whereas the waiting period for bypass surgery in Canada has been as high as six months. Though some waiting periods have shortened, this is in part due to the recognition by physicians that expensive procedures must be rationed. In the United States the elderly with kidney disease will be given dialysis as long as they are physically able to stand it (lengthening life by a year or more). A similar English patient cannot schedule routine dialysis treatments under the British, government-run system.

Another important area that would be lost if the United States were to go to a single-payer system would be in the area of innovation. Prescription drug, medical device, and medical procedure innovation has been highly concentrated in the United States, largely because the innovator makes money that cannot be made in the single-payer countries. Furthermore, the innovation that takes place abroad is likely motivated by profits that can be made in the United States. As a result, very few health care economists believe that turning the United States into a single-payer environment would be good for health care innovation.

Last, because doctors are typically immune from lawsuits in countries with single-payer systems, accountability for mistakes is left to professional standards boards. While these mechanisms can work, very often they end up being a system for physicians to protect their own.

Summary

You should now understand how the system of health care finance seriously alters the market for health care services. You also understand that in the United States 43 percent of the health care tab is picked up by the taxpayer, with the remainder being picked up either by patients directly or through their insurance companies. You understand why health care is not like most other goods that economists study but that we can look at it using the same supply and demand tools discussed earlier. You understand that both taxpayer-financed health care and private insurance–financed health care increase the overall price of health care. Last, you understand why a single-payer, taxpayer-financed health care system would have both advantages and disadvantages.

Key Terms

copayment, 197
deductible, 197
lifetime maximum, 197
maximum out of pocket, 197

Medicaid, 196
Medicare, 196
moral hazard, 200
primary care physician (PCP), 197

risk averse, 196
risk neutral, 196
single-payer system, 201
third-party payer, 200

Quiz Yourself

1. The primary motivation for the purchase of any insurance lies in the fact that most people are
   a. Risk lovers.
   b. Risk averse.
   c. Risk neutral.
   d. Risk tolerant.

2. The risk-averse person will buy health insurance
   a. Only if the expected health costs equal the insurance premium.
   b. Only if the expected health costs are greater than the insurance premium.
   c. Even if the expected health costs are less than the insurance premium.
   d. Under no circumstances.

3. The government, in the form of Medicare, Medicaid, and the Children's Health Insurance Program pays for _____ of health care costs.
   a. Less than 10 percent.
   b. Slightly less than half.
   c. About 75 percent.
   d. All.

4. If you have a $2,000 covered health expense, have a deductible of $500, and a 20 percent co-pay then you pay _____ and the insurance company pays _____.
   a. $1,500, $500.
   b. $1,000, $1,000.
   c. $800, $1200.
   d. $700, $800.

5. Which of the following forms of private insurance is likely to have the lowest premiums and least doctor choice flexibility?
   a. Medicare.
   b. An HMO.
   c. A PPO.
   d. A fee-for-service plan.

6. Medical care inflation is likely to be easily overstated (if you look simply at the increase in the cost of a hospital stay) because that calculation ignores
   a. The original costs.
   b. The new costs.
   c. Quality increases.
   d. Quality decreases.

7. The problem of the "third-party payer" arises in health care in the form of
   a. Doctors having to pay part of the own expenses.

   b. Government and/or private insurance paying a significant part of the costs.
   c. Patients having to pay a significant part of the costs.
   d. Hospitals not being able to collect from many patients.

8. One significant feature of a "single-payer" system lacking in the U.S. system is
   a. Government involvement in health care.
   b. Coverage for the elderly.
   c. Coverage for the poor.
   d. Universal coverage.

Think about This

List the pro's and con's associated with the U.S. system of financing health care relative to the U.K. system. Do the same relative to the Canadian system. Use your understanding of opportunity cost to think about why we can't have "the best of both worlds."

Talk about This

In the United States a terminally ill patient can decide to decline extraordinary medical treatment but in all cases the patient, or the spouse, is the one who makes that decision (either with prior instructions or by making his or her wishes known to the health care provider). In the United Kingdom, the government can, and does, limit the availability of extraordinary medical treatment. Thus, though care is free (or nearly free) to the patient, it can be limited against their will. The U.K. government's contention is that health care resources are scarce and they would be wasted extending the life of a terminally ill patient by a few days. Which is worse, the aspect of the U.S. system where people are denied care when they are unable to pay, or the U.K. system where they are denied care because their treatment would not lead to a significant increase in the quality of life?

For More Insight See

Health Care Finance Association statistical tables— http://www.hcfa.gov/stats/.

Phelps, Charles E., *Health Economics* (Reading, MA: Addison-Wesley, 1997).

http://www.census.gov/prod/2004pubs/04statab/health. pdf. International Comparisons of Types of Health Care Finance Systems—http://www.nao.org.uk/publications/ Int_Health_Comp.pdf

Behind the Numbers

International Comparisons of Vital Statistics and Health Care Expenditures, 2002.

Statistical Abstract of the United States; comparative international statistics—http://www.census.gov/prod/2004pubs/04statab/intlstat.pdf.

Health care expenditures; Centers for Medicare and Medicaid Services; historical tables—http://cms.hhs.gov/statistics/nhe/historical/

Health Insurance Coverage, 2003.

U.S. Census Bureau; health insurance coverage— http://www.census.gov/prod/2004pubs/04statab/health.pdf; http://www.cdc.gov/nchs/nhis.htm.

Medicare premiums, 2005; Centers for Medicare and Medicaid Services—http://www.cms.hhs.gov/publications/trusteesreport/tr2005.pdf.

Number of Americans with and without health insurance, 2004—http://www.cdc.gov/nchs/data/nhis/earlyrelease/insur200506.pdf.

Chapter **19**

Government-Provided Health Insurance: Medicaid, Medicare, and the Child Health Insurance Program

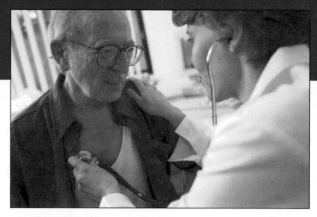

Medicare helps pay health care expenses for the elderly.
Source: © Royalty-Free/CORBIS

Chapter Objectives

After reading this chapter you should be able to

Understand that Medicaid is a program that covers medical expenses for many of this nation's poor.

Understand that Medicare is a public insurance program for the elderly.

Distinguish Medicaid from Medicare and understand their relationship.

Understand that the Child Health Insurance Program serves the children of the working poor.

Chapter Outline

Since the early 1900s the United States has been subsidizing medical care for citizens whose incomes are extremely low. The number of people who were covered by some form of federal medical care increased until 1967, when the Medicaid program came into full fruition. From that point on, millions of Americans have benefited from free medical care. Today, 19 million children and another 22 million adults have nearly all of their medical expenses paid for by Medicaid.

In this chapter we describe the Medicaid program in full, and we provide information about the people who are eligible for its benefits and what coverage they receive. We also discuss the groups that draw most heavily on Medicaid benefits. We describe the relationship between the federal government and the states in funding and administering the Medicaid program. We outline how doctors and hospitals are reimbursed when they work with patients whose costs are paid through Medicaid. We move on to use our supply and demand model to explain why Medicaid costs so much, and we focus attention on Medicaid's treatment of two very different populations: the very old and the very young. Then we consider provisions in Medicaid that are intended to keep costs down.

Medicare and Social Security are the centerpieces of the United States' policy toward its elderly. Social Security ensures an income for the retired, and Medicare guarantees heavily subsidized health insurance for everyone over 65, retired or not. Social Security began in the New Deal 1930s, Medicare in the second great wave of social programs during the Johnson administration's Great Society of the 1960s. In its first full year in operation, 1967, the cost of its benefits totaled $2.7 billion; by 2003 it cost $278 billion.

Medicare comprises two programs: Medicare, Part A, a mandatory program that covers expenses derived from hospital stays; and Medicare, Part B, a voluntary program that covers doctor visits. This section begins by laying out why a government health insurance program for the elderly makes economic sense, and we review the problems that such health insurance programs inevitably face. After discussing how each part of Medicare works, we focus on ways that each part has attempted to control costs. We then look at the Medicare Trust Fund and its projected problems in staying solvent, and we suggest ways Medicare can stave off bankruptcy. As part of that discussion we talk about the relationship between Medicaid and Medicare, the program for Americans 65 or older.

Finally we take up the relatively new Child Health Insurance Program and its function of providing health insurance to the children of working families where the parents have no employer-provided health insurance.

MEDICAID: WHAT, WHO, AND HOW MUCH

Medicaid was established in 1964 to consolidate and expand existing programs that had been charged with providing health care to those who could not otherwise afford it. In 2003 the program cost the federal and state governments $278 billion. We begin our discussion of the Medicaid system by describing who is eligible, what is covered, who is enrolled, which groups cost the most, what relationship federal government has to the states, and how doctors and hospitals are reimbursed.

People who are eligible for Medicaid must meet one of many criteria. In general, anyone who is in a family that is eligible for cash assistance under Temporary Aid to Needy Families (TANF) or Supplemental Security Income (SSI) is automatically eligible for Medicaid. Others eligible include any children under 19 whose parents' income is less than 133 percent of the appropriate poverty line for their family size. Pregnant women and children under a year old whose family income is less than 185 percent of that poverty line are also eligible, as are relatively few others who are affected by a variety of other rules. It is important to note that adults who do not have children who are under the age of 19 can have very little income and not be covered by Medicaid because their wealth makes them ineligible for TANF or SSI. This means that although Medicaid enrolls more than 40 million, only half of those whose incomes are below 150 percent of the poverty line receive its benefits.

Medicaid pays for nearly everything that is considered necessary from a medical standpoint, and it pays for some things that can be questioned. Doctor visits, emergency room visits, surgery, outpatient procedures, medicines, birth control pills, permanent and semipermanent birth control procedures and devices, long-term care—you name it, Medicaid probably pays for it. Literally, the only things that are not covered are most abortions, cosmetic surgeries, and drugs for weight loss and hair growth. Abortions are paid for by Medicaid in only a few states, and in those states the state must pay the whole fee. Whenever a pregnancy is the result of rape or incest, or threatens the life of the mother, Medicaid pays as it would for any other procedure.

Far more women and young people are served by Medicaid than their proportion in the general population. Whereas 51 percent of the population is female, nearly 60 percent of the Medicaid population is. Only 28 percent of the population is under 20, yet 55 percent of the Medicaid population is under 20. If you look at simply the adults on Medicaid, 70 percent are female. Additionally, though the population of Medicaid recipients is disproportionately young, we will show that the dollars spent are disproportionately allocated to care for the elderly.

In racial makeup, Medicaid recipients mirror the population of those who live in poverty nearly perfectly: 44 percent white, 25 percent black, and 20 percent Hispanic. Another 11 percent are racially or ethnically mixed to a degree such that Medicaid classifies their race as "unknown."

Medicaid is a cooperative effort of federal and state governments. The federal government mandates that the states enroll all people who are eligible, and it gives them guidelines to use if they wish to enroll others. States have the option of covering or denying coverage of certain specified expenses (like the previously mentioned abortions), as they wish.

The federal mandates are partially covered by federal matching money, and states are reimbursed according to their relative GDPs. Poorer states are given greater reimbursement rates, and richer states are given smaller ones. Twelve states get the minimum 50 percent matching percentage from the federal government, while 6 other states and the District of Columbia get at least a 70 percent match. In this way Medicaid is less of a burden for poorer states to fund.

Some states make it is easier to get on Medicaid than others. States have different income and wealth standards for TANF, and people who are eligible for Medicaid in New York and Wisconsin, for example, would not be eligible in states like Texas and Arkansas. This difference is effective only for adults, since children under one year of age are eligible, regardless of the state they live in, under a federal standard that makes them eligible if their family's income is less than 185 percent of the poverty line. All other children are similarly eligible as long as their family income is less than 133 percent of the poverty line.

When they treat patients whose bills are paid by Medicaid, doctors and hospitals are reimbursed at widely varying rates. States pay different amounts for the same procedures. These variations come about because Medicaid payments start at the state level with the federal government matching the state's payments. States must set reimbursement rates high enough that there are enough physicians and hospitals in all areas to treat Medicaid patients adequately. When many physicians are in competition with one another, rates can be lower; when there are few, rates must be higher.

For doctors and hospitals, Medicaid is an all-or-nothing proposition. When doctors and hospitals agree to take Medicaid patients, they agree to accept the state reimbursement rate as payment in full. They also agree to take any and all Medicaid patients who show up for treatment. They cannot limit their practice to a certain percentage, and they cannot accept patients with one disease and not another. Finding these restrictions to be unreasonable and reimbursement rates too low, many private hospitals and prestigious doctors do not take Medicaid patients.

WHY MEDICAID COSTS SO MUCH

Medicaid is an expensive program. To examine why it costs as much as it does, it will be helpful to put it into our supply and demand context. In 2003 the federal and state governments spent $278 billion to provide health care for the 41 million Americans eligible for Medicaid. That amount translates to more than $6,800 per recipient. The 251 million Americans who are not on Medicaid account for a little less than $5,665 per citizen in health spending, for a total expenditure that comes to around $1.7 trillion. Why is it that the expenses of people who pay their own health care are less than the expenses of people whose health care is paid through Medicaid?

Let's turn to our supply and demand model for an explanation. As it is with any other good, the demand for health care is downward sloping. This is because when the price is high, people forgo care for ailments that are not all that troubling. Although price is always a concern, there are ailments that people will have treated pretty much regardless of cost. Keeping our upward-sloping supply curve makes sense because it takes more money to get doctors and hospitals to provide the greater quantities of care we desire and the higher quality of care that we also desire.

Figure 19.1 differs from every other supply and demand diagram you have seen, though, in that we have separated the demand by people in poverty from the demand by the people whose incomes are above the poverty line. The demand curve $D_{nonpoor}$ for the nonpoor is further to the right than the demand curve D_{poor} for the poor. To get the market demand curve $D_{poor + nonpoor}$, we must add the quantities of care that both the nonpoor and poor want at each

FIGURE 19.1   The supply and demand for health care without Medicaid.

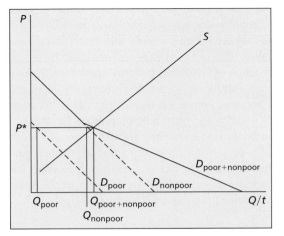

FIGURE 19.2   The supply and demand for health care with Medicaid.

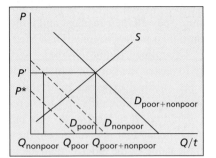

price. At some prices the poor cannot afford any health care, and they therefore do not demand any health care. As prices fall, the poor begin to demand health care, and the nonpoor begin to demand more health care. To find where the market demand curve cuts the horizontal axis, you add the quantity of health care that each would want if it were provided free of charge. This horizontal adding of demand curves gives us the market demand curve.

Where the market demand curve $D_{poor + nonpoor}$ crosses the market supply curve S, we get the equilibrium price P^* and quantity $Q_{poor + nonpoor}$. When we take that price over to the nonpoor person's demand curve, we can read off the quantity of health care the nonpoor person will get as $Q_{nonpoor}$. Taking it further, to the poor person's demand curve, we can read off what the poor person wants as Q_{poor}. If the health care system is such that the poor cannot get access to care at affordable prices, there will be a disparity between the health care received by the nonpoor and that received by the poor that some people will consider to be unacceptable.

If the poor are provided health care free of charge, as they are with Medicaid, a different problem arises. The market demand curve does not stay as it was in Figure 19.1 but moves to its position in Figure 19.2. This new demand curve is made up by adding the quantity Q_{poor} of care poor people will want if it is free to the demand curve $D_{nonpoor}$ for the nonpoor. At the intersection of market supply and market demand, the price rises to P', which is substantially above its old price at P^*. It also results in greater access for the poor and less access for the nonpoor. Figure 19.2 exaggerates this effect, but in the real world Medicaid recipients consume more health care

than those who have private insurance. In any event, it costs more to provide health care to Medicaid patients than it does for those who are able to pay the costs out of their pocket or who can afford insurance.

Why Spending Is Greater on the Elderly

In terms of expenses, Medicaid dollars are spent disproportionately on the elderly. This stands to reason in that older people need care that tends to be more expensive, and they need it more often than do those who are younger. The average Medicaid recipient utilized $4,560 in medical care in 2001. The average child under 5 who was covered by Medicaid cost the government only $1,454, while the average covered person over 65 cost $12,691. Thus, though children make up slightly less than half of Medicaid's population, they account for only 16 percent of the bills, and although those over 65 (and not disabled) make up less than 10 percent of its population, they account for 26 percent of the bills. This is in addition to the $278 billion that they account for in Medicare bills.

As mentioned previously, the central reason for Medicaid's spending more on the elderly than it does on the young is that older people tend to get illnesses that cost more than those of younger people. However, there is a reason that comes in a close second: nursing home care. Nursing home care is not part of either Medicare Part A or Part B. People who are elderly must therefore pay for this care themselves, unless, of course, they cannot. When elderly people's incomes are low enough that they qualify for assistance, Medicaid will pick up the tab for nursing home care. This can cost anywhere between $30,000 and $70,000 a year, constituting a substantial outlay for Medicaid. In the final analysis, Medicaid spends 35 percent of its total budget on long-term care, of which about three-quarters is on care for the aged.

The problem that this generates for elderly Americans is that they have to qualify for Medicaid before Medicaid will start paying. For widows and widowers this is not that difficult; they simply pay all their medical and nursing home expenses until their money is gone. Then Medicaid starts paying. Oftentimes, adult children with power of attorney try to hasten the point at which Medicaid pays their parents' medical expenses by draining the wealth of their parents by making gifts of it to themselves and their own children. It is legal to do this but only up to a point. Any money that is given to children and grandchildren in the name of the elderly relatives in the two-year period leading up to their enrollment in Medicaid is treated as a semifraudulent way of avoiding paying for nursing home care. The government monitors this and takes back any money that was given away within that period.

Giving away an elderly person's assets does not solve the nursing home problem entirely, in any case, because many times an elderly married couple has one partner who needs care and another who does not. This is especially true when an otherwise healthy person gets Alzheimer's disease. Medicaid used to require that the entire household's wealth be spent down before it would pay anything to a nursing home. This left many healthy spouses destitute because of the need to finance health care for their partner. At the time the only alternative for the couple was to file for divorce the minute one of them was placed in a nursing home. That way, the assets were divided in half so that only half would be spent down, and the other half would be available for the healthy spouse. The needless emotional trauma of divorcing a long-time spouse is now avoided because the law now allows the assets of the couple's household to be divided equally between what will be spent down and what will be left untouched when one member of the married couple is admitted to a nursing home.

Cost Saving Measures in Medicaid

During the early 1990s Medicaid costs were rising by more than 10 percent a year. This trend, coupled with other welfare concerns, motivated many of the welfare reform measures of the middle part of that decade. During that time states began to shift their Medicaid systems from individual doctors reimbursed for expenses to health maintenance organizations (HMOs). From 1990 to 2004, doctors in HMOs went from treating fewer than 5 percent of Medicaid patients to treating 60 percent of them.

When HMOs are in place, people are denied coverage unless it is authorized by the doctors who have been designated as their primary care physicians. Under HMOs, primary care physicians are charged with providing basic care, and they are the only people who can refer patients to specialists. The use of HMOs has stemmed the unfortunate practice of Medicaid patients' use of emergency room treatments for basic care. Nonemergency Medicaid patients are now counseled that if they show up at an emergency room for treatment of nonserious matters, they may be turned away. They are also counseled about the benefits of having a physician who follows their particular health needs. In this way HMOs are saving the state and federal governments money and, at the same time, are helping to improve the health of the people they are serving.

MEDICARE: PUBLIC INSURANCE AND THE ELDERLY

Why Private Insurance May Not Work

There are two main arguments for government provision of health insurance for the elderly: equity and efficiency. While it was appropriate in earlier times to argue that it was only fair to provide for the elderly in that the elderly were poorer than younger people, such arguments are less appropriate today. Today's elderly are among the least likely of our citizens to be in poverty, due in some measure to these programs. What remains are arguments that the market cannot provide health insurance efficiently to people who are not in groups.

The problem with health insurance, in general, is that people who really need it, those who are sick, are more than willing to pay very high prices for it; and those who are healthy are only willing to pay low prices. Most people have in mind two kinds of health expenses when they are thinking about buying insurance, the expenses they are rather sure they will incur and expenses of which they are not as certain. They will buy insurance readily if the expenses they expect are greater than the premiums they have to pay. People will pay for insurance that covers them in areas they are not certain they will need, but if premiums are too high, only the sickest will want to buy insurance. If this group were to become the only one that buys insurance, the expenses to the insurance company would be greater than the premiums received and premiums would have to rise. This would make the problem worse, as only the

FIGURE 19.3   Real Medicare spending in billions of 2000 dollars.

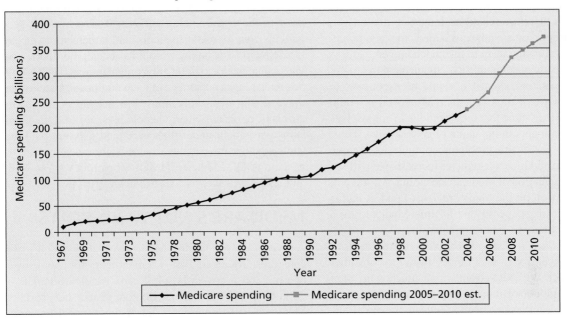

sickest of the sick would buy the insurance. This problem is referred to by economists as adverse selection.

This vicious cycle would go on and on until there was no insurance at all. Fortunately, this is not much of a problem in the United States because most private health insurance is group insurance that employers buy for their employees. In each group there are undoubtedly some people who are sick, some who are healthy, and many who are somewhere in between. The healthy subsidize the sick. Because being part of a group affords such important benefits both to the insurance companies and to members of the group, people who buy health insurance as individuals always run into problems not encountered by people who buy into group health insurance.

This would not be a problem if the elderly were still with their employers. They are not; they are retired, and many employers do not offer membership in company health groups to retirees. With the efficacy of offering health plans to people in groups, and with millions of individual retirees needing health insurance, it has made sense for the government to offer such insurance, and it does so through Medicare.

What remains debatable about Medicare is who pays for it—its beneficiaries (as with normal health insurance), or all taxpayers, or a combination of these groups. At the outset it was intended that the cost split would be about 50–50, proportions that offered the elderly a substantial subsidy. Today the subsidy is such that about

three-quarters of the total expenses are paid out of tax dollars and only about a quarter by its beneficiaries.

Why Medicare's Costs Are High

All government health insurance programs suffer from problems of cost control, problems that are compounded in an era of rapid advances in medical technology that vastly improve health care but increase costs as well. Anytime the consumption of a good is subsidized via insurance, several basic problems ensue. The first problem is that you risk increasing its consumption to an inefficient level. The second problem, referred to by economists as the third-party payer problem, is that by insuring consumers and thereby insulating them from costs, neither consumers nor producers have incentives for holding down costs. These and other insurance problems were explained in detail in Chapter 18 on health care.

As with all other government health insurance programs, then, the costs of Medicare have escalated dramatically. Figure 19.3 shows the increase in the costs of Medicare since its inception in 1967.

For most programs, spending can rise only because prices rise or beneficiaries become more numerous. Medicare spending has risen for these reasons and one other: increases in numbers of available medical services. Medicare beneficiaries are not limited to the medical procedures that existed in 1967. They can avail themselves of the best that medical science has to offer in the 2000s. This means that some patients who would have died 20 years ago, and who therefore would no longer be drawing on Medicare's resources, are now given medicines and procedures that are allowing them to live much longer.

It would be unconscionable to deny medical treatment to Medicare patients, even if it would be expensive, to improve their life or their life span. Moreover, it would be unrealistic to assume that they would deny themselves expensive treatments in the name of cost savings. Thus, as treatments for health problems continue to become more effective and life expectancies increase, we will see a continued escalation of Medicare spending. As you will see in our section on the Medicare Trust Fund, it is this quickly increasing expense that has put Medicare on a course that is likely to lead it to bankruptcy.

One of the ways to deal with this kind of problem is to transfer the incentive to save money from the consumer to the producer. While it is usually consumers who want to limit the amount of money they pay, with insurance this incentive is either drastically reduced or even eliminated. As discussed above, if no one has an incentive to keep expenses down, no one will keep expenses down. It is possible, though, to make producers the costconscious parties by paying them prospectively rather than retrospectively.

Retrospective payment is what people are used to when they buy services. When a person has a car repaired, a garage worker finds the problem, asks whether the customer wants it fixed, tells what it will cost, and fixes it. At that point the retrospective payment is made. Under normal circumstances, this is not a problem because the customer still has the incentive to keep costs down. Problems arise when retrospective payments are used with insurance. When you have an accident that is someone else's fault, it is the other person's insurance that is paying the bill. Here you want everything fixed perfectly, with original parts, and the repair shop is only too happy to oblige because the mechanic can rack up the charges. If you had to pay for the repair, you would be more likely to be satisfied with "good enough" and to accept substitute parts. That is why either you are required to get two or three estimates before the work starts, or the single estimate and the repairs must be preapproved by an insurance adjuster. Both multiple estimates and insurance adjusters' oversight serve to keep repair shops competing with one another and prevent or lessen overbilling.

In health care it is unusual for an insurance company to have you go to several doctors to get estimates, though some may require second opinions. This is why some

insurance companies and Medicare have gone to a system of prospective payments. Prospective payments are made prior to the service being performed. The hospital gets paid up front to treat its patients, and it then has an incentive to keep costs below what it has been paid. In the private arena, health maintenance organizations (HMOs) are designed to take advantage of such payments. Gatekeeper doctors, who are usually family practice physicians, pediatricians, or obstetrician/gynecologists, are paid specified sums per patient under their care, and they are paid the sums whether the patients require a great deal of care or no care at all. Medicare HMOs work this way as well, and, as we will see, so does Medicare Part A.

MEDICARE'S NUTS AND BOLTS

As we discussed before, Medicare is divided into two categories. Medicare Part A is mandatory for people over age 65, and it covers hospital care. Medicare Part B is voluntary, and it covers doctor visits. No part of Medicare covers common out-of-the-hospital prescription drugs or long-term nursing home care.

Provider Types

The first choice a Medicare recipient has to make is whether to choose traditional Medicare or a Medicare HMO. Medicare HMOs are approved by the government, and doctors who participate in them are paid per patient under their charge. The government pays less per HMO patient than per non-HMO patient on average, probably because healthy elderly people are more likely to enroll in an HMO. The cost controls that HMOs offer are usually enough that HMO premiums are significantly lower than normal Medicare premiums. People who opt for traditional Medicare are automatically enrolled in Part A; they may choose to enroll in Part B.

Part A

For people who work 10 years before reaching 65, Medicare Part A has no premium. For everyone else the premium charged for Medicare Part A differs, depending on how long they worked. In 2005 the deductible was a relatively high $912 for the first day in the hospital. The costs for the next 60 days were paid by Medicare. After 60 days in the hospital patients paid $228 per day, Medicare paid the rest, and after 90 days patients paid $456 per day. From day 91 on, patients have a 60-day reserve of days upon which to draw. When that reserve is gone patients must pay the rest themselves.

From the hospital's position, Medicare is paying amounts that it has settled on for specific diagnoses. These payments, and they are prospective payments, are determined by where the patients' ailments put them on a list of more than 500 diagnosis-related groups (DRGs). All Medicare patients who enter the hospital are placed in a DRG, and rather than paying for specific expenses that are incurred, Medicare pays the hospital a predetermined amount that is considered appropriate for that DRG. This motivates the hospital to keep costs down. Medicare had paid for every bandage, meal, and service until the mid-1980s, when it found that hospitals were racking up costs of questionable medical value just to increase their profit margins. Under fixed payments for DRGs, Medicare has kept much better control of cost increases. This policy has also led to a significant shortening of average hospital stays for specific problems. The current system also provides an incentive for hospitals to discharge patients as soon as possible.

Part B

Medicare Part B, the voluntary insurance program that pays for visits to doctors, has a monthly premium and an annual deductible. In 2005 the premium was $78.29 and the deductible was $110. Because neither the premium nor the deductible has increased at the rate of inflation, this part of the program is now being subsidized at a rate approaching 75 percent. What this means is that for every dollar a patient pays, Medicare Part B pays 3 out of tax revenues. Accordingly, there is virtually no reason for an elderly person not to enroll in Part B. For those who cannot afford the premium, Medicaid, the parallel program that provides health insurance for the poor, typically steps in. For everyone else, that $78.29 premium is a small enough amount that nearly 100 percent of the non-Medicaid eligible elderly are enrolled.

From a doctor's perspective, Medicare Part B pays a regional standard for each treatment. Unlike Part A, Part B is billed expense by expense with retrospective payment. Medicaid pays a fixed amount for each service, but each service is billed individually rather than being grouped in a DRG.

The reason that prospective payments do not work for non-HMO Medicare Part B is that, with a huge range of possible ailments, there are many potential doctors a patient may want to see. In a Medicare HMO, a gatekeeper is in charge of referrals to specialists, but non-HMO patients can go at any time to the doctors of their choice. It would be impossible to predict such choices in advance,

and since no single doctor, HMO, or hospital is in total charge of their care under Part B, prospective payments cannot be made to work.

In the 2003 reauthorization of Medicare, a new wrinkle—means testing—entered. For the first time, Medicare, Part B premiums will depend on income. For seniors with income less than $80,000, premiums will still account for 25 percent of costs. For seniors with incomes between $80,000 and $200,000 premiums will rise to ultimately cover 80 percent of average program costs.

Prescription Drug Coverage (Part D)

As part of the 2003 reauthorization of Medicare, the costs of prescription drugs are now covered. Prior to this change, health care economists were of two minds. First, they saw a distortion of the market when surgery was covered but medicines were not. Second, they noted Medicare's precarious financial state and worried that the additional benefit would make it that much worse.

As expensive as most drugs are, drug-based treatments are less expensive than their surgical alternatives. Because Medicare did not cover prescription drugs and it did cover surgery, patients may have elected surgery even though it may have been more expensive.

On the other side of the debate were the concerns over the cost of any prescription drug program. Initial estimates in the 2003 Medicare reauthorization placed the cost of such a program at $400 billion over 10 years. Those estimates were quickly revised. Currently the program is anticipated to cost at least $720 billion over 10 years. What must be understood about any such estimates is that they are highly sensitive to assumptions about price elasticity for drugs. If the estimator uses data on the number of prescriptions filled and multiplies that number by the cost per prescription covered by the government (assuming perfectly inelastic demand), this would seriously underestimate costs. There are people who will benefit from prescriptions who did not go to the doctor because they knew they would get a prescription slip they could not afford to fill. Additionally, there were elderly who used to get multiple prescriptions and fill only a fraction of them because they could not afford to fill them all. Taking this into account, cost estimates are likely to be exceeded and higher deficits will ensue.

The 2003 reauthorization also introduces means testing to Medicare. The Republican-authored bill made premiums and coverage dependent on income and will still require most seniors to pay as much as $3,600 out of pocket. Premiums will run $420 per year, there will be a $275 deductible, and there will be a 25 percent co-pay up to $2,200. Between $2,200 and $3,600 there will be no coverage and catastrophic coverage will resume at $3,600 with a small 5 percent co-pay. Democrats sought universal coverage for all drug expenses in a way that would have been unrelated to income because they worried that making the benefit more generous to the poor would weaken Medicare's political support.

Cost Control Provisions in Medicare

Medicare has been attempting to keep costs under control since its inception, but, unfortunately, it has enjoyed little success. Ultimately the reasons for this lack of success boil down to two:

1. Medical care is increasingly sophisticated, with continually improving success rates, and it is therefore more costly.
2. There is no economic incentive for either patient or doctor to control costs.

While the aforementioned DRGs have helped control costs in Part A, and Medicare HMOs have helped control costs in Part B, neither has been foolproof. The DRGs, however, have succeeded in doing a couple of important things with regard to costs. First, basing the payments on DRGs has given hospitals the incentive to take many procedures that used to require one night in the hospital and turn them into outpatient procedures. Second, hospitals have put pressure on doctors and patients to shorten the average length of stay of many multiday procedures.

Given that DRGs pay a fixed amount for a procedure, hospitals have the incentive to cut costs. Since one of a hospital's greatest costs is keeping someone in a bed overnight, converting a procedure that formerly involved a hospital stay to one that is done on an outpatient basis helps to raise profits. Heart bypass surgery is not likely to be an outpatient procedure anytime soon, but many other procedures are candidates. While many people are concerned about the health consequences of turning out patients who would have stayed a night, there has been little medical evidence that sending people home right away has had adverse effects.

A second area where costs have come down is the shortening of the length of stay for many multiday procedures. Surgeries that used to require a three- or four-day stay in the hospital to recuperate now require only two or three. In part this is because surgeons are better at

limiting the trauma to the body from surgery, and in part it is because postsurgical rehabilitation has improved.[1]

THE MEDICARE TRUST FUND

One of the greatest concerns today is the fiscal health of the Medicare program that provides for our elderly's physical health. The Medicare Trust Fund enjoyed assets of $303 billion in 2005. This trust fund was set up to handle the anticipated medical expenses of the baby boom generation. Like the Social Security Trust Fund, it deliberately collected more in taxes than was necessary in order to build savings for the period between 2015 and 2035, when it was anticipated that the high numbers of the baby boom generation were likely to strain the system. Like the Social Security Trust Fund, the Medicare Trust Fund is invested only in U.S. government debt. In 1997, however, the trustees of the Medicare Trust Fund issued an alarming report. They estimated that long before the serious crisis hit, the trust fund would be bankrupt. While later trustees' reports have been somewhat more optimistic about the fiscal health of the program, eventual bankruptcy remains its conclusion.

The annual reports of the trustees have been based on three different projections of the future: one very optimistic, the second very pessimistic, and the third on what the trustees judged to be the most realistic assumptions. Assumptions have been made about two economic variables and two demographic variables. The economic considerations have been the growth in inflation-adjusted wages and the real interest rate. The demographic variables have been the fertility rate and life expectancy. The higher the projected growth rate in wages, the more projected tax revenues would be; the higher the projected real interest rate, the better return on the trust fund would be; and because it is held that greater numbers of children will produce more tax revenue, the higher the projected fertility rate, the greater the projected tax revenues. Last, longer projected life expectancy would be anticipated to create greater Medicare expenses.

---

[1]While the data on length of stay have not shown a decline, this is misleading because of the aforementioned outpatient substitution. Since the length-of-stay data are based on the number of days a patient stays in a hospital, the procedures that are now outpatient do not count at all. If length of stay for the other procedures had remained the same as it was before the outpatient substitution, then the overall average would have risen substantially since whenever you remove short stays and leave only the longer stays, the average rises. Since the overall average has remained constant, we know the length of stay for longer-stay procedures has fallen.

FIGURE 19.4   The Medicare Trust Fund under alternative assumptions.

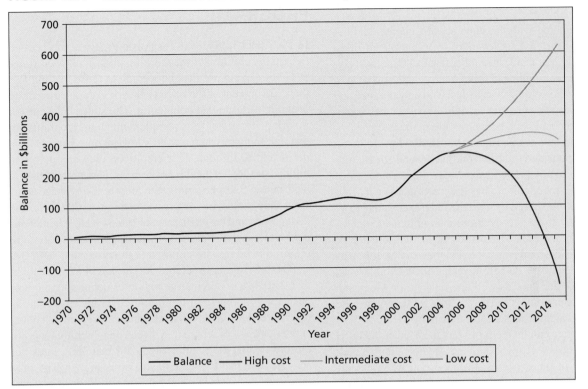

Figure 19.4 shows the actual balance of the Medicare Trust Fund from 1985 to 2005 and the projected balance of the trust fund until 2014 under the alternative assumptions just outlined. The estimates of low costs are based on the following assumptions: real wages will grow quickly, at a rate of 1.6 percent; real interest rates will be a high rate of 3.7 percent; and fertility will be high, at 2.2 children per woman. The figures that reflect the estimate of high costs are just the opposite: real wages will grow at 0.6 percent; real interest rates will be 2.2 percent; and fertility will be 1.7 children per woman. The intermediate cost projections are that real wages will rise at 1.1 percent; real interest rates will be at 3.0 percent; and the average woman will have 1.95 children.

If the assumptions leading to high costs are correct, Medicare is genuinely on the verge of bankruptcy. If the costs turn out to be low, the year of bankruptcy is beyond the immediate projections of the report, but it still happens in the middle of the 21st century. The 1997 report used the intermediate assumptions and projected bankruptcy in 2008. The 1999 update of the report projected that the system would be bankrupt in 2015. The 2000 through 2005 versions have produced a relatively stable projection for around the 2020s.

To forestall the projected bankruptcy, it seems reasonable to consider simply raising taxes along the way in a pay-as-you-go format. This would presuppose that nothing is done to alter the current program. If we go to a pay-as-you-go system where taxes have to increase each year to meet the health care needs of the elderly, tax rates may rise substantially.

Under current law, the payroll tax that funds Part A of Medicare is 2.9 percent. That is, you and your employer each contribute 1.45 percent of everything you make on the job. (The self-employed contribute the full 2.9 percent.) Under the most likely scenario the rate would more than double to 3.3 percent each.

If raising taxes to the necessary levels is unacceptable, other solutions may be explored. The age at which people become eligible could be raised, premiums and deductibles could be raised to their inflation-adjusted 1970 level or beyond, all beneficiaries could be required to have gatekeeper physicians (as in HMOs), and it could be mandated that at certain income or wealth levels the elderly would get reduced subsidies. Many people are dissatisfied with these alternatives, and none meet with the approval of the main lobbying organization for the elderly, the American Association of Retired Persons.

The Relationship between Medicaid and Medicare

Besides beginning with the same act of Congress and besides sharing the first six letters of their eight-letter titles, Medicare and Medicaid share other features. The most significant is a commingling of tasks when people are both old and poor. Medicare was set up to deal with only the aged and Medicaid was set up to deal with only the poor. When someone is both old and poor, both programs come into play.

When a person is of an age to be eligible for Medicare and is also poor and qualifies on that ground for Medicaid, the first to pay is Medicare. Medicaid is the payer of last resort. Since Medicare has two parts and since Medicaid's costs are shared by both the federal and state governments, the story gets even more complicated.

All elderly are required to participate in Medicare Part A, which covers hospital expenses, and they can elect to participate in Medicare Part B, coverage for doctors' visits. When people are poor as well and qualify for Medicaid, the Medicare premiums and deductibles for Part A are paid by Medicaid and the remainder are paid by Medicare. For Part B, the state can then elect to pay the Medicare Part B premiums and deductibles and have Medicare Part B pick up the bulk of the expenses. In any event, when elderly people are eligible for Medicaid, there is significant overlap between Medicare and Medicaid.

CHILD HEALTH INSURANCE PROGRAM

In 1997 the Child Health Insurance Program was created to help the children of the working poor. It allowed states to either expand Medicaid coverage to those making less than 200 percent of the poverty line or to create a separate program to serve that population. The states have chosen a variety of strategies to implement their programs. In general, though, when a child's low-income parents have no insurance through their employer, they can purchase highly subsidized health insurance. The premiums are held below $20 per family per month, a tiny fraction of what they would be for private insurance. Similarly, the deductibles and co-payments are low as well. An interesting feature is that well-baby visits and immunizations are required to be free for children in the program.

The program is structured very much like Medicaid in that there is a matching rate for states depending on their per capita income and minimum coverage expectations to ensure that all covered children are given adequate care regardless of where they live. The matching rates are closely tied to the regular Medicaid matching rates but are, on average, 12 percentage points higher. The program now serves more than 5 million children at a cost of $6 billion per year.

Summary

At this point you understand that Medicaid is a program that covers medical expenses for a subset of this nation's poor. You understand that eligibility for Medicaid benefits is tied to family income and the age of dependent children, and, as a result, there are many people who are in poverty and not covered by the program. You understand that the beneficiaries are disproportionately women but that in other demographic dimensions they mirror those who are in poverty.

You understand how much the program costs, and you know why those costs are high relative to the costs of those who are covered by private insurance. You know that a disproportionate amount of money is spent on the elderly, and you are able to articulate why that is the case. You understand the relationship between Medicaid and the companion program for the elderly, Medicare. Last, you are aware of the cost-saving measures that have been put in place for Medicaid.

Quiz Yourself

1. A five-year-old child from a family making more than 133 percent but less than 200 percent of the poverty line is
   a. Ineligible for any health care assistance.
   b. Eligible for Medicare's prescription drug plan only.
   c. Eligible for all of Medicare.
   d. Eligible for Medicaid.

2. When a 65-year-old goes to the hospital, the part of Medicare that pays for the hospital bill is
   a. Part A.
   b. Part B.
   c. Part C.
   d. Part D.

3. When a program like Medicaid is introduced the market demand curve for health care will
   a. Increase and flatten.
   b. Increase and become more steep.
   c. Decrease and flatten.
   d. Decrease and become more steep.

4. Medicaid spending per recipient is
   a. Twice that of the average citizen's use of health care.
   b. Somewhat less than the average citizen's use of health care.
   c. Somewhat greater than the average citizen's use of health care.
   d. Half that of the average citizen's use of health care.

5. The DRG system controls Medicare expenses by
   a. Preventing doctors from using particular procedures.
   b. Paying hospitals after they submit bills.
   c. Paying hospitals on the basis of a disease or injury rather than expenses.
   d. Paying the patient who then pays the hospital.

6. The Medicare Trust Fund is necessary because
   a. Current expenses are greater than current revenues.
   b. Current expenses are less than current revenues.
   c. Future expenses will be greater than future revenues.
   d. Future expenses will be less than future revenues.

7. Medicare's prescription drug coverage will likely
   a. Cost substantially more than it was estimated to cost in 2003.
   b. Cost substantially less than it was estimated to cost in 2003.
   c. Cost slightly less than it was estimated to cost in 2003.
   d. Cost about what it was estimated to cost in 2003.

Think about This

One of the suggestions for providing the working poor with health insurance has been to require employers to provide health insurance benefits for all workers by having employers "buy them into Medicaid." Requiring this would raise the cost to employers of hiring new workers. Under what circumstances would this be good for workers? Under what circumstances would it not be good?

Talk about This

When public provision of health care is discussed in most political arenas, providing more coverage (e.g., prescriptions and long-term care) for the elderly typically garners more attention than expanding coverage to the working poor. Why is that? Is this the right priority in your mind?

For More Insight See

Garrett, Major, "Medicare: Healthier for Now." *U.S. News & World Report,* April 12, 1999, p. 29.

Lee, Ronald, and Jonathan Skinner, "Will Aging Baby Boomers Bust the Federal Budget?" *Journal of Economic Perspectives* 13 (Winter 1999), pp. 117–140.

Miller, Matthew, "Premium Idea." *The New Republic,* April 12, 1999, pp. 24–27.

Newhouse, Joseph, "Policy Watch: Medicare." *Journal of Economic Perspectives* 10 (Summer 1996), pp. 159–168.

Phelps, Charles, *Health Economics* (Reading, MA: Addison-Wesley, 1997), esp. Chapter 13.

"Survey: Health Care." *The Economist,* July 6, 1991.

2000 Annual Report of the Board of Trustees of the Federal Hospital Insurance Trust Fund.

Behind the Numbers

Historical data.
   Federal Medicare Spending 1967–2004.
      Budget of the United States Government, 2006; historical tables—http://www.gpoaccess.gov/usbudget/fy06/pdf/hist.pdf.
   Historical and Projected Medicare Trust Fund Assets, 1970–2012.
      Centers for Medicare and Medicaid Services; 2003 Trustees Report—http://www.cms.hhs.gov/publications/trusteesreport/tr2005.pdf.

Medicaid Spending and Population Characteristics, 2002. Statistical Abstract of the United States; health—http://www.census.gov/prod/2004pubs/04statab/health.pdf.

Medicaid and Medicare recipients, eligibility and costs; Centers for Medicare and Medicaid Services—http://www.cms.hhs.gov/.

Medicare Trust Fund, 2005.
   Budget of the United States Government, 2006; Department of Health and Human Services—http://www.gpoaccess.gov/usbudget/.

Number of Americans with and without health insurance, 2004—http://www.cdc.gov/nchs/data/nhis/earlyrelease/insur200506.pdf.

Chapter 20

The Economics of Prescription Drugs

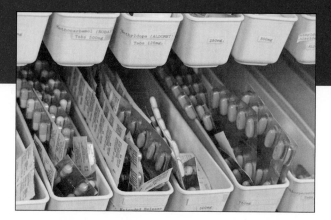

Prescription drug prices are an important issue for people with health conditions, particularly older Americans. *Source: Royalty-Free/CORBIS*

Chapter Objectives

After reading this chapter you should be able to

Apply the concepts of monopoly as well as consumer and producer surplus to the economics of prescription drugs.

See why most health economists view prescription drugs as relatively inexpensive, even while most noneconomists view them as very expensive.

Understand why it is that most health economists do not favor price controls on prescription drugs.

Understand the consequences of an approval process that is too stringent or too lax.

Chapter Outline

Profiteers or Benevolent Scientists?

Monopoly Power Applied to Drugs

Important Questions

Summary

When people go to the doctor because they are sick or injured, they want the doctor to make them better. For certain injuries they may expect active treatments, like surgery. It is just part of the human psychological makeup to want to know that "everything is being done" to restore the patient's health. The same holds for the treatment of illnesses. Nothing is more frustrating to patients than to be told they have a "virus," because they accurately translate that to mean "go home and go to bed because there is nothing we can do for you." On the other hand, if patients go home having filled a prescription for a drug, they feel better simply because they think that taking medicine will make them well. In part they think

this because the prescription drug industry has been so successful in treating everything from infections to impotence. When we have a virus and there is no prescription forthcoming, we lose hope for a quick end to our illness. In this sense we go to the doctor hoping for prescriptions because it is usually a drug the doctor prescribes, rather than something the doctor actually does, that makes us better.

It seems all the more strange to economists, then, that prescription drugs get as much criticism as they do when it comes to expense. The amount of money spent on prescription drugs is actually trivial relative to all health spending. In 2003, for example, all U.S. health spending amounted to more than $1.7 trillion dollars, and 10.5 percent of that was spent on prescription drugs.

This chapter has several purposes. We look at the degree to which prescription drug manufacturers are profiteers or good Samaritans. We use our monopoly model to discern why drugs are so costly, and we examine some of the new drugs and discuss whether they are expensive necessities or relatively inexpensive godsends. In doing this we will see the fundamental reasons why prescription drug companies are likely to remain unpopular even as they continue to provide important medicines. Last, we look at how other countries control prescription drug prices, and we offer a perspective on whether the United States should follow suit.

PROFITEERS OR BENEVOLENT SCIENTISTS?

Among the more interesting advertisements of the 1990s were the pharmaceutical industry's feel-good television spots that focused on a variety of hardworking scientists endeavoring to conquer a disease. These ads differed somewhat from the ads that commonly try to get us to go to the doctor to ask about problems like hair loss, seasonal allergies, or other afflictions. Just as McDonald's wants to sell burgers, so also the pharmaceutical ads are trying to sell us a particular drug. The feel-good ads are there, not to have us buy any particular product, but to persuade us to feel better about the industry in general.

Usually, the earlier ads discussed an emotional attachment the scientists had with curing the disease they were working on. A friend, spouse, relative, or parent had the disease and this, we were supposed to believe, motivated the scientist to spend long nights crouched over a microscope in search of a cure. With no attempt to criticize the scientists' sincerity, however, we know deep down that whether or not something altruistic motivates the scientist, what motivates the drug company is profit.

As with any invention, the fundamental economic problem is how to reward the inventor. Unless the inventor is given exclusive rights to his or her idea once the item has been invented, copycats can steal it. Knowing this, inventors will have little economic incentive to innovate. This is why we have laws that govern copyrights and **patents.** Within existing laws, a patent-holding inventor is

patent
A right granted by government to an inventor to be the exclusive seller of that invention for a limited period of time.

the only person who can sell the invention for as long as the patent exists.

Monopoly power is particularly important in the so-called **orphan drug** industry, an industry that deals with diseases that afflict few people. Sales of therapies that benefit small numbers of patients cannot hope to generate sufficient profits during normal patent lives for companies to justify research. For this reason drugs that are labeled orphan drugs are granted very long patent lives so that profits, though small, can be expected to last long into the future. Without this aspect of the patent law, research on such diseases would never be instituted by scientists working in the private sector.

orphan drug
A drug that treats someone with a disease that afflicts few people.

In economic terms what this monopoly power does is give the inventor total control. As you recall from Chapter 5, monopoly means that there is one seller. It means, in turn, that there are no other companies producing the particular drug. When the drug is one-of-a-kind, as AZT was in the early 1990s, and it is the only hope a patient has, its monopoly power is dramatic. It is all the more dramatic when the disease it treats is fatal. Since most drugs cost very little to produce but may, as in the case of AIDS drugs, cost billions to discover and test, we are conflicted about high prices. We know that companies need to be rewarded for their investments, but we also find it troublesome that money has the power to determine whether a person gets a drug and lives or does not get a drug and dies.

On the other hand, when the drug is one of many, and it treats a non-life-threatening condition, as do the anti-heartburn medications Nexium and Zantac, we are not at all conflicted. The problem is not life and death, and the power the companies have to charge high prices is limited only by competition and consumers' willingness to suffer through ailments that are merely annoying.

Whether we view drug companies as profiteers or benevolent scientists rests on whether they, in the end, do good and whether they charge what are perceived to be fair prices. Drug companies make a great deal of money, but they incur a great deal of risk. Much economic research has gone into studying whether their profits are out of line in comparison with those of similar industries. Although that research has not settled on a definitive answer, it does suggest that the rate of return to stockholders in the pharmaceutical industry is either at or slightly above that of similar industries. What is clear is that prescription drugs have both improved the quality of life for millions and made companies billions in profit.

FIGURE 20.1 The prescription drug monopolist.

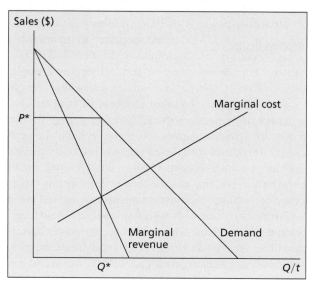

FIGURE 20.2 Comparing monopoly and perfect competition in prescription drugs.

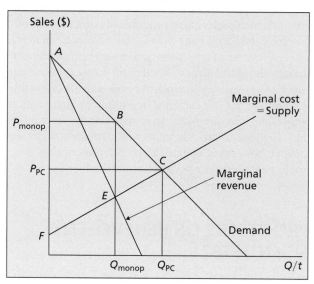

MONOPOLY POWER APPLIED TO DRUGS

As stated previously, the key economic attribute of the prescription drug industry is monopoly. While patents do run out and competition takes place in the form of generic drugs, monopoly reigns for several years at least. Figure 20.1 is the same graph that we saw in Chapter 5 for a monopolist's decision on price and production. As you know, a monopolist is the only seller of a good. This means that the demand curve that a monopolistic firm faces for its goods is the entire market demand curve. For such a firm, this has good and bad aspects. In contrast to perfect competition, the seller does not have to worry about other firms. On the downside, if the firm wants to sell more goods, it not only has to lower the price to the people who will buy the extra goods; it has to lower the price to everyone else as well. This includes the people who would have purchased their goods at high prices, so the money gained from increasing sales is partially offset by the money that is lost from having to lower prices. The good news for the firm is that raising the price does not cause all customers to leave, as it does under perfect competition.

Figure 20.1 depicts a drug company that is the sole provider of a certain drug. It indicates that the marginal revenue curve, the curve that represents the additional revenue to the firm associated with the sale of one more unit of the good, is downward sloping rather than flat, as it would be under perfect competition.

Using the tools of consumer and producer surplus we can show that with the price equal to P^* and the quantity equal to Q^*, relative to the societal optimum, the price is too high and the quantity too low. This can be seen by looking at Figure 20.2 and the assumptions that go along with it. For a moment suppose that the proper comparison to make with regard to the monopolistic production of prescription drugs is perfect competition.[1] As you saw in Chapter 5, the marginal cost curve for a perfect competitor—out of the minimum of average variable cost—was the supply curve. If you adapt that notion here, the marginal cost curve for this monopolist in Figure 20.1 is also what the supply curve would be if the market were under perfect competition.

In Figure 20.2, monopoly is compared with perfect competition. The perfectly competitive market would produce Q_{PC} at a price of P_{PC}, because this is where supply crosses demand. The monopolistic producer charges much more, P_{monop}, and produces less, Q_{monop}, because this is where marginal cost equals marginal revenue. Our consumer and producer surplus analysis, then, allows us to show that companies profit not only at the expense of sick people, but also at the expense of society as a whole.

Figure 20.2 indicates that the consumer surplus (the area under the demand curve but above the price line) at the perfectly competitive price–quantity combination is

---

[1]Because of the large innovation costs, this is a poor assumption for the industry at all stages of production but a reasonable one after the drug has been invented and approved.

$P_{PC}AC$, and the producer surplus (the area above the supply curve but under the price line) is $FP_{PC}C$. Under monopoly, the consumer surplus shrinks to $P_{monop}AB$, and the producer surplus rises to $FP_{monop}BE$. This means that producers are better off but not by as much as consumers are worse off. Stated differently, the

deadweight loss

The loss in social welfare associated with production being too little or too great.

deadweight loss, or loss to society of producing at the wrong price–quantity combination, can be shown as the difference between the sum of consumer and producer surplus between the perfect competition and monopoly situations. That area is depicted as *EBC* in Figure 20.2.

IMPORTANT QUESTIONS

Expensive Necessities or Relatively Inexpensive Godsends?

In addition to the fact that we can show prices to be "high" in a theoretical sense, the data show they are also high in real life. In the United States in particular, drugs are often priced at 10 times their marginal production costs. In addition, drug prices are increasing far more rapidly than the overall inflation rate. As a matter of fact, from 1986 to 2005 drug prices went up more than 204 percent at a time when overall inflation increased general prices 78 percent. While some difference could have been expected, this difference is remarkable given that nonprescription drugs saw only a 51 percent price increase over the same period.

The reasons for increased prescription drug prices are many and varied, but they boil down to a few important issues: development costs, regulation, and litigation. There is also a problem with the mismeasurement of inflation in drug prices.

Development of new drugs costs a great deal of money, and drug companies need to recoup costs before they can make a profit. Since the "easy" diseases already have cures or treatments, we are left with some very difficult diseases to research. The training required to even understand how to start researching drug therapies takes several years after a researcher has earned a doctorate or a medical degree. People who get that kind of education for that long a period of time are going to command very high salaries once they start working. In addition to high labor costs, the equipment needed for this kind of work is specialized and expensive.

The capital and labor costs of drug research are extended even further by the years required to take a drug from successful trials to government approval. Typically, new drugs are first tested on small animals. They are then tested on primates. These tests are followed by small-scale human trials, designed primarily to gauge safety. Finally, a large-scale human trial requires that the drug be shown to work effectively while not causing unacceptable side effects. This lengthy process is expensive and it significantly extends the time before the company's revenue stream starts.

The concept of present value can shed light on how this contributes to the high costs of drugs. Let's use a numerical example to illustrate these issues. Assume a drug company sees that 1 million patients with a particular ailment are willing and able to pay for a treatment. Suppose it costs $10 million a year for 10 years to invent a drug. Suppose it then takes another $10 million a year for another five years to test it and get it through the approval process. The law on how long a drug company has monopoly power over a drug is somewhat complicated, but we will assume that the company has that power for 10 years; after that, perfect competition takes hold and all economic profits disappear,[2] Add to this scenario the fact that few drugs make it from the scientist's lab to the pharmacy. Drug companies claim that the number of unsuccessful attempts is very high and that this is an additional reason for high costs.

Let's examine a hypothetical situation drug companies might face. Assume for every five drugs that reach the testing phase another five do not make it that far. Further, suppose that only one of every five that is tested is shown to be safe and effective. Thus for every 11 that incur invention costs there are five that also incur testing costs. Only one produces revenue. Suppose at the very beginning of this process the manufacturer does not know which of these 11 plausible ideas will pay off, but it does know that one of them will. Also suppose that the manufacturer has a good idea that marginal production costs will amount to $10 per patient per year. Given all that, at a 10 percent real rate of return the anticipated profit to the manufacturer from this one drug would have to be $520 million per year for the drug company to make back its initial investment. Thus, even if you ignore all of the markups that wholesalers and retailers charge from the manufacturer to the patient, the price per patient per year for our hypothetical example will have to be $530 dollars ($520 million dollars in profit/1 million patients +$10 in production costs).

---

[2]Manufacturers typically will make some economic profits on drugs after the expiration of the patent because of brand loyalty among physicians and patients. Drug company representatives encourage that loyalty with gifts. Sometimes these gifts are as innocuous as drug company pens while at other times they are expensive company-sponsored vacations.

In addition to all the preceding considerations, drug prices are made higher by our society's propensity for suing pharmaceutical companies. Americans sue each other more than any other group of people. Pharmaceutical firms have deep pockets. They produce products that do not work all the time and that sometimes do more harm than good. To cite a recent example, Vioxx and other Cox-2 inhibitors were approved and later had their safety called into question because they were shown to cause heart problems. Subsequent multimillion-dollar lawsuits were filed against their makers and, if upheld, they will completely wipe out the profit from the sale of these drugs. With the fear of such judgments in mind, pharmaceutical firms will increase their prices so they have enough money on hand to account for such judgments and to have profit left over. In countries where lawsuits and judgments are limited, the prices of drugs tend to be commensurately lower.

Another phenomenon we must account for in analyzing the prices of drugs is that drug price indexes suffer from all of the problems that other price indexes suffer from. The consumer price index's lapses, discussed briefly in Chapter 6, are especially problematic with drugs. For an illustration of this you need look no further than birth control pills. The pills your grandmother took in the early 1960s are nothing like those that are available now. The side effects of the early pills were much more severe than today. Part of the increase in the current price of birth control pills can be attributed to the improvement of quality rather than to the effects of inflation.

Taking all of the preceding into account, we are left with the fact that either drug prices are high or they seem to be high. The problem of the high expenses of drug therapies is shown very clearly in the cost of AIDS treatment. The drugs necessary to keep AIDS under control cost more than $12,000 a year. The "drug cocktail," a combination of AZT and protease inhibitors, can render AIDS a manageable disease in many. Instead of simply sedating patients as they die painfully, the only therapy in the middle 1980s, doctors can now offer many AIDS patients hope that they can manage the disease in a manner that is similar to the way patients with high blood pressure deal with their disease. That is to say, although the disease may eventually still kill them, the length and quality of their lives will be greatly enhanced. This is quite literally a life-saving cocktail of drugs, but it is one that forces many people into debt or requires that they quit work in order to qualify for Medicaid's health coverage. While bankruptcy is better than death, we can safely say that for AIDS patients this is an expensive necessity.

To counter some of the preceding negative characteristics, it must be said that the prescription drug industry can also lay claim to lowering health costs in some areas and to improving lives in nearly all areas. Drugs treat some diseases that either used to require surgery or, worse, that simply went untreated. There are drugs, also, that improve the quality of life and do so in a number of important areas. Some nonemergency heart conditions can now be treated with drug therapies rather than $30,000–$50,000 bypass or $5,000–$10,000 catheterization surgeries. Although the drugs are expensive and cannot be used when a patient is suffering from near-complete arterial blockages, they can slowly open up the arteries, and they have been shown to have a success rate that is comparable to more invasive alternatives.

In other areas new drugs have simply improved life. From ailments as irritating as seasonal allergies to those as trivial as heartburn, to those as debilitating as asthma, new drugs have made the lives of people of all ages much better. While seasonal allergies and heartburn are never life-threatening, people's lives are changed when they are successfully treated.

Before the invention of nonsedating antihistamines such as Seldane[3] and Claritin, allergy sufferers like me were hard pressed to accomplish much out of doors in the spring and fall. These medications let allergy sufferers play golf, mow the lawn, and do many other enjoyable and productive things that used to only induce fits of sneezing. Claritin was also shown to be safe enough that the FDA allowed the drug to go "over the counter" (meaning no prescription is required) in 2003. Before the new antiheartburn medications such as Nexium,[4] spicy, high-acid, or rich dishes were simply off-limits for many middle-aged people. While it may seem trivial to the young, being unable to eat favorite foods affects people's quality of life. Being able to eat pizza, Cajun wings, or a piquant sauce does not rank high in the sphere of important medical issues, but being able to indulge once in a while does make life a little more enjoyable.

These latter cases are also not life-threatening, but they do represent serious quality-of-life issues. The drugs that treat these ailments may not be critical to life but they represent significant advances for people. Some would classify them as luxuries, but compared to not having the treatments available, others consider them to be inexpensive.

---

[3]This drug was pulled from the market because it was shown to interact in potentially fatal ways with heart medications.
[4]In extreme cases this drug has reduced the risk of esophageal cancer.

Why then do prescription drugs get such a bad rap? It is the reality that drug prices have increased significantly faster than inflation along with perceptions that economists claim are not well-founded. Our perceptions tell us that the costs of prescription drugs are much higher than the actual 10 percent of medical spending for which they are responsible. For every dollar of expense incurred in hospital or doctor visits, less than 25 cents is paid by the patient in out-of-pocket expenses. On the other hand, more than 50 cents on the dollar is picked up by the patient for prescription drugs. This leaves the patient more aware of and sensitive to increases in drug costs than increases in the costs of hospitals and doctors.

Price Controls: Are They the Answer?

Another of the facts that must be faced with regard to drug prices is that they are higher in the United States than anywhere else in the world. That is because in most other countries drug prices are regulated. Whether the drug prices themselves are controlled or the profits from their sales are controlled, people in other countries pay much less for drugs than we do. Go to El Paso, Texas, and price a drug, and you will find it at half price or less across the border in Mexico. You find the same thing in Detroit relative to Windsor, Canada. The drug is not safer in El Paso or Detroit; it is only more expensive. As a matter of fact, it is often in exactly the same package. Prices are lower in other parts of the world and one of the reasons is certainly price controls.

Would we be better off if the government controlled the price of drugs? Probably not. The world's drug inventors eye the profit that they get in the United States when they pour billions into their scientists and laboratories. If they could not make a profit in the United States, there would be no place to make one and they would not put the money into innovation. To mix metaphors, the United States is the drug industry's cash cow; by controlling prices, we would be killing the golden goose just as she is producing some very important life-improving and life-saving eggs.

The law with respect to prescription drugs is in flux. It has been against the law for companies to buy prescription drugs in a foreign country and resell them in the United States. Otherwise, a drug company could sell its products to a Canadian company at a low price determined by Canadian law. That Canadian company would then resell them to a U.S. retailer, thereby avoiding the high price in the United States. This would have the same effect as allowing Canada to control U.S. prices. This law has been under review for some time.

FDA Approval: Too Stringent or Too Lax?

The approval for, and the regulation of, prescription drugs is performed by the Food and Drug Administration (FDA). In the early 1990s the FDA was under scrutiny for not allowing drugs to come to market quickly enough. The issue then was magnified by the excruciatingly slow process of getting AIDS drugs approved. As described earlier, the FDA's process is a multistage one where a drug is tested first for its safety and then for its effectiveness. A drug can be marketed only if both meet a high scientific standard.

While this sounds very good, the problem is that people will die of afflictions for which there are already existing drug therapies. For example, in the early 1990s the AIDS-combating protease inhibitors had been shown to be safe but scientists had not yet had the time to show their effectiveness. Reasoning that unforeseen drug interactions were the least of their worries, dying AIDS patients wanted the drugs immediately. The problem of overly stringent FDA regulation is that people die when they could be saved with a less stringent process.

During the middle 1990s the FDA began to experiment with a fast-track approval process. Here, drugs that are shown to be safe get an expedited review for effectiveness. The problem is that the initial safety review is conducted using a relatively small sample of people, while the effectiveness review is conducted using a much larger one. Adverse drug interactions and relatively rare and unforeseen safety issues come to light during this effectiveness testing. Expediting the effectiveness testing causes some safety issues to be missed, and as a result the FDA sometimes has to subsequently pull drugs off the shelves. This was Fen-Phen's fate and may end up being the fate of all Cox-2 inhibitors.

This is a prime example of how the marginal analysis of economics can be used to aid in decision making. The marginal benefit of increasing FDA stringency is the decrease in the health problems accruing to those who take approved drugs that later are found to be unsafe. The marginal cost of increasing FDA stringency is the foregone increase in the health of people who could have been treated who were not. The optimal degree of FDA stringency is where the marginal cost equals the marginal benefit.

Whether a particular drug goes over the counter is also a matter for FDA approval. When a new drug shows that it is sufficiently safe that it can be used by consumers with little or no consultation with a doctor, the FDA will approve it for use over the counter. When that occurs, the price of the drugs falls precipitously because it can be more easily mass-marketed. Whether that translates into consumers saving money is another story. It is ironic that when Claritin went over the counter in 2003, consumers without prescription drug coverage on their health insurance saw the price fall from more than $100 per month to around $35 per month, while those with insurance saw

the cost to them rise because no insurance companies cover over-the-counter drugs. Former Claritin users with insurance were then motivated to seek more expensive prescription solutions such as Allegra. Insurance companies have since responded to this trend by requiring over-the-counter options be tried before prescription options are tried.

Summary

You are now able to apply the concept of monopoly as well as consumer and producer surplus to the analysis of the costs of prescription drugs. You are able to apply those concepts to see the reasons most health economists view prescription drugs as relatively inexpensive even while most noneconomists view them as very expensive. You also understand why it is that most health economists do not favor price controls on prescription drugs. Last, you understand how economists see the issue of FDA approval and the appropriate degree of stringency.

Key Terms

deadweight loss, 221   orphan drug, 219   patent, 219

Quiz Yourself

1. The prescription drug industry is characterized by products that have
   a. Low fixed costs and low marginal costs.
   b. Low fixed costs and high marginal costs.
   c. High fixed costs and low marginal costs.
   d. High fixed costs and high marginal costs.

2. A patent is necessary to motivate innovation in areas where the innovation is
   a. Costly to figure out and easily copied.
   b. Cheap to figure out and difficult to copy.
   c. Costly to figure out and difficult to copy.
   d. Cheap to figure out and cheap to copy.

3. The reason orphan drug laws were created was that the motivation to invent drugs for these diseases was
   a. Much greater than normal because prices could be high.
   b. Much less than normal because prices would be too low.
   c. Much less than normal because firms anticipated few sales.
   d. Much greater than normal because firms anticipated high sales.

4. The market form for a new drug in an area where there are no competitors is
   a. Perfect competition.
   b. Monopolistc competition.
   c. Oligopoly.
   d. Monopoly.

5. The market form for a new drug in an area that has one other drug is
   a. Perfect competition.
   b. Monopolistc competition.
   c. Oligopoly.
   d. Monopoly.

6. The approval process for new drugs, if governed by economic thinking, should set stringency standards so that the _____ equals the _____.
   a. Total cost; total benefit.
   b. Average cost; average benefit.
   c. Marginal cost; marginal benefit.
   d. Cost of production; revenue from sales.

7. When an existing prescription drug goes over the counter
   a. Everyone wins.
   b. Drug companies win but consumers lose.
   c. Drug companies lose but consumers win.
   d. Drug companies likely win because of the increase in sales and consumers may win depending on whether prescriptions are covered by insurance.

Think about This

Vioxx and other Cox-2 inhibitors were invented because the existing pain medications (when taken for persistent pain) did damage to the lining of the stomach. After years of clinical trials they were determined to be safe. It was only after use by millions of people that we become aware of the fact that they affected the heart. Under what conditions should their makers be legally liable for these side effects?

Talk about This

When a disease has no cure, people with the disease have no options. Suppose a prescription drug is invented but is so expensive that some patients cannot afford it. Are we better off with a drug being available, but only to those with insurance? What are the social consequences of this?

For More Insight See

Scherer, F. M, "Pricing, Profits, and Technological Progress in the Pharmaceutical Industry," *Journal of Economic Perspectives* 7, no. 3 (Summer 1993), pp. 97–115.

Behind the Numbers

Health expenditure, 2003; Statistical Abstract of the United States; health and nutrition—http://www.census.gov/prod/2004pubs/04statab/health.pdf.

Chapter **21**

The Economics of Crime

Convicted criminals often wind up in maximum-security prisons. *Source: © Hank Morgan Photo Researchers, Inc.*

Chapter Objectives

After reading this chapter you should be able to

Understand how economics can contribute to the debate over crime and crime control.

Know who generally commits crime and why.

Understand why economists who study crime often assume that criminals are rational.

Analyze the cost of crime to society and whether we are currently spending the right amount, focusing on the right criminals, emphasizing the right crimes, and enforcing the right sentences.

Understand how an economist looks at issues of crime control.

Chapter Outline

Who Commits Crimes and Why

The Rational Criminal Model

The Costs of Crime

Optimal Spending on Crime Control

Summary

Crime is a problem that does not naturally spring to mind as one for which economists would have much of value to contribute. Other than early work on crime by Nobel Prize–winning economist Gary Becker, we have not used much of our research time and money on this subject. Still, there are areas where economic analysis is uniquely suited to deal with the problems of crime. For instance, a potential criminal makes a decision to commit a crime based on the income potential of legal work, the booty to be gained from the crime, and the chance and consequence of getting caught. Couched in different words, this is not all that different from an investment decision in which small gains in safe assets are compared to large gains in risky assets. When looked at this way, economics and criminology have some important links.

The first thing we do in exploring the economics of crime is to look at who commits crime. We then see what a theoretical "investment-like" decision would tell us about who we should expect will commit crimes. Next, we use cost–benefit analysis to discuss how the noncriminal public should devote resources in the areas of crime prevention, detection, apprehension, and punishment. Last, we use economics to study whether the goals of life imprisonment and the death penalty have the desired effects of deterring or preventing future crime.

WHO COMMITS CRIMES AND WHY

Most crime is committed by young men who are socially and economically disadvantaged. The victims of their crimes are disproportionately from the same group. Young black men, for example, overwhelmingly commit crimes against other young black men. Moreover, when we examine the disadvantages attributed to racism and compound them with the economic disadvantage of poor job opportunities, the problem seems to magnify. For instance, while white people are killed by other whites in about the number that would be predicted by the overall population (86 of 100), 94 of every 100 murdered blacks are killed by other blacks. In this case the number predicted by the distribution of the population as a whole would be 12 out of 100, rather than 94 out of 100.

Crime statistics generally come to us from two sources: police reports and surveys of crime victims. Those who view the police to be racially biased may argue that statistics that come from police reports are racially biased, but it is hard to believe that crime victims would have an interest in biasing their reports. Falsely reporting an attacker to the police would diminish the likelihood that the perpetrator would be caught and doing so in a survey would not serve any useful purpose. No matter whether you measure crime by looking at arrest reports sent to the FBI or by looking at victimization surveys, the data indicate conclusively that minorities commit far more crimes than their 24 percent proportion of the populace. The question is not whether poor blacks, Hispanics, and other needy members of minority communities commit more crimes, but why.

THE RATIONAL CRIMINAL MODEL

In the late 1960s Gary Becker came up with a model of criminal behavior that explained crime in terms of a simple investment decision. According to Becker, the decision to commit a crime is one of risk versus return. The low-return investment, work at a legal job, has a low return, but the worker carries no risk of being arrested. On the other hand, the high-return investment, stealing or selling illegal goods, has a high return, but it puts the thief or drug dealer at risk of being caught and punished. In this context, a criminal is no different from an investment banker who is deciding whether to invest in tried-and-true U.S. Treasury bonds or a risky initial public offering of an Internet stock. Just as investors have a portfolio that contains a mix of risky and safe assets, you would expect to see that most criminals would have legitimate jobs as well. This is, in fact, the case.

We should take some time to explain what economists mean when they use the word "rational." To an economist, if people know what it is they want, know the constraints they face, know the costs of getting what they want, and choose to proceed with getting it, then they are rational. This does not mean that these rational people will do what society thinks is best for them. It means only that their actions are consistent with their goals, constraints, and costs. By this standard all but the insane are rational.

Crime Falls When Legal Income Rises

If a person has the potential for earning a higher income through legal means than illegal ones, then the person would be just plain stupid to pick the risky and lower-earning alternative of a life of crime. If you have the skills to be a doctor or lawyer and have a six-figure salary, the alternative of clearing $50,000 while selling cocaine is not all that attractive. Thus the rational criminal theory correctly predicts that people with high legal incomes are not likely to be prevalent in the criminal and prison population.

This conclusion may seem trivially easy to come to, but what is not trivial is how a person with a set of intermediate skills, earning $10 an hour, or about $20,000 a year, would treat the issue. To be at that level of income in today's society, most people have completed high school. It is therefore significant that less than half of those in the prison population graduated from high school, and 33 percent were not working at a legal job just prior to being arrested. Weighing a $20,000 a year job against a high-risk, high-income criminal life is hard, and the decision could go either way.

A full-time minimum-wage worker, earning approximately $10,500 a year, would see the opportunity of earning a high criminal income as a significantly greater temptation than would a person making much more. We would expect that greater economic alternatives in the legal realm would translate into less crime, and fewer opportunities would lead to more crime. Why, then, did crime escalate during the sustained economic growth in the middle to late 1980s and fall during the sustained growth of the middle to late 1990s? The answer lies in the placing of economic opportunities.

If our rational criminal theory is accurate, raising a middle-, upper-middle-, or high-income person's economic prospects should have little to no effect on crime. Even without a growth in income, such a person would have virtually no incentive to turn to crime. An increase in income would simply lessen a trivially small temptation and would have no appreciable impact on crime. On the other hand, if the economic prospects changed at the low end of the economic scale, the effect on crime would likely be substantial.

In the decade and a half from the mid-1970s to the early 1990s, income inequality rose. Average income rose because the upper half of the income scale did very well, while people with little education and few job skills saw their real spending power remain stagnant or fall.[1] What you would expect to see from our rational criminal model did, in fact, happen. Crime increased substantially through the period, and it did so more in the lower-income groups than in the higher-income groups.

After the recession of 1990–1991, however, when crime was at a near-term high, the economic prospects of low-skill workers began to increase. The minimum wage was raised from $3.35 to $5.15 during the period, and both the overall unemployment rate and the unemployment rate for minorities and for low-skill workers fell. At the same time, either because of coincidence or because the model is right, crime fell, and it fell quickly.

The rational criminal model has a more difficult time explaining the general increase in crime during the 1960s, when incomes rose both in general and within the poor communities. This highlights an important thing to keep in mind when it comes to using economics to explain complex social phenomena. Sometimes a change in social norms, an area better left to sociologists, or a change in moral values, an area better left to the clergy, is at the heart of these social phenomena. Economics is then less capable of explaining them.

Crime Falls When the Likelihood and Consequences of Getting Caught Rise

The other variable that can change things in this rational criminal model is the probability and consequences of getting caught. We know that crime pays when you do not get caught. We also know that choosing to become a criminal becomes less attractive when the chances of getting away with crime diminish and when the potential punishment becomes more severe. It is usually true that if you knew you would get caught, you would choose a legal occupation. Sometimes, however, this is not true. For women who possess low levels of education and few marketable skills, for example, the occupation of prostitute entails getting caught regularly and going to jail for a few days as a part of the cost of doing business. The important thing here is that even given the lost time in jail, for such women, prostitution pays better than legal work.

To deter potential criminals from committing crimes, there are two things that we can do. We can make the chances of meeting punishment greater, and we can make the punishment more severe. In its simplest terms, the first implies that by having more police, judges, and jails we can increase the likelihood that criminals will be caught, be convicted quickly, and go to jail. The second suggests that we make the sentences longer or the fines greater.

Though these may seem like two aspects of the same approach, in part because we are talking about increasing spending on the same kinds of people, they are really distinct in their intent. The first is intended to make criminals less confident that they will get away with their activities. Depending on where in the judicial system the money is

---

[1] Of course, the material in Chapter 6 lays out the case that because the CPI overstates the effects of inflation, real incomes for the poor did not fall but rose slightly.

spent, this can provide additional funding for cops on the street, making detection and apprehension more likely, or it can provide funds for greater numbers of effective prosecutors, who may garner greater numbers of postarrest guilty verdicts. This differs from spending more money on prisons and allowing judges to sentence convicted criminals to longer terms.

Problems with the Rationality Assumption

Criminologists and sociologists have a hard time granting the assumption that the decision to become a criminal is a rational economic decision made by people capable of evaluating complex choices. In support of their view, you only have to look at the percentage of crime that is seemingly senseless. School shootings are not explainable using economic methods. One of the main criticisms of economic models is that they assume too much intellectual capacity on the part of humans. For instance, it might be argued that if criminals could evaluate the options as rationally as economists claim they can, they probably would be smart enough not to have to turn to crime. In any event, economists use the idea of the "rational criminal" when looking at criminality; and, as was seen above, the rational criminal model is often consistent with what we know about crime.

THE COSTS OF CRIME

We spend a total of $147 billion a year on the police, the judiciary, and prisons. Every year 14 million persons are arrested and some 360,000 of that number get jail time. Currently there are more than 2.1 million Americans in state or federal jails and prisons. This is all done in response to the 1.4 million violent and 10.4 million nonviolent crimes that are reported each year. When we see these numbers, we wonder whether the money we spend is worth it and whether the distribution of spending on police, justice, and prisons is a good one.

If we put any faith in the model we have been discussing, we are convinced that by spending money in this arena, we can change the probability of a criminal's being punished and the extent of the punishment. Of course, we could also talk about spending the money to raise the legal income potential of people. Some people argue, for example, that we should take money that is earmarked for building new prisons and put it into education and social programs like Head Start and employment training programs that might help people to get out of poverty legally. Others point to data that indicate that these programs do not work and suggest that building prisons is the best of a set of bad alternatives.

On the central questions of whether we are spending the right amount of money on crime control and whether we are spending on the right mix of control mechanisms, we need to examine how much crime there is and how much it costs us. Using a variety of criminological surveys, we know that, of the 11.7 million crimes reported annually, more than twice that number are actually committed. Though most murders get reported, robberies, rapes, and other crimes tend not to be universally reported. Some of this may be attributed to the rationality of crime victims. If the chances of catching the perpetrator of a crime are low and the psychological and monetary costs of testifying are high, then it is quite likely that some victims will not report crimes committed against them.

How Much Does an Average Crime Cost?

When a crime is committed there are several different kinds of costs to consider. If we could put a dollar value on the average crime, we could, at least theoretically, come to an estimate of the cost of crime in general. The first and most obvious cost of crime is the value of items taken or stolen. This is fairly easily measured but it is not always very important, especially if the crime is a form of assault rather than a form of theft. The victim's loss of actual or potential income is harder to estimate, since data on the number of work days lost owing to crime are rarely gathered. Moreover, there is no way of knowing whether a crime causes people to be less ambitious or productive than they would have been. The monetary value of psychological trauma that comes with victimization is also difficult to estimate. Though some try to assess psychological costs by looking at settlements in civil suits, economists are not usually comfortable extrapolating this far. By far the most controversial aspect of this accounting for the costs of crime are attempts to put dollar values on the human lives lost to murder and manslaughter.

If we simply ignore all of the estimated costs of pain and suffering and lives lost, then the cost of the average crime has been estimated at a little more than $500. Adding at least the "pain and suffering" costs, some economists have estimated the costs at between $2,000 and $3,000 per average crime.

How Much Crime Does an Average Criminal Commit?

We can use these figures to estimate the cost of letting criminals go free and compare that to the cost of keeping them in jail. If we know how many crimes the average criminal commits, we can multiply the average cost per crime by the average number of crimes committed in a year to come up with the costs imposed on society by the early release of a still violent criminal. Looked at another way, we can compute the average cost of not catching and imprisoning a criminal.

Even when we interpret sophisticated criminological surveys, we find that the average number of crimes committed by the average criminal ranges all the way from 180 down to 12. Most economists are comfortable with estimates in the range of 15 to 20 crimes. If we assume for a moment that crime would stay the same if we eliminated all expenditures on law enforcement, the average savings from keeping average criminals off the street would range from 15 crimes per criminal times $500 per crime, or $7,500, to 20 crimes per criminal times $3,000 per crime, or $60,000.

OPTIMAL SPENDING ON CRIME CONTROL

What Is the Optimal Amount to Spend?

The average cost of holding a criminal in jail is $27,000 per year. Assuming that crime rates would rise if we eliminated all expenditures on law enforcement—either by the average criminal's committing more crimes or because otherwise law-abiding citizens turned to crime—it is quite clear that the money we spend on prisons is worth it. Even though more than 2 million people are in jail and prison at a cost of $33 billion a year, this may be a good expenditure.

The question of whether we spend the optimal amount on keeping people in prisons, however, remains to be answered. At this time, there are far more than double the number of felons on the street than in prison. These are people who have served their sentences, been released on parole, or were never imprisoned in the first place. If they are committing crimes at a rate similar to the 15 to 20 crimes a year that incarcerated criminals were committing, then we have too few people in prison.

Of key concern to economists is not necessarily whether the total amount spent on crime control exceeds the total amount saved from preventing crime, but whether

we are spending the correct amount. At its heart, the problem is exactly the same as the profit-maximizing problem for a business firm. The mere fact that a firm's revenues exceed its costs does not mean that profit is as high as it could be. That means we are less interested in the costs and benefits of capturing, trying, and incarcerating the "average" criminal than we are in incarcerating the "marginal" criminal.

Think of it this way. Suppose we catch a prolific thief who costs society $100,000 a year, and it costs $27,000 a year to lock him up. Now suppose we catch a part-time thief who costs society only $10,000 a year, and it still costs $27,000 a year to lock him up. The intermediate or average thief costs society $55,000 each year, and we spend $27,000 per year keeping him locked up. This does not mean we should not have locked up the part-time thief. The marginal benefit to society of locking him up was less than the marginal cost.

Applying this information to the problem of optimal crime control means that we would need to look at who the people are who get arrested and put away when we increase spending on criminal justice. The practical problem is much harder to figure out than it is for a firm. In business we can see how much extra material and labor costs go into producing another unit of output and judge whether that is greater than the price, but we cannot easily determine which extra criminals are caught as a result of our spending more on police. Are these criminals more or less prolific than the average criminal caught before the spending increase? For this reason, much of the research on crime assumes that the "marginal" criminal is just like the "average" criminal.

Is the Money Spent in the Right Way?

Whether we spend the right amount of money is interesting but equally interesting is whether we spend the money in the right way. Again, marginal analysis is of use. If we spend $167 billon on the system, the allocation between police, justice, and incarceration should depend on how effective the marginal dollar is in combating crime in each category. If the optimal distribution is accomplished, the marginal benefit of a dollar should be equal in the three areas.

Are the Right People in Jail?

Of course there is the related issue of whether the right people are in jail. Of the more than 2 million people who are in prisons, just under half are there for violent crimes. The remainder are there for nonviolent crimes

Things That Matter in Crime

An interesting investigation of this issue was conducted by economist Steven Levitt. What he found was that "community policing," whereby police are in constant communication with the communities and subcommunities that they patrol, was less effective than simply increasing their numbers. What this implies is that visibility deters crime more than anything the police actually do.

Similarly, he found that stiffening the sentence for crime had little deterrent effect, but having more criminals locked up longer decreased crime. The reason for this is deceptively obvious. He argues that the patterns of drug dealers, for instance, flies in the face of the rational criminal model. These criminals are less apt to react to increases in potential punishment when they have already chosen an occupation where death at the hands of competitors is an occupational hazard. What he found was that longer and more certain sentences worked because they prevented the convicted criminal from offending again any time soon.

In terms of economics and crime, what Levitt found was that the significant decrease in crime in the 1990s was less associated with the growing economy of the time, than it was of higher degree of "wantedness" of the children born 15 to 20 years before. In one of those conclusions that only an economist could come up with (see the discussion of how smokers help Social Security in Chapter 16), Levitt argues that the legalization of abortion in the 1970s increased the proportion of children born into homes where they were wanted. The argument, that some economists have taken issue with, is that children born into homes in which they are not wanted will grow up to commit more crime than children born into homes in which they are wanted.

such as burglary, drug possession, and drug distribution. If these prison spaces are being used for drug offenders rather than violent criminals or thieves, perhaps the wrong people are in jail. If we release violent criminals in order to make room in prisons for drug users, we will have to either build more prisons or let the drug users go.

In recognition of this choice, state and local governments decided to go on a prison-building spree. In Texas,

FIGURE 21.1   Marginal cost and marginal benefit analysis and crime.

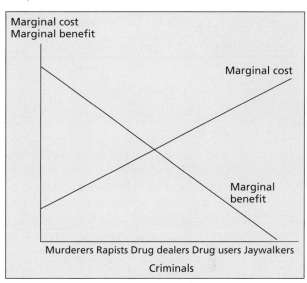

for example, prison capacity during the 1980s and 1990s was nearly doubling every four years. This phenomenon was certainly not confined to any one state, as state after state went to "truth in sentencing" laws that required criminals to serve at least 85 percent of their sentence. In Florida and Texas felons had been serving less than a third of their sentences, a disparity these states and others found unacceptable.

What Laws Should We Rigorously Enforce?

In a formal way, economists look at crime control measures from a cost–benefit point of view. In Figure 21.1 the vertical axis represents the amount of marginal benefit and marginal cost associated with catching, adjudicating, and imprisoning an additional criminal. We will make three assumptions:

1. The marginal benefits are decreasing for each additional criminal.
2. We will deal with serious crimes first and petty crimes last.
3. The dollar benefits of preventing these crimes will fall.

Furthermore, we will assume that the marginal cost of dealing with criminals increases because the petty criminals violating trivial laws are assumed to be more expensive to catch and convict than are criminals whose crimes are more serious. This assumption is predicated on the idea that we would have to have very many and, most important, less competent police[2] to catch such violators.

Figure 21.1 indicates that it makes sense to spend the money to catch, prosecute, and imprison all murderers, rapists, and high-end drug dealers. It also indicates that it makes no sense to do the same for jaywalkers, drug users, and low-end drug dealers. Though this picture is simplistic in its assumptions, you can see, roughly, how an economist reasons on the issue of crime control. Spend the money on the really bad guys and do not spend it on the not-so-bad guys.

That leaves one last issue to deal with in determining how we spend our law enforcement dollars: How do we divide the money among the various sectors? States, for example, have spent a growing part of their budgets to deal with crime and in doing so have changed the percentage that they allocate to the different sectors. The increase in resources has gone mainly to prisons and police, with a smaller percentage of money allocated to adjudication. Competent police are more effective in deterring criminals and apprehending criminals who have not yet been deterred. It also means that people sentenced stay in jail longer. The downside of this is that more cases are plea-bargained than ever before.

Since the increases in spending have not funded all sectors of the system evenly, criminals are more likely to be caught, plea to a crime that is less severe than the one they actually committed, and go to jail. The length of term they face has probably increased because 85 percent of a short sentence is often longer than 33 percent of a long one. Part of the reduction in crime since the early 1990s is also attributable to this policy of sending greater numbers of criminals to prison. A small minority of criminals (6 percent) commits a majority (50 percent) of the crime, and they now must stay in prison longer. Though estimates vary, an increase of 10 percent in the prison population has been shown to result in a 4 percent to 6 percent decrease in crime. Whereas some of this may be deterrence, it is likely that simply holding criminals prevents them from committing the crimes they would have committed had they been left on the streets.

What Is the Optimal Sentence?

One of the major debates of our time is whether criminals convicted of murder and other of the most heinous crimes should be put to death or be locked up with no opportunity for parole. While many religious leaders and lay persons alike approach this as a moral issue, economists again tend to look at it from the standpoint of the costs and benefits. If you sentence men and women to death, the sentences are carried out only after a long and drawn-out appeal process. Even then, many death row inmates die in their prison cots rather than facing injection, asphyxiation, or electrocution. In economic terms we have to decide whether spending a lot of money over a 10-year period is worth the savings in imprisonment expenses. Life sentences, which are routinely given in murder cases, also have cost issues to face. If a 75-year-old is released from prison, is he or she likely to again become a menace to society?

To examine whether the death penalty saves money or costs money we need to recall the Chapter 7 concept of present value. Suppose it would take $1 million invested now to make the payments to house, adjudicate appeals, and put to death a condemned inmate. Suppose it would cost less than $1 million invested now to simply house the inmate from the time he or she is sentenced to the time that inmate would have died if given a life sentence. In such a circumstance the death penalty costs money. Otherwise it saves money. This of course assumes that the death penalty is not a deterrent. It may also be that it costs $1 million in present value to execute a person and $900,000 to imprison the same person for life but that we get $100,000 or more worth of satisfaction knowing that the worst of the bad guys got his or her due.

The cost–benefit trade-off is important also in establishing sentence length. Since nearly no crime is committed by 80-year-olds, does it make sense to sentence people to life in prison? Why not let them out when the chances of their committing a crime have gone away? It is not hard to figure that, as time goes on, a person violent enough to kill at age 18 is not as likely to commit murder at 50 and is even less likely to at 70. This point may not be worth considering since the life expectancy in a prison is such that few inmates sentenced to life live long enough to outlive their own violent tendencies. Prison life is hard and the food and medical care are not geared to keeping people healthy in their "golden years." Ironically, this makes the death penalty even less economically sensible since the "lifer's" life is not going to be that long.

---

[2]We assume they are likely to be less competent because cities hire the more competent of their applicant pool first and these are all gone when it comes time to hire more.

Summary

You should now understand how economics, and in particular the use of marginal benefit–marginal cost analysis, can contribute to the debate over crime and crime control. Besides knowing who it is that generally commits crime and why, you have seen that economists often model criminals as rational human actors who are influenced by the risks and rewards of their decisions. You have seen how much crime costs society and how much we spend to control it. You have seen how an economist looks at issues of crime control to answer questions about whether we are spending the right amount on the right criminals and the right crimes and enforcing the right sentences.

Quiz Yourself

1. If judges had to be trained as economists before taking their position, they might use _____ analysis when deciding on the right sentence.
   a. Marginal.
   b. Punitive.
   c. Religious.
   d. Average.

2. The optimal level of police protection would compare the _____ with the _____.
   a. Marginal cost of hiring an additional officer; marginal benefit of crime reduction.
   b. Average cost of all officers; average benefit per officer of crime reduction.
   c. Total cost of all officers; average benefit of crime reduction.
   d. Length of the average sentence; history of sentences, per crime.

3. Economist Steven Levitt has drawn an unexpected connection between crime and _____.
   a. Obesity.
   b. The political party in office.
   c. Abortion rights.
   d. Global warming.

4. The average cost per crime has been estimated at between
   a. $500 and $2,500.
   b. $1,000 and $10,000.
   c. $10,000 and $100,000.
   d. $100,000 and $1,000,000.

5. To an economist, the correct distribution of money among police, the justice system, and prisons is one that
   a. Sets an equal amount to each.
   b. Sets the amount each gets equal to its average benefit.
   c. Sets the amount each gets so that none is wasted.
   d. Sets the amount each gets so that no other element could get better use (in terms of crime reduction) of the marginal dollar.

6. The rational crime model explains crimes of
   a. Passion.
   b. Stupidity.
   c. Profit.
   d. Love.

7. The rational criminal model draws a parallel to the thought processes of
   a. Investors.
   b. Educators.
   c. Law enforcement officers.
   d. Politicians.

Think about This

The rational criminal model is often invoked to explain the behavior of drug dealers and their pushers. Economist Steven Levitt disputes this by suggesting that drug dealers engage in behaviors that are just as irrational as those who play the lottery. Is drug dealing rational?

Talk about This

Under what circumstances would you engage in a criminal activity? Would your actions be rational?

For More Insight See

Journal of Economic Perspectives 10, no. 1 (Winter 1996). See articles by John J. DiIulio; and Richard B. Freeman and Isaac Ehrlich, pp. 3–8.

Levitt, Steven D., *Journal of Economic Perspectives* 18, no. 1 (Winter 2004), "Understanding Why Crime Fell in the 1990s: Four Factors that Explain the Decline and Six that Do Not."

Behind the Numbers

Federal justice system statistics on crime; Federal justice system expenditures—http://www.ojp.usdoj.gov/bjs/eande.htm.

Number of arrests and inmates, Bureau of Justice Statistics—http://www.ojp.usdoj.gov/bjs/prisons.htm.

Characteristics of victims, criminals, and types of crime committed, U.S. Department of Justice; Bureau of Justice—Statistics; crime and victim statistics—http://www.ojp.usdoj.gov/bjs/cvict.htm; http://www.ojp.usdoj.gov/bjs/homicide/race.htm.

Chapter **22**

Education

By funding this young girl's education, the government is investing in human capital. *Source: © Ellen B. Senisi/ Photo Researchers, Inc.*

Chapter Objectives

After reading this chapter you should be able to

Understand that education is an investment and that this investment not only pays dividends to the person getting the education, but also positively affects society at large.

Participate in the debate over whether spending more on education will yield more significant returns.

Understand the economics behind the school reform issues and why many economists argue that the current structure of education prevents more money from doing any good.

See why a college education is more costly than a K–12 education and why for most college students it is a wise investment.

Chapter Outline

Investments in Human Capital

Should We Spend More?

School Reform Issues

College and University Education

Summary

From a strictly economic perspective, the amount of time and money we spend on educating ourselves and our fellow citizens is amazing. Required to stay in school until we are 16, we are strongly encouraged to graduate from high school, and, when we do, we are offered substantial subsidies to get some form of higher education. Some of us even press on to earn graduate degrees. In the end, it is easily possible that we have spent the first third of our lives acquiring an education. Our parents and our government have encouraged us to invest in ourselves even while contributing nothing of substance to society during that time. Since most people retire before they die, the typical postgraduate educated person has fewer than 40 years to earn enough to pay back, figuratively, what he or she invested in formal education.

In general, parents and grandparents are staunch supporters of schools, at least financially. People without children in school have other reasons for supporting them. In this chapter we explore some of the reasons people give for supporting education. We try to determine whether society is getting its money's worth for elementary and secondary education. We also examine whether you and other college students are getting a reasonable return on your investment in higher education.

In considering the elementary and secondary level, we look at how much money is spent on education and attempt to determine whether taxpayers are getting what they pay for. To that end we plot measures of cost, and we look at the ratio of the numbers of students to teachers. Next we examine measures of success such as students' performances on standardized tests and the numbers of degrees that are granted. Finally, we ask why college costs so much and whether it is worth it to get a degree.

INVESTMENTS IN HUMAN CAPITAL

In Chapters 4 and 5 we spoke of capital as though the concept were confined to machines. In this chapter we

human capital
The ability of a person to create goods and services.

turn to another form of capital, **human capital.** This refers to the ability of a person to create goods and services. Education and training play an important role in developing human capital.

Present Value Analysis

In Chapter 7's discussion of present value and investments we learned it is possible to invest too little or too much in anything, including human capital. Determin-

net present value
The difference between the present value of benefits and the present value of costs.

ing the right amount depends on the value of the **net present value,** the difference between the present value of benefits and the present value of costs.

The investment we make in the education of our own children we do out of love for them, but it also makes sense from an economic point of view. If there were no

"free"[1] public schools, we would look first at the present value of costs of educating a child from kindergarten through high school. We would then subtract that from the present value of the child's increased earning potential because of that education. If at that point we found that the net was positive, then we would conclude, that for the parent, the investment would be a wise one.

Again, from the view of the parent, an even more refined look at this analysis would subtract out those costs that would occur anyway. Consider the modern family with two working parents or a single parent. If there were no public school, they would have day-care expenses whether or not the child were educated. That means, at the margin, a cost of educating the child is the difference between the tuition to the school and the day-care costs. This reduces the relevant costs, and it makes education an even better investment.

External Benefits

Of course, K–12 education is public and it has been for so long that we may not even think of asking why. There are societal as well as economic reasons for having free public education. Societally, benefits accrue to us all from having children become educated, whether or not they are our own children. Economically, benefits accrue to us because people who are educated are less likely to be on welfare or commit crimes against us and are more likely to be productive citizens who pay more in taxes than they cost in government benefits. An additional benefit that we derive from public school education is that having children of all races, ethnic groups, religions, and

external benefits
Benefits that accrue to someone other than the consumer or producer of the good or service.

income classes in the same schools may foster social stability. Thus the **external benefits** of K–12 education justify having a considerable subsidy to that education.

We can use our supply and demand diagram to illustrate the inefficiency of just having unsubsidized private education. Consider Figure 22.1 and what it suggests the price of education should be to the parents of the children to be educated. The price is the annual tuition and the

---

[1]Free is in quotes for two reasons. First, some states require a textbook rental fee that, in Indiana at least, is more than $100 per student per year. This fee is waived for students qualifying for the Federal School Lunch program. Second, the taxpayer pays for this public education. Thus "free" should be read as "free to the parents except for any fees that might be involved."

FIGURE 22.1   External benefits of K–12 education.

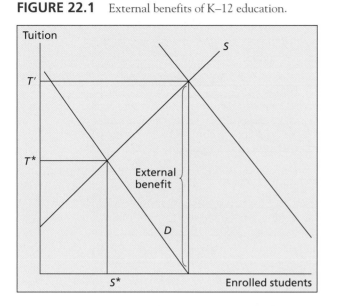

quantity is the number of kids educated in a year. At low tuition rates, more will invest in education, and when it is free, everyone will take advantage of it. The resulting demand curve is downward sloping, but if tuition is low, schools will be willing to educate fewer students.

The equilibrium tuition $T*$ and the equilibrium number of enrolled students $S*$ are what the unsubsidized market would yield. If there is an external benefit of the size shown, then the optimal number of students is much greater than the market amount. In this case the optimal number of students is everyone and the optimal price is zero. This means that taxpayers will have to pay the T' per student. From a theoretical point of view, this does not necessarily mean that the school must be government-owned and operated. In the United States, except for some experiments in Milwaukee and other cities, this is precisely what it means.

Specific estimates of the magnitude of this external impact have started to emerge. Economists Lance Lochner and Enrico Moretti estimate that the impact of crime reduction is between 12 and 26 percent of the private benefit to education.

SHOULD WE SPEND MORE?

The Basic Data

We spend a great deal of money on elementary and secondary education. In so doing we are hoping that the tax money we are spending nets us a return of smart, educated, and productive future taxpayers. In this section we

look at how much is spent and how it is spent, measures of performance, and reasons why our dollars apparently are not buying us what they used to. We also explore the alternatives to public elementary and secondary schools and ask whether the near monopoly that is our current public school system is serving our interests adequately.

As of 2003 the United States was spending more than $440 billion to educate 54 million elementary and secondary students. In exploring whether this amount of money is justified, we can look at how inflation-adjusted spending per pupil has tracked over time and compare the amounts that have been spent with outcomes such as test scores and graduation rates. It is important that we look at things in this way because as the number of students rises, the number of classrooms needed rises too. This not only raises construction and maintenance costs; it also increases the number of teachers that are needed. Thus, whether or not spending increases, it is spending per pupil that matters. In addition, because inflation makes a 1960 dollar more valuable than a 2001 dollar, we need to adjust the spending figures for inflation. Though a flawed measure, the CPI is what we typically use to perform that adjustment.[2]

From Figure 22.2 you can see that even when it is adjusted for inflation, spending per student increased dramatically over the last 40 years. Although it leveled off in the 1990s, there is, nonetheless, a marked increase from $2,275 (2001 dollars) per student in 1960 to $8,203 in 2002. While that spending went for many other things as well, it served to decrease average class size dramatically. As can be seen in Figure 22.3, in 1960 there were more than 26 students per class; there are currently 16. If the demands on what needs to be taught have remained constant, such a significant reduction in the number of students in a class would be expected to have a similarly significant impact on the success of students. By some measures it has, and by others, it has not.

Figure 22.4 indicates students' scores on the SATs over the same period did not respond in proportion to the reductions in class sizes, and there is no clear evidence that reducing class size led to an improvement in SAT scores for college-bound students. If anything, the opposite happened. Average math SATs plummeted while class sizes were falling and have rebounded during the time when class sizes have leveled off. The decline in verbal SATs bottomed out later and the rebound was less dramatic. These scores are more than 30 points below where they had been 40 years earlier.

---

[2]See Chapter 6 for a brief review of this issue.

FIGURE 22.2   Spending per pupil, in 2001 dollars.

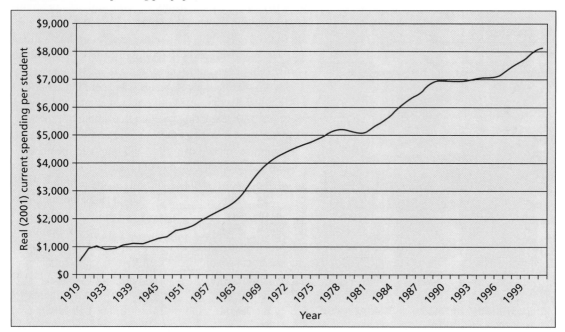

Sources: *Digest of Education Statistics;* http://nces.ed.gov/programs/digest/d03/tables/dt166.asp.

FIGURE 22.3   Student-to-teacher ratios.

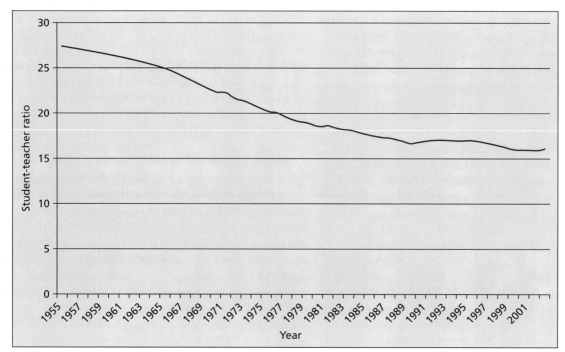

Sources: *Digest of Education Statistics;* http://nces.ed.gov/programs/digest/d03/lt2.asp#c2.

FIGURE 22.4   SATs for college-bound students.

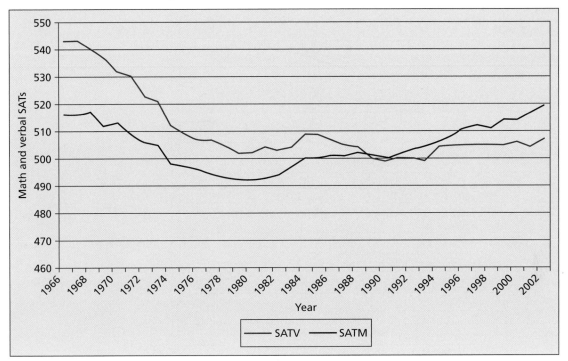

Sources: *Digest of Education Statistics;* http://nces.ed.gov/programs/digest/d03/tables/dt132.asp.

On the other hand, high school graduation rates have been rising dramatically. As you can see in Figure 22.5, this is especially true for African Americans and Hispanics. High school graduation rates showed marked increases over the last 40 years, doubling for whites and Hispanics and more than tripling for blacks.

Cautions about Quick Conclusions

Before you draw any conclusions from these figures about whether schools are doing a good job, you need to consider some mitigating issues. The data, which on the surface indicate that there has been more than a doubling of real spending per pupil, are easily misinterpreted because much of the increase has gone for noninstructional purposes and special education. Though it is depressing on the surface, the low SAT scores can be accounted for in part by the increasing proportion of students from low socioeconomic groups taking the SAT. The high school graduation rate, which on the surface shows improvement, should be looked at in light of the fact that General Equivalency Degrees (GEDs) are included in the data. In addition, whether it is accurate or not, the perception is that it is easier to graduate today because the standards

that teachers use to evaluate students are not as high as they used to be.

While real spending per pupil has almost tripled since 1960, an increasing proportion of the amount of increase has been going for noninstructional needs. The proportion of dollars spent on people who have only a tangential impact on student learning, for example, has gone from 32 percent of total spending in 1960 to 40 percent in 1991. Employees like janitors, bus drivers, secretaries, and administrators do not teach children, and therefore we should not count the money spent on them as though it has an impact on learning. The proportion of the total staff in the classroom has fallen from 70 percent in 1960 to just over half in 2001. If the proportion of total spending on noninstructional employees had remained constant, then the overall rate of increase could be telling us something about whether we have been getting what we paid for. It has not remained constant so we cannot. It is still the case, however, that real instructional spending per pupil has doubled.

Some of the real instructional spending per pupil that has doubled since 1960 has been devoted to legally mandated special education instruction. In 2002, 12 percent of the student population was labeled with disabilities and thus eligible for help that was subsidized through various

FIGURE 22.5   High school graduation rates.

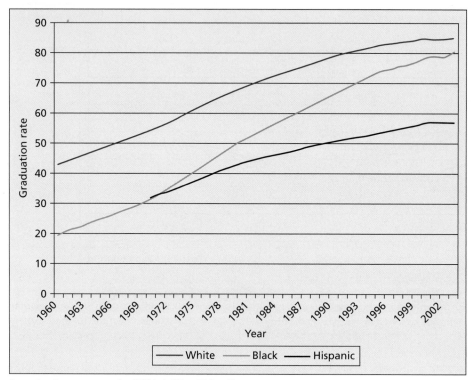

Source: http://www.census.gov/prod/2004pubs/04statab/educ.pdf.

state and federal programs. Most students who have been labeled as having physical disabilities do not require many extra resources, but some require quite expensive services. Although the Americans with Disabilities Act requires that the school provide all necessary assistance to such children while they are in school, the money that it costs to do so should not be called a spending increase for purposes of deciding whether annual costs per pupil are too high. Such spending does not directly benefit students without disabilities, and it therefore should be netted out of the analysis. Doing so reduces the per-pupil spending by around $650.

If we include the spending that funds special education programs in our analysis, the figures on class sizes are understated. Because the figures are derived by simply dividing the number of students by the number of teachers, and because many of the additional teachers focus on only a few special education children, the correct number for analysis should be the number of non–special education students divided by the number of non–special education teachers. When we do that computation we see that classes are not as small on the average as we thought. The student-to-teacher ratio has not fallen to 16 but only to 19.5.

In the past 40 years real total spending per pupil has increased, real total instructional spending per pupil has increased, and real total instructional spending has increased for students without eligible handicapping conditions. The SAT and other test scores are lower today than they were 40 years ago. While we would not expect increased spending on bus drivers or students with severe academic problems to increase SAT scores, we have every reason to expect a real increase in spending on instruction of students without disabilities to increase test scores. Because spending has increased and the test scores have decreased, it seems logical to conclude that we are not getting what we pay for in education spending. That conclusion may not be warranted, though, because the number of students taking the tests has increased and the number going to college has increased. If we look at the entire range of students, moreover, we will see that greater numbers of those who earn lower scores are represented than used to be the case. For instance, if a high school senior class of 10 has 5 going to college and they averaged a combined score of 1,000, is that better than a class of 10 where the first 5 average a 1,000 and the sixth, less qualified student, gets an 800? Since more people are taking the SAT now than in 1960, and since the quality of the students who would not have taken it then but take it now is lower than the quality of students who would have taken it anyway, we should expect average SAT scores to decrease. Even a level SAT average would indicate that today's schools are doing a better job.

Test scores have fallen as spending has increased, and we have speculated about why increased spending has not resulted in higher test scores. Let's look now at graduation rates. Though graduation rates have risen substantially over the decades, there is an open question as to whether this can necessarily be viewed as an improvement. For one thing, more people earn a GED diploma today than at any other time in our history. Some of them have dropped out of school for various reasons. Others are prisoners who have learned that completing a GED shaves time off their sentence. It is admirable that they do this, regardless of who they are, but even though the "E" stands for equivalence, few employers consider it to be the equal of a high school diploma. The best evidence for this assertion is that the income of GED holders is far closer to the income of high school dropouts than it is to high school graduates who have not gone to college. We need to consider this when we make positive statements about the marked increase in graduation rates for blacks. Because blacks hold a vastly disproportionate number of the GEDs, we have to be careful to interpret the increases in graduation rates.

Additionally, there is the common perception that high schools engage in what is referred to as "social promotion," that is, the granting of diplomas for survival rather than for achievement, a trend that critics say has increased in recent years. States have begun implementing exit exams for students to combat this perception, but the data are not yet in on whether graduation rates will fall as a result. If they do, the evidence will show that standards have indeed been lowered and that social promotion, rather than anything to be proud of, is responsible for increased graduation rates.

Literature on Whether More Money Will Improve Educational Outcomes

There is a vast literature written by economists on whether increases in spending can be counted on to increase educational outcomes. The premise that "you get what you pay for" and that more money will make things better can be traced to the production function that we outlined in Chapter 4. Recall that this function maps the relationship between inputs and the resulting outputs. We used workers as the example for that chapter. We showed that more

FIGURE 22.6   Educational production function.

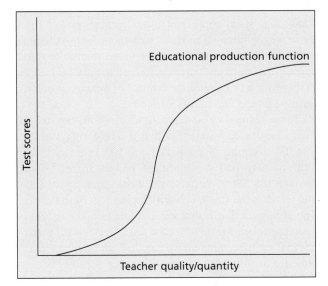

inputs translated into more outputs until the point where the limited capital stock or the structure of the business prevented the new workers from having a positive impact on output.

Applying that idea to education, let's assume that the input is teachers and the output is some agreed-on measure of education outcomes. Each of these assumptions requires some clarification. First, whether it is best to hire more teachers (a higher quantity) to reduce class size or whether it is best to pay teachers more to get better ones (a higher quality) or both is certainly an open question. For the purposes of our graph, we will simply assume quality and quantity are interchangeable concepts. Second, while standardized test scores do not necessarily qualify as an agreed-on measure of outcome, for simplicity of explanation we will assume that they do. Given all that, Figure 22.6 shows the relationship between teachers and test scores.

Eric Hanushek, a leading economist on the issue of education, summarized 377 studies where one or more measure of input like student-to-teacher ratio (the quantity of teachers), teacher education, and teacher experience (the quality of teachers) was used to explain test scores. He reported that most of these studies found no relationship between test scores and these inputs and that nearly as many found a negative one as a positive one. This stunning conclusion, however—that money does not matter and that spending more is a waste of taxpayer resources—is in some dispute by other economists. These economists contend that test scores are less important than the earnings of the graduates. They state that over the last century graduates of schools in states that spent more had more earning power than those who graduated in states that spent less. All economists who study the issue have found, moreover, that educational outcomes are determined mostly by factors that are largely beyond the control of schools, such as family income and family structure.

These results are not as contradictory as they might seem. Figure 22.6 indicates that it might very well be that the structure of public schools has been such that more money had a significant impact in the 1940s through the 1960s because we were spending so little and were on the steep, upward-sloping part of the curve. The argument that Hanushek and others make is that it appears that we are now "on the flat of the curve," meaning that we have done all we can do with more teachers. Now we need to look at something else.

SCHOOL REFORM ISSUES

If we are in fact on the flat part of the educational production function and more money will not help until the structure is changed, it is reasonable to ask what the structure is and why it is limiting. There are two separate issues with regard to the structure that we explore in this section. The first is that the public education system operates as a monopoly and as such tends not to be responsive to the desires of individual students and parents. The second is that teachers' salaries are usually not dependent on their performance. The debate about whether private schools and vouchers to pay for them might help to improve formal education makes up the remainder of this section.

The Public School Monopoly

In Chapter 5 we saw that in industries dominated by monopolies, prices are higher and output is less than it would be under perfect competition.[3] Public schools operate in most communities as a monopoly. Though there are private schools and home schooling, these are not real options to most parents. Even more interesting is that this monopoly charges you, in the form of state and local taxes, whether or not you use the schools. It would be as if your electric company could continue sending you a bill even after you decided to buy your own electric generator.

There are reasons for this. If you believe that the external benefits of K–12 education are so great that they

justify being subsidized, then parents who choose to send their children to private schools should have to continue paying school-related taxes because they are getting those external benefits.

Ultimately, the problem that seems to come to the fore with a monopoly is that it becomes unresponsive to the needs and desires of its customers. In the case of public schools, there is no compelling monetary incentive for the school to help a child with a particular need or to foster excellence in another child. Consider the following problem that exists at the beginning of every school year in nearly every school in the country. Every school has teachers of varying quality and many parents know who the better ones are. Parents want the teachers they consider to be better, and the principal must disappoint some of these parents. Under competition, a disappointed parent could threaten to move to another school. Under competition, the principal would have at least a budgetary incentive to make bad teachers better. Under the current system in most school districts, the parents are simply told, "That's the way it is."

Merit Pay and Tenure

One of the areas that distinguishes teachers from other professionals is the lack of economic performance incentives and lifetime job security. One recent study has found that individual teacher quality does matter. Economist Jonah Rockoff, in particular, found that he could isolate the impact of individual teachers and found that you could identify the better ones statistically by carefully matching student achievement to their past teachers. The reason is that most teachers in the United States are represented by a union that is an independent union, an affiliate of the National Education Association, or the American Federation of Teachers. Unions in general, and teachers' unions in particular, prefer that pay be based solely on education and seniority.

This means that a poor teacher with more experience earns more than a good teacher with fewer years in the classroom. This is a problem because energetic teachers can become discouraged by the lack of monetary recognition for their efforts. Any time pay is based strictly on who you are rather than what you do, there is an incentive to do as little as possible.

The other serious obstacle to rewarding good teachers and getting rid of bad ones is teacher tenure. Much like the institution of tenure in colleges and universities, K–12 educators are often granted tenure after they have successfully met certain criteria and taught for a set number of years. This means that, short of some abusive

---

[3]This conclusion is further reinforced in Chapter 32, "Antitrust."

behavior, they cannot be fired. This further adds to the lack of performance incentives in older teachers.

Many teachers and their union representatives argue several points in defense of this system. First, they argue that as professionals they are above economic considerations and teach to the best of their ability all the time. Second, they argue that granting a principal the power to fire senior teachers and hand out merit pay would foster cronyism. Only those who did the principal's bidding would keep their jobs or get large pay increases. Last, they argue that pay in general is low relative to other professionals and that any additional money should raise all teachers' pay to a higher level.

An additional obstacle facing the current educational system is the degree to which talented women have fled teaching jobs. Economists Caroline Hoxby and Andrew Leigh have identified a frightening degree of movement of brighter women away from teaching and an even more frightening shift of less bright women toward teaching. This, combined with the fact that very few men, bright or otherwise, choose teaching as a profession, means that salaries will have to rise in order to reattract bright men and women to the profession of teaching. Teachers' salaries, although they have risen with inflation, have fallen relative to the salaries of equally credentialed occupations. These economists argue that economics has overcome the sociological tendency of women to be attracted to teaching as a profession and only more pay will reverse this trend.

Private versus Public Education

In the presence of failed or failing public schools, many have come to ask whether private schools should be allowed to receive public funds. In general, students from private schools perform dramatically better and have far fewer discipline problems than students in public schools. This happens even though most private schools exist with funding that is far less than that of public schools.

When private schools outperform public schools it can be attributed to a variety of factors. Because the parents pay tuition to private schools out of their own pockets, we can surmise that the students come from homes where education matters, they are wealthier on average than their counterparts in public schools, and it is unlikely they possess academic or physical disabilities.

The question is whether, after separating out these factors, private schools do outperform. The answer is an equivocal "yes." If you look at public school students who fit a profile similar to private school students, private schools do a little more with a little less. The difference is

not as dramatic as it is without this filter, but it still exists. The primary reason is that parent involvement is higher and administrative costs are lower in private schools.

School Vouchers

The question raised by the preceding analysis is whether parents should be allowed to take their children out of a public school and have them placed in another public school or a private school that is then given the taxpayer money that would have gone to educate the child in the first public school. This would amount to about $2,500 per year for an "able" student. With cost savings and a general dislike of teachers' unions in mind, this option is popular among Republicans. Democrats, strict believers in the "public" part of public education, generally oppose attempts at privatization.

There are, however, ongoing experiments with school vouchers. The school system in Milwaukee, Wisconsin, for example, has been operating a school choice program since 1990. In this system low-income parents can obtain vouchers to send their children to secular (i.e., nonreligious) private schools. The degree of parental disgust with public schools can be seen in the fact that there was space for only a third of those who applied for the vouchers.[4]

The results of this experiment and others like it are mixed. Until recently, only a research team at the University of Wisconsin had access to the data and they concluded that, compared to all other Milwaukee public school students, children did no better. Research that ensued after the data were released to the general academic community suggests that those in the program for three or more years did better (3 to 5 percentile points on reading and 5 to 12 on math) than those who applied but could not get in.

The debate continues on the wisdom of school vouchers from a variety of perspectives, political, ethical, and economic. Research conducted separately by Helen Ladd and Derek Neal suggests that vouchers and charter schools have not performed so well, or so badly as to settle the issue from the perspective of effectiveness. Part of the problem in such analysis is that parents who show an interest in getting their children out of failing public schools are likely to nurture their children in either setting. If those that succeed in getting their children out of the failing schools and into charter schools are highly motivated parents, then any success in the charter schools is likely to be overstated with simple analysis.

---

[4]State law mandated that in such a circumstance the awarding of vouchers would be determined at random.

FIGURE 22.7   College graduation rates.

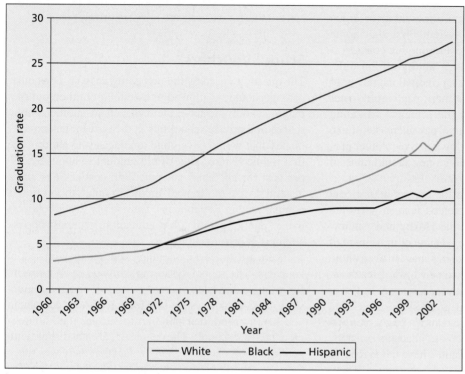

Source: http://www.census.gov/prod/2004pubs/04statab/educ.pdf.

These researchers found that controlling for that bias, the impact of charter schools is modest at best.

COLLEGE AND UNIVERSITY EDUCATION

Why Higher Education Costs So Much

In the preceding section we raised questions about the costs and effectiveness of education through grade 12. Here we explore whether students in colleges and universities are receiving good value for their money. In 2000 a little more than $233 billion was spent educating 16 million college students, which works out to $14,840 per student, per year. Obviously it costs substantially more for higher education than it does for students in elementary or secondary schools. Moreover, tuition, room, and board have increased 228 percent over the last 20 years—a period when overall prices increased only 87 percent. To find out why this is so, we examine some of the economic issues for higher education. We include a discussion of why it costs more and whether those costs are worth it to the college student consumer.

Figure 22.7 shows that if we measure the success of higher education by looking at degrees granted, there is success. There, again, is a question about whether standards have been reduced. The rates of increase are less pronounced than they are for high school diplomas. With nearly a quarter of our adult population college-educated, it seems as if higher education succeeds on behalf of its constituents.

The reasons why college costs more than high school per student are both obvious and hidden. First the obvious. On the average, college professors' average salaries are almost twice those of elementary and secondary teachers. Colleges have libraries that dwarf what we might see in a high school, and librarians have no choice but to subscribe to wildly expensive journals, including many in the sciences that have five-figure subscription prices. If you have not already noticed, college professors teach far less than high school teachers do. A professor at a research-oriented university may teach only 3 to 6 hours a week, while a professor in a teaching-oriented community college may average 12 to 15 hours a week. High school teachers are in the classroom from around 8 or 9 A.M. to around 3 P.M., with time off for lunch and preparation. They may teach five or six hour-long classes, five days a week. In net, a high school teacher is in class more in a single day than some professors are in a week.

Exploring reasons for the disparities between K–12 and college teachers gets us into some less obvious reasons why per-pupil college costs are more than the costs for high school students. Educators at all levels must maintain a high level of expertise in their field. At the college level, it is accepted that professors need time for reading and studying. Professors who teach at the higher end of a discipline need particularly great amounts of time for scholarly study. Many professors are also judged by the degree to which they advance knowledge in their academic discipline. This research commands most of a professor's time at most universities, whether or not they are regarded as prestigious. A sad fact of life in modern college education is that for a professor to advance within an institution, or to advance from a less prestigious school to a more prestigious school, research and other scholarly activity is more important than teaching.

Research costs money, and lots of it. Research for an English professor requires a well-stocked library and a state-of-the-art computer. This is cheap compared to what it costs to set up a biologist to do advanced research. Not only do biologists require the well-stocked library, they require a fully stocked laboratory, with equipment that can separate out DNA and that can magnify samples so that individual cells can be seen. The cost of some of this equipment is so high that if you used the money to equip high schools, you could equip the labs of high schools in a medium-sized city for what it costs to fund the laboratory of a single professor at Harvard, MIT, or Stanford.

Other disciplines, too, are very expensive because of their teaching methods. Music, nursing, and medicine are areas that cost colleges and universities vastly more money than students pay in tuition. This is mainly due to the one-on-one or, at most, small group nature of the learning. You need many more professors of music, nursing, and medicine to teach 100 students than you do in the fields of psychology, sociology, or economics.

What a College Degree Is Worth

Now that we have seen a few reasons why college costs so much, we can ask whether it is worth the expense. To explore this question, we need again to understand and to use the concept of present value.

How We Pay for College

One of the interesting changes over the last three decades has been the change in the way students pay for higher education. In the 1940s World War II veterans received the GI Bill, which allowed many former soldiers to go to college. Not only was their tuition paid but they were also granted a stipend upon which to live. In the 1960s and 1970s the federal government instituted programs such as the Pell Grant, which provided a similar benefit to children of poor families. In the 1980s President Reagan shifted the focus to making student loans available at subsidized rates. In the 1990s President Clinton reformulated the loan process by increasing federal government involvement and sponsored educational income tax deductions and credits. Taken together, these transformations have allowed more students to access some form of aid, but the aid is now more likely to come in the form of a subsidized loan.

Nationally, between 1990 and 2000 the percentage of students on some form of aid has increased from 58 percent to 73 percent, the percentage borrowing to pay for college increased from 32 percent to 45 percent, while the percentage receiving federally funded education grants has remained constant at roughly 30 percent.

If the interest-adjusted amount of money you spend on your education, the present value of the costs, is less than the interest-adjusted amount of the extra money you earn as a result of your education, the present value of the benefits, then your college education is worth the money you pay for it.

Assume for a moment that your four years of college costs you $10,000 a year in out-of-pocket expenses and you give up another $12,000 a year in what you would have earned had you worked full time. The total cost of your education is then $22,000 a year, or a total of about $88,000. Since the expenses incurred in the second, third, and fourth years are in the future, you must discount them by the appropriate interest rate.

Now assume that instead of making $12,000 a year without a degree, you will earn the degree and then make $30,000 a year. The benefit from going to college is the extra $18,000 you earn a year. We use $18,000 because this is roughly the difference in median income of households headed by people who have college degrees over that same figure for households headed by people with only a high school education. We must again discount these benefits, as they will happen in the future. If we assume that all of these dollar figures are inflation-adjusted and the real interest rate is 3 percent, then the present value of the costs is roughly $82,000 and the present value of 40 years of $18,000 extra a year is roughly $415,000. The net present value of a college degree is $333,000. Dropping out of college is likely to be the most expensive mistake you ever make. Conversely, doing well in college may be the most lucrative thing you ever do.

Many college students recognize the benefits of education but cannot see themselves paying for them. While we have just shown that it makes sense to complete college even if you have to borrow all of the money to do it, you

know that merely racking up student loans does not mean you get a degree. This means that there is some risk involved. You have to weigh the risk of having the only thing you take away from college be debt against the benefit that you get the $333,000 in net present value. In addition, though it seems as if a college degree costs you a lot of money, consider the fact that at a public university you are getting a subsidy of $2 for every $1 you spend. The subsidy of $1 for every $1 at a private university is less, but it is still substantial. Subsidies to universities are computed from the value of interest-reduced loans and gifts to the universities. Whether you are a student at a public or private university, you are paying great sums of money, sums that would be even greater were it not for subsidies from national, state, and private sources.

Summary

You now understand that education is an investment in human capital and that this investment not only increases the earnings of the person being educated but has positive externalities as well. You also understand that spending more money will not necessarily yield even more returns. Moreover, you are well aware of the debate centering on whether, with the current education structure, we are on the "flat" of the education production function. You now understand the economics behind the school reform issues, and, finally, you know why a college education is more costly than a K–12 education and that the net present value of a college education is substantially positive for most college students.

Key Terms

external benefits, 236   human capital, 236   net present value, 236

Quiz Yourself

1. The evidence on the impact of spending on K–12 education outcomes suggests that, ceteris paribus,
   a. The more a school district spends, the better it does.
   b. The more a school district spends, the worse it does.
   c. The more a school district spends on expensive buildings, the better it does.
   d. The amount of money a school district spends has no consistent positive or negative impact on outcome.

2. The fact that education benefits not just the person being educated, but society as a whole suggests that there is a
   a. Positive externality.
   b. Negative externality.
   c. Congestion.
   d. Monopoly.

3. The argument that spending more money on teachers has little impact on educational outcomes in K–12 is
   a. Inconsistent with any economic model.
   b. Consistent with the upward-sloping nature of a production function.
   c. Consistent with the downward-sloping nature of a demand curve.
   d. Consistent with the flat part of the production possibilities frontier.

4. The institution of teacher tenure is meant to
   a. Ensure job security for teachers with 10 years of experience.
   b. Ensure that teachers do not get fired for political reasons.

c. Allow teachers to engage in any behavior they wish.

d. Allow the easy firing of incompetent teachers.

5. The evidence on charter schools is that they
   a. Have had no impact in any locations they have been tried.
   b. Have had an enormously positive impact on education generally.
   c. Have had a negative impact on students.
   d. Have had some impact in some locations, but there is no generally obvious positive impact.

6. The economic tool that proves the value of an expensive college education is
   a. Production possibilities.
   b. The yield curve.
   c. Supply and demand.
   d. Present value.

7. The cost of educating a college student
   a. Is less than the cost of educating a high school student because college classes are generally large.
   b. Is equal to the cost of educating a high school student because although college teachers make more money their classes are generally larger.
   c. Is less that it used to be.
   d. Is much greater than the cost of educating a high school student because college professors make more money and teach fewer hours per week.

Think about This

Your education, from kindergarten through college, benefited you and it benefited society. The proportion of a typical college education paid by the student has risen in recent years. How much of your college education do you pay? (Consider the state appropriation to your school if it is public, the federal and state financial aid that you get, the value of the guarantee on any of your student loans). Is this the right division of the burden?

Talk about This

How did cost figure into your choice of school? Did you have lots of options? If you could have gotten a "full ride," where would you have gone?

For More Insight See

Greene, P., Paul E. Peterson, Jiangtao Du, Leesa Boeger, and Curtis L. Frazier, *The Effectiveness of School Choice in Milwaukee: A Secondary Analysis of Data from the Program's Evaluation,* http://hdc-www.harvard.edu/pepg/op/evaluate.htm.

Lochner, Lance and Moretti, Enrico, *American Economic Review* 94 no. 2, "The Effect of Education on Crime: Evidence from Prison Inmates, Arrests, and Self-Reports."

Hoxby, Caroline M., and Andrew Leigh, *American Economic Review* 94 no. 2, "Pulled Away or Pushed Out? Explaining the Decline in Teacher Aptitude in the United States."

Journal of Economic Perspectives 10, no. 4. (Fall 1996). See articles by Francine D. Blau; Eric Hanushek; David Card and Alan B. Krueger; and Caroline Minter Hoxby, pp. 3–72.

Journal of Economic Perspectives 16, no. 4 (Fall 2002). See articles by Helen Ladd and Derek Neal, pp. 3–44.

Rockoff, Jonah E., *American Economic Review* 94 no. 2, "The Impact of Individual Teachers on Student Achievement: Evidence from Panel Data."

Behind the Numbers

Historical data.
   Per-student spending 1959–2001
   Pupil/teacher ratio 1959–2001
      Graduation rates and SAT scores.
      Instructional and noninstructional staff.
      National Center for Education Statistics; *Digest of Education Statistics*—http://nces.ed.gov/programs/digest/d03/index.asp.

Revenues and Expenditures for Public Elementary and Secondary Education: School Year 2002–2003—http://nces.ed.gov/pubs2005/2005353.pdf.

Chapter 23

Poverty and Welfare

Some poverty-stricken families are forced to live in dire conditions. *Source: © Peter Turnley/CORBIS*

Chapter Objectives

After reading this chapter you should be able to

Understand how poverty is measured, who is poor in the United States, and how the percentage of the population that is poor has changed through the last 40 years.

Be aware that the federal government's official poverty rate causes some significant problems.

Understand the myriad programs that exist for the poor.

Know why the government prefers programs that grant the recipient goods and services rather than money.

List the incentives and disincentives of welfare.

Know the welfare reform issues that we currently face.

Chapter Outline

Measuring Poverty

Programs for the Poor

Incentives, Disincentives, Myths, and Truths

Welfare Reform

Summary

Welfare and the reforming of welfare have been political issues from the time when the first "relief" bills were passed by Congress in the 1930s. In more recent times, President Bill Clinton vowed to "end welfare as we know it," and in 1996 a compromise was reached between his administration and the Republican majority in Congress. Shortly thereafter the welfare rolls were significantly cut and welfare programs in general were significantly changed. Even so, there are myriad programs that provide assistance to people in need, and we review them in this chapter. Some of these programs, such as TANF, and WIC, read like an alphabet soup; others have catchy names, like Head Start and Medicaid; still others have more straightforward names, like Food Stamps and the School Lunch and Breakfast program. Each program is designed to help poor people in specific ways. Some disburse cash; others provide goods or services at little or no cost.

After defining what constitutes a state of "poverty," we describe the people who meet the criteria. We present and discuss some of the modern history of poverty, and we discuss why the measure of poverty we outlined might not be adequate to the task of ascertaining who needs assistance and who does not. We then describe the programs that are available to the poor. We divide the programs into those that provide cash and those that provide goods and services. We discuss why we make such a division. Last, we discuss, in general terms, the incentives and disincentives endemic to welfare programs, and we show why it is so difficult to solve the problems of those who live in poverty.

MEASURING POVERTY

What does being "poor" really mean? Are you poor only if you are on the verge of starvation? This absolutist position would suggest that poverty in the United States is almost entirely gone. As we will see later in our discussion, one of the most significant health problems of America's poor is that they are obese rather than starving. On the other hand, there is the position that poverty is a relative concept. We note that someone who has the living standard of a median-income Somalian is in poverty in the United States but not in Somalia, and an American today with an average income has a living standard that 100 years from now will likely be considered unacceptably poor. To see this point note that the poor of today live in larger homes than all but the very richest Americans did in 1900.

The Poverty Line

Surveys have established reasonably well that low-income families of four spend roughly a third of their income on food. Defining the **poverty line** as that level of annual income sufficient to provide a family with a minimally adequate standard of living, we created the first poverty line by multiplying the cost of a minimally sufficient diet by 3, the reciprocal of one-third. In successive years, the amount has been raised by the amount of increase in the consumer price index. For other family sizes, a similar process takes place where the reciprocal of the fraction of income spent on food by low-income people of that family size is multiplied by the cost of the minimally sufficient diet. In 2003 these numbers were $9,373 for one person, $12,015 for two people, $14,640 for three people, and $18,810 for four people.

The **poverty rate** is the percentage of people in households whose incomes are under the poverty line. In 2003 the poverty rate in the United States stood at 12.5 percent.

Another important measure of poverty is the **poverty gap,** a representation of the total amount of money that would have to be transferred to households below the poverty line in order for them to get out of poverty. The poverty gap in the United States was $58 billion as of 2003.

poverty line
That level of income sufficient to provide a family with a minimally adequate standard of living.

poverty rate
The percentage of people in households whose incomes are under the poverty line.

poverty gap
The total amount of money that would have to be transferred to households below the poverty line for them to get out of poverty.

Who's Poor?

Table 23.1 displays indicators of who is poor and compares that to their general portion of the population. Many people think that most poor people are African American. While many academics are quick to dispel that myth, they often perpetuate another with a counterassertion that most poor people are white. Neither is true if you separate European Americans from Hispanic Americans. Table 23.1 shows disproportionate numbers of blacks and Hispanics are in poverty and that they, together with American Indians, Asians, and Pacific Islanders, comprise a majority of the Americans living below the poverty line. It is obvious that there is a significant degree of racial and ethnic distinction in U.S. rates of poverty.

The data indicate that women are more likely to be in poverty than men; and, if we define "families" as not including single adults, then of families in poverty, half are in female-headed households while half are families of

TABLE 23.1   *Who's poor, 2004.*

	General Population (in millions)	Percentage of the General Population	Percentage of Those in Poverty	Poverty Rate (%)
White, non-Hispanic	197.3	67.9	44.6	8.2
Hispanic	39.9	13.7	25.0	22.5
Black, non-Hispanic	37.1	12.8	24.7	24.4
Other race	16.5	5.7	5.7	11.8
Male	143.0	49.1	43.8	10.9
Female	147.8	50.9	56.1	13.3
Under 18	73.0	25.1	35.0	17.6
18–24	28.9	9.9	13.1	16.5
25–64	153.0	52.6	41.4	9.5
65 and over	35.9	12.4	10.3	10.2
Female-headed household, no husband present	46.9	16.1	30.0	25.6
High school dropout*	26.9	9.3	27.6	21.3
High school graduate (no college)*	58.1	20.0	21.6	11.3
College (without a degree)*	45.7	15.7	13.9	8.5
Bachelor's degree or greater*	49.0	16.9	6.6	4.2

Sources: http://www.census.gov/prod/2004pubs/04statab/pop.pdf; http://www.census.gov/prod/2004pubs/p60-226.pdf; http://pubdb3.census.gov/macro/032004/pov/new29_100_01.htm.

married couples. Given that female-headed households with children make up only 16.1 percent of the general population, poverty is clearly a women's issue.

It is also true that children under 18 make up 35.0 percent of those who are poor, though they comprise only 25.1 percent of the general population. This is a poverty rate among children of 17.6 percent. Whether this indicates that the poor have more children or that raising children can itself lead families into poverty can be debated. Clearly, the picture of poverty is this: minorities, women, and children are poor in numbers vastly out of proportion to their numbers in the general population.

Another key indicator of poverty is education or, more properly, the lack of it. Those with a bachelor's degree experience poverty at one-twelfth the rate as high school dropouts. Simply completing high school cuts chances of being in poverty by almost two-thirds, and simply attending college reduces the chance of being in poverty from 11.3 percent to 8.5 percent. Completing college reduces the rate even further. Only 1 in 50 households headed by a college graduate is in poverty.

Poverty through History

Figure 23.1 indicates that although the number of people in poverty is roughly the same as it was in 1959, the poverty rate has fallen dramatically. As we will discuss later, the poverty rate shown fails to account for the many government benefits. This means that the reduction in the poverty rate since 1959 can be attributed to an economic strengthening for those whose incomes are at the bottom of the economic scale.

In considering the decline in the general trend in poverty, be aware of the following caveats. The poverty rate has remained largely unchanged since the middle 1960s when the "war on poverty" actually began. From that time to the present it has neither fallen below 11 percent nor gone above 15 percent. The systemic reduction, as a matter of fact, occurred between 1959 and 1969, before the enactment of many of the antipoverty programs. Noting that the lighter bars in Figure 23.1 indicate recessions, it can be seen that the poverty rate has increased during recessions and lessened during periods of growth. Democratic presidents Kennedy and Johnson get much of the credit for the pre-1969 reduction in the poverty rate. However, this was a result more of a strong economy's providing excellent economic opportunities than anything these administrations did for the poor. The bulk of the pre-1969 decline took place prior to 1965 when these programs first began to become law. Since 1969 Democrats and Republicans have nearly identical records with respect to poverty. Generally speaking, the poverty rate is a reflection of the health of the overall economy.

FIGURE 23.1   Poverty since 1959.

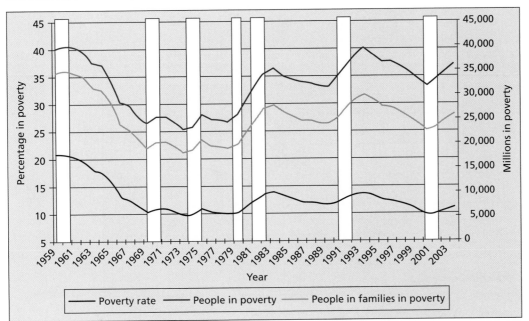

Source: http://www.census.gov/hhes/www/poverty.html.

Problems with Our Measure of Poverty

There is a host of reasons why using three times the cost of a minimally sufficient diet as a measure of poverty is inadequate to the task of measuring who is poor. First, it does not distinguish among families that are intact with one income earner and families that are either not intact or for other reasons have day-care costs. Since nearly 34 percent of families living in poverty are headed by single women with children under 18, this is potentially a significant problem. Since the one-third fraction that was used in the original poverty measure came from a survey conducted when there were fewer such female-headed households, the poverty line could be understated by all or part of the cost of day care. Since day-care costs can be between $3,000 and $5,000 per year per child under 12, this is a substantial area of mismeasurement.

Although this indicates that poverty is understated, there are problems with the measure that indicate that poverty may be overstated. Robert Rector of the conservative Heritage Foundation repeatedly updates statistics that purport to show that poverty is not a problem in the United States.[1] He uses government surveys and published statistical documents to show that 38 percent of households considered poor own their homes, nearly half have air conditioning,

62 percent own a car, and 14 percent own two or more cars. He notes that the square footage of living space of America's poor is greater than the square footage of the average western European, and the diet of the average poor American equals or exceeds the recommended daily allowances of important nutrients. As a matter of fact, one of the singular features of the poor in the United States is their rate of obesity, which implies that few are actually starving.

Specifically on the point of wealth, nearly a million poor families own homes worth more than $150,000. There are hundreds of thousands of people in the United States who have little income but who are worth hundreds of thousands of dollars. Some are even millionaires. Admittedly, it is a small number of people like this who are rich, but called poor. However, it is important to note that the poverty line only measures people's income relative to a fixed standard that ignores measures of wealth.

Another shortcoming of the formula that is used to determine the poverty line is that it only includes income that is in cash. Thus programs that the poor take advantage of that are not cash-driven are incorrectly and absurdly omitted as if they have no value. For instance, the $200 in food stamps that a family might get a month is not counted and, if they found a subsidized rental apartment and free medical care, these also would not be counted. Depending on the study you believe, this failure to include income that is in forms other than cash overstates poverty by between two and four percentage points.

---

[1]A recent version is available at http://www.heritage.org/Research/welfare/BG791.cfm.

FIGURE 23.2   Poverty line with and without CPI adjustment.

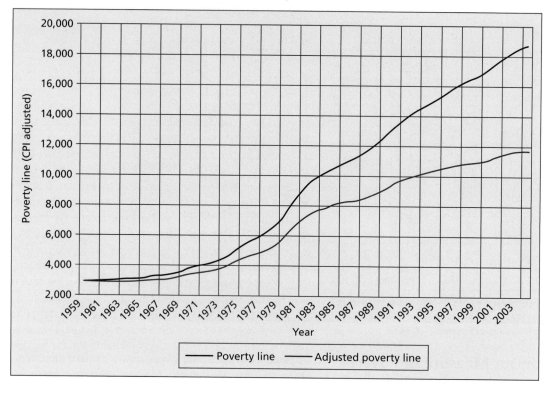

As we saw in Chapter 6, the consumer price index that is used to update the poverty line each year has many shortcomings. Best estimates are that it has overstated the cost of living by at least a full percentage point a year. Since the increase in the poverty line is generated using this flawed measure, it is likely that the poverty line has long been overstated relative to its real value in the 1960s. Figure 23.2 indicates that although the lower line, the adjusted version, tracks the upper line throughout the 1960s, the spread is significant enough that if you take the 1959 poverty line as the base on which to build the adjusted poverty line, you see that instead of being $18,104 in 2001 it should have been $11,607.

Besides the possible overstating of poverty that we have seen up to this point, there are additional problems with this measure that result in mislabeling some people as poor and others as not poor. As we mentioned specifically in the previous paragraph, the general CPI is used to adjust the poverty line. Because the CPI is a general indicator of the prices of many goods, it does not necessarily reflect the goods that are bought by people living in poverty. To the degree that poor people buy things that have increased in price more than the overall CPI, the "true" poverty line probably would fall between the two shown in Figure 23.2.

The way costs of living vary from area to area leads to yet another source of mismeasurement of the numbers of people who live in poverty, and it is a source about which there is uncertainty of the direction of the bias. Because it is much more expensive to live in San Francisco, California, than in Appleton, Wisconsin, for example, families of four in San Francisco with incomes that are a single dollar over the poverty line figure of $18,104 are significantly worse off than families of four in Appleton with incomes one dollar under the poverty line. In this way the poverty rate underestimates both urban poverty and poverty on the coasts. It overestimates the incidence of poverty in rural areas, small cities, in the South, and in the Midwest.

There is a final reason to doubt official poverty numbers, and that is a missing $2 trillion. In Chapter 6, when we talked about national income accounting, we briefly explained the sources of the numbers that make up the gross domestic product. It turns out that data used by the Census Bureau add up to substantially less, $2 trillion less, than the source numbers for personal income used in GDP calculations. While much of the missing $2 trillion is the in-kind transfers mentioned above, this certainly does not account for all of it. It is clearly true that most of that probably goes to the nonpoor. Some of it must also be in the hands of the poor, so there are clearly some who are labeled poor who are not.

PROGRAMS FOR THE POOR

In Kind versus In Cash

The programs available to the poor are many and complicated. They are better understood as varying from state to state rather than being one consistent program across the country. Further, these programs are best understood as being divided between cash payments and provisions of **in-kind subsidies** goods and services in forms other than cash. Economists refer to the latter types as **in-kind subsidies**.

in-kind subsidies
Provisions of goods and services in forms other than cash.

Table 23.2 describes the different programs, the functions, and the populations they serve, as well as the restrictions placed on eligibility to receive them.

Why Spend $471 Billion on a $58 Billion Problem?

Given the preceding information on the extent of poverty and the dollar costs of poverty programs, the following should strike you: If the poverty gap is $58 billion, why do the various levels of government spend more than six times that on poverty programs? The answer is twofold: (1) there are people above the poverty line in need whom we choose to help; and (2) poverty programs must be terribly inefficient if it genuinely takes $471 billion to cure a $58 billion problem.

Table 23.2 shows that billions more are spent on goods and services than are spent in cash benefits. Including some minor programs not mentioned in Table 23.2, cash benefits total around $91 billion, whereas in-kind benefits total $381 billion. Clearly the government spends far more money on programs that give it control over recipients' behavior. For instance, we think the poor do not have enough to eat, adequate medical services, adequate housing, and so on. Instead of providing them with enough money to pay for these things, the government provides them with what it thinks they need.

If there is a family whose members enjoy good health, it is conceivable they would rather have more money spent on food and less on medical care. They cannot make that substitution. People who live in poverty are denied the ability to make basic decisions when they are given specific goods and services rather than money. In many studies of the poor, it is clear that they value cash more than the goods they are provided. Some food stamp recipients show exactly how little they value food stamps and WIC vouchers by selling them on the black market for 50 cents on the dollar. Why haven't programs been designed so that people in need receive cash and are then encouraged to make their own decisions on how to spend it?

There are several reasons, but three are obvious. First, through their elected officials, voters have made it clear they do not trust the judgment of the people who receive government benefits concerning what goods they buy. Many believe that if the poor could make good decisions, they would not be poor to begin with.

Second, people are more concerned with the welfare of needy children than with the welfare of adults. If you look at the programs with this in mind, you will see that nearly all of them require the presence of a child for an adult to be eligible. If we want to guarantee services for children, it makes more sense to give the adult access to such services rather than cash. This minimizes the likelihood that the money will be diverted by adults away from the targeted children.

Third, some welfare benefits seem designed more to provide those who tender them with a feeling of magnanimity than to benefit the poor. If it is our own happiness we are maximizing and if our happiness is enhanced by the knowledge that we provided the poor with enough to survive, it may be even more important to us that we ensure that the poor are consuming what we think is good for them rather than what they want.

INCENTIVES, DISINCENTIVES, MYTHS, AND TRUTHS

While no one has ever intended this to be the case, many of the programs designed to help the poor are blamed for ensuring that people who live in poverty and who receive benefits have no incentive to become self-sufficient. The existence of welfare is accused of giving people a reason not to work. It is blamed for encouraging young women both to get pregnant and to carry the pregnancy to term. Welfare is indicted for encouraging recipients to have more children so that their WIC will be extended and their food stamps and TANF payments increased. The structure of TANF's predecessor, Aid to Families with Dependent Children (AFDC), was blamed for breaking up poor families by giving them the incentive to have the father leave. Together, these problems created the concern that welfare was becoming a way of life and that people were getting used to it.

From a theoretical perspective, each of the preceding arguments has merit, but the evidence from economic studies is not one-sided. First, there are several counterclaims. Birth rates among teenagers climbed steadily from the 1960s through the early 1990s and leveled off when the states and then the federal government instituted welfare reforms designed to curb

TABLE 23.2   Programs for the poor and their characteristics, 2006.

Program	Function	Cash or In Kind and Annual Federal + State Cost ($ billions)	Population Served	Eligibility Requirements
Temporary Aid to Needy Families (TANF; formerly called AFDC)	Cash income to the poor (the welfare check)	Cash, $17	Poor parents and their children under 18	Though this varies from state to state, the following generalizations can be made: recipients (1) have to have children; (2) cannot have much wealth (usually less than $5,000 net) including house and car; (3) can remain on the program for 24 consecutive months only
Women, Infants and Children (WIC)	Food, formula, and diapers	In kind, $4.9	Pregnant women and new mothers	Low wealth and income; cutoffs depend on the state
Food Stamps	Vouchers that can only be spent on food	In kind, $27.2	All poor	Low wealth and income; cutoffs depend on the state. Recipients can remain on the program for 24 consecutive months only
Medicaid		In kind, $303	All poor	Low wealth and income; cutoffs depend on the state
Section 8 or Housing Authority Apartment	Reduced rent or low-cost housing	In kind, $29.6	All poor	Low wealth and income; cutoffs depend on the state
Head Start	Day care; preschool	In kind, $6.7	Poor with children under 5 years	First come, first served for anyone below 1.25 poverty line
School Lunch	Lunch and breakfast	In kind, $9.4	Poor with school-age children	Anyone below 1.25 poverty line
Supplemental Security Income (SSI)	Cash assistance to "deserving poor"	Cash, $40.8	Disabled and widow(er)s and orphans	Someone (a parent, guardian, or spouse) must be disabled or must have died
Earned Income Tax Credit (EITC)	Negative tax; boost low pay to workers	Cash, $33.1	Working poor	Based on family size: phases in at incomes up to $10,350, then phases out for incomes between $15,050 and $34,458; family of four maximum now $4,300

Sources: http://www.acf.hhs.gov/opa/fact_sheets/tanf_factsheet.html; http://www.cms.hhs.gov/publications/trusteesreport/tr2005.pdf; http://www.fns.usda.gov/pd/wisummary.htm; http://www.fns.usda.gov/pd/fssummary.htm; http://www.fns.usda.gov/pd/concosts.htm; http://www.ssa.gov/notices/supplemental-security-incom/text-eligibility-ussi.htm; http://www.whitehouse.gov/omb/budget/fy2006/pdf/appendix/ssa.pdf; http://www.gpoaccess.gov/usbudget/fy06/sheets/25_12.xls; http://www.irs.gov/pub/irs-pdf/p596.pdf.

benefits. The truth is that the real dollar value of benefits per recipient is lower today than it was in the late 1960s. Thus if poor teenagers were really considering the value of welfare in making decisions about having children, teen pregnancy rates would have fallen from the mid-1970s on as the real value of the benefits fell. It is more likely that the culture and teen sex drives had more to do with teen pregnancies than the prospect of receiving welfare checks.

Second, although it was and still is true that the more children you have, the more benefits you get, there is no systematic evidence that people on welfare had more children because they were on welfare. If welfare mothers were concerned only for themselves and the benefits they could get, it would make sense that they would have children so they would be eligible for more benefits. What had to have been evident to them, however, is that the increase in benefits does not cover any more than the increased cost of

Welfare's Best Urban Legend

The world of welfare is replete with urban legends. My favorite goes something like this: "I was standing in line at the grocery store one day behind a nicely dressed woman who was buying beer, steak, shrimp, and a whole bunch of stuff I couldn't afford. She had them put the steak and shrimp on her food stamp card and used her cash to buy the beer. She packed up her groceries and went to her brand new SUV." In teaching this subject for years I have heard this story in countless renditions from students who were either customers or grocery employees. The story is almost always the same. While the story may be about fraud, it is also quite likely about them misinterpreting the actions of a foster parent.

Most states give foster families Medicaid cards and an allotment on a food stamp card to pay for the food and medical expenses of the children in their care. That some of these families are wealthy enough to afford nice meals and nice vechicles does not diminish our obligation to pay them for the service they are providing us by caring for orphaned, discarded, or abused children or those children whose parents are in prison.

raising an additional child. Unless we want to claim that the poor do not care about their children, there is little likelihood that rational women would get pregnant and do the work of raising an additional child in order to keep a few extra dollars a month. They could make more money with less effort if they cleaned houses on the side.

Third, it is true that families on welfare are far more likely to have absent fathers, but it is hard to say whether the father's leaving was caused by the need to be welfare-eligible or the family became welfare-eligible because the father left. In order to accept the argument that welfare caused a rash of absent fathers, you must hold the cynical belief that a well-meaning father would abandon his children so they could receive benefits. Although this might have been the case prior to 1996, today, after welfare reform, the abandonment would have to be complete. A mother now has to name and state the last known location of absent fathers to get benefits. Clearly, whether the need to apply for welfare leads to the breakup of families that would have stayed together is debatable. The reason that some welfare programs are contingent on a parent's being absent stems from the conviction that if there are two able-bodied adults in a house-

hold, one of them should be working. Either the problem of absent fathers is a coincidence or it is the price society is paying for building welfare requirements around a view that families with both parents present should not be eligible for assistance unless one is disabled.

Fourth, under AFDC, that is, prior to the welfare reforms of 1996, welfare dependency had been growing at an alarming rate. Some 26 percent of recipients had been receiving benefits from the program for 10 years or more at the same time that the percentage of families that had been on welfare for very short periods of time was falling. In addition, daughters of recipients were tending to become recipients themselves. These circumstances and others like them led Congress and the president to agree to change welfare programs to incorporate limits on the length of time people could receive benefits and to require that recipients become gainfully employed.

WELFARE REFORM

Is There a Solution?

To be successful, a social safety net must meet three goals:

1. The program that is designed cannot be so expensive that the taxpaying public will not sustain it.
2. The program must have an incentive built in that makes beneficiaries want to leave it.
3. The program must provide enough of a level of basic necessities that recipients have a socially acceptable standard of living.

The problem facing policy analysts in the United States has always been that these goals cannot be satisfied simultaneously.

Any program must have a phaseout level of income. If the phaseout is too quick, meaning that for every dollar you earn you lose significant welfare benefits, the disincentive to work will be too profound. The AFDC program reduced benefits by nearly a dollar for every dollar the recipient earned. This nearly 100 percent take-back rate meant that without a salary at least twice the minimum wage in a job, a single parent with two small children requiring day care would be far better off on welfare than working.

If the phaseout is too slow, then too many people will be getting welfare benefits and not enough will be paying taxes. Though this is possible, it violates the first goal, that of having a program that does not cost too much money. On the other hand, the phaseout could be slow and of low cost to taxpayers. The problem would then be that there would not be enough money for recipients to survive on.

The implicit choice made by policy makers prior to the reforms of welfare that were instituted in 1996 was to give up on providing incentives to leave the program. The increase in long-term dependency on the program can, at least in part, be blamed on this decision. The near 100 percent take-back rate on AFDC left people with no earned income better off than people making $10,000 a year. The result was that only those recipients who could invest in an education could ultimately afford to leave the program.

Welfare as We Now Know It

In the 1996 reforms, the problem of welfare dependency was tackled by simply ordering people to leave welfare. The institution of time limits was an acknowledgment of the concern that dependency was wrong and that monetary incentives for relinquishing benefits were too expensive. Instead of being offered incentives to leave the program, people are now told how long their benefits will keep coming. States are given block grants of money (TANF) that

they are supposed to use to aid their poor. Instead of having to give it away in cash benefits, as they did under AFDC, they can now spend it on job training, child care, or tax breaks for businesses that are willing to hire welfare recipients. States must set time limits of 24 months or less and they must establish work requirements for some programs. Supplemental Security Income rules for disability have changed such that some people who were once eligible for full benefits are now eligible for only partial benefits.

By 1999, welfare caseloads had fallen to their lowest point in three decades. Though it is difficult to tell how much of this was due to the robust economy of the 1990s, it is clear that the reforms that were instituted have had some effect. Economists Rebecca Blank summarized the growing research that has been conducted on this issue by noting that the reforms of providing assistance to work, monetary incentives to work, and requirements to work, the current array of programs is raising incomes and increasing employment in ways previous programs did not.

Summary

You now understand how poverty is measured, who is poor in the United States, and how the percentage of the population that is poor has changed through the last 40 years. You are able to describe some of the significant problems presented by the official poverty rate. You understand the myriad programs that exist for the poor, note that most of the programs grant the recipients goods and services rather than money, and understand why it is that government does this. Last, you are aware of the incentives and disincentives in the welfare state, and you know the welfare reform issues that we currently face.

Key Terms

in-kind subsidies, 253	poverty line, 249	poverty rate, 249
poverty gap, 249		

Quiz Yourself

1. Poverty is a _____ concept in that a person with that income in the U.S. may be considered in poverty while a person with that same income in Somalia may be in the upper quarter of income earners.
   a. relative
   b. absolute
   c. irrelevant
   d. ficticious

2. In a simple 300 million person world of all four-person families, if the poverty line is $12,500 and half of the 10 million families (with 40 million poor people) earn $10,000 and the other half earn $7,500 then the poverty gap is
   a. $125 billion (= 10 million * $12,500).
   b. $250 billion (= 20 million * $12,500).
   c. $150 billion (= 20 million * $2,500 + 20 million * $5,000).
   d. $37.5 billion (= 5 million * $2,500 + 5 million * $5,000).

3. In a simple 300 million person world of all four-person families, if the poverty line is $12,500 and half of the 10 million families (with 40 million poor people) earn $10,000 and the other half earn $7,500 then the poverty rate is
   a. 3.33% (10 million/300 million)
   b. 13.33% (40 million/300 million)
   c. 16.66% (50 million/300 million)
   d. 96.33% ((300 million – 10 million)/300 million)

4. Using a poverty line of $12,500, under the current system of calculating the poverty rate, which of the following people is not considered in poverty and probably ought to be.
   a. a rural family who's sole income earner is from a minimum wage ($10,300)
   b. a rural family who's combined income is $15,000
   c. a New York City family who's combined income is $13,000
   d. a retired couple who's multi-million dollar estate yields them no income.

5. Using a poverty line of $12,500, under the current system of calculating the poverty rate, which of the following people is considered in poverty and probably ought not to be.
   a. a rural family who's sole income earner is from a minimum wage ($10,300)
   b. a rural family who's combined income is $15,000
   c. a New York City family who's combined income is $13,000
   d. a retired couple who's multi-million dollar estate yields them no income.

6. The distribution of aid to the poor between in-kind and in-cash is
   a. roughly equal.
   b. weighed heavily toward in-cash benefits
   c. weighted slightly toward in-kind benefits
   d. weighted heavily toward in-kind benefits.

7. The most obvious pattern in poverty rates is the degree to which they are higher during
   a. Democratic administrations.
   b. wars.
   c. odd years.
   d. recessions.

8. The evidence is that welfare reform in 1996 resulted in _____ welfare rolls
   a. a substantial increase in
   b. a slight increase in
   c. a substantial decrease in
   d. no impact on

Think About This

The wealth of one person, Bill Gates, is about equal to the annual poverty gap in the United States in one year, $58 billion. The United States has a more significantly unequal division of income than any industrialized country. What are the consequences of that unequal distribution?

Talk About This

What other "urban legends" exist about the poor and welfare? What research could be conducted to dispel these legends or prove them to be factual?

For More Insight See

Blank, Rebecca M., "Evaluating Welfare Reform in the United States," *Journal of Economic Literature* XL (December 2002).

Journal of Economic Perspectives 11, no. 2 (Spring 1997). See articles by Peter Gottschalk; George Johnson; Robert Topel; and Nicole Fortin and Thomas Lemieux, pp. 21–96.

Journal of Economic Perspectives 12, no. 1 (Winter 1998). See articles by Dale Jorgenson; and Robert Triest, pp. 79–114.

Wolff, Edward, "Recent Trends in the Size Distribution of Household Wealth," *Journal of Economic Perspectives* 12, no. 3 (Summer 1998).

Behind the Numbers

Historical data.
   Poverty tables 1959–2003.
      Statistical Abstract of the United States; historical poverty tables—http://www.census.gov/hhes/poverty/histpov/hstpov2.html.

   Poverty line 1959–2003.
      Statistical Abstract of the United States; population—http://www.census.gov/prod/2003pubs/02statab/pop.pdf.

Poverty rate and income, 2002.
      U.S. Census Bureau; publications, 2003—http://www.census.gov/prod/www/titles.html.

Characteristics of people in poverty.
      Statistical Abstract of the United States; list of tables—http://www.census.gov/prod/www/statistical-abstract-02.html.

Poverty Gap—http://pubdb3.census.gov/macro/032004/pov/new28_001_01/htm.

Federal spending on programs for the poor.
      Fiscal year 2002 spending on programs for the poor.
         Budget of the United States Government, 2004; detailed functional tables—http://w3.access.gpo.gov/usbudget/fy2004/sheets/fct_2.xls.

   School lunch program.
      Food and Nutrition Service; National School Lunch Program—http://www.fns.usda.gov/cnd/Lunch/default.htm.

Statistics of those in poverty.
      The Heritage Foundation; paper by Robert Rector—http://www.heritage.org/Research/Welfare/BG791.cfm.

Chapter 24

Social Security

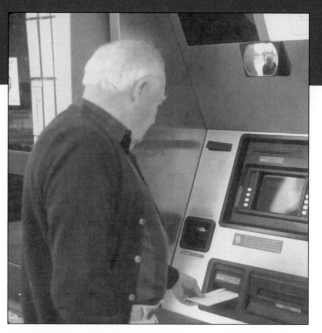

An elderly man deposits his Social Security check at an ATM.
Source: © David Young-Wolff/PhotoEdit.

Chapter Objectives

After reading this chapter you should be able to

Understand what Social Security is and its basic tax and benefit structure.

Be aware of changes to the program since its inception.

Understand the economic rationale for having such a system.

Know the effects of the program on work and savings.

Understand how economists use present value analysis to aid in determining for whom the program works and for whom it does not.

Understand what the Social Security Trust Fund is.

Be aware of present estimates that the system will be bankrupt by 2042 and the options for fixing the system.

Chapter Outline

The Basics

Why Do We Need Social Security?

Social Security's Effect on the Economy

Whom Is the Program Good For?

Will the System Be There for Me?

Summary

When most people think about Social Security, they envision retirement checks for the elderly. Social Security has a much broader scope, including benefits for eligible widows and orphans in addition to medical and disability insurance. In this chapter we concentrate on retirement benefits.

We begin by reviewing the history of Social Security as a government pension program, and we include its tax, benefit, and retirement age structure. We then turn to why it is needed. We discuss the effects of Social Security on the economy in general and show that as a retirement program, it is better for retirees who are poor than for those who are rich and much better for those who retired before 1960 than after 1980. Last, we discuss why bankruptcy is likely without reform and what reform might look like.

THE BASICS

The Beginning

In 1935 the Social Security Act was passed and signed into law by President Franklin Roosevelt. The stock market crash of 1929 and the Great Depression of the 1930s had caused great upheavals in people's financial circumstances. Unemployment had reached a high of 25 percent. People who had been wealthy investors before the crash were lucky if they had a job that would allow them to at least live from paycheck to paycheck after the crash. Many banks closed when, as a result of the stock market crash, their investments were insufficient to pay their depositors. In this circumstance, even people who had saved diligently and invested prudently for their retirement found themselves without savings. Social Security guaranteed a safety net, come good times or bad, to generations who retired from the late 1930s on. At the time, it was not intended that Social Security be the only income on which a person lived. To nearly a third of recipients today it is just that.

Today, Social Security provides guaranteed retirement benefits averaging about $900 a month to 32 million American people over the age of 62. Social Security is a **pay-as-you-go pension** system where current workers' taxes are used to pay pensions to current retirees. This is unlike a traditional **fully funded pension** system where, for every benefit dollar it is required to pay in the future, there is an offsetting amount currently invested that is sufficient

pay-as-you-go pension
A system where current workers' taxes are used to pay pensions to current retirees.

fully funded pension
A system that has an amount currently invested that is sufficient to pay every benefit dollar it is required to pay in the future.

to pay off that dollar. It is the pay-as-you-go aspect that allowed money to go to the elderly right away (the first checks went out in 1936) but, as we will see, it is also this aspect that currently puts Social Security in the most jeopardy.

Taxes

Social Security taxes (technically called FICA, or Federal Insurance Contribution Act taxes) are **payroll taxes.** That is, the amount workers pay is based on what workers earn from their work. This is different from an income tax in that interest, dividends, and other forms of unearned income are not subject to this tax. In addition, not all payroll is taxed; taxes are paid only up to a limited amount of income called the **maximum taxable earnings.** In 2003, this amount was $87,000, which means that workers did not have to pay the old-age portion of the Social Security tax for income they earned beyond that point. Both the employer and employee pay an equal amount of this tax so that if you have to pay $1,000 in tax, so does your employer. The self-employed pay both parts of the tax.

payroll taxes
Taxes owed on what workers earn from their work.

maximum taxable earnings
The maximum of taxable earnings subject to the payroll tax.

Benefits

On the benefit side, eligible retirees get benefit checks that are based on what they made during their working years. The **average index of monthly earnings (AIME)** is the monthly average of the 35 highest earnings years adjusted for wage inflation. The AIME is put into a formula that generates the **primary insurance amount (PIA).**[1] Single people are paid the PIA and married couples get 1.5 times the highest of their PIAs, or the sum of their individual PIAs, whichever is higher. For full benefits workers cannot begin

average index of monthly earnings (AIME)
The monthly average of the 35 highest earnings years adjusted for wage inflation.

primary insurance amount (PIA)
The amount single retirees receive in a monthly check if they retire at their retirement age.

---

[1]The formula for 2003 was 90 percent of the first $606 plus 32 percent of the next $3,047 plus 15 percent of the remainder up to a maximum benefit. This formula is adjusted yearly for inflation. For more information, see http://www.socialsecurity.gov.

retirement age
The age at which retirees get full benefits.
to collect until they reach the **retirement age,** though they can collect partial benefits at age 62.

Although the payroll tax structure is such that everyone with income under the maximum taxable earnings pays the same rate of tax, the benefit structure is such that, in net, Social Security redistributes income to the lower end of the income scale. To see this, consider the following example. Assume, inflation-adjusted, a person makes \$5,000 per month for 35 years, so that person's AIME is \$5,000. Inflation-adjusted, the employee and the employer each pay \$382.50 (7.65% × \$5,000) per month in taxes. That person would get a monthly Social Security check of \$1,722. If someone else were in a similar situation with one-fifth the income, that person and his or her employer would combine to pay one-fifth the tax but the benefit would be \$691 per month. Thus this employee pays one-fifth the tax but receives one-third the benefit. This means that the person at the lower end of the income scale has a benefit dollar–to–tax dollar ratio that is twice that of the upper income person. This is by design, and, as such, the program serves to redistribute money down the income line.

Changes over Time

Since its inception Social Security has added benefits. Payments to widows and orphans, called survivor benefits, have been part of Social Security from its inception. Disability insurance, for workers who are unable to work for long periods of time, was added in 1956, and basic, highly subsidized health coverage (called Medicare) was added in 1966.

Table 24.1 shows how the tax rate, the maximum taxable earnings, and the retirement age have changed since the program began. This table shows how Social Security's components have been changed to ensure its survivability. As you can see, tax rates have risen, in part to pay for the other benefits described previously, but also to guarantee that retirement benefits would be there for each generation. The tax rate has risen from 1 percent to 7.65 percent while the maximum amount subject to tax has risen from \$3,000 to \$87,000. The retirement age has also risen. People born before 1938 can retire with full benefits at 65; those born after 1960 must wait until they are 67. A somewhat complicated transition formula determines the retirement age of

TABLE 24.1   History of Social Security's components at selected points in time.

Year	Maximum Taxable Earnings ($)	Old-Age and Disability Tax Rate (% of payroll)	Medicare Tax Rate (%)	Total Tax Rate That Both Employers and Employees Pay (%)	Retirement Age* Year of Birth	Age	Benefits[†]
1937	$ 3,000	1.000%	0%	1.000%	1937	65	OA, S
1950	3,600	1.500	0	1.500	1950	66	OA, S
1955	4,200	2.000	0	2.000	1955	66 + 2 months	OA, S
1960	4,800	2.250	0	2.250	1960	67	OA, S, DI
1965	4,800	3.625	0	3.625	1965	67	OA, S, DI
1970	7,800	4.200	0.600	4.800	1970	67	OA, S, DI, HI
1975	14,100	4.950	0.900	5.850	1975	67	OA, S, DI, HI
1980	25,900	5.080	1.050	6.130	1980	67	OA, S, DI, HI
1985	39,600	5.700	1.300	7.000	1985	67	OA, S, DI, HI
1990	51,300	6.200	1.450	7.650	1990	67	OA, S, DI, HI
1995	61,200	6.200	1.450	7.650	1995	67	OA, S, DI, HI
2000	76,200	6.200	1.450	7.650	2000	67	OA, S, DI, HI
2003	87,000	6.200	1.450	7.650	2003	67	OA, S, D, HI

*Until 1983 the retirement age was 65. In 1983 the law was changed to increase it depending on year of birth. 1938, =>65 + 2 months; 1939, =>65 + 4 months; 1940, =>65 + 6 months; 1941, =>65 + 8 months; 1942, =>65 + 10 months; 1943–1954, =>66; 1955, =>66 + 2 months; 1956, =>66 + 4 months; 1957, =>66 + 6 months; 1958, =>66 + 8 months; 1959, =>66 + 10 months; 1960 on, 67.

[†]OA = old age; S = survivor; DI = disability; HI = health insurance (Medicare).

those born between 1939 and 1959. In short, in contrast to the view that Social Security has been a monolithic and unalterable program, there have been many changes that have both broadened its scope and ensured its survivability.

WHY DO WE NEED SOCIAL SECURITY?

If you have worked through other issue chapters in this book by now, you know that it has been mentioned before that economists believe that government intervention in private enterprise must be justified on at least one of the following three grounds:

externalities
Effects created by an unregulated market on people other than the buyer or seller.

1. The need to control **externalities,** that is, effects created by an unregulated market on people other than the buyer or seller, such as pollution, secondhand smoke, and drunk driving.
2. Concern about significant moral or ethical problems associated with the good being sold, for example, drugs, prostitution, and pornography.
3. Sellers or buyers are incapable of making rational decisions, because people either cannot be counted on to do the smart thing or have inadequate information upon which to base a decision.

It is a combination of the first and third reasons that makes some form of compulsory-saving/retirement-benefit program necessary in the eyes of economists.

Ideally, rational and wise people will be able to save money for their own retirements based on their own preferences for consuming now versus consuming later. They will realize that money spent now has an opportunity cost, namely, money that cannot be spent later. Investment markets allow people to save or borrow as they please. If all the assumptions about well-functioning markets are valid in the investment market, then there is no reason for government to force people to save. They will save the right amount for themselves.

In opposition to the rationale put forth by economists is the contention that people may not be able to save the right amount for themselves. This is an argument that has little appeal among economists. Many economists maintain that if the government were not taxing workers for this purpose, workers could be saving the money on their own, and saving or not saving would therefore be their choice.

On the other hand, two arguments against a completely free market approach have some appeal among economists. First, our humanity prevents us from letting others starve. If people do not save for themselves, someone else will be forced to bail them out. Their decision not to save affects others. These "others" could be children, relatives, friends, or government. Social Security prevents people from not saving the right amount, and it protects others from having to bail them out.

Second, our rationality stems from our ability to learn from our mistakes. In most situations, and especially in most markets, we learn from our mistakes. For instance, if the first time you go grocery shopping for yourself you buy nothing but marshmallows and Red Bull, you will quickly learn that you need vegetables and fruits in your diet. If you do not save enough for retirement, you cannot just decide to live the first 65 years of your life over again. Government often prevents us from this sort of mistake. There are few guarantees that we will always do the right thing ourselves. There are other examples of this: (1) you cannot borrow money before age 18 without a cosignature; (2) you cannot drop out of school before you are 16; and (3) you cannot drink until you are 21. Society fears that you might suffer irreparable bankruptcy, poverty, or alcoholism, respectively, and it wants government to ensure that you will not make mistakes that cannot be undone. For these reasons, the question among economists is not whether some form of government-run retirement is needed but what form that system takes and how to fund it so that it is financially stable.

SOCIAL SECURITY'S EFFECT ON THE ECONOMY

Effect on Work

Before Social Security was implemented, 51 percent of men over age 65 worked. Today, that number is 15 percent. While there is much dispute on the degree to which Social Security itself caused this to happen, Social Security has clearly made it easier for people to retire. This has good as well as bad aspects. Though the retired may be happier being retired, the economy is deprived of their labor and the fruit of their labor. On the other hand, as more people retire, positions are opened up throughout the labor scale as everyone moves up to fill vacated positions. Paradoxically, this is a circumstance in which the economy is hurt even though everyone in it is happier. (If this seems odd revisit Chapter 6 and the section "Real Gross Domestic Product and Why It Is Not Synonymous with Social Welfare.")

Effect on Saving

Most economists believe that if people had to save for their own retirement, they would save more than they do now. Though these economists disagree on the magnitude of this effect, they have concluded that the existence of Social Security reduces the amount of money that is saved in the economy. This is primarily due to the **asset**

asset substitution effect
Government is saving for you; thus you will save less for yourself.

substitution effect. If the government is taxing you on your earnings now and promising a pension payment later, the government is, in effect, saving

for you. If the government is saving for you, you will save less for yourself.

Two counteracting effects to this are the **induced re-**

induced retirement effect
People need to save more if they are going to retire earlier than they would have without Social Security.

tirement effect and the bequest effect. As mentioned, people are clearly retiring earlier than they did in the past. If Social Security did not exist, and people had no hope of ever retiring, they might not save anything. On the other

hand, since Social Security makes retirement a possibility, people may save so as to retire. The induced retirement effect thus increases national savings because people need to save more if they are going to retire earlier than they would have without Social Security.

Another impact of Social Security is that it may increase national savings if the elderly are putting aside more money for bequests, that is, money that will go to younger family members when their elders die. It may be that Social Security provides a stable enough income for the elderly that they choose to save enough to pass on a larger inheritance than they would have if there had been

bequest effect
People save more to give larger gifts to their descendants, thus increasing national savings.

no such program. The **bequest effect** thus increases national savings because people save more so as to give larger gifts to their descendants than they would have without Social Security.

Economists dispute the net effect of Social Security on savings. Martin Feldstein, in particular, was the first to estimate the effect of Social Security on savings. In 1974 he concluded that there was a dramatic reduction in savings. This was disputed by other economists, led by Alicia Munnell in 1977 and Dean Leimer and Selig Lesnoy in 1982, all of whom estimated that the net effect was zero. Not to be silenced, in 1996 Feldstein published revised estimates for 1992, when personal savings

were actually $248 billion, indicating that it would have been $646 billion without Social Security. The upshot is that there is little agreement except for a middle ground that appears to indicate a small net negative impact of Social Security on savings.

WHOM IS THE PROGRAM GOOD FOR?

With a spreadsheet, a few assumptions, and some specialized terminology, you can compute whether Social Security is a good deal for you. To do this you will need to draw on the present value discussion of Chapter 7. We can then compare the taxes we pay today with the benefits we anticipate getting 40 or 50 years from now.

There is much literature on the present value of Social Security. C. Eugene Steuerle and Jon Bakija provide detailed present value estimates for different categories of people born in different generations. Though exact estimates vary by marital status, by earners, and by age, the results show unequivocally that the program was a net winner across the income scale for those retiring before 1980. However, because of the rapid increases in FICA taxes, this situation has steadily eroded, leaving only married couples, with only a single, low-income earner, to benefit.

To get a flavor of what this kind of analysis entails, consider the following example. First, we need to make some basic assumptions. To estimate the present value of your Social Security taxes and benefits we need to know your age, your marital status, the starting salary you can expect upon graduation, the rate at which your income will grow, an assumption of yearly inflation, your age at retirement, and, finally, your age at death. For Table 24.2 we will assume the following: you are 19; you will graduate at age 23; you will not get married; you will work until you are 67; you will die at 88; inflation will be 3 percent every year; your income will grow at 4 percent per year; and 8 percent is the appropriate interest rate. Though the old age and disability tax rate is 6.2 percent, the old age part is only 5.3 percent. This tax is on both the employer and employee, so we will assume that your old age Social Security contributions amount to 10.6 percent of your earnings (up to, of course, the maximum taxable earnings).[2]

Table 24.2 indicates that today's 19-year-olds would do better if their Social Security taxes were invested at

---

[2]We assume that employees bear the entire burden of the Social Security tax because empirical estimates of labor supply elasticity are nearly zero.

TABLE 24.2 Present value analysis of Social Security.

Income ($)	Present Value of Social Security Taxes at 8% ($)	Present Value of Social Security Benefits at 8% ($)	Net Present Value of Social Security at 8% ($)	Real Rate of Return (%)
$10,712	$18,411	$ 9,373	−$ 9,038	3.0%
15,000	25,780	11,434	−14,346	2.6
20,000	34,374	13,836	−20,538	2.3
25,000	42,968	16,239	−26,729	2.1
30,000	51,561	18,446	−33,115	1.9
35,000	60,154	19,572	−40,582	1.7
40,000	68,748	20,698	−48,050	1.5

8 percent per year (inflation plus a 5 percent real rate of return) than they would do under Social Security. The first column shows the income assumed for the calculations, and the second indicates the present value, at 8 percent, of all taxes to be paid. The third column shows the present value, again at 8 percent, of all the benefits that people will be entitled to from their retirements at age 67 until their deaths at 88. The last column indicates the appropriate real interest rate that equalizes the present value of taxes and benefits.

As can be seen from the first two columns, as people make more money, they also pay more taxes. Starting with people making minimum wage ($5.15/hour × 2,080 hours in a year) and ending with people starting their working life with a $40,000 salary, the present value of their taxes increases from $18,411 to $68,748.[3] Also apparent from the table is that the present value of benefits for high-income people is greater than that for low income people. This is because the more you make and contribute to the system, the bigger your benefit checks are at retirement. Note here that although the high earner makes much more than three times what the lower earner makes, the benefit check the high earner gets is a little more than twice that of the lower earner.

The fact that the net present value is negative means that Social Security will not pay as well as a private investment making 8 percent. As can be seen from the fourth column, everyone in your generation will do better if your money is privately invested. For those of you

who are going to be high earners, this loss is significant. The last column shows that, as an investment, Social Security is a better deal, in terms of the real rate of return, for a low earner than for a high earner.

Two conclusions can be drawn from Table 24.2: (1) For no members of the current generation of college students is Social Security likely to beat their private alternatives; (2) the more money people are likely to make over their lifetimes, the worse the discrepancy between private investments and Social Security is likely to be.

There are a couple of logical questions that could be asked at this point so I'll ask them for you: (1) You assumed a 5 percent real interest rate. What would happen if you assumed something like 3 percent? In this case, the net present values would be near zero for the low earner and −$41,693 for the high earner. (2) What if I live until I'm 100? Can I beat the system? The power of compounding interest dwarfs your ability to live long enough to make the system work for you. Even though a high earner would get benefits in excess of $100,000 a year, at age 90 the present value of this is around $2,000 a year.

If your parents, grandparents, and great-grandparents had run these numbers when they were your age, the outcomes would have been markedly different. For those retiring in 1960 the real rate of return averaged 15 percent while those retiring in 1980 saw an average 7 percent real rate of return. The basic reason for the difference in real rates of return between you and previous generations is that the Social Security tax rates they paid were much lower than the rates you can expect to pay. Those retiring in the 1960s faced tax rates of less than 3 percent for much of their working lives. Those who retired in the 1980s saw tax rates rise from 1 percent to 5 percent while they worked. You will

---

[3]The reason that the increase in taxes paid is less than proportional to the increase in income is that people with starting salaries of $40,000 and 4 percent growth per year will hit the maximum taxable earnings before they retire. So, whereas the taxes that a poor worker will pay will go up 4 percent every year, the taxes a richer person will pay will go up only 3 percent a year once they have hit that limit.

FIGURE 24.1   Workers per retiree history and projections.

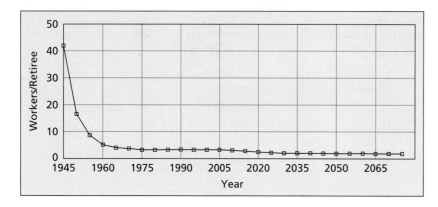

face Social Security tax rates (old age) of at least 5.3 percent for your working life.

In part Social Security has been viewed as a successful program because, until recently, it has been a good deal for everyone. For people alive when Social Security was introduced, it was an example of the great things that government can do. For people born between 1935 and the mid-1950s, Social Security provides a guaranteed retirement income that is about equal to, for married average wage earners, what they would have gotten in the stock market.[4] For those born after the mid-1950s, the real rate of return on Social Security is likely to be dwarfed by private investment opportunities. For those who are single people, for married dual-income earners, or for higher income earners, the year of birth for a breakeven status was as long ago as 35 years earlier. For such people, Social Security has returned to them much less than private investments would have.

The whole question of who benefits from Social Security is often seen as a loaded one. Simply asking it sometimes causes people to think that you favor its elimination. So given that this section may have struck you as a sales pitch for its elimination, remember that Social Security is part of what economists call "social insurance." It is not intended to be a good investment. It is intended to provide a secure source of income during retirement. As you will see when we discuss the reform question, that is where the debate centers.

Those who favor some form of privatization judge the program using a yardstick, like rate of return, that others reject.

WILL THE SYSTEM BE THERE FOR ME?

Why Social Security Is in Trouble

There has always been a concern about whether Social Security could survive. Tax rates have always risen faster than benefits have been added because the retired population has grown faster than the working population. In 1982 a significant concern was raised that the pay-as-you-go system could not handle the demographic bulge of the post–World War II baby boom. In the years following World War II, until around 1960, some 2.5 percent of all women gave birth each year. The advent of the birth control pill, the increased availability of abortion, and the social unrest of the 1960s and 1970s significantly altered America's birth rate. By 1976 only 1.5 percent of women gave birth each year.

As a result, the baby-boom generation, 39 to 57 years old in 2003, represents 26 percent of the current population. A comparable group before them, those between 55 and 69, are now only 12 percent of the population. Because of this, the number of taxpaying workers per benefit-receiving retiree will continue to fall precipitously. In 1950, there were more than 16 workers paying taxes for every retiree who was collecting benefits. Today, the number is 3.3, and current projections say it will drop to 2.2 by 2030. Figure 24.1 presents an overview of this situation.

---

[4]Because the system has a built-in transfer from high-income earners to low-income earners, though the average earner would break even, the low-income earner would get more than the present value of taxes. A high-income earner would get less.

The Social Security Trust Fund

To combat the demographic problem the **Social Security Trust Fund** was established in 1982 to collect more taxes than were needed to pay current benefits. In later years there would thus be money enough to pay benefits to baby-boom retirees. In 2002, there was approximately $1.4 trillion in U.S. government debt in this fund. As you may recall from Chapter 12, "Monetary Policy," or Chapter 10, "Federal Deficits, Surpluses, and the National Debt," the federal government owes itself more than $2 trillion.

Whether this actually constitutes a true trust fund is debatable. It is a collection of debt that will either be issued for the first time or reissued to the public when there is less in Social Security tax revenues than benefits to pay. One way of looking at this issue is that the trust fund is money that was collected using the Social Security tax, rather than the income tax. This was begun in the 1980s and early 1990s to reduce what would otherwise have been a much larger deficit. If you look at it this way, the national debt that grew to $6.2 trillion by 2002 actually only grew to just under $4.8 trillion. As a result, should surpluses come in, we would be reducing the true national debt to allow ourselves the ability to borrow much more later. Either way it is essentially the same. Reissuing debt and borrowing money are functionally identical.

The Social Security Trustees periodically issue reports that attempt to project how long this trust fund will suffice. They issue three different predictions based on three different sets of assumptions. The "optimistic" report is based on assumptions that economic growth will be higher than we have seen in the recent past, life spans will be shorter than current health trends are likely to yield, and interest rates will be lower than they are likely to be. The "pessimistic" report is based on assumptions of slow growth, long lives, and high interest rates.

The "intermediate" report is the most widely quoted, and it indicates that the Social Security system will continue to collect more in taxes than it pays in benefits until about 2018. Between 2018 and 2042 there will be less collected in taxes than paid in benefits, and the difference will come out of this fund. By 2042 the fund will run dry and the annual deficit could be as much as 27 percent of the benefits owed. It is at

that point that the system will be **bankrupt,** that is, having insufficient assets to pay off its obligations.

This intermediate view of whether Social Security will survive has to be balanced by the fact that much of it is based on assumptions that may or may not materialize. For instance, if the optimistic view holds, and the economy grows a single percentage point a year more than predicted, the problem is mostly solved. Changes, for example, in immigration policies that allow more workers to enter over the next 20 years, could help solve the remainder of the problem. Additionally, if inflation and interest rates are slightly less than predicted, Social Security bankruptcy is far from certain.

Of course things could be worse, too. A significant recession, or high inflation, could each seriously damage the system's solvency. If we have a period like the one we had from 1974 to 1983, where there were three recessions, high inflation, and high interest rates, the system might be bankrupt earlier than expected. As a matter of fact, an increase in something as unrelated as the divorce rate would make the problem worse. Husbands and wives typically get less in benefits married than they do if they are divorced.

The long and the short of it is that economists cannot be sure that Social Security will be bankrupt. Significantly altering what many consider to be the nation's greatest social program on the basis of economic assumptions that may or may not come true strikes many as foolhardy. This is especially true, from the point of view of economist and Social Security expert, Peter Diamond. He notes that even if the trust fund is exhausted in 30, 40, or 50 years, the taxes paid will be sufficient to cover 75 percent of benefits. On the other hand, the possible solutions that we next describe also require several years to be effective if the goal is to make the program 100 percent solvent into the future.

Options for Fixing Social Security

The options for saving Social Security are plentiful, and they range from radical to timid. They all include a mixture of the following elements: raising payroll taxes, raising the retirement age further, cutting benefits to upper-income recipients, changing the target from indexing benefits using wage inflation to indexing using price inflation investing the trust fund in corporate stocks and bonds, or carving out some of the payroll tax for privatized individual accounts.

Raising taxes is the option most preferred by those who like Social Security the way it is. This could be accomplished by raising the tax rate as well as raising or eliminating the maximum taxable earnings lid on what an individual has to pay. Estimates vary, but eliminating this provision so that the upper-income people would have to pay taxes on more than just the first $87,000 of their earnings would solve about a third of the problem. Raising the overall payroll tax rate for the old age part from 5.3 percent to 6.3 percent would probably be sufficient to deal with the remainder.

Another alternative would be to raise the retirement age. Typically those who like this option argue that Social Security's original retirement age was pegged at life expectancy, which in 1935 was 65. If the retirement age is exactly life expectancy, then people who die at or before expectancy pay a lifetime of taxes and get no benefits. This ensures that there is enough money to pay for those who die after expectancy. Currently life expectancy is 77. For those who make it to 65, men can expect to live another 16 years, women 19 years. Though people are living much longer, the problem is that there is less Social Security retirement money to go around. Depending on how quickly we did it, raising the retirement age to 70 would also solve about a third of the problem.

One of the great successes of Social Security is that it has brought the poverty rate among the elderly down greatly. On the other hand, many retirees have enjoyed financial success in their own right. Some have succeeded so well in this area that they are getting Social Security checks but have no need for them. The median net worth for a Social Security recipient is currently about twice that of a nonrecipient. One proposed

means test
Determination of the amount of one's government benefit on the basis of income or wealth.

solution to Social Security's problems is to subject its beneficiaries to a **means test.** Those with high incomes or great wealth would get less of their PIA than those who depend on the monthly check. Depending on how much a wealthy person's check is reduced, this could go a long way to staving off bankruptcy. Denying Social Security to anyone whose other income is greater than $50,000, for example, would eliminate the solvency issue altogether. Less radically, means testing could be introduced into the system by using a hybrid form of indexing espoused by economists Pozen, Schieber, and Shoven. They suggest indexing benefits

for upper-income retirees using price inflation rather than wage inflation. Since the former is usually one percentage point lower than the latter, this would have the effect of slowly reducing the benefits paid to upper-income retirees. On the other hand, this could create problems. If benefits to the wealthy are reduced too much, this could seriously discourage savings among the upper- and upper-middle-income earners. Also, political support for the program might be seriously jeopardized, as it would resemble a welfare program more than a universal retirement program.

Another way to save the system would be to invest the Social Security Trust Fund in corporate investments that yield higher rates of return. As mentioned above, the trust fund buys government debt and this debt "yields" between 5 percent and 6 percent. In this sense the government (the Treasury) owes the government (the trust fund) money and has to pay itself interest. Proponents of this solution contend that if the government invested the money in corporate stocks and bonds, the higher rates of return would generate enough to pay retirees' benefits.

There are problems with the approach. First, government would be in the business of picking stocks and might not do very well. Second, the process of picking government investments might be unduly politicized. Given politicians' penchant for succumbing to special interests, it is not beyond the realm of possibilities that such investment would not be in the general interest. Third, though corporate securities do better in the long run than government bonds, they are also riskier.

The last option suggests that individuals be allowed to invest part of their taxes themselves. In the 2000 presidential election candidate George W. Bush made this a cornerstone of his solution to the Social Security crisis. The precipitous declines in global stock markets that began in 2000 and did not abate until 2003 seriously undercut the political support such an option was beginning to build, but with his reelection in 2004, President Bush again pushed this option front and center. What he suggested was a system by which younger workers would have a portion of their taxes placed in an account under their control. Opponents of the president's plan focused on the fact that the guaranteed Social Security benefit would be significantly reduced while supporters countered that the proceeds of the accounts, if investments returned their normal historical rates, would more than make up the difference.

Summary

You now understand what Social Security is. You know its basic tax and benefit structure as well as the changes that have been made to the program since its inception. You understand the economic rationale for having the system to begin with, and you know the effects of the program on work and savings. You understand how economists use present value analysis to aid in determining for whom the program works and for whom it does not. You understand that, under present estimates, the system will be bankrupt by 2042, what the Social Security Trust Fund is, and what the options are for fixing the system so that it will not only be there for you but be good for you as well.

Key Terms

asset substitution effect, 262
average index of monthly earnings (AIME), 259
bankrupt, 245
bequest effect, 262
externalities, 261

fully funded pension, 259
induced retirement effect, 262
maximum taxable earnings, 259
means test, 266
pay-as-you-go pension, 259

payroll taxes, 259
primary insurance amount (PIA), 259
retirement age, 260
Social Security Trust Fund, 265

Quiz Yourself

1. Social Security's revenue emanates from taxes on
   a. All income.
   b. Payrolls.
   c. Capital.
   d. Estates.

2. One of the reasons a government-run annuity system such as Social Security may be better for society than simply relying on private savings is that
   a. No one would save for themselves.
   b. People, being overly risk averse, will save too much.
   c. People, being risk neutral, will save too much.
   d. People, having imperfect foresight, will save too little.

3. The average index of monthly earnings are indexed
   a. For wage inflation.
   b. For consumer price inflation.
   c. For producer price inflation.
   d. Via a combination of wage and price inflation.

4. Since its inception, the portion of earnings that have been subject to the social security tax has
   a. Remained roughly contact.
   b. Increased substantially.
   c. Decreased slightly.
   d. Decreased substantially.

5. In 2005, a worker who earned $95,000 would have _____ in Social Security taxes taken out of their pay and _____ would also be paid by their employer.
   a. $14,535; $14,535 (both equal to $90,000*.153).

   b. $6,957.50; $6,957.50 (both equal to $90,000*.0765+.0145*$5,000).
   c. $6,957.50 ($90,000*.0765+.0145*5,000); ($95,000*.0765).
   d. $7,267.50; $7,267.50 (both equal to $95,000*.0765).

6. The asset substitution effect implies that Social Security will _____ from where it would have been without it
   a. Increase savings.
   b. Increase work.
   c. Decrease work.
   d. Decrease savings.

7. The question of whether Social Security increases or decreases savings depends mostly on whether the _____ effect outweighs the _____ effect or visa versa.
   a. Bequest; asset substitution.
   b. Bequest; induced retirement.
   c. Asset substitution; induced retirement.
   d. Interest; asset substitution.

8. When compared to people of your grandparents' generation, you can expect the net present value of Social Security to be
   a. Much better.
   b. About the same.
   c. Slightly worse.
   d. Much worse.

Think about This

How much risk is appropriate for a government-run annuity system? Is there an appropriate risk-return calculation to be made? Is Social Security risk free? What about political risk?

Talk about This

Defenders of the status quo in Social Security note the extremely low administrative costs of the system relative to those associated with private investment houses. Critics of the status quo note that the real rate of return to future recipients is so much less than the long-term historical average of stocks that paying the extra administrative costs would be worth it. Who's right? Given the methods of saving Social Security described in this chapter, which combination would you employ to save it?

For More Insight See

Aaron, Henry, "The Myths of Social Security Crisis: Behind the Privatization Push," *NTA Forum* 26 (Summer 1996).

Clark, Robert, "Social Security Financing: Facts, Fantasies, Foibles and Follies," *America Economic Review* 94, no. 2.

Cogan, John F., and Olivia S. Mitchell, "Perspectives from the President's Commission on Social Security Reform," *Jounral of Economic Perspectives* 17, no. 2.

Diamond, Peter, "Social Security," *American Economic Review* 94, no. 1.

Feldstein, Martin, "Social Security and Saving: New Time Series Evidence," *National Tax Journal* 49, no. 2 (June 1996), pp. 151–163.

Hyman, David, *Public Finance: A Contemporary Application of Theory to Policy,* 7th ed. (Fort Worth TX: Harcourt College Publishers, 2001).

Journal of Economic Perspectives 10, no. 3 (Summer 1996). See articles by Edward M. Gramlich; and Peter A. Diamond, pp. 85–88.

Leimer, Dean, and Selig Lesnoy, "Social Security and Private Saving: New Time Series Evidence," *Journal of Political Economy* 90, no. 3 (June 1982), pp. 606–642.

Pozen, Robert, Sylvester J. Schieber, and John Shoven, "Improving Social Security's Progressivity and Solvency with Hybrid Indexing," *American Economic Review* 94, no. 2.

Rosen, Harvey, *Public Finance,* 5th ed. (Boston, MA: Irwin/McGraw-Hill, 1999).

Steuerle, C. Eugene, and Jon M. Bakija, *Retooling Social Security for the 21st Century: Right and Wrong Approaches to Reform* (Washington, DC: Urban Institute, 1994).

Behind the Numbers

Social Security information.
    Components, taxes, and bankruptcy.
        Social Security Administration; fast facts and figures—http://www.ssa.gov/policy/docs/chartbooks/ fast_facts.

    History and projections.
        Social Security Administration; 2005 Trustees Report—http://www.ssa.gov/OACT/TR/TR05/.

    Trust Fund debt, 2002.

    Recipient age requirements and benefits.

Labor force characteristics, 2002.
    Percentage of those over 65 in the labor force.
        Statistical Abstract of the United States; labor—http://www.census.gov/prod/2004pubs/04statab/labor.pdf.

Chapter 25

Head Start

Head Start provides early childhood education for children in low-income families. *Source: © Mark Richards/ PhotoEdit*

Chapter Objectives

After reading this chapter you should be able to

Understand that Head Start is a program that provides early childhood education to nearly a million children.

See that the premise of the program is similar to any investment premise, that money spent now will yield results in the future.

Analyze Head Start using present value concepts.

Understand that evidence that the program works is rather scant, concentrates on the time the child is in the program, and cannot be used to affirm that Head Start's effects last into adulthood.

Understand that there is an opportunity cost to the $6 billion program.

Chapter Outline

Head Start as an Investment

The Head Start Program

The Current Evidence

The Opportunity Cost of Fully Funding Head Start

Summary

Established in 1965, the Head Start program serves more than 900,000 children under the age of five at an annual cost of more than $6.8 billion dollars. It began on the seemingly sound premise that early intervention in the lives of children can pay dividends later in the form of improved educational outcomes, reduced crime rates, and other socially desirable outcomes. Thus Head Start has enjoyed broad political support, despite a vigorous debate over whether it has engendered a long-run positive influence.

We explore the premise that undergirds the notion that early intervention in the lives of children is worth the investment. We offer a cautionary note concerning the effectiveness of a short-term investment in early childhood education. We fully describe the program and show the increase in enrollment and funding that Head Start has enjoyed. Additionally, we describe its mission, its faculty, and its client children. We examine the evidence of the success of Head Start as well as the evidence of its shortcomings, and we offer a final thought on the opportunity cost of fully funding it.

HEAD START AS AN INVESTMENT

The Early Intervention Premise

When social scientists looked at the problem of poverty in the 1960s, many hoped that with enough money, poverty could be significantly reduced and perhaps permanently eliminated. Early evidence gave them great hope. The poverty rate fell from more than 20 percent in 1960 to less than 11 percent a decade later, but it never fell below that. Though more than $300 billion has been spent each year on poverty programs, the official poverty rate has continued to hover between 11 percent and 15 percent ever since.

More troubling has been the degree to which people whose annual incomes are lower than the poverty line have settled into habits that almost guarantee they will remain in poverty permanently. The poor are far more likely than the nonpoor, for example, to drop out of school, father children or become pregnant as teens, use illegal drugs, or get arrested. At the inception of Head Start people thought that early intervention in the lives of children could lessen or even eliminate some of the sources or causes of poverty. Theoretically, children given academic skills, life skills, and health care to promote a "head start" on life would be more likely to succeed.

The early intervention premise suggests two things about money spent on a quality early education. By interrupting a cycle of poverty, we save future taxpayers money. This can be analyzed using the Chapter 7 concept of present value. What is also implied about this premise is that people other than the child and the parent benefit when a child gets high-quality care. We examine this aspect as well.

Present Value Analysis

Those who founded Head Start hoped that money invested early in the education of young children would pay for itself in the long run: Students who were not judged among the likely to succeed would graduate from school, live with good standards of hygiene, earn respectable incomes, and pay taxes. Ideally, using the economic concept of present value, we would be able to prove that, like any good investment, such early childhood education would pay for itself. As you know, present value is arrived at by discounting future payments by projecting interest rates in a way that puts future and present dollar figures on an even basis. Because human nature is to want things now rather than later, dollars paid now are more valuable to people than dollars paid in the future. Therefore, if the present value of the dollars spent on early education is less than the present value of the stream of benefits, then any such early education program is a good investment.

Suppose it could be shown that having a child in Head Start reduced a child's likelihood of dropping out of school, of getting pregnant, and of committing crimes for which jail time was required. Suppose it could also be shown that Head Start increased the likelihood that the child would grow up to be a fully functional taxpayer.[1] If all that were true it still would not necessarily justify the investment. From a strictly economic perspective, the present value of the increased costs associated with Head Start would have to be exceeded by the present value of the benefits as measured by the increased taxes and reduced welfare and imprisonment costs.

External Benefits

When people other than the consumer or producer of a good get a benefit from a good, economists refer to this as a **positive externality.** The argument here is that when parents choose the child care for their child, people other than themselves, their child, or their daycare worker are affected. By choosing a high-quality option, other parts of society stand to benefit because the presumption is that the child is more likely to be a productive citizen in the future. Whenever there are such external benefits, economists will generally concede that some form of subsidy is warranted.

positive externality
The benefits that go to someone other than the consumer or producer of a good.

The Early Evidence

The efficacy of the premise underlying the desirability of early intervention was fortified by studies from the 1960s through the 1980s that showed how effective early childhood education could be. The most prominent of these studies followed several hundred young, poor children, half of whom were given an excellent preschool experience free for two years, and half of whom were given nothing. The half that got the schooling not only performed better on IQ tests when they entered school, but also they performed better in school, they were less likely

---

[1]Later in this chapter you will see that there is an open debate over whether Head Start has had any of these effects.

to commit crimes as teens, and they graduated at far higher rates than the group that did not get that early education. By nearly every measure the children given the "head start" stayed ahead.

Advocates of Head Start maintained that for every dollar spent on early childhood education, five dollars would be returned in increased tax revenues and reduced welfare spending. While not reported in present value terms, recalculating it that way using reasonable interest rates suggests that such an investment would be a good one. Armed with that early evidence, Head Start began with great hope that in a generation or two, early childhood education would make significant inroads into poverty in the United States.

The Remaining Doubts

Even in the early years, some people questioned the premise that the investment in early childhood education could have the kind of return that was projected. These doubts were based mainly on the implausibility that a few years of preschool could enable children to overcome the effect of poverty and other social problems. Although most Head Start programs are offered for half days during the school year, even children in the all-day, all-year form of Head Start spend only 4,600 hours in the enriching environment. The rest of their childhood, 153,000 hours, is spent in poverty-stricken homes, crime-ridden neighborhoods, and educationally deficient schools. Regardless of how good the 4,600 hours is, it is hard to imagine that its influences would be strong enough to enable children to prevail over all the other influences in their lives.

Critics also point to flaws in the original study that showed the great potential for early intervention. Children in the original study were placed in a classroom that was nearly ideal, and their teachers were better equipped, physically and educationally, than any national program could ever hope to be. Critics doubted whether the program could be duplicated and used for the rest of the country.

THE HEAD START PROGRAM

Ever since its beginning in 1965, Head Start has enjoyed significant growth in appropriations but has never had a budget sufficient to be called "fully funded." A fully funded program would have enough money, staff, and facilities to handle all children who are eligible for the program. In reality there have been long waiting lists in some cities for Head Start services.

Head Start is much more than day care, and it is not merely a preschool. Under reforms enacted in the early 1990s, it has become a center of learning for the entire family. Teachers are charged not only with creating a wholesome environment for children, but also with making sure parents know of the available social resources for economically troubled families. The teachers make sure that immunization and health records are up to date, and they advise parents on a host of other matters related to child rearing as well.

The evidence is that Head Start centers are performing these tasks very well. Professional accreditation agencies have found that centers are well within the standards for early childhood education, certifying the vast majority of centers as "good" or better.

By 2005 there were more than 900,000 children enrolled in Head Start, at an average cost per child of nearly $7,554. As can be seen from Figure 25.1, inflation-adjusted spending and enrollment stayed relatively flat from 1965 to 1990. Though enrollment began at nearly 750,000 and fell through the 1970s to a low of 333,000, it rebounded through the early 1980s to a half million, where it stayed until 1990. Similarly, inflation-adjusted spending on the program stayed between 750 million and 1 billion 1982 dollars from its inception through 1990.

Beginning in 1990 President Bush (George Herbert Walker) and Congress attempted to change Head Start. They sought either to fund it fully or to open slots for many more students. By 1997 enrollment reached 800,000, with the stated goal for 2000 being 1 million children. While it fell short of that goal, enrollment has continued to rise. In that same year new standards came into place that required teachers to attain a higher degree of certification. This in turn was the impetus for increases in teachers' salaries. These reforms increased the cost of the program substantially. Though enrollments increased a substantial 67 percent, spending increases were even more substantial. Inflation-adjusted spending increased by more than 204 percent from 1990 to 2001.

The children who are enrolled in Head Start do not mirror those who are in the general population, and they do not mirror the population living below the poverty level. While just about three-quarters of the general population and just under half the people living in poverty are white, non-Hispanic, less than a third of the children in Head Start are white. While only 13 percent of the overall population and 24 percent of the poverty population are black, non-Hispanic, 31 percent of the Head Start population is black. Similarly, Hispanics are overrepresented, in that they comprise only 14 percent of the

FIGURE 25.1   Head Start spending and enrollment.

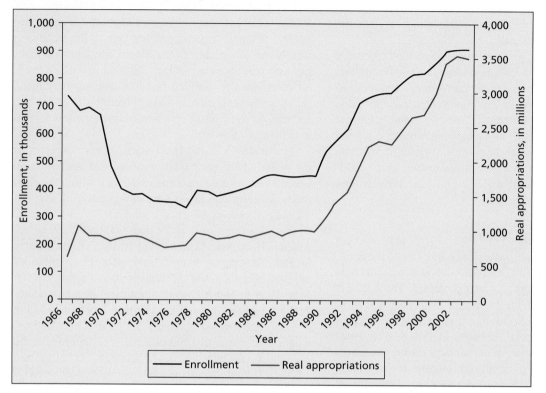

general population and 25 percent of the poverty population but constitute 31 percent of the Head Start population.

Groups that are significantly overrepresented in Head Start are the physically and mentally disadvantaged. Though fewer than 5 percent of children are disadvantaged in this way, children with such disparities represent 13 percent of the children in Head Start.

The families of Head Start children are overwhelmingly poor and their levels of educational attainment are low. On average they have more than one child, and they tend to receive some government assistance besides Head Start. Forty-four percent of Head Start families have yearly incomes that are lower than $9,000, and 60 percent have incomes below $12,000. Some 35 percent are headed by women who never married, and another fifth are headed by women who are separated, divorced, or widowed. Only 1 percent of Head Start families are headed by single men. Only 22 percent of the families whose children are in Head Start have only one child; a fifth have four or more. Only 16 percent of the families exist without any other form of government assistance than Head Start itself. Two-thirds are eligible to either receive Medicaid or participate in the Child Health Insurance Program, half receive Food Stamps or are eligible for the Women, Infants, and Children (WIC) program, and a quarter get a welfare check from the Temporary Aid to Needy Families program. Taken together, Head Start children are clearly in need of some sort of help.

In a third of the Head Start families no one in the household has a job. In these cases Head Start serves an augmented preschool function only. In one-fifth of households both parents are present and both have jobs. In these cases Head Start also provides a significant and free day-care service. In the remaining half, one parent, perhaps the child's only custodial parent, works. Again, whether the parents view the day-care function as more important than the preschool function, the child nevertheless gets good care and an education simultaneously. Moreover, parents are assisted in being better parents.

One of the more disturbing facts of life in the poor communities that are home to most Head Start children is that crime rates are much higher than they are in communities that are more affluent. Nearly a third of Head Start families are within eyesight or earshot of at least one violent crime every year. A quarter know a recent violent crime victim, and 6 percent have been victimized themselves by a violent crime that has usually taken place near home.

The 198,000 paid staff members of the program closely mirror the racial makeup of the children in the program. The median teacher is almost certainly a woman in her forties, she has more than 10 years of teaching experience, and she has been with Head Start for more than 5 years. Although only a third have college degrees, another third have some college credits. Ninety-five percent have a professional accreditation degree for child development (CDA), which is similar to a two-year technical degree. Typically the staff are better paid and have a better benefits package than a typical day-care worker, though the pay and benefits are somewhat lower than those of kindergarten teachers with a similar level of education.

THE CURRENT EVIDENCE

Evidence that Head Start Works

The evidence that Head Start works comes mostly from myriad studies which test Head Start children at or near their exit from the program. Head Start children do dramatically better on IQ tests than equally situated[2] non–Head Start children on entrance into kindergarten. Virtually all of the studies that examine the program have found some significant advantage for these children in the year or so after they exit the program.

The improvements can be seen in lower numbers of children being retained in the first grade and in higher reading and verbal test scores. In addition, Head Start children are healthier than equally situated non–Head Start children, in large measure because part of Head Start is parental education and because children in Head Start are fed nutritious meals while they are in the program. In the teacher–parent contacts, immunization records are reviewed and, when necessary, doctor and dentist referrals are made. Parents of Head Start children are more aware of the many services available to them and their children, an awareness which explains, in part, why 59 percent of them are enrolled in Medicaid.

---

[2]Not all studies of Head Start compare children's abilities adequately. For instance, if you put a child of educated, financially well-off parents in a dilapidated building with a lousy teacher, you will probably get better results than you will if you put a poor child of a single, uneducated teen-age mother in a new building with a great teacher. The home environment is remarkably important. This means that unless you control statistically for home environment variables, you get study results that are not indicative of the effectiveness of the program. Good studies of Head Start must compare "equally situated" children.

Individual studies continue to show success of programs in particular states, in specific areas of short- and medium-term areas of achievement, or using particular Head Start curricula. Recently, a study produced by Oden, Schweinhart, and Weikart showed that children who participated in a Head Start program in the 1970s in Colorado and Florida were, 17 years later, less likely to drop out of high school and less likely to commit crime. Several others have shown that there is a demonstrable decrease in repetition of kindergarten and first grade and early placement in special education. Both of these are costly to school districts.

Evidence that Head Start Does Not Work

Head Start's detractors have evidence to support their position as well. While there are limited studies that show success for Head Start education that extends beyond the second grade, there are companion studies that show that it does not. As the General Accounting Office (GAO), the investigative wing of Congress, reported in 1997, there are no national studies that show, in a compelling way, that anything long lasting is achieved in Head Start. A study by Janet Currie and Duncan Thomas put it quite well: "In summary, despite literally hundreds of studies, the jury is still out on the question of whether participation in Head Start has any lasting beneficial effects."

Although some studies do show that using some measures of success, some types of students do better, the patterns in the literature on Head Start are not consistent. Some show lasting effects for black children and others do not. Some show lasting effects for white children and others do not.

The basic premise of Head Start is that it is literally an educational "head start" and that the students who graduated from it ought to do better down the road than similarly situated students who did not participate. There is very little evidence, however, that suggests that test scores, dropout rates, graduation rates, or any other measure of educational achievement in later years is enhanced when students have Head Start in their background. Most of the studies that show a waning influence find that most of the benefit of Head Start is gone by the third grade and that none is evident by the sixth grade.

Note, however, that the GAO report and the Currie and Thomas study found that none of the more than 200 academic studies on Head Start used a national representative sample. Therefore, there are none upon which to make positive or negative claims.

More Evidence Is Coming and Some Is In

In its 1994 and 1998 reauthorizations of the law that created Head Start, Congress commissioned a national study on the long-term benefits of the program. By 1999 a highly regarded committee of scholars settled on a methodology and a set of goals for collecting the relevant data. That process is ongoing and a final report is due to Congress in 2006. In the meantime, Janet Currie, one of the authors of the study pointing to the dearth of long-term evidence supporting Head Start's effectiveness, produced an additional study that shows that even if there are no long-term benefits to Head Start, the program may be worthy for its short- and medium-term benefits. Specifically, even many program detractors concede the statistical evidence is sufficient to demonstrate that participants are less likely to have to repeat kindergarten or first grade and are less likely to be placed in special education during that time. If you further concede her point that half of the program's costs would be spent anyway on subsidizing day care, then, Currie maintains, the cost reductions from diminishing grade repetition and the use of special education are nearly sufficient to cover the other half.

In a newer study she, and other economists, found that for whites, participation as a child increased their likelihood of graduating high school and attending college, as well as increasing their income as young adults. For African Americans, participation as a child decreased their likelihood of being charged with a crime. Interestingly, the spillover benefits also extend to the child's non-participating siblings who also are less likely to be charged with a crime as young adults.

THE OPPORTUNITY COST OF FULLY FUNDING HEAD START

If tax money had no opportunity cost, Head Start would not be controversial. In the tradition of the medical profession's Hippocratic oath, Head Start clearly does no harm. Whether it does any good and, if so, whether that good is enough to justify the costs are other questions. Head Start costs $7,554 per year per student, more than most day-care centers charge for a year of service, even though most day care is nine hours a day, all year, and Head Start is only four days a week during the school year. According to the census bureau, day-care costs per child range between $4,000 and $6,000 per year, though costs vary widely by location.

If the federal government wants to provide free day care for poor children, it can do it for less money than it spends on Head Start. If Head Start genuinely provides a measurable head start, it should show up in the congressionally commissioned study.

Make no mistake about it, the opportunity cost would exist whether or not Head Start was effective. The worst billion-dollar-a-year government program and the best billion-dollar-a-year program have the same opportunity cost: a billion dollars of other programs or tax cuts.

What differentiates an effective program from an ineffective one is that when we fund a program that does not perform, we do not consider alternatives designed to meet the same goal which might perform better. The conventional wisdom among politicians is that Head Start is living up to its billing. They think that it is a good net present value investment. This 2006 study may prove that case, but until then this thinking prevents anyone from coming up with more effective long-term ways of utilizing the funds. The lost opportunity to experiment with a better alternative program cannot be ignored.

Summary

You now understand that Head Start is a federally funded program that provides early childhood education to nearly a million children at a cost of $6 billion per year. You are able to use investment and net present value thinking to understand the premise of the program. You know that despite the efforts of economists and others to verify the worth of the program, the evidence that the program works is rather scant and is the subject of ongoing research. You can see that, as with any other expenditure, there is an opportunity cost to the program.

Key Term

positive externality, 270

Quiz Yourself

1. From an economic perspective the tool one would use to analyze the costs and benefits of Head Start would be
   a. Present value.
   b. Supply and demand.
   c. Production possibilities.
   d. Marginal net benefit.

2. If Head Start were a good long-run investment from a strictly economic perspective, for current children enrolled in the program it would
   a. Make them happier.
   b. Help their parents with subsidized day care/preschool.
   c. Increase the likelihood of future success as adults.
   d. Increase the likelihood that they knew the alphabet going into kindergarten.

3. Though the high-quality preschool experience is a private benefit for the children and their parents, the economic justification for Head Start is based on
   a. External costs.
   b. Its low total cost.
   c. The increase in reading ability of participants going into kindergarten.
   d. The external benefits to society.

4. The early evidence on programs like Head Start made it clear that
   a. The rate of return to these programs was very low.
   b. The net present value of the external benefits was positive.
   c. The short-run benefits were not worth the costs.
   d. The long-run benefits were not worth the costs.

5. The typical Head Start teacher is
   a. An ill-trained minimum wage worker.
   b. A professional credentialed worker making more than the typical day-care worker.
   c. A college graduate making $30,000 a year or more.
   d. A professional with a master's degree or higher.

6. Current evidence suggests that the long-term benefits of Head Start are
   a. Sufficiently positive to make the net present value positive.
   b. Sufficiently positive such that when added to the short- and intermediate-term benefits, the net present value is positive.

   c. Nonexistent.
   d. Curiously negative.

7. The intermediate-term external benefits of Head Start
   a. Focus on reducing the likelihood of the children ending up in prison.
   b. Focus on reducing the likelihood that the children will become pregnant as teenagers.
   c. Are significant if you know that the children would qualify for subsidized free day-care anyway.
   d. Are significant in that they reduce the likelihood of the children needing expensive special education in elementary school.

Think about This

The notion of calculating the present value of external benefits and comparing that to the present value of extra costs in evaluating Head Start is a purely economic way of looking at the program. Is this the only way? Is it the right way? Whether or not society benefits from their participation, does society owe these underprivileged children such a program?

Talk about This

Suppose the evidence was that Head Start was completely ineffective from a present value perspective. What would you do with the money that is spent on the program? What programs are we forgoing?

For More Insight See

Congressional Budget Office, *Research Provides Little Information on Impact of Current Program*, April 1997.

Currie, Janet, *Early Childhood Intervention Programs: What Do We Know?* April 2000, http://www.brook.edu/dybdocroot/es/research/projects/cr/doc/curie20000401.pdf.

Currie, Janet, and Duncan Thomas, "Does Head Start Make a Difference?" *American Economic Review* 85, no. 3 (June 1995), pp. 341–364.

Garces, Eliana, Duncan Thomas, and Janet Currie, "Longer-Term Effects of Head Start," *American Eco-nomic Review* 92, no. 4. (Sept. 2002)

National Head Start Impact Research, U.S. Department of Health and Human Services, http://www.acf.dhhs.gov/programs/core/ongoing_research/hs/nhs_impact/nhs_impt.html.

Oden, Sherri, Lawrence Schweinhart, and David Weikart, *Into Adulthood.* (Ypsilanti, MI: High/Scope Press, 2000).

Behind the Numbers

Historical data.
>Head Start data, 1980–2003.
>>Statistical Abstract of the United States; Social Insurance and Human Services—http://www.census.gov/prod/2005pubs.

Head Start enrollment and families, 2005.
>Administration for Children and Families; Head Start Bureau—http://www.acf.hhs.gov/programs/hsb/research/2005.htmI.

Head Start Program Information, 2005.
>Administration for Children and Families; Head Start Bureau FACES 2000 Survey—http://www.acf.hhs.gov/programs/opre/hs/faces/.

Chapter **26**

The Economics of Race and Sex Discrimination

A racially diverse classroom engages in discussion.
Source: © image 100 Ltd.

Chapter Objectives

After reading this chapter you should be able to

State how economists measure the income disparity between the races and sexes.

Understand what discrimination is, how it is measured, and how it is detected.

See how economists model discrimination in the labor market and what they can say about it in the markets for real estate, automobiles, and lending.

Understand what affirmative action is; how, why, and when it came about; and what forms of it exist today in the United States.

Chapter Outline

The Economic Status of Women and Minorities

Definitions and Detection of Discrimination

Discrimination in Labor, Consumption, and Lending

Affirmative Action

Summary

African Americans and women have been subjected to discrimination throughout history. That discrimination exists is not a surprise, but its precise detection and measurement is not as simple as it may seem. Some of the differences in income and wealth are diminishing over time but nontrivial gaps remain. This chapter explores the economic status of women and minorities, discusses the varieties of discrimination economists recognize and moves to explain them. In so doing, the chapter discusses the means of detecting discrimination and seeks to model its impact on wages. The chapter progresses to explain why, absent legally sanctioned discrimination, some economists thought wage gaps would cease to exist and then explains that those gaps have not been eliminated. Finally, the chapter ends with a discussion of affirmative action, its economic justification and machinations.

THE ECONOMIC STATUS OF WOMEN AND MINORITIES

Women

Women are becoming an ever-growing part of the U.S. economy. Economists call the percentage of people in a particular category who are over 16 and working the

labor-force participation rate

The percentage of the population of a group that is employed or seeking employment.

labor-force participation rate. The rate for women has been rising steadily for decades, from 38 percent in the early 1960s to 60 percent today. While the rate for men is higher than that for women, 76 percent, it has been steadily decreasing. Demographers, the people who study population trends, adjust the labor-force participation rate to reflect the fact that as the U.S. population ages, more people are in age groups likely to be retired from work. For this reason, they suggest the real importance of women in the workplace is even greater than the raw participation rate suggests.

What is also important from an economic perspective is that though men and women are approaching equality in income and wealth, men still have 73 percent more income than women, make 24 percent more in wages for full-time employment, are 5.4 percent (3.5 percentage points) more likely to be covered by pensions, and are less likely to be in poverty. Though more couples file for bankruptcy than single men or single women, the incidence of single women filing for bankruptcy has

increased substantially, while the incidence of couples or men filing alone has remained steady. Finally, single men have 31 percent more wealth than single women. The differences are summarized in Table 26.1.

This is not to suggest that the economic status of women is not improving. Figure 26.1 shows that the ratio of women's to men's weekly wages for full-time employment and the similar ratio for money income from all

TABLE 26.1   Economic differences between men and women.

	Men	Women
Income from all sources	$29,931	$17,259
Average weekly wages for full-time employment	$713	$573
Mean net worth (singles)	$111,951	$85,319
Covered by a pension	43%	40.8%
Poverty rate	10.9%	13.3%
Percentage of single-filing bankruptcies	46%	54%

Sources: http://www.census.gov/prod/2004pubs/04statab/socinsur.pdf; http://www.bls.gov/cps/cpsaat39.pdf.

FIGURE 26.1   Ratio of women's income to men's.

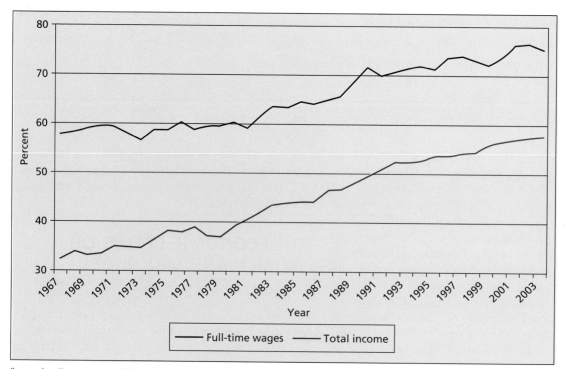

Sources: http://www.census.gov/hhes/www/income/histinc/p40.html; http://www.census.gov/hhes/www/income/histinc/p54.html.

TABLE 26.2   Median full-time wage earnings, 2003: selected occupations.

Occupation	Women's Earning's as a Percent of Men's
Physicians	59.0
Lawyers	87.3
Managers/Executives	69.9
Teachers (elementary)	89.8

Source: http://www.bls.gov/cps/cpsaat39.pdf.

sources continue to increase. Still, as Table 26.2 suggests, even when you look at identical professions, women currently make less than men.

Minorities

There are two clear trends in the data on economic and social conditions affecting the races. Inequality within the races is clearly documented, and the degree of inequality is lessening. The clearest sign of this phenomenon of shrinking-but-not-yet-zero inequality can be seen in the data on median family income for white and black families. Figure 26.2 shows us that since 1967 median family income has risen from $8,234 to $55,768 for white families and from $4,875 to $34,369 for black families.

Figure 26.3 indicates that while the gap in income between black people and white people is widening in ab-

solute terms, the ratio of white median family income to black median family income is narrowing. This means that while white families still enjoy the benefits of more income, the income of black families is increasing at a faster rate than that of white families. The ratio of white family income to black family income remains significantly less than 1.0 (its value if perfect equality existed), but it has grown from .52 in 1950 to .62 in 2003.

Other economic measures provide us with additional data on the inequalities that exist between African Americans and whites. For instance, in 2003 for salaried and full-time hourly workers, median weekly earnings is $636 for white workers and $514 for black workers. In this arena, the ratio of .81 shows we are closer to equality, but since this ratio has remained constant for nearly 20 years, we are not seeing significant improvement.

Although there remain many signs of astonishing economic inequality, there are also signs of significant progress. Nevertheless, only 24 percent of African Americans are in the top 40 percent of income earners, whereas 57 percent are in the bottom 40 percent; moreover, unemployment rates across age categories are between 2.5 and 4.5 percentage points higher for blacks than whites. Encouragingly, the growth in the number of businesses owned by members of minority groups has been astounding. Between 1987 and 1996 the number of such firms grew by 46 percent and their receipts by 63 percent. Sociologically the story is similar. We

FIGURE 26.2   Median family income.

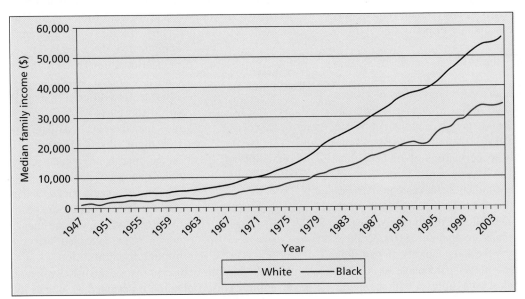

Source: http://www.census.gov/hhes/www/income/histinc/f06b.html.

FIGURE 26.3   Ratio of black to white family income.

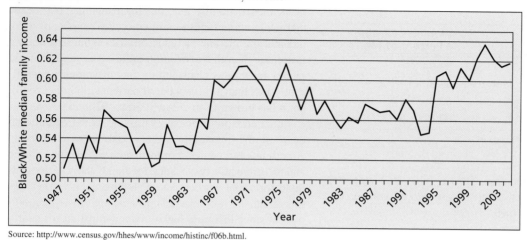

Source: http://www.census.gov/hhes/www/income/histinc/f06b.html.

cannot escape the fact that in the United States there are the same number of blacks on parole, in prison, or on probation (1.9 million) as in college. These figures highlight two problems: there are not enough African Americans in college and there are too many in prison. Both statistics are even more pronounced when you look at African American men. Of blacks, there are nearly 50 percent more women in college than men and nearly 10 times more men in prison than women.

Also, we cannot escape the fact that black children are more than twice as likely as white children to be in a female-headed household. Because family structure is a key determinant of economic well-being, this social problem of single-parent (overwhelmingly female) households is a major cause of the economic disparity that African Americans face.

It must be noted, too, that African Americans are disproportionately the victims of crime. In any given year, 5.5 out of 100 African Americans are victims of violent crime, whereas only 4 out of 100 whites are so victimized. The racial distinction is greatly highlighted by the difference in rates of robbery victimization. Blacks are three times more likely to be victims of robbery than whites.

In the arena of educational achievement, African Americans are graduating from high school at a much faster rate than they were in 1960. Unfortunately, the rate at which African Americans are graduating from college is not growing with nearly the same rapidity. In part, this could be because a much higher percentage of African Americans get their high school diploma with a general equivalence degree (GED) than whites. Many colleges,

moreover, are less enthusiastic about GEDs than actual high school diplomas. Further, white or black, the average incomes of GED recipients are closer to those of high school dropouts than of high school graduates.

DEFINITIONS AND DETECTION OF DISCRIMINATION

Discrimination, Definitions, and the Law

On the surface, it would seem that defining discrimination would not be that difficult. If you treat people in a certain way because they are women, African American, or Hispanic, you are discriminating. To make matters more complicated, there are two types of discrimination rather than just one. If you treat two otherwise equal people differently and do so on the basis of their sex or race, then this is called **disparate treatment discrimination.** If, on the other hand, you do something that is not necessarily discriminatory on its face but that impacts some groups more negatively than others, you are engaging in what is called **adverse impact discrimination.**

disparate treatment discrimination
Treating two otherwise equal people differently on the basis of race.

adverse impact discrimination
Doing something that is not necessarily discriminatory on its face but that impacts some groups more negatively than others.

While both forms of discrimination are usually illegal, adverse impact discrimination is accepted as long as the persons or companies doing the discriminating can show

Sociology or Economics: Why Women Earn Less Than Men

A multitude of studies compare women's pay to men's. Many economists do the comparison by controlling for education, full- or part-time status, experience, job requirements, and a host of other factors to determine whether men and women earn the same money for the same work. Sociologists and nearly all feminists view this as fallacious because they see these as symptoms of continued mistreatment of women, rather than economic phenomena that should be statistically controlled for. The issues are:

- All income versus earned income: As shown in Table 26.1, if you focus on the broad issue of relative incomes, women earn only 57.7 percent of what men do but if you focus more narrowly on the differences between what women and men earn when they both work full time, the ratio is narrower: women earn 78 percent of what men do.

- Experience with the same employer: Men have been with their current employer for a median 3.9 years; the comparable figure for females is 3.4 years.

- Different professions: Only 28 percent of lawyers, 30 percent of doctors, and 14 percent of engineers are women. On the other hand, women account for 97 percent of secretaries, 90 percent of nurses, 82 percent of elementary school teachers, 95 percent of day-care workers, and 80 percent of social workers.

- Pregnancy and child rearing: While it is illegal to discriminate based on pregnancy, any opportunity that a woman loses and a man gains can result in young professional fathers being promoted more quickly than young professional mothers. Since only women can give birth and 98 percent stay-at-home parents are women, women lose opportunities.

- Flexible employment: For reasons that are primarily sociological, women rather than men pick flexible employment so that they can deal with their family's needs. Flexible jobs also happen to be lower-paying.

Are these legitimate economic consequences of choices that people make freely and knowingly or are they manifestations of discrimination itself? That is a debate for you to have with your fellow students and your professors of economics and sociology.

that what they are doing makes sense for their needs. For instance, if whites sued the National Football League (NFL) on the basis that defensive backs were disproportionately black, there would be two legal hurdles. The first hurdle would be for whites, the group at whom the discrimination had supposedly been aimed, to show the "adverse impact." They could do this easily, by showing that the United States is 70 percent white and that less than 1 percent of defensive backs are white. In actuality, in the 1997–1998 season there was one white defensive back. With adverse impact proved, the burden of proof would be transferred to the accused, in this case the NFL. The NFL would have to show a "business necessity" that led the teams to make the choices they made. The NFL would win in court if the teams could then point to their tests of speed, strength, and conditioning and show (1) that these tests did predict the ability to cover receivers, and (2) they chose defensive backs on the basis of these tests. Thus while differential treatment discrimination is always illegal, adverse impact discrimination is illegal only when it cannot be defended on the grounds that it stems from a business necessity.

The more common example of differential treatment discrimination arises when an employer uses a rule-of-thumb approach to hiring. Rules of thumb are useful in that they can be simple guidelines for people making complex decisions. Some economists who study this kind of discrimination assert that rules of thumb for hiring are generally perpetuated long past the time when they are relevant. Furthermore, they suggest that many of those rules of thumb never really were very good predictors of performance. One that was propagated in the world of broadcasting was that men, being generally more interested in sports, would make better sports broadcasters. Although it may be true that men watch more sports, that does not say anything about whether a particular man or a particular woman would be better for a particular job. Furthermore, many rules of thumb, like the notion that men are better drivers, never were good predictors of performance on the job.

Even when there is a concretely accurate rule of thumb, discrimination is illegal. This form of discrimination is the economic equivalent of racial profiling, which we hear about with regard to police tactics. In economics, such discrimination is labeled by some as **rational or statistical discrimination** because it is based on sound statistical evidence. It is referred to

rational or statistical discrimination
Unequal treatment of classes of people that is based on sound statistical evidence and is consistent with profit maximization.

as "rational" only because it is consistent with the recognized goal of firms maximizing profit. For instance, it is a fact of life in the United States that when a bank consults with the best statisticians and economists, it finds that African Americans are 2 percent more likely to default on a home loan. This is true even when the study holds income, occupation, and a host of other important variables constant. If lenders use this information to charge blacks a higher interest rate for mortgages, or if they use this information to set a higher standard for blacks to qualify for a loan, they are guilty of "statistical" discrimination.[1] Regardless of whether it makes economic sense, it is illegal to use race in any part of the lending decision.

Detecting and Measuring Discrimination

Detecting and measuring the extent of discrimination in an authoritative way is not always easy. If a Hispanic female high school dropout and an affluent white male college professor each went into a bank to ask for a loan, and the high school dropout was denied the loan and the professor got one, we would not automatically assume we were looking at a case of gender or race discrimination. We would have to separate out the reasons why one person got the loan and the other did not.

There are two ways that economists try to do this. First, they use the statistical technique called "regression" to look for systematic patterns in the data. Once they figure the appropriate values using a statistical computer program, regression analysis tells them the impact of one variable on another holding the effects of other variables constant. It allows them to say, with degrees of certainty, that a variable like race or sex has a specific impact on another variable, like whether or not a loan was approved, even when they hold other variables like income constant. When many different people, from many different backgrounds, with different incomes and debt histories seek loans from many different banks, the regression technique can, when correctly applied, determine whether being African American or female makes an applicant less likely to get a loan.

The second technique involves creating fake identities for people who are exactly alike except for their race or sex. These "auditors" approach a situation one after the

other to see if they are treated differently. Since everything other than race is held constant, any differences in the way the auditors are treated must be related to race. A fascinating example of this work was conducted by economists Bertrand and Mullainathan. They showed that on purely fictitious and functionally identical resumes, applicants with names like "Emily" and "Greg" were statistically, substantially, and depressingly more likely to be called for an interview than applicants with names like "Lakisha" and "Jamal."

These two techniques have their critics. This may, at least in part, be because of the somewhat different conclusions the techniques have led economists to make. Generally, regression techniques expose a smaller race bias problem across the board than is exposed by audit techniques. Typically, those who advocate regression measurement rather than using auditors say that the fictitious auditors themselves may create part of the disparity by the way they act. They also say that the exactness of the match is less than reliable. On the other hand, the advocates of auditing suggest that variables included in regressions, like intelligence scores, are themselves biased or indicative of other past discriminatory practices and therefore always understate the true problem.

DISCRIMINATION IN LABOR, CONSUMPTION, AND LENDING

Keeping these basics in mind, we turn now to three areas of the economy in which professional economists have studied discrimination in some depth. These areas are the labor market, where people sell their labor to firms; the goods market, where people buy things; and the lending market, where people borrow money.

Labor Market Discrimination

We can start exploring the effect of discrimination in the labor market by assuming a world, like the 1960s, where it is legal and openly practiced. In Figure 26.4, suppose there are two kinds of jobs: jobs that only whites are allowed to do and jobs that whites are allowed to do but blacks must do if they want jobs.[2] In a world where there is no discrimination, the nondiscriminatory supply curve S_{ND} crosses the demand curve at a wage W_{ND} that is equal for blacks and whites. In the world where such discrimination is legal and binding, the supply of workers available to perform tasks limited to whites only (left panel)

---

[1]Another interpretation of this finding is that it is actually whites who are being discriminated against since, all else being equal, they are defaulting less frequently than blacks. This implies that they are being turned down too often.

[2]This analysis works the same for modeling sex discrimination.

FIGURE 26.4   The effect of racism on white and black wages..

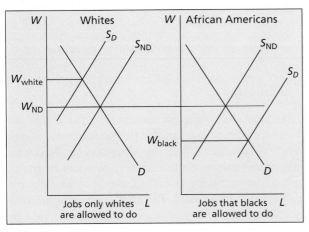

is less, S_D, and therefore the wage that must be paid to whites is greater. Because blacks must perform the other tasks, the supply of workers available in that market (right panel) is greater and therefore the wage is lower.

Thus with discrimination that is legal, whites make more than blacks. The question is: If discrimination is held to be illegal, is that sufficient to eliminate the wage differential? Beginning with the work of economist Gary Becker, the profession showed theoretically that without a legal basis, discrimination and wage differentials would go away. In the 1960s the economics profession was confident that profit-oriented but open-minded business owners would want to make as much money as possible and would therefore ignore skin color. If employers employed people to do what used to be considered "a white man's job" and were right in assuming that the only reason blacks had been previously prevented from doing the job before was racism, then the African Americans would be able to do the job just as well as whites. That, in and of itself, however, would not motivate profit-oriented business owners to hire blacks. What would motivate them would be that they could offer blacks a little bit more than their other jobs paid but less than they were currently paying whites. In Figure 26.4 this would be between W_{black} and W_{white}.

If profit-oriented managers were to hire African Americans at just above the W_{black} wage that is depicted in the right panel of Figure 26.4, they could get all the labor they need at much lower cost than they would have had to pay white workers, W_{white}. Thus the business manager's desire to make money can serve to narrow the wage gap, at least a little.

As other managers see the advantage of hiring lower-paid, equally skilled African American labor, the wages among African Americans would continue to rise as firms seeking cheaper labor attempt to outbid each other. Thus a traditional economist argues that in time nothing more than removing legal impediments is required to achieve equality. The idea that greed prevails over bigotry remains steadfast in the minds of many economists.

Considering that wages are not equal 30 years after the civil rights movement's heyday, however, there must be obstacles that simple economic incentives have not been able to overcome in equalizing wages. The first thing to consider with regard to whether economic profit incentives will overcome racism is that people will pay extra, when they want to, to satisfy their bigoted nature. Managers will pay a little extra not to have to work with "them," regardless of whether "them" is women, blacks, gays, whites, or anyone else. Presumably bigots are willing to pay to support their bigotry.

Another problem is that some people will patronize only businesses where not any of "them" are around. Even if you are an open-minded, profit-oriented manager, if you see that your business decreases whenever you hire more African Americans, you may decide to hire only whites, and you will pay more to attract them. You may do this even though you know it is illegal and morally wrong. It is a fact of life that if you are a manager and your livelihood depends on satisfying your customers, you may do things you would not otherwise do.

It is for these reasons that, even though the wage gap between whites and blacks has shrunk, it has not disappeared. Regression analysis shows that it remains at between 12 percent and 15 percent.[3] Remember that the regression results hold constant things that are supposed to determine pay such as education and occupation. Because African Americans have attained a lower average level of education and because they are less prevalent in high-income occupations, you would expect that they would be paid less. What this also means is that the actual difference in pay is much greater than the 12 percent to 15 percent that these regression studies indicate. In an apparent contradiction, studies limited to well-educated professionals show that being a black woman actually pays a premium. This is interesting but it lacks practical

---

[3]Some economists have found that when they include standardized tests of intelligence, this remaining difference disappears. These tests and their use in this context are hotly debated by economists. The economists who employ the results of the tests believe the tests are truly tests of intelligence, whereas others contend that the tests are racially biased and therefore of no value.

significance since most African American women are not well-educated professionals.

Consumption Market and Lending Market Discrimination

While it is easy to imagine discrimination in the labor market, where people either are denied positions or are hired for lower pay, it is harder to imagine in the market for goods. You never see a Wal-Mart charge a white man $65 for a car battery and then charge a Hispanic woman $75. There are areas in the goods market, however, and especially in the services market, where the races can be and are treated differently.

At first it would seem rather silly for a business to discriminate and turn away profitable sales. What you have to consider, though, is that audits performed by various economists and government investigators have shown that discrimination is in fact quite prevalent in real estate sales, rentals, and car sales.

In real estate, audits show that real estate agents of both races tend to show white clients more houses. Moreover, they show white families houses in all-white neighborhoods while diverting black families to houses in black or integrated neighborhoods. The same results were evident when auditors looked for rentals. Why would real estate agents do this? Why, in particular, would black real estate agents do this? There appear to be a couple of explanations.

The first possibility is that agents are simply trying to make the clients happy, and they think they are doing this—and may in fact be doing this—by showing housing in areas where they think the clients want to live. Salespeople make judgments all the time about what will make their clients happy, and they do so with very little to go on. The economists who uncovered this form of discrimination attribute this behavior to racism and call it discrimination. If a significant segment of African Americans really do want to live in already-integrated neighborhoods rather than move in to another neighborhood to become the only minority family in the area, the economists are incorrect when they label this behavior as discrimination.

The second possibility is that both the black and white agents have regular clients in the neighborhoods that contain the apartments or houses that are available, and they do not want to anger their regular clients by upsetting the racial "balance" in the neighborhood. The audits do not include interviews of the agents, so the data do not show whether either of these scenarios accounts for the discriminatory practices that exist when realtors are showing properties to their clients. If you live in a neighborhood originally developed before 1975 you might be shocked to find the covenants for your property probably include a line like the one I recently found in mine:

> No person of any race other than Caucasian shall own, use or occupy any lot or building in this subdivision, except that this covenant shall not prevent domestic servants or employees of a different race domiciled with an owner tenant.

Another area where economists have found race and sex discrimination in the market for goods is in automobile sales. Auditors found that even when they used the same bargaining strategy, made it clear they would be paying cash, and were talking about the same car, dealers charged blacks and women more. The usual method of the audit had blacks and whites, men and women going into the same dealership within a short period of time and asking a salesperson to tell them the asking price for a specific car. In each case the auditors would then offer a price they had previously decided to offer and then they would use a "split the difference" bargaining technique until the salesperson and they arrived at a final price. What happened was that the initial offer made by both black and white car dealers was lower for whites than it was for blacks. The dealers also agreed to sell cars to whites for lower prices than those for blacks. The economists who performed these audits concluded that on the average black women pay $1,000 more, black men pay $800 more, and white women pay $400 more for a car than do white men.

Why would dealers do this? Though the bias was less evident when the dealers themselves were women or minorities, they still discriminated against blacks and women. It seems as if either the dealers did not want the sales or dealers have preconceived notions of sales resistance and bargaining strategies. It may be they believe they can outmaneuver African American and female customers.

Another area where economists have investigated and found serious race discrimination is the area of mortgage lending. Because it is rare that banks offer anything but a single interest rate, the question is whether blacks are more likely to be turned down for loans than are whites. Again, audits found that given nearly identical economic characteristics, blacks were somewhat more likely than whites to be turned down for a loan. It seems likely here that, short of bigotry, banks, which use both objective standards and subjective standards in making their decisions, have discriminatory prejudice in their subjective standards. As we said before, it has been shown that blacks and whites of equal economic standing have different default rates on mortgage loans. It may be that the loan officer who denies a mortgage to a black couple that would have been approved for a white couple is doing so in a "rational" sense. Nevertheless, this discrimination remains a violation of law, and banks are currently being monitored and penalized for such practices.

Some economists claim to have noted sex discrimination in retirement annuities. Whether it is actually discrimination, men have better choices than women because women live longer than men by more than half a decade. Insurance companies that offer annuities have to charge women more than men, offer fewer benefits to women than men, or split the difference in some other way so that women end up paying somewhat more and being paid somewhat less. Making it illegal to charge women more than men for such annuities would not change these facts. It would merely force companies to indulge in what would amount to a redistribution of wealth from men to women.

AFFIRMATIVE ACTION

The Economics of Affirmative Action

As you saw in the preceding discussion, there are conditions under which discriminatory behavior can continue long after it is declared illegal. Either because employers may be bigoted or because employers may have customers who are bigoted, discrimination in employment exists even in a perfectly competitive market. This means that the perfectly competitive market may fail to arrive at the socially optimal level of employment for minorities. Minorities will be underemployed and underpaid and whites and men will be overpaid for the work they are doing and get jobs for which they are not as qualified.

Anytime a market fails to achieve a situation where consumer and producer surplus combined are maximized, economists are interested in actions that can correct that market's failure. Though corrective policies for failed markets have costs, they are seen by economists as necessary investments that will ultimately pay dividends. In this con-

affirmative action
Any policy that is taken to speed up the process of achieving equality.

text the corrective policies are called **affirmative action**. Affirmative action is any policy that is taken to speed up the process of achieving equality.

The costs of affirmative action policies range from the costs of more thorough searches for employees to the cost of monitoring fair hiring practices with a fully staffed human resources office. These costs can be seen in the same context as any costs associated with cor-

recting a failed market. For example, though it costs industry money to clean up pollution, expenditures to do so by industry which are mandated by the government make us better off in the aggregate than we would be without them. When affirmative action is utilized to correct an inequality that is seen as permanent, affirmative action supporters view it very much like scrubbers on coal-fired plants: It is money spent to fix a market failure. If affirmative action exists to speed up a transition from inequality to equality that would have happened eventually anyway, these are seen as costs that diminish the market failure by shortening the time it exists.

On the other hand, if the market differences between minorities and whites and between men and women only reflect the differences in the skills of the groups, then the market is not failing. If this is the case, then any attempt at affirmative action imposes a cost on, rather than a benefit to, the economy. In such a case, the costs of affirmative action should be viewed as buying "fairness" rather than fixing a market failure.

What Is Affirmative Action?

Even if traditional economic models correctly predicted that pay gaps between men and women and between whites and minorities would eventually be eliminated without needing such influences as affirmative action, there is the problem of time. Affirmative action came about because proponents wanted to achieve equality more quickly. To the degree that equality is not arriving fast enough through economic incentives, advocates have asserted that further affirmative action be taken to speed up the process.

Gradations of Affirmative Action

Affirmative action's many forms range from the inconsequential to the highly consequential. For instance, many citizens hold as conventional wisdom that affirmative action consists of quotas that mandate the number of people who must be hired, promoted, or admitted. As a matter of fact, explicit quotas are rare and, unless they have been ordered through a court decision, they are illegal. On the other hand, many other policies can be engaged in that stop far short of quotas.

One form of affirmative action is simply to make sure that all potentially qualified employees know about a particular job. So, for instance, if you were hiring production workers in a southwestern city, affirmative action could consist of your advertising in both the English- and Spanish-language newspapers. If you were hiring in a city that had a radio station whose audience was primarily African American, under this form of affirmative action you would advertise there alongside radio stations where audiences were predominantly white. This form of affirmative action requires that employers cast the net wide when looking for new hires. It places very little burden on employers and it gives no one any sort of unfair advantage. The only people who might be perceived as disadvantaged would be those who previously had an unfair advantage. These might be those who were less qualified but got jobs because minorities were not aware particular jobs were available.

Another form of affirmative action has held that if two applicants are judged to have equal qualifications for a position, then the one who is a member of a minority should automatically be hired. Just as in baseball where "tie goes to the runner," this form of affirmative action suggests that "tie goes to the minority." The advantage to the minority group members here is that once they have shown they are equally qualified, their chance of being hired goes from 50–50 to 100 percent, and the disadvantage to the member of the majority is that the chance of being hired goes from 50–50 to 0 percent.

A third, higher level of affirmative action is one in which an employer sets a level of qualification that is appropriate for a job, hires all minorities who meet the standard, and then fills out the remaining slots with non-minorities. When universities make decisions about whom to admit, and they use criteria to further affirmative action, they often conduct them in the following way: a school will decide that an SAT of 1,000 is sufficient to make graduation likely and admit all minorities that meet that standard. The remainder of the student body is then generated from the best of the rest, a pool of students whose SATs may well be above 1,000.

A fourth version of affirmative action, just short of a quota, is establishing a guideline that employers should try to meet. The idea behind this is to ensure that employers can be somewhat flexible while also ensuring that the proportion of minorities not be allowed to drop too low. In military promotions, for example, if the racial, ethnic, and gender proportions of those promoted are not roughly equal to the racial, ethnic, and gender proportions of those eligible for promotion, the promotions board must file a report justifying the discrepancy. That means that though there is no specific number that must be promoted, any deviation from the guideline is suspect.

The final version of strictness associated with affirmative action is quotas. Surprisingly, the quotas that most people think of when they think of affirmative action are actually against the law as a general practice. Quotas are legal only when court-mandated, either through a verdict or a consent decree. Sufficient grounds must exist to show that a particular employer or university has been guilty of discrimination in the past to make quotas legal. What troubles some economists is the degree to which businesses engage in quotalike hiring practices designed to protect themselves from legal troubles.

Summary

You now understand the economic implications of discrimination. You know how economists measure the impact of discrimination, detect its existence, and explain its importance. You know how labor market discrimination can be modeled, which implies that discriminatory pay gaps should close over time but the reality is that the rate of closure is slow. You know what affirmative action is in its various machinations.

Key Terms

adverse impact discrimination, 280
affirmative action, 285

disparate treatment discrimination, 280
labor-force participation rate, 278

rational or statistical
discrimination, 281

Quiz Yourself

1. How academics look at the evidence on how much women make relative to men is an issue that very much depends on
   a. Which year you look at.
   b. Which state you look at.
   c. Whether you take some variables as "choices" or as "further evidence of discrimination."
   d. Which court you are in.

2. The earnings of African Americans relative to whites has
   a. Increased from 40 percent in the 1920s to 90 percent today.
   b. Increased from 50 percent in the 1950s to around 60 percent in the 1970s, remaining in that area since.
   c. Remained constant since the 1950s.
   d. Decreased steadily since the 1960s.

3. The method of detecting sex discrimination most likely to minimize it would be to use
   a. Simple differences in income between men and women.
   b. Simple differences in full-time wages for men and women.
   c. Regression techniques.
   d. Auditing techniques.

4. The method of detecting sex discrimination most likely to maximize it would be to use
   a. Simple differences in income between men and women.
   b. Simple differences in full-time wages for men and women.
   c. Regression techniques.
   d. Auditing techniques.

5. If a women does not get an interview for a job requiring heavy lifting because the manager has noted that the average women can lift less than the average man, this is
   a. A legal example of statistical discrimination.
   b. An illegal example of statistical discrimination.
   c. A legal example of adverse impact discrimination.
   d. An illegal example of adverse impact discrimination.

6. Those who believe that wages paid to minorities will rise without government intervention believe that bosses are primarily motivated by
   a. Profit.
   b. Religion.
   c. Doing right.
   d. Helping the downtrodden.

7. Affirmative action
   a. Can take many forms.
   b. Is almost always a racial quota.
   c. Applies only to women.
   d. Has typically been declared unconstitutional.

Think about This

Think about your chosen major, your favorite restaurant, the place you live. Are they predominantly male, female, black, or white? Would you feel comfortable going outside the social norms in your choices? Are those social norms limiting?

Talk about This

Who is going to raise your children? Who is going to sacrifice a career for their care, an illness, their after-school activities, etc.?

For More Insight See

Bertrand, Marianne, and Sndhil Mullainathan, "Are Emily and Greg More Employable than Lakisha and Jamal? A Field Experiement on Labor Market Discrimination," *America Economic Review* 94, no. 4. (Sept. 2004)

Blau, Francine, Marianne Ferber, and Anne Winkler, *The Economics of Women, Men and Work,* 3rd ed. (Upper Saddle River, NJ: Prentice Hall, 1998).

Curry, George E., ed., *The Affirmative Action Debate* (Reading, MA: Addison-Wesley, 1996).

Feiner, Susan F., *Race and Gender in the American Economy* (Englewood Cliffs, NJ: Prentice Hall, 1994).

Journal of Economic Perspectives 12, no. 2 (Spring 1998). See articles by John Yinger; William A. Darity, Jr., and Patrick L. Mason; Helen F. Ladd; and Kenneth J. Arrow, James J. Heckman, and Glenn C. Loury, pp. 23–126.

Sowell, Thomas, *Race and Economics* (New York: David McKay, 1975).

Waldfogel, Jane, "Understanding the 'Family Gap' in Pay for Women with Children," *Journal of Economic Perspectives* 12, no. 1 (Winter 1998), pp. 137–156.

Behind the Numbers

Historical data.
   Median family income, 1947–2003.
      U.S. Census Bureau; historical income tables— http://www.census.gov/hhes/income/histinc/f06.html.

Population and earnings, 2003.
   Median earnings for salaried and full-time workers by race.
      Statistical Abstract of the United States; labor— http://www.census.gov/prod/2004pubs/04statab/labor.pdf.

Population by race.
  Statistical Abstract of the United States; population—http://www.census.gov/prod/2004pubs/04statab/pop.pdf.

Corrections data.
  Parole, probation, and prison statistics. Bureau of Justice Statistics; Sourcebook of Criminal Justice Statistics, 2001—http://www.albany.edu/sourcebook/.

Income by gender, 1980–2002.
  U.S. Census Bureau; historical income tables—http://www.census.gov/hhes/income/histinc/p02.html.

Gender data on income, wealth, and pensions income and pension coverage, 2004.
  Statistical Abstract of the United States—http://www.census.gov/prod/2004pubs/04statab/income.pdf.

Wealth, 1998.
  U.S. Census Bureau; asset ownership of households, 2000—http://www.census.gov/hhes/www/wealth/1998_2000/wlth00-5.html.

Earnings and education.
  Bureau of Labor Statistics; annual demographic survey, 2004—http://census.gov/population/socdemo/education/cps2004/tab084.xls.

Median earnings and ratio of men's to women's income, 2001.
  Bureau of Labor Statistics; highlights of women's earnings in 2003, May 2004—http://www.bls.gov/cps/cpsaat39.pdf.

Chapter 27

Farm Policy

Many farms would not survive without help from the government. *Source: C. Borland/PhotoLink/Getty Images*

Chapter Objectives

After reading this chapter you should be able to

Understand that economists generally are not in favor of price supports in agriculture.

See why price variation is the leading economic justification for such support, although even price variation has few supporters among economists.

Use a supply and demand diagram and consumer and producer surplus analysis to analyze economists' reasoning.

Understand the mechanisms that are typically used to enforce price supports, and know some of their history.

Chapter Outline

Farm Prices since 1950

Price Variation as a Justification for Government Intervention

Consumer and Producer Surplus Analysis of Price Floors

Price Support Mechanisms and Their History

Kick It Up A Notch

Summary

Farm policy in the United States has been schizophrenic. Sometimes farmers are depicted as strong, independent men and women who simply need the government to stay out of their way. At other times they are depicted as desperate victims in need of help. In political speeches, family farms are spoken of with the same reverence as motherhood and apple pie, and to hear politicians talk, you would think farmers were demigods.

It is ironic, then, that without almost continuous government grants and low-interest loans, many farmers would have declared bankruptcy long ago. Help for farmers has come from government in many forms. The government

has bought and stored excess production, bought and given away excess production, bought livestock to prevent oversupply, and paid farmers not to farm.

We look here at the history of farm prices since 1950, and we draw on that history to discuss why government has and will probably continue to feel motivated to intervene in agriculture. We use our basic supply and demand model and our consumer and producer surplus knowledge to discuss the impact of farm price supports. In that discussion, as we said, we review the history of farm price supports and the various ways that farmers have received assistance.

FIGURE 27.1   Farm prices relative to their 1982 levels.

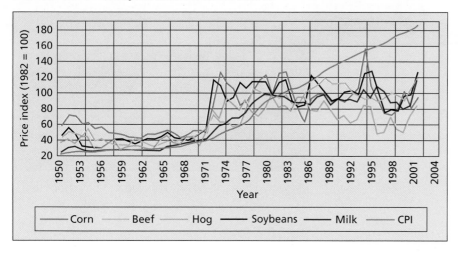

FARM PRICES SINCE 1950

A look at Figure 27.1 quickly tells you that farm prices are anything but stable. While beef, hogs, milk, corn, and soybeans are sold in different units, by displaying prices relative to where they were in 1982, we can show all of them on one graph. A number higher than 100 indicates a price in a selected year for that commodity that exceeds its 1982 level. A number below 100 indicates the opposite.

Whereas the prices of all the products shown in Figure 27.1 were higher in 2004 than they were in 1950, two of the five were lower in 2004 than in 1982. Since, according to the CPI, overall inflation was 89 percent from 1982 to 2004, farmers who produced the same crops in the same amounts and with the same costs would have experienced a 53 percent (100/189) loss in real income. Hog prices in particular took a beating between 1998 and 2000, yielding at times less than 45 percent of their 1982 levels. Any farmers who had not gotten more productive by this time would have seen a standard of living only 33 percent of their 1982 level. On a positive note, though, it can be seen that prices in general have risen much faster than the prices of these basic commodities.

If you look carefully at Figure 27.1 you will see that there was a sharp jump in all of these commodity prices in the early 1970s. Corn, soybean, and hog prices doubled in the four years from 1972 to 1975. Before 1975, corn, soybean, and milk prices had been the most stable, but since 1976, corn has joined beef as a commodity whose price is not stable. We are defining stability here as the ratio of the standard deviation of real prices to their mean.

PRICE VARIATION AS A JUSTIFICATION FOR GOVERNMENT INTERVENTION

Economists agree on few things, but one area where there is wide agreement is on the inadvisability of government intervention in agriculture. As a result, appeals for intervention tend to be based on sentiment rather than analysis. Although such sentimental appeals have not persuaded many economists, they have swayed politicians. The family farm is so revered in America, even by people who have never lived on or even near one, that economists have had little success forestalling farm bailouts. That said, there are reasons for government intervention in agriculture that a few academic economists, particularly agricultural economists, accept.

The Case for Price Supports

The most compelling of the reasons for government intervention in this market is that price variability makes farming a necessarily economically risky occupation. Supporters think that farmers whose farms are small need some government action to survive the aforementioned variability. The government's assistance in this might take the form of buying and storing excess crops when prices are too low and selling them out of inventory when prices rebound. This would do nothing to change the long-term price of crops, but it would stabilize prices. When the government does this for farmers, it acts as it does when it controls the value of its own currency.

There are two sources of price instability for any good: supply uncertainty and demand uncertainty. Sources of supply uncertainty are obvious: the weather and other natural phenomena like diseases and insect damage. The source of demand variability is mostly the unpredictability of international markets and whether there is demand for American crops by other countries.

The weather and other aspects of nature determine whether crops will do well, and there is not a great deal farmers can control once the planting is done. They can plant different varieties of corn and soybeans based on the lateness of the planting season, but once the seeds are sown, most of the economic decisions are made. Grain farmers, for example, are powerless to do anything if market conditions change after planting. At harvest time they will reap what they sowed—no more, no less.

On the demand side, variability comes from the quantities of goods foreigners will buy. In part this is supplyside variability in other nations. For instance, if the weather is bad in the other major exporting countries of Argentina, Australia, Canada, and Russia, then demand will be high in the importing countries for American grain. The United States is the largest source in grain production, but prices in the United States are usually somewhat higher than in other countries. For this reason, food importers buy all they can from these other countries; then they buy the rest of what they need from the United States. If the weather in these other exporting countries is bad, then importing countries will need great quantities of U.S. grain. If their weather is good, importing countries will not need much U.S. grain. With the weather and other forces of nature as variable as they are, there are few goods whose prices fluctuate as much as basic farm prices.

The Case against Price Supports

Though price variability is the most compelling reason for government interference in agriculture, it is not a persuasive reason for many economists. Option markets for agricultural goods exist and offer many opportunities to ensure that prices at harvest time are known in advance. Such markets serve as insurance to farmers on prices.

To see how using an option market might work, suppose you planted your crop in May and expected it to yield 10,000 bushels. At planting time in May you can buy an option to sell 10,000 bushels at harvest time for a specific price. If the price at harvest time is lower than the price specified in the option, you can exercise the option and sell your harvest at the higher contract price. If the price is higher, you do not need the option. This is comparable to buying automobile insurance. You will use it if you have an accident; you will not if you avoid a wreck.

If you fear your crop might fail, you can protect yourself by buying crop insurance. Crop insurance will pay off if crops fail. With these two forms of insurance (options and crop insurance), farmers can deal with the aspects of farming over which they have no control without government help. If farmers do not buy options or crop insurance, it is because they cost money. Even when things go well, profit margins on farms are low enough that some farmers believe they cannot afford insurance.

CONSUMER AND PRODUCER SURPLUS ANALYSIS OF PRICE FLOORS

One Floor in One Market

All of the many forms of support that government can give to farmers can be modeled with our supply and demand model, and we can discuss their implications using the consumer and producer surplus language that was introduced in Chapter 3. This section quickly reviews that language and uses Figure 27.2 to look at the impact of farm price supports on the economy.

Chapter 3 told us that consumer surplus is the difference between how much consumers value a good and the price they have to pay for it. It also told us that producer surplus is the difference between the amount producers

FIGURE 27.2   Price floors in a supply and demand model.

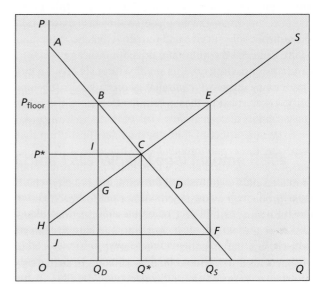

get from consumers and the variable cost of production. The demand curve represents what consumers are willing to pay for a good, and we interpret that as how much they value the good. In Chapter 5, we saw that the supply curve in a perfectly competitive market is made up of the marginal cost curves of the many entities that comprise the market. The area under the supply curve thus represents the variable costs of production.

At equilibrium, $P^* - Q^*$, consumers have a consumer surplus of P^*AC. Similarly, the producer makes out well, too. The firms net a producer surplus of HP^*C. The combined surpluses make up the value to society of the exchange, a value represented as HAC.

If the government sets a **price floor** of P_{floor}, it will

price floor
Price below which a commodity may not sell.

have to enforce it somehow. While we will not talk until the next section about how government might enforce the floor, assume for the moment that it is possible. Since consumers will want only Q_D, this is all that will be sold to consumers. The consumer surplus will shrink (to $P_{floor}AB$) while firms' producer surplus will grow (to $HP_{floor}BG$), but the combined surpluses are less than without the floor by GBC. Economists label this deadweight loss. To see why this is the case, turn to Kick It Up A Notch at the end of the chapter.

Variable Floors in Multiple Markets

Support for farmers and their price supports dates back to the Great Depression, when dairy farmers could not sell their products, and they convinced the government to set minimum prices. The so-called Eau Claire Rule came about at this time. Put in place so that farmers outside Wisconsin could survive and remain in business, the Eau Claire Rule sets the minimum price for milk as a function of a farm's proximity to this small Wisconsin city. To this day, a dairy farmer in central Wisconsin gets a substantially lower subsidy than a similar farmer in the other dairy capitals of central New York or northern California.

To see the effect of this, consider for illustration that there are three geographically distinct areas. Suppose two of these are rural areas where dairy products are both produced and consumed and the third area is a city where these products are consumed but not produced. Suppose one rural area, call it Eau Claire, has a production advantage over the other, call it Vermont, and this advantage overwhelms the fact that a consuming city, say New York, is closer to Vermont than Eau Claire. In such a circumstance Vermont dairy farmers would sell only to

those living in Vermont, and Eau Claire farmers would sell to those in New York as well as Eau Claire. This is the economically efficient scenario.

If, on the other hand, there is a rule that says that the lowest price that can be charged in New York is higher than the market equilibrium, it might be high enough that Vermont rather than Eau Claire produces the dairy for New York. Thus not only do New Yorkers have to buy milk at high prices, but the fact that they do tends to reward less efficient means of production. This is, unfortunately, precisely what the Eau Claire Rule does in the United States.

What Would Happen without Price Supports?

If there were no price supports, how low could prices go? The first thing to understand is that like everyone else, farmers have options other than farming. If prices go low enough, they will sell out and work somewhere else. In this sense farmers are like any other small businesspersons who must decide when they have had enough. While being your own boss has clear advantages, they must also be weighed against risks and the frayed nerves associated with being in charge.

For most farmers, the lack of a boss outweighs the frayed nerves. Even with lower income, they would rather continue farming than work for someone else. On the other hand, there is a price for which the rate of return to farming is just too low. When that point is reached, farmers auction off their assets, pay their debts, and move on. As a result, prices cannot fall below the level where farmers are better off not farming. If they did, the farmers would leave the market thereby reducing the number of sellers, and that would put upward pressure on the price.

PRICE SUPPORT MECHANISMS AND THEIR HISTORY

Price Support Mechanisms

As we noted in the previous section, there are many ways of enforcing a price support. The reason an enforcement mechanism is required in agriculture and not in other price floor situations is that production happens and most costs are incurred well before sales are made or even arranged. For instance, the minimum wage is a form of price floor. The buyer of labor, the boss, cannot pay the seller of labor, the worker, any less than the minimum wage, just as the buyer of the agricultural product cannot pay the farmer any less than the price floor. The supply and demand analysis in the minimum wage shows that more people want to work than there are jobs available. This is not as much of a problem in normal working situations as it is in farming because, unlike farming, the workers are not working and then looking to see if the boss will pay them. They are hired and then they do the work. Farmers, on the other hand, grow and harvest their crops before they have a known buyer. Raising the price that farmers get to P_{floor} will not do farmers any good if many of them end up having truckloads of grain to sell and no one willing to buy them. They will have incurred all of the costs of working but they will not derive any revenue from their work.

For this reason, the government has to enforce the price floor in a manner that makes sure that either only Q_D is produced or that Q_S is wanted. There are several ways that this can be done. The government can limit what farmers produce by allocating rights to sell among farmers. With rights to sell, farmers can sell only what their rights allow. The government can pay farmers to participate by allowing anyone to sell at $P*$ while allowing only those who agreed to limit production to sell at P_{floor}. The government can then buy all that farmers want to produce. At its discretion it can then give the good away to foreign or domestic recipients that could not afford to buy it at P_{floor} or the government can buy and store all that farmers want to produce at P_{floor}.

The government's least expensive option to keep prices high, however, is to limit the amount that a farmer can produce. It can do this by allowing only licensed farmers to produce specific quantities. Peanuts and chewing grade tobacco are two crops that are produced under licensing. You cannot grow and sell these products unless you have a license. If you examine Figure 27.2 again, you will see that by limiting the number of farmers and the amount of acreage that can be devoted to this production, the P_{floor} price can be maintained and farmers will produce only Q_D.

The government's next least expensive option is to pay farmers not to produce as much as they might otherwise choose to. In the past the government paid farmers not to plant in certain fields, and it even paid them not to farm altogether. Moreover, to affect the price of milk, the government bought dairy herds and sent them off to slaughter. The government, of course, keeps production down when it pays farmers not to produce. The effectiveness of this method is lessened, however, by increases in productivity and by new people becoming farmers. In the case of milk, farmers who had their herds bought were not allowed to get back into dairy farming for several years, even if they wanted to, but that did not prevent others from becoming farmers. It did not prevent remaining farmers from increasing their herds, and it did not prevent others from increasing the productivity of their cows, using artificial hormones. Grain farmers also experienced this form of price support. Many were paid to have idle fields, fields that could be used for hay but not for cash grains like wheat, soybeans, or corn. In general, the government subsidies have had the effect of persuading significant numbers of farmers either to do something else or to limit production.

An expensive option for the government has been to let farmers grow all they want and either pay them the difference between the market price and the price floor or simply buy up whatever was not purchased by consumers. Figure 27.2 shows that it is very expensive for the government to choose either of these options. If it chooses the former, it will have to pay farmers the difference between P_{floor} and the price that Q_S will sell for on the open market, shown in Figure 27.2 as J, for all Q_S. This totals $JP_{floor}EF$. If the government chooses the latter option, it will have to buy the difference between Q_S and Q_D for the P_{floor} price. That totals Q_DBEQ_S.

If it buys up what is left by consumers, the government still has to figure out what to do with the excess. There are three options here: let it spoil, give it away, or store it. The first does not cost anything more than trucking the surplus to a place where it can be dumped. Giving the excess away sounds more appealing, but if you give people something that they would have ordinarily paid for, you still are not solving the agriculture price problem. You are reducing demand even further by the amount you are giving away. You can only give the good to people who are so poor they would have gone without, and you are most likely to find such people in the developing world. It may sound somewhat cynical, but the government of the United States is a leading contributor of foodstuffs to victims of starvation and natural disaster in the developing world in part because the United States has an excess that it needs to dispose of.

Even though the most expensive option for the government is to store the excess, it has, at various times, stored milk and grains. Milk has been stored either as a powder or in the form of block American cheese. While both can be stored at near room temperature, a cool, dry environment is more conducive to long-term storage. Abandoned salt mines have served that purpose well.

Storing grain is somewhat easier. It does not require any processing, the way milk does, but it is still subject to rotting if it gets wet. However it is stored, storing food is very expensive.

History of Price Supports

At various times the United States has employed every imaginable way of supporting agriculture prices. At one time it could have idled all grain farms in the United States for a year and still had enough in storage to process into food and to feed livestock. In the middle of the 1982 recession, there was enough excess dairy in storage that the government gave every poor person who showed up for it several pounds of cheese and several boxes of powdered milk. In the middle 1980s, thousands of dairy farmers around the country went into early retirement when the government paid top dollar to buy up their herds.

As we said before, the support for agricultural price supports grew out of the depression of the 1930s. Agricultural prices fell so far so fast that farm bankruptcies skyrocketed. Politicians reacted by putting price floors on a number of agricultural products, most notably dairy. In the middle 1980s, the Reagan administration tried to lessen the cost of agriculture subsidies by limiting supply, rather than serving as a buyer of last resort. First it sold off and gave away much of the government's excess stocks of grain and dairy products. Then it offered farmers payments not to farm. The ultimate act in this regard was the middle 1980s policy to thin dairy herds. This led to nearly a 10 percent reduction in farmland under active cultivation since 1988. While we proceed down a path of restricting output rather than buying up excess, many thousands of farmers still are paid many billions of dollars not to farm many millions of acres.

The 1996 Freedom to Farm Act began yet another long phase of practices leading away from agricultural price supports. By 2002 the United States was supposed to exist without supports for milk or grain, but alas, support continued with the federal government spending $26 billion in 2005. Farming is still considered as sacrosanct as motherhood and apple pie, so if mom or the pie gets in trouble, politicians will always be strongly tempted to help them out.

Kick It Up
A Notch

Referring back to Figure 27.2, at equilibrium, $P^* - Q^*$, consumers pay the producers OP^*CQ^*, but they value what they get at $OACQ^*$. This means they have a consumer surplus of P^*AC. Similarly, the producer makes out well, too. The producer receives the OP^*CQ^* in revenue and the variable costs are only $OHCQ^*$. This nets the producer surplus of HP^*C. The combined surpluses make up the value to society of the exchange, a value represented as HAC.

If the government sets a price floor of P_{floor} consumers will want only Q_D. They will pay the $OP_{floor}BQ_D$ to producers. Consumers will value this at $OABQ_D$ and will net a consumer surplus of $P_{floor}AB$. It will cost producers $OHGQ_D$, so their producer surplus will be $HP_{floor}BG$. The combined surpluses are $HABG$. The deadweight loss is the difference between the combined surpluses with and without the floor, GBC.

Summary

Now that you have plowed your way through this chapter you understand why economists generally are not in favor of price supports in agriculture. You understand that though price variation is real, there are mechanisms that farmers can use to deal with that sort of government intervention. You are now able to employ consumer and producer surplus analysis to demonstrate the inefficiency caused by price floors. Last, you understand how price floors work in practice, and you have an appreciation for their history.

Key Term

price floor, 292

Quiz Yourself

1. The economic rationale for farm price supports is generally
   a. Weak, but relies on price variability.
   b. Weak, but relies on the unavailability of crop insurance.
   c. Strong, and relies on the fact that prices are too high.
   d. Strong, and relies on the importance of Iowa in presidential elections.

2. Price supports in the United States have
   a. Always relied on the government paying farmers to set aside land.
   b. Always relied on the government buying excess crops.
   c. Always relied on forbidding production above certain levels.
   d. Utilized a wide variety of means to raise prices and reduce output.

3. Farm price supports are typically for
   a. Basic commodities like raw milk and grain.
   b. Fruits and vegetables.
   c. Refined products like flour.
   d. Manufactured products like breakfast cereals.

4. A price support mechanism
   a. Can only regulate supply.
   b. Can only regulate demand.
   c. Must involve government purchases.
   d. Can involve government manipulation of the supply or demand of the good.

5. Looking at Figure 27.2, maintaining P_{floor} as the target minimum price (rather than equilibrium) would
   a. Raise consumer surplus more than it would decrease producer surplus.
   b. Raise producer surplus more than it would decrease consumer surplus.
   c. Involve creating deadweight loss.
   d. Enhance the welfare of consumers and producers.

6. Looking at Figure 27.2, maintaining P_{floor} as the target minimum price (rather than equilibrium) by having the government purchase how much of the product farmers wished to produce would cost the government _____ dollars.
   a. OP^*CQ^*.
   b. $Q_D BEQ_S$.
   c. $OP_{floor}BQ_D$.
   d. BCG dollars.

Think about This

How much does it matter from the perspective of market form (monopoly, oligopoly, perfect competition) if there are 100, 1,000 or 1,000,000 farms producing raw grain?

Talk about This

Farm price supports are intended to help "the family farmer" but in reality often help multimillion-dollar farms. When Congress limited the size of the check that any particular farm could receive, farmers divided their farms into separate entities with different family members owning different farms so that they could continue to collect money. The "family farmer," defined as a simple farm with one house and the occupants of that house working the land, no longer produces a significant portion of the raw grain, cattle, or milk in the United States. Is the family farm more of a social myth than an actual entity?

For More Insight See

Gardner, Bruce L, "Changing Economic Perspectives on the Farm Problem," *Journal of Economic Literature* 30, no. 1 (March 1992), pp. 62–101.

Behind the Numbers

Farm product prices.
   Bureau of Labor Statistics; archived news releases— http://www.bls.gov/schedule/archives/ppi_nr.htm.

Chapter 28

Minimum Wage

The federal minimum wage was last raised on September 1, 1997, to $5.15 an hour. *Source: Ryan McVay/Getty Images.*

Chapter Objectives

After reading this chapter you should be able to

Understand what a labor market is, what a minimum wage is, why it has come about, how it alters the outcome of a labor market, and why the minimum wage must be higher than the equilibrium wage in order to be relevant.

See how most economists use the consumer and producer surplus argument to justify their belief that the minimum wage increases unemployment.

Use this argument to help identify real-world winners and losers of a minimum wage increase.

Understand that some economists have taken a new look at the issue and disagree with the conclusion that an increase in the minimum wage results in lower employment.

Understand that there is an alternative to a minimum wage that focuses more money on the working poor.

See that the consensus among economists on the issue of the minimum wage has recently been called into question.

Chapter Outline

Traditional Economic Analysis of a Minimum Wage

Rebuttals to the Traditional Analysis

Where Are Economists Now?

Kick It Up A Notch

Summary

The **minimum wage** is the lowest wage that may legally be paid for an hour's work, subject to government restrictions. In 1938 the first minimum wage was set at 25 cents per hour, and the amount has been increased periodically over the years. In July 2005 it stood at $5.15 per hour.

minimum wage
The lowest wage that may legally be paid for an hour's work.

The minimum wage has traditionally been justified as a mechanism to ensure a **living wage,** that is, a wage sufficient to keep a family out of poverty. As you can see in Figure 28.1, the minimum wage was always sufficient to keep an individual above

living wage
A wage sufficient to keep a family out of poverty.

the poverty line.[1] It has been less successful for families. Since 1985 the minimum wage has been insufficient to maintain a one-earner, minimum wage family (constituting more than an individual) above the poverty line. For instance, to accomplish the feat of keeping a family of four above the poverty line, the minimum wage for a single full-time earner would have to be more than $9.50 an hour.

Figure 28.2 indicates that although the minimum wage itself has been increased several times over the

[1]The poverty line used here is the official poverty line, with which there are many problems. Review Chapter 23, "Poverty and Welfare," to understand this issue.

FIGURE 28.1   The ratio of the earnings of a full-time minimum-wage worker to the poverty line for various family sizes.

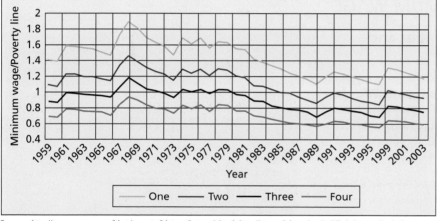

Sources: http://www.census.gov/hhes/poverty/histpov/hstpov1.html; http://www.dol.gov/esa/public/minwage/main.htm.

FIGURE 28.2   The nominal and real minimum wage, 1938–2003, in 1999 dollars.

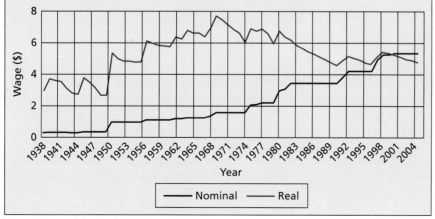

Source: http://www.dol.gov/esa/public/minwage/main.htm.

last 60 years, its real value, that is, the value adjusted for inflation in 1999 dollars, has not fluctuated much. Since 1950, the lowest it has been in inflation-adjusted dollars is $4.50 per hour, the amount in 1989, while the highest level it reached was $7.65 per hour in 1968.[2] At $5.15 in 2005, its inflation-adjusted value is approaching its 1989 low. Without an increase, at present rates of inflation, it will soon surpass the 1989 low and approach its lowest value in 50 years.

Over time, economists have tended to argue against the minimum wage. In this chapter we explain those arguments along with the reasons why, until recently, most economists thought raising the minimum wage wrongheaded. We also look at the arguments that suggest it may have been economists who were wrongheaded.

TRADITIONAL ECONOMIC ANALYSIS OF A MINIMUM WAGE

Labor Markets and Consumer and Producer Surplus

Most economists have had few good things to say about the idea of establishing a minimum wage, and they have based that opinion on a traditional supply and demand analysis of the issue. Figure 28.3 represents a market for low-skill minimum-wage labor. The good being sold in

---

[2]As stated in Chapter 6, this measure of inflation overcorrects for inflation.

FIGURE 28.3   Labor market.

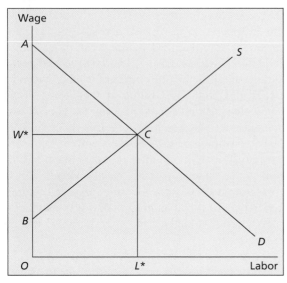

States and Cities Increase the Minimum Wage on Their Own

Because the federal minimum wage has remained constant for nearly a decade, states and cities have begun to take the initiative to impose a higher minimum wage within their jurisdictions. Below is a list of states and cities that imposed a higher than federally mandated minimum wage as of July 2005. Cities with minimum wage laws typically apply those laws only to themselves and firms receiving benefits or doing some business with the city.

States	Cities
New York	Baltimore, MD
Delaware	Boston, MA
Florida	Chicago, IL
Hawaii	Cleveland, OH
Maine	Denver, CO
Illinois	Detroit, MI
District of Columbia	Los Angeles, CA
Rhode Island	Minneapolis, MN
Massachusetts	San Antonio, TX
California	San Fransisco, CA
Vermont	
Connecticut	
Oregon	
Washington	

this market is labor, and the price at which it is sold is the wage. The supply is made up of workers who will want to work more at higher pay, implying an upward-sloping supply curve; demand is made up of bosses seeking to hire that labor. The employers are assumed to want fewer laborers at higher wages, implying a downward-sloping demand curve. Without a law that sets its actual dollar amount, the wage would be set in this market at the point where the supply and demand curves meet. At this point there would be no shortage and no surplus. The wage would be W^* and there would be L^* work. Being a market clearing equilibrium, this is a wage at which no one who wants a job at that wage is without one, and no employers who want workers at that wage are unable to get them.

In this situation workers would be paid a total of OW^*CL^* dollars. When we addressed the notion of consumer and producer surplus in Chapter 3, we stated that the consumer surplus is the area under the demand curve but above the price line, while the producer surplus is the area under the price line and above the supply curve. Of course, in this case the price is the wage.

The key difference here is that businesses are getting the consumer surplus W^*AC, because it is they who are buying the good, that is, hiring the labor. We interpret consumer surplus here as the money that businesses make from the work of their employees that exceeds the amount they have to pay workers.

The producer surplus BW^*C is also different in that it is what workers get, since it is they who are doing the selling. The interpretation here is that it represents the amount of money that workers get in excess of what they would have worked for. So, just as in any other market, the consumer gets something and the producer gets something.

A Relevant versus an Irrelevant Minimum Wage

If a minimum wage is set below W^*, would businesses pay the minimum wage rather than the higher W^*? Surprisingly, the answer is no, they would not: To get workers in the numbers that are most profitable to the business, employers have to pay the higher W^*. They would rather pay more than the minimum because, even though their labor costs then rise at a higher rate, the output of the extra workers will generate enough additional revenue to pay workers and to produce an increased profit as well. In addition, it is in their best interests to pay W^*, because otherwise their competitors will outbid them for labor. Thus any minimum wage set below W^* is irrelevant, because firms make more profit offering W^* rather than a lesser amount.

If you are not yet convinced that setting a minimum wage may be irrelevant, consider what would happen if your professors told you that you would fail if you showed up to class naked. Unless you had planned to do this anyway, an unlikely event since you would be kicked out of school, the rule would not affect your behavior in the least. Any rule that tells you that you

FIGURE 28.4 Minimum wage.

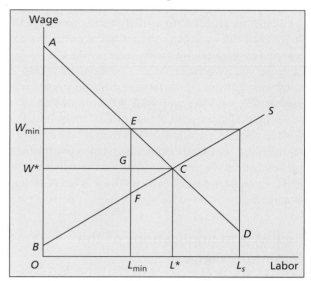

cannot do something that you had no intention of doing anyway is not much of a rule. It does not alter your behavior, and it is therefore irrelevant. For the minimum wage to be relevant, it has to be an amount that is set above the equilibrium wage.

What Is Wrong with a Minimum Wage?

As seen in Figure 28.4, a minimum wage that has been set above the equilibrium wage has several effects. First, it raises the wage from W^* to W_{min}. Second, it reduces the amount of labor sold from L^* to L_{min}. Third, as long as the money gained from raising the wage to workers is greater than the money lost as a result of having fewer people working, workers in general have more money than they had before. From your earlier study of the concept of elasticity, you will recognize the condition for this is that the demand for labor has to be inelastic. Finally, the imposition of a minimum wage will raise the unemployment rate for workers in this market. This will happen because either more workers will want to work or existing workers will want to work more hours. With a minimum wage set above the equilibrium wage, workers want to provide L_s labor, whereas they used to want to work only L^*. Further complicating this is that employers now want to hire labor only up to L_{min} rather than the L^* they had wanted previously.

In the end, the consumer surplus shrinks to $W_{min}AE$ and producer surplus grows. The sum of the consumer and producer surpluses is less than it was without the minimum wage, by the triangle *FEC*.

What this all leads to is that under this economic analysis of the minimum wage, there are winners and losers. The winners are those workers who get a wage increase and who are still able to continue working as much as they want. The losers are men and women who used to be working and who are now unemployed $(L^* - L_{\min})$. The important part of this analysis is that what is gained by workers is less than what employers lose. We are thus confronted with what economists label deadweight loss, the net loss to society by the area *FEC*. To see this precisely go to "Kick It Up A Notch" on page 302.

Real-World Implications of the Minimum Wage

Though rather elegant as a mechanism to analyze the impacts of a minimum wage, consumer and producer surplus analysis does not put it in terms easy for the average person to see. The winners are the more than 4 million people who work for the minimum wage and get a pay increase because they keep their jobs.

The losers are the people who lose their jobs. Research on the subject has led economists to use the rule of thumb that a 10 percent increase in the minimum wage results in a 1 percent to 3 percent drop in the number of jobs held by teens. That translates to a loss of 90,000 to 268,000 jobs lost by teens as a result of the increase in the minimum wage from $4.25 to $5.15 an hour. Economists who study those unlucky teens find that they are disproportionately black, Hispanic, and uneducated. That is, they are among the very people that an increase is trying to help. This point must not be missed. An increase in the minimum wage may very well hurt the poor more than it helps them.

Other losers include small business owners who have to pay the higher wage with perhaps a very small profit margin to do so. Small independent restaurateurs are especially hard-hit because the industry is such that many such new entrepreneurs constantly teeter on the edge of bankruptcy and can afford to pay only minimum wage. That means that an increase in the minimum wage may destroy not only the jobs these entrepreneurs are creating, but also the entrepreneurs themselves.

Finally, the losers include anyone who buys goods or services produced by minimum-wage workers, because part of the increase is passed on to them in the form of higher prices.

Alternatives to the Minimum Wage

It is for all of these reasons and more that until recently most economists could not endorse increases in the minimum wage. Those who took the position that the minimum wage was an inappropriate cure to the problems of poorly paid workers highlighted the fact that most workers who made the minimum wage were under 24. Nearly a third of these were under 19 and therefore very unlikely to be supporting a family. Combine this with the fact that many of those who earn the minimum wage and are over age 24 are spouses who work only to supplement the income of the family's primary income producer and are nowhere near poverty.

In the eyes of many economists a better alternative is the Earned Income Tax Credit (EITC). Low-income working families with children are eligible for up to $4,140 that arrives in the form of a tax refund. The benefits of the EITC are concentrated on the people who actually need the money to feed their families. More than 70 percent of the money goes to households that are or would otherwise be in poverty. This contrasts dramatically with the minimum wage, where upwards of 70 percent of the benefits accrue to households not in poverty.

The EITC, while born in the 1970s, saw great increases starting during the administration of President Ronald Reagan. It was during this administration that the minimum wage saw a long period of real decline in its value. It was President Reagan's view that the minimum wage was a poor mechanism to help the poor and that the EITC could help working poor families without hurting businesses. While President Clinton's first budget increased taxes for many, it also greatly increased the EITC. Moreover, though he pushed through an increase in the minimum wage as well, the increased level of the EITC has had a greater effect on the working poor.

REBUTTALS TO THE TRADITIONAL ANALYSIS

In contrast to the preceding section, important points of rebuttal to the traditional analysis have gained respectability in recent years among economists. They center on three main lines of argument. Macroeconomic analysis suggests, first, that the effect of a decrease in income by owners of businesses is somewhat offset by the effect of an increase in income by the lower-income people. Low-income people spend more and high-income people save more. A second line of argument is that the good in question, labor, is not as definable as most other goods and that with better pay, workers can be induced to work harder. If they do so, the increase in the wage becomes less of a burden on employers. The remaining argument is that the elasticity of demand for labor may be so low that the traditional analysis needs to reflect this fact. If it does, the negative aspects of the minimum wage will be small.

The Macroeconomics Argument

The first argument in rebuttal to the traditional analysis relies on an aspect of macroeconomics that suggests that if you track all of the times a particular amount of money is spent, you can figure up the total impact of new spending. Or, as is appropriate in this case, you can examine the net effect of money's being spent by different people. If, for instance, business owners save most of their profit rather than spend or invest it, then something less than the entire profit of the business works its way through the economy in the form of additional spending. On the other hand, if the business owners have to relinquish more of that profit to workers because of the imposition of a higher minimum wage, then almost all of that money will be spent. Men and women who are paid the minimum wage save very little, and they spend nearly all of their additional income. Because money is spent rather than saved, total consumption in the economy rises. From a macroeconomic standpoint, any negative effects of a minimum-wage increase range from being offset, to being nonexistent, to being positive.

Suppose, for example, that the result of an increase in the minimum wage is to increase the incomes for workers by $75 while creating a $100 loss in profit to businesses. Remember that it is not simply a direct transfer; workers' gains are offset by losses to business that are greater. The $25 difference, the deadweight loss, is the amount of damage to an overall measure of economic activity like the gross domestic product. This gap can be made up if the effect of low-skill workers' spending it is greater than the effect of bosses spending it. If low-skill workers spend all of their increased income, and bosses spend or invest only 80 percent of theirs, the net effect of raising the minimum wage is that the GDP shrinks by $5 rather than $25. This is because 80 percent of $100 is only $5 more than 100 percent of $75. This is, of course, predicated on the assumption that a higher minimum wage has the net effect of increasing the income of minimum-wage workers.

The Work Effort Argument

The second argument is probably correct in assuming that people adjust the effort they put in at work depending on how happy they are with their employer. This means that the graphs in Figures 28.3 and 28.4 are not as stable as we previously thought them to be. The good "labor" is not as fixed in its meaning as are most other goods for which we use this supply and demand model. People can work hard or slack off, and there is not a great deal that an employer can do to force slackers to work harder. If higher pay translates into workers who are happier and who do more work per hour, it may be the case that some if not all of the impact of forcing wages to rise will be mitigated. In this way the minimum-wage increase may pay for itself. On the other hand, if it did pay for itself, we would have to assume that employers were either ignorant of this fact or not maximizers of profit. Neither of these assumptions sits well with most economists. It is more plausible that such an increase merely lessens the negative impact.

The Elasticity Argument

The last argument used to rebut traditional analysis simply tweaks the traditional analysis a little to suggest that the negative impact of an increase in the minimum wage is very small. Any increase can thus be interpreted as simply a transfer of money from business owners to workers. Comparing Figure 28.5 to Figure 28.4, you

FIGURE 28.5 The minimum wage in the short run.

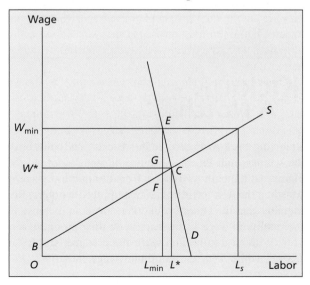

will find that the only real difference is that the demand curve is steeper, that is, more inelastic, in Figure 28.5. The net amount that workers gain is very great, and the resulting unemployment of those who had jobs before, $L^* - L_{min}$, is very low. As we said when we discussed elasticity in Chapter 3, there are two things that will influence elasticity: the number of close substitutes and time to invent them.

Given that in the short run there are very few substitutes for having workers on the job, this rebuttal seems, of the three mentioned, the most persuasive to traditional economists. Most economists still believe that the existence of a minimum wage will reduce employment in the long run. They maintain that the only reason the gain to workers is great and the net loss to society is small is that this is an analysis that works only in the short run.

They argue that in the long run business owners will search until they find substitutes for labor such as easier-to-use machines and self-serve devices. If you look at the fast-food industry and the equipment that it uses, you will find that the companies involved are always looking for new ways to reduce the need for employees, and they have had great success in their endeavors. Putting the drink machines in the lobby and using chain ovens or broilers that cook the food for exactly the correct amount of time without needing employee monitoring are just a couple of examples of how employers of minimum-wage workers have substituted capital for labor.

WHERE ARE ECONOMISTS NOW?

If the more recent, nontraditional analysis is correct, it is probably because in the short run there is not much deadweight loss to be made up. The combined impact of the macroeconomic effect and the harder worker effect is therefore enough to completely eliminate the problem. The data on whether recent minimum-wage increases have had a net negative impact on unemployment for the 1990 and 1996 increases are mixed. Two influential economists, David Card and Andrew Krueger, published a study of the minimum wage utilizing data on fast-food employment. They surveyed establishments in two neighboring states in a period where one increased its minimum wage and another did not. They found that the increase did not negatively impact, and perhaps positively impacted, employment in the state that raised its minimum wage.

Since this study ran against the conventional wisdom of labor economists, many were quick to try to duplicate their results. The attempts to replicate the work of Card and Krueger turned up serious data and methodology problems with their work. As a result of the newer work casting doubt on the Card and Krueger conclusion, most labor economists have not moved much from their earlier assessment. In particular, many still use the teen employment rule of thumb mentioned earlier but concede that a 10 percent increase in the minimum wage translates to a 1 percent or 2 percent decrease in teen employment. In any event, economists have expended considerable time rethinking an issue that they thought they had put to bed a long time ago.

Kick It Up
A Notch

Referring back to Figure 28.4, we can firmly establish the winners and losers and more rigorously defend the claim that the gain to workers from a minimum wage is less than the loss to firms and unemployed workers. Remember that the benefit to workers from an increase in the minimum wage is the increase in their producer surplus. Without a minimum wage the producer surplus is BW^*C, while with the minimum wage it is $BW_{min}EF$.

The consumer surplus is the benefit to firms hiring the labor. They go from having a consumer surplus of W^*AC without the minimum wage to a consumer surplus of $W_{min}AE$ with it. The gain to workers is $W^*W_{min}EG - GFC$, while the loss to firms is $W^*W_{min}EG + GEC$. The net effect is the gain to workers minus the loss to firms, which is $-FEC$. Because the net effect is negative, this is a loss, one that economists call the deadweight loss.

Summary

After this exploration of the minimum wage, you understand why it exists in the first place and what its implications are for our supply and demand model for labor. You know how to use our consumer and producer surplus techniques to identify the winners and losers of any minimum wage increase and then apply real-world observations. You understand the diversity of opinion among economists on the subject, and you know the Earned Income Tax Credit is an alternative to it.

Key Terms

living wage, 297

minimum wage, 297

Quiz Yourself

1. Between 1998 and 2005 the real minimum wage
   a. Rose rapidly.
   b. Rose slowly.
   c. Remained constant.
   d. Fell rapidly.
2. In order for the minimum wage to reach its 1968 high in real terms, it would have to rise to approximately _____ per hour.
   a. $6.
   b. $7.
   c. $8.
   d. $9.
3. The last time the minimum wage alone was sufficient to keep a family of three above the poverty line was
   a. 1979.
   b. 1985.
   c. 1990.
   d. 1998.
4. The argument that the minimum wage is worse than the earned income tax credit is based on the idea that
   a. The people who earn the minimum wage are really poor.
   b. The minimum wage applies to all workers not just the working poor.
   c. The earned income tax credit goes to all workers.
   d. The minimum wage applies only to those younger than 25.
5. The argument that the minimum wage does not significantly increase unemployment is based on
   a. Producer surplus.
   b. Consumer surplus.
   c. Elasticity.
   d. Aggregate demand.
6. The argument that the minimum wage hurts society more than it helps is based on _____ analysis.
   a. Consumer and producer surplus.
   b. Production possibilities.
   c. Aggregate supply–aggregate demand.
   d. Marginal.
7. The argument that employers would actually not lose money if the minimum wage were raised is based on
   a. The idea that workers would spend the extra money buying goods from their employer.
   b. The idea that workers would work overtime without having to be paid.
   c. The idea that workers would be more productive if they felt they were adequately compensated.
   d. The elasticity of demand for labor.

Think about This

Several states have set the minimum wage in their states higher than the federal minimum wage. If doing so places them at a competitive disadvantage for new business this might be counterproductive. On the other hand, the minimum wage is typically only relevant in low-paid service jobs. Who makes the minimum wage in your community? Would your community be better off with a higher minimum wage?

Talk about This

One of the principal opponents to minimum wage increases is the umbrella organization for small business. Many states with higher minimum wages than the federal level exempt businesses with few employees. Should small businesses be exempt from minimum wage laws?

For More Insight See

Brown, Charles, "Minimum Wages Laws: Are They Overrated?" *Journal of Economic Perspectives* 2, no. 3 (Summer 1988), pp. 133–146.

Brown, Charles, Curtis Gilroy, and Andrew Kohen, "The Effect of the Minimum Wage on Employment and Unemployment," *Journal of Economic Literature* 20, no. 2 (June 1982), pp. 487–528.

Card, David, and Alan Krueger, *Myth and Measurement: The New Economics of the Minimum Wage* (Princeton, NJ: Princeton University Press, 1995).

Behind the Numbers

Historical data.
Minimum wage, 1959–2005.
　　U.S. Department of Labor; Employment Standards Administration—http://www.dol.gov/esa/public/minwage/main.htm.
Poverty line, 1959–2005.
　　U.S. Census Bureau; historical poverty tables—http://www.census.gov/hhes/poverty/histpov/hstpov1.html.

EITC eligibility and amount.
　　Internal Revenue Service—http://www.irs.gov/individuals/article/0,,id=96406,00.html.

Adams, Scott, and David Neumark, "A Decade of Living Wages: What Have We Learned?" Public Policy Institute of California—http://www.ppic.org/content/pubs/EP_605SAEP.pdf.

Chapter **29**

Rent Control

Rent control protects tenants from large rent increases.
Source: © image 100 Ltd.

Chapter Objectives

After reading this chapter you should be able to

Use the principles of supply and demand to model the effect of rent control.

Understand that the reasons for controlling rents are typically short term in nature.

See why economists generally oppose rent controls.

Understand that the consequences of controlling rents vary with the time horizon: the short-term benefits to the renter are usually offset by longer-term losses to landlords and other renters.

Use the supply and demand model to explain why eliminating rent control can be in a city's general interests but not in the interests of the voters of that city.

Chapter Outline

Rents in a Free Market

Reasons for Controlling Rents

Consequences of Rent Control

Why Does Rent Control Survive?

Summary

Several cities in the United States have enacted laws that control the amount of rent that a landlord can charge. Some, like New York City, have laws that date from World War II and the price controls that were instituted at that time because of the war. When the general price controls expired, New York City chose to extend them for rents in the city. Others, like the more than 100 New Jersey cities with such laws, began their excursion into rent control by simply extending the price controls imposed by President Nixon in 1971. San Francisco, Los Angeles, and San Jose adopted controls when skyrocketing land prices drove rents up in California in the late 1970s and early 1980s.

Rent control laws typically specify how often rents can be increased and by how much. Some rent control laws prevent rents from being increased as long as a tenant continues to rent the same apartment. As we analyze the issue of rent control, the first thing we examine is how rents are established in a free market. Then we look at what might motivate governments to control rents, and we examine the long- and short-term consequences of preventing rent increases.

RENTS IN A FREE MARKET

In a free market, rents are determined in the same manner as the price of any other good or service. The supply of apartments is determined by how much it costs landlords to build them and how their profitability compares with that of other investments. The demand for apartments is based on the number of people seeking apartments, how much it costs to rent in the city as opposed to buying or renting in a neighboring community, and the income of the potential tenants.

When landlords choose to invest their money in apartment buildings, they are motivated by exactly the same things that motivate all other investors. They look for the highest possible rate of return on their investments subject to a limited amount of risk. The costs associated with being a landlord are more varied and variable than they are with most other investments. The most prominent cost is the cost of the building itself. If the investor borrows money to build or buy the building, the building's cost is the interest portion of the monthly mortgage payment. If the investor buys the building without borrowing, the cost of the building is the interest rate that the investor could have received in his or her next best investment. In this sense the costs involved in investing in rental properties are not all that different from those in other investments.

Other costs in owning rental property, though, are considerably more variable than those of other investments. Landlords have to fix all of the problems in a building. They have to deal with tenants who do not pay their rent on time. They have to deal with tenants who leave before their lease is up and tenants who cause more damage to their apartments than their security deposits will cover. It is for this reason that people who are handy find investing in apartment buildings highly profitable. They use their skills to save money on maintenance.

People looking for a place to live have a similar set of concerns. They must decide whether to buy or rent. If they buy, they need to come up with a down payment, and they have to pay for their own repairs. If they rent, they must decide where to rent. In a large city the cost of renting close to work is greater, but the time and expenses involved in commuting are avoided. If rents in the city are low, people are more likely to live in the city. If they are high, people are more likely to live farther away.

Figure 29.1 shows us that a market for rental apartments generates an equilibrium number of apartments rented Q^* and an equilibrium rent R^*. Such a market can be affected by a number of factors. If interest rates rise,

FIGURE 29.1 The market for rental apartments without rent control.

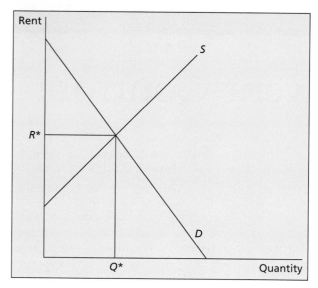

for example, the cost to landlords rises and more people want to become renters. This is because the home mortgage payments that represent the cost of alternatives to renters increase. Increased costs to landlords and greater numbers of potential tenants both lead to higher rents.

It is important to insert at this point that there are several rental markets for different types of rental housing. For instance, landlords who rent to young college-age people anticipate having repair costs at the end of the lease that landlords who rent to older people do not anticipate. Landlords who rent apartments of low quality must deal with the probability that some of their tenants will always be late paying their rent. Landlords who rent apartments that command higher rents will not.

With such a dichotomy of rents and quality it is often the case that renters are self-segregating. Apartments close to colleges and universities have higher rents than similar apartment buildings elsewhere, because college students value the lower transportation costs and are willing to pay higher rents so they can take advantage of them. People who are not college students do not value being close to the school. Because they have a homogeneous population, a landlord will require security deposits that are higher than typical for such apartments. This is important because it would be illegal to have a differential security deposit for different types of people. For instance, landlords know that they will have to pay more in repair costs after a college-age male tenant leaves than they will after a college-age female leaves. They cannot set rents that are based on gender, race, religion, or age whether or not these factors are predictive of repair costs.

REASONS FOR CONTROLLING RENTS

When landlords face increased costs, they need to raise rents to make the rate of return on their investments of rental apartments equal to that of other, comparable investments. Few people begrudge landlords such increases. On the other hand, like all other owners of businesses, landlords want to increase prices to increase profits. What prevents landlords from raising rents is exactly what prevents any business from raising prices: their competition will take their customers. In this area, though, landlords have an advantage over businesspeople who sell other goods.

When you switch brands of toothpaste, beer, or anything else, no cost is involved. When you change apartments the costs may be staggering. First you have to find a new place. This may or may not cost you money, but since it is a pain in the neck, its opportunity cost is high. Then you have to disconnect all utilities and have them reconnected at your new place, you have to inform everyone of your new address, and you have to pack all your stuff and move it. Even if you know someone with a pickup and have buddies to help you move, it still costs you plenty of time and money to move. Since the threat of switching apartments is essentially the only leverage you have against the landlord, the costs of moving diminish that leverage.

Landlords know your leverage is diminished by moving costs, and they know they can increase rents each year by just a little bit less than those costs. If they increase rents by more than the moving costs, you will move; but if they make sure to keep the year's increase to less than moving costs, you will decide it is in your economic interest to stay put and pay the extra rent. This process cannot continue forever, since that would imply that rents always go up faster than other prices. If they did, investors would build new apartments in hopes of getting the higher-than-average return on investment. With new apartments, there would be a rent war, and renters would be its winners. On the other hand, it is possible for a rent war not to start for a few years. This in turn may be all that is required for politicians to mistake a temporary situation for one that's permanent and that can

be solved only through the imposing of rent controls. As we will see later, once rent control is imposed in a city, it is nearly impossible to discontinue it.

CONSEQUENCES OF RENT CONTROL

Rent control is a form of **price ceiling** where the price is not allowed to rise above a specified level. Once rent control is in place, the market for rental apartments is no longer governed by supply and demand alone, but also by the often obscure rules that politicians have written into the legislation. The consequences of any price ceiling in general, and of rent control laws in particular, depend on the elasticity of the supply and demand curves. Those elasticities are dependent on the number of close substitutes and on time. Since close substitutes can be better developed over time, the two are closely related. We will subsume them both under the idea of time and discuss the consequences in the short run as being different from the consequences in the long run.

price ceiling
The level above which a price may not rise.

Note that for a price ceiling to be relevant it must be lower than the equilibrium price. Imagine what would happen if the ceiling were, in fact, above the equilibrium price. If landlords charged more than equilibrium, their renters would move to other landlords' buildings. Since landlords do not find it in their best interest to do this, setting rents by law at a rate lower than equilibrium has the effect of telling landlords that they cannot do something that is not in their best interests anyway. It is exactly as if a professor were to tell you that you cannot attend her class naked. You were not going to partake of class in the buff anyway, so having her tell you not to do so is irrelevant.

We can analyze the consequences of rent control more systematically by examining Figure 29.2. First note that in Figure 29.2 there are two panels. The panel on the left indicates the consequences of rent control in the short run, while the panel on the right indicates the consequences in the long run. There are important long-run and short-run differences because, if you recall from Chapter 3, an important determinant of the elasticity of supply and demand is time.

The inelasticity of the supply and demand curves in the short run makes sense because renters and landlords have little time or ability to change what they do. Apartment owners are going to rent most of their units regardless of what the rent is. It is only with apartments that need some

FIGURE 29.2 The short- and long-run consequences of rent control.

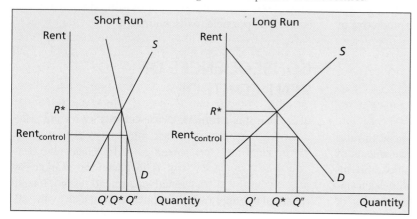

attention that landlords will base the decision on getting them ready to rent on the amount of money they can get for them. Again, in the short run, this is likely to be a very small percentage of the units under their control.

Focusing on what they have in common for a moment, we see that the equilibrium rent R^* is being superseded by a legal limit $R_{control}$. The first consequence of this is the one legislators intended: Rents are lowered, landlords make less than they would without rent control, and renters either pay less in rent or get more for their money.

Reducing the rent also results in the quantity demanded Q'' exceeding the quantity supplied Q'. The quantity of apartments rented decreased because a certain number of apartments $(Q^* - Q')$ that would have been rented before rent control are not being put up for rent after rent control. To see why this is the case, imagine yourself a landlord with a building of apartments of varying difficulty to maintain. The more difficult ones, say, basement apartments that require more frequent painting because humid conditions cause early deterioration, will not be rented unless at least R^* rent is paid. Thus the second consequence of rent control is that the number of apartments that would ordinarily be rented is decreased.

The final obvious consequence of rent control, which happens regardless of whether we are talking about the short run or long run, is that people will seek apartments in the rent-controlled community who had not sought to rent there before. Specifically, there will be $Q'' - Q^*$ apartments demanded at $R_{control}$ that had not been demanded at R^*.

The magnitude of these consequences and the reactions of people to the consequences determine whether they hold for the short or long run. In the short run, for instance, the rent reduction comes at a fairly small cost. Only a few people lose out on the ability to rent apartments, however, because in the short run, both the supply curve and demand curve are likely to be inelastic.

Likewise, renters who live in the community are not likely to want to move to a better apartment immediately following the introduction of rent control. Renters who live outside a community, on the other hand, are not likely to want to move into the community until there is a substantial difference between their current rents and those in the rent-controlled city.

With all the preceding having been said, though, the short-run changes are actually likely to last quite a while, since most rent control laws do not lower rents but simply prevent them from increasing. If overall inflation runs at 2 percent a year and rents are not allowed to rise, it takes several years for a significant difference between equilibrium rents and controlled rents to develop. It is only when that difference becomes large enough so that landlords do not fix up apartments and tenants start moving that the full effect of rent control will even start to be felt.

Once this long-run scenario begins to develop, the serious flaws in rent control begin to overwhelm the benefits. The difference between Q' and Q^* in Figure 29.2 begins to widen significantly as landlords who would have built or refurbished apartment complexes in the community decide not to. The gap between Q'' and Q^* also grows as commuters who live outside the community seek to rent in town, attracted by the lower rents.

Where the system goes from here depends on its rules. For instance, one set of problems is generated if rents can increase by only a fixed percentage each year regardless of who lives there. If, on the other hand, rents cannot increase at all for the duration of a tenant's stay, another set of problems is created. Rules with regard to subletting and eviction tend to exacerbate the problems.

Some rent control laws allow modest yearly increases in rents. Usually, though, these increases do not keep up with either inflation or what equilibrium would have been. In New York City, the difference has had more than 60 years to build up, so that rent-controlled apartments are very inexpensive places to live. They can be had for a third or less of their free-market rent. This makes for a perverse scenario in which those looking for an apartment turn not to the newspaper's real estate section but to the obituaries.

When markets are controlled, they will sometimes go underground. These shadow markets, as they are called by some economists, are generated because there are people who have legal rights to something of value—an apartment, say, whose rent is below equilibrium—and there are people who want them. It is illustrative that in New York City more transactions for rent-controlled apartments happen in the shadow market than out in the open. The evidence for this is the paucity of rent-controlled apartments advertised in the newspapers. Though more than 60 percent of the rental housing in New York is rent-regulated, only 3 percent of the ads in the major city newspapers list housing that is rent-controlled.

To illustrate how the shadow market works, suppose you know someone who has a loved one die and no local relatives are looking for a cheap apartment. You can go to the funeral, pretend to be sad, and see if you can get the dead person's apartment. Of course everyone knows this, so, on the sly, the dead tenant's executers attempt to sell the right to the apartment to the highest bidder. It is a common occurrence, in cities with laws such as this, for people to pay what amounts to a bribe to rent a rent-regulated apartment.

The law in other communities is even more strict: rents cannot increase until the lease expires, and since the renter can perpetually renew the lease, this happens only when the owner dies unexpectedly. If the heirs of a deceased renter can swing it, they sublet with the original renter's name still on a lease that is decades old. Again, the right to sublet an apartment is sold to the highest bidder, sometimes through multiple generations.

Typically the only recourse that owners of buildings whose rents never increase have is to make the buildings miserable places in which to live. This is a well-trod path. Because rents are so low, there is little money for repairs, and repairs simply are not made. Additionally, if owners can get every tenant in a building to leave, they can gut the building and start over again. Refurbished buildings are treated as new ones, and the owners can set charges that are subject only to the market. The other alternative that the owner has once the building is empty is to refurbish and sell the apartments as individual condominiums. Renters know this and will fight moving out as long as they can. They do not do this to spite the owner. They do it because they know that finding a rent-controlled apartment is difficult. Without one, they would be one of many (Q'') wanting to rent one of the few (Q') available apartments. This is why in rent-control communities tenants often do their own repairs or pay for them out of their own pockets. They know they have a good thing going and they do not want to see it stop. The only recourse that tenants have against landlords who do not pay for necessary repairs is to report them to the city health department. Sometimes the health department can get a court order for the landlord to fix the place up, sometimes they cannot. This sort of pressure rarely works. Owners simply abandon the buildings, leaving tenants worse off than if they had not reported the problem.

Thus one reaction of landlords is to reduce the quality of the apartment they are renting. Charging the same rent for a lesser apartment is the same as raising the rent. As a result, economists suggest that, in the long run, rent controls are ineffective because landlords raise rent on the sly, not by explicitly raising rent, but by lowering quality. Finally, rent control makes racial, ethnic, age, and other forms of housing discrimination more likely. If there are more people interested in an apartment than there are apartments to rent, landlords can pick, albeit illegally, their next tenant based on their own bigotry. Under free market pricing, the landlord's bigotry battles the landlord's wallet. Under rent control, bigotry has no such countervailing force with which to contend.

WHY DOES RENT CONTROL SURVIVE?

With all of these strange long-run consequences, it makes sense to ask why cities continue controlling rents. The answer is simple, and it can be traced to the ballot box. Let's start with the obvious: you do not get to vote in a community unless you live there. People who live in a suburb cannot vote in a city's election, even though the result of the election directly affects them. Add the fact that many of the people who live in the rent-controlled city benefit from rent control almost by definition.

Figure 29.2 helps to make this clear. The people hurt by rent control are (1) landlords and (2) people who can no longer find an apartment in the city ($Q^* - Q'$). The first group is a minuscule number whose plight is not treated that seriously by candidates.[1] The second group had to move out of town to find a place to live. Either way the majority of the people left in the community (Q') are simply better off than they would be were rent control to be discontinued.

In Boston, though, repeal of rent controls led to none of the problems that rent control supporters had predicted. Rents in previously controlled apartments did rise, but new construction ensued. This had the effect of holding down increases in rents.

---

[1]This is not to say that these landlords have no influence. Through campaign contributions landlords, particularly the high-profile ones, are able to make their case and have received consideration on a number of development issues of concern to them. Nevertheless, this influence has not led to the undoing of rent control in New York.

Summary

You are now able to use the model of supply and demand we introduced in Chapter 2 to show the effects of rent control. You understand that though there are reasons for controlling rents, these are typically short term in nature and economists generally are against rent controls. You understand that the consequences of controlling rents differ given the time horizon and that the short-term benefits to the renter are usually offset by long-term losses to landlords and renters who cannot get housing in a community. Last, you are now able to use the supply and demand model to explain why eliminating rent control can be in a city's general interest but not in the interests of the voters of that city.

Key Term

price ceiling, 307

Quiz Yourself

1. The principal argument against rent control is that
   a. Landlords and all tenants are made worse off.
   b. Landlords and a few tenants are made worse off by less than the majority of tenants that are made better off.
   c. Landlords and a few tenants are made worse off by more than the majority of tenants that are made better off.
   d. All tenants are made better off, not just poor ones.

2. In the long run, rent control has _____ impact because, over time, supply and demand become _____ elastic.
   a. An increasing; more.
   b. A decreasing; more.
   c. An increasing; less.
   d. A decreasing; less.

3. Rent control is an example of a _____
   a. Price ceiling.
   b. Price floor.

   c. Price irrelevancy.
   d. Price equalization.

4. If the equilibrium rent is _____ the controlled level, then rent control laws are _____ .
   a. Above; necessary.
   b. Above; irrelevant.
   c. Below; necessary.
   d. Below; irrelevant.

5. Which of the following is likely to occur after several years of relevant rent control?
   a. Rents exceeding equilibrium.
   b. An increase in available housing.
   c. A decrease in available housing.
   d. Rents equaling equilibrium.

6. History suggests that rent control laws
   a. Tend to be declared unconstitutional.
   b. Tend to be overturned soon after they are adopted.
   c. Tend to become a permanent fixture of a community.
   d. Are incredibly unpopular.

Think about This

Rent control laws, like minimum-wage laws apply to everyone, not simply the poor. Should there be provisions to apply rent control only to those who need the lower rent?

Talk about This

In smaller cities, being a landlord is a way for handy men and women to invest in property, fix it up, and rent it out. It allows them to save and invest some of their own sweat. Should rent control laws exempt these type of landlords?

For More Insight See

Keating, W. Dennis, Michael Teitz, and Andrejs Skaburskis, *Rent Control: Regulation and the Rental Housing Market* (New Brunswick, NJ: Center for Urban Policy Research, 1998).

Chapter **30**

Ticket Brokers and Ticket Scalping

A ticket scalper looks for buyers at the Olympics.
Source: © Robert W. Ginn/PhotoEdit

Chapter Objectives

After reading this chapter you should be able to

Understand what ticket scalping is and why it exists.

Locate the market for tickets within the monopoly model.

Understand why the marginal cost curve presented in Chapter 4 is not appropriate for ticket sales.

See why promoters may rationally charge less for an event than they could, and that the result of this is a shortage of tickets.

Understand why the conditions of a shortage typically create a scalping market, where people buy tickets below, at, or above their face value and sell them for a profit.

Understand that economists generally value the scalping market, see very little reason to make laws regulating it, and see very little functional distinction between the legal and illegal forms of scalping that exist across the country.

Chapter Outline

Defining Brokering and Scalping

An Economic Model of Ticket Sales

Why Promoters Charge Less than They Could

An Economic Model of Scalping

Legitimate Scalpers

Summary

If you want to see a concert, a game, a race, or any other event that is sold out, you probably know that you can always get a ticket—for a price. Some events are "once in a lifetime," while others are just something many people want to see. In recent years, tickets to events like Michael Jordan's last game as a Chicago Bull and the game in which Mark McGwire hit his home run number 62 in St. Louis commanded prices many times their face value. There are other events, not once in a lifetime, where demand continues to be extraordinarily high. The Super Bowl, the World Series, and the NASCAR Bristol night race are events that are important enough to some people that they are willing to pay more than face value for a ticket.

While in many cities it is illegal to sell a ticket for more than face value, in every major city there is a way of getting such tickets when they are the only ones available. Economists are almost always against laws that prevent people from selling things they possess. They reason that if one person would rather have $500 than a ticket to a game and another person would rather have a ticket to a game than $500, then both are better off with the trade than without it.

This chapter defines ticket scalping and offers an economic explanation for it. We begin that explanation by using our monopoly pricing model from Chapter 5 to understand the promoter's ticket-pricing scheme. We show that for scalping to exist, promoters have to be underpricing their tickets, and we consider why they do this. We use our supply and demand model and our consumer and producer surplus language to see how scalping helps consumers and scalpers alike. We talk about the mechanism by which scalpers become "legit" by calling themselves "brokers" or by offering packages that combine the tickets with other amenities.

DEFINING BROKERING AND SCALPING

Brokering tickets is the act of buying a ticket and selling it at a price higher than its face value when such a transaction is legal. **Scalping** tickets is the act of buying a ticket and selling it at a price higher than its face value when such a transaction is illegal. Thus the practice is scalping only when it is done illegally. Regardless of semantic differences, for many fans and performers, scalpers and brokers

brokering
The act of buying a ticket and legally selling it at a price higher than its face value.

scalping
The act of buying a ticket and illegally selling it at a price higher than its face value.

are the worst form of predator; they obtain large blocks of tickets before other people get them and then they sell the tickets at prices that net them a profit. They do not produce anything. Those who engage in this trade view themselves as simply providing a service from which they make a living. To others, they are simply leeching off the talents of others.

For economists, scalpers perform a function that "fixes" pricing that promoters get wrong. As we will see, scalping can exist profitably only when enough fans are willing to pay more for tickets than the face value of the ticket and there are more buyers willing to pay face value than there are seats.

This does not necessarily mean the performance is a sellout. If some seats are really good and others are really terrible, then the good ones, at courtside, say, might be scalped while those in "nosebleed territory" might remain unsold. What is true is that there cannot be unsold seats right next to seats for which scalpers wish to charge more than face value. When traditional ticket outlets that sell for face value have open, decent seats, these will be sold out before scalpers can sell any.

AN ECONOMIC MODEL OF TICKET SALES

The question we can pose at this point is, "Why would a promoter charge less for a ticket than it is worth?" To answer the question we need to look at what determines the price a promoter should charge. To model that, we need to go back to Chapter 5 to see which model of the market is more appropriate for ticket sales, perfect competition or monopoly. Because there is ultimately only one seller of the tickets, the promoter, our monopoly model is clearly more appropriate to this than the perfect competition model, in which there are many sellers.

Marginal Cost

To complicate things somewhat more, remember the shape of the marginal cost curve that was introduced in Chapter 4. It is a check-shaped curve, as seen in the left panel of Figure 30.1. For ticket sales to a sporting event or a concert, the marginal cost looks a little different. The right-hand side of Figure 30.1 shows that up to the capacity of the stadium, the marginal cost is probably more likely to be a constant. The costs of printing and selling the tickets and the costs of cleaning up after each additional fan remain relatively constant. These extra costs are likely to be the same for the thousandth fan as the hundred-thousandth fan. At capacity,

FIGURE 30.1   Marginal cost.

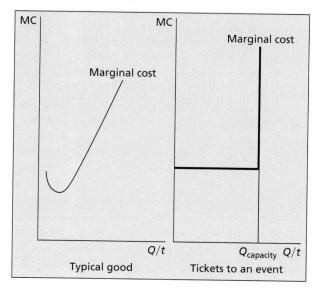

FIGURE 30.2   The profit-maximizing promoter's choice of price and ticket sales.

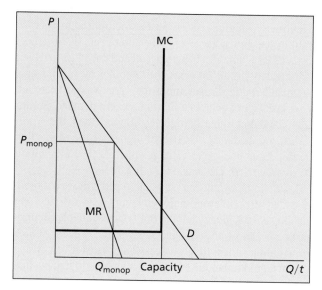

The Promoter as Monopolist

When promoters are attempting to maximize profits and are trying to figure out what price to charge for events, they have to gauge what the demand will be for the event. Once they have done that, they can look at this problem as any other monopolist would. Recall that we have always assumed that firms are profit maximizers. Though revenue would be maximized where marginal revenue cuts the horizontal axis, this is not where the profit-maximizing promoters operate. As is depicted in Figure 30.2, they project the number of sales and set the price so that marginal revenue equals marginal cost. This means that they would sell Q_{monop} tickets for P_{monop} each.

An interesting aspect of this is that it may make sense for promoters to see that the arena is only partially filled. Promoters hold back tickets when they would have to lower the price too far in order to sell out the facility. You should not be surprised by this conclusion, especially if you are at a school that does not have a popular athletic program. Consider a school whose men's basketball team draws between 4,000 and 6,000 fans a game, while the women's team draws fewer than 1,000 a game. If the athletic department were to price tickets to sell out the arena, tickets would be nearly free for the men's games

and the department would have to pay people to see the women. That is not a slam at the women; it is just a fact of life at a school without a national sports reputation. Clearly, it makes sense for this university to charge more for the men's games and to charge something for the women. The university makes the most money possible that way, even with only one sellout per decade.

The Perfect Arena

To a promoter, the size of the facility is significant. In a promoter's eyes, the perfect facility would be represented as seen in Figure 30.3, where the capacity is exactly the number of seats that the promoter wants to sell anyway. That is, the facility with perfect capacity is the one where marginal cost intersects marginal revenue at the quantity that is exactly the capacity of the facility. Of course, promoters cannot always find the perfect facility. Most medium and small cities have only one or two places to hold an event like a concert, and even in other places, the perfect arena or concert hall may not be available.

In a big city with many venues of many different sizes, a promoter should seek the facility whose size ensures that the marginal cost will cross marginal revenue at exactly the capacity. On the assumption that facilities that are unnecessarily large cost the promoter more to rent, booking this "perfect" facility maximizes profit.

FIGURE 30.3 The perfect arena.

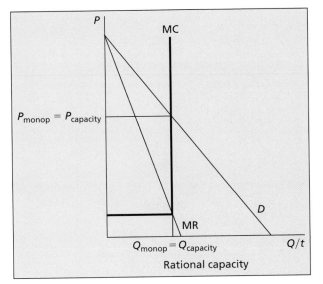

Rational capacity

FIGURE 30.4 Capacity versus profit-maximizing prices.

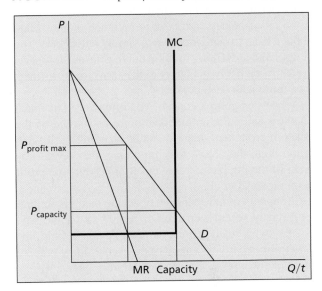

In each case mentioned so far there is no market for scalpers because the face value of the ticket is the price at which it is sold. Scalping makes sense only if the market price of the ticket is greater than the face value. The only way for that to happen is if the promoter charges less than the profit-maximizing amount. This is seen in Figure 30.4, where the ticket is priced at or below the price that would sell out the facility rather than the price that would maximize profits for the promoter.

WHY PROMOTERS CHARGE LESS THAN THEY COULD

Why might promoters sell out a facility rather than maximize profits? First, they may not have good information on the price they ought to charge. This uncertainty might motivate them to err on the safe side and charge a lower price. Second, there may be some "excitement" factor to a full stadium that appeals to the performers and that is worth the loss of profit. Third, the performers may want a reputation of charging a "fair price" for their events and be willing to forgo maximum profit in order to further that reputation. Fourth, the performers may want some mechanism other than price to separate the "real fans" from those who go to events simply because they have money. Fifth, ancillary sales of shirts and other memorabilia are important sources of revenue for performers and promoters alike. Since it may be that the revenue gained by these sales exceeds that lost by hav-

ing low ticket prices, low ticket prices may lead to increasing audience size and may therefore maximize profit after all. Last, it may be in the long-run best interest of the performers to charge a low price for tickets so that the largest possible audience can provide word-of-mouth advertising for them and generate interest for their talent.

Sometimes promoters do not have an exact idea of what price to charge for an event. More often than not, promoters of a new act must guess what the market will bear for the ticket. If they guess too low, scalping may ensue. In addition, promoters may want to play it safe and not run the risk of pricing too high, thereby purposefully pricing less than even their best guess. This might also result in scalping.

There is an excitement to being at a sold-out event in a large arena. The sound and feel are different for a sold-out event than for one in a half-full auditorium. The performer enjoys it more and the fans enjoy it more. Although this may not seem like an important function for a promoter, consider that promoters are hired by athletes or performers to promote the event as effectively as possible. It may be in the promoters' best interests to cater to the performer, regardless of what maximizes profit.

Some performers try to establish a closeness with their fans. Some try to signal their empathy by making sure ticket prices are low enough that "ordinary" fans can afford to go. This means that performers and promoters are willing to accept less money for the good feeling that charging "fair" prices gives them.

Performers may appreciate fans who are willing to camp out for tickets more than those simply willing to pay a lot of money. You have to be much more excited about a band to camp out than to simply buy tickets. The people who are willing to camp out to get front-row seats are far more likely to convey enthusiasm for performers than those with deep pockets.

When you go to a concert, you often spend as much on shirts and other promotional items as you did on the ticket. If promoters keep you out by charging a price that is too high, they forgo that important other revenue as well. In the big picture, low ticket prices may be profit maximizing after all.

Promoters of new bands may decide that it is in their long-run interest to keep ticket prices low so that the band is seen by as many people as possible. By setting low ticket prices early in a performer's career, they may be more likely to turn a one-hit wonder into a star.

For any one of the reasons just outlined promoters may choose to sell their tickets at prices below their monopoly market value and perhaps even below the price that would guarantee a sellout. In any event, a price below what they see as the free market value will cause scalpers to buy tickets at the lower price in order to sell them at a higher price.

AN ECONOMIC MODEL OF SCALPING

A market characterized by ticket scalping is going to have a typical demand curve. It will reflect the demand by those who do not get tickets by normal means. For many events, such as the Brickyard 400 NASCAR race in Indianapolis, tickets are distributed to those who subscribe. Because this particular event was fully subscribed within 10 days of the announcement of the inaugural event, and subscribers have the first opportunity to buy tickets every year, there is no way to get tickets the normal way for subsequent races. Anyone else who wants tickets to this event must buy tickets from people who already have them.

The demand curve for these tickets is downward sloping just as it is for any other good. If the event is a "must see," then you expect a demand curve further to the right or perhaps more inelastic, or steeper, because tickets for a "once-in-a-lifetime event" have fewer substitutes than tickets for events that will be repeated. The elasticity of demand will be expected to be less.

The supply curve for this market is upward sloping (and not vertical), not because the number of tickets is not

FIGURE 30.5   A scalper's market.

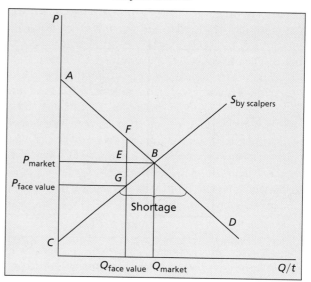

limited but because in order to get tickets away from those who have them, you have to give up more and more to persuade more and more rabid fans to give up their tickets. Figure 30.5 reflects the market for scalped tickets.

If the price is required to stay at the face value of the ticket, then there will be fewer tickets than potential buyers. To an economist this is the very definition of a shortage. Note that the supply curve may start below $P_{\text{face value}}$ or above it. In Figure 30.5 it starts below. To understand why, consider that there are people who have tickets for an event who are willing to sell them for less than they paid because they do not want to go to the event. Why would you buy a ticket for an event you did not want to go to? Suppose you had season tickets to the Los Angeles Lakers and a ticket to the California 500 NASCAR race. Suppose the L.A. Clippers were playing the Lakers on the day of the race. You paid face value for the ticket, and you are willing to take almost anything for that game's ticket because you have decided to go to the race.

If scalping is illegal, only $Q_{\text{face value}}$, the tickets that people are willing to unload for the face value, will be sold. If those are the only tickets that are sold, then the people who are willing to pay more than face value will not find any to buy. Some people will go to the game when they would rather have received P_{market} and stayed home. Others will stay home, when they would rather have paid P_{market} and gone to the game.

Without scalping, there is a shortage and a loss of societal benefit. That loss, measured by the loss in consumer and producer surplus, can also be seen in Figure 30.5. The loss of welfare to people who want to see the game at the scalper's price is *EFB,* while the loss to people who would like to have sold their tickets is *GEB.* The total loss to society when scalping is forbidden is *GFB.*

In this circumstance, is the permission to scalp tickets creating a problem or solving one? Economists posit that scalpers are solving the shortage by taking tickets from those who have them and who value them least and transferring them to those who do not have them and who value them most. For this the scalper takes a cut. Performers take a dim view of this. They view it as a practice in which people profit from something they had no hand at all in creating.

LEGITIMATE SCALPERS

In some states, all forms of scalping are legal; in others, none are. In a growing number of states scalping remains illegal but "brokers" are allowed to sell tickets for more than they pay for them. The only difference between a scalper and a broker is that the scalper walks around an event's perimeter trying to sell tickets, while the broker does it from a desk and a phone. The scalper demands cash; the broker takes credit cards.

Another way that scalpers have become legitimate is by pairing their services with that of a travel agent. It is legal in nearly every state for travel agents to create packages with hotel rooms, cab rides, and the like, and then offer these along with the tickets. Suppose you want a ticket to the latest "fight of the century." If it is in a no-scalping state and you cannot get tickets the normal way, you can still get the ticket because travel agents now can combine a $100 ticket with a $100 hotel room and a $10 dollar cab ride and call it a $500 "excursion." (Do the math!) This is legal nearly everywhere, even when "scalping" is not. It is also what an economist would call a distinction without a difference.

It must be reinforced, therefore, that economists generally disapprove of antiscalping regulations. Whether as legal brokers or illegal scalpers, the sellers are providing services. They are not only fixing the market shortage left over by the promoter; they are also providing convenience. The hours of ticket offices at major arenas are not always amenable to customer desires. Lines at the ticket booth or at "will call" windows are often very long the day of the event. Because scalpers and brokers provide us with a convenience and harm no one in the process, there is little economic reason to ban their activities.

Summary

You now understand what ticket scalping is and why it exists. You understand that the market for tickets falls within the monopoly model and that the marginal cost curve presented in Chapter 4 is not appropriate for ticket sales. You understand why promoters may rationally charge less for an event than they could and that the result of this is a shortage of tickets. You understand that under the conditions of a shortage there is typically a place for a scalping market in which people buy tickets below, at, or above their face value and sell them for a profit. Last, you understand that economists generally value such services, see little reason to make laws regulating them, and see little functional distinction between the legal and illegal forms of brokering or scalping that exist across the country.

Key Terms

brokering, 313   scalping, 313

Quiz Yourself

1. Ticket scalping is a symptom of
   a. Stupid promoters.
   b. Market prices being greater than the face value of the ticket.
   c. Market prices being less than the face value of the ticket.
   d. Stupid consumers.

2. Economists _____ the activities of ticket brokers and scalpers.
   a. Draw no distinction between.
   b. Separately model.
   c. Draw a stark between.
   d. Ignore.

3. The optimal venue for an event is one where
   a. The number of seats exceeds the number where marginal cost equals marginal revenue.
   b. The number of seats is less than the number where marginal cost equals marginal revenue.
   c. The number of seats is exactly the number where marginal cost equals marginal revenue.
   d. Marginal revenue exceeds marginal cost for all seats.

4. The distinct feature of the marginal cost curve in the analysis of venues is that they are
   a. A vertical line.
   b. A horizontal line.
   c. A check-shaped curve.
   d. A backward L.

5. The model for a promoter is _____ whereas the model for scalpers is that of _____.
   a. Monopoly; monopolistic competition.
   b. Monopolistic competition; perfect competition.
   c. Monopoly; oligopoly.
   d. Monopoly; perfect competition.

6. If antiscalping laws are perfectly enforced, it will result in
   a. Deadweight loss.
   b. A significant increase in consumer surplus.
   c. A significant increase in producer surplus.
   d. A significant loss to people who are going to the event.

Think about This

There are laws in many states and communities against scalping. Many promoters will let people buy only a limited number of tickets for fear that the buyer will simply resell them later. Why would a promoter care who buys the tickets? If you became a performer, would you care?

Talk about This

Some scalpers will pay college students who have camped out for a concert to buy extra tickets for them so that they can later resell them. Because this is against the law in some places, there is some risk for the scalper in that the student could simply resell the tickets themselves. If you were standing in line for tickets, what would you do?

For More Insight See

Happel, Stephen, and Marianne Jennings, "The Folly of Anti-Scalping Laws," *The Cato Journal* 15, no. 1 (Spring/Summer 1995), pp. 65–76.

Chapter **31**

Personal Income Taxes

A clerk at the Internal Revenue Service sorts through piles of tax returns. *Source: AP Wide World Photo*

Chapter Objectives

After reading this chapter you should be able to

Understand the rudiments of how taxes work.

Describe the concepts of horizontal and vertical equity and how they apply to the issue of taxation.

Understand the trade-off that exists between simplicity and horizontal equity when people are making tax policy.

See how taxes can alter the incentives of people to work and save.

Know how taxes have been used to motivate socially desirable outcomes.

Understand in a greater context the debates over taxes that took place during the 1990s and continue today.

Chapter Outline

How Income Taxes Work

Issues in Income Taxation

Incentives and the Tax Code

Who Pays Income Taxes?

The Tax Debates of the Last Decade

Summary

In 2004 income taxes accounted for $858 billion of the $1,853 billion that made up federal revenue. As Figure 31.1 suggests, the rest came from payroll (FICA), corporate, customs, excise, estate, and miscellaneous taxes. Personal income taxes make up almost a majority of the revenue government takes in. These taxes also provoke many of the disagreements between Republicans and Democrats. Each party fights for policies it believes are best for the nation and that help its constituencies.

Usually the political fights surrounding the personal income code boil down to whether the rich pay their "fair share." To look at these controversies with any insight we will need to understand the way taxes work and who pays them before we get into which party has the better claim on taxes.

This chapter leads off with a discussion of how income taxes work in the United States. Following that we discuss whether and how income taxes alter the willingness of people to work and save and how capital gains fit into this picture. We then introduce surprising news about who actually pays taxes. At the end we lay out some of the interesting tax debates of the 1990s and beyond.

FIGURE 31.1 Federal taxes and their sources in billions.

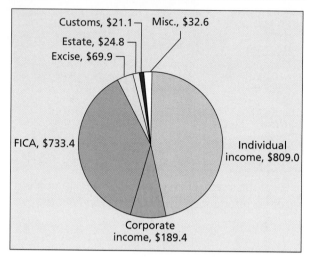

HOW INCOME TAXES WORK

Federal income taxes in the United States are collected through a series of guesses that are corrected on April 15 of the year after the tax year. When you get a new job, you have to fill out a W-4 form on which you specify how many exemptions you are taking. Usually, your exemptions are yourself and the others in your household, but you can adjust the number by as many as necessary to improve the guess on the taxes you will owe. The number you provide is used by your employer to figure out how much tax should be withheld from each

withholding
Deduction from your paycheck to cover the estimated amount of taxes you are going to owe during a year.

of your paychecks. **Withholding** is the deduction from your paycheck in which you and the government estimate how much tax you are going to owe during a year so you can pay it a little at a time rather than all at once. On April 15 you use the amount you actually earned, as reported to you on a W-2 or a 1099 form, to compute what you actually owe. People who have had too much withheld get a tax refund. If they have too little withheld, they have to make it up by April 15.

As you can see from Figure 31.2, the amount of tax you owe looks complicated. In reality tax computations are simple for most people because, thanks to a 1986 law, most people can skip the most complicated step, the deductions, and fill out as few as 10 lines on their tax forms. Still, for many others, tax forms, rules, and procedures are complicated and jargon-filled. To understand

how taxes affect people, we must first take a crack at understanding those forms, rules, procedures and jargon.

The tax you owe is, of course, influenced by how much you earn. The **adjusted gross income (AGI)** is

adjusted gross income (AGI)
Total net income from all sources.

the total net income from all sources. To get that number, add together all of your income from the traditional sources (wages, salaries, tips, interest, and dividends). Then add in any net profit from businesses and rental apartments, any profit you have from asset sales (called **capital gains**), and, finally, adjust that for net alimony received. (If you paid alimony, this is a negative.)

capital gains
Any profit generated by selling an asset for more than was paid for it.

To figure out how much of that adjusted gross income is taxable you first have to adjust that number by two other numbers. The first, **exemptions,** is an amount by

exemptions
An amount by which AGI is reduced which is determined by the size of the family.

which AGI is reduced that is determined by the size of your family. These exemptions are similar to, but not the same as, the exemptions you compute for form W-4. For that form you can essentially create fictitious people in order to make your withholding correct. Here, the exemptions have to be real. Each person in the household counts as one. Each person over 65 counts as one more, as does each blind person. For the 2004 tax year, each exemption reduced AGI by $3,200. For example, a married couple, both of whose members are old and blind, would have had six exemptions, whereas a husband and wife with two small children would have had four. In the first case the total exemption is 6 × $3,200, or $19,200. In the second example it is 4 × $3,200, or $12,800.

Deductions are also amounts by which AGI is

deductions
Amounts by which AGI is reduced; the greater of either the standard deduction or itemized deductions.

reduced. These are complicated by the fact that they are the greater of either a minimum level or the sum of particular expenditures, the value of which is money that will not be taxed. The minimum level of deduction is called the **standard deduction,** and this is the amount that most people take. **Itemized deductions** are for particular expenses on which government does not want taxes paid. The reason most people can compute

standard deduction
The minimum level of deduction.

itemized deductions
Deductions for particular expenses on which the government does not want taxes paid.

FIGURE 31.2 Federal income taxes, 2004.

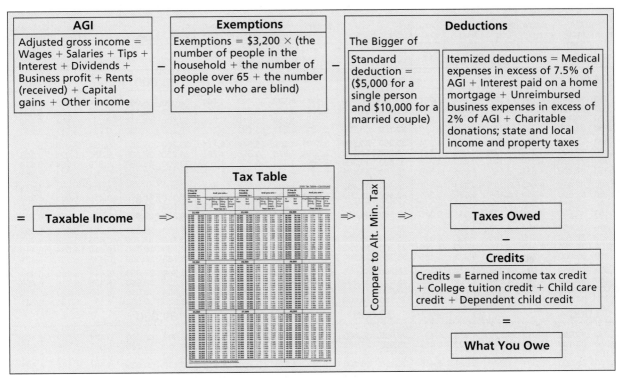

their taxes relatively easily is that they skip this complicated step. Rather than itemizing deductions, they accept the value of the standard deduction.

When people itemize (that is, "list"), they add up those things that are **deductible** (approved types of expenses) and instead of reducing their taxable income by a fixed amount, they reduce it by the sum of those expenses. For instance, when people buy homes they typically have mortgage payments. In the early years of paying a mortgage, the payment is almost entirely interest. That interest is deductible. Other deductible items that are listed include state and local income and property taxes, charitable donations, certain employment expenses, and certain (usually very high) medical expenses.

deductible
Approved types of expenses for income tax purposes.

Most people do not itemize their deductions because if they did, the total would not equal the standard deduction. This is especially true for those who rent their residences, because renters cannot deduct mortgage interest and property taxes. Only those who own the properties are entitled to take these deductions.

The standard deduction simplifies taxes for most people, and it reduces the amount of tax that they owe. Those people who itemize have at least one, if not many more, forms than the people who take the standard deduction. In addition, since the standard deduction gives the people who take it a larger reduction off income than they would otherwise get, it reduces their tax burden. **Taxable income** is therefore adjusted gross income minus personal exemptions minus (the greater of either the standard or itemized) deductions.

taxable income
Adjusted gross income minus personal exemptions minus (the greater of either the standard or itemized) deductions.

Another thing people must know in order to compute the tax they owe is their **filing status.** A person's filing status can be one of four things: single, married filing jointly, married filing separately, and single head of household. Single people without children file as singles, whereas those singles with kids in the household file as a single head of household.

filing status
Classification of taxpayers based on household; can be single, married filing jointly, married filing separately, and single head of household.

FIGURE 31.3 Tax table for 2004.

2004 Tax Table—Continued

If line 42 (taxable income) is— At least	But less than	Single	Married filing jointly *	Married filing separately	Head of a house-hold	If line 42 (taxable income) is— At least	But less than	Single	Married filing jointly *	Married filing separately	Head of a house-hold	If line 42 (taxable income) is— At least	But less than	Single	Married filing jointly *	Married filing separately	Head of a house-hold
		Your tax is—						Your tax is—						Your tax is—			
32,000						**35,000**						**38,000**					
32,000	32,050	4,744	4,089	4,744	4,294	35,000	35,050	5,494	4,539	5,494	4,744	38,000	38,050	6,244	4,989	6,244	5,194
32,050	32,100	4,756	4,096	4,756	4,301	35,050	35,100	5,506	4,546	5,506	4,751	38,050	38,100	6,256	4,996	6,256	5,201
32,100	32,150	4,769	4,104	4,769	4,309	35,100	35,150	5,519	4,554	5,519	4,759	38,100	38,150	6,269	5,004	6,269	5,209
32,150	32,200	4,781	4,111	4,781	4,316	35,150	35,200	5,531	4,561	5,531	4,766	38,150	38,200	6,281	5,011	6,281	5,216
32,200	32,250	4,794	4,119	4,794	4,324	35,200	35,250	5,544	4,569	5,544	4,774	38,200	38,250	6,294	5,019	6,294	5,224
32,250	32,300	4,806	4,126	4,806	4,331	35,250	35,300	5,556	4,576	5,556	4,781	38,250	38,300	6,306	5,026	6,306	5,231
32,300	32,350	4,819	4,134	4,819	4,339	35,300	35,350	5,569	4,584	5,569	4,789	38,300	38,350	6,319	5,034	6,319	5,239
32,350	32,400	4,831	4,141	4,831	4,346	35,350	35,400	5,581	4,591	5,581	4,796	38,350	38,400	6,331	5,041	6,331	5,246
32,400	32,450	4,844	4,149	4,844	4,354	35,400	35,450	5,594	4,599	5,594	4,804	38,400	38,450	6,344	5,049	6,344	5,254
32,450	32,500	4,856	4,156	4,856	4,361	35,450	35,500	5,606	4,606	5,606	4,811	38,450	38,500	6,356	5,056	6,356	5,261
32,500	32,550	4,869	4,164	4,869	4,369	35,500	35,550	5,619	4,614	5,619	4,819	38,500	38,550	6,369	5,064	6,369	5,269
32,550	32,600	(4,881)	4,171	4,881	4,376	35,550	35,600	5,631	4,621	5,631	4,826	38,550	38,600	6,381	5,071	6,381	5,276
32,600	32,650	4,894	4,179	4,894	4,384	35,600	35,650	5,644	4,629	5,644	4,834	38,600	38,650	6,394	5,079	6,394	5,284
32,650	32,700	4,906	4,186	4,906	4,391	35,650	35,700	5,656	4,636	5,656	4,841	38,650	38,700	6,406	5,086	6,406	5,291
32,700	32,750	4,919	4,194	4,919	4,399	35,700	35,750	5,669	4,644	5,669	4,849	38,700	38,750	6,419	5,094	6,419	5,299
32,750	32,800	4,931	4,201	4,931	4,406	35,750	35,800	5,681	4,651	5,681	4,856	38,750	38,800	6,431	5,101	6,431	5,306
32,800	32,850	4,944	4,209	4,944	4,414	35,800	35,850	5,694	4,659	5,694	4,864	38,800	38,850	6,444	5,109	6,444	5,314
32,850	32,900	4,956	4,216	4,956	4,421	35,850	35,900	5,706	4,666	5,706	4,871	38,850	38,900	6,456	5,116	6,456	5,321
32,900	32,950	4,969	4,224	4,969	4,429	35,900	35,950	5,719	4,674	5,719	4,879	38,900	38,950	6,469	5,124	6,469	5,331
32,950	33,000	4,981	4,231	4,981	4,436	35,950	36,000	5,731	4,681	5,731	4,886	38,950	39,000	6,481	5,131	6,481	5,344
33,000						**36,000**						**39,000**					
33,000	33,050	4,994	4,239	4,994	4,444	36,000	36,050	5,744	4,689	5,744	4,894	39,000	39,050	6,494	5,139	6,494	5,356
33,050	33,100	5,006	4,246	5,006	4,451	36,050	36,100	5,756	4,696	5,756	4,901	39,050	39,100	6,506	5,146	6,506	5,369
33,100	33,150	5,019	4,254	5,019	4,459	36,100	36,150	5,769	4,704	5,769	4,909	39,100	39,150	6,519	5,154	6,519	5,381
33,150	33,200	5,031	4,261	5,031	4,466	36,150	36,200	5,781	4,711	5,781	4,916	39,150	39,200	6,531	5,161	6,531	5,394
33,200	33,250	5,044	4,269	5,044	4,474	36,200	36,250	5,794	4,719	5,794	4,924	39,200	39,250	6,544	5,169	6,544	5,406
33,250	33,300	5,056	4,276	5,056	4,481	36,250	36,300	5,806	4,726	5,806	4,931	39,250	39,300	6,556	5,176	6,556	5,419
33,300	33,350	5,069	4,284	5,069	4,489	36,300	36,350	5,819	4,734	5,819	4,939	39,300	39,350	6,569	5,184	6,569	5,431
33,350	33,400	5,081	4,291	5,081	4,496	36,350	36,400	5,831	4,741	5,831	4,946	39,350	39,400	6,581	5,191	6,581	5,444
33,400	33,450	5,094	4,299	5,094	4,504	36,400	36,450	5,844	4,749	5,844	4,954	39,400	39,450	6,594	5,199	6,594	5,456
33,450	33,500	5,106	4,306	5,106	4,511	36,450	36,500	5,856	4,756	5,856	4,961	39,450	39,500	6,606	5,206	6,606	5,469
33,500	33,550	5,119	4,314	5,119	4,519	36,500	36,550	5,869	4,764	5,869	4,969	39,500	39,550	6,619	5,214	6,619	5,481
33,550	33,600	5,131	4,321	5,131	4,526	36,550	36,600	5,881	4,771	5,881	4,976	39,550	39,600	6,631	5,221	6,631	5,494
33,600	33,650	5,144	4,329	5,144	4,534	36,600	36,650	5,894	4,779	5,894	4,984	39,600	39,650	6,644	5,229	6,644	5,506
33,650	33,700	5,156	4,336	5,156	4,541	36,650	36,700	5,906	4,786	5,906	4,991	39,650	39,700	6,656	5,236	6,656	5,519
33,700	33,750	5,169	4,344	5,169	4,549	36,700	36,750	5,919	4,794	5,919	4,999	39,700	39,750	6,669	5,244	6,669	5,531
33,750	33,800	5,181	4,351	5,181	4,556	36,750	36,800	5,931	4,801	5,931	5,006	39,750	39,800	6,681	5,251	6,681	5,544
33,800	33,850	5,194	4,359	5,194	4,564	36,800	36,850	5,944	4,809	5,944	5,014	39,800	39,850	6,694	5,259	6,694	5,556
33,850	33,900	5,206	4,366	5,206	4,571	36,850	36,900	5,956	4,816	5,956	5,021	39,850	39,900	6,706	5,266	6,706	5,569
33,900	33,950	5,219	4,374	5,219	4,579	36,900	36,950	5,969	4,824	5,969	5,029	39,900	39,950	6,719	5,274	6,719	5,581
33,950	34,000	5,231	4,381	5,231	4,586	36,950	37,000	5,981	4,831	5,981	5,036	39,950	40,000	6,731	5,281	6,731	5,594
34,000						**37,000**						**40,000**					
34,000	34,050	5,244	4,389	5,244	4,594	37,000	37,050	5,994	4,839	5,994	5,044	40,000	40,050	6,744	5,289	6,744	5,606
34,050	34,100	5,256	4,396	5,256	4,601	37,050	37,100	6,006	4,846	6,006	5,051	40,050	40,100	6,756	5,296	6,756	5,619
34,100	34,150	5,269	4,404	5,269	4,609	37,100	37,150	6,019	4,854	6,019	5,059	40,100	40,150	6,769	5,304	6,769	5,631
34,150	34,200	5,281	4,411	5,281	4,616	37,150	37,200	6,031	4,861	6,031	5,066	40,150	40,200	6,781	5,311	6,781	5,644
34,200	34,250	5,294	4,419	5,294	4,624	37,200	37,250	6,044	4,869	6,044	5,074	40,200	40,250	6,794	5,319	6,794	5,656
34,250	34,300	5,306	4,426	5,306	4,631	37,250	37,300	6,056	4,876	6,056	5,081	40,250	40,300	6,806	5,326	6,806	5,669
34,300	34,350	5,319	4,434	5,319	4,639	37,300	37,350	6,069	4,884	6,069	5,089	40,300	40,350	6,819	5,334	6,819	5,681
34,350	34,400	5,331	4,441	5,331	4,646	37,350	37,400	6,081	4,891	6,081	5,096	40,350	40,400	6,831	5,341	6,831	5,694
34,400	34,450	5,344	4,449	5,344	4,654	37,400	37,450	6,094	4,899	6,094	5,104	40,400	40,450	6,844	5,349	6,844	5,706
34,450	34,500	5,356	4,456	5,356	4,661	37,450	37,500	6,106	4,906	6,106	5,111	40,450	40,500	6,856	5,356	6,856	5,719
34,500	34,550	5,369	4,464	5,369	4,669	37,500	37,550	6,119	4,914	6,119	5,119	40,500	40,550	6,869	5,364	6,869	5,731
34,550	34,600	5,381	4,471	5,381	4,676	37,550	37,600	6,131	4,921	6,131	5,126	40,550	40,600	6,881	5,371	6,881	5,744
34,600	34,650	5,394	4,479	5,394	4,684	37,600	37,650	6,144	4,929	6,144	5,134	40,600	40,650	6,894	5,379	6,894	5,756
34,650	34,700	5,406	4,486	5,406	4,691	37,650	37,700	6,156	4,936	6,156	5,141	40,650	40,700	6,906	5,386	6,906	5,769
34,700	34,750	5,419	4,494	5,419	4,699	37,700	37,750	6,169	4,944	6,169	5,149	40,700	40,750	6,919	5,394	6,919	5,781
34,750	34,800	5,431	4,501	5,431	4,706	37,750	37,800	6,181	4,951	6,181	5,156	40,750	40,800	6,931	5,401	6,931	5,794
34,800	34,850	5,444	4,509	5,444	4,714	37,800	37,850	6,194	4,959	6,194	5,164	40,800	40,850	6,944	5,409	6,944	5,806
34,850	34,900	5,456	4,516	5,456	4,721	37,850	37,900	6,206	4,966	6,206	5,171	40,850	40,900	6,956	5,416	6,956	5,819
34,900	34,950	5,469	4,524	5,469	4,729	37,900	37,950	6,219	4,974	6,219	5,179	40,900	40,950	6,969	5,424	6,969	5,831
34,950	35,000	5,481	4,531	5,481	4,736	37,950	38,000	6,231	4,981	6,231	5,186	40,950	41,000	6,981	5,431	6,981	5,844

* This column must also be used by a qualifying widow(er).

(Continued on page 65)

Take the amount of taxable income, $32,550, and find the column labeled single. The person with that taxable income owes $4,881.

Almost all married people file jointly, though those going through a separation or a divorce typically file separately. Most married couples pay less tax if they file jointly, though some couples file separately because they balk at sharing financial information with one another.

In the 2004 tax year, for married couples the standard deduction was $10,000; for single people it was $5,000. As a result, for those married couples with two children who took the standard deduction, the first $22,800 ($3,200 × 4 + $10,000) they earned was tax-free. For single people the first $8,200 was tax free.

The tax tables show the amount most people owe in tax. To read tax tables, find the column that contains the filing status. Then read the row to find the amount of taxable income. As an example, take a single person who does not own a home and whose only income is salary. The taxes she or he owes are very simple to compute. Say such a person earns $40,750 a year and takes the standard deduction. The taxable income is $40,750 − $5,000 (standard deduction) − $3,200 (personal exemption), or $32,550. A 2004 tax table is duplicated here in Figure 31.3, and circled on that form is the tax amount of $4,881.

An increasingly important part of the tax calculation process is the alternative minimum tax. This tax, invented in the 1960s to prevent the superrich from accumulating so many deductions that they could avoid taxes altogether, has begun to hit ordinary middle-class taxpayers. The alternative minimum tax is doubly frustrating for taxpayers who do their own taxes because after they have completed their federal return, if they come under its provisions, they have to refigure their taxes using its provisions. There is no obvious way to know this until you are almost entirely finished completing your 1040.

The alternative minimum tax has enormous policy implications because, as can be seen from Figure 31.4, the alternative minimum tax is currently projected to hit 30 million taxpayers and account for $90 billion in tax revenue by the year 2010. By 2050 it will reach 70 percent of taxpayers and add 20 percent to their average person's tax bill. There are two reasons it will become increasingly important to taxpayers. First, while most of the federal income tax system is indexed for inflation, the alternative minimum tax thresholds are not. As a result, simple inflation will drive more and more taxpayers into this complicated system. Second, while the tax cuts of 2001 and 2003 lowered tax rates for both the regular system and the alternative minimum tax, for 2005 and beyond the alternative minimum tax rates rise back to their old levels.

FIGURE 31.4   The impact of the alternative minimum tax.

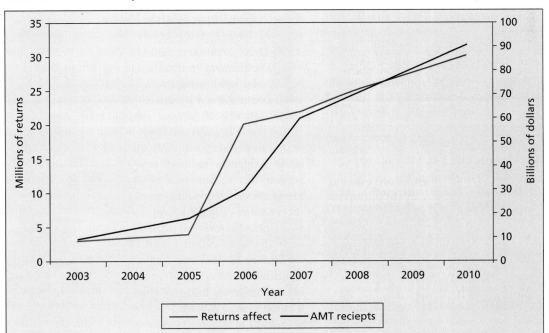

Source: Congressional Budget Office, May 2005 testimony of Director Douglas Holtz-Eakin, http://www.cbo.gov/showdoc.cfm?index=6370&sequence =0#figure1.

TABLE 31.1   Tax brackets for taxable income, 2004.

Status	10%	15%	25%	28%	33%	35%
Single	$0–7,300	$ 7,300–29,700	$29,700–71,950	$ 71,950–150,150	$150,150–326,450	$326,450–
Single head of household	$0–10,450	$10,450–39,800	$39,800–102,800	$102,800–166,450	$166,450–326,450	$326,450–
Married filing jointly	$0–14,600	$14,600–59,400	$59,400–119,950	$119,950–182,800	$182,800–326,450	$326,450–
Married filing separately	$0–7,300	$ 7,300–29,700	$29,700–59,975	$ 59,975–91,400	$ 91,400–163,225	$163,225–

The tax rates in the United States are **progressive** in that with higher income you pay a higher rate of tax. Table 31.1 shows the so-called tax brackets in the United States for 2004. The **marginal tax rate** is the percentage of each dollar in that bracket that must be paid in tax. This means that our single person making $40,750, with taxable income of $32,550, has a tax rate of zero on the first $8,200 of income, pays 10 percent on the next $7,300, pays 15 percent on the next $22,400, and pays 25 percent on the remaining $2,850 ($32,550 − $29,700).

progressive taxation
Those with higher income pay a higher rate of tax.

marginal tax rate
The percentage of each dollar in a bracket that must be paid in tax.

Even after you have figured your tax, this is not what you actually owe. There are four important tax credits that now go into the computation. The first, the earned income tax credit, is designed for the working poor. This can be a substantial increase in your take-home pay if you have children and do not make a lot of money. For those with at least two children, the credit amounts to as much as $4,300. The second important credit is the child credit. For those married couples that make less than $110,000, this credit amounts to $1,000 per child. The third major credit is the child (and elder) care tax credit. For the majority of families with child care expenses, this credit allows for between 20 percent and 30 percent (again, depending on AGI) of those expenses to come off the tax bill. The last of the major credits is a tuition tax credit. This allows for up to $1,500 of college-related expenses to come off the tax bill.

There is an important distinction between tax credits and deductions. A tax deduction comes off taxable income, so the savings to taxpayers are whatever their marginal tax rate is times the amount of the deduction. For example, if a person is in the 15 percent tax bracket, a $1,000 deduction is worth $150. A $1,000 credit, on the other hand, is $1,000 off the tax bill. Tax credits are therefore better than deductions if the two are in equal amounts.

There is another aspect of the distinction between credits and deductions that is important. During tax debates there is often a discussion of whether there should be a tax deduction for something or a tax credit for it. Since credits are more costly to the government than deductions, we can imagine that the choice facing policymakers for the tax cut would be a $2,500 deduction or a $500 credit. For people in the 15 percent tax bracket a $2,500 tax deduction is worth between nothing (because they still end up with insufficient deductions to get over the standard deduction) and 15 percent of $2,500, or $375. For people in the 28 percent bracket a $2,500 deduction is worth up to $700. The net result of this is that credits are better than deductions when they are in equal amounts and that for tax reductions of equal cost to the government, credits are better than deductions for the poor. For the rich the opposite is true: Tax deductions are preferred over tax credits.

For people with a variety of income sources and many deductions, the rules are very complicated. The vast majority of people are not in this predicament. You have to own a farm or business, have a significant and actively changing investment portfolio, have significant medical expenses that you have to pay yourself, work in an environment where you get high pay but have to pay for lots of work expenses (like a truck driver), or have some other strange source of income in order to have overly complicated income taxes.

ISSUES IN INCOME TAXATION

Horizontal and Vertical Equity

One question that always arises with regard to income taxes is whether they are fair. The very definition of "fair" requires some thought. To be fair, it seems clear that equal people should be treated equally. This concept, called **horizontal equity,** is not much disputed. People who make the same income, from the same sources, with the same family structure, and who are the same in every other dimension should pay the same taxes.

horizontal equity
Equal people should be treated equally.

Where the controversy lies with most people is the issue of **vertical equity.** That is, are people across the income scale treated fairly with regard to their ability to pay? As you saw with Table 31.1, people at the upper end of the income scale pay much more in tax and much higher percentages of tax than people at the lower end.

vertical equity
People across the income scale are treated fairly with regard to ability to pay.

Equity versus Simplicity

There is a distinct trade-off between horizontal equity and simplicity. This is because it is difficult to nail down the question of "sameness" that is at the heart of the definition of horizontal equity. Most economists who study the issue of taxation want the tax code to be **neutral.** For instance, to ensure neutrality, income earned from work must be treated the same as income made from investments. The problem is that in order to accomplish neutrality, the tax code would have to be very complicated. Consider capital gains income.

neutral
When applied to a tax code, the implication that it does not favor particular forms of income or expenditure.

When assets are bought and later sold at a profit there is capital gain. Under the principles of neutrality that capital gain should be taxed—the question is how much? This question arises because there are problems with capital gains that do not affect earnings from work. First, much of the increase in the value of an asset is simply the compensation for inflation. We tax all gains rather than just the inflation-adjusted gains because this is easier. Second, some assets are difficult to evaluate, so capital gains are taxed only on realization (when you actually have the profit in hand) rather than accrual (when the asset price increase happened).

This undertaxes capital gains by letting the holder of them defer the tax.

Taxing on realization rather than accrual is simple, but it creates a different problem whose solution only creates another problem. Because there is no tax until an asset is sold, when a person dies while in possession of an asset, there are capital gains. Perhaps there is no paperwork to find out when it was bought, so there is no way of finding out exactly how big the capital gain is. To solve this, all capital gains, and therefore all taxes owed on those gains, are forgiven at death. This creates yet another problem. There is an incentive for the elderly to hold assets with large capital gains rather than sell them, because doing so avoids the capital gains tax.

Thus the problem is that there is a trade-off between simplicity and equity. In order to be simple we will violate equity and in order to be fair, this will cost us simplicity.

INCENTIVES AND THE TAX CODE

There is an active debate among politicians and among economists about the effects of income taxes on the behavior of people. Two of the most interesting of these issues are how such taxes affect people's willingness to work and save. Republican politicians and conservative economists are convinced that income taxes cause people to work and save less. Democratic politicians and liberal economists are convinced that people do not work and save any less and may, in fact, work and save more.

This is because there is a fundamental disagreement between economists concerning the relative importance of what economists call the **substitution effect** and the **income effect.** Any time you change the price of something, in this case either the take-home wage rate or the after-tax interest rate, you create these two effects. The substitution effect moves people toward the good that is now cheaper or away from the good that is now more expensive. As an example, if there are only two goods, apples and oranges, and the price of apples increases, you would move toward oranges. This is not the end of the story, though. There is also an income effect. This can go either direction and depends on the Chapter 2 concepts

substitution effect
Purchase of less of a product than originally wanted when its price is high because a lower-priced product is available.

income effect
An increase in price lowers spending power; if the good is normal, this further lowers consumption; if it is inferior, it can increase consumption back toward where it was (or even further). This effect works in either direction.

of normal and inferior. If a good is inferior, the increase in price lowers your real spending power and you would move back toward that good.

Do Taxes Alter Work Decisions?

One of the most well-researched questions in economics is the effect of take-home pay on the number of hours worked. To the untrained observer this may not seem like a very difficult question, but it actually is. The substitution effect is the more obviously seen effect. Since taxes reduce the take-home pay for every hour worked, the incentive to work, rather than stay home and relax, is lessened. Thus you reduce your work effort. The other side of the story, though, is the reduction in income. If you do the work that is necessary to generate a certain standard of living, then you will have to work more hours to have the income to sustain that standard of living. The empirical research suggests that if taxes do alter the work decision it is only very slightly. Most estimates suggest that the substitution effect is exactly countered by the income effect. That is, an increase in taxes has no effect on work effort, though some have found the effect to be that it takes an 8 percent reduction in after-tax wage rates to generate a 1 percent reduction in work hours. Either way, taxes do not substantially alter the incentive to work.

Do Taxes Alter Savings Decisions?

A similar result has been found on after-tax interest rates. Though there is disagreement in methodology that generates a disagreement in the conclusion, many economists also believe that an increase in tax rates has little or no effect on saving behavior. This also suggests that the substitution effect and income effect completely counter each other. There are, though, estimates that suggest that the net is not zero. In particular, Michael Boskin estimated that a 2.5 percent decrease in the after-tax interest rates results in a 1 percent decrease in savings.

Taxes for Social Engineering

If taxes do not substantially alter the incentive of people to work or save, then you might think that policy makers would have given up on using taxes to get people to do other desirable things. If you thought that, you would be wrong. President Clinton proposed and Congress enacted a plan to use tax credits to provide an incentive to go to college. Tax deductions and credits for a variety of desirable outcomes have been tried at a variety of different

TABLE 31.2   Distribution of taxes, 2001.

Percentile of Taxpayers, Bottom x% of Returns*	Cumulative Percentage of Adjusted Gross Income	Cumulative Percentage of Taxes Paid
10	1	0
20	2	0
30	5	1
40	9	2
50	13	4
60	19	8
70	27	12
80	43	22
90	57	35
100	100	100

*Example: The bottom 40 percent of taxpayers earn 9 percent of adjusted gross income and pay 2 percent of all federal income taxes.

Source: Statistics of Income: Individual Income Tax Returns 2001, Internal Revenue Service, Washington, DC.

times. Typically the breaks do not end up causing more of the desired outcome, but simply subsidize the people who were already engaging in it. If the research on college tax credits that is published in the next few years duplicates the results of the research on work and savings, the tax deductions and credits will probably not increase the number of people going to college but will merely be a special tax break to those who would have gone to college anyway.[1]

WHO PAYS INCOME TAXES?

A vastly misunderstood concept of income taxation is who it is that pays. For years Republicans and Democrats alike have perpetuated the myth that middle Americans pay this tax and the rich do not pay their fair share. A look at Table 31.2 should begin to dispel that myth. The first column indicates the percentile of tax returns; the second and third columns indicate the percentage of income earned and taxes paid by everyone at or below that percentile. For instance, the bottom 40 percent of earners account for 9 percent of income and 2 percent of taxes paid.

From this table you can draw several myth-breaking conclusions. First, the bottom half of taxpayers pays only 4 percent of the income tax while the top half pays the

---

[1] Another effect of this subsidy is that it gives colleges and universities an increased ability to raise tuition.

FIGURE 31.5 Income and tax distributions.

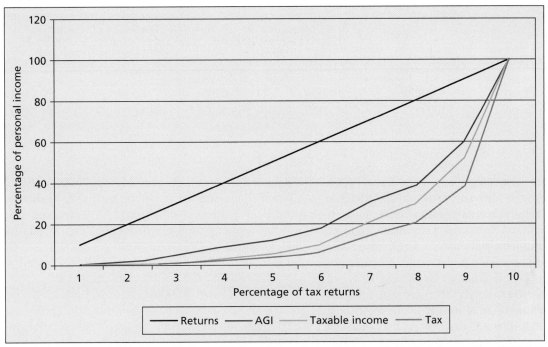

Source: Statistics of Income: Individual Income Tax Returns 2001, Internal Revenue Service, Washington, DC.; http://www.irs.gov/pub/irs-soi/01in11si.xls.

remaining 96 percent. Second, the top 10 percent of taxpayers accounts for 65 percent of federal income taxes paid while the rest of us account for only 35 percent. Third, if it were true that the rich were not paying as much as the middle class, the second column would not always exceed the third. It does; and the rich pay far more tax than do the rest of us.

Figure 31.5 portrays the same information graphically. If all income and taxes were earned and paid equally it would represent a straight line. The degree to which the income earned, shown as AGI, is bowed is the degree to which income earned is unequal. If taxes were paid mostly by the middle class, then the tax curve would be above the income curve. Since the opposite is true, it should be clear that there is significant effective progressivity in the tax code.

THE TAX DEBATES OF THE LAST DECADE

One of the central themes of the political debates of 1990s and 2000s was whether tax cuts should be across-the-board or targeted tax. Republican presidential candidates offered across-the-board tax cuts, whereas Democratic presidential candidates offered tax cuts that were targeted to specific populations. The difference in philosophy boils down to essentially two differences of opinion: whether most of the tax cuts should go to the people who pay most of the tax or whether the tax code should be used to encourage particular behaviors and help people with the least income.

On the first difference of opinion, it is clear that any across-the-board tax cut must go mostly to the rich since it is they who pay the vast majority of income taxes. Thus an across-the-board tax cut by definition favors the rich. Whether this is fair criticism is relative. If you look at where most of the dollars go in such a cut, it is indisputable that the rich get most of the money. On the other hand, this is because they pay the most. Giving a tax cut to the poor gives a tax cut to people who do not pay any federal income taxes to begin with.[2]

Because of the progressivity of the tax code, simply reducing the tax rate by a fixed percentage not only gives more of a tax break to upper-income taxpayers, it also

_____
[2]Tax cuts to the poor typically result from increasing the earned income tax credit. This credit often exceeds the amount of tax owed by a substantial amount. Many low-income families pay "negative taxes," so a tax cut to them simply makes this more negative.

TABLE 31.3   Hypothetical example of the effect of a 10 percent cut in tax rates on income distribution.

	Before Tax	Tax Code where Tax = 10% of the First $50,000 and 20% of the Rest		Tax Code after a 10% Cut in Tax Rates where Tax = 9% of the First $50,000 and 18% of the Rest	
		Tax	After Tax	Tax	After Tax
Lower-income person	$10,000	$1,000	$9,000	$900	$9,100
Upper-income person	$100,000	$15,000	$85,000	$13,500	$86,500
Ratio	10	15	9.44	15	9.51

changes the income distribution in a way that favors upper-income Americans. To see how, consider Table 31.3. The second column indicates before-tax income, showing a circumstance where the upper-income person makes 10 times what the lower-income person makes. The third column indicates the tax that would be paid under the simple hypothetical tax code where 10 percent of the first $50,000 and 20 percent of the rest is paid in tax. The progressivity of the income tax is displayed here in that the upper-income household makes 10 times as much as the lower-income household but pays 15 times as much tax. The fourth column shows the after-tax income. Again, note the effect of the progressive income tax is to reduce the ratio of spending power of the high-income to lower-income person from 10 to 1 to 9.44 to 1. The fifth and sixth columns show the effect of a 10 percent reduction in tax rates. The 10 percent tax rate becomes 9 percent and the 20 percent tax rate becomes 18 percent.

Republicans and Democrats will interpret Table 31.3 in two entirely different ways. The Republicans will say that under both tax codes the upper-income people are paying 15 times the taxes that the lower-income people are paying. Moreover, they will claim that any tax cut that helps the poor will change the distribution of taxes to be even further slanted to upper-income people. Democrats will focus on the distribution of after-tax income figure and note that an across-the-board tax cut increases the ratio of an upper-income person's after-tax income to a lower-income person's after-tax income from 9.44 to 9.51. As a result, though an across-the-board tax cut keeps the percentage of government funded by each group the same, it changes the after-tax income distribution in favor of the rich.

Another great debate of the last decade centered on unraveling the 1986 tax reform law that eliminated most social engineering from the tax code. Prior to that year thousands of provisions were included to induce people to do a variety of things. The law passed in 1986

eliminated almost all of them. Slowly, but steadily, the Clinton administration sought provisions to again urge people in particular directions. For instance, they sought and got partial tax deductions and credits for higher education. Vice President Albert Gore, while campaigning for the presidency in 2000, argued to make those deductions and credits complete.

After his election in 2000, George W. Bush sought and got two substantial personal income tax cuts. The first, in 2001, cut marginal tax rates, phased in an increase in the dependent child credit, and phased out the estate (inheritance) tax. The second, in 2003, sped up the timetable on the 2001 tax cuts and reduced the tax rate on corporate dividends.

Taken together, the beneficiaries of these tax cuts were middle-income and higher-income families with children and the wealthy. Middle-income families with children saw dramatic declines in their effective rates as the per-child tax credit jumped from $200 per child to $1,000 per child. The wealthy saw a sizable reduction in their taxes as well with the reduction in marginal income tax rates by 3 to 5 percentage points (depending on bracket), the reduction in the rate at which dividends are taxed, and the phasing out of the estate tax.

Of particular concern with regard to the 2003 tax cuts is their sunset provisions. What this means is that all the significant tax cuts put in place in 2003 will, if no law changes this, be undone in 2011. Making those tax cuts permanent, something President Bush repeatedly argued for in 2005, would widen deficit projections for 2011 and beyond.

Referring back to the alternative minimum tax, a looming tax debate centers on dealing with the its ever-expanding grip. Democrats and Republicans alike agree that a separate and even more complicated system that affects 4 percent of taxpayers may be acceptable, but one that affects more than one-third of taxpayers is not. The underlying problem is that, left alone the Congressional

Budget Office projects it will raise trillions of dollars over the course of the next 20 years. This means that correcting it will require a redistribution of those taxes to other people; those other people tend to make less than $100,000.

Regardless of the politics of the time, taxes are always going to be the focal point for debate. Because the federal government accounts for more than a fifth of the economy, who pays for that fifth and who gets the benefit of that fifth will always be the subject of debate.

Summary

You now understand how taxes work and are able to apply that knowledge and the concepts of horizontal and vertical equity to the U.S. tax code. You understand the trade-off that exists between simplicity and horizontal equity and understand that in theory taxes can alter the incentives of people to work and save but that little effect has actually been shown. You know that this has not stopped policy makers from using taxes to motivate socially desirable outcomes. Last, you should be able to understand in a greater context the debates over taxes that began during the 1990s and continue today.

Key Terms

adjusted gross income (AGI), 320
capital gains, 320
deductible, 321
deductions, 320
exemptions, 320
filing status, 321

horizontal equity, 325
income effect, 325
itemized deductions, 320
marginal tax rate, 324
neutral, 325
progressive taxation, 324

standard deduction, 320
substitution effect, 325
taxable income, 321
vertical equity, 325
withholding, 320

Quiz Yourself

1. The tax brackets have higher tax rates for more taxable income. This makes the federal income tax
    a. Proportional.
    b. Regressive.
    c. Progressive.
    d. Integrative.

2. Because there are _____ adjusted gross income is always _____ taxable income.
    a. Deductions and exemptions; less than.
    b. Deductions and exemptions; greater than.
    c. Credits; greater than.
    d. Credits; less than.

3. The alternative minimum tax has the effect of limiting
    a. Income.
    b. Taxable income.
    c. Deductions.
    d. Exemptions.

4. If Congress wants to use $100 billion on tax cuts, the version that would help a family of four making

$40,000 a year would
    a. Lower marginal tax rates by one percentage point.
    b. Increase the standard deduction by $2,000.
    c. Increase the child credit by $1,000.
    d. Index the alternative minimum tax to inflation.

5. If someone is in the 25 percent tax bracket, this means that _____ is owed in taxes.
    a. 25 percent of his or her salary.
    b. 25 percent of his or her adjusted gross income.
    c. 25 percent of his or her taxable income.
    d. Less than 25 percent of his or her taxable income.

6. Which of the following would immediately be more valuable for most people?
    a. A $1,000 increase in the child credit.
    b. A decrease in the degree to which brackets are inflation-indexed.
    c. An indexing of the alternative minimum tax.
    d. A $2,500 increase in the standard deduction.

Think about This

If current law is not changed, the alternative minimum tax will affect 30 percent of taxpayers. The problem with fixing it is that doing so only helps the top end of taxpayers. One solution would be to simply index the current point at which the AMT kicks in. The longer we wait, the greater the pressure will be to do something because the impact will start to affect people who are not that wealthy. This is what happens when you do not index brackets for inflation. When should they fix this?

Talk about This

The Democrats tend to work toward tax code adjustments that help those at the lowest end of the income scale, Republicans do the opposite. As a college graduate you are likely to start at the low end and become part of the high end. Are your attitudes about a political party going to stay the same or change as your income circumstances change?

For More Insight See

Citizens for Tax Justice, *The Hidden Entitlements* (Washington, DC: Robert S. McIntyre, 1996).

Hyman, David, *Public Finance: A Contemporary Application of Theory to Policy,* 6th ed. (Fort Worth: Dryden Press, 1999), esp. Chapters 13 and 14.

Slemrod, Joel, "Do We Know How Progressive the Income Tax Should Be?" *National Tax Journal* 36, no. 3 (September 1983), pp. 361–369.

Slemrod, Joel. *Do Taxes Matter? The Impact of the Tax Reform Act of 1986* (Cambridge, MA: MIT Press, 1991). All tax forms can be found at http://www.irs.gov.

Behind the Numbers

Fiscal Year 2002.
>   Federal revenue and income taxes.
>   >   Budget of the United States Government, 2006; historical tables—Michael J. Boskin, "Taxation, Saving and the Rate of Interest," Journal of Political Economy, vol. 86, no. 2, pt. 2 (April 1978).

Federal tax data.
>   Income and tax distribution, 2001.
>   >   Statistics of income—http://www.irs.gov/taxstats/indtaxstats/article/0,,id=98123,00.html.

Tax tables, rates, exemptions, and deductions, 2004.
>   Internal Revenue Service; publications—http://www.irs.gov/formspubs/lists/0,,id=97817,0.html.

The alternative minimum tax; Congressional Budget Office—http://www.cbo.gov/ftpdocs/53xx/doc5386/04-5-AMT.pdf.

Chapter 32

Antitrust

Bill Gates testifies before the Senate Judiciary Committee on anticompetitive issues and technology.
Source: © Reuters NewMedia Inc./CORBIS

Chapter Objectives

After reading this chapter you should be able to

Understand why economists worry about monopolies and why some monopolies are inevitable and even good for society.

Be aware that laws regulate the existence and pricing behavior of monopolies.

See how antitrust law has been applied to specific industries within the United States.

Chapter Outline

What's Wrong with Monopoly?

Natural Monopolies and Necessary Monopolies

Monopolies and the Law

Examples of Antitrust Action

Summary

When a business treats us badly, most of us get a high degree of satisfaction by announcing that we will never be back. When the business is the phone, gas, electric, or water company, though, it is frustrating because in most cases we cannot get our phone, gas, electricity, or water somewhere else. We all buy goods or services from businesses that are monopolists. It is likely that you have only one source of cable television, local phone service, electricity, water, or natural gas. When a representative of a monopolistic company makes you mad, you know and the representative knows that you have no alternatives; you are stuck. You can scream and complain, but in the end you have to go back to the same company for service. For capitalism to function, these situations work best when there is both a carrot of high profits and a stick of bankruptcy to keep firms working in the consumer's best

interest. Without such incentives, a company's profit motive tends to work against consumers rather than in their best interests.

It is for this reason that we have laws that inhibit firms from becoming monopolies through merger, and we have laws that prevent the monopolies that do exist from using their power to the detriment of consumers. That said, this chapter reviews what it is about monopoly that concerns economists and we also discuss situations where monopolies may be necessary evils. We then turn to laws that are in place to protect consumers from the problems that monopolists cause. We attempt to figure out how many competitors are needed for competition to work, and we provide a few examples of firms that have been accused of using their monopoly power to the detriment of their customers.

WHAT'S WRONG WITH MONOPOLY?

High Prices, Low Output, and Deadweight Loss

A survey of economists published in 1992 suggests that 72 percent agree, in whole or in part, with the idea that "laws should be rigorously enforced to reduce monopoly power"[1] and that it is a proper role for government to prevent monopolies from charging excessive prices for shoddy products. Figure 32.1 illustrates the core of the problem with monopolies.

Chapter 5 told us that a monopolist controls an entire market. That is, when we diagram the monopolistic situation, the market demand curve will be the demand curve for the firm's output. What follows from this is that to sell more of its good, the firm has to progressively lower the price it charges. When the firm lowers prices, the resulting graph shows that the marginal revenue curve is not flat, as it is under perfect competition, but is downward sloping. In particular, it has the same vertical intercept as the demand curve, and it cuts the horizontal axis at exactly half where the demand curve does. (Refer back to Chapter 4 and the discussion of marginal revenue to see why this is the case.)

Assuming that its goal is to maximize profits, a monopolistic organization will sell its output at a price that is determined by the point on the graph at which marginal cost and marginal revenue are equal. In Figure 32.1 that output level is $Q_{monopoly}$. The price a monopolistic firm would charge for that output can be found by going up from $Q_{monopoly}$ to the demand curve and over to the price axis to get $P_{monopoly}$.

To compare this monopoly outcome to what would exist in an industry made up of many firms in perfect competition, we need to recall that the supply curve for each individual perfect competitor is its marginal cost curve. To find the industry supply curve, we would horizontally add the individual supply curves together. When we do that we find that we have also created the marginal cost curve for an industry ruled by one firm. That is why, in Figure 32.1, the supply curve for the industry of perfect competitors is also labeled as the marginal cost curve for the monopolist. It is simply a

FIGURE 32.1   Perfect competition versus monopoly.

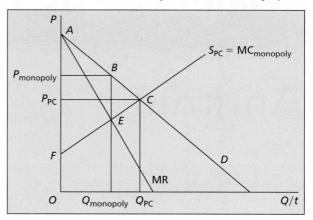

different interpretation of the same information. It is not, however, the monopolist's supply curve. There is no such thing because monopolists do not take the price as given; they search for the price that makes them the most money.

Given that, we can say that if an industry is characterized by many perfectly competitive firms rather than a monopolistic firm, then the price–quantity combination will be where supply equals demand: P_{PC}, Q_{PC}.

Under perfect competition we know that the consumer surplus, depicted as the area under the demand curve but above the price line, would be $P_{PC}AC$ and the producer surplus, depicted as the area under the price curve but above the supply or marginal cost curve, would be $FP_{PC}C$ for a combined social benefit of FAC. (See Chapter 3 if you need to review consumer and producer surplus.) In an industry that is ruled by just one firm rather than many, the consumer surplus is much smaller and the producer surplus somewhat larger. To be precise, the consumer surplus shrinks to $P_{monopoly}AB$ and the producer surplus grows to $FP_{monopoly}BE$. The combined area is $FABE$. This is smaller than the combined area under perfect competition by the triangle EBC. Economists call this area deadweight loss because it represents the loss in economic benefits to society that results from carrying a deadweight—that is, a monopolist.

The desire to eliminate deadweight loss is at the heart of why economists, usually reluctant to let government control markets, generally accept the need for government to intervene in monopoly cases.

Reduced Innovation

Another problem with monopolies—both those subject to price control by government and those that are government-owned, like the post office—is the reduction in the motivation to innovate. When there are no competitors to keep a business on its toes, it can easily get lax. Monopolies like your local telephone company are much less likely to engage in cost-saving or service-enhancing innovation when they are not threatened with competition. Even worse, since they use their costs to justify their prices to regulators, they have an incentive to pad costs that make their own jobs easier.

This problem is not limited to privately held monopolies. The U.S. Postal Service is a government-held monopoly for letters. It did not consider overnight delivery important until Federal Express and United Parcel Service developed the business. Cost-saving or service-enhancing technology is less likely to come from the U.S. mail than it is from the private package delivery companies.

NATURAL MONOPOLIES AND NECESSARY MONOPOLIES

Natural Monopoly

Many of the monopolies that we deal with every day are inevitable. The utilities—electricity, natural gas, local telephone service, sewers, and cable television—are monopolies where there are very high fixed costs and diminishing marginal costs. On an intuitive level you understand that you would not want several hundred wires or pipes coming in and out of your house. It would be ugly and expensive for there to be many different electric companies vying for your business. Changes in technology and reforms of the regulatory structure are rapidly changing the way these utilities do business. Still each locale typically has only one provider of these services.

If you look at Figure 32.2, you can see the problem in the context of Chapter 4's cost curves. Instead of the marginal cost curve's sloping up and the average total cost curve's being U-shaped, both are downward sloping and steadily flattening out. In a typical monopoly, the fixed costs of stringing wires or burying pipes are so great that output levels never get to where marginal costs are rising.

barrier to entry
A legal or economic mechanism that prevents firms from competing in an industry.

It is the large fixed costs that represent a potentially insurmountable economic **barrier to entry.** Recall from Chapter 5 one of the four requirements for perfect competition is freedom

FIGURE 32.2   Natural monopoly.

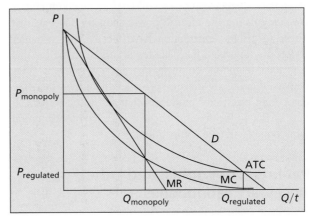

of entry and exit. When fixed costs are high, it is nearly impossible for a firm to get a foothold in the market. If the fixed costs are significant, then having more than one firm bearing them is not cost-efficient. A carefully regulated monopoly in this case may save money for the consumer. The quality of regulation is definitely the key, because the company will want to charge P_{monopoly} and produce only Q_{monopoly}. The monopolist wants to exploit the power it has, and it is part of the government's job to provide the regulation that prevents that from happening.

Government regulators will allow monopolies *normal profit,* the profit consistent with what a similar investment would get them in another industry. This is depicted in Figure 32.2 as the point at which the average total cost curve ATC crosses the demand curve D. It should be clear that the difference between what an unregulated natural monopoly would charge, P_{monopoly}, and what a regulator would let it charge, $P_{\text{regulated}}$, is substantial. For this reason, it is argued that we are better off with one utility company that is prevented from exploiting its position, and we know that most local telephone, electrical power, and natural gas is provided through regulated monopolies in the United States.

This need not be the end of the story. Technology and a revised legal structure are changing the competitive nature of many of these utilities. Satellite dishes are doing as much to keep cable TV rates down as regulation ever did. Cable companies are now selling phone and Internet access that was once provided only by a monopoly telephone company. An additional challenge to local phone companies is coming from the wireless phone industry. Many young people no longer have a home phone; they simply use cellular phones.

Though the poorly thought-out California electricity deregulation experiment was a disaster, some communities are deregulating the electric power industry successfully. These forms of deregulation have the existing provider charge a wire access fee. This fee is similar to the fee that your local telephone company charges you to use its lines with a different long-distance provider. In this way there are competing electricity producers that sell to customers. It may be that in the near future these once inevitable natural monopolies will face competition.

Patents, Copyrights, and Other Necessary Monopolies

Copyrights and patents are examples of other legalized monopolies that we have decided are needed for the economy to work well. The only way singers, authors, or moviemakers make money on their creative work is through their exclusive right to sell it. If you electronically copy a CD, a book, or a movie, you know the cost is usually much lower than if you buy it in the store at full retail price. Monopoly power is given to record companies, publishers, and movie producers so they can make enough money to inspire their efforts.

Consider the recent history of Internet music providers Napster and Kazaa. Many of you discovered for yourself the ability you had to download music and listen to it on an MP3 player or your computer. This meant that you could get all the latest music without paying for it. Many in the music industry believed that you were in violation of the copyright laws. They were correct and a federal court shut Napster down. The economic issue in such a case is how this type of service affects the motivation to produce new music. If musicians are not paid for their music, they will not produce new music and this will be a net loss to society.

Patents are given to inventors of new things for the same reason that copyrights are given to writers and performers. Patents expire after a number of years, depending on the type of invention. While the patent is in force, however, the inventor is the only one who has the right to sell his or her invention. Whether the invention is a new drug, or the proverbial better mouse trap, it belongs to the inventor. In the modern era, scientists usually work for a big company that retains the right to buy their ideas for $1 each. Although this may seem unfair, scientists are often part of a team that jointly creates ideas. In addition, since inventing is a risky business with inventions only rarely striking it big in the marketplace, the companies guarantee the scientist an income. For that, they get to keep the high returns.

In any event, the exclusive right to sell something creates the incentive to be creative or innovative, as the case may be. The author of the book you are reading right now would like to think he would have written this book for the good of his own students' understanding, but the truth is he is working for money, too. Lest you think I am the only one, ask yourself whether you too are not motivated to work by money. Writers, singers, moviemakers, or inventors need the protection accorded monopolies to make money at their endeavors.

The rationale for other monopolies is that they provide a social good. The U.S. Postal Service performs the social service of providing equal mail service at an equal price to everyone anywhere in the United States. Though its detractors suggest that a privatized system would be more efficient and cost less, its defenders believe that the "social good" is sufficient to justify any monopoly inefficiencies.

MONOPOLIES AND THE LAW

The Sherman Anti-Trust Act

Under the law it is not illegal to be a monopoly. It is not even against the law for a company to establish itself as a monopoly. The Sherman Anti-Trust Act of 1890, however, makes it illegal for a company to use its monopoly power in one market to enhance its position in another.[2] According to the Sherman Act it is also illegal to attempt to control a market in all of its stages of production.

As we saw above, there are cases where monopoly power is a good thing. As a matter of fact, it is the ultimate carrot for a business. If a manufacturer is so good that it makes a product so much better than that of its competition, then it will, of course, benefit by having no competition. As long as the company is that good and as long as it continues to price its product low enough that other firms see no point in joining in, there is no demonstrable harm from having a monopoly. Concomitantly, there is no violation of antitrust law. Later in the chapter we will see that Microsoft claims to be a company that has performed so well that it became a monopoly in the operating system business.

As we said previously, it is against the law to use monopoly power in a given area to generate business in another area. For instance, if a telephone company with a monopoly in a particular region sells cellular telephone

---

[2]While a number of important laws amending and clarifying the Sherman Act have been enacted since 1890, for simplicity and brevity we will consider this one body of antitrust law.

service where it does not have a monopoly, it cannot require that its local telephone customers subscribe to its cellular service.

Antitrust law also forbids a company from controlling the entire production-to-sales process for a particular good. This is what got Standard Oil in trouble with the government in the early 1900s. At one time, Standard Oil dominated the oil and gasoline industry through its ownership and control of drilling equipment, oil wells, refineries, pipelines, distribution networks, and gas stations. This was found at the time to be illegal, and it is still illegal.

Other parts of the law work toward preventing companies from becoming monopolistic by merging. It is very much against the law for two separate companies, in an industry of only a few, to share information or to collude on setting prices. This is called "price fixing," and local gasoline stations are accused of it all the time. Just as someone realized that companies could fix prices if they merged, Congress gave power to the Federal Trade Commission (FTC) to allow or to deny proposed mergers. When two airlines merge and it is a merger that would lead to a monopoly at an important airport, the FTC steps in. It can simply say no to the merger, or it can require that the airline sell its gate access to another airline.

What Constitutes a Monopoly?

One of the new areas of economic research asks an interesting question: How many firms does it take to ensure competition? We have assumed that we needed many, but we have not produced a number. Some economists have begun to argue that one is actually enough. They argue that if the one entity that comprises the monopoly is afraid of potential competition, and prices its goods low enough that no one decides to enter the market, we have what ordinarily comes only with perfect competition. In this hypothetical example, however, it has come with but a single firm.

To see this at work, imagine an airport that is served by only one major airline. Speculate on how it will price its tickets, as a monopolist or as if it had many competitors. It turns out that under certain conditions, it will be sufficiently frightened at the prospect of another carrier coming in that it will price its tickets very close to a competitive level and significantly below the potential monopoly level.

As a concrete example, Southwest Airlines has a reputation of causing other airlines to lower their fares when they are in competition with Southwest and in some places where they are not. Southwest is an airline that is always depicted as being run by a group of happy people working hard. The man who started the airline pays himself a salary that is much lower than his counterparts in other airlines and he treats his employees well. In return, they have chosen not to insist on some of the typical union-induced work-rule inefficiencies that plague other airlines.

You may be able to see examples of Southwest's efficiency for yourself. The next time you have a long layover at an airport observe a Southwest gate. Time a plane from the moment it pulls into the gate to the moment it leaves again. Then repeat what you have done at American, United, Delta, USAir, or Northwest. More often than not you will see a turnaround time for Southwest that is considerably less than that of any of the others. This means that Southwest can get at least one additional flight, if not two more flights, out of a plane and crew each day. This means it can outcompete everyone else on the price of tickets.

Suppose you are in charge of pricing tickets for another airline and you have a monopoly in a particular city. You know that Southwest chooses its next target city on the basis of its ability to charge much less than the price that is currently being charged. What will you do? You keep your price low in hopes that Southwest will ignore you.

contestable markets hypothesis
One firm is all that is necessary for competitive prices to exist as long as that firm is threatened by hit-and-run entry.

To its firm believers, this **contestable markets hypothesis** means that the answer to the question of how many firms it takes to have competitive prices is *one,* as long as it is one that is scared.

EXAMPLES OF ANTITRUST ACTION

Standard Oil

When John D. Rockefeller established Standard Oil, no one knew how petroleum would change the world. By the time the huge monopoly that was Standard Oil was broken up, Rockefeller had become the richest man the world had ever known. If you measure personal wealth as the percentage of all U.S. wealth, Bill Gates would have to more than double his to come close to Rockefeller's. Rockefeller got as rich as he did by controlling the entire petroleum production process. He owned the oil fields, all the drilling equipment, all the pipelines and trucks that distributed it, and he licensed all the retail outlets that sold his gas, oil, and kerosene.

trust

A single company having ownership of all stages of production in a particular industry.

This kind of monopoly, called a **trust,** involves the single ownership of all stages of production, and it has been accomplished to this degree only a few times. A comparable situation would occur if Bill Gates owned not only Microsoft, but also Intel, Dell, Gateway, and all other computer hardware manufacturers, and he licensed franchises to all of the retail outlets that sold computers.

In Rockefeller's case he used the total control he had over the oil production business to gain control over the pipelines and the retail outlets. He did this by simply refusing to use pipelines that refused to sell to him, and he refused to sell his products to stations that he did not license. He then used this power to make even more money by buying the pipelines at low prices and by selling his products to filling stations at high prices. Our debt to Rockefeller is that much of the law making trusts illegal simply makes illegal what he did so well.

The breakup of Standard Oil made several companies out of one. Each competed with the others for pipeline services and to sign up gas stations. Among others, we know these companies today as Exxon, Amoco, and Standard Oil. The lessons that Rockefeller taught the world were learned very well and most developed countries now have laws that make it illegal to use monopoly pressure to limit competition.

IBM

International Business Machines, better known as IBM, came into the world as a producer of typewriters and adding machines. Your grandparents may remember working in an office where the secretary's IBM Selectric was the most sophisticated machine in the place, because it could erase a typo. By the 1960s, however, IBM was well into the business of computers. Back then a state-of-the-art mainframe computer with the computational capacity of a current Palm Pilot would fill several rooms. Moreover, if you needed that kind of computing you had one choice, IBM.

As the monopolist in mainframe computers, IBM could use this power to get a leg up on the companies that produced mainframe software as well as other hardware. In 1969 the Justice Department sued, arguing that IBM was using its monopoly in one area, the central processing units for mainframes, to develop a monopoly in other mainframe areas.

This lawsuit dragged on in court for years. By 1977 an upstart company, Apple, developed the first personal computer, and somewhat later IBM decided to join in this market and began to make computers for the home and office. These computers were novel and they possessed far more power than the computers that flew to the moon. By the early 1980s it became apparent that the mainframe market was dying as the PC's popularity grew. In 1982 the case was dropped because even if IBM had a monopoly in mainframe processors, which it no longer had, it was no longer an important area.

One of the reasons that IBM had lost any chance of generating a monopoly in PCs was that it had licensed the operating system of that original PC, called DOS (disk operating system), to a little-known company in Washington State called Microsoft. Further, it was buying its microprocessors, so named because they were physically much smaller than the processors developed for the mainframes, from another little-known company called Intel. When others found that they too could put parts together to make a computer and use Microsoft's DOS to run it, all chances of an IBM monopoly were gone.

Microsoft

In the mid-1980s, Apple Computer introduced a new personal computer, called a Macintosh. It used pictures, called icons, on a monitor screen and a pointing device, called a mouse, instead of using typed-in commands to tell the computer what to do. Microsoft followed shortly thereafter with its own changes that relied on a mouse. It called its new operating system Windows. While the first two versions of Windows were terrible and could have lost Microsoft its advantage in operating systems, Windows 3.1 took over the industry in short order.

Since that time, Windows (in its 3.1, 95, 98, 2000, XP, or NT form) has dominated the operating system market. The only serious threat that Windows faced during this time was IBM's introduction of OS/2 and its follow-on Warp. Both offered multitasking, an attribute that Windows 3.1 did not possess. Multitasking allows a computer to divide its resources so that it can work on more than one task at a time. Because that is what mainframes do, IBM got it working first, Apple struggled to get it to work, and Microsoft's Windows 95, which included multitasking, was more than a year from being released.

If the Justice Department and many of Microsoft's critics are to be believed, this made Microsoft very nervous. Critics charged that it was at this point that Microsoft began using its preeminence in the industry to pressure software companies to write exclusively for the soon-to-be released Windows 95. The Justice Department also charged that Microsoft pressured the vendors of such hardware as modems, sound cards, disk drives, and network cards not to provide software for OS/2. If Microsoft did those things, it was in flagrant violation of the law.

In another questionable practice, Microsoft offered manufacturers a low price on its versions of Windows—but with a catch. The manufacturers would pay Microsoft a fixed fee per machine it sold, whether the customer wanted Windows or not. That way people who bought PCs had to pay for Windows even if they wanted a different operating system. Since most people did not have a good reason to pick another operating system, no other operating system succeeded in getting past this initial stage. Again if Microsoft did this to eliminate competition, it was in violation of the law. In any event, the threat that OS/2 posed to Windows evaporated.

Later Microsoft was to run into other problems. The Internet grew to a degree that Microsoft had seriously underestimated, and Netscape grabbed well over three-quarters of the market for Internet browsers. On top of that, Sun Microsystems created Java, a programming language that is compatible with Windows, Apple, or any other computer. This threatened not only the Windows stranglehold, but the domination of the Windows Office Suite as well. In reaction to these events, Microsoft created Internet Explorer as its alternative to Netscape Navigator and, in Windows 98, integrated it into the operating system.

Even more troubling to the Justice Department was its contention that Microsoft was insisting that PC makers not put any product on their PCs that competed with a Microsoft product. Specifically, it was alleged that Microsoft would not sell Windows to PC makers if they also bundled their PC with Netscape or Corel's WordPerfect Suite.

Last, it was believed by many in the industry that there were secret parts of Windows 98 that made computers using non-Microsoft products crash. If this was true, users of these non-Microsoft products would conveniently blame the makers of those products and want the "more reliable" Microsoft software.

What the Justice Department charged in the trial of 1998 and 1999 was that Microsoft had used and was using the tactics of Rockefeller to drive out other competitors. On April 3, 2000, the judge for the case, Thomas Penfield Jackson, ruled first that the evidence showed that Microsoft wanted to monopolize a variety of areas of software, that it used its monopoly in Windows to further a monopoly in Office Suite, to build one for the Internet Explorer, and to prevent competition from, among others, Sun's Java. He further ruled that Microsoft had harmed consumers in the process. In his June 7, 2000, ruling ordering a breakup of the company into an operating system business and an applications business, he also showed that he believed that Microsoft had indeed used secret parts of Windows to cause other software to crash. By ordering that it "shall not take any action it knows will interfere with or degrade the performance of any non-Microsoft" software and by ordering that it disclose the "interfaces," the software that allows applications to talk to the operating system, he was clearly implying that at some point in time Microsoft had done both. On appeal to a U.S. Court of Appeals, the important finding of facts with regard to the illegal activities of Microsoft was upheld but the breakup remedy was not. Prior to September 11, 2001, the Department of Justice was intently focused on settling the case and had taken the breakup off the table.

In November of that year, with other matters to attend to, the Department of Justice ended the fight with Microsoft on terms quite friendly to the software giant. While some of the states that had sued alongside the federal government stuck to their guns, by 2003, when California settled for $1.1 billion in vouchers to the state's citizens and AOL Time-Warner (the parent of Netscape) settled for $750 million, the battle was pretty much over.

Summary

You now understand why economists worry about monopolies, and why some monopolies have been seen as inevitable and even good for society. You know that laws were enacted to regulate the existence and pricing behavior of monopolies. Last, you saw how that body of law was applied to Standard Oil, IBM, and Microsoft.

Key Terms

barrier to entry, 333   contestable markets hypothesis, 335   trust, 336

Quiz Yourself

1. Antitrust law is designed to limit the impact of
   a. Monopoly.
   b. Oligopoly.
   c. Monopolistic competition.
   d. Perfect competition.

2. One of the concerns about monopolies is that they
   a. Reduce the motivation to innovated.
   b. Reduce the motivation to make a profit.
   c. Hire people at an excessive level.
   d. Waste resources in pursuit of the next invention.

3. Monopoly creates prices that are _____ which would exist under perfect comptetion.
   a. Lower than that.
   b. Equal to that.
   c. Greater than that.
   d. More volatile than that.

4. Using the monopoly power in one area to compel customers to buy goods in another area
   a. Is a violation of the Sherman Anti-Trust Act.
   b. Is legal, but bad business practice.
   c. Is illegal but would be bad business practice anyway.
   d. Is legal and a recommended strategy.

5. Standard Oil's trust involved monopolizing
   a. Gas stations only.
   b. Oil exploration only.
   c. Refining.
   d. All aspects of the petroleum industry.

6. The suit against Microsoft accused it of
   a. Using its own innovation to thwart competition.
   b. Using its Windows monopoly to foster other monopolies.
   c. Incorporating more innovations into the Office Suite.
   d. Charging more than Windows was worth.

Think about This

Those that opposed the Department of Justice suit against Microsoft argue that the company was responsible for great innovation. They argue that the "next Microsoft" would be reluctant to be as successful. Does this criticism make sense to you? Would a multibillion-dollar corporation be limited in innovation for any reason?

Talk about This

If Apple used the high market share in iPods to generate a monopoly in music downloads via iTunes would that be a concern to you?

For More Insight See

Journal of Economic Perspectives 1, no. 2 (Fall 1987). See articles by Steven C. Salop, Lawrence J. White, Franklin M. Fisher, and Richard Schmalensee, pp. 3–54.

Online Newshour, "The Microsoft Antitrust Case," http://www.pbs.org/newshour/bb/cyberspace/july-dec99/microsoft_index.html.

Chapter 33

Energy Prices

In August 2003, a major power outage occurred in the northeastern United States, forcing these New York City commuters to return home on foot. *Source: AP Wide World Photo*

Chapter Objectives

After reading this chapter you should be able to

Understand what a cartel is, why cartels work to make their members large sums of money, why they are not stable, and why they sometimes seem to come back from the dead.

Put OPEC into perspective as a major oil-producing cartel.

See that the price of oil and gasoline, when adjusted for overall inflation, has been historically unstable as a result of both geopolitics and the inherent instability of cartels.

Understand that though it takes months for oil to go from the well to the gas tank, it is perfectly consistent with our economic model of supply and demand for events in the Middle East to cause prices at the pump to change in days.

Understand that the market for residential electricity has been characterized by regulated monopoly.

Chapter Outline

The world runs on petroleum products. Whether it is gasoline for automobiles, diesel fuel for trains and trucks, or home heating oil, modern society could not survive without oil. With proven oil reserves at just over 1,000 billion barrels, roughly 500 billion barrels more believed to be yet undiscovered, and oil consumption running at a little over 77 million barrels a day, it is likely that oil reserves will run out in the second half of the 21st century.

This chapter reviews the history of oil and gasoline prices, discussing the causes and effects of significant changes. We consider the Organization of Petroleum

Exporting Countries (OPEC) and how it developed and collapsed as an effective oil cartel. We also talk about why gasoline prices seem to rise and fall much more quickly than supplies would justify and use the 1999–2005 period as our primary focus. We look at electricity prices and why the industry lends itself to monopoly, why this has led to government price regulation, and why the California experience with deregulation was so problematic. Last, we look at the future and try to get an idea of where the oil industry might be 50 to 100 years from now.

THE HISTORICAL VIEW

Oil and Gasoline Price History

Gasoline prices, which were never stable, skyrocketed in the 1970s. Although several events coincided during that decade to increase prices, many politicians declared that this period was the beginning of a general, long-term "energy crisis." A brief look at Figure 33.1 suggests that the crisis was actually short run in nature. As a matter of fact, by 1998, the prices of crude oil and gasoline had fallen to a point at or near their 30-year lows. Crude oil prices doubled in the 1999–2000 time frame, doubled again in the 2003–2005 time frame and non-inflation-adjusted gasoline prices reached all-time highs in the early summer of 2005. In inflation terms, by early 2005 gasoline prices were rapidly approaching their all-time highs, and in the aftermonth of Hurricane Katrina surpassed their all time highs.

The top curve in Figure 33.1 shows the path of gasoline prices (GDP deflator adjusted for inflation) since the general conversion to unleaded fuel in 1978. The middle curve tracks the price of domestically produced crude oil, and the bottom curve shows the price of imported crude. Though oil prices are usually quoted in barrels, the prices have been converted to gallons for use here, and the prices have been adjusted for inflation.

Geopolitical History

Some geopolitical history here will provide insight into why oil prices changed as they did. As you can see from Table 33.1, oil is not evenly distributed throughout the world. You can surmise from this that the politics of the Middle East, and the Persian Gulf in particular, have been important in determining oil supplies.

TABLE 33.1   Global reserves by region.

Group	Barrels in Reserve (in billions)	Percentage of World Reserves
Persian Gulf OPEC	710	61
Non-Persian Gulf OPEC	157	13
Rest of the world	304	26

Source: U.S. Department of Energy, http://www.eia.doe.gov.

FIGURE 33.1   Inflation-adjusted gasoline and domestic and imported crude oil prices, 1973–2005 (2000 dollars).

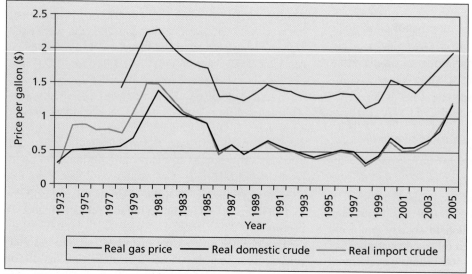

Source: U.S. Department of Energy, http://www.eia.doe.gov.

The Arab–Israeli wars of 1967 and 1973 generated a great deal of animosity between Arab nations and the Western world. The United States in particular was castigated because it supported Israel. The United States provided both substantial intelligence and support in material that helped the Israelis to prevail in taking (in 1967) and then holding (in 1973) the West Bank of the Jordan River from Jordan, the Golan Heights from Syria, and the Gaza Strip and Sinai peninsula from Egypt.

After this, Arab nations, angered by U.S. aid to Israel, refused to sell oil to the United States and much of the rest of the Western world. Though this did not lead to the rationing of gasoline in the United States, it did in Great Britain. This embargo also resulted in marked increases in prices. Figure 33.1 indicates that these first jumps in oil prices occurred in 1973 and 1974.

The significant price increases that came about in the late 1970s resulted from the economic power that OPEC wielded as an oil cartel. How cartels come about and how they can raise prices substantially will be thoroughly explained later in this chapter; but, suffice it to say, in inflation-adjusted terms, crude oil and gasoline prices reached record highs during this time. Gasoline hit $1.40 a gallon, the 2004 equivalent of $2.94, and crude oil hit $40 a barrel, the 2004 equivalent of $84.

During this time in Iran, the Ayatollah Khomeni took over from the deposed Shah, making neighbors such as Iraq, Kuwait, and Saudi Arabia very nervous. There is some dispute as to who the aggressor was, but these fears proved to be well founded, when in 1980 Iran and Iraq went to war. Although this war had many impacts more morally significant than its effect on the price of oil,[1] the impact on the price of oil changed the business of oil forever.

Because modern weapons are expensive, because both Iran and Iraq were strapped for cash, and because each country had only one realistic way of raising money, each began to sell as much oil as it could. While their official production figures do not show it, likely because they had to lie to fellow OPEC members, greater production allowed them to purchase more and better weapons.

As oil prices rose through the 1970s, Iran and Iraq began to pump more oil. Additionally, other nations engaged in efforts to find new sources of oil. New reserves were found in the North Sea, in Mexico, and in many other countries, and these reserves began to be exploited. In 1982 and 1983 a major recession rocked the United States and Europe, depressing demand for oil. As a result of these factors, the price of oil collapsed. Ultimately, by 1986 the price per barrel of oil fell to less than $10, and the average price of oil at the end of the year was $12.51.

When the Iran–Iraq war ended in 1988, oil prices began to recover but reached only the $15 level—a little more than 30 cents a gallon. At the end of the war, Iraq owed Saudi Arabia and Kuwait $40 billion each, as it had borrowed feverishly to buy weaponry. At $15 a barrel Iraq could not afford to both pay these debts and rebuild its war-torn country. Adding to the insult that Iraq felt, Kuwait and Saudi Arabia were not budging on OPEC production quotas, and Iraq felt that it had done Kuwait and Saudi Arabia a favor by fighting Iran in the first place. As we will see later when we discuss cartels, production quotas must be held down to keep prices high.

On August 2, 1990, Iraq invaded Kuwait, and the United States was convinced it was poised to continue the attack into Saudi Arabia. The fear of another war in the Persian Gulf sent oil prices to nearly $30 a barrel very quickly, which caused the average price for the year to be $20 per barrel. With the American- and British-led victory in the Gulf, prices calmed down and until 1998 fluctuated between $10 and $15 a barrel.

Since that time OPEC has reasserted itself with a series of production cuts that led the price of crude oil to top $30 a barrel in the spring of 2000. Another politically inspired set of price swings occurred in the run-up to and aftermath of the Iraq war in 2003. Gas prices spiked at over $2.00 per gallon in many U.S. cities in the month before the war. Once the conventional aspect of the war ended without major petroleum shortages, the price of gasoline came back to a more normal level. Between 2003 and 2005 the Iraqi insurgency prevented a continuous flow of oil from that country and, coupled with increased worldwide demand for oil, prices spiked once again. Historical highs were set in 2004 and 2005 in nominal terms and for the first time in 25 years, the inflation-adjusted record price for oil began to be challenged. Inflation-adjusted gasoline prices briefly exceeded record levels in the weeks following Hurricane Katrina.

The Middle East in general and the Persian Gulf in particular have proven that they can rival the Balkans in the old adage that "they produce more history than they can consume locally." The price of oil is inextricably tied to the political, military, and religious tensions of the

---

[1]Iraq first used poison gas on Iranian soldiers and its own citizens, Iranians recruited children to serve as soldiers, the Reagan administration sold the Iranians weapons while using the profits to fund the Nicaraguan contras, and the CIA gave intelligence support to Iraq.

region, tensions that are historically significant but would likely be dismissed in the West were it not for the oil.

OPEC

What OPEC Does

In the preceding historical survey of the price of oil, we alluded to the important part OPEC has played. OPEC is

cartel
An organization of individual competitors that join to form a single monopolist.

a **cartel** (an organization of individual competitors that join to form as a single monopolist) that is composed of Algeria, Indonesia, Iran, Iraq, Kuwait, Libya, Nigeria, Qatar, Saudi Arabia, United Arab Emirates, and Venezuela: countries that export oil. Taken together, they have, as Table 33.1 shows, 74 percent of the proven oil reserves in the world. There was a time when this gave them enormous political power to wield. Through the 1990s, however, oil prices were such that the cartel seemed to be powerless, only to be revived in 1999 and 2000. How did all this happen?

When groups of people, firms, or countries have little power as individuals but perceive their joint power as great, they hypothesize themselves as a joint force. If something exists or arises that binds them together and there are not too many of them to organize, there is a chance they can pull it off. These ingredients were present when, in the late 1960s and early 1970s, Middle Eastern oil-exporting countries saw that together they could punish Israel's main supporters and make a profit at the same time.

This turned a loose organization, OPEC, into a powerful oil cartel. Cartels can exist in many different industries where a small number of competitors make up the vast majority of the suppliers of a commodity. The trouble is all cartels have a self-destructive tendency and OPEC was no different.

How Cartels Work

Cartels work because the individual perfect competitors join forces to act like a monopolist. In order to do this they must agree on a mechanism to withhold their goods from the market. In OPEC's case, that means they must, together, agree on a plan to reduce oil production. That plan usually means that each country must limit its production to a fraction of what it was producing before they formed the cartel. If they succeed in getting that agreement, prices will rise. Recall from Chapter 5 that in the long run and under perfect competition the price of a good will equal both the marginal cost and the average

cost. If prices rise, profits rise and all of the members of the cartel are happy.

Why Cartels Are Not Stable

This is not the end of the story, though, because cartels such as these are not stable. Let's look at an intuitive reason why. Suppose your teacher in this class announced, at the beginning of the semester, that grades on exams would be granted on a curve. This would mean that regardless of how well people did on exams, a predetermined percentage of students would be assigned As, Bs, Cs, Ds, and Fs. A clever class of students would band together to make a joint promise not to study. They would reason that if they all studied, they would end up ranking exactly the same (based on their aptitude for economics) as they would if they did not study at all.

Let's add here the outlandish assumption that students have no desire to study economics for fun and that they just want the grade for as little effort as possible. What would happen then? Would no students study? The scheme might work for the first quiz, but it would start falling apart as one or more students eventually sneaked off to study. They would see that it was in their interest to study because they could get better grades. Eventually, other students would notice that some were cheating. They would see their own grades drop in relation to those of their peers as the cheaters passed them by. Noncheaters would then start to cheat—that is to say, they would study. If, as we speculate, everyone ends up studying as they would without the prior agreement, then the agreement has become meaningless.

This is rather close to what happened with OPEC. Countries saw that they could make money by cheating even a little. A country committed to cheating would see that cheating paid because at their agreed-upon production their marginal revenue (the new high cartel price) was greater than the marginal cost so the country could make a profit. That profit would greatly exceed the profit previously received at the cartel's imposed quota. As in our previous example, using grading on a curve where everyone schemed together, individual greed induced cheating on the collective and this caused all gains to evaporate. Cheating by OPEC members led not only to the disappearance of the large profits, but also to the evaporation of all economic profits.

Putting another nail in the coffin of OPEC was the introduction of other, non-OPEC countries into the mix. A large importer, Great Britain, motivated by high prices to find its own sources, found oil in the North Sea. Moreover, it found

FIGURE 33.2   Worldwide oil production, 1970–2004.

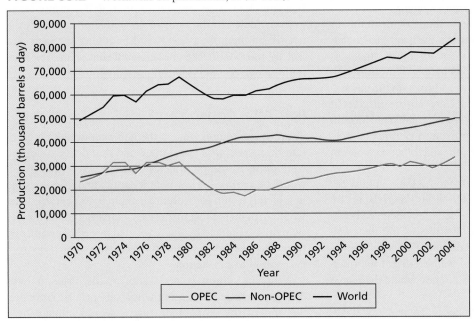

Source: U.S. Department of Energy. http://www.eia.doe.gov.

enough to both solve its own problems and become an exporter. Mexico and other countries also found oil and began selling it in large quantities. Although OPEC tried to persuade these countries to join in a larger, more powerful cartel, none agreed. They reasoned that they could still sell at or slightly below the cartel price, and they could do so without any production quotas. Figure 33.2 highlights this fact by showing that, as a percentage of total world production, OPEC is no longer the biggest producer. Other nations are producing oil and taking market share from OPEC.

Back from the Dead

The 1990s saw oil prices fall dramatically and remain below historical averages until 1999, when prices took a sudden jump higher. How did OPEC, which seemed dead, come back to life? In fact, the potential profitability of OPEC never disappeared. It was only the behavior of the individual countries that dissipated potential profits. Throughout 1998 and 1999 OPEC began a series of production cuts that eventually totaled 4.3 million barrels a day. They thus drove up world prices. Unlike previous oil price spikes, they chose to let up before a major inflation episode struck the United States. Thus OPEC seems back in the saddle again, controlling world oil prices. Will it last? It might, but only if OPEC learns from its past mistakes. In the long run, after all the political issues in Iraq

are settled, if OPEC is to maintain its pricing power, it must settle on a price that does not motivate non-OPEC countries to explore for additional oil. Even if it accomplishes this, there will still be the tendency for self-interest on the part of OPEC members to exceed their quotas.

WHY DO PRICES CHANGE SO FAST?

It takes months for an empty tanker to leave the United States, arrive in the Persian Gulf, be loaded with crude oil, arrive back in the United States, be offloaded, and for the crude oil to be refined into gasoline. If that is true, how is it possible that the price of gasoline at a neighborhood gas station can change by 20 percent in a week? The answer takes us back to Chapter 2 and the determinants of supply and demand. Remember that the expectations of the future price of a good affect both the current supply curve and the current demand curve.

Remember, too, that if the price is expected to rise, then on our supply and demand diagram there will be little to no delay in the demand curve's moving to the right and the supply curve's moving to the left. This is because consumers will want to stock up before any price increase fully takes effect and producers will want to hang on to what they have in hopes of being able to sell it for more later. The impact of this is that prices will rise now in anticipation of price increases later.

To see how this works in the oil industry recall the reaction in the United States to Iraq's invasion of Kuwait. Within days gasoline prices went up by as much as 25 cents per gallon. How did this happen? Starting with the oil-importing companies and ending with the gas stations, each wanted to buy and store all the product it could before the prices went up. Normally, no one in gasoline production keeps significant quantities in storage. It costs money to store oil and other petroleum products.

The oil companies thus hurried to fill their tankers before the price went up too far. Refineries got in the act by rushing to get tankers lined up to sell them their crude before the price went up too far, distributors did the same thing, and so did gas stations. At every stage, the demand for product rose because firms wanted to put as much cheap input in storage as possible. They would then have more when the prices rose.

Also true in such circumstances is that at every stage, firms do not want to sell out of their storage to provide someone down the line with product to store—that is, unless the buyer is willing to pay more. Prices rise and storage tanks fill up. If there were an actual gasoline shortage, this would not be bad: it would be beneficial to have the extra oil in storage.

When prices are anticipated to fall, the opposite happens: Firms attempt to get rid of product. Because firms will want to get as much as possible for the gasoline that is in storage and will empty storage tanks only when it is clear that prices will in fact fall, prices decrease more slowly than they increase. Prices did fall after the Gulf War, and they fell by more than the 25 cents they had increased, but the decrease took much longer than the increase had taken.

The ultimate example of rapid price swings based on price expectations occurred the afternoon and evening of September 11, 2001. In response to concerns, both real and imagined, over the availability of gasoline, prices at some stations tripled. Some stations, particularly in the Midwest, were charging $1.40 per gallon in the morning hours prior to the terrorist attacks and were charging more than $4.00 per gallon later that day. While some price increase could be explained by changes in wholesale prices (they increased between 5 and 10 cents per gallon that day), the bulk of the price jump occurred because of a rumor-fed fear that prices would dramatically rise if refineries were shut down or oil imports stopped. While consumer advocates and attorney generals were upset, consumers in particular were not blameless. Two-hour gas lines were not uncommon that afternoon and evening fueled by the same rumor-fed fear that if they did not fill up then, the price would be higher the next day. But by morning it became apparent that refineries were not in jeopardy, and prices fell to previous levels.

Is It All a Conspiracy?

There is a common view in the general public that gasoline prices are all a conspiracy and that deals are cut in backrooms to set the price of gasoline. Were that true it would be against the law both federally and in every state in which it occurred. Absent an explicit conspiracy, what would explain the fact that prices increase not just rapidly (which is explained by the "expected price" phenomenon from Chapter 2) but at almost exactly the same time from gas station to gas station?

When a station gets its supply, the price it pays changes to reflect changing wholesale prices. Were that the end of the story, then prices would change only when stations got a new supply. The twist is that the cost of the gasoline in the ground is quite literally "sunk" and therefore ignored. Remember from Chapter 5 that fixed/sunk costs are ignored when setting the profit-maximizing price. It is only the cost of replacing that gasoline, its opportunity cost, that concerns the profit-maximizing gas station. Since that price changes daily, even if the gasoline in the underground is a week old, gas stations will adjust their price daily to reflect the cost of replacing it.

Why would the prices at neighboring gas stations change within minutes of one another and why would it take only hours for price increases to be reflected across town? The answer to these questions revolves around the fact that the industry is governed by oligopoly. The neighboring stations must keep their prices at or below one another so when wholesale prices change there is a natural tendency for the resulting retail prices to come out close. In most communities, though there are many gas stations, there are but a few wholesale suppliers. The wholesale suppliers face rapidly changing national spot markets for gasoline and keep their prices in line with their competitors (few as they may be) in order to maintain their gas station customer base. Since only a few wholesalers are selling to the same set of retailers at the same wholesale price, and since those retailers are pricing according to the replacement cost of the gasoline, it should not be surprising that gas prices seem to change at the same time across a community.

TABLE 33.2 Crude oil prices, various types, April 8, 2005.

Variety of Oil	Price of Oil
West Texas Intermediate	$51.71
Indonesia Minas	$58.60
Brent Sea (U.K.)	$54.43
Mexico Maya	$40.04
Saudi Light	$50.85
Saudi Heavy	$45.45
OPEC Countries Spot Price	$50.95

Source: http://eia.doe.gov.

From $1.00 to $2.50 per Gallon in Six Years?

We need to take a step back to understand something about the "price" of oil. As Table 33.2 shows, there is not one price. Every grade and type of crude oil has a price based on the ease with which you can refine it into saleable products like gasoline. As a result there can be a 25 percent difference in the crude oil price between the output of countries and even within countries. When oil prices are referred to on the news they typically choose a representative type. The most often-quoted oil prices are Brent Sea, Saudi Light, and West Texas Intermediate.

Still, by whatever measure, the price of oil skyrocketed between December 1998 and 2005. For data consistency purposes the U.S. Department of Energy produces a weighted average of imported oil prices that it calls the Refiner Acquisition Cost of Imported Oil. Figure 33.3 shows how that measure increased over the six-year period from late 1998 to 2005.

What caused this rapid increase in prices? The short answer is increased world demand coupled with problems in the world oil-supply chain brought about by increased OPEC discipline, political unrest in oil-producing countries, and the U.S.-led war in Iraq. Gasoline prices, which tend to closely follow crude oil prices, were also impacted by limited U.S. refining capacity.

The main factors in increasing demand between 2002 and 2005 were the global economic expansion coming out of the 2001 recession; the significant increase in miles driven by the typical American; the substitution by Americans from more-fuel-efficient cars to less-fuel-efficient vans, pickups, and SUVs; and the long-term expansion of demand in India and China.

FIGURE 33.3 Refiner acquisition cost, December 1998–February 2005.

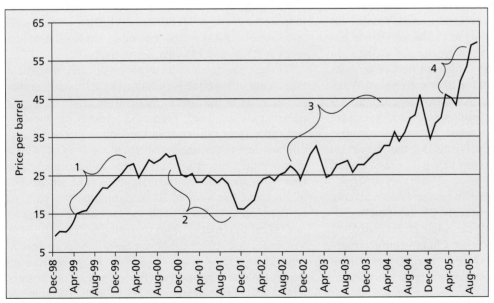

1—OPEC production cuts; low stocks of oil; bad weather.

2—Release of oil from the Strategic Petroleum Reserve; recession.

3—Political unrest in oil-producing Venezuela and Nigeria; war in Iraq.

4—Hurricanes Damage Platforms in the Gulf of Mexico.

Source: http://eia.doe.gov.

FIGURE 33.4   Gasoline prices, December 1998–Oct 2005.

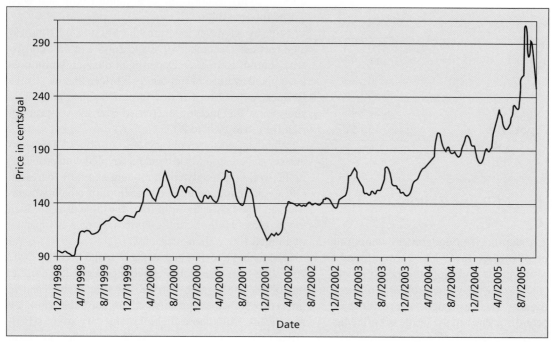

Source http://eia.doe.gov.

Americans have steadily migrated to less fuel-efficient vehicles. Whereas cars made up 70 percent of the U.S. fleet in the late 1990s, they now make up 60 percent. Though the fuel efficiency of cars has increased and the fuel efficiency of vans, pickups, and SUVs have increased, the impact of moving to the larger vehicle has totally eliminated the benefit of greater gas mileage. In net, the fuel efficiency of the American fleet of vehicles has remained essentially flat for 10 or more years. When combined with the fact that Americans are driving 2.9 trillion miles, up from 2.1 trillion miles 15 years ago, gasoline demand in the United States has jumped markedly. As you can see from Figure 33.4, this increase in demand, combined with a variety of supply issues, caused gasoline prices to spike.

Chinese demand for petroleum has increased markedly as well. Once a net exporter of fuels, China is now a leading importer. Over the last 10 years while global petroleum demand has increased 16 percent, China's petroleum demand increased 94 percent. Over the next 10 years China is expected to account for 40 percent of the increase in world oil demand.

Just as there is more than one variety of oil, there is also more than one variety of gasoline. Gasoline is not simply "regular," "plus," or "premium." For environmental reasons gasoline is formulated for the particular climate and environmental conditions of local areas as well as state and local law. Gasoline prices are also impacted by state and local taxes. These taxes average 20.7 cents per gallon with Rhode Island, Pennsylvania, and Wisconsin topping the charts at 31, 30, and 29.1 cents, respectively, and Georgia, Alaska, and Wyoming having the lowest taxes at 7.5, 8, and 14 cents, respectively.

Though gasoline can be imported directly, more than 90 percent of gasoline is produced by a limited number of refineries in the United States from crude oil that is increasingly imported. Figure 33.5 shows the location and capacity of refineries in the United States. Of significant note is that the refineries along the Gulf Coast of the United States are susceptible to hurricanes. The four hurricanes that hit the area in the summer and fall of 2004, and five more in 2005 highlighted this particular bottleneck. In 2004, with the hurricanes coming in one after the other, ships carrying crude oil from Venezuela and Africa could not make it to port thereby constraining U.S. supplies of gasoline. Hurricane Katrina decimated the Port of New Orleans and in the process dramatically affected gasoline prices in the late summer and early fall of 2005.

Who is to blame for all this? Mostly ourselves. The United States government has chosen to limit new exploration and the creation of more refining capacity,

FIGURE 33.5   Refinery locations and capacity in the United States.

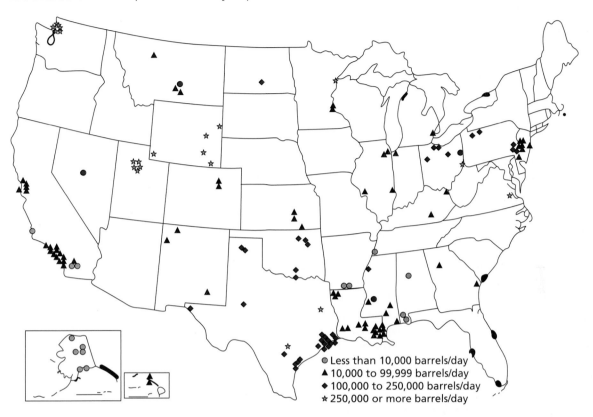

Less than 10,000 barrels/day
10,000 to 99,999 barrels/day
100,000 to 250,000 barrels/day
250,000 or more barrels/day

largely for environmental reasons. Americans generally are to blame for driving more miles and driving less-fuel-efficient cars. The war in Iraq cut supplies coming from that country. Blaming the Chinese for increasing their appetite for driving is the "pot calling the kettle black" but they are, so we can blame them too. Finally, OPEC has become far more disciplined in its management of cartel prices. In the end, we are running on a global energy system where, if anything goes wrong, prices escalate rapidly, and for six years many things have gone wrong.

ELECTRIC UTILITIES

Electricity Production

While it took more than a century for Edison to capitalize effectively on Benjamin Franklin's dreams for electricity with his lightbulb, it did not take that long for the United States to become dependent on it. Similarly, while the motivation for building the Hoover Dam may

have been economic stimulation, flood control, and irrigation, the by-product of cheap electricity was credited with allowing millions to live and find work in southern California.

For the most part, electricity is produced by regulated utility companies. These companies incur substantial fixed costs that present nearly insurmountable barriers to entry. These fixed costs include the power plant itself as well as the transmission lines and transformers that get the electricity into homes so that consumers can use it.

Their variable inputs are sometimes nearly free, as is the case with hydroelectric, wind, and solar power, but more typically, oil, natural gas, coal, or nuclear fuel must be purchased. Where you live often determines how your electricity is produced. Nationally, burning coal to produce electricity through steam turbines accounts for more than half of electricity produced. Nuclear power accounts for 21 percent of electricity production, while natural gas accounts for 16.5 percent and hydroelectric power accounts for 6 percent.

The distribution of that reliance varies substantially across the country. The Pacific and Mountain West regions produce 15 to 20 times the amount of electricity through the turbines of their dams than does New England. Nuclear power provides almost 70 percent of the electricity usage in Connecticut, but nothing in Washington State and less than 10 percent in Maine. Not surprisingly, burning coal is a main source of electricity where coal is abundant.

Why Are Electric Utilities a Regulated Monopoly?

Because of the high fixed costs of production, the residential electricity market is characterized by monopoly because these costs tend to deter entry. Whether or not the proper model for this market is that of a natural monopoly or a simple monopoly depends on the type of electricity produced and the distance of transmission.

A **natural monopoly** exists when there are high fixed costs and diminishing marginal costs. In nuclear and hy-

natural monopoly

Exists when there are high fixed costs and diminishing marginal costs.

droelectric power the variable costs are low. In nuclear power the rods themselves are cheap, relative to the amount of coal that would have to be purchased to produce the same electricity. On the other hand, the personnel that are required at a nuclear facility are highly trained and compensated. In hydroelectric power, the variable input is free as the water that drives the turbines does so because of gravity. In both cases the cost of the facility is enormous relative to the costs of the variable inputs. Even when coal, oil or, natural gas are burned to generate electricity, the market tends toward monopoly because of the high fixed costs of the transmission network.

One factor that plays into whether the market for electricity is a natural or simple monopoly is the distance from the generator to the user. Half of all electricity produced in the country fizzles out on its way to the end user. The longer the power lines, the greater the degradation. For this reason, if greater production is being sent to farther distant locations (rather than more being consumed by the existing consumers) marginal costs rise.

Figure 33.6 shows what the price-output combination would be in an unregulated market for electricity in the case of a simple monopoly while Figure 33.7 shows the price-output combination for an unregulated natural monopoly. In either case the price is substantially above the marginal cost. This, combined with the fact that people

FIGURE 33.6   A simple monopoly.

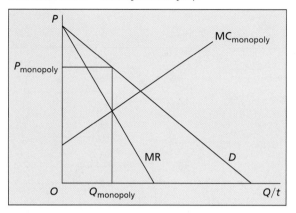

FIGURE 33.7   A natural monopoly.

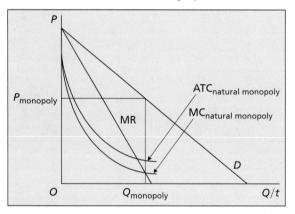

need electricity to live a modern life, led to the widespread regulation of prices for electric utilities.

Figures 33.8 and 33.9 show the likely regulated prices that would exist if the regulators sought to allow the electric companies normal profits.

The California Experience

During 2000 and 2001 California experienced a substantial increase in electricity prices. Average wholesale electricity prices went from $26.56 per megawatt hour in April 2000 to $575 per megawatt hour a year later. While prices cooled during the late spring and summer of 2001 (to $385 by May 18 and under $100 during July), the search for a villain heated up. While some economists looked to collusive behaviors on the part of natural gas suppliers and electricity generators, others looked to a changed regulatory scheme.

FIGURE 33.8   A regulated simple monopoly.

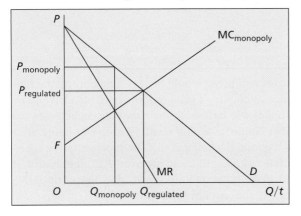

FIGURE 33.9   A regulated natural monopoly.

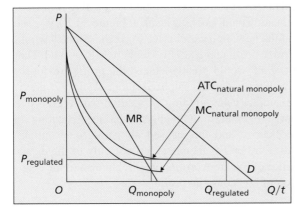

Prior to 2000, California operated under a similar set of regulatory rules as the rest of the country where the large utilities would seek price increases from a government body. The utilities owned the electricity generators and the transmission lines. In 2000, new regulations came to full fruition and the utilities were required to divest themselves of their generating capacity. The logic was that a myriad of new generating companies would sell their electricity to the utility at competitive rates, and the utility would then sell that electricity to consumers at regulated rates.

The problem with this scheme was though wholesale market prices and prices to industrial users were deregulated, residential prices remained regulated. This meant when there was a spike in the price of natural gas (the burning of which is a key method of generation in California) causing the price of a major input to more than double during the period, wholesale electricity

prices shot up. California's biggest utility could not afford the higher prices because they could not raise residential rates. They began to borrow money to buy power and when that ability ran out, generators refused to accept their promissory notes. The result was a scarcity of electrical power and rolling blackouts.

While the spike in the price of natural gas has been explained by some economists in collusion terms as well as strictly economic ones, it is clear that the California version of "deregulation" could not adapt to it.

WHAT WILL THE FUTURE HOLD?

Oil reserves are likely to be almost entirely depleted before the end of the 21st century. What will happen? Will we revert to the Stone Age once all the oil is gone? No. There are no perfect substitutes for oil and gas today, but there are some serviceable ones. We already use vegetation-based fuels; and we produce electricity with geothermal and solar power and with wind. As supplies decrease, more efficient uses of petroleum will be invented. Why are economists less worried about the end of fossil fuels than are people in other fields? Economists, who are not usually accused of making Pollyannaish predictions, are convinced that normal human self-interest will be more than adequate to spur on the important innovations that will be needed.

A lot of money will be made as we find substitutes for fossil fuels. As these fuels become more scarce and we exhaust all sources of them, they will become more and more expensive. Moreover, prices will not fall in the latter half of the 21st century. This will spur investment and investment will spur innovation. It always has and it always will.

Consider this: If you were an oil company, and you anticipated the end of your current form of business, you would spend as much money as it took to figure out a way to continue to sell fuels to your current customers. You would spend money on a variety of promising leads. You would try, for example, to figure out how to use renewable corn or soybeans to fuel existing cars, and, if that did not work, you would experiment with high-power, quick-charge batteries that you could sell so cars could run on electricity without the current problems of slow acceleration and long recharge times.

Nearly any problem can be solved with the proper incentive, and profit is one of the oldest and most effective incentives of all.

Kick It Up
A Notch

Going back to the question of how cartels work, consider Figure 33.10. On the left panel is the market for oil. If the market were governed by perfect competition, then the price–quantity combination would be P_{comp}, Q_{comp}. This price would be carried over to the right panel, which would show the cost functions of a representative oil-producing country. Recall from Chapter 5 that the long-run equilibrium in such a market would mean that the price line would come tangent at the bottom of the average total cost (ATC) curve, where it would also intersect marginal cost (MC). Thus the representative oil-producing country would sell q_{comp}, because this is where marginal revenue (MR) intersects marginal cost (MC). At this level of production, they would make only normal profit, that is, the profit consistent with the return expected in other industries.

If they joined a cartel with other, similar countries, then the model for the market would be monopoly rather than perfect competition. If that were the case, then the cartel would jointly produce only Q_{cartel} and would charge P_{cartel} because that's where marginal revenue (MR) intersects marginal cost (MC) on the left panel of Figure 33.10. Since total production of all countries combined would be less than before, the representative country's production would also have to be less than it was before. Some negotiations between the member countries would result in each one being allocated a quota, labeled q_{quota}. If the representative country produced q_{quota} line and received P_{cartel} per barrel, it would make an economic profit, that is, profit above normal, in the amount of *abcd*.

Cartels are not stable because cheating pays. The right-hand panel of Figure 33.10 shows this; see that q_{quota} marginal revenue MR′ was greater than the marginal cost MC. Countries that cheated did so hoping that no one would notice. A country committed to cheating would see that cheating paid. Looking again at Figure 33.10, you see that at the new high cartel price P_{cartel} the country would maximize profit at q_{cheat}. This is where MR′ = MC. That profit, *gaef,* would greatly exceed the profit previously received at the cartel's imposed quota. As in our previous example, using grading on a curve where everyone schemed together, individual greed induced cheating on the collective and this caused all gains to evaporate. Cheating by OPEC members led not only to the disappearance of the large profits (*gaef*), but also to the evaporation of all economic profits.

FIGURE 33.10   A model of a cartel.

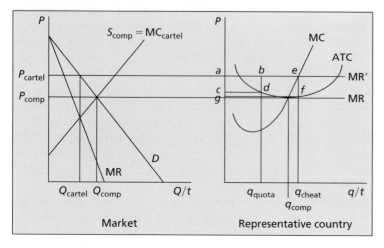

Summary

Now that you have completed this chapter, you know what a cartel is, that OPEC is a major oil-producing cartel, why it is that cartels work to make their members large sums of money, why it is that they are not stable, and that they seem to be able to rise again from the dead. You know that, inflation adjusted, the price of oil and the price of gasoline have been historically unstable and that this instability has been a consequence of geopolitics and the inherent instability of cartels. You understand why it is that events in the Middle East can alter prices at the pump within a few days.

Key Terms

cartel, 342

natural monopoly, 348

Quiz Yourself

1. In order to compare the price of gasoline in the 1970s with the price in 2005, you have to adjust for
   a. The availability of oil.
   b. The price of oil.
   c. Overall inflation.
   d. Unemployment.

2. The heaviest concentration of proven oil reserves is found in
   a. Alaska.
   b. The North Sea.
   c. The Persian Gulf.
   d. Texas.

3. When a group of competitors joins together to form a monopoly, they are forming a
   a. Cartel.
   b. Coalition.
   c. Union.
   d. Trust.

4. Cartels are considered _____ because each participant is motivated to _____.
   a. Stable; work with each other cooperatively.
   b. Stable; work in their own interest to produce more.
   c. Unstable; work with each other cooperatively.
   d. Unstable; work in their own interest to produce more.

5. Gasoline prices in early 2005 were above $2.10. Theae were
   a. The highest nominal prices and highest inflation-adjusted prices in American history.
   b. The highest nominal prices but were not the highest inflation-adjusted prices in American history.
   c. Neither the highest nominal prices nor the highest inflation-adjusted prices in American history.
   d. The highest inflation adjusted prices but were not the highest nominal prices in American history.

6. California electricity deregulation involved the deregulating _____ prices while regulating _____ prices.
   a. Wholesale; retail.
   b. Retail; wholesale.
   c. Real; nominal.
   d. Nominal; real.

Think about This

All energy consumption involves externalities that are recognized. Given that we have spent billions of dollars militarily defending access to oil, should we consider that an externality too? Aren't the consumers of energy indirectly compelling increased spending on the military?

Talk about This

Oil prices are highly sensitive to output changes. Hurricanes, terrorist acts, and other unexpected occurrences regularly cause the price of oil to increase by 10 percent within the course of a month, only to fall again when the trouble subsides. Should the federal government use its strategic petroleum reserve to counter these effects or should it use the reserve only in a true emergency?

For More Insight See

Adelman, Morris, *Genie Out of the Bottle: World Oil Since 1970* (Cambridge, MA: MIT Press, 1995).

Behind the Numbers

Global energy resource data, 2001.

Oil consumption per day.

Global oil reserves by region.

World crude oil production.

Energy Information Administration; Monthly Energy Review, September 2003—http://www.eia.doe.gov/emeu/mer/pdf/mer.pdf.

Energy prices.

Oil and gasoline prices.

Energy Information Administration; petroleum—http:// www.eia.doe.gov/aer/pdf/pages/sec5.pdf.

Domestic and imported crude oil and gasoline prices.

Energy Information Administration; International Energy Annual 2001, March 2003—http://www.eia.doe.gov/pub/pdf/international/021901.pdf;http://www.bts.gov/publications/national_transportation_statistics/2004/.

Chapter 34

If We Build It, Will They Come? And Other Sports Questions

Screaming fans fill the Rose Bowl in Pasadena, CA.
Source: © Jerry Cooke/Photo Researchers, Inc.

Chapter Objectives

After reading this chapter you should be able to

Understand how economic principles can be applied to the issues of sports.

See that despite the obvious attempts of cities to acquire sports franchises through league expansion and by other means, no economic evidence suggests that having a franchise enhances a city's economic stature.

Understand that owners are on the opposite side in negotiating with cities.

Analyze how owners decide, when negotiating with players, whether they wish to make more money or win championships, since it is clear that teams in small markets cannot do both.

Understand the basics of sports labor economics history and the vocabulary that is central to it.

Understand how monopolies work with sports.

Chapter Outline

The Problem for Cities

The Problem for Owners

The Sports Labor Market

The Vocabulary of Sports Economics

Summary

Sports offers an interesting venue in which to ask economic questions. For instance, if you are the mayor of a city whose citizens want a sports franchise, are you better off if you get one from another city, or do you mount a campaign to garner an expansion franchise? If it will enhance the chances of getting a franchise, do you build a multimillion-dollar stadium and hope you get a team to put in it? Now suppose you are a mayor of a city that already has a franchise whose owner is threatening to leave. Do you build the franchise owner a stadium, even though the one the team is in is only 25 years old? The question that underlies all these decisions is whether a sports franchise is an important economic attraction for a city. Mayors make deals all the time to attract other kinds of major employers. Why not a sports franchise?

To change perspective, suppose now that you are an owner of a franchise. What would make you want to move your team to a different city or to hold your own city hostage to build you a stadium? How do you decide whether to bid for high-priced talent? Can you compete in the financial arena if you do? Can you compete on the field, or the ice, or the basketball court if you do not?

These are all questions that arise in all sports, and they are all economic in their nature. We answer each by looking at them from two perspectives: the city's and the team owner's. Since no discussion of the economics of sports today would be complete without a discussion of labor, we include that, too. We try to figure out how we went from sports as games to sports as business.

THE PROBLEM FOR CITIES

Expansion versus Luring a Team

One of the emerging trends of the 1990s, like the 1950s, was the sudden increase in the desire among owners of sports franchises to move their teams from one city to another. Compared to other sports, baseball has been relatively stable. It has increased in numbers of teams, but existing teams have tended not to move. Other sports, however, have seen teams move all over the place. Some of that movement, such as baseball's movement west, occurred with the Dodgers and Giants relocating from New York to California during the 1950s. That made good economic sense for the sport at the time. The movement of the Rams and Raiders out of Los Angeles, on the other hand, made little economic sense for the National Football

League.[1] In nearly all of the recent franchise shifts, movement has resulted from a city's offering enticements to owners. In each case, the franchise owner has made millions.

A city has to decide on its strategy when it seeks to attract a team. While each sport has added new teams in the last several years, such expansion is not always the surest way for a particular city to get a team. In part, this is because there's no guarantee that a given sport will expand or will choose that city. Football and baseball added only two teams each between 1970 and 1990. Though the 1990s have seen increased expansion in both sports, many cities have waited in line for an expansion franchise, only to be spurned. When cities lose patience, they may turn their attention to finding teams that are in financial trouble and offering their owners the lure of millions of dollars as well as profit guarantees.

Cities that have been spurned in the expansion process and have subsequently sought out financially troubled teams have succeeded in getting them, but at a high cost. After St. Louis lost the football Cardinals to Arizona, it sought, but was denied, an expansion team while franchises were granted to Jacksonville and Charlotte instead. It turned, then, to luring an existing team. The Los Angeles Rams wanted a stadium built in Los Angeles containing revenue-producing luxury boxes, and the owner threatened to move if demands were not met. As part of its expansion bid, St. Louis was already in the process of building such a stadium. When Los Angeles refused to build one, the Rams moved to St. Louis. Before their Super Bowl year, the team drew fewer fans than it had drawn in Los Angeles. Nevertheless, the owner made more money because corporations paid hundreds of thousands of dollars for luxury boxes. Nashville has the same story to tell as the Oilers moved from Houston. In each case, a city stood in line, was denied a place at the table, and managed to buy its way in anyway.

In its pursuit of a team, a city has to decide whether it should build a stadium in hopes that a team and a franchise will come. This "if you build it, they will come" strategy is fraught with uncertain payoffs. St. Louis built it, and the Rams did come. St. Petersburg built it, and no one came.

---

[1]The only economic aspect of the decision not to have a team in the second largest city in the United States that makes sense is that the Rams and Raiders rarely sold out the Los Angeles Coliseum. This meant that not only were their games blacked out during that time, but also the network slated to cover the game could not cover any other game during that time. With no team in Los Angeles, there are no game blackouts and that means more ad revenue to the networks, which could potentially mean a higher bid for broadcast rights.

In hopes that the Chicago White Sox would move, the Tampa–St. Petersburg area built a new stadium but, at the last minute, the city of Chicago and the state of Illinois agreed to build the White Sox a new Comisky Park. The White Sox are still in Chicago. Though the Tampa Bay area ultimately got an expansion franchise, the wait lasted 10 years, and the city may have to build another new stadium because the facility in which the team plays is considered one of the worst places to see a baseball game in the major leagues. Building in hopes of getting a franchise sometimes works and sometimes does not. Since it rarely happens that a city gets a franchise without either a good stadium or one that is already under construction, building a new facility may be the only chance a city has, even though it may not be a very good bet.

Does a Team Enhance the Local Economy?

From a rational perspective, a city needs more reasons for having a franchise than just wanting to have one. To this end, the justification that most proponents give for getting a team is that doing so is an investment in the city's future. If that were true, the jobs gained, the tax income generated, and the prestige gained from having a team would genuinely be enough to pay for the costs of building the stadium. Because most mayors consider economic development a vital responsibility of their terms in office, you might think that enticing a team to move in would be the same as enticing any other major employer to move in. Does it not make sense for a mayor who seeks to draw a major employer to an area to also seek out a sports franchise that will employ many people?

While the reasoning sounds good, sports franchises simply do not generate very good jobs for people other than the athletes. Whether the jobs are created in the facility or are in surrounding restaurants, their pay scale is relatively low, and they provide few benefits. Moreover, though each baseball team has 81 home dates, in basketball the number is 40, and in football it is a mere 8. You cannot build a local economy with only a few workdays a year.

It turns out that whether a sports franchise can be an economic cornerstone is a well-researched question. You may be surprised to know, though, that in nearly every study on the subject, economists have concluded that sports teams do next to nothing to improve economic activity in a city. The research has focused on whether cities that have lost franchises did any worse economically than they would have had they not lost the team. Research also questioned whether cities that were granted a franchise did any better than they would have without one. The conclusion that was consistently drawn was that a city's economic activity was almost totally unrelated to whether it had a franchise.

The reason that sports teams do not add much to a local economy is that money spent on tickets, parking, and memorabilia is mostly local. This is referred to as **local substitution,** and it means that local people are going to games instead of eating out or going to movies or other things they would have done locally with their money. In the larger picture, sports is just a branch of the entertainment industry. Having a team changes how entertainment dollars are spent, but it does not change the amount that is spent. In this sense, arguing whether a city should attract a sports team is like arguing whether a city should fight to attract a Super Wal-Mart. Both produce about the same gross revenue and employ large numbers of people at low wages. The difference is that for a Wal-Mart, much of the money leaves the local area in payment for the store's goods, and for a team, huge amounts of money go to a few rich stars.

local substitution
The effect of the substitution of one economic activity for another within a community, so the net effect is zero.

Although some cities may not feel they have "arrived" or are "major league" until they have at least one baseball, basketball, hockey, or football team, they pay a very high price for that honor. Some cities grow in population to the point where a team is justified, but they have none. The Norfolk–Virginia Beach area of Virginia is now the largest Standard Metropolitan Statistical Area without any major league football, basketball, hockey, or baseball franchise. When people in Norfolk–Virginia Beach look at the attention that a small city of less than 100,000 gets each year with the Packers in Green Bay, they may conclude that they will not be living in an important area until they have one. If image is everything, then it may be worth it to assess citizens millions in taxes to get a franchise. Otherwise such outlays of money are highly questionable.

Why Are Stadiums Publicly Funded?

That outlays for stadiums are questionable as a means of creating economic growth does not prevent the issue from coming up. Public funding of stadiums can be explained in terms of **positive externalities** and bargaining power.

positive externalities
The benefit that a person other than the buyer or seller receives as a result of a transaction.

The positive externalities here are the benefits to the fans of having a team in the city which are in excess of what they get from going to the games. There are millions of sports fans who enjoy having a team in their city whether or not they ever go to a game or watch it on television. They enjoy following the team in the newspaper and talking about the team with their friends. Because they value that experience, voters, having decided that they want to keep a team, are willing to pay taxes to keep the team. This is similar to their willingness to pay taxes to support the arts when they do not attend concerts or museums.

Having seen why voters may be willing to pay taxes to keep a team, we need to look at why they end up having to pay to keep a team. Because teams have demonstrated a willingness to move, and cities have demonstrated a willingness to lure the teams of other cities, all of the bargaining power belongs to the team owner. One of the things that we assumed in Chapter 5 when we discussed perfect competition was that there were many buyers and many sellers and that none had any market power. Here the market power is concentrated with the owner, who can move the team if voters do not pay for the stadium.

THE PROBLEM FOR OWNERS

To Move or to Stay

Owners are the big winners in sports when teams play musical chairs with their locations. Owners understand that an individual team's worth is based on how much it can rake in from memorabilia sales, luxury boxes, and, in the case of baseball, local TV revenue. They also know that it is to their advantage to have many suitors for their teams and to do little to discourage talk of moving.

Unfortunately, owners are often at cross-purposes with their leagues since it may be in the best interests of the leagues to have stable teams. Each owner knows that the sport is harmed by movement. Each owner knows that the owner of the team that is moving makes a great deal of money. As a result, it is in the communal best interests of sports that teams do not move around too much. However, it is in every individual owner's best interests to consider moving, to threaten to move, and sometimes to actually move. This is why baseball and football have ownership rules that require agreement of two-thirds to three-quarters of the other owners for a team to move or be sold. Though the owners of the Minnesota Twins, the Pittsburgh Pirates, and the Chicago White Sox threatened to move their baseball

teams, none have. In football, the owners have seen the money that others have made in moving. To keep the option open for themselves they have routinely approved other owners' moves.[2]

When teams relocate it is because the owners want to make more money. Some relocations lead to the need for new team mascots; new mascots mean vast increases in sales of shirts, hats, and other memorabilia. The Browns reaped such benefits when they moved to Baltimore and became the Ravens; and the Oilers did also when they moved to Nashville and became the Titans. Even teams that should have changed their mascots but did not reaped revenue from the sales of memorabilia. For instance, the Jazz moved from New Orleans to Utah, and the Lakers moved from Minneapolis to Los Angeles. Each move meant sales to a whole new set of fans in the new city.

Football teams usually move to gain stadiums with luxury boxes. Such boxes provide a significant source of extra revenue for a team. Though television contracts for football are admittedly large, the NFL spreads the revenue equally among the teams. The teams therefore get the same amount, whether they are in New York or Green Bay. Since the league's contract with the players dictates salary costs for all the teams, owners are left with small margins of profitability and a motivation to look for alternative sources of revenue. Luxury boxes make the difference. Because luxury box revenue is not shared between the teams the way ticket revenue is, potential revenue from such boxes has been enough of an incentive for the Rams to move from Los Angeles to St. Louis, enough for the Oilers to move from Houston to Nashville, enough for the Browns to move from Cleveland to Baltimore, and enough for the New England Patriots to nearly move from the Boston area to Hartford, Connecticut. Oddly enough, in each case, luxury boxes improved team finances enough to warrant movement from a larger metropolitan area to a smaller one.

To Win or to Profit

Some teams are worth very little where they are and would be worth much more if they moved. The Kansas City Royals and Minnesota Twins are two baseball teams that cannot simultaneously field consistently competitive clubs and make a profit. In baseball, team revenues are

---

[2]An exception to this was the refusal of the NFL to let the Seahawks move from Seattle to Los Angeles. This location was too lucrative to just let someone have. It will likely be the location of an expansion franchise, and all owners will get a cut of the franchise fee.

largely affected by local television deals. The Yankees' TV deal, for example, dwarfs that of the combined size of the Royals, the Twins, the Mariners, and a number of other "small-market" teams. The Royals were sold for $96 million in 1996 on the condition that the team not leave Kansas City for at least 10 years. Had the owners been able to at least threaten to move to another city, chances are good that they would have sold for many times $96 million. A move to someplace like Charlotte, Orlando, or another large, growing city would generate a lucrative local TV deal. It may be, however, that the only owner with sensitivity toward his city and the team's fans was the late Ewing Kaufman, whose will required that anyone who bought the team be required to keep it in Kansas City for a decade. For a prospective owner, nothing can be better than to be able to buy a struggling team for under $100 million and to sell it 10 years later for a half billion. This is probably a temptation that a living owner will not pass up, and, unless things change, the Kansas City Royals will go down in history with the Washington Senators, who moved and became the Texas Rangers, and the Seattle Pilots, who moved and became the Milwaukee Brewers.

This is not to say a small-market team cannot win. Some such teams will win if they construct a superior farm system and are lucky enough to see their players all mature at exactly the right time. This happened with the Royals in the late 1970s, with the Twins in the middle 1980s, and with the Mariners in the middle 1990s. Unfortunately, if a team is that lucky, free agency will limit the time that the team can win and remain profitable. The Braves, Yankees, and Dodgers will always be ready to buy up the talent as soon as the players are eligible for free agency. As further evidence of this problem, a special committee appointed by the commissioner of baseball noted that, from 1994 to 1999, no team whose payroll was in the bottom half of major league baseball won a playoff game.

Don't Feel Sorry for Them Just Yet

While it may be tempting to feel sorry for the "poor" owners who lose money each and every year on their franchises, you can probably leave the Kleenex in your pocket. As Tables 34.1 and 34.2 indicate, even though baseball and football franchises may claim to lose money each year, the return on their investment is still substantial. How? Because history suggests that the team will sell for substantially more than the owner paid for it. Economist Rodney D. Fort specializes in sports economics, even writing a textbook devoted to it. Having collected financial data on NFL and MLB franchises over the years, he has come to the conclusion that it is the capital gain that makes these investments truly valuable.

You might expect there to be high real rates of return on owning powerhouse franchises like the Yankees, Cardinals, and Dodgers in baseball and the Cowboys, Raiders, and Steelers in football. On the other hand, even baseball's lowly Royals and Expos, and football's futility champions Cardinals and Saints earned substantial

TABLE 34.1 Purchase prices, current values, and rates of return on selected major league baseball franchises.

Team	Purchase Price (Year)	*Forbes* Magazine 2003 Estimate of Value	Real Annual Rate of Return
New York Yankees	$10 million (1973)	$849 million	11%
St. Louis Cardinals	$3.75 million (1953)	$308 million	5
Los Angeles Dodgers	$347,000 (1944)	$449 million	9
Kansas City Royals	$96 million (1996)	$153 million	5
Montreal Expos	$50 million (1999)*	$113 million	20

*In 2003 MLB purchased the Expos for $120 million so as to be able to contract or move them. This was part of an agreement that allowed the former owner to buy the Florida Marlins.

Source: http://users.pullman.com/rodfort/PHSportsEcon/Common/OtherData/DataDirectory.html.

TABLE 34.2   Purchase prices, current values, and rates of return on selected national football league franchises.

Team	Purchase Price on Most Recent Sale	*Forbes* Magazine 2002 Estimate of Value	Real Annual Rate of Return
Pittsburgh Steelers	$2,500 (1933)	$555 million	15%
Dallas Cowboys	$150 million (1989)	$784 million	10
Oakland Raiders	$180,000 (1972)	$421 million	23
Phoenix Cardinals	$50,000 (1932)	$374 million	9
New Orleans Saints	$71 million (1985)	$481 million	8

Source: http://users.pullman.com/rodfort/PHSportsEcon/Common/OtherData/DataDirectory.html.

profits for their owners. For comparison, it should be noted that these real rates of return are better than typical alternatives. Specifically, real stock market returns average between 5 and 8 percent.

THE SPORTS LABOR MARKET

What Owners Will Pay

When we think about the market for talent in any sport we have to recognize that it is fundamentally no different from any other labor market. Firms will hire the marginal laborer as long as the contribution of the employee to revenue equals or exceeds the money that must be paid to that employee. This concept, called the **marginal revenue product of labor,** is im-

marginal revenue product of labor
The additional revenue generated from hiring an additional worker.

portant in any firm. In sports, the marginal revenue product of labor is the money that the team generates in revenue because a particular player is on the team. It would include any increase in revenue that results directly from their performance as well as all that revenue that results indirectly, say in the form of memorabilia sales, from the player being on the team. So a star may make a team win, which causes it to draw more fans. But the star's presence may also cause sales of team logo jerseys to increase. In deciding whether to sign a player to a large contract, therefore, an owner must decide whether the player is worth the money. If the player brings in at least as much in revenue to the team as the salary that the player commands, then the player is worth it.

What Players Will Accept

The issue for players is whether the pay they are offered to play for a team exceeds their next best offer. This next best offer is a player's **reservation wage.** It is the least that the player will sign for, because anything less makes an offer from some other team or some other job more desirable. Before the days of lucrative sports contracts, players quit their sports before they otherwise would have because their outside offers were better. Depending on the institutional structure of the sport, a player's reservation wage can be very high because he[3] will have offers from other teams, or it can be very low because the player is able to offer his services to only one team. In the latter case, the reservation wage is the next best job, but outside of the sport.

reservation wage
The least amount that a player will accept because it is the next best offer.

The pay that a player will end up getting will thus be between the most it can be, the marginal revenue product, and the least it can be, the reservation wage. This gap can be enormous.

THE VOCABULARY OF SPORTS ECONOMICS

Franchise owners, of course, spend their time attempting to increase revenues and fighting increases in expenditures. We have dealt with the revenue side and the luxury-box

---

[3]"He" is appropriate here as long as big money is associated only with men's professional team sports.

solution, but the expenditure side is stickier. The problem owners face is players who are **free agents.** It is increas-

free agent
A player who is able to offer services to the highest bidder.

ingly difficult to compete in the major sports without an ability to buy talent. Total revenue for the average "small-market" major league baseball team is between $30 million and $40 million. No team with a payroll under $48 million, however, was in the playoffs in 1998. The 1997 Florida Marlins lost millions winning the World Series and the owner proceeded to sell all of the team's high-salaried players the following year. Though this practice occurs most often in baseball, it is done in other sports as well. In basketball, for example, once Michael left the Bulls, the owner of the now Jordanless team traded, sold, or decided not to renew contracts on Pippen, Rodman, and a host of others. As a result,

draft
The process by which new talent is assigned to teams.

the Bulls became the first team to win a championship in basketball and follow that with a season in which they were eligible for the **draft** lottery.

The draft is a mechanism designed to provide competitive balance. By allowing teams that finished poorly to draft first, the leagues infuse the poorer teams with the best of the young talent. One problem with such a draft is that it motivates teams to play badly to vie for the first pick. This was the accusation in the NBA when, in hopes of getting Ralph Sampson with the first pick in the 1983 draft, the Houston Rockets played very badly. While never proven conclusively, the concern was they were playing badly intentionally. In 1985 the NBA created a system whereby the teams that did not make the playoffs were entered into a lottery. In 1990 the system was changed so that the chance of winning was higher for the poorer performing teams.[4]

It is difficult, if not impossible, for a team to win without great talent; and unless it manages to find that talent through the draft, it must bid for the talent of players who are free agents. With the single exception of the 1998 NBA lockout, the ultimate winners in labor negotiations during the last several years have been the players. Athletes have successfully negotiated for greater access to free markets for their talent. Free agency has driven average salaries up faster than revenues from TV or ticket sales so that today, a single player can make more in a

year (though only in nominal terms) than it cost to build Yankee Stadium in 1923.

Quite often today's owners must decide whether to make money or to win games. It is unfortunate that for more than a few teams, in more than a few sports, these are conflicting goals. Owners within each of the major sports have complained about their inability to turn a profit or to at least break even. Because only a few players are on the free agent market each year and because many teams consider themselves just a few wins short of either contending for the playoffs, or better, winning a championship, the price that players are able to command is quite high.

Sports franchise owners have attempted to institute

salary cap
The maximum in total payroll that a team can pay its players.

salary caps in order to protect themselves from themselves. That is, they want to protect themselves from being tempted to bid against one another. Other than baseball, each major professional team sport has some form of salary cap in place. The owners hope to lessen their costs at the expense of players by limiting the amount of money they can bid against each other for talent. Sometimes it is not in the best interests of the owners to have strict salary caps. During the 1980s the NBA allowed teams to have one player's salary not count against the cap as long as any further signings were done at the minimum. This rule, called the Larry Bird exemption, was instituted so that teams could keep a marquee player.

Another avenue for allowing small-market teams to succeed is to put into place a general sharing of revenues, or at least a sharing of the television revenues. Since foot-

revenue sharing
The process by which some revenues are distributed to all teams rather than simply the teams that generate them.

ball does **revenue sharing** well and baseball does not, you would expect a more fluid mix of winners and losers in football than in baseball. That is in fact what we saw in the 1990s. Two baseball teams dominated the decade, the Atlanta Braves and the New York Yankees, both of which had a "local" television market via cable that was, in fact, thoroughly national. Neither, of course, shared the revenue it got with the other baseball teams, and this gave them an absurd advantage in bidding for high-priced talent.

In a simpler time sports were games played by men who were happy to be paid at all. Owners were happy to oblige them by hardly paying them at all. There were no women's professional leagues and no laws requiring high schools and colleges to fund women's athletics. Without a doubt there was grumbling among players about their pay, but not until 1977 did business considerations come

---

[4]Specifically, of the 29 teams in the NBA, 13 do not make the playoffs and are in the lottery as a result. Like the lotto, each team's logo is printed on Ping-Pong balls. A team has one ball plus one for each team they were behind in the race to the playoffs. Thus the worst team in the league has 13 of the 91 balls in the hopper. As a result, their probability of getting the first pick is 14.3 out of 100.

into play. In that year baseball had an epiphany. An arbitrator declared two players free agents and the sport was forever changed. Within a few years other sports also gained forms of free agency and players who had had virtually no right to the economic benefits of the free competitive market began to get rich.

Prior to 1977 all players in all team sports were bound to the team they played for the previous year. Having this

reserve clause
A contract clause that requires that players resign with the team to which they belonged the previous year.

so-called **reserve clause** in contracts meant that the only choice players had was to either play for what the owner offered or retire. Whereas star players in their later years had the sort of leverage that was afforded by the support of public opinion, lesser players did not. Even when Joe DiMaggio, considered by many the best right-handed hitter of all time, held out for a better contract by going home to San Francisco to open a restaurant, he ultimately came back to the Yankees for much less than he was worth. Going back to our discussion on the reservation wage, with the reserve clause in place, the reservation wage for players bound by it was very low.

From 1977 on, each sport has engaged in collective bargaining agreements that have given players more and more freedom of movement and contracts that are much more lucrative in terms of salaries and incentives. These agreements usually require teams to pay a minimum salary. The lowest minimum salary in the big-money sports is the $100,000 per season in hockey. The highest is the more than $250,000 per season in basketball. In each sport players are bound to the team they played for the previous year for a period of time that ranges from four to six years, depending on the sport. These collective bargaining agreements have decidedly raised the reservation wage of players with the requisite experience to have earned free agency. For free agents, the reservation wage is the next best offer from another team. That is usually very close to their marginal revenue product.

Thus free agency and other aspects of collective bargaining agreements have raised average salaries in all sports far faster than inflation. Though there is dispute among economists as to how much credit for this change goes to free agency, in some sports, average salaries have increased more than tenfold in 20 years. This increase may be attributed to an increase in the marginal revenue product of players, which has come about in part because the sports are more popular, they draw larger gates and television audiences, and sales of memorabilia have grown. For

whatever reason, consider this: In the 1920s Babe Ruth became the first player to earn more than the president. Before the 2001 governmental pay hike, the major league baseball minimum salary exceeded the president's.

Of course when you change a system, good and bad outcomes ensue. Along with higher

strike
An action by labor to deny employers the services of the employees.

pay and benefits for players arrived at through collective bargaining agreements, professional sports has had to endure **strikes** and **lockouts.** Each sport has lost

lockout
An action by employers to deny employees access to their jobs.

at least part of a season to this sort of work stoppage. A strike, a refusal by the players to work, is usually voted for when the players want something in a new contract that is quite different from the status quo. A lockout, a refusal by the owners to let the players work, is usually instituted when the owners want to make extensive changes in existing contracts.

Baseball owners have tried other avenues to get around the competitive nature of bidding on free agents. After 1986 baseball free agents found that owners were no longer willing to bid on their services. The change was so abrupt that it caught many off-guard. Subsequently, players began to suspect that it could only have resulted from the collusion of the owners not to bid on each other's players. In 1987 the first case went to an arbitration. The owners offered the "How could we possibly collude?" defense, arguing that such an arrangement would have been impossible to enforce among themselves. It was not lost on millions of baseball fans or the arbitrator that, in a different era, a different set of owners had managed to collude to keep blacks and Hispanics from the game until 1946. Various arbitrators found that baseball owners had in fact colluded and were ordered to pay $280 million in damages.

What differentiates team sports like baseball, football, hockey, and basketball from individual sports like golf and tennis is that individual sports have no "owners" with whom to negotiate. Players can make as much as they want. They just have to win.

One problem with team sports is that it is under the control of a small number of self-serving owners. They pay the talented players. Unfortunately, anytime only a few bosses bid on talent, the bosses are usually satisfied, and the talent usually grumbles. In golf and tennis there are no owners, so golfers and tennis players never grumble. They accept the direct relationship that exists between winning and income. While I am a fan of

The National Hockey League's 2004–2005 Lockout

In 2004–2005 the National Hockey League became the first sports league to lose an entire season to a work stoppage. The NHL owners chose to lock out the players after negotiations failed to produce an agreement to lower salaries. The players refused an owner demand that the league adopt a salary cap that would have cut players' salaries by 30 percent. In the end, after a completely lost season, the owners got almost exactly what they wanted. This stands with a football strike in the 1980s and a basketball strike in the 1990s as the only cases in sports history in which owners unambiguously won a labor dispute.

many sports, auto racing, and, in particular, National Association of Stock Car Auto Racing (NASCAR),[5] is interesting to me as an economist. It is something like golf and tennis in that individual achievement is vital. It is also something like team sports in that an individual driver must rely on a host of others doing their jobs. In auto racing there are so many different owners and so many different drivers that something like perfect competition exists. Moreover, there is easy entrance and exit from the market because anybody with sufficient capital can start a new team and attempt to qualify for major events like the Daytona 500 or Indianapolis 500. Additionally, there are enough buyers and sellers of talent that the prices arrived at for talent seem fair to all concerned. The only issue that could upset this balance would be if NASCAR, Championship Auto Racing Teams (CART), Indy Racing League (IRL) or Formula 1[6] got so lax with safety that drivers were forced to band together to fix a problem. Thus they would become adversaries instead of part-

ners with the owners and sponsors.[7] Unless something like this happens, racing will probably remain an example of how, under perfect competition, all parties get what they are worth and are worth what they get.

What a Monopoly Will Do for You

Motor sports offers an interesting lesson in the power of monopoly. Three of the major series (NASCAR, the IRL, and Formula 1) are owned by a single person or family. The France family, the Hulman-George family, and Bernie Ecclestone control their respective series with iron fists. Moreover, many of the venues in which the series operate are owned by these people as well. To the never-ending frustration of the track owners who attempt to host races at other sites, these series owners control the destiny of their sport to a degree that no baseball or football owner can imagine.

The IRL, which has all but driven its principal competitor (CART) out of business, is owned by the family that controls the Indianapolis Motor Speedway. In 2002, excepting a race in Denver, CART's total attendance was less than that of the Indy 500. From the time when the two series split in 1996, the IRL has been able to use the family-owned Indy 500 to bully CART and television networks.

The France family, which owns several tracks (including a track outside Miami, Florida), has driven the owner of the Texas Motor Speedway nuts in his appeals for a second race. The Miami race, held in November, has never been able to draw more than 75,000, while the March Texas race consistently draws more than 200,000. In 2003 the family announced a schedule that grants southern California a second race. Not coincidentally, the family owns an interest in that track as well.

Formula 1 racing has rarely been able to maintain the same race schedule two years in a row. The problem here is that the owner, Bernie Ecclestone, requires such a high advance fee to hold a race in a particular location, that promoters cannot afford to build a fan base for this worldwide form of racing.

As in all economics, market power, and especially monopoly power, determines who the winners and losers are.

---

[5]NASCAR is the governing body of the most notable of several stock car racing circuits. Stock cars are called "stock" because they look vaguely like regular passenger cars that you can buy at your local dealer.

[6]The IRL and CART are competing leagues for cars that you see running the Indianapolis 500. Formula 1 is an international racing circuit with cars that are similar in shape to the IRL and CART cars but that go much faster.

[7]This happened in NASCAR when the speedway at Talladega, Alabama, opened. Speeds were so great that many blowing tires were causing life-threatening crashes. It also was threatened in the 2000 NASCAR season when two drivers died nine weeks apart at the New Hampshire International Speedway. In the latter case NASCAR partially acquiesced by using devices to slow the cars.

Summary

You now understand how economic principles can be applied to the issues of sports. In particular you understand that, despite the obvious attempts of cities to acquire franchises through expansion and by luring others, there is no economic evidence to suggest that having a franchise enhances a city's economic stature. You understand that owners are not only on the opposite side of this particular bargain, they also face a problem of their own. They must negotiate with players; if they are doing so in a small market, they must often decide whether they wish to make money or win. Last, you now understand the basics of sports labor economics history and the vocabulary that is central to it.

Key Terms

draft, 359
free agent, 359
local substitution, 355
lockout, 360

marginal revenue product of labor, 358
positive externalities, 355
reservation wage, 358

reserve clause, 360
revenue sharing, 359
salary cap, 359
strike, 360

Quiz Yourself

1. The value of a sports franchise to a city's economy depends greatly on
   a. The sale of memorabilia to citizens.
   b. The degree to which non-ticket-based sales increase.
   c. The degree to which restaurant revenues rise.
   d. The degree to which noncitizens spend money in the city.

2. Most baseball franchises have _____ over the years while the sale price of the typical team has _____.
   a. Made a profit; fallen.
   b. Lost money; fallen.
   c. Made a profit; risen.
   d. Lost money; risen.

3. The typical problem for generating parity in sports leagues is that
   a. There is no mechanism for bringing in new talent in a way that helps the bad teams.
   b. There is no means by which players on one team can move to another.
   c. With no salary cap and with unlimited free agency, big city, high-revenue teams have an advantage.
   d. No one wants it.

4. The motorsports industry is dominated by independent teams running in series operated as
   a. Monopolies.
   b. Oligopolies.
   c. Monopolistic competitors.
   d. Perfect competitors.

5. Economists note that a reason exists for policy makers to subsidize sports stadiums and it is that
   a. They bring in billions of dollars to their communities.
   b. They result in large increases in city payrolls.
   c. They result in enormous increases in taxes.
   d. The teams make people happy; even those that don't go to the games.

6. When the National Hockey League had its 2004–2005 work stoppage, it was
   a. A Player strike over salaries that were too low.
   b. A Player strike over a limited ability to move to another team.
   c. An owner lockout over reducing salaries.
   d. An owner lockout over union work rules.

Think about This

Formula 1 may never compete again in the United States as a result of a problem with tires at the Indianapolis Motor Speedway. Michelin's tire was simply too dangerous for the teams to safely run the 2005 U.S Grand Prix. Because there are two competing tire companies supplying tires to competitor teams, neither would agree to the other's posed solutions. This would never happen in NASCAR or the IRL because they use only one tire manufacturer. Once a problem was identified it would have been in everyone's interest to find a solution. What does this tell you about the benefits and costs of oligopoly over monopoly?

Talk about This

The Indianapolis Colts used an implied threat to move as a means by which to induce the state of Indiana and the city of Indianapolis to build them a new stadium. This is somewhat ironic since the same family used the fact that Indianapolis built them a stadium in the 1980s to leave Baltimore. To what degree are the combined threats by owners to leave their respective cities a conspiracy?

For More Insight See

Kahn, Lawrence M., "The Sports Business as a Labor Market Laboratory," *Journal of Economic Perspectives* 14, no. 3 (Summer 2000).

Sheehan, Richard, *Keeping Score: The Economics of Big-Time Sports* (South Bend, IN: Diamond Communications, 1996).

Siegfried, John, and Andrew Zimbalist, "The Economics of Sports Facilities and Their Communities," *Journal of Economic Perspectives* 14, no. 3 (Summer 2000).

Chapter **35**

The Stock Market and Crashes

Traders and clerks work the floor of the Chicago Mercantile Exchange. *Source: Tim Boyle/Getty Images*

Chapter Objectives

After reading this chapter you should be able to

Understand how stock prices are determined and what stock markets do.

Know the fundamental elements of stock prices and understand how prices can get out of line with their fundamental value.

See these issues at work in the technology-laden NASDAQ in 2000.

See that bankruptcy is an important feature in corporate business but that many of the bankruptcies of 2001 and 2002 involved a level of deception on the part of their accountants that was potentially quite damaging.

Chapter Outline

Stock Prices

Efficient Markets

Stock Market Crashes

The Accounting Scandals of 2001 and 2002

Summary

Even to many of the people who invest in it, the stock market is a mystery. Investors buy stocks, that is, shares of the value of a company. As stockholders they have the right to vote in shareholders' meetings and a right to a pro-rated share of dividends. The questions of what makes the prices of stocks go up and down in general and why prices actually soar or plummet on any particular day have perplexed both stockholders and economists for many years.

Figures 35.1, 35.2, and 35.3 show the values of three important measures of the stock market. You can see that each has grown over time, and though each saw a major dip in 2000 and 2001, that dip was small, given the substantial

FIGURE 35.1   The Dow Jones Industrial Average, 1896–2004.

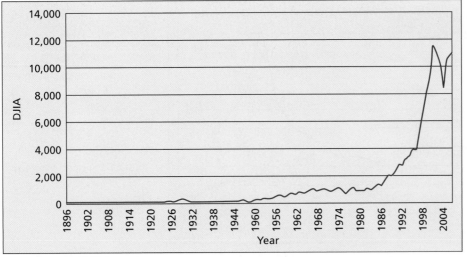

Source: http://www.globalfindata.com/.

FIGURE 35.2   Standard and Poor's 500, 1870–2004.

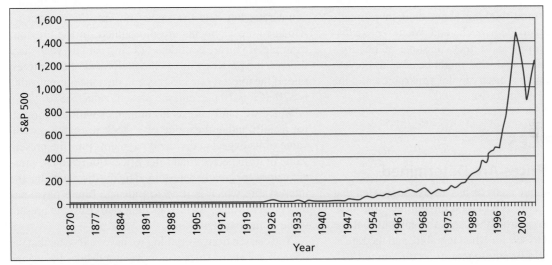

Source: http://www.globalfindata.com/.

runs of the previous 20 years. Looking back through time you will also see that in August 1982, for instance, the Dow Jones Industrial Average stood at less than 800 points. By December of that year it was over 1,300, a figure that showed the price of stocks in general had risen significantly. What could cause stocks to go up by more than 50 percent in four months? Even more perplexing was the 1987 stock market crash. In one day the stock market lost nearly 20 percent of its value. Assuming that the price of a share of stock does, in fact, represent the value of that share of the company in question, how can the value of anything change so fast?

The ultimate question of what actually determines stock market prices is the focus of this chapter. We explore what traditional economic theory has to say on the subject of how stock prices are determined. We discuss how a stock market can advance economic growth by helping to transfer financial capital into the hands of

FIGURE 35.3   NASDAQ Composite Index, 1980–2004.

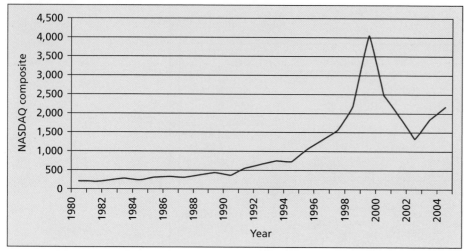

Source: http://bigcharts.marketwatch.com.

the people who can use it best. We show that if a stock market is "efficient," small investors—investors who invest relatively small amounts of money—do not need to take a lot of time thinking about their investments because it will not do them much good. We move to a discussion of the causes and effects of some of history's stock market crashes and what might be done to prevent them. We finish with a discussion of bankruptcy and the accounting scandals of 2001 and 2002.

STOCK PRICES

How Stock Prices Are Determined

Traditional economic analysis has always suggested that the value of any asset is based on three things: the flow of returns that come from the asset, the amount that the asset is expected to sell for when it is sold, and the rate at which the future flow of those returns is "discounted." To compute the value of a stock, we add up payments that come in at different times. To put those payments on an even playing field, we use the concept of present value that we introduced in Chapter 7.

Although the math for computing present value is somewhat complicated, the concept is not hard to understand. If there are 1 million shares of a company and the company profits are exactly $1 million, then the earnings per share is exactly $1. How much would you pay for a share of stock that would yield earnings of $1/year forever? What it is worth is the present value of that $1 each

year. Recall that you learned in Chapter 7 that one of the components of present value is the interest rate. Sometimes we change the jargon a bit and refer to it as the discount rate, but it is the same concept: the amount by which future payments are discounted. In the previous example, if you are confident of being paid $1/year/share forever, the present value is the reciprocal of the interest rate. If the interest rate is 5 percent, then the present value is $20. If it is 10 percent, the present value is $10.

Since we rarely act as if companies will last forever, we usually judge the value of a stock to be the present value of its expected dividend payments plus the present value of its expected final sales price. Both of these present values are greatly determined by the discount rate, the interest rate which is used to translate future payments into present value. As the discount rate rises, the present value of the payments falls.

You can see from everything we have said so far that the price of a share of stock can move as a result of a change in any of the three variables. A change in the profit expectations will change both dividend expectations and final sale price expectations. These in turn will change the price of the stock. A change in interest rates will also change the stock price. In the end, though, the ultimate long-term value of a stock is determined by its profit expectations and the interest rate. These are known as **fundamentals,** elements that go into a stock's price that make long-term economic sense.

fundamentals
Elements that determine stock prices that make long-term economic sense—profit expectations and interest rates.

What Stock Markets Do

Stock markets exist as an efficient way of getting available financial capital to whichever investors can make the best use of that financial capital. Stock markets set share prices, thereby providing investors information about which companies are doing well and which are not. Stock markets allow firms that need new influxes of money to get what they need, and they allow investors to invest their money in places that provide good returns.

Though most of the shares traded on any particular day are stock issued many years before, an important function of a stock market is to support new companies with investors' funds. When a company sells stock for the first time in an attempt to raise money for expansion, this

initial public offering (IPO)

initial public offering (IPO)
A company's first sale of stock to the public in an attempt to raise money for expansion.

turns what is typically a small, privately held firm into one that now has stockholders, issues dividends, and has a board of directors.[1] It allows companies to grow far beyond what owners can borrow or otherwise raise themselves. Though such firms can incorporate and sell stock among a limited number of people,[2] an IPO opens up the possibility that an unlimited number of people, or even other corporations, can become its investors.

For stocks that are not IPOs, the market has two effects. First, it has the effect of spreading risk equally across all stocks to all stockholders. In economic terms, it equalizes the risk-adjusted rates of return across investments. If one company is going to yield a return on equity that is greater than another, the market price of the share of stock of the better company will rise until the return is equal to any new investors. In this way the stock market provides a way of signaling value to all future investors.

An additional important effect of the non-IPO market is that it provides liquidity to those shares of stock that were previously issued. IPOs only have value when their owners know that they can sell them if they wish to turn their investments into cash. Without a market for previously issued securities, it would be overly costly to issue new ones.

[1]Sometimes IPOs are not so small. When AT&T spun off its hardware division, Lucent, that IPO was very large.
[2]Such an entity is called an S-corporation.

EFFICIENT MARKETS

A market is labeled **efficient** by economists if all available information is accounted for in the market. For instance, if markets are efficient, the price of a share of stock will encapsulate everything that investors know about that stock. If investors are concerned that a product that a company sells is likely to generate cumbersome lawsuits, for example, the market price will fall by the value that the market places on the uncertainty it is feeling about the company and on the expected legal exposure.

efficient market
All information is taken into account by participants in a market.

What this "efficient market hypothesis" means for everyday investors is that they do not have to worry about outsmarting the market. The Wall Street gurus who spend every waking minute looking for new information on the market will bid prices up and down in appropriate ways as new information on profits, risks, and interest rates comes in. Since all of that information will be absorbed into the market long before most other investors find out about it, most other investors cannot take advantage of it. As unlikely as it may seem, new investors can simply invest in whatever they like, knowing that the chances are good that anything they pick will have the same chances of doing as well as anything else a professional outside Wall Street might pick.

While maintaining a diverse portfolio of investments is less risky than picking a specific stock, investors do not always have enough money to buy a variety of different stocks. Such investors can avail themselves of index funds, which buy stocks in exact proportion to their value in a commonly known **stock index,** like the Dow Jones Industrial, Standard and Poor's, and NASDAQ (see Figures 35.1 to 35.3). Since a stock index is simply a weighted average of stock prices in a particular group, buying shares of an index fund provides diversity and an expected return that is on a par with any other investment involving similar risk.

stock index
A weighted average of stock prices in a particular group.

The best evidence that markets are efficient is the stories you hear about how well monkeys do when picking stocks. Newspapers often compare the hypothetical monetary returns earned from a monkey's random choices with the returns generated by professional investors. Unhappily for the professionals, monkeys have been known to hold their own.

STOCK MARKET CRASHES

The American stock market "crashed" twice in the 20th century, once in October 1929 and again in October 1987. In both cases a loss of at least 25 percent of the stock market's total value was experienced in a matter of days. The real question that economists who believe that stock markets are rational have to answer is this: Is it possible that expectations of things that are fundamental can change for everyone simultaneously and by amounts necessary to change stock prices that much?

If the answer to that question is "no," that things that are fundamental cannot change that much or that fast, then the stock market is not much more socially useful than a casino. On the other hand, if you can explain everything that goes on in a stock market in terms of changes in fundamental economic variables, then, as we explained before, the stock market is socially useful.

Bubbles

It is crucial for us to know how a stock market, or how any market for anything else, crashes. If people invest their savings for retirement, college, or anything else, and their investments are going to be subject to wild swings, then it is important to know whether increases in stock prices happen because of increases in value or because of what economists call **bubbles.** A bubble of any kind grows slowly and looks very nice while it exists, but, when bubbles break, they break fast and ugly. The metaphor of a bubble is often used to describe an asset market that grows beyond all economic reason.

bubble

The state of a market where the current price is far above its value determined by fundamentals.

The two fundamentals that go into the formula for the value of an asset are the flow of payments it produces and the interest rate. The price of a stock can change a great deal if either of these changes a great deal. Economists are not overly concerned about this, and their lack of concern becomes justified when the stock prices of companies that are believed to generate losses in the short run and great profits in later years vary quite a bit with a change in interest rates. This variability does not bother economists much even if the stock price can change by a large percentage in a short time. The expected flow of payments, or profits, also is not likely to change quickly enough to change the price of the stock greatly or quickly.

The main source of crashes and the bursting bubbles is more likely to be abrupt changes in the sale price that is projected for the future. This is especially true if our expectations of future prices are based, at least in part, on current prices. For instance, because today's price is $90, you may think the price next year will be $100. If the price today were $80, you might expect that the future price might be $90, and so on.

The bubble bursts when a stock price falls and you think this indicates that it will be worth less next year. That makes you think that its value today is lessened. Now you start thinking that its value will be even less next year, and its current value becomes even less in your mind. This vicious cycle spirals the value of the stock down, and it can all happen very fast. As we discussed earlier, nearly every stock in the world lost in the neighborhood of 25 percent of its value within hours of the start of the October 1987 crash.

If stock market crashes had no impacts other than hurting some of the investors who hung on too long, there would be no issue of concern. The problem is that stock market crashes have real impacts on average families. When stocks are doing very well, people feel richer, and they are richer. They do not have to save as much because their previous savings are doing so well. As a result, they feel comfortable buying new homes, cars, major appliances, and furniture that they would not have purchased if things were not as good.

Homes, cars, appliances, and furniture are all goods that have to be made by industry, and industry runs on its workers. When the demand for their labor is high, workers get more hours, better pay, and a host of other benefits. With better pay, workers are richer, and they buy more and more. This is an economically virtuous cycle in which good times create more good times. A good stock market causes a good economy and a good economy fosters an even better stock market. Unfortunately, we cannot avoid the reality that what goes up can also come down. When the stock market falls, people lose wealth, and they then buy fewer goods. Stock values fall even lower; consumption drops even further.

The doldrums within Japan's stock market lasted for all of the decade of the 1990s. Japan's equivalent to the Dow Jones Industrial Average, the Nikkei Index, remained depressed during a time in which the American stock market values tripled. The virtuous cycle that existed in the United States during the 1990s and the vicious cycle that existed in Japan during the same period give testimony to two important conclusions: (1) a stock

FIGURE 35.4   NASDAQ Composite Index, 1999–2003.

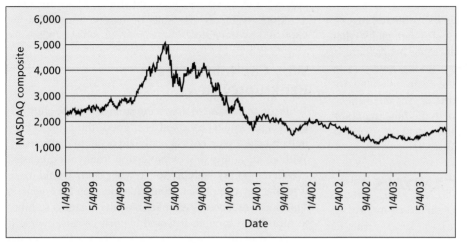

Source: http://moneycentral.msn.com.

market's health influences the rest of the economy and (2) stock prices can rise and fall very quickly.

Example of a Crash: NASDAQ 2000

In 1999 the NASDAQ (National Association of Securities Dealers Automated Quotations) increased 84 percent from 2,208 to 4,069 on the back of a technology sector that seemed to grow without bound. By March 10, 2000, the NASDAQ was above 5,000. That same index reached a low of 2,340 on December 21, 2000, for a 53 percent fall from its peak (see Figure 35.4).[3] What happened?

There are a number of explanations. Some of them revolve around our notion of the bubble while others are more fundamental. The technology sector in general, and some of the hottest companies in particular, were operating with staggering losses while being touted as leaders of the "new economy." As a matter of fact, for the dot-coms, making a profit was a sign of "stagnant thinking." New-economy thinking led firms to plow everything they made into improving name recognition and market share. To this end, the 1999 and 2000 Super Bowl broadcasts were filled with elaborate multimillion-dollar-per-minute dot-com ads.

Expectations for these companies were such that losses now would be more than made up for with massive profits later. If you do the math, and we will avoid that here, you will see that anytime you have losses early on

and profits much later, the net present value of this investment can change quite rapidly with reasonably small changes in interest rates or profit expectations.

To see this, take a hypothetical dot-com that is expected to lose $1 per share for 10 years and then make $5 per share thereafter. If the appropriate interest rate on a comparably risky investment is 10 percent, then, using the fundamentals, the stock would be worth $14.44. If you increase the interest rate to 11 percent, the stock's value would drop to $11.23. A 10 percent increase (1 percentage point) in the interest rate would translate to a 22 percent drop in the value of the stock. If the expected profit to the company had been spread out evenly throughout the lifetime of a company of equal value, an increase in the interest rate of 1 percentage point would only decrease the value of the stock to $13.13. Thus one explanation of the drop in the NASDAQ is that interest rates rose during the period.

A second explanation of the drop in the NASDAQ is diminished profit expectations. Again, because the profits were expected to come much later in the process, small changes had large effects. Continuing with our hypothetical dot-com, a drop in profit expectations to $4 per share, even keeping interest rates constant at 10 percent, would drop the value of the share of stock to $10.22. Thus a 20 percent drop in profit expectations drops the share price 29 percent.

The final explanation for the 1999 run-up and the 2000–2001 tumble is the bubble explanation. Recall that a bubble is the metaphor for an asset whose value has stretched far beyond its fundamental value, based

[3]It later fell below 1,500 as a result of the September 11, 2001, terrorist attacks. It had not recovered beyond its early 1999 level through 2003.

on the notion that expected increases in the asset price are self-fulfilling. Whether the NASDAQ in March 2000 was in a bubble state is in some dispute because of the aforementioned changes in fundamentals that occurred during the period. On the other hand, there is little doubt that the buying frenzy among investors in 1999 and early 2000 was fed by the desire by many not to be left out of "the next Microsoft" or "the next Intel." Thus, if people buy without regard to the fundamentals, a bubble is created, and when fundamentals are reexamined, bubbles burst.

THE ACCOUNTING SCANDALS OF 2001 AND 2002

In the aftermath of the September 11, 2001, attacks on New York City's World Trade Center buildings and the recession of 2001, the Enron Corporation declared bankruptcy. Enron, the United States' seventh-largest corporation in terms of revenue, declared **bankruptcy,** owing more than $5 billion and lacking the ability to pay the interest on that debt. Companies or individuals declare bankruptcy when they lack the necessary funds to pay their **creditors.** While Kmart and Global Crossing also declared bankruptcy during the same period of time, the Enron bankruptcy made far more news. Why? Kmart served many more customers, and Global Crossing was more in debt ($12 billion), but Enron's demise was potentially far more damaging.

bankruptcy
A legal status entered into when a company or individual cannot pay its debt.

creditors
The people or institutions to which a company or individual owes money.

Bankruptcy

When a corporation cannot pay its creditors, it must either renegotiate the repayment schedule that it has with its creditors or it must declare bankruptcy. When a company declares bankruptcy, it has two choices: It can try to reorganize and go forward or it can simply give up. The former, called Chapter 11 bankruptcy, protects a company from its creditors so as to give the company time to get its financial affairs back on track. The latter, called Chapter 13 bankruptcy, lets the company sell off its assets in an orderly fashion so as to preserve as much value as possible for the last-in-line stock holders. Nearly every case of corporate bankruptcy you hear on the news is of the Chapter 11 variety.

When a company declares bankruptcy, a judge is appointed to oversee its financial affairs. Major financial decisions, such as the sale of assets, must first be approved by the judge.

Why Capitalism Needs Bankruptcy Laws

While on the surface it may seem strange that the ability to avoid debts would be viewed as a "good" thing, under capitalism bankruptcy laws actually aid economic efficiency. Without the ability to seek protection from your creditors, even a temporary inability to pay your debts would make it so that any one of them could foreclose on the business. This could reduce or even eliminate the business's ability to turn things around. It would happen because, while it would be in the collective interest of the creditors for the company to get back on its feet, it would be in their individual interest to be the first in line to get their money back.

Suppose, for example, that a company owes money to three different banks. Suppose, too, that the company has insufficient funds to pay these creditors this year but that, given the chance, it can probably make enough money over the next few years to pay them what it owes. Further suppose that if the company sells its assets, it can pay what it owes to only two of the three banks. Without the protection of Chapter 11 bankruptcy, it would be in the interests of each of the banks individually to foreclose because each would not want to be the one bank that wasn't paid. In an apparent contradiction, it might easily also be in the banks' interests for the company to be allowed to continue without anyone foreclosing. Bankruptcy laws enable firms to continue under judicial supervision and afford all concerned the hope that they will pay off their debts.

The Kmart and Global Crossing Cases

When Kmart and Global Crossing filed for Chapter 11 bankruptcy in 2002, economists found the reasons to be familiar and not all that troubling. Kmart, in the middle of a discount store sandwich with Wal-Mart and Target, went bankrupt because it was not able to discount as deeply as Wal-Mart, nor was it able to market to upscale consumers as effectively as Target. Global Crossing took a gigantic gamble borrowing billions to string fiber-optic cable under the oceans, connecting Europe, Asia, and North America with Internet-friendly broadband connections.

Bankruptcies like these do not trouble economists in the way they appear to disturb people in the press, bankers, and shareholders. Economists hold that when companies get outcompeted, it's right that they lose money. Further, when they do it long enough, they should go out of business. They maintain that capitalism works only when the promise of profit is countered by the threat of bankruptcy. Incompetence and risky business decisions that turn out badly must have consequences, and in the cases of Kmart and Global Crossing this is exactly what happened. Kmart suffered from management and marketing strategies that were not up to those of the competition. Global Crossing operated on the premise that intercontinental bandwidth would be a hot commodity, and it used debt to finance its decision. AT&T, which is in the same market and raised its money with sales of stock and reinvested profits, also made little money in this market. It survived because its losses resulted only in disappointing earnings to stockholders. Global Crossing, on the other hand, could not generate enough profit to pay the interest on its $12 billion debt.

Both Kmart and Global Crossing declared bankruptcy even though they possessed more in assets than they owed their creditors. Kmart had $16 billion in assets and $2 billion in debts while Global Crossing had $22 billion in assets and $12 billion in debts. There were two problems, though: The assets were listed at book value rather than market value, and the assets were not such that they were producing revenue.

Two examples may illustrate the problem. When Kmart builds a store and outfits it with the Kmart logo and colors, it may cost $10 million, but there is no one who will pay $10 million for it after it is built. Similarly, it may have cost Global Crossing $20 billion to lay fiber-optic cable from one end of the ocean to another, but that by no means suggests that anyone will buy it from Global Crossing for that amount of money.

To illustrate further the circumstance in which there are many assets and no revenue from those assets with which to pay creditors, suppose someone is worth $5 billion and borrows $10 billion to buy gold coins. The person has an asset worth $10 billion but has no revenue coming in to pay the interest on the debt. Now suppose the person takes those coins and drops them one by one in the ocean between New York and London. Our hypothetical person now has $15 billion in assets on his or her books, but the coins that are apparently worth $10 billion may actually be worth next to nothing. There is genuinely $10 billion worth of debt with no revenue in sight to pay for the interest that is accruing on it.

What Happened in the Enron Case

Usually it is not that difficult to say what a business does. Wal-Mart, for example, is a discount retailer; GM makes cars; and State Farm sells insurance. To get a handle on what happened in the Enron case, you have to understand Enron's actual business activities. What does Enron do to make money? It is an energy trading company. It buys electricity, oil, natural gas, gasoline, and other energy sources from producers, with the intent of reselling them to industrial companies and utilities. It makes money by "buying low and selling high." It did this rather well for several years during the 1990s. Later it started getting into sideline businesses such as the buying and selling of bandwidth for the Internet.

"Buying low and selling high" is always good business practice, but it is hard to sustain because economic profit always induces entry (i.e., new competition), especially when there are few barriers. Enron had few competitors in this industry in the early 1990s, but when other companies saw that profits were achievable in this arena, they jumped in. With no barriers against getting into the arena, Dynegy Inc., Reliant Energy, El Paso Energy, Duke Energy North American, and Calpine Corp. joined the competition, and they raided Enron for valued employees who knew the game. Had this been the end of the story, there would not have been much of a story at all. It would have been the typical "company has idea, milks it for as long as it can, and then settles in for a run of normal profits."

What happened with Enron was that its management wanted to keep things going and its executives were paid almost exclusively in stock and stock options. One of the classic problems in corporate capitalism is called the

principal–agent problem

The problem that occurs when the owner of an asset and the manager of that asset are different and have different preferences.

principal–agent problem, a problem that occurs when the owners of the company (the shareholders) are motivated by long-term profitability for the company and the managers are motivated by monetary gain for themselves. When chief executive officers (CEOs) are paid high salaries, they may avoid potentially lucrative business avenues that might be accompanied by some level of risk. The problem is that the agent, in this case the CEO, is not making decisions consistent with the principals', in this case the stockholders', wishes. The primary concern in this example of the principal–agent problem is that salaried CEOs will avoid risking their jobs and will err on the side of caution.

For years it has been taken on faith that the best way for stockholders to get the CEO to do their bidding was to tie the CEO's compensation to stock performance. One version of this has the CEO paid only in stock. Thus, when stock prices are low the CEO is paid less than when the stock price is high.

An extreme version of this scheme is in place when management is paid in stock options. Stock options are authorizations that allow those who hold them to buy a specific number of shares of stock at the price stated on the option. They are enormously valuable when the stock price is above the option price but have no value when the underlying stock price is below the option price. Enron's compensation package for its managers was a combination of stocks and options.

Enron's management compensation was thus tied to stock performance, and in the eyes of Enron shareholders, this was good. Their perception was that management decisions that affected the company in good ways were rewarded while those that affected the company in bad ways were punished. It unfortunately also put management in a position such that if it could deceive the *markets* into thinking that it was doing better than it actually was, then management could enrich itself. This is not new. This is the primary reason why accounting firms exist. They are supposed to guard against such deception by going over the corporate financial statements of the companies they audit so as to certify to the public that when a company says it earned $1 billion, it actually did.

Enron's deception took the form of high-debt, off-the-books gambles. Enron created several subsidiaries, named, for whatever reason, for "Star Wars" characters, and it saddled each with millions in debt. Each subsidiary had a high-risk, high-return niche market. None of this would be interesting except for the fact that the debt of these firms was secured by assets of the larger corporation. That in turn would not be interesting except that this debt was deceptively noted in Enron financial statements.

Enron would state that it was owed money by other companies; it would report this as an asset but would not mention that it was also a debt. Even more troubling, the smaller subsidiaries would borrow from banks to pay Enron the interest, thus raising Enron's reported profits. In the final analysis, Enron was overstating its profits by $1.2 billion and its assets by even more.

When the whole thing collapsed in the fall of 2001, there were two fatally wounded companies: Enron and its accounting firm, Arthur Andersen. Andersen had certified Enron's books to be accurate when they demonstrably were not. It had participated in the creation of the subsidiaries and had gone along with the attempt to cover things up by issuing a reminder to employees working on the Enron account to shred "unneeded" documents. Though this "reminder" was technically a simple restate-

ment of company policy, everyone at Andersen who worked on the Enron case knew that it meant to shred the evidence. Why would an accounting firm participate in such fraud? It again boils down to the principal–agent problem. The lead accountant in any firm wants to please his or her clients. The clients pay the firms millions in fees per year for which the lead accountants are handsomely rewarded. The *principal,* the accounting firm, must trust the action of its *agent,* the lead accountant. Their interests are sometimes at odds because the accounting firm is worthless without a reputation for honesty. That reputation was effectively sold by the lead accountant, without Andersen's knowledge or consent. The upshot of all this is that Andersen may well be destroyed by the actions of its lead accountant in the Enron case.

Why the Enron Case Matters More than the Others

The Kmart and Global Crossing cases really do not have much influence on the economy as a whole, but the Enron debacle is an ominous sign of a systemic problem. Economically speaking, Kmart's loss is Wal-Mart's and Target's gain. Global Crossing rolled the dice and it came up "snake-eyes." The risk associated with buying Global Crossing stock was pretty well understood, and if international bandwidth markets had taken off, Global Crossing stockholders would have made a fortune. Because they did not, and because the firm was very much in debt, the stockholders were left with nearly worthless stock. Enron stockholders were simply lied to. Investors must be able to rely on the veracity of financial statements.

Investors take calculated risks. They assemble the information and make decisions based on that information. The area of uncertainty that investors expect is that of the return to be received from their investments. Some companies make a profit and others do not. They seek to avoid the uncertainty over the veracity of financial reports by insisting on independent audits. If accounting firms aid the company's deceptive tactics rather than uncover them, then investors are left with two areas of uncertainty: (1) Will the company make money? and (2) Will the financial statements tell me the truth? The additional uncertainty about the accuracy of audits raises the required rate of return on stocks and results in inhibiting some profitable business avenues.

As a direct result of problems evidenced by Enron and Andersen, other companies began to reveal their own "overstatements" of profits. One by one, Xerox, World-Com, and other corporate giants came out with earnings "corrections." As a result, investors continued to lose confidence through 2002 and stock values dropped an additional 20 percent from levels that were already 20 percent to 60 percent below the levels of March 2000. It was not until the early spring of 2003 that the markets began to shake off the effects of these scandals.

Summary

You now understand how stock prices are determined and what stock markets do. You should understand the fundamental elements of stock prices and understand how prices can get out of line with their fundamental value. You were able to see these concepts at work as you read about the Asian financial crisis of the late 1990s and the NASDAQ of 2000. You understand the economic need for bankruptcy law and the consequences of the accounting scandals and bankruptcies of 2001 and 2002.

Key Terms

bankruptcy, 370
bubble, 368
creditors, 370

efficient market, 367
fundamentals, 366
initial public offering (IPO), 367

principal–agent problem, 371
stock index, 367

Quiz Yourself

1. The fundamental value of a share of stock is based on the present value of expected future
   a. Dividends.
   b. Revenues.
   c. Profits.
   d. Costs.

2. A stock index is
   a. Essentially the weighted sum of stock prices.
   b. The simple sum of stock prices.
   c. The geometric average of stock prices.
   d. The consensus view of professional economists.

3. If you invested in 20 different companies and chose those companies at random, you would be counting on the _____ market hypothesis and its implication that you would do as well as you would with any other investment strategy.
   a. Random
   b. Complete
   c. Stock
   d. Efficient

4. Stock market crashes tend to result when stocks get _____ their fundamental values.
   a. Too far below.
   b. Too close to.
   c. Too far above.
   d. Confused with.

5. A stock market exists
   a. Only to service the sale of new issues, called IPOs.
   b. To provide liquidity to all stocks, including recent ipos.
   c. Help policy makers predict the future.
   d. To make the rich richer.

6. The principal–agent problem centers on the separation of
   a. Supply and demand.
   b. Investors and savers.
   c. Owners and managers.
   d. Interest and dividends.

Think about This

Not all asset bubbles are related to stocks. In 2005 there was a concern about housing prices on the coasts exceeding all rational prices. One of history's bubbles involved tulip bulbs. The problem is that bubbles are easier to recognize in retrospect. Are there any assets you can think of that currently look like a bubble?

Talk about This

Stock markets are designed to allow corporations to raise initial capital. In providing liquidity to previously issued securities, they enhance that aspect. For that benefit we devote some of our best and brightest financial minds. Is that a good use of resources?

For More Insight See

Journal of Economic Perspectives 4, no. 2 (Spring 1990). See articles by Joseph E. Stiglitz; Andrei Schliefer and Lawrence H. Summers; Peter M. Garber; Robert J. Schiller; Eugene N. White; and Robert P. Flood and Robert J. Hodrick.

Behind the Numbers

Historical data.

Dow Jones Industrial Average, 1896–2004.
Global financial data—http://www.globalfindata.com.

Standard and Poor's 500, 1870–2004; Standard and Poor's—http://www2.standardandpoors.com.

NASDAQ Composite Index, 1980–2004; big charts; NASDAQ Composite Index—http://bigcharts.marketwatch.com/javachart/javachart.asp?symb_nasdaq&time_8.

NASDAQ Composite Index, 2003.
Money Central; investor—http://moneycentral.msn.com/investor/charts.

Chapter **36**

Unions

A carpenters' union holds a demonstration.
Source: © Mark Richards/PhotoEdit

Chapter Objectives

After reading this chapter you should be able to

Understand why labor unions exist and how they alter the bargaining relationship between employers and employees.

Distinguish between a competitive labor market and one where there is market power only with the employer, only with the employee, and when both have power.

Understand the difference between labor unions that seek to raise wages by reducing supply and those that seek to raise wages by using collective bargaining as a monopolist.

Be able to draw on your knowledge of the history of unions in the United States to predict the future of unionization in the United States.

Chapter Outline

The role of labor unions in the United States has been the subject of some controversy for more than 100 years. As the economy developed from agriculture to industrial manufacturing, labor issues came to the forefront. Although the struggle to organize labor to demand better treatment began much earlier, it was not until the 1930s that legislation was enacted giving workers the right to bargain collectively and to join unions. Unions grew in influence and membership, with their representation in the work force peaking at nearly 30 percent in 1975. That year saw the beginning of a long and rapid decline, and unions now represent less than 15 percent of the total work force and less than 10 percent of the private work force.

On a theoretical level, we discuss here why unions are usually desirable in a manufacturing economy, and we show how they can serve the best interests of both laborers and the economy as a whole. We then survey the early struggles, the pertinent laws, and the successes and failures of unions. We use two measures of union power to illustrate the health of labor in the United States, and we conclude with some insights into the ways unions are making the transition to the 21st century.

WHY UNIONS EXIST

The Perfectly Competitive Labor Market

When the United States was almost entirely agrarian in nature, aside from those who were enslaved, indentured, or otherwise beholden to masters of one sort or another, people worked mainly for themselves. Obviously, if you work for yourself, and outside influences are not at work, your pay and working conditions cannot be unfair since your own productivity determines your own wealth. As the United States grew throughout the 19th century, however, it evolved into an economy where fewer and fewer people worked for themselves. The industrial revolution came to the fore, and more and more people began to work for companies that manufactured goods. The supply and demand model of the economy supports us in concluding that any time one person buys something from another person, there are gains to both sides. This applies to labor as well.

Figure 36.1 indicates that if the good being sold is labor, and the price at which it is sold is the wage, then, like any market in perfect competition, there is an equilibrium wage and an equilibrium amount sold that makes both parties better off than they were before the transaction took place. In Figure 36.1, at equilibrium the wage paid is W^* for L^* labor. The firm that hires the labor pays it OW^*CL^*,

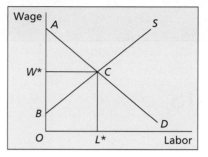

FIGURE 36.1   A labor market under perfect competition.

values it at (i.e., generates revenue from the sales of output from it of) $OACL^*$, and therefore gets the difference that is its consumer surplus (or profit) of W^*AC. The workers get paid OW^*CL^* when it costs them only $OBCL^*$ in opportunity cost to provide their efforts. As a result, they get producer surplus of BW^*C. There is no other wage–labor combination that provides as much surplus to the combination of both workers and firms as this one.

In a fairly subtle way, we conditioned all this on the assumption that there was perfect competition in the labor market. This means that there are many independent firms and many independent—that is, nonunion—workers, so that neither buyers nor sellers of labor have any control over the wage. Perfect competition also requires that all parties involved have good information about their alternatives.

A Reaction to Monopsony

We can safely assume that there is perfect competition if we are talking about a very large city and a field that is not particularly specialized. For instance, there are many carpenters in large cities, and there are many contractors who hire them. On the other hand, competition can be a lot less than perfect for two reasons, which both boil down to whether the number of firms buying labor is limited. The most extreme example of this would be a so-called company town, where only one firm buys labor in a particular area. Though company towns tend to be rare today, towns like Redmond, Washington, with Microsoft, and State College, Pennsylvania, with Penn State University, are close. On the other hand, history is replete with companies that literally owned entire towns. Mining towns were especially likely to be company towns, with all the problems of paternalistic control and subjugation of workers with which they have been associated.

The case where the specialization is so narrow that there are at most only a few potential buyers of that skill is one that is somewhat different in cause but similar in effect. This is fairly common in high-skill specialties where there is only one employer in a large area. You may be actually sitting at a chair in such a location. While assistant, associate, and full professors in colleges earn pretty good salaries, adjunct professors at colleges and universities are paid very little. Faculty at midlevel universities often earn in the neighborhood of $60,000 and teach four to six courses per year. Though there are research and service obligations to their jobs, their salaries translate to between $10,000 and $12,000 per course. Adjuncts are often paid less than $3,000 for a semester-long course. Many colleges are in towns where they are the only employer of people with masters and doctoral degrees (especially in the arts and humanities). For that reason, for people who are in the college town as a result of their spouse's work, a college can offer to pay them very little and still get relatively high-quality instruction.

Regardless of the reason, if it is the case that there is only one employer in an area, that employer has power that is very similar to the monopoly power enjoyed by utilities. Recall that under monopoly there is only one seller of a good and that seller can charge very high prices.

monopsony
A market with only one buyer.

When the market has only one buyer, a **monopsony** exists. In a monopsony the seller rather than the buyer is exploited.

Figure 36.2 shows how monopsony alters the perfectly competitive markets depicted in Figure 36.1. Before going into the detail of the graph, though, we need to step back and deal with a little labor vocabulary. As we mentioned briefly in the explanation of Figure 36.1, the demand curve for labor represents how much money an additional worker can generate for the firm as that worker increases production and therefore sales revenue. This is called the **marginal revenue product of labor,** and it is equal to the demand curve, because the firm will be willing to pay up to the amount of money it can make from its workers' efforts in order to squeeze all possible profit out of its labor force.

marginal revenue product of labor
The additional revenue generated from hiring an additional worker.

In addition, since there is only one buyer of labor, the firm is not looking at an equilibrium wage that it must pay its employees. The firm decides how much labor it wants, and it pays the minimum required to get that labor. To get more workers, it not only has to pay the new workers more, but also it has to pay all workers more. Thus if

FIGURE 36.2   A company town and a monopsony market for labor.

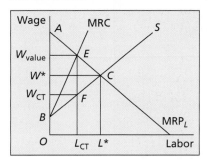

the firm wants to hire more workers, its costs do not rise along the supply curve; they rise faster. The cost of increasing hiring is therefore not the supply curve but the curve that is labeled the **marginal resource cost (MRC)** in Figure 36.2. This shows the increase in total labor costs to the firm of buying increasing amounts of labor.

marginal resource cost
The increase in total labor costs to the firm of buying increasing amounts of labor.

To solidify this in your mind consider Table 36.1. The first column represents the wage that is paid. The second is the quantity supplied. The third, the total cost to the employer, is the product of the first and second. The final column is the difference in the total cost from one worker to the next. Notice that it rises substantially faster than the first column.

The monopsonist firm maximizes profit when it hires at the point where the marginal revenue product of labor equals the marginal resource cost. In Figure 36.2 this is L_{CT} (i.e., in a company town) rather than L^* workers. To find what these workers are paid, we take L_{CT} up to the supply curve to get W_{CT}. If we want to know what these workers are worth, we go up to the demand curve to find that the amount of money they are making for the company is W_{value}. It should be clear that under monopsony

TABLE 36.1   Relationship between supply and marginal resource cost.

Wage	Quantity Supplied	Total Cost to the Employer	Marginal Resource Cost
5	1	5	
6	2	12	7
7	3	21	9
8	4	32	11
9	5	45	13

FIGURE 36.3 The impact of licensing.

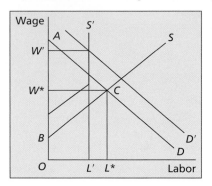

workers do not earn what they are worth. As a check, note that under perfect competition, at L^*, workers earn their marginal revenue product; that is, they earn exactly what they are worth.

A Way to Restrict Competition and Improve Quality

Some unions and professional organizations enhance the pay of their members by restricting the supply of workers and by increasing the value of their members. Thus Figure 36.3 alters Figure 36.1 by reflecting the reduction in potential workers as a changing of the shape of the supply curve. First, the supply curve moves to the left because there is a cost to the employee of learning how to become skilled in this area. The costs to the newly licensed employees are reflected in the general movement of the supply curve to the left. Since the number of openings for training in the field, here noted as L', is limited, the supply curve is perfectly inelastic at that point. Because there is an improvement in skills of the workers and the quality of their work, there is a movement of the demand curve to the right. This raises the wage to those who ultimately work in the field. Among others, the American Medical Association, the American Bar Association, the International Brotherhood of Electrical Workers, and the Plumbers and Steamfitters[1] all follow this pattern.

By restricting the ability of people to become workers in a particular field, these types of unions keep the supply of workers down. You cannot practice medicine or law without a license, and that license serves as a mechanism to restrict competition. While you can wire your

[1]The United Association of Journeymen and Apprentices of the Plumbing and Pipe Fitting Industry of the United States and Canada.

own house or do your own plumbing, in many communities you cannot sell these services to others without a license.

The other side of Figure 36.3 is the increase in demand. Because of the training that union plumbers and electricians get, we can model their increased productivity and quality as an increase in the demand for their services. Thus having a certification process also increases the pay of these workers, because an increase in the demand occurs for their services. As you can see, the net result is an increase in the price of these services and an uncertain effect on the numbers of these services that are provided.

If, on the other hand, the net effect of unionization of this form is that the labor sold is reduced, then unionization of this type detracts from economic efficiency. Otherwise, unionization is neutral or good for it. Though there is considerable debate among labor economists on this point, they tend to suggest that the net impact of licensing is generally negative.

A Reaction to Information Issues

Another reason that the actual market for labor may not be the perfectly competitive version is that workers may not have good information about other positions they might fill. Workers who explore other prospects tend to be viewed as disloyal by their bosses and co-workers. To avoid this perception as well as the effort of looking for a new job, people may not know what they are worth elsewhere. Though it was not stated above, one of the things that makes the perfectly competitive labor market perfect—workers earn what they are worth—is that workers who are paid less than market wages know it and will move on to other, better-paying jobs. If they do not know about the other jobs, they are not likely to move even when they are poorly paid or poorly treated.

There are a couple of ways that this works to hurt workers. The first, as stated above, is that there is a tendency for employers and co-workers to distrust people seeking better jobs, especially when those better jobs are with the competition. Therefore, there is sociological "peer pressure" that stands in the way of workers finding out what they are worth. Second, employers are not above conspiring with one another to strike fear into workers. This works when there is a limited number of firms and they collude in agreeing not to bid against one another for workers. When this works, each of the firms can threaten "disloyal" workers with statements like "you will never work in this town again."

A UNION AS A MONOPOLIST

Unions exist to ensure that workers get at least what they are worth in a perfectly competitive market and possibly more. In economic-speak, laborers band together in unions so they can force employers to provide them with wages that are equal to their marginal revenue product. They do this by countering the market power that firms have with market power of their own. Unions are most effective when they are the single seller to a firm's single buyer. Sometimes unions such as the United Auto Workers, the United Mine Workers, and the Teamsters[2] provide labor to many different buyers of labor. In such cases it is the union that possesses the sole market power.

The formal model of unions is the same as the model of monopolies. In Figure 36.4 you see the impact of having a union control all labor. The marginal revenue to the union is set equal to the supply curve to find the amount of labor the union wishes to provide. This occurs at L_{union}. That means that wages are higher than before, as W_{union} exceeds W^*. If we look at unions as if they existed in a vacuum, it would appear they are bad for the economy, since the consumer surplus falls by less than producer surplus grows, so unions appear to hurt the economy.

Unions did not arise and they do not exist in a vacuum. In some cases, poor treatment, poor pay, or both poor pay and poor treatment encouraged workers to organize. For others, Figure 36.4 depicts the end of the story. When unions simply use their monopoly power to sell labor to different competitive firms, then the existence of the union detracts from economic efficiency. We can see, though, that some workers lose opportunities to work, because L_{union} is less than L^*. We also see that the gain to those who keep their jobs is greater than the loss to those who lose theirs, because the producer surplus increases. Clearly the firms that do the hiring are worse off as their consumer surplus is reduced. The net effect is that unions reduce the total amount of the surplus.

To compare those unions that exist as a reaction to monopsony power to the case without the union, we need to combine Figures 36.2 and 36.4. In Figure 36.5 we can find out where the battle lines are drawn. In its monopolistic form the union will want to set the wages at $W_{highest}$. This is what the union would demand if it was bargaining

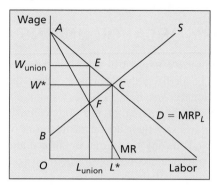

FIGURE 36.4   A union's effect on wages in a perfectly competitive labor market.

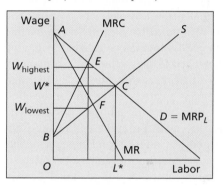

FIGURE 36.5   The union fights the one-company town, or monopoly versus monopsony.

with many different employers. The "company" that rules the company town will want to pay what it would have paid if it were bargaining with many independent workers, W_{lowest}. There are some sophisticated economic models that are designed to predict the outcome of bargaining between unions and firms, but at this point we have difficulty making good predictions about where within the range the wages will ultimately settle.

Once a wage has been agreed on in this range, the number of workers the employer will hire depends on the supply and demand curves. To find out exactly how many will be hired, remember that since we are not going to be at equilibrium, it will be the lower of quantity demanded and quantity supplied at that wage. To find quantity demanded at that wage, take that wage to the demand curve. Similarly, to find quantity supplied, go over to the supply curve. As long as the bargaining process works out between what unions want and what firms are willing to pay, the economy is better with a union in a company town than it is without a union in a company town.

[2]The United Automobile, Aerospace, and Agricultural Implement Workers of America; the United Mine Workers of America; and the International Brotherhood of Teamsters, Chauffeurs, Warehousemen and Helpers of America, respectively.

The result of the bargain is that the loss of consumer plus producer surplus is limited.

THE HISTORY OF LABOR UNIONS

Labor organizations have existed in the United States since shoemakers banded together near the end of the American Revolutionary War. Labor's battle was largely unsuccessful until the beginning of the 20th century, though, because courts saw their actions as restraint of trade or conspiracy. Thus any union that organized and struck an employer for better conditions or better wages had these actions stopped by the courts.[3]

Before laws began to support laborers' attempts to form unions, and before unions had any rights under the law, there were court rulings that were decidedly antiunion. At one point, in a dispute between workers and a company that made railroad cars, sympathetic railroad workers refused to handle cars made by that particular company. The company retaliated by having U.S. mail cars attached to the "offending" company's cars. When railroad workers then uncoupled the mail cars from the company's cars in sympathy for the company's workers, they were jailed for conspiracy to tamper with the U.S. mail. From the end of the Civil War to 1914, the courts, Congress, and most presidents were beholden to large corporate interests, interests that saw that union members were fired, jailed, beaten, and killed. Seldom were they successful in getting pay increases.

All that began to change in 1914 when President Woodrow Wilson, a Democrat, was able to work with a Congress controlled by the Democrats. In that year, laws were enacted to grant labor rights. Although one of these laws, the Clayton Act, was overturned by the Supreme Court, its passage marked a clear dividing line between the political parties. Republicans sided with management and Democrats with organized labor.

Through the 1920s Republicans held both the presidency and Congress and nearly no headway was allowed for labor unions. The Great Depression, which started in 1929, changed the economic and political landscape. As millions of workers lost their jobs, Democrats were voted into office; and, under the presidency of Franklin Roosevelt, Congress enacted the Norris–La Guardia

Act, the National Industrial Recovery Act, and the Wagner Act, among others. These laws reestablished labor rights that had been granted under the Clayton Act, and they created new ones. Under these acts, workers were given the right to organize and to bargain collectively. Additionally, they stipulated that exercising these rights could no longer be construed as conspiracy to restrain trade. The law now stated that whenever a majority of workers voted for union representation, the union was held to represent all workers, whether nonunion workers wanted to be represented or not. In actuality, it was often the case that when a firm's workers were represented by a union, membership in that union was required as a condition of employment for all the employees.

These rights did not apply to everyone. Most notably, government employees were still forbidden from striking, but the new laws did give labor a great deal of muscle. As the economy surged out of the depression and into World War II, strikes were becoming commonplace. Strikes were considered serious enough that, during World War II, Congress temporarily gave the president power to seize control of industries in which strikes were considered to be jeopardizing the production of war material.

In the year following Japan's surrender in World War II, nearly 120 million workdays, 1.9 percent of all potential work time, were lost to strikes. In part, this was because a wide disparity existed between where wages were going before the war and where they were as a result of a wartime freeze. Since wages were frozen for much of the war, workers wanted to at least be paid what they would have been paid had the freeze not been in place. Management liked the low current wages and argued that the health insurance benefits that were put in place to balance the wage freeze were sufficient to make up for the freeze.

As a result of depression-era laws, labor was still holding nearly all of the cards and was quite successful in achieving its aims. Organized labor was so successful that to keep its power in check, a Republican Congress passed the Taft–Hartley Act over President Harry Truman's veto.

The Taft–Hartley Act amended the Wagner Act in ways that gave management back some of the cards it had held in previous years. It allowed states to determine whether they would allow workers who did not want union representation to work for a company for whom a majority wanted union representation. It also allowed the president to order a cooling-off period, temporarily ending any strike that threatened the economic health of the nation.

---

[3]See Campbell R. McConnell, Stanley L. Brue, and David A. MacPherson, *Contemporary Labor Economics,* 6th ed. (New York: Irwin/McGraw-Hill, 2003), Chapter 10.

FIGURE 36.6 Union membership as a percentage of the work force.

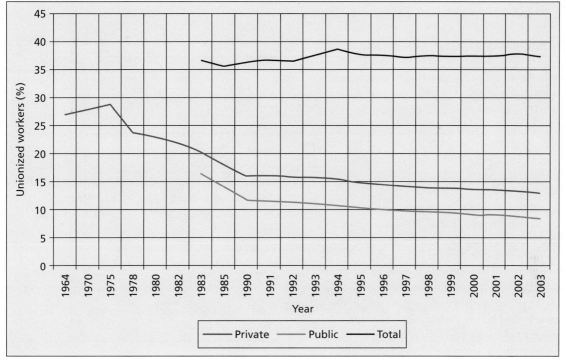

Source: http://www.census.gov/prod/2004pubs/04statab/labor.pdf.

In 1962 President John Kennedy issued an executive order that gave federal employees the right to unionize and to bargain collectively in ways they had not been able to do under the Wagner Act. Though still unable to strike, they were granted grievance procedures. Other protections were instituted that led greater numbers of public employees to form and to join unions.

A look at Figures 36.6 and 36.7 shows that since the time of President Kennedy, there has been a general decline in the number of workers who belong to unions. Though union power peaked in the middle 1970s, the decline has been long and consistent. The exception has been the relative health of public employee unions. Figure 36.6 shows that the percentage of all workers who are unionized and the percentage of private-sector employees who are unionized have fallen dramatically since the 1980s. It further shows that the percentage of public employees who are unionized has stayed at a relatively constant 35 percent to 40 percent.

This difference between the health of public and private employees' unions is most clearly seen in just a few unions. The United Auto Workers lost nearly half of its 1.5 million members between 1978 and 1995. The United Steelworkers of America once numbered 1.3 million; today membership is only 400,000. On the other hand, the American Federation of State, County, and Municipal Employees Union has had membership more than triple since 1968.

Similarly, if you look at work stoppages as a measure of labor unions' confidence (that they can win in a situation in which workers either strike or are locked out by management), you find that unions have been running scared since the early 1980s. The drop in the number of strikes is generally attributed to President Reagan's firing of the striking air traffic controllers in 1981.

In one of the more ironic events in labor history, the only president of the United States who had ever belonged to a union or had been a president of a union became the president most identified with labor's downfall. President Reagan had been a member of, and eventually president of, the Screen Actors' Guild. When the Professional Air Traffic Controllers Organization (PATCO), the union representing the air traffic controllers, struck in the summer of 1981, President Reagan followed the law, which unambiguously stated that public employees who engaged in strikes were to be terminated. At the time, hardly anyone thought he

FIGURE 36.7   Lost time from strikes and lockouts.

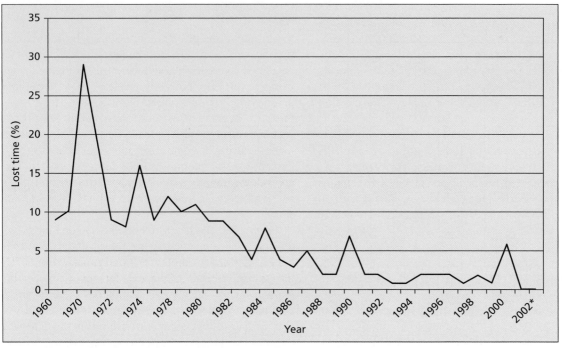

*In 2001 and 2002 less than 0.05 percent of work time was lost to strikes or lockouts.

Source: http://www.census.gov/prod/2004pubs/04statab/labor.pdf.

would actually follow through and fire the controllers, and virtually everyone thought he would hire them back after the strike was settled. When they struck, he fired them. He then ordered his secretary of transportation not to negotiate with them, since they were fired and no longer held legal status as employees. Instead, he ordered every available air traffic controller in the military to fill in until new controllers could be recruited and trained.

The events of this single week in 1981 are given inordinate weight by many, but it does serve as a timepost. Though PATCO was a small union and though unions were beginning to lose many of their battles in the late 1970s, the outcome of this strike is viewed by many in the labor movement as singularly important. For the first time since the 1930s the government was perceived to be as much a foe of unionized labor as was management. It is even more ironic, then, that President Reagan garnered more union votes than any other 20th-century Republican president.

It was not until 17 years later, when the Teamsters Union struck the United Parcel Service (UPS) in 1998, that a major union won major concessions from an employer. Whether this strike serves as another turning point or simply magnifies labor's difficulties by serving as the exception that proves the rule will not be known for several years. For more than 15 years nearly every major strike left workers worse off than they had been when the strike started. The only exception to this generalization is strikes by already highly paid professional athletes, which succeeded in making them even more highly paid. Less than one-tenth of 1 percent of all work time was lost to strikes over the late 1990s, a consequence that can be attributed to the realization on the part of labor that they would lose any confrontation.

The ultimate reasons that organized labor won the UPS strike are the same as the reasons that any union wins a strike. The workers were not easily replaceable and the company that employed them had competitors that were taking its market share. The labor market of the late 1990s was such that finding dependable workers was difficult. This contrasts with strikes such as the strike by Caterpillar's Peoria, Illinois, workers in the early 1990s. In that period of time dependable workers willing to take jobs at $15 to $25 an hour were not difficult to find. In 1998 such workers were much more difficult to find. Thus the Teamsters would demand higher wages. Another difference was that UPS saw its market share in the overnight delivery business disappear. The fear that customers would not return after the strike induced the company to settle. Conversely, Caterpillar had less of a concern that competitors would or could take market share for long because of Caterpillar's dominance in the heavy construction equipment industry.

In July 2005, the AFL-CIO had its most significant defections in decades as the Teamsters and other unions abandoned the umbrella organization. The dispute centered on whether the financial resources of the unions should be devoted to electing politicians sympathetic to union concerns or whether they should be devoted to increasing union membership by unionizing previously unorganized industries.

WHERE UNIONS GO FROM HERE

Unions composed of men and women who work in the public sector will likely survive long into the future, as there are far fewer pressures on them than there are on unions in the private sector. For instance, if a car company decides it can no longer afford its union's pay demands, it can move its production facilities to a location where the workers are only too happy to take the jobs at whatever the company is offering. On the other hand, if a city cannot afford its firefighters' wage demands, it must negotiate. It cannot move to a location where it can hire other firefighters and pay lower wages.

Unions in the private sector are likely to have continuing difficulty. Because employment growth has been most evident in service and retail industries where many employers hire only a few employees each, unions have found it much more difficult to organize these workers. For this reason the picture for private-sector unions is rather bleak. Further, since old-line manufacturing in areas like automobiles and steel is susceptible to international trade pressures to keep costs down, unions will have a hard time winning concessions even in industries in which they are still strong.

In general, the health of private-sector unions will depend greatly on whether we return to the days when only a few major employers hired most workers. The information age has seen many start-up companies lure workers away from larger companies. The wages of computer engineers, programmers, and the employees who actually make computers are pretty close to what these workers are worth. If, on the other hand, the computer industry begins to centralize around only a few major employers and start-ups become rare, unions may finally make inroads into information-age industries. Unless that happens, public-sector unions may dominate the labor movement by the end of the 21st century.

Kick It Up A Notch

Referring back to Figure 36.2 and using the notions of consumer and producer surplus introduced in Chapter 3, we can see that monopsony is worse than perfect competition. Firms do better because they pay less, and workers do worse because they make less. The net to society is reduced by EFC because the consumer surplus to firms is $W_{CT}AEF$ while the producer surplus to workers shrinks to $BW_{CT}F$. That combined area is less than the optimal level by EFC. We can conclude from the preceding that if the problem that unions combat is monopsony, then unions can make things better by moving the market toward its original equilibrium.

In Figure 36.4 we see that the fall in consumer surplus is $W_{union}AE$ and the increase in producer surplus is $BW_{union}EF$. As a result, in combination there is a net reduction, and unions appear to hurt the economy. Remember from the body of the chapter, unions do not exist in a vacuum and are typically a reaction to something operating against workers.

Summary

You now understand why labor unions exist and how they alter the bargaining relationship between employers and employees. You understand how a competitive labor market differs from one where there is market power with only the employer, with only the employee, and when both have power. You understand that labor unions differ in that some seek to raise wages by reducing supply, whereas others seek to raise wages by using collective bargaining as a monopolist. Last, you now understand how unions came about in the United States, and you have enough knowledge of recent history to be able to project where unionization is going in the United States.

Key Terms

marginal resource cost, 377

marginal revenue product of labor, 377

monopsony, 377

Quiz Yourself

1. When there is only one employer in a city, the model that economists use is one for
   a. Monopoly.
   b. Monopsony.
   c. Perfect competition.
   d. Monopolistic competition.
2. When there are many employers in a city and one union, the model that economists use is one for
   a. Monopoly.
   b. Monopsony.
   c. Perfect competition.
   d. Monopolistic competition.
3. Under perfect competition marginal resource cost _____ supply; under monopsony marginal resource cost _____ supply.
   a. Equals; equals.
   b. Equals; is greater than.
   c. Equals; is less than.
   d. Is greater than; is less than.
4. A union that trains and restricts supply has an effect on the supply curve that moves it to the _____and, at a point, makes it _____.
   a. Left; vertical.
   b. Left; horizontal.
   c. Right; vertical.
   d. Right; horizontal.
5. Labor unions have greater representation in _____ employees.
   a. Public.
   b. Service

   c. Manufacturing
   d. Retail
6. In the past 30 years work stoppages have
   a. Plummeted.
   b. Remained constant.
   c. Increased slowly.
   d. Increased rapidly.

Think about This

The ability of unions to have their demands met has decreased markedly since the 1981 PATCO strike. Work stoppages have also decreased since that time. Are unions just not trying to make their influence known or do they not strike knowing they have little chance of winning?

For More Insight See

McConnell, Campbell R., Stanley L. Brue, and David A. MacPherson, *Contemporary Labor Economics,* 6th ed. (New York: Irwin/McGraw-Hill, 2003), esp. Chapters 10, 11, and 13.

Behind the Numbers

Union and private workforce information.
   Statistical Abstract of the United States; labor—http://www.census.gov/prod/2004pubs/04statab/labor.pdf.

Chapter 37

The Cost of War

A U.S. army soldier atop his jeep guards the main entrance of the U.S. administration office in Baghdad, Iraq, Saturday, July 5, 2003. *Source: Photo courtesy of U.S. Army Chief Petty Officer Edward Martens*

Chapter Objectives

After reading this chapter you should be able to

Apply the concept of opportunity cost to the decision to go to war.

Understand that economists use the concept of present value to estimate the value of a human life.

Understand that the economic and accounting cost of going to war are substantially different.

See that GDP is affected positively by wartime expenditures but negatively by wartime uncertainty.

Note that, in addition to the strictly economic issues, war has environmental and cultural consequences that must be accounted for.

Chapter Outline

Opportunity Cost

Present Value and the Value of a Human Life

Economic vs. Accounting Cost

How GDP Was Affected

Environmental and Cultural Costs

Summary

A war, however how well or poorly justified, costs a great deal of money. Whether you view a particular war as "worth it" or not depends greatly on your ethical and political values, but it should also depend on whether the war aims are significant enough to justify the expense in lives and money. Putting aside the question of whether the war in Iraq was justified or unjustified, this chapter will look at how an economist would estimate the cost of a war using that particular war as its primary example.

In so doing, this topic serves as a useful example of the Chapter 1 concept of opportunity costs, the Chapter 5 distinction between economic and accounting costs, the Chapter 6 discussion of GDP accounting, the Chapter 7 concept of present value in calculating the dollar value of lost lives, and, finally, the environmental and cultural cost of such a war.

Before the war began, the Bush administration, the media, and policy analysts placed the cost at between $75 billion for a short war with a short occupation and more than $1 trillion for a lengthy war with a 10-year postwar occupation. While the conventional aspect of the war was hardly lengthy, lasting about 20 days from the first attempt to kill Saddam with a bombing run on one of his palaces until the fall of Baghdad, the length of the occupation can only be estimated at this point. In 2004, the Congressional Budget Office estimated the annual cost of the operations in Iraq and Afghanistan at $64 billion. At that rate, the cost in terms of both lives and treasure of the occupation phase of these operations vastly exceeded the relatively low costs of conventional wars themselves.

OPPORTUNITY COST

Chapter 1 referred to the economic concept of opportunity cost as the "forgone alternative of the choice made." Unless attacked directly, war is always a choice. Though we had war thrust upon us in World War II, we chose to go to war in Europe in World War I, and chose to fight in Korea, Vietnam, Grenada, Panama, Kuwait, Bosnia, and Iraq. Whether going into Iraq was a good choice or a bad one, it was clearly a choice. France, Germany, Russia, and China, and by prewar poll numbers a sizable minority of the American population, believed that continued weapons inspections were a better option than war. President Bush believed that such a choice left America vulnerable to a chemical, biological, or nuclear attack by terrorist organizations. Whomever you agreed with at the time and whoever seems to be right in retrospect, a choice was made and there are costs to that choice.

More than 250,000 men and women from the Army, Navy, Air Force, and Marines were deployed to the Persian Gulf in the months leading up to the March 2003 attack, and an additional 150,000 were deployed after hostilities commenced. Though the conventional invasion aspect of the war was surprisingly short, more than 150,000 troops will remain in the area for years after the fall of Baghdad.

The fact that regular troops were no longer at their U.S. bases meant that whatever they could have accomplished there, they were unable to accomplish because they were in Kuwait, Iraq, Qatar, or at sea. Their fighting power, both in terms of damaged equipment and exhausted personnel, was degraded because of their constant use such that if they had been needed elsewhere they would have been unable to respond with their previous ability. At the beginning of the conflict, North Korea was posturing itself in such a way that at least some of these American forces might have been usefully deployed in and around eastern Asia in response. At least some of the forces used in the Gulf were diverted from the hunt for Al-Qaeda suspects in the horn of Africa. Finally, after Baghdad fell, but before all was secure, a crisis in Liberia erupted. Unlike the situation in Iraq, members of the United Nations, and France and Germany in particular, were clamoring for U.S. forces to head there to keep the peace. Though a small force was sent, the primary reason for limiting the scope of U.S. involvement was the degree to which forces were stretched too thin across the globe. In large part this was because so many were in Iraq.

Similarly, more than 150,000 reservists were called up to active service. As a result, they were providing, and to an unprecedented level continue to provide, military service rather than producing goods and services for sale in the private marketplace. Putting aside for a moment the cost of having reservist called to duty for the invasion, the burden on reservists during the occupation phase of the operation has been significant. The military's "stop loss" policy allows it to continue to compel service long past the contractual end of a soldier's tour of duty. In terms of economic costs suppose, for example, that a community's local National Guard or reserve unit specialized in small unit operations, a task sorely needed in an insurgency. Suppose further that the unit was disproportionately composed of the community's police officers and firefighters. If the unit was called to active duty and these officers were not replaced, the increase in crime or the delay in response times in the community that resulted from inadequate staffing is a cost of the occupation. If reservists called to active duty would have been producing automobiles, the lost production was a cost of the war and occupation. A final opportunity cost to consider is the impact of the deployment on families here at home. Fathers, mothers, husbands, wives, sons, and daughters spent the months of March and April under extreme stress worrying about their deployed loved ones. That stress was only compounded by the daily news of attacks by Saddam loyalists through 2003. Worse yet was the success of the insurgency through 2004 and 2005 in making everyday one in which the safety of loved ones was in doubt. Although it is not easy to establish a monetary value for these costs, they are costs nevertheless.

This is not to say that the war was not, at least potentially, worth the cost. The defeat of Saddam Hussein's regime was greeted with the gratitude of many Iraqi people. In the end, though, figuring all of the costs of the war is an important part of that calculation.

PRESENT VALUE AND THE VALUE OF A HUMAN LIFE

In war, people die. Soldiers die, pilots die, and civilians die. While many of the costs of war are difficult to estimate, economists have for quite some time felt comfortable giving an estimate of this loss. This is because we have much practice at doing it. When someone dies at the hands of a drunk driver or as a result of someone's or some company's negligence, economists are called upon to estimate how much money their loved ones would need as compensation.

A forensic economist computes the net loss for each year the person would have likely been alive. This net loss is the income the person would have made had they not died, minus the portion of that income they would have spent on their own consumption plus the value of their nonmarket activities to their families. Once that data are in place, then the present value of the net loss is taken at a low-risk market interest rate. Jury awards for economic damages in wrongful death cases tend to vary between $500,000 and $2 million for a young person. Juries will often add to that figure punitive damages or amounts for pain and suffering. These damages vary widely. You may choose to be skeptical of the technical or moral validity of any of these calculations, but for every 100 American soldiers who died as a result of the war and the occupation, between $50 million and $200 million is added to its cost. As of mid-2005, near 1,800 military personnel died in Iraq and Afghanistan.

When Iraqi dead are included, the total is likely to grow substantially higher. How much higher depends to a degree on how many Iraqis died but also on the present value calculation for the average Iraqi. Early estimates of between 4,000 and 5,000 Iraqi civilians were based entirely on local hospital records. Those who died and remain unaccounted for because they died and never got to hospitals surely make that number small by comparison. It is important to note that the amorality of the present value calculation has the average American being worth substantially more than the average Iraqi because the average American will earn substantially more money.

ECONOMIC VS. ACCOUNTING COST

Chapter 5 stressed the difference between economic and accounting costs in the context of a person quitting a job and starting a new business. In that example, accounting costs were those "costs that must be explicitly paid." The idea was that costs such as those for personnel, supplies, and equipment count toward the cost of doing business. Economic costs represented "all costs of a business: those that must be paid as well as those incurred in the form of forgone opportunities." In that chapter, the example used to illustrate the cost of

forgone opportunities was the cost associated with giving up a salary and benefits and the loss of interest on savings invested in the business. As a result, the accounting costs were only a portion of the total costs. A war is a case where certain accounting costs are not counted by economists, and certain economic costs are not counted by accountants.

Personnel, Food, and Supplies

What appears to be the most obvious cost of the war may not be a cost of a war at all in an economic sense. Paying the regular soldiers their regular pay is not necessarily an economic cost of the war because they would have been paid in their home bases. When more soldiers have to be recruited to fill in the gaps or reservists must be called up, these costs are economic. If a mission that would otherwise have been undertaken is impossible because the forces are elsewhere, at least some of the personnel costs of the deployment are economic as well.

There are some aspects of a soldier's salary that clearly count under any circumstance. Soldiers in a war zone get "imminent danger/hostile fire pay" of $225 per month and a "family separation allowance" of $250 per month. As a result, for every month soldiers are deployed to combat areas, they get $475 per month more than their regular pay. For perspective, consider that a brand new recruit's (E-1) basic pay is $1,143 per month, a sergeant (E-5) with six years of military service receives $2,205 per month, a newly minted officer (O-1) receives $2,344, while a division commander/ship's captain with 20 years in the military makes more than $10,000 per month. So, although the cost of paying 400,000 soldiers is approximately $1 billion per month, as little as $200 million of that may be a cost of the war in terms of explicit personnel costs. Of course, if these soldiers would have been put to use elsewhere had they not been deployed in this fashion, the economic cost may again rise to the $1-billion-per-month figure.

The costs of feeding, housing, and supplying soldiers are substantially increased when they are a half a world away from home. While the soldiers must also be fed at home, they can be fed in efficient cafeterias at a relatively low per-soldier cost, or they can feed themselves in their own homes. On the frontlines a soldier is eating prepackaged MREs (Meals Ready to Eat). Production costs of MREs amount to between $1 and $2 per pouch. If you assume that producing and delivering food in this form increases costs from $5 per soldier per day to $10 per soldier per day, the cost of food is $60 million per month.

Once the conventional fighting ended and the occupation began, food costs dropped because less expensive methods of food preparation were used. But a significant number of soldiers continued to eat MREs as they went about their patrols in occupied Iraq.

Of course, soldiers also need other nonammunition supplies such as water, razors, changes of uniform, and other miscellaneous items. Getting soldiers what they need is much more expensive when it needs to be shipped thousands of miles, especially when the last 300 or so miles are along a supply line that is under threat of ambush as it was in the first two weeks of the war. Though these things are needed at home too, the cost of getting them to the soldiers in the field costs at least an additional $60 million per month.

Because 150,000 service men and women were called to active duty from the guard and reserve units to fill roles that the deployed regular units would have filled, this is a cost of the war because if the war had not occurred they would not have been called up. Strangely enough, as we will learn when we discuss GDP accounting, this substantial cost may not show up as a loss to the economy as it is measured. Assuming that the ranks represented in these units are proportional to the ranks in regular units, this call-up costs $340 million per month.

Cost of Munitions

Attempting to figure out how much expended ammunition costs is difficult at best. From "smart" bombs that cost more than $1 million apiece to bullets that cost less than 10 cents, we have to account for the cost of munitions. Obviously, a bullet is not just a bullet anymore. For instance, had your grandfather or greatgrandfather served in an armored unit in World War II, the tank shell he would have fired would have essentially been a big bullet that was lucky to hit what it was pointed at. Today, a tank shell has a guidance system. Furthermore, it doesn't blast through the enemy's armor—it melts through it. So while it may take fewer shells to destroy an opposing tank, the shells themselves are far more expensive.

The bullets fired by 30-caliber machine guns are no longer simply bullets either. Made from depleted uranium, each bullet coming from an A-10 "Warthog" can cost $50. When the pilot fires the nose-mounted Gatling gun for one second, she can expel $1,000 in ammunition. It is expensive but effective. A single burst from an A-10 can take out a multimillion-dollar tank.

Bombs are also far more expensive than those from past wars. If you look at the first Gulf War, $2.7 billion worth of bombs were dropped. Of the 227,000 bombs and missiles used, only 7.5 percent were "smart" in that they were guided to their targets. Though many more of the munitions this time around were of the more expensive "smart" variety, presumably fewer of them were needed to destroy a particular target.

Estimates suggest that we used approximately $7 billion to $10 billion worth of ammunition in the approximately 21 days of active fighting. In the first Gulf War, the unguided bombs used were taken from inventories and to a large extent not replaced. This was because a strategic decision was made to focus procurements of new munitions on the "smart" variety. Nowadays, each smart bomb used will likely end up being replaced with a new one.

Cost of Getting Personnel and Equipment in Position

Though precise estimates for getting the force in place have not come out for this war, we can assume again that costs are proportional to the costs from the previous Gulf War. A "round-trip" ticket for this volume of personnel and equipment is likely to cost between $5 billion and $10 billion.

Fuel

A significant line item in this war was the cost of fuel. An M1A1 Abrams tank has a gas tank that holds 500 gallons of fuel and gets less than half a mile per gallon. One of the riskiest ventures of the opening week of the war was getting fuel across a 300-mile supply line that was constantly subject to ambush. Fuel costs for the first Gulf War totaled more than $30 billion. In that war, the fuel was provided free of charge by the Saudi Arabian government. Such was not the case this time around. Estimates suggest that fuel costs ranged between $10 billion and $15 billion for the combat phase and $1 billion or more per month in the occupation phase.

HOW GDP WAS AFFECTED

Because GDP accounting doesn't distinguish between paying someone to be a soldier and paying someone to make something that consumers will buy, the way in which we count GDP will miss the degree to which the economy is affected by a war. GDP is simply the sum of the money spent by consumers, businesses, the government, and foreign buyers (minus imports) on their purchases of goods and services. What the good or service is, whether it is in pursuit of something wise or unwise, is irrelevant to the accounting.

To see how this works, suppose a civilian reservist is capable of producing $50,000 worth of stuff in her private job. Suppose she is called up as a $28,000-per-year sergeant to take a role at a military base that was being performed by a soldier currently deployed to the war. If she is not replaced in her private job, there is a loss of consumption of $50,000 as the goods she would have produced for her boss's customers don't materialize. Consumption falls by $50,000 and government spending increases by $28,000, so the loss to GDP ends up being $22,000. Nevertheless, there is a loss of $50,000 worth of consumer goods.

If she is replaced, the impact on the economy depends on what that person was doing before being hired to take the place of the called-up reservist. If the person was not working, and is as capable as the called-up reservist, then the $50,000 in goods is not lost and we still have the $28,000 gain. If her replacement was previously in another job, then this other production was lost or must be replaced. Depending on the degree of unemployment or underemployment prior to the war, the effect on GDP of civilians being called to the military may in fact be positive, negative, or zero. This is not to say that we are necessarily better off or worse off. If the replacement for the reservist is less capable than the reservist, then the quality of the goods may be worse.

On issues of significant economic importance, the war had several impacts for which the cost is hard to calculate. First, during the run-up to war, American consumer confidence was dropping quickly such that in the weeks just prior to the war, one measure had consumer confidence at a decade low. Second, the increase in crude oil prices from $30 per barrel to more than $40 per barrel placed a heavy burden on energy-sensitive sectors of the U.S. economy. Third, businesses were reluctant to invest in new plant and equipment in the months leading up to the war. Fourth, President Bush requested $75 billion, for war-related expenses and $87 billion in occupation and rebuilding expenses. This added to an already bleak budget deficit picture that could, in the longer term, mean the end of historically low interest rates.

Though only three weeks passed from the beginning of war to the fall of Baghdad, we did not know that on March 19, 2003, when the bombs started to fall. The $1 trillion figure of the cost of the war was produced by William Nordhaus, a respected economist who based his estimate on the possibility that the war would drag on, that it would potentially spread, that oil prices would

spike, and that the United States would have to occupy Iraq for 10 years with 100,000 troops. While the conventional war itself went well from the perspective of the American and British militaries and did not spread, at this writing the occupation appears likely to last years. While oil prices have soared to record nominal levels, and historically high inflation-adjusted levels, not all of that impact is the war.

It is worth knowing what we were risking by going to war. Consider that a reduction in the projected growth rate of as little as one percentage point means a loss of $100 billion to the U.S. economy per year. Oil prices are higher than they would have been without the war but they could have gone much higher. If combat had continued for months, the deficit would have ballooned by several hundred billion a year and interest rates would have increased, adding to mortgage costs and diminishing consumers' willingness to borrow and businesses' willingness to invest. The choice to go to war put the economy at risk. Because the war was relatively short, the macroeconomic costs will likely be muted.

ENVIRONMENTAL AND CULTURAL COSTS

From a military perspective, the war went well, but it is also important to consider the environmental costs. These come from a variety of sources. First, while oil fires were substantially less numerous and severe than during the first Gulf War, they nevertheless fouled the air around Basra and Baghdad. Second, the depleted uranium-based ammunition eventually leaches into the soil of the area in which it is used. Third, the use of heavy tracked vehicles can break up the thin layer of crust that forms on the desert sand. This crust diminishes the severity of sandstorms.

Estimating the damage caused by each of these is very difficult, especially when the impacts are very much in doubt. The volume and severity of the oil fires were substantially less than prewar fears, which were largely based on the oil fires in the first Gulf War. During the time of the first Gulf War, there were acute respiratory difficulties throughout the Middle East. Lung cancer rates in and around the Basra area spiked in the 1990s with the most plausible cause being those fires. The oil fires from this war were extinguished within a month, while some of the fires from the first Gulf War went on for more than a year.

While several hundred tons of depleted uranium weapons were fired during this war, the health impact of this is not certain. The increase in cancer rates in the Basra region of Iraq following the first Gulf War could have been from the volume of depleted uranium in the area, the oil fires lit by the Iraqi army, or the use of chemical weapons by the Iraqi military during the Iran–Iraq war of the 1980s. A World Health Organization study of Bosnia commissioned after the U.S. role there in the middle 1990s revealed few identifiable health impacts from the use of depleted uranium. The concern is that as time passes the depleted uranium will leach into the groundwater.

While a desert looks devoid of all life, it is an ecosystem that relies on a top layer of crusted sand. When it is broken up by heavy armored vehicles, the result can be increased sandstorm activity. Quantifying any of these impacts into a dollar figure is an imprecise art.

Finally, while establishing the cost to the environment is difficult, it is simple relative to establishing the cost of lost cultural artifacts. The combined result of the military strategy of using relatively few soldiers in lightening-fast raids into Baghdad and the relatively light resistance in the capital itself was that looting was rampant in the days following the fall of the city. Conceivably one could establish the cost of the looting to shop owners and civilian agencies in Iraq. On the other hand, the world lost some of its earliest known works of art and historical treasures when Baghdad's museums were looted of artifacts dating to thousands of years prior to the birth of Christ.

Summary

Whether or not you think the war with Iraq was wise from a political, moral, or environmental standpoint, the economic cost will be significant. It cost $5 billion to get the soldiers in position; nearly a billion dollars a month to pay, feed, and sustain them over and above the amount it would have cost to do those things in their home bases; and between $10 billion to $15 billion worth of fuel per month of battle. It will cost more than $60 billion per year in occupation costs and when all is done another $5 billion to bring the soldiers and their equipment back home. Whether the final cost ends up at the low end or at the high end still depends on the length of the occupation and whether the transition to civilian control in Iraq occurs soon or drags into the next president's term. What we bought is also still in dispute. At a minimum, we bought a Saddam-free Iraq. We may have gotten far more. You have to decide if what we paid, plus what we risked, made that a bargain or not.

Quiz Yourself

1. One opportunity cost of the war in Iraq was
   a. Soldiers still needed to be fed.
   b. Soldiers still needed to be paid.
   c. Soldiers enjoyed the experience of battle.
   d. The degree to which the deployed soldiers could not be devoted to other crises.

2. In war
   a. Economic and accounting costs are identical.
   b. All economic costs are ignored.
   c. All accounting costs are ignored.
   d. Economic and accounting costs count depending on whether they would have occurred had the war not occurred.

3. The pay soldiers receive in wartime is an accounting cost of that war
   a. But never an economic cost of it.

   b. But only the "combat pay" ever counts as an economic cost.
   c. And may be an economic cost if the soldiers had other missions to which they could have been deployed.
   d. But only during the combat phase of the war.

4. If soldiers are deployed to a war, the cost of feeding them is an accounting cost
   a. But never an economic cost of it.
   b. But only the excess cost of getting the food to them in the field over the cost of feeding them in their bases is an economic cost.
   c. And an economic cost as well.
   d. But only during the combat phase of the war.

5. The method of accounting for the cost of lost lives during a war described in this chapter
   a. Evaluates all lives equally.

b. Evaluates an Iraqi life as worth more than an American one.

c. Evaluates an American life as worth more than an Iraqi one.

d. Suggests that economists never attempt to place a dollar value on lost lives.

6. GDP

a. Accounts for all of the costs of war correctly.

b. Counts some costs of war as being positive when they clearly are not.

c. Ignores all cost of war.

7. When depleted-uranium weapons are fired, economists are concerned

a. With the cost of the weapons themselves and nothing else.

b. That the weapons cost too much.

c. That the weapons are too ineffective.

d. With the potential environmental cost whether or not they are cost-effective weapons.

Think about This

Economists are often consulted about the cost of activities that have mainly political goals (like winning a war) and give dollar estimates of those costs. How would you put a dollar estimate on the benefits that accrue from the achievement of those political goals? Suppose that a country is made safer because its enemy is beaten and is no longer a threat. Is there a dollar value for that?

Talk about This

In the months after the fall of Baghdad no evidence of weapons of mass destruction (WMD) were found and little evidence was found tying Iraq to Al-Qaeda. While the ruthless oppression of the Iraqi people at the hands of Saddam ended, it is unlikely that we would have gone to war without the WMD argument. Given that, how does this impact what the opportunity costs for the war were?

For More Insight See

Congressional Budget Office, "Estimated Costs of Continuing Operations in Iraq and Other Operations of the Global War on Terrorism," http://www.cbo.gov/ftpdocs/55xx/doc5587/Cost_of_Iraq.pdf.

House Budget Committee Democratic Staff, "Assessing the Cost of Military Action Against Iraq: Using Desert Shield/Desert Storm as a Basis for Estimates."

Nordhaus, William. "The Economic Consequences of a War with Iraq," NBER Working Paper No. 9631.

President Bush's Request for $74.7 billion for war-related expenses: http://www.whitehouse.gov/news/releases/2003/03/20030325.html.

World Health Organization Report on the Health Impact of Depleted Uranium: http://www.who.int/ionizing_radiation/pub_meet/ir_pub/en/.

Poast, Paul. *The Economics of War.* McGraw-Hill, 2006.

Chapter **38**

The Economics of Terrorism

This U.S. Embassy in Dar es Salaam, Tanzania, was one of the targets of nearly simultaneous 1998 bombings of two U.S. embassies in Africa that killed 224 people. *Source: AP Wide World Photo*

Chapter Objectives

After reading this chapter you should be able to

Understand the economic impact of the September 11, 2001, terrorist attacks.

Use an aggregate supply–aggregate demand diagram to model the impact of the attacks.

Understand how insurance works and why the increased uncertainty after the attacks affected insurance markets.

Understand the concept of the "rational" terrorist.

Chapter Outline

The Economic Impact of September 11th and of Terrorism in General

Modeling the Economic Impact of the Attacks

Terrorism from the Perspective of the Terrorist

Summary

This chapter explores the impact of terrorism and its continuing threat on the U.S. and world economy, as well as why economists look upon the terrorist as we would look upon any "rational" economic actor. In doing so, we will review the economic impact of September 11th. As we progress, you will understand how economists apply the notions of uncertainty, risk, and insurance when exploring the economic impact of terrorism and why self-protection against terrorism negatively affects those that do not protect themselves. Further, you will see why economists look upon the terrorist in the same way we look upon the drug dealer or the Mafia hit man: as a rational economic actor seeking to maximize benefits to himself at a minimum of costs.

THE ECONOMIC IMPACT OF SEPTEMBER 11TH AND OF TERRORISM IN GENERAL

Osama Bin Laden's Al-Qaeda operatives claim that the damage inflicted by their attacks on the United States total more than $1 trillion. While that figure is hard to justify, true damage estimates are, nonetheless, difficult to construct. In order to tally up the damage, you have to begin with the costs associated with the demolition and the ensuing cleanup of World Trade Center and Pentagon debris. Then you have to add the costs of rebuilding the affected portion of the Pentagon and replacing the WTC commercial and transportation facilities. You must also include the lost earning potential of the more than 3,000 victims. You cannot stop there. The war on terrorism, and the ancillary increases approved in defense spending because of that war, have added $100 billion annually to the federal budget. Adding the cost of the war and occupation of Iraq[1] to the mix sends the total much higher.

There are other costs you must include as well: any and all other money you have to spend because of the attacks that you would not have had to spend had the attacks not occurred. When that is complete, you have to add the money that could have been earned that might not now be earned. Thus when survivors seek counseling because of their trauma; when we all demand greater security at airports, large sporting events, and other potential targets; or, whenever we forgo an opportunity to travel because of the risk that we feel is present, these expenses must be included among all the other economic impacts of the attacks.

Starting at the top, the World Trade Center and the adjacent buildings were insured for $4 billion. The damage to the Pentagon cost another billion to repair. Next, the four planes were worth between $50 million and $100 million each. These are costs related to the direct damages that resulted from the attacks, but they are by no means either the only costs or the only damages.

There was income lost as a result of these buildings being attacked. Those in the WTC and surrounding buildings who did not perish did not produce goods and services for several days as their employers sought new facilities in which to operate. Many of the people and companies housed in the WTC towers were engaged in offering financial services, and they had purchased insurance against loss of income. Estimates of these losses suggest that upwards of $10 billion was paid to these companies to compensate them for that lost income. Total insurance estimates of the cost of the New York attacks total between $25 billion and $30 billion. As a result, many of the victims of the attacks received some form of monetary compensation, either from employers or from organizations like the Red Cross.

In economic terms, accounting for the loss of those who died is somewhat more difficult, depending as it does on estimating the value in money that a victim would have been worth over his or her entire projected lifetime. Economists have little trouble coming up with a dollar figure

that we can justify, but it is clear that saying that the life of Mary the secretary was worth $750,000 and that of Sally the investment banker was worth $3.6 million raises controversy.

A first pass at estimating what was lost to the economy as a result of the deaths of 3,000 people is to establish the present value of their future earnings. These were highly trained and highly paid people. If you assume that the average person killed earned $75,000 in salary and benefits, was 40 years old, and had a life expectancy of 35 years, then such a calculation would have each person worth approximately $1.7 million. With 3,000 dead that comes to a little over $5 billion.

In addition to what we have presented so far, there is the lost production of those 100,000 or more New York residents who would have been producing goods and services in the weeks following the attacks but were not able to because their bosses were still attempting to find new office space, reestablish phone and computer connections, and regain electric power. This includes the inhabitants of the World Trade Center itself as well as the people who worked in surrounding buildings that had to be evacuated because of the damage done to them.

Now consider the losses outside of New York and Washington that must be associated with the attacks. Airlines in particular were hard hit. The resulting drop in passenger flights led them to lay off more than 100,000 employees. Nationwide, in all sectors of the economy from mid-September through the end of 2001, new filings for unemployment insurance increased from just over 300,000 per week to nearly 650,000 per week. Although these numbers diminished to between 400,000 and 450,000 for most of 2002 and 2003, the employment outlook remained weak during this period.

All of the preceding examples are clearly costs to society, but in what will appear to be quite contradictory, GDP accounting will score some of these losses as economic positives. The money it cost to tear down the damaged buildings and begin rebuilding the New York WTC site and Washington's Pentagon came from two main sources. The federal government put forward $40 billion for this effort, and insurance companies were responsible for another $25 billion. The resulting increase in government spending will likely have a positive impact on GDP in the future, and because the insurance companies footing the bill were mostly foreign rather than domestic—while the demolition and rebuilding efforts occurred in the United States—this, too, had the effect of boosting GDP.

Increases in military spending, government spending on internal security, and spending on airport security has and

---

[1]Setting aside whether the war in Iraq was really about terrorism, it is unlikely Iraq would have been invaded had there not been the terrorism argument in the background.

will also continue to lead to increases in GDP. Of course, none of this is likely to make us better off than we were on September 10. We only hope that by spending this extra money we will be as secure today as we thought we were on September 10. Spending more to accomplish the same thing boosts reported GDP but does not make us better off.

MODELING THE ECONOMIC IMPACT OF THE ATTACKS

If you have studied Chapter 11, "Fiscal Policy," you are familiar with what economists call aggregate-demand shocks. Let me remind you that aggregate-demand shocks are unexpected events that change aggregate demand. Clearly, the attacks of September 11th qualified as "shocks" under any definition. Retail sales during the week of September 11th were dramatically lower than they otherwise would have been. This, and a variety of other indices of consumer confidence, all took very serious hits in the fall of 2001. Complicating things further, business confidence, which is typically measured by looking at businesses' hiring, layoff, and investment plans, was also adversely affected by the aftermath of the attacks. These effects in combination created the clearest example of an aggregate-demand shock in decades. Figure 38.1 shows the impact of these shocks on the aggregate demand–aggregate supply model. Lower aggregate demand reduces equilibrium, real gross domestic product, and overall prices.

As we will see in the section on insurance later, premiums paid by businesses in high risk areas rose substantially as well. That would lead to an aggregate-supply shock. Though this effect was likely less than the relative

FIGURE 38.2   The post-9/11 aggregate-supply shock.

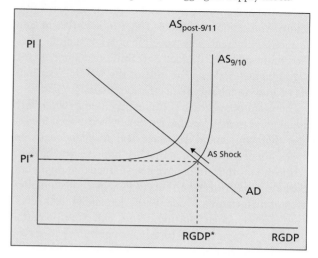

importance of the aggregate-demand shock, it is important to note, and Figure 38.2 depicts that aspect.

Insurance Aspects of Terrorism

When dealing with a world of uncertainty, rational people can seek out insurance because they view themselves as better off if they can pay something upfront to minimize the financial consequences of a foreseeable, but not necessarily predictable, problem. We insure our cars and our homes because, although the likelihood of a financially catastrophic incident is low, the consequences of a problem could be so severe that we are better off avoiding them by paying an insurance company to take the risk for us. The insurance company is only too happy to sell us the insurance because they get more money than they expect to have to pay out, and the uncertainty in their payouts is relatively low because they are spread out over so many people. They have actuaries who tell them how many homes are likely to be damaged in fires or how many automobiles they are likely to have to repair or replace.

Terrorism insurance in a place where terrorist acts are somewhat predictable (like Israel) is likely to be very expensive but also likely to be available because insurance companies can anticipate the number of buses and restaurants that will be destroyed. These many small-scale attacks are insurable because no single one of them jeopardizes the long-term survival of the insurance company. September 11th changed much of that thinking. It was the worst insurance outcome in American history, easily surpassing the previous record set by Hurricane Andrew.

FIGURE 38.1   The post-9/11 aggregate-demand shock.

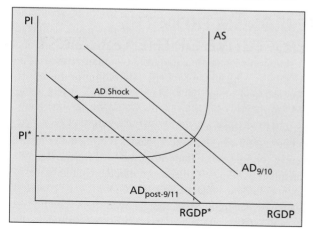

In the post–September 11th world, insurance companies have become leery of insuring major commercial landmarks. A major attack of a nuclear, biological, or chemical nature, or even another airliner hijacking directed at a major population center, is enough to cause insurance companies to fear for their own survival. For a while they refused to offer insurance on major new construction projects, did not renew policies on major commercial landmarks, and insisted that acts of terrorism be excluded from the policies' payout provisions.

This is not without precedent. After Hurricanes Andrew and Hugo in the late 1980s and early 1990s, insurance companies began pulling out of the Gulf Coast region of the United States for fear that they could not survive another hurricane. They stayed because they were able to buy **reinsurance** and pass the cost on to their customers. Reinsurance is like insurance itself except it is bought by insurance companies from other larger insurance companies (or from consortiums of insurance companies). The provisions of these reinsurance policies state that if a loss exceeds a certain level (usually in the multiple millions of dollars) for any one major event (such as a hurricane or terrorist attack), then the reinsurance company pays the insurance company and they, in turn, pay the claims of the victims of the incident.

reinsurance
The form of insurance where one insurance company promises to pay another if the first company has a large (usually multiple million dollar) loss from a single event.

September 11th was so big that the reinsurance companies were concerned for their own financial survival. Of course, at the time they did not know whether September 11th would be followed by several more attacks or not. The anthrax scare of late 2001 and early 2002 only added to the uncertainty. Insurance works well when the level of uncertainty to the party doing the insuring is somewhat low. Reinsurance works well when the uncertainty to the insurance company is large but is manageable to a reinsurance company. Nothing works when no one has any level of confidence in the risks involved.

The solution was re-reinsurance, where the U.S. federal government became the insurer of last resort. No one buys terrorism insurance from the government; there are no re-reinsurance agents selling to homeowners or businesses. The government will sell reinsurance to insurance companies and re-reinsurance to reinsurance companies. Few pieces of legislation initiated by the George W. Bush administration passed with as much support as the bill authorizing the government's involvement in the reinsurance market. This was partly because much of the financial community and labor unions were on the same side of the issue.

Buy Insurance or Self-Protect or Both

When faced with any uncertainty, a rational economic actor can do one or both of the following: protect himself or buy insurance against the loss. We have already extensively discussed the latter, so let's talk a bit about self-protection. Suppose you live in a community in which automobile theft is rampant. You can buy a car with an electronic alarm, an ignition that will start only with a special key (such that the car cannot be "hot-wired"), or a tracking system like "Lo-Jack" that allows a stolen car to be located from a satellite. You can also buy a product like "The Club" that prevents a car from being driven when it is attached to the steering wheel.

If you protect yourself against such a loss, you are simultaneously making your car less attractive to a thief and your neighbor's car relatively more attractive. This, like the problem of pollution or secondhand smoke, is a negative externality. Your actions hurt someone else who was not part of your decision to take action. With terrorism, if one business were to install devices or employ personnel to deter terrorist acts against it, a neighboring business becomes a relatively more attractive target. If you have flown since September 11, 2001, especially if you have flown during a code "Orange" elevated state of alert, you know that U.S. airports are substantially more secure than they were prior to that time. In the aftermath of the heightened security at airports and the USA Patriot Act, which allowed substantially more intrusive surveillance of foreigners in the United States, a terrorist is unlikely to attempt an attack on a target in the United States, let alone a U.S. airport, and far more likely to target Americans or American interests in other, less secure locations. That puts Americans in those locations in more danger than they would have been had these security measures not taken place in the United States.

TERRORISM FROM THE PERSPECTIVE OF THE TERRORIST

Economists who study terrorism look upon these folks in the same manner as economists who study crime look upon hit men: as rational people behaving in their own self-interest. You can quarrel with this interpretation if you like, and many people have a hard time calling a suicide bomber "rational" in this sense, but terrorists are in it for something. That "something" is usually political. Irish Republican Army (IRA) terrorists want Northern Ireland returned to Irish control or at least want the English out. Palestinian terrorists want some, most, or all of what is now Israel as a Palestinian state. Sudanese, Filipino, and antiabortion terrorists have political goals. Whether you are a terrorist or a freedom fighter often depends on which side of the power structure you are on.

This "rational terrorist hypothesis," like the "rational criminal hypothesis," suggests that terrorists have a goal, that they devote resources to achieving that goal, that they weigh benefits and costs, and that the best way of reaching the goal is to take all such actions where the marginal benefit equals or exceeds the marginal cost. Since the goals are political, the actions must have a political impact, which means they must garner media attention. They garner the most media attention when attacks are gruesome, affect innocent people, and occur where the media exist. They are the least costly to the terrorist when the targets are relatively unguarded and easy to get to. That means that from the perspective of Al-Qaeda, the September 11th attacks were nearly perfect. The lax security at U.S. airports; the high-profile nature of the World Trade Center, the Pentagon, and the Capitol Building or White House (whichever building Flight 93 was destined to attack) in the media meccas of New York and Washington; and the obvious innocence of the people on the planes and in the buildings made them the perfect targets for terrorism.

The worldwide reaction, the wars in Afghanistan and Iraq, and the public's willingness to give up some degree of its freedoms and privacy combined to make the costs of terrorism to the terrorist substantially greater. The substantial increase in the counterterrorism budget of the CIA and the FBI and the new powers granted to these organizations make a terrorist act in the United States far more expensive to pull off. The lack of any attack in the United States between September 11th and the writing of this edition suggests that terrorists may have weighed the costs and benefits and taken the stance that attacks on U.S. interests in the United States are not worth it. On the other hand, terrorists have clearly not given up. Attacks around the globe, embassy bombings, assassinations of U.S. diplomats, and attacks on places where Americans congregate overseas suggest terrorists are targeting easier, though less media dense, locations. Economists refer to this, and any other occurrence where one alternative gets more expensive so that the other is chosen, as the *substitution effect*.

The Madrid train bombing in 2004 and the London subway bombings in 2005 illustrate this substitution effect very well. Because terrorists apparently thought it was easier to get into Spain and the United Kingdom than it was to get into the United States, they chose targets that were "less expensive."

Unprecedented expenditures on security increase security generally but also motivate the terrorist to find the softest, most high-profile targets. This does not mean that the United States is immune from further attack, but it makes it predictable that the terrorist target selection process will focus on less secure cities and facilities. For this reason, it is reasonable to fear that the next target for a terrorist attack within the United States will be focused on our water supply, chemical plants, or refineries.

Summary

In this chapter, you have seen that economists' estimates of the damage inflicted by Al-Qaeda on September 11, 2001, encompass a wide variety of issues, from the loss of the buildings, to the loss of economic output, to the economic consequences of the loss of lives. You have also seen that insurance issues become more complicated as the level of uncertainty rises but that reinsurance helps to resolve those issues. Finally, you now see that economists view terrorists as rational economic actors attempting to get the biggest result for the least expense in the same way that any other goal-oriented person would. As a result, we can predict that as we tighten security in one area in response to an attack, they will seek other targets.

Key Term

reinsurance, 395

Quiz Yourself

1. This chapter suggests that many economists generally
   a. Accept the notion that a human life is worth the value of the chemicals that can be extracted from it.
   b. Argue that a human life is worth the sum of the person's future income.

c. Argue that the loss to society resulting from "wrongful death" is the present value of the person's income.

d. Reject the notion that any dollar value can be used to estimate the value of a human life.

2. The destruction of the World Trade Center and damage to the Pentagon and the accompanying work to rebuild and repair led to _____ to the insurance companies and _____ in GDP.

a. Gains, gains.

b. Losses, losses.

c. Losses, gains.

d. Gains, losses.

3. Economists call the reduction in consumer confidence that resulted from the September 11th attacks an _____ shock which leads to the _____.

a. Aggregate demand, aggregate demand curve shifting left.

b. Aggregate demand, aggregate demand curve shifting right.

c. Aggregate supply, aggregate supply curve shifting left.

d. Aggregate supply, aggregate supply curve shifting right.

4. Economists call the increase in insurance costs that resulted from the September 11th attacks an _____ hock which leads to the _____.

a. Aggregate demand, aggregate demand curve shifting left.

b. Aggregate demand, aggregate demand curve shifting right.

c. Aggregate supply, aggregate supply curve shifting left.

d. Aggregate supply, aggregate supply curve shifting right.

5. The chief effect of reinsurance is that

a. Insurance premiums are higher.

b. Insurance companies are prevented from engaging in fraud.

c. Insurance companies can offer insurance without fear of a major event causing them to go out of business.

d. Consumers are protected against easily anticipated occurrences.

6. The government's role in terrorism insurance is that of

a. A primary provider.

b. A reinsurance provider of last resort/re-reinsurer.

c. Innocent bystander.

d. Disinterested observer.

7. The negative externality associated with self-protection from terrorism suggests that

a. Terrorists cause more damage than they think they will.

b. People engage in less self-protection than they should.

c. People engage in the right amount of self-protection.

d. A person who self-protects makes someone else relatively more vulnerable.

8. Under many economic models of terrorism, the terrorist is assumed to act

a. Without regard for incentives, costs, or benefits.

b. In a predictable way, since they maximize costs subject to minimizing benefits.

c. In a predictable way, since they maximize benefits subject to minimizing costs.

d. With no predictable nature.

9. Substitution in the context of the "rational terrorist model" suggests that a clampdown at airports will

a. End terrorism.

b. Cause terrorists to target airports even more as they attempt to show their strength.

c. Cause terrorists to seek alternative targets.

d. Foment even more terrorism around the globe because it will show them they have succeeded.

Think about This

One of the things that counterterrorist intelligence agents must do is put themselves in the position of the terrorist. Take 10 minutes and think about your hometown. What action could terrorists take that would have the maximum impact for the least cost to themselves? Would that action necessarily be suicidal?

Talk about This

Do you agree with the contention that terrorist actions can be viewed as "coldly rational." Would you characterize the actions of terrorists who kill themselves in conducting their operations as rational?

For More Insight See

Brauer, Jurgen, "On the Economics of Terrorism," *Phi Kappa Phi Forum* 82, no. 2 (Spring 2002).

Chapter 39

Wal-Mart: Always Low Prices (and Low Wages)—Always

Source: © McGraw-Hill Companies/John Flournoy, Photographer

Chapter Objectives

After reading this chapter you should be able to

Understand the importance of Wal-Mart in the U.S. economy.

Understand that the grocery sector continues to have a variety of competitors with monopolist competition being an adequate model to explain it.

Understand that consumers tend to benefit when Wal-Mart enters a community but that labor may win or lose, that other businesses may win or lose, and that the net impact is not always easy to compute.

Chapter Outline

The Market Form

Who Is Affected?

Summary

Depending on who you talk to Wal-Mart is either one of the great American success stories and the driving force behind the upsurge in American productivity, or it is the emblem for low-wage, no-benefit, dead-end jobs, and the destroyer of small business. The reality is that it is all of that. Begun by Sam Walton as a small discount store in Bentonville, Arkansas, it has grown over the last 30 years to become the largest nongovernmental employer in the United States responsible for more than 2 percent of U.S. GDP. With nearly every new store there is a debate about whether a new Wal-Mart is good or bad for the community. Several communities, and one state, Vermont, have banned large discount stores on the argument that what Wal-Mart brings, low-priced merchandise

and low-wage jobs, is not worth the cost in terms of other lost jobs and lost local character. This chapter explores the pros and cons of "big-box stores" in general and Wal-Mart in particular.

THE MARKET FORM

Most communities that have Wal-Mart Supercenters have other large grocery-chain-affiliated stores as well. Also in the mix are individually owned stores, some of which are affiliated with what was once called the International Grocers Association but is now known as the familiar IGA. Your prototypical community will have stores of all varieties. From warehouse stores like Sam's and Costco to

FIGURE 39.1   Store locations of the top 10 grocery store outlets in the United States.

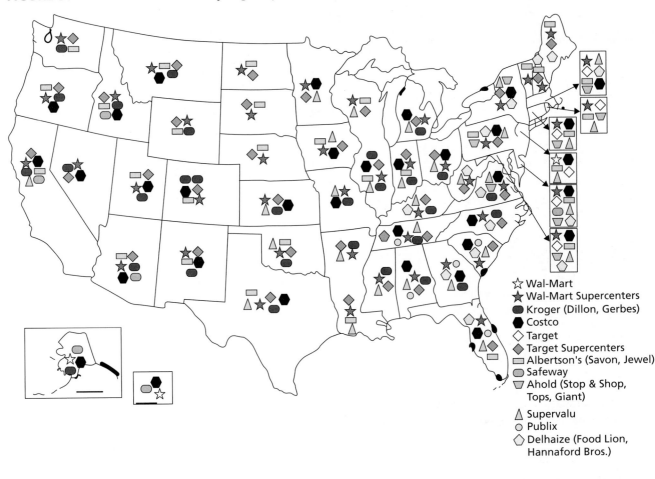

☆ Wal-Mart
★ Wal-Mart Supercenters
⬬ Kroger (Dillon, Gerbes)
⬢ Costco
◇ Target
◆ Target Supercenters
▭ Albertson's (Savon, Jewel)
⬭ Safeway
▽ Ahold (Stop & Shop, Tops, Giant)

△ Supervalu
○ Publix
⬠ Delhaize (Food Lion, Hannaford Bros.)

the "supers" (Kmart, Wal-Mart, and Target), to the national chains (Kroger, Safeway, etc.), to the national holding companies (for example Ahold is a holding company with regional stores like Stop & Shop and Giant), to the regional chains (Wegmans, Winn-Dixie, and Publix, etc.) to the IGA-affiliated stores, the grocery business is large and diverse. The market form that best describes this set of conditions is monopolistic competition. Though very small towns may have only one grocery store (monopoly) and small cities may have just two or three (oligopoly), the vast majority of Americans live in a community in which three of the four types of stores are present.

Every grocery store has a monopoly of sorts based on its location but is faced with competition from other stores as consumers are willing to travel short distances past one store to go to another. Many people have a preference for stores that include or do not include some goods. While some are intimidated by a "super" store,

others are attracted to them because they can do grocery shopping, have their pharmacy needs met, and pick up a power tool and a new-release DVD all in one location. Some consumers want the "hometown proud" feeling of an IGA affiliate because they want to be on a first-name basis with their meat cutter and appreciate the fact that the owner sponsors a local Little League team. Monopolistic competition fits this market quite well.

A look at Figure 39.1 clearly shows that the top 10 grocery store companies and holding companies are widely dispersed throughout the United States with little likelihood that any one firm could gain a monopoly in any but the smallest of communities. Table 39.1 shows the percentage of total grocery sales by the top 10 firms. These top 10 grocery chains (and holding companies) account for three-quarters of all such sales. However you slice the data, the concern that Wal-Mart is establishing a monopoly is not supported.

TABLE 39.1   Top 10 grocery store chains.

Rank	Company	Annual Sales (billions)	% of Total Grocery Sales ($755 billion)	% Top 10 Grocery Sales ($566 billion)
1	Wal-Mart Stores	$284	36.65	50.19
2	Kroger Company	$56	7.25	9.93
3	Costco Wholesale Corp.	$47	6.09	8.34
4	Target	$47	6.04	8.27
5	Albertsons	$40	5.12	7.02
6	Safeway	$36	4.62	6.33
7	Ahold USA Retail	$27	3.54	4.84
8	Supervalu	$20	2.52	3.45
9	Publix Super Markets	$19	2.40	3.29
10	Delhaize America	$16	2.04	2.79

Source: http://supermarketnews.com/.

A similar concern is the degree to which Wal-Mart affects its suppliers. To many firms, large and small, Wal-Mart is their largest buyer. Were Wal-Mart to become its only potential buyer the problem of monopsony would occur. In that circumstance, companies are forced to reduce the prices to Wal-Mart for fear that Wal-Mart will shut them out. Just as Wal-Mart can "make" a company by vastly expanding the market for a company's products, it can just as easily break it by compelling the firm to produce goods more cheaply. This can, and often does, result in the company outsourcing production to another country, reducing wages and benefits at its U.S. production facilities, or making products from less expensive and less durable materials.

WHO IS AFFECTED?

There are many stakeholders when any "super" comes to town and, especially in the Northeast and West, local city and county authorities have developed zoning laws that are clearly aimed at keeping "supers" at bay. In examining why some object to the introduction of a Wal-Mart Supercenter into a community it helps to look at who wins and who loses. First, as a group consumers unambiguously win because Wal-Marts tend to charge substantially less for identical items when comparisons are made between its prices and those of other big national or regional grocery stores like Kroger, Safeway, Food Lion, or Albertsons. Often Wal-Mart can sell its staple items (like milk and bread) for less than IGA affiliates pay their suppliers. Second, workers may win or lose depending on two things: (1) whether there is a net increase in jobs or

whether the jobs gained at the Wal-Mart are countered by lost jobs at competitors, and, (2) what Wal-Mart pays its employees. Third, taxpayers may win or lose depending on whether or not there is a net addition to sales in the community that results in a net increase in sales taxes. Finally, some of the owners of small businesses and other, existing corporate retailers may be affected negatively, while others may benefit from such an endeavour. Let's examine some data.

Most Consumers Stand to Gain— Some Lose Options

We'll take each set of stakeholders in turn, starting with the buying public. The gain to consumers from paying less for their groceries is substantial. The average Wal-Mart Supercenter sells between $75 and $125 million worth of goods in a year. Estimates vary considerably, but a trade association of mass marketers suggests that Wal-Mart's prices are 15 percent to 22 percent lower than national averages. Suppose the average consumer saves 15 percent. The gain to the consumers that voluntarily switch from an average store to a Super Wal-Mart is (per store) between $11.25 and $27.5 million annually.

Whatever these consumers do with the saved money, it is clear that they benefit from this perspective. Whether or not the local economy benefits depends on what consumers do with the saved money. If they consume more locally produced goods and services then the local community benefits. If they put the money in their Wall Street managed investment accounts, the local community does not benefit as much.

There may be some locations where a "super" drives an IGA-type store out of business and in so doing makes some consumers worse off because they now have their optimal grocery option removed from their set of choices. To ballpark that loss, suppose a family used to pay $1,000 more a year on groceries at an IGA than they would have at a Wal-Mart and did so because they liked the personalized service available at the IGA store. They have shown through their "revealed preferences" that this option is worth at least $1,000. For every 1,000 consumers so affected, the loss would be $1,000,000. What seems likely is that consumers as an aggregate are better off though some may be worse off.

Workers Probably Lose

It's hard to tell what the impact will be on workers because it is unclear whether there will be any net addition (or net loss) to the work force. If there is a net addition, it may not be great enough to offset the loss associated with the fact that nationally, Wal-Mart's pay is $5 to $10 less per hour (including benefits) than the typically unionized grocery store it is challenging. Nearly every supercenter that has opened in the last two years has employed approximately 450 people. However, there are problems with that number: first, about a third of the jobs are part-time, and second, the literature on displacements suggests that between 75 percent and 133 percent of such jobs will be displaced elsewhere in the community.[1] If we assume that a work year contains 2,080 hours, and, further, if we assume Wal-Mart pays its employees $8 per hour and its competitors pay $18 per hour there will be a loss to the community of workers that is somewhere between $4 million and $10 million per store.

Sales Tax Revenues Won't Be Affected Much

The question of whether taxpayers will gain or lose depends on whether the net sales in the state increase. The literature on the degree to which new supercenters increase total sales in a community suggests that between 70 percent and 80 percent of their sales displace sales that would have taken place in that community anyway. The problem with saying that sales taxes would therefore increase is that (1) a sizable portion of the sales are for tax-exempt items like food and (2) very little of the taxable sales would go to people who would have spent their money outside the state.

The latter point is important because sales taxes in many states go directly to the state. Therefore, whether the sales are in the particular community or in one of the neighboring counties, the sales taxes collected are the same. So, though more sales taxes would be collected in the community, there would be little effect on total sales tax collections.

Some Businesses Will Get Hurt, Others Will Be Helped

The impact of Wal-Mart and other "supers" on other stores in the area is not clear. IGA affiliates follow a strategy of not trying to "out-Wal-Mart" Wal-Mart. They "believe that a good grocery store isn't a sprawling, impersonal example of cookie-cutter commerce, but a community hub owned and operated by the very people who know the area best—the citizens." As a result they support local charities, sponsor many local children's athletic teams, stock food products not often stocked at a "super," happily take special orders for meats not typically carried by the "supers," cut meat on-site rather than having it delivered already packaged, and their owners are on-site and part of their communities. At least some of Wal-Mart's growth has been at the expense of these stores.

What is also important in the mix is that Wal-Marts tend to lead to the creation of complementary businesses. This "pull-factor" has been estimated to increase the creation of other retail business and other economic activity. A new Wal-Mart is likely to "pull" retail sales from neighboring counties. That also leads to new fast-food and chain sit-down restaurants and other "big-box" retailers like Home Depot, Circuit City, and Staples which often follow "supers." Wal-Mart can be the instant critical mass for an undeveloped or depressed area to become economically vibrant.

Community Effects

Sociologists have entered the Wal-Mart discussion by pointing out that the introduction of "supers" has the impact of displacing stores that are owned by people who are also community leaders. This suggests that there is a further external cost to Wal-Marts in that they damage a community's noneconomic fabric. They also argue that after controlling for a host of other variables, shortly after a Wal-Mart enters a market, local rates of poverty rise.

---

[1]One nonacademic source suggests that Wal-Mart gets so much more work out of an employee that the total number of workers falls when a Wal-Mart comes to town.

Summary

The net result of any new Wal-Mart is what you would expect. Consumers mostly win and workers mostly lose, some businesses win, others lose, with the net being somewhat positive depending on the particulars of the community. If the new store simply replaces sales that would have occurred in the town anyway and the gain in employment is offset completely by the closing of other businesses then what consumers gain is approximately equal to what workers lose. If, as is more likely, there is some net addition to employment and complementary businesses grow alongside the Wal-Mart, then it is a net addition to the community. The local business leaders will gain or lose depending on whether they try to go head-to-head with Wal-Mart (a suicidal venture) or they attempt to complement the Wal-Mart by selling what Wal-Mart does not, service.

Quiz Yourself

1. The impact of a new Wal-Mart on a community's consumers is
   a. Significantly positive for those that get lower prices.
   b. Somewhat negative for those that prefer a personal touch (if stores offering it close).
   c. Substantially negative in all aspects.
   d. A combination of *a* and *b*.

2. The impact of a new Wal-Mart on a community's workers is
   a. Only positive in that new jobs are created.
   b. Only negative because better-paying jobs at competitors are lost.
   c. Positive and negative because new jobs are created, but they often displace better-paying ones.
   d. Only positive because Wal-Mart pays better than their competitors.

3. We can measure how much someone values the personal touch of a small grocery store by using the amount extra they pay at that store even when there is a Wal-Mart in town. Economists call that
   a. Revealed demand.
   b. Revealed preference.
   c. Parsing the preference.
   d. Noting the demand.

4. The impact of Wal-Mart on its suppliers is
   a. Unambiguously positive.
   b. Unambiguously negative.
   c. Positive and negative in that Wal-Mart enlarges the market for their products but demands a much lower price than they typically receive.
   d. Negligible.

5. The predominant market form for the grocery business in the majority of U.S. cities is one of
   a. Monopoly.
   b. Oligopoly.
   c. Monopolistic competition.
   d. Perfect competition.

6. Wal-Mart's entry into the grocery business in the 1990s
   a. Turned it into a monopoly.
   b. Had no impact on the market form; it remained perfectly competitive.
   c. Had no impact on the market form; it remained monopolistically competitive.
   d. Had no impact on the market form; it remained an oligopoly.

Think about This

Wal-Mart's entry into the grocery business in the 1990s had an important effect in lowering the price of groceries to poor people. Should this be taken into account when establishing the poverty line?

Talk about This

Major American companies that used to manufacture their goods in the United States, are now manufacturing their goods in China because Wal-Mart puts enormous pressure on the company to lower prices. This is because its practice is to tell a manufacturer what it will pay for a good. If the company wishes to sell its goods in a Wal-Mart it will lower prices. This is good for you in that you get goods at a lower cost. It is bad for the U.S. employees of the business because they lose their jobs. What is the net good/bad in your mind?

For More Insight See

Boyina, Manjula, "An Examination of Pull Factor Change in Non-Metro Counties in Kansas: A Study of the Economic Impact of Wal-Mart Construction," *Kansas Policy Review* 26, no. 2.

Franklin, Andrew W., "The Impact of Wal-Mart Super-center Food Store Sales on Supermarket Concentration in U.S. Metropolitan Areas." Paper presented at the USDA conference "The American Consumer and the Changing Structure of the Food System, Arlington, Virgina, May 3–5, 2000.

Stone, Kenneth E., Georgeanne Artz, and Albert Myles, *The Economic Impact of Wal-Mart Supercenters on Existing Businesses in Mississippi:* http://www.seta.iastate.edu/retail/publications/ms_supercenterstudy.pdf.

Chapter 40

The Economic Impact of Casino Gambling

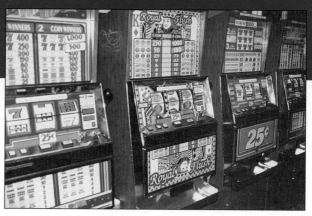

Source: Jack Star/PhotoLink/Getty Images

Chapter Objectives

After reading this chapter you should be able to

Understand potential economic impact of casino gambling in the context of the local substitution problem.

Understand the externalities problem as it relates to casino gambling.

Understand that the overall picture of the local economic impact of casino gambling depends greatly on where the casino is located.

Chapter Outline

The Perceived Impact of Casino Gambling

Local Substitution

The "Modest" Upside of Casino Gambling

The Economic Reasons for Opposing Casino Gambling

Summary

When state and local governments run into financial difficulties one of the first solutions brought to the table is casino gambling. Whether it be the introduction of gambling to the state or its expansion to a new part of the state, the argument goes something like this: "If we open a new casino, gaming companies will hire people to build it, more people to run it, and in the end they will all be paying more in taxes." This "everyone wins" scenario is plagued with the same logical flaw as the "if we build it they will come" argument for publicly funding the construction of a new sports stadium. This is in addition to the negative externality that is created for casino communities.

THE PERCEIVED IMPACT OF CASINO GAMBLING

The perception that gambling has an enormous economic impact on a community is understandable. More than 50 million Americans set foot in a casino each year, leaving nearly $30 billion. The Casinos themselves employ 370,000 people while paying more than $4 billion in taxes. That, in a nutshell, is why gambling became one of the "answers" to state budget crises that stemmed from the 2001 recession.

LOCAL SUBSTITUTION

The problem with the argument that a casino is an economic boon to its host community is that the money that goes into the casino came out of the pockets of some other businesses and therefore does not increase total economic activity in the community. To explain why, I will use my hometown as an example.

Terre Haute, Indiana, is known for two things: it was the college town for Larry Bird and it is the home of the U.S. penitentiary that housed and then executed Timothy McVeigh. It is also home to economic and population decline. Once considered a major city in the state, it currently struggles to be noticed by the state's leaders. Some local leaders proposed that the solution to Terre Haute's economic woes included a riverboat on the Wabash River that defines the city's western edge.

It is unambiguously true that such a facility would have cost in the neighborhood of $100 million to construct and that many of those construction jobs would have gone to citizens of the city. It is also true that once operational, a casino in Terre Haute would employ hundreds of workers at all levels of pay and responsibility. The problem is that money would have, in large part, come from people who already spend their entertainment dollars in the city.

The confusion over whether casinos are an economic answer to a community's problems results from the fact that the thing right in front of you often masks the equally sized but more dispersed negative impacts. This is true even if there are not the negative social consequences associated with gambling.

When properly examined, the bulk of the money that is spent on gaming in a community is money that usually comes from inside the community. The only substantial impact comes when a casino is located in a relatively rural area with a major market unserved by an existing casino. Thus residents of Cincinnati will drive to Indiana's neighboring Aurora to gamble when they otherwise would not have gone across the Ohio River to spend their entertainment dollars. Chicago, Illinois, is on the Illinois and Indiana border. Three cities on the Indiana side of the border, Gary, Michigan City, and Hammond, all have casinos but these mostly serve the Chicago metropolitan area.

A Terre Haute casino might draw Indianapolis residents but it is not close enough to make it a slam-dunk success. The other problem with relying on the Indianapolis market is that if the issue of casinos is opened up again in the Indiana Legislature, other towns much closer to Indianapolis will certainly want in on the game. In the end, the people most likely to patronize a Terre Haute casino are people who already spend their entertainment dollars in Terre Haute.

This Indiana example is playing out in many states. Whether it be gambling in Wisconsin, Missouri, or anywhere else, the names change but the idea stays the same.

THE "MODEST" UPSIDE OF CASINO GAMBLING

Senior Economist Thomas A. Garrett of the St. Louis Federal Reserve notes that, "Although economic development is used by the casino industry and local governments to sell the idea of casino gambling to the citizenry, the degree to which the introduction and growth of commercial casinos in an area leads to increased economic development remains unclear." The evidence, as Dr. Garrett puts it, favors a "modest impact." In particular, the impact depends on where the casino is (rural or urban) and whether there is a large unserved market nearby.

Were there no externalities associated with casino gambling, the Garrett data would suggest that it is no different than any other recreational activity. That it is no ticket to an economic panacea would preclude it from being part of the larger solution of economic growth. Again, looking at my state's experience shows that the impact of casino gambling is quite modest. From 1991 to 2001, the period of significant casino growth in the state of Indiana, the annual growth rate in personal income in counties with a casino was 5.3 percent whereas in counties without a casino that annual growth rate was 5.2 percent.

Further, the notion that casinos are a boon to community tax coffers is partly wrong and partly deceiving. Much of the revenue that gets attributed to the casino would have been paid by other entertainment operators were there no casino. Concentrating the dollars paid into one source doesn't make them any greater. The real increase in tax revenue attributable to casinos exists because the effective tax rate on a gambled (and lost) dollar is substantially higher than the effective tax rate on a dollar spent at a restaurant or a dollar spent at a bowling alley. It is a tax increase that brings in the revenue to local governments, not an increase in economic activity. No wonder politicians fall for casino industry promises of money, they offer the possibility of raising taxes without the negative political consequence.

THE ECONOMIC REASONS FOR OPPOSING CASINO GAMBLING

The economic reasons to oppose this modest economic growth opportunity are the same as the reasons to oppose or limit the sale of tobacco, alcohol, drugs, and prostitution. Gambling is quite clearly addictive. Addicts of all varieties will do anything to satisfy their desires. Gambling addicts will run up credit card debt, mortgage their homes, and put their families in terrible financial condition before seeking help. This leads to another problem: gambling is associated with costs borne by someone other than the gambler or the casino. In the presence of **externalities,** free markets produce more of the good or service (including gambling entertainment) than is consistent with economic efficiency.

externalities
Effects of a transaction which hurt or help people who are not part of that transaction.

Psychologists who study gambling addicts contend that most inveterate gamblers became attracted to it because they won significant sums of money their first time. This creates such an emotional high in the same centers of the brain that drug addicts get and, like drug addicts, they continually try to repeat that high. Of course, gamblers can't win over the long run. Casinos make money; money that used to belong to gamblers. To a statistician, gambling has a negative "expected value." That means that the average person who brings in $100 to a casino will leave with less than $100. This is because the gambles themselves are never "fair." Whether it's craps, poker, blackjack, or any other game the "house" has a **"vig,"** or percentage of the average gamble that is its take.

vig
The expected percentage of any gamble that a casino will keep.

The "vig" is what pays for the employees, the facility, and the profits to the casino company. This is why there are few gamblers who made their money gambling.

This, of course, is no different than any other form of entertainment. You never leave a movie theater with more money than you went in with. Assuming the movie was good, you do not complain because you got to see the movie. The allure of gambling is that you will win. When your first experience gambling is like mine (I fed $40 in quarters into a slot machine in 20 minutes and won nothing), casino gambling has no appeal. On the other hand, psychologists insist that when you win big your first time out, there is a "high." It is a high that could potentially lead to addiction. As a result, you can make an economic argument against casinos on the same grounds you argue that cocaine or methamphetamine should be illegal.

That addiction can also create other negative behaviors by the gambler and those behaviors can affect innocent third parties. When gamblers borrow extensively to support their addiction to gambling, the result can be high rates of bankruptcy. Higher bankruptcy rates lead to higher interest rates for the rest of us because credit card companies cannot distinguish people using their credit cards to buy food, clothing, or pay hotel bills from those who use their cards to support a gambling addition. In addition, the money that a gambler uses to support their habit could have been put to better use on food, clothing, or other goods for their family. When gamblers divorce leaving spouses and their children on public assistance, those consequences are an external cost of gambling. Left unregulated or untaxed, any such market that produces external costs will produce too much.

Summary

You now understand that it is easy to overstate the impact of a new casino on the economy of a community. The impact is "modest" because of the degree of local substitution. There is no panacea of better jobs, higher incomes, and greater tax revenues. You also understand that gambling is addictive and that economists consider addictive goods worthy of regulation. Finally you understand that a casino produces external costs and, like any good where that happens, an unregulated, untaxed market will produce too much gambling.

Quiz Yourself

1. The argument that casinos have little economic impact on a community is based on the notion of
   a. Supply.
   b. Demand.
   c. Opportunity cost.
   d. Local substitution.

2. Economists generally believe that a new casino in a city that already has them would likely have————————economic impact.

   a. An enormously negative.
   b. A modestly negative.
   c. An enormously positive.
   d. A modestly positive.

3. Which one of the following communities would likely see the greatest economic impact from a new casino?

   a. Plainfield, IN (just outside Indianapolis).
   b. Gary, IN (outside Chicago and already has one).
   c. Terre Haute, IN (Indianapolis is 70 miles away, no other population center is closer than 180 miles).
   d. Las Vegas, NV.

4. The percentage that casinos make on the average bet is called the

   a. Vig.
   b. Rip.
   c. Take.
   d. Rob.

5. The argument that increasing the number of casinos in a state will increase overall tax revenue in the state is

   a. Substantially correct, because they pay substantial taxes.
   b. Overstated but still partially correct, because there is tax substitution but gambling profits are taxed more heavily than other profits.
   c. Understated because they pay more taxes than is generally known.
   d. Wrong because casino profits are not taxed.

6. The concern that gambling affects not only the gambler and casino but others is called a _____ and suggests that there would be too _____ production in an unregulated or untaxed market.

   a. Positive externality; much.
   b. Negative externality; much.
   c. Positive externality; little.
   d. Negative externality; little.

Think about This

Casino companies, Wal-Mart, and sports teams make the same case with regard to economic development and they are mostly wrong for the same reasons: local substitution. Why do they still succeed in overstating their economic impact?

Talk about This

The effect of gambling addiction is similar to the effect of other addictions though it is less apparent to others. Alcoholics, drug addicts, and so on, are easier to spot. Part of the problem is that inveterate gamblers can be successful at their addiction (winning a televised poker championship) or unsuccessful (and losing everything), while no one becomes a successful meth addict. Is gambling only a problem for the losers? Should casinos only allow people to lose a particular amount of money?

For More Insight See

Garrett, Thomas A., *Casino Gambling in America and Its Economic Impacts,* Federal Reserve Bank of St. Louis: http://research.stlouisfed.org/regecon/CasinoGambling.pdf.

Garrett, Thomas A., and Mark W. Nichols, *Do Casinos Export Bankruptcy?* Federal Reserve Bank of St. Louis: http://research.stlouisfed.org/wp/2005/2005-019.pdf.

Evans, W. N., and J. Topoleski, "The Social and Economic Impact of Native American Casinos," NBER Working Paper No. 9198: http://papers.nber.org/papers/w9198.

Chapter 41

Why College Textbooks Cost So Much

@Royalty-Free/CORBIS

Chapter Objectives

After reading this chapter you should be able to

Understand the process by which textbooks come to market.

Understand that, depending on the subject, competition among publishers considers whether the models of monopoly, oligopoly, or monopolistic competition are appropriate.

Understand the impact that the Internet has had on the used book market and how the used book market impacts the new book market.

Understand that the book selection process often does not involve price.

Chapter Outline

The Process

Textbooks and Market Forms

Technology and the Impact of Used Books

When Price Matters and When It Does Not

So Why Do They Cost So Much and Who's to Blame?

Summary

The market for college textbooks is a good example of a great many economic concepts: fixed and variable costs, the impact of patents and copyrights on the market for a good, the fuzziness of the line between oligopoly and monopolistic competition, and the degree to which increased technology increases supply.

THE PROCESS

Before we get too deep into the analysis you should understand how a textbook comes to market. In the beginning there is a void, or at least a perceived void. That is, either a publisher or a college professor decides that there is some niche not being adequately covered, some market share to gain with an alternative approach, or all the books in the field are so poorly written that any improvement would garner great interest. This spawns sample chapters. Either solicited or unsolicited, a faculty member will write a chapter or two to show a publisher why this new book would be better than those that exist. These sample chapters take a few months to write, refine, and edit. When finished they are sent to the publisher. Very few of these make it past this step.

Those sample chapters that meet with the publisher's expectations are sent out to faculty who, when the book is published, might consider using the book for their course. Typically the publisher will pay four to eight selected faculty between $200 and $600 to read and comment on the book chapters. If the comments are positive, then a book is ready to be written. A contract is drawn up that specifies how the author is to be paid. Typically the author will get a percentage of the sales (in the neighborhood of 15 percent) to bookstores (based on the whole-sale price net of returns). An **advance** is usually offered to the author against future **royalties.** The book takes at least a year to write, revise, edit, and publish. Often a first edition takes much longer than subsequent editions because it is typically reviewed by a different collection of faculty around the country.[1]

advance
The amount of money paid to authors prior to a book's publication. This is typically counted against future royalties.

royalties
The amount of money paid to authors. Typically paid on a percentage basis.

Once available for sale the book is mailed, free of charge, to faculty all around the country that teach a course in which the book might be used. This could be thousands of books, as is the case when there is a rollout of a principles of economics book (that which is appropriate for business and economics majors) or a few hundred (when the book has a more limited audience). Faculty place their orders with their respective bookstores and the bookstores order them in the month leading up to the beginning of the semester.

To see where the money goes on the sale of a new book, consider the one you are reading. As shown in Figure 41.1 the previous edition of this book sold for $80 as a new book in my university's bookstore. The book was sold to the bookstore for $60 so its expenses and profit come out of their $20 markup. I get 15 percent of the amount that the publisher gets, or $9. The publisher keeps the remaining $51. The publisher's costs include fixed costs such as the payments they have made for supplements (the test-bank, the instructor's manual, the Web site material, the study guide, the Powerpoints, etc.), the share of the editorial staff's time turning my work into its final form, and the share of the marketing staff's time selling the book. The variable costs also include the cost of the paper, ink, and printing of the book itself. Textbook paper is not cheap and, depending on whether the book is black and white, two-color (which means black and white plus various shades of another color), or multicolor, the ink can be costly too. In all, the marginal production cost of a textbook is less than $10 sometimes as little as $5. When all is said and done the $51 margin that the publisher makes must cover all the fixed costs of production.

Here it gets tricky because the publisher, and by extension the author, makes money only when a new book is sold. You do not have to be in college very long to know that you can buy used textbooks for much less than new ones and that you can sell your books back to the bookstore at the end of the semester. Typically a book that sells new for $80 will sell used for $60. The bookstore will have purchased that used book from a previous student for around $40. The bookstore then stocks both new books and used books and makes a profit on either. There is some risk for the bookstore in overstocking a new book since they have to pay a restocking fee to return new books to the publisher but there is enormous risk in overstocking used books. This is because if there is a new edition of the book, the old edition is worthless.

This brings us to the new edition scam. Calculus hasn't changed since Newton figured it out so why would anyone need to write a new edition? Because publishers and authors make money only when the new edition sells for the first time. Publication cycles typically run for two to four years between editions.

---

[1]The first edition of this text was begun in 1999 and sold its first copy in 2002.

FIGURE 41.1   Where the money goes.

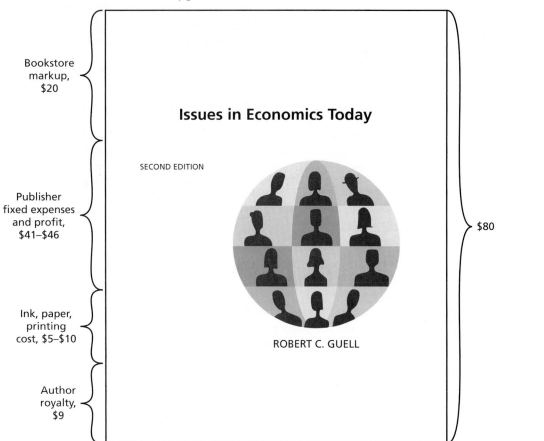

Bookstore markup, $20

Publisher fixed expenses and profit, $41–$46

Ink, paper, printing cost, $5–$10

Author royalty, $9

$80

Who's to blame for all this? Everybody. . . . including your professors. Faculty, especially those that teach large classes, want a testbank (a computer-generated set of questions they can ask on multiple-choice tests). They want these tests to have a mix of easy and hard questions and they want the questions to have only one good answer. That costs money. Also, remember that your faculty member got the book for free. His or her office is either full of textbooks (some with the wrapper still on them), or he or she has either given them away or sold them. Suppose Professor X writes a new book and Professor Y uses it but Professor Z does not. Professor X makes money on the royalties but Professor Z also makes money by selling the free copy. This is one of those things that you see all the time but you may not recognize. Textbook buyers will walk the halls of faculty office buildings looking to buy sample copies from faculty. They will themselves resell them online and at regular college textbook stores. Your $80 book may have been purchased by a bookbuyer for $28 from a faculty member,

sold to a textbook wholesaler for $35 and then sold to a bookstore for $50. Finally, you buy it for $60. When a book is sold this way the author gets nothing.

Figure 41.2 illustrates this recycling of textbooks. Note that the only time the publisher or the author make money is shown in the upper-left-hand corner: when the bookstore buys the book from the publisher. In every other transaction noted here, someone else is making money.

Alas, you are also to blame. You want your professors to teach from books with well-articulated Web sites, books that have study guides, and books that have Powerpoints. These ancillaries cost serious money to produce. The ancillaries budget for a new book depends significantly on the number of books the publisher believes can be sold. A book like the one you are reading has a budget of between $15,000 and $20,000 depending on how much work needs to be done.

The bottom line for publishers is that they are in business to make money. The break-even point on a book such as this one is around 7,000 units. We can use basic

FIGURE 41.2   The textbook recycling process.

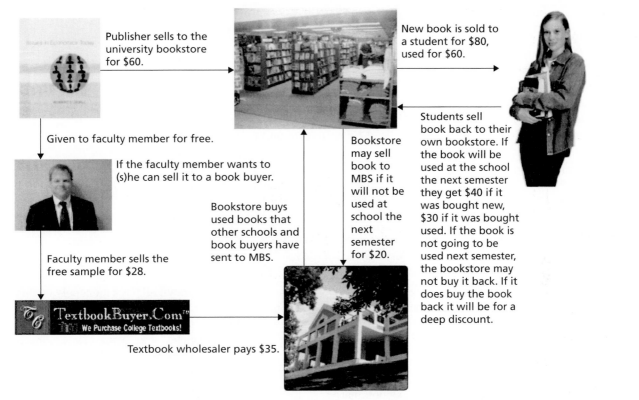

Publisher sells to the university bookstore for $60.

New book is sold to a student for $80, used for $60.

Given to faculty member for free.

If the faculty member wants to (s)he can sell it to a book buyer.

Bookstore may sell book to MBS if it will not be used at school the next semester for $20.

Students sell book back to their own bookstore. If the book will be used at the school the next semester they get $40 if it was bought new, $30 if it was bought used. If the book is not going to be used next semester, the bookstore may not buy it back. If it does buy the book back it will be for a deep discount.

Bookstore buys used books that other schools and book buyers have sent to MBS.

Faculty member sells the free sample for $28.

Textbook wholesaler pays $35.

Textbook wholesaler (MBS) collects and sorts books to be sold back to bookstores.

math to figure how the bottom line is affected by sales. This is done in Table 41.1. Increasing sales adds quickly to the bottom line because, for each book sold, there are only $14 in costs and $60 in revenue.

The book you are reading is the intellectual property of its owner. I gave that intellectual property to the publisher in exchange for the royalties they pay me for sales on the book. What the copyright does is it gives McGraw-Hill the exclusive right to sell this material. It also prohibits you from walking down to Kinko's and running off copies for your friends. Copyrights are necessary to bring intellectual property to market because

TABLE 41.1   A simple analysis of textbook profitability.

Economic Concept	Detail	Assuming Break-Even Sales of 7,000 units@$60	Assuming Sales of 15,000 units @$60
Revenue	Price to the bookstore × number of books sold	$420,000	$900,000
Fixed costs	Payment for ancillaries (Powerpoint, Web, testbank, instructor's manual, study guide)	20,000	20,000
	Editing, typesetting, graphics, payment for reviews, marketing	300,000	300,000
Variable costs	Royalties	65,000	135,000
	Materials	35,000	75,000
Profit	Revenue—fixed costs—variable costs	0	370,000

TABLE 41.2   The market for common economics textbooks.

Discipline	Number of Books	Lowest Price	Highest Price
Essentials (general education)	23	$80.51	$103.55
Principles (combined macro and micro)	23	107.30	133.00
Principles of macroeconomics	23	87.35	97.95
Principles of microeconomics	23	87.35	97.95
Intermediate macroeconomics	15	90.25	129.20
Intermediate microeconomics	15	115.85	126.35
International economics*	17	96.71	123.95
Money and banking	7	101.33	119.13
Mathematical economics*	10	99.95	126.35
Econometrics*	28	96.85	126.35
Labor economics	6	112.81	121.55
Public finance	4	116.80	121.55

*Includes books that are billed as meeting the needs of "advanced undergraduates and graduate students."

Source: http://barnesandnoble.com.

without them producers of the books, songs, and inventions would have no financial motivation to do so.[2]

TEXTBOOKS AND MARKET FORMS

In some disciplines there is one standard textbook that everyone uses while in others there are multiple texts that look very much the same. In this section we will use the market for economics textbooks to illustrate some of these market form concepts and learn why college texts have risen in price so greatly.

Once you understand the structure of the textbook market it becomes easier to see why the books cost so much. There are hundreds of textbooks on the market but most are not good substitutes for another. It does little good to bring your economics text to your poetry class. In the end, your professor probably had a relatively small number of books from which to choose. If you are using this book while taking a general education economics course for nonmajors, your professor had to decide whether to cram a bunch of theory in or do an issues approach. Having chosen this book your professor chose the issues approach. There are four books that really

work in this niche. McGraw-Hill has a monopoly on this book but it is a competitor in this area. The market form best suited to this area is monopolistic competition.

The market for principles of economics texts is much greater and there are many more choices. There are four really big sellers and several scattered players. This is also an example of monopolistic competition. The differences between books is quite slight (mostly in presentation and emphasis) but the publishers still retain their monopoly rights.

For an example of an area in which there are fewer sellers, consider the market for graduate-level textbooks in mathematical economics. For all intents and purposes, there are two. One has been around since dirt and the other one is a few years old. This is an example of oligopoly. Some areas of economics are so narrow, with such a small market that there is only one book.

In Table 41.2 the number of books that exist for specific economics courses are listed, along with the range of new prices.

TECHNOLOGY AND THE IMPACT OF USED BOOKS

Consider the predicament of a college student without a robust used book wholesale market. A student at the University of Florida may have purchased this book in August only to discover in December that because the faculty member using it was moving to a different school, the book would not be used on that campus again. That student's bookstore would be reluctant to buy the book back because they would have no assurance that the book

---

[2]A copyright lasts for a long period of time, 95 years after publication or 70 years after the death of the creator, which ever is longer. Chances are quite good that no one will be interested in this book at that time. On the other hand you can pick up a copy of Marx's *Das Kapital* or Adam Smith's *The Wealth of Nations* for less than $10 because the copyright has expired and the book is in the public domain.

would be used again at the University of Florida. Now suppose the same faculty member adopts the book in the spring at the University of Washington. Those students would be stuck buying a new version of the book because the student with the perfectly good used book to sell does not know about the student looking for a book to buy.

Technology bridges that information gap. Computers, computer networks, and, more recently the Internet, have allowed the two students to meet up through textbook buyers and the used textbook wholesalers. Today a textbook is easily recycled throughout the system and throughout the publication cycle of the book. The turn-around time from December to January is now the only bottleneck. Those with books to sell can find buyers quickly and easily using either direct locating Web sites (like eBay) or through Internet buyers and sellers (like textbookbuyers.com).

Though the Internet has significantly increased the availability of used books, it has also contributed to the increased cost of new ones. Remember that the publisher and author will produce the book only if they are sufficiently compensated. The technology-enhanced used book market has cut into sales of new books by increasing the rate of reuse. The result is that publishers have to raise the new book price and shorten (sometimes artificially) the publication cycle for new editions in order to make money for themselves and to compensate authors.

WHEN PRICE MATTERS AND WHEN IT DOES NOT

When you buy a car, go to a restaurant, go shopping, or take a trip you consider price because you are the one making the decision. Textbooks are chosen for you and by a faculty member who is often completely oblivious to the price that will be charged for the book. Faculty get the book for free and rarely inquire as to the price that will be charged. When students go to the bookstore and get their books they cannot choose which book to buy (beyond their choice of used versus new), they have to decide to buy the book or not. Thus the price of the book is irrelevant in the adoption decision. Under good circumstances the adoption decision is typically made after a professor has looked at the choices in the area and selected the one that goes best with the course and the way the professor teaches. In the end, faculty often pick books that have the supplements they are looking for, have illustrations that simplify the subject, and are pleasing to the eye. All of these add to the price of the book but the price simply does not enter into the decision to adopt the book.

The student is then made to choose between buying the book or not. Faculty consider buying the book the first real test of whether students are serious about their course. When students ask questions and the professor indicates that the answers can be found in the book, if the students indicates they did not buy the book, professors are typically unsympathetic.

SO WHY DO THEY COST SO MUCH AND WHO'S TO BLAME?

Taken together, the reasons listed above give rise to very expensive books. Faculty take time to write them on the premise that they will be rewarded. They take an enormous amount of time and money to write, edit, and publish. The supplements necessary to generate adoptions are expensive to create. The fact that only the first sale generates revenue for the publisher and royalties for the author means that new editions have to be regularly produced. In some areas, books are expensive because there is little or no competition. Finally, professors choose to adopt textbooks and rarely think about textbook prices in the process. The student is given a take it or leave it option.

In every case each person makes a seemingly simple economic calculation and acts in his or her own interest. An author decides whether or not to take the time to write a book based on what she or he views as a reasonable expectation of compensation. Faculty pick the books they think will work best for their courses and students. Publishers work with authors to put the best ("best" here means most marketable) book they can on the shelves. Bookstores stock the books that faculty indicate they are requiring for their courses. Students try to buy books as cheaply as possible. Add in book buyers and wholesalers realizing that there is money to be made by buying up unwanted books and getting them to where they are wanted and you have a recipe for the conclusion that "the free market is to blame."

In the end the problem of textbook prices is the same as the problem for prescription drug companies: enormously high fixed costs and very low variable costs. Compound that with the similarity to the music industry and imagine a world where pirated textbooks could be downloaded in PDF form for free? The market for textbooks is undergoing enormous change and by the time you send your children to college, the textbook may be as quaint as the vinyl LP and 8-track tape. The content will still be important but it may not come to you on paper.

Summary

You now understand why this particular textbook cost you as much as it did. You understand the process by which a book comes to the market and the high fixed cost–low marginal cost aspect of the industry. You understand that the market form that governs a particular textbook can vary from monopolistic competition to oligopoly to monopoly. Finally, you understand the importance of the used textbook market and how it affects new book production cycles and costs.

Key Terms

advance, 409   royalties, 409

Quiz Yourself

1. In a course like principles of economics (macro, micro, or combined) the market form for textbooks is
   a. Monopoly.
   b. Oligopoly.
   c. Monopolistic competition.
   d. Perfect competition.

2. The textbook production industry has a great deal in common with the pharmaceutical industry in that there are _____ fixed costs and _____ marginal costs.
   a. High; high.
   b. High; low.
   c. Low; high.
   d. Low; low.

3. Authors are typically paid for their work
   a. Based on a percentage of the sales at college bookstores.
   b. Based on a percentage of the sales from publishers to bookstores.
   c. According to a fixed rate.
   d. On a per-page basis.

4. Which of the following make no money in the system that buys and sells used books?
   a. Publishers.
   b. Textbook buyers.
   c. Textbook resellers.
   d. Bookstores.

5. The buying and selling of used textbooks has been around since the 1920s. This market has been more active recently thanks to
   a. Cell phones.
   b. Bookstores.
   c. Publishers.
   d. The Internet.

6. The typical $100 college textbook will net the author _____ in royalties.
   a. $5.
   b. $12.
   c. $25.
   d. $50.

Think about This

Imagine yourself in the position of a professional where it is common practice to send goods to you unsolicited. Imagine further that the reason they do this is so that you will recommend the purchase of the goods by the people with whom you deal. Also imagine that you are legally entitled to sell the sample goods and that there is a market for them. Would you sell them?

Talk about This

Some instructors are told by their department chair (or a committee) which book they have to use. Ask your instructor if she or he had a choice. Ask the instructor if she or he knows how much you paid for this book. Ask if the process for textbook choice for this course considered price.

Glossary

absolute advantage   The ability to produce a good, better, faster, or more quickly than a competitor.

accounting costs   Only those costs that must be explicitly paid by the owner of a business.

adjusted gross income (AGI)   Total net income from all sources.

administrative lag   The time it takes for Congress and the president to agree on a course of action.

advance   The amount of money paid to authors prior to a book's publication. This is typically counted against future royalties.

adverse impact discrimination   Doing something that is not necessarily discriminatory on its face but that impacts some groups more negatively than others.

adverse selection   The problem in insurance in which those who need it most are the only ones willing to pay for it, thus driving the price up and driving out those who need it somewhat less.

affirmative action   Any policy that is taken to speed up the process of achieving equality.

aggregate demand (AD)   The amounts of real domestic output that domestic consumers, businesses, governments, and foreign buyers collectively will desire to purchase at each possible price level.

aggregate demand shock   An unexpected event which causes aggregate demand to increase or decrease.

aggregate supply (AS)   The level of real domestic output available at each possible price level.

aggregate supply shock   An unexpected event which causes aggregate supply to increase or decrease.

asset substitution effect   Government is saving for you; thus you will save less for yourself.

attainable   Levels of production that are possible with the given resources.

average fixed cost (AFC)   Total fixed cost divided by output, the average fixed cost per unit of production.

average index of monthly earnings (AIME) The monthly average of the 35 highest earnings years adjusted for wage inflation.

average total cost (ATC)   Total cost divided by output, the cost per unit of production.

average variable cost (AVC)   Total variable cost divided by output, the average variable cost per unit of production.

bankrupt   The state of having insufficient assets to pay obligations.

bankruptcy   A legal status entered into when a company or individual cannot pay its debt.

barrier to entry   A legal or economic mechanism that prevents firms from competing in an industry.

barter   The direct trade of goods for other goods and without money.

base year   Year in which the market basket is established and year to which all other prices are compared.

baseline budgeting   Using last year's budgeted figure to set this year's budgeted figure.

bequest effect   People save more to give larger gifts to their descendants, thus increasing national savings.

brokering   The act of buying a ticket and legally selling it at a price higher than its face value.

bubble   The state of a market where the current price is far above its value determined by fundamentals.

budget deficit   The amount by which expenditures exceed revenues.

budget surplus   The amount by which revenues exceed expenditures.

business cycle   Regular pattern of ups and downs in the economy.

CAFTA   Central American Free Trade Agreement

capital budget   That part of the federal budget devoted to spending on goods that will last several years.

capital gains   Any profit generated by selling an asset for more than was paid for it.

capitalism   An economic system where markets, in particular markets for financial resources, are free.

cartel   An organization of individual competitors that join to form a single monopolist.

causation   A change in one variable makes another variable change.

ceteris paribus   Latin for other things equal.

common property   Property that is not owned by any individual but is owned by government or has some other collective ownership.

communism   An economic system where governmental authorities determine the allocation, use, and distribution of financial resources.

comparative advantage   The ability to produce a good at a lower opportunity cost of the resources used.

concentration ratio   A measure of the market power held by the top firms in an industry. For a specific number of firms (n) it is the percentage of total sales in the industry accounted for by top n firms.

consumer price index (CPI)   The price index based on what average consumers buy.

consumer surplus   The value you get that is in excess of what you pay to get it.

consumers   Those people in a market who want to exchange money for goods or services.

contestable markets hypothesis   One firm is all that is necessary for competitive prices to exist as long as that firm is threatened by hit-and-run entry.

continuing resolution   A bill passed by Congress and signed by the president that allows the government to temporarily spend money in a fashion identical to the previous year.

copayment   Either a set amount or the percentage of the bill after the deductible has been taken out that you have to pay.

cost   The expense that must be incurred to produce goods and services for sale.

cost function   A graph which shows how much various amounts of production cost.

cost of living adjustment (COLA)   A device that compensates people for the fact that changes in inflation change the spending power of their income.

cost-push inflation   Inflation caused by a decrease in aggregate supply.

creative destruction   The notion that people need to lose their jobs involuntarily in order to seize better opportunities.

creditors   The people or institutions to which a company or individual owes money.

cross-price elasticity of demand   The responsiveness of quantity of one good to a change in the price of another good.

crowding out   The opportunity cost of government deficit spending is that private investment is reduced.

current-services budgeting   Using an estimate of the costs of providing the same level of services next year as last.

cyclical deficit   That part of the deficit attributable to the economy's not being at full employment.

cyclical unemployment   State that exists when people lose their jobs because of a temporary downturn in the economy.

deadweight loss   The loss in societal welfare associated with production being too little or too great.

deductible   The amount of health spending a year that you have to pay before the insurance company pays anything (from Chapter 18).

deductible   Approved types of expenses for income tax purposes (from Chapter 31).

deductions   Amounts by which AGI is reduced; the greater of either the standard deduction or itemized deductions.

default risk   The risk to the investor that the borrower will not pay

deflation   A general reduction in prices.

demand   The relationship between price and quantity demanded, ceteris paribus.

demand-pull inflation   Inflation caused by an increase in aggregate demand.

demand schedule   Presentation, in tabular form, of the price and quantity demanded for a good.

depression   Severe recession typically resulting in a financial panic and bank closures, unemployment rates exceeding 20 percent, prolonged retrenchment in RGDP on the magnitude of 10 percent or more, and significant deflation.

diminishing returns   The notion that there exists a point where the addition of resources increases production but does so at a decreasing rate.

direct correlation   A higher level of one variable is associated with a higher level of the other variable.

discount rate   The rate at which the Fed itself loans money to banks.

discouraged-worker effect   Bad news induces people to stop looking for work, causing the unemployment rate to fall.

discretionary fiscal policy   Government spending and tax changes enacted at the time of the problem to alter the economy.

discretionary spending   Budget items for which an annual appropriations bill must be passed so that money can be spent.

disparate treatment discrimination   Treating two otherwise equal people differently on the basis of race or gender.

division of labor   Workers divide the tasks in such a way that each can build momentum and not have to switch jobs.

draft   The process by which new talent is assigned to teams.

dumping   The exporting of goods below cost to drive competitors out of business.

economic cost   All costs of a business: those that must be paid as well as those incurred in the form of forgone opportunities.

economic profit   Any profit above normal profit.

economics   The study of the allocation and use of scarce resources to satisfy unlimited human wants.

economies of scale   The aspect of production where per-unit costs decrease as production increases.

efficient market   All information is taken into account by participants in a market.

elastic   The circumstance when the percentage change in quantity is larger than the percentage change in price.

elasticity   The responsiveness of quantity to a change in another variable.

encouraged-worker effect   Good news induces people to start looking for work, causing the unemployment rate to rise (until they succeed in finding work).

entitlement   A program where if people meet certain income or demographic criteria they are automatically eligible to receive benefits.

equilibrium   The point where the amount that consumers want to buy and the amount firms want to sell are the same. This occurs where the supply curve and the demand curve cross.

equilibrium price   The price at which no consumers wish they could have purchased more goods at the price and no producers wish that they could have sold more.

equilibrium quantity   The amount of output exchanged at the equilibrium price.

excess demand   Another term for shortage.

excess supply   Another term for surplus.

exemptions   An amount by which AGI is reduced which is determined by the size of the family.

expansion   The part of the growth period of the business cycle from the previous peak to the new peak.

external benefits   Benefits that accrue to someone other than the consumer or producer of the good or service.

externalities   Effects of a transaction which hurt or help people who are not a part of that transaction (from Chapter 17).

externalities   Effects created by an unregulated market on people other than the buyer or seller (from Chapter 24).

fallacy of composition   The mistake in logic that suggests that the total economic impact of something is always and simply equal to the sum of the individual parts.

federal funds rate   The rate at which banks borrow from one another to meet reserve requirements.

filing status   Classification of taxpayers based on household; can be single, married filing jointly, married filing separately, and single head of household.

fiscal policy   The purposeful movements in government spending or tax policy designed to direct an economy.

fixed costs   Costs of production that cannot be changed.

fixed inputs   Resources that do not change.

foreign exchange   The conversion of the currency of one country for the currency of another.

foreign purchases effect   When domestic prices are high relative to their imported alternatives, we will export less to foreign buyers and we will import more from foreign producers. Therefore, higher prices lead to less domestic output.

free agent   A player who is able to offer services to the highest bidder.

frictional unemployment   Short-term unemployment during a transition to an equal or better job.

fully funded pension   A system that has an amount currently invested that is sufficient to pay every benefit dollar it is required to pay in the future.

functional finance   That part of the budget attributable to programs designed to get an economy out of a recession.

fundamentals   Elements that determine stock prices that make long-term economic sense—profit expectations and interest rates.

gatekeeper   Doctor who treats general afflictions and refers patients to specialists.

GATT   General Agreement on Tariffs and Trade, a world trade agreement.

GDP deflator (GDPDEF)   The price index used to adjust GDP for inflation, including all goods rather than a market basket.

Gini coefficient   A measure of economic equality ranging from zero to one.

gross domestic product (GDP)   The dollar value of all of the goods and services produced for final sale in the United States in a year.

hard currencies   Currencies easily converted to U.S. dollars or gold.

hedging   Taking an investment position so that changes in prices or exchange rates do not alter the advisability of a business decision.

horizontal equity   Equal people should be treated equally.

human capital   The ability of a person to create goods and services.

incentives   Something that influences a decision we make.

income effect   An increase in price lowers spending power; if the good is normal, this further lowers consumption; if it is inferior, it can increase consumption back toward where it was (or even further). This effect works in either direction.

income elasticity of demand   The responsiveness of quantity to a change in income.

induced retirement effect   People need to save more if they are going to retire earlier than they would have without Social Security.

inelastic   The circumstance when the percentage change in quantity is smaller than the percentage change in price.

inflation rate   The percentage increase in the consumer price index.

initial public offering (IPO)   A company's first sale of stock to the public in an attempt to raise money for expansion.

in-kind subsidies   Provisions of goods and services in forms other than cash.

interest rate   The percentage, usually expressed in annual terms, of a balance that is paid by a borrower to a lender that is in addition to the original amount borrowed or lent.

interest rate effect   Higher prices lead to inflation, which leads to less borrowing and a lowering of RGDP.

inverse correlation   A higher level of one variable is associated with a lower level of the other variable.

itemized deductions   Deductions for particular expenses on which the government does not want taxes paid.

labor-force participation rate   The percentage of the population of a group that is employed or seeking employment.

law of demand   The statement that the relationship between price and quantity demanded is a negative or inverse one.

law of diminishing marginal utility   The amount of additional happiness that you get from an additional unit of consumption falls with each additional unit.

law of supply   The statement that there is a positive relationship between price and quantity supplied.

lifetime maximum   The most that an insurance company will pay on your health expenses over your lifetime.

living wage   A wage sufficient to keep a family out of poverty.

local substitution   The effect of the substitution of one economic activity for another within a community, so the net effect is zero.

lockout   An action by employers to deny employees access to their jobs.

logrolling   The trading of votes to generate sufficient support for projects that are not in the general interest of the country.

Lombard System

long run   The period of time where a firm can change things like plant and equipment.

Lorenz curve   A graph that maps the cumulative percentage of population against the cumulative percentage of another variable like income.

loss   The money a firm makes is less than its costs (costs − revenue).

M1   Cash + coin + checking accounts.

M2   M1 + saving accounts + small CDs.

M3   M2 + large CDs.

macroeconomics   That part of the discipline of economics that deals with the economy as a whole.

mandatory spending   Budget items for which a previously passed law requires that money be spent.

marginal benefit   The increase in the benefit that results from an action.

marginal cost   The increase in the cost that results from an action.

marginal resource cost   Additional revenue the firm receives from the sale of each unit.

marginal revenue (MR)   The increase in revenue associated with increasing sales by one unit.

marginal revenue product of labor   The additional revenue generated from hiring an additional worker.

marginal tax rate   The percentage of each dollar in a bracket that must be paid in tax.

marginal utility   The amount of extra happiness that people get from an additional unit of consumption.

market   Any mechanism by which buyers and sellers negotiate an exchange.

market basket   Those goods that average people buy and the quantities they buy them in.

market risk   The risk that the market value of an asset will change in an unanticipated manner

maximum out of pocket   The most that a person or family will have to pay over a year for all covered health expenses.

maximum taxable earnings   The maximum of taxable earnings subject to the payroll tax.

means test   Determination of the amount of one's government benefit on the basis of income or wealth.

Medicaid   Public health insurance in the United States which covers the poor.

Medicare   Public health insurance in the United States which covers those over age 65.

Medicare Part A   The compulsory part of Medicare that pays for hospitalization expenses.

Medicare Part B   The voluntary part of Medicare that pays for doctor visits.

microeconomics   That part of the discipline of economics that deals with individual markets and firms.

minimum wage   The lowest wage that may legally be paid for an hour's work.

model   A simplification of the real world that can be manipulated to explain the real world.

monetary aggregate   A measure of the quantity of money in the economy.

monopolistic competition   A situation in a market where there are many firms producing similar but not identical goods.

monopoly   A situation in a market where there is only one firm producing the good.

monopsony   A market with only one buyer.

moral hazard   Having insurance increases the demand for the insured good.

NAFTA   North American Free Trade Agreement, involving the United States, Mexico, and Canada.

national debt   The total amount owed by the federal government.

natural monopoly   Exists when there are high fixed costs and diminishing marginal costs.

net benefit   The difference between all benefits and all costs.

net present value   The difference between the present value of benefits and the present value of costs.

neutral   When applied to a tax code, the implication that it does not favor particular forms of income or expenditure.

nominal interest rate   The advertised rate of interest.

nondiscretionary fiscal policy   That set of policies that are built into the system to stabilize the economy.

nontariff barriers   Barriers to trade resulting from regulatory actions.

normal profit   The level of profit that business owners could get in their next best alternative investment.

normative analysis   A form of analysis that seeks to understand the way things should be.

off-budget   Parts of the budget designated by Congress as separate from the normal budget. Programs that operate with their own revenue sources and have trust funds; Social Security, Medicare, and the Postal Service are examples.

oligopolistic market   A situation in a market where there are very few discernible competitors.

on-budget   Parts of the budget that rely entirely or mostly on general revenue.

open-market operations   The buying and selling of bonds, which, respectively, increases or decreases the money supply, thereby influencing interest rates.

operating budget   That part of the federal budget devoted to spending on goods and services that will be used in the current year.

operational lag   The time it takes for the full impact of a government program or tax change to have its effect on the economy.

opportunity cost   The forgone alternative of the choice made.

optimization assumption   An assumption that suggests that the person in question is trying to maximize some objective.

origin   The point on the graph where both the variables are zero. (0, 0)

orphan drug   A drug that treats someone with a disease that afflicts few people.

output   The good or service produced for sale.

patent   A right granted by government to an inventor to be the exclusive seller of that invention for a limited period of time.

pay-as-you-go pension   A system where current workers' taxes are used to pay pensions to current retirees.

payroll taxes   Taxes owed on what workers earn from their work.

peace dividend   Money that was freed for other spending priorities when the Cold War was over.

peak   The highest point in the business cycle.

perfect competition   A situation in a market where there are many firms producing the same good.

perfectly elastic   The condition of demand when price cannot change.

perfectly inelastic   The condition of demand when price changes have no effect on quantity.

political business cycle   Politically motivated fiscal policy used for short-term gain just prior to elections.

positive analysis   A form of analysis that seeks to understand the way things are and why they are that way.

positive externalities   The benefits that a person other than the buyer or seller receives as a result of a transaction.

positive externality   The benefits that go to someone other than the consumer or producer of a good.

poverty gap   The total amount of money that would have to be transferred to households below the poverty line for them to get out of poverty.

poverty line   That level of income sufficient to provide a family with a minimally adequate standard of living.

poverty rate   The percentage of people in households whose incomes are under the poverty line.

present value   The interest-adjusted value of future payment streams.

price   The amount of money that must be paid for a unit of output.

price ceiling   The level above which a price may not rise.

price elasticity of demand   The responsiveness of quantity demanded to a change in price.

price elasticity of supply   The responsiveness of quantity supplied to a change in price.

price floor   Price below which a commodity may not sell.

price gouging   The pejorative term applied to the circumstance when firms raise prices substantially when demand increases unexpectedly.

price index   A device that centers the price of the market basket around 100.

price of the market basket in the base year   National average of the total cost of the market basket, abbreviated P_{MB}^{BY}.

primary care physician   Physician in managed care operations charged with making the initial diagnosis and making referrals. Also called a *gatekeeper*.

primary credit rate

primary insurance amount (PIA)   The amount single retirees receive in a monthly check if they retire at their retirement age.

principal-agent problem   The problem that occurs when the owner of an asset and the manager of that asset are different and have different preferences.

procyclical   Situation that renders good times better and bad times worse.

producer surplus   The money the firm gets that is in excess of its marginal costs.

producers   Those people in a market who want to exchange goods or services for money.

production function   A graph that shows how many resources are needed to produce various amounts of output.

production possibilities frontier   A graph which relates the amounts of different goods that can be produced in a fully employed society.

profit   The money that a firm makes: revenue − cost.

progressive taxation   Those with higher income pay a higher rate of tax.

quantity demanded   Amount consumers are willing and able to buy at a particular price during a particular period of time.

quantity supplied   Amount firms are willing and able to sell at a particular price during a particular period of time.

quota   A legal restriction on the amount of a good coming into the country.

rational or statistical discrimination   Unequal treatment of classes of people that is based on sound statistical evidence and is consistent with profit maximization.

real-balances effect   When a price increases, your buying power is decreased, causing you to buy less (from Chapter 2).

real-balances effect   Because higher prices reduce real spending power, prices and output are negatively related (from Chapter 8).

real gross domestic product (RGDP)   An inflation-adjusted measure of GDP.

real interest rate   The rate of interest after inflation expectations are accounted for; the compensation for waiting to consume.

recession   The declining period of at least two consecutive quarters in the business cycle.

recognition lag   The time it takes to measure the state of the economy.

recovery   The part of the growth period of the business cycle from the trough to the previous peak.

reinsurance   The form of insurance where one insurance company promises to pay another if the first company has a large (usually multiple million dollar) loss from a single event.

reservation wage   The least amount that a player will accept because it is the next best offer.

reserve clause   A contract clause that requires that players re-sign with the team to which they belonged the previous year.

reserve ratio   The percentage of every dollar deposited in a checking account that a bank must maintain at a Federal Reserve branch.

resource   Anything that is consumed directly or used to make things that will ultimately be consumed.

retirement age   The age at which retirees get full benefits.

revenue   The money that comes into the firm from the sale of goods and services.

revenue sharing   The process by which some revenues are distributed to all teams rather than simply the teams that generate them.

risk   The possibility that the investor will not get anticipated payoffs

risk averse   A characteristic of a person who would pay extra to guarantee the expected outcome.

risk neutral   A characteristic of a person who would not pay extra to guarantee the expected outcome.

risk premium   The reward investors receive for taking greater risk.

royalties   The amount of money paid to authors. Typically paid on a percentage basis.

runs   Panicked withdrawal of money by worried depositors.

salary cap   The maximum in total payroll that a team can pay its players.

scalping   The act of buying a ticket and illegally selling it at a price higher than its face value.

scarce   Not freely available and lacking a finite source.

seasonal unemployment   State that exists when people lose their jobs predictably every year at the same time.

shock   Any unanticipated economic event.

shortage   The condition where firms do not want to sell as many goods as consumers want to buy.

short run The period of time where a firm cannot change things like plant and equipment.

simplifying assumption An assumption that may, on its face, be silly but allows for a clear explanation.

single-payer system The government collects (usually very high) taxes to pay for everyone's health care.

slope The increase in the value of the *y*-axis variable for a one-unit increase in the value of the *x*-axis variable.

social cost The true cost of production and consumption of a good that includes the effects on innocent bystanders.

Social Security Trust Fund A fund established in 1982 to hold government debt which will be sold as necessary when tax revenues are less than benefits.

socialism An economic system where a significant part (but not all) of the decisions regarding the allocation of financial resources are made by a governmental authority.

special drawing rights (SDRs) A made-up currency of the IMF that is composed of a weighted average of the four major currencies of the world.

standard deduction The minimum level of deduction.

stock index A weighted average of stock prices in a particular group.

strategic trade policies Policies designed to get more of the benefits from trade in a country than would exist under free trade.

strike An action by labor to deny employers the services of the employees.

structural deficit That part of the deficit that would remain even if the economy were at full employment.

structural unemployment State that exists when people lose their jobs because of a change in the economy that makes their particular skill obsolete.

substitution effect Purchase of less of a product than originally wanted when its price is high because a lower-priced product is available.

sunk costs Expenses that do not change whether you produce zero or any other amount.

supply The relationship between price and quantity supplied, ceteris paribus.

supply and demand The name of the most important model in all of economics.

supply schedule Presentation, in tabular form, of the price and quantity supplied for a good.

supply-side economics Government policy intended to influence the economy through aggregate supply by lowering input costs and reducing regulation.

surplus The condition where firms want to sell more goods than consumers want to buy.

tariff A tax on imports.

taxable income Adjusted gross income minus personal exemptions minus (the greater of either the standard or itemized) deductions.

terms of trade The amount of a good one country must give up to obtain another good from the other country, usually expressed as a ratio.

third-party payer An entity other than the consumer who pays part of the costs.

total expenditure rule If the price and the amount you spend both go in the same direction, then demand is inelastic, whereas if they go in opposite directions, demand is elastic.

trough The lowest point in the business cycle.

trust A single company having ownership of all stages of production in a particular industry.

unattainable Levels of production that are not possible with the given resources.

underemployment The state of working significantly below skill level or working fewer hours than desired.

unemployment A situation that occurs when resources are not being fully utilized.

unemployment rate The percentage of people in the work force who do not have jobs and are actively seeking them.

unitary elastic The circumstance when the percentage change in quantity is equal to the percentage change in price.

variable costs Costs of production that can be changed.

variable inputs Resources that can be easily changed.

vertical equity People across the income scale are treated fairly with regard to ability to pay.

vig   The expected percentage of any gamble that a casino will keep.

withholding   Deduction from your paycheck to cover the estimated amount of taxes you are going to owe during a year.

work force   All those nonmilitary personnel who are over 16 and are employed or are unemployed and actively seeking employment.

WTO   The World Trade Organization, an institution that arbitrates trade disputes.

***x*-axis**   The horizontal axis.

***x*-intercept**   The value of the *x*-axis variable when the *y*-axis variable is zero.

***y*-axis**   The vertical axis.

***y*-intercept**   The value of the *y*-axis variable when the *x*-axis variable is zero.

Yield curve   The relationship between reward and the time until the reward is received.

Index